HTML 3.2 PLUS HOW-TO

David Kerven

Jeff Foust

John Zakour

Waite Group Press™
A Division of
Sams Publishing
Corte Madera, CA

Publisher: Mitchell Waite
Associate Publisher: Charles Drucker

Acquisitions Manager: Jill Pisoni
Acquisitions Editor: Joanne Miller

Editorial Director: John Crudo
Project Editor: Kurt Stephan
Technical Reviewer: Eric Sinclair
Software Specialist: Dan Scherf
Copy Editor: Bruce Tracy/Creative Solutions

Production Director: Julianne Ososke
Production Manager: Cecile Kaufman
Production Editors: Kate Talbot, K.D. Sullivan/Creative Solutions
Senior Designer: Sestina Quarequio
Designer: Karen Johnston

Production: Carol Bowers, Jennifer Dierdorff, Dana Rhodes, Shawn Ring, Kevin Fulcher

Printed in the United States of America
97 98 99 • 10 9 8 7 6 5 4 3 2 1

Library of Congress Cataloging-in-Publication Data
Kerven, David.
    HTML 3.2 Plus how-to / David Kerven, Jeff Foust, John Zakour.
      p.   cm.
    Includes index.
    ISBN 1-57169-091-3
    1. HTML (Document markup language) I. Foust, Jeff.   II. Zakour, John.   III. Title.
    QA76.76.H94K4713   1997
    005.7'2--dc21   96-52454
                                                                  CIP

DEDICATION

I would like to dedicate this book to my mother, Sheila Yoskowitz; my wife, Jenny Kerven; and my family.

—David Kerven

To Mom.

—Jeff Foust

To my parents, as after all, if it weren't for them, I wouldn't be here.

—John Zakour

David Kerven was born in Jersey City, New Jersey, in 1967 and was raised in Livingston, New Jersey. He received his B.S. in electrical engineering from Johns Hopkins University and his Ph.D. in computer science from the University of Southwestern Louisiana. Dr. Kerven is currently living in Atlanta with his wife Jenny. He is an assistant professor of computer science at Clark Atlanta University, where he teaches courses in software engineering and object-oriented programming principles. For the past six years, he has participated in hypermedia research and development, in the development of four hypermedia environments, and the development of CGI applications for World Wide Web-based adaptive tutorial/training systems. He currently serves as Webmaster of the Clark Atlanta University Computer Science Web server.

Jeff Foust is a graduate student in planetary astronomy at M.I.T. A native of Council Bluffs, Iowa, he holds a B.S. in planetary science from Caltech. He has been exploring the Web and creating pages for it since the fall of 1993. His Shoemaker-Levy 9 impact page, with information and images of the impact of the comet on Jupiter, received national attention in *Astronomy, Macworld,* and *Wired* magazines. When not working on his thesis or using the Web, he has been active in a number of space-related ventures, including serving as editor of *SpaceViews,* a monthly space journal, and he is a former co-chair of Students for the Exploration and Development of Space (SEDS). Jeff is also a (frustrated) Boston Red Sox fan.

John Zakour is currently an HTML consultant and a freelance writer. Some of his writing—daily computer cartoons, the novel *The Doomsday Brunette,* and a new novel *Plutonium Blond*—can be found on Prodigy On-Line Service's World Wide Web pages. John majored in Computer Science at Potsdam State University. Upon completion of his studies at Postdam, he worked as a database programmer for Cornell University. Upon his return to New York, he was a Web page designer for Cornell University's New York State Agriculture Experiment Station. As an HTML consultant, John also has a Web page. You can see it at http://www.psnw.com/~jmz5/.

TABLE OF CONTENTS

CONTENTS

ACKNOWLEDGMENTS

I would first like to thank my wife Jenny for her loving forbearance and support throughout the entire writing process. In addition, I would like to thank the editors at Waite Group Press for their diligence and uncommon perseverance in wading through my unpolished drafts. Special thanks go to Troy Downing, who contributed How-To 13.8 on how to set up the MacHTTP server security. Finally, I would like to acknowledge the support of God, my family, and my department at Clark Atlanta University.

—David Kerven

Chris Lewicki and others at the University of Arizona chapter of Students for the Exploration and Development of Space (SEDS), who have created a first-class Web site (http://www.seds.org/) and provided me with space to experiment with Web designs for some time.

—Jeff Foust

To my wife Olga and my son Jay, who put up with me during those "one or two days" I was running behind schedule. To Ron, who was always there with computer advice. To Tom, who's always there with grammatical advice. To my ex-boss Linda, who would always let me take an hour or two off when I needed it.

—John Zakour

PREFACE

Welcome to World Wide Web authoring. Surfing the Internet through the World Wide Web has escaped the confines of academia and is quickly becoming a common sport in board rooms and family rooms. *HTML 3.2 Plus How-To* will provide you with a road map to enter the dynamic environment of Internet publishing on the World Wide Web. Unlike existing HyperText Markup Language (HTML) documentation, *HTML 3.2 Plus How-To* presents many real world document development problems, along with specific step-by-step solutions, explanations, and examples. With *HTML 3.2 Plus How-To* as your guide, you can concentrate on developing your information rather than your implementation. To give you a jump start on the information superhighway, all example documents, program code, and multimedia objects presented in the book are included on the CD-ROM.

The World Wide Web is expanding at an incredible pace. Approximately ten new Web servers are emerging online everyday with no end in sight. The basic building blocks of the World Wide Web are documents developed using HTML. The Internet traffic devoted to the retrieval of HTML documents is likewise increasing; in fact, high traffic servers currently receive in excess of one thousand accesses every hour. Both small and large-scale HTML projects are being initiated daily by both individuals and large commercial entities. With this kind of volume usage, HTML has become the de facto development language for network-based hypermedia information.

From purchasing flowers in Maine to ordering a pizza in California, you will find more commercial ventures are beginning to enter this arena. Financial institutions, retailers, publishers, and other corporations are only beginning to explore the potential of the worldwide electronic community. *HTML 3.2 Plus How-To* is not another manual, nor is it a technical specification; it is a guide that will provide direction for entering this rapidly growing environment and enhancing existing documents.

Each How-To in the book states a problem; describes the circumstances leading to the problem; develops a step-by-step solution; and delineates relevant tips, comments, warnings, and, occasionally, alternative solutions. Each How-To will walk you through the solution to a common development problem. *HTML 3.2 Plus How-To* is not another style manual; rather, it is a user-oriented, goal-driven guide that will change the way you develop HTML documents. *HTML 3.2 Plus How-To* provides everything you need to know to begin developing world-class HTML documents. So, jump into *HTML 3.2 Plus How-To* and share your vision with the world.

Chapter 1, Web Basics, introduces several key concepts about the World Wide Web. Most of this information should be familiar ground to prospective authors. The information serves as a review and a reminder while potentially filling gaps. Finally, the How-To's set the stage for the HTML 3.2 details to come.

Chapter 2, *HTML Basics,* deals with the basic concepts of authoring documents in HTML 3.2. You will learn how to identify and construct simple HTML documents. The How-To's tell you how to begin developing HTML documents. They will also introduce you to several of the key HTML elements.

Chapter 3, *Adding HTML Physical Character Effects,* continues by describing the various physical character effects possible with HTML 3.2. Each How-To walks you through the use of these character effects. Documented examples demonstrate the proper use of these elements while also addressing relevant stylistic issues.

Chapter 4, *Adding HTML Logical Character Effects,* carries you beyond the physical effect to HTML 3.2's logical character effects. Although these effects do not require a visible change in your Web pages, many Web browsers do provide a visible indication of these elements. This chapter's How-To's demonstrate the effective usage of the logical character elements supported by HTML 3.2

Chapter 5, *Tables,* looks at the management, organization, and formatting of data using HTML 3.2 tables. HTML 3.2 provides a significant improvement in these areas over earlier versions of HTML. Tables also support strict formatting of desired elements, such as images and text, by providing row/column alignment. The How-To's in this chapter instruct you in the use of HTML 3.2 table elements.

Chapter 6, *Lists,* leads you through the myriad of list types supported by HTML 3.2. Lists serve an essential function in the organization of many HTML documents. The How-To's explain the different types of lists and styles available and provide step-by-step instructions on inserting each type of list into your pages.

Chapter 7, *Managing Document Spacing,* takes a close look at the management of space in HTML 3.2 documents. How you space the information in your Web page substantially affects the impact of the page upon a viewer. HTML 3.2 provides several elements to control spacing. The How-To's in this chapter provide clear instructions on the use of these spacing elements.

Chapter 8, *Establishing Links,* covers the creation of links in HTML 3.2 documents. Links are the glue that connect HTML documents around the world. Links potentially connect your Web page to both other Web pages and a variety of other Internet-based information. The How-To's in this chapter examine the creation of links to other Web pages and other network-based information.

Chapter 9, *Using Images in Your Documents,* jumps into the topic of images. HTML 3.2 allows the incorporation of images directly into your Web pages in both the foreground and the background. This chapter also introduces the creation and use of imagemaps. Imagemaps allow you to click upon a particular location within the image and trigger a link associated with the location. The How-To's in this chapter step you through the process of image inclusion and imagemap construction.

Chapter 10, *Adding Externally Linked Multimedia Objects,* delves further into the multimedia arena. This chapter examines how HTML 3.2 supports the inclusion of a variety of multimedia data types. The How-To's provide stylistic and technical information on the inclusion of these data types. Even though the information in this chapter concentrates on the development and inclusion of multimedia objects accessed indirectly through links and external helper applications, much of the information is relevant in developing multimedia objects suitable for direct inclusion through the non-HTML 3.2 standard methods discussed in Chapter 18, Direct Inclusion of Multimedia Objects.

Chapter 11, *HTML Interactive Forms,* begins the examination of HTML forms. Authors use HTML forms to request data from viewers of pages. HTML provides a variety of input styles, such as text entry windows and lists of selections. The How-To's in this chapter explain the use of those HTML elements in form creation.

Chapter 12, *Server Basics,* examines how to make HTML 3.2 documents available on the World Wide Web by establishing your own Web site. The How-To's in this chapter outline the various tasks required to accomplish this goal.

Chapter 13, *Handling Server Security,* addresses the issue of providing security for your HTML documents. If you wish to restrict access to a selection of your Web pages, you will likely find your answer in this chapter. Several of the procedures discussed may require the actions of your Web site administrator; however, many of the How-To's in this chapter provide instructions that you may use to restrict access to your Web pages.

Chapter 14, *The Common Gateway Interface (CGI),* offers information on gateway applications. Gateway applications process the data gathered by HTML forms, as described in Chapter 11. These applications generally produce dynamic documents based upon the information available both on the server and through forms. The How-To's in this chapter examine the issues involved in creating gateway applications and provide instructions on and examples of how you can develop such applications.

Chapter 15, *Navigator and Internet Explorer HTML Extensions,* presents a variety of features supported by Netscape's Navigator and Microsoft's Internet Explorer, two of the most popular Web browsers. These features allow you to extend beyond the bounds of the HTML 3.2 standard. However, these additional features are not without some cost in cross-browser compatibility. The How-To's in this chapter not only detail the use of these additional features but also discuss ways to minimize cross-browser incompatibility.

Chapter 16, *Cascading Style Sheets,* explores the use of HTML cascading style sheets. Style sheets provide another means of specifying formatting constraints in Web pages. Further, they allow for a differentiation of style among instances of a particular HTML element. Thus, Web pages might utilize multiple versions of the same HTML element with each particular use having a different style. Currently, only Microsoft's Internet Explorer and several experimental Web browsers support style sheets. However, in the near future, you may see them incorporated into the HTML standard. This chapter's How-To's cover the creation, use, and incorporation of HTML style sheets in your Web pages.

Chapter 17, *Web Programming with Java™ and JavaScript™,* introduces the use of Java and Javascript in your Web pages. Java applets are small programs that you may download via the Web. These applications run within browser environments that support Java, such as Navigator and Internet Explorer. Javascript allows the incorporation of scripted functions within your Web pages. While HTML 3.2

supports the inclusion of Java applications, scripted functions are not yet a part of the standard. The How-To's in this chapter describe the current mechanisms for adding both Java and Javascript elements to your Web pages.

Chapter 18, *Direct Inclusion of Multimedia Objects,* discusses the mechanisms currently used to support the direct inclusion of multimedia objects within a Web page. Both Netscape and Internet Explorer allow you to directly include multimedia objects within your Web pages. The How-To's in this chapter present methods of including various types of multimedia objects. Since these mechanisms are not HTML 3.2 standard as yet, these How-To's provide information on minimizing cross-browser incompatibilities, as well as on the proper use of these features.

Chapter 19, *Frames,* addresses this advanced means of controlling Web page layout. Frames allow you to control different portions of a "page" presented by a frames-capable browser using multiple HTML documents. This chapter's How-To's present the tricks and practices of using frames in Web page development.

Chapter 20, *Unsupported, Proposed HTML Features,* presents many speculative HTML elements. The HTML language generates a wide variety of discussion leading to much speculation about the proper elements of the standards. The How-To's in this chapter examine a host of HTML elements that have been proposed or tested and that are not part of the HTML 3.2 standard but may eventually become part of the HTML standard or may end up in various browser HTML dialects.

Chapter 21, *Some of the Best Sites on the Web,* takes you on a brief tour of Web pages where the author has taken advantage of the unique aspects of HTML. There is a surfeit of pages on the Web that are cool; this chapter mentions the cream of the crop.

Just two years ago, few had heard of the World Wide Web and still fewer knew of HTML. Now these terms have become almost commonplace, appearing in advertising and even nationally syndicated comic strips. Commensurate with this exposure, the Web has experienced, and is still experiencing, a rapid growth in size and usage.

Individuals and businesses who wish to keep pace with technology must learn the valuable skills necessary not only to use this medium but also to actively participate in the evolution of this medium through authoring. In the clearly defined, explicit how-to format, this book equips you to enter that arena confidently.

INSTALLATION

The companion CD-ROM contains all the code for the How-To's in the book, as well as shareware and freeware programs to view and edit graphics, HTML, audio, and video.

What follows is the top-level directory structure of the CD.

```
\
 ┌ARCHIVES
 ├SOURCE
 │   ┌CH02
 │   ├CH03
 │   ├CH04
 │   ├CH05
 │   ├CH06
 │   ├CH07
 │   ├CH08
 │   ├CH09
 │   ├CH10
 │   ├CH11
 │   ├CH14
 │   ├CH15
 │   ├CH16
 │   ├CH17
 │   ├CH19
 │   └CH20
 ├3RDPARTY
 └EXPLORER
```

All of the utilities, viewers, and browsers can be found in their own subdirectories under 3RDPARTY. It is best to copy the programs from the CD-ROM to your hard drive before using them. To do this, see the next section, Installing to Your Hard Drive.

Since all the software in this book is shareware or freeware, we have included a compressed file that contains many programs for distributing to your friends in ARCHIVES.

The directories CHAP02, CHAP03, etc., contain the source code used in the chapter, broken down by How-To subdirectories such as HT01, HT02, and so on. Contained within these subdirectories are all the files that make up the How-To.

If you don't already have a World Wide Web browser, you will find Microsoft's Internet Explorer 3 included in the EXPLORER directory. Please refer to Appendix I for installation instructions.

Installing to Your Hard Drive

Since all the code for the How-To's in this book is on the companion CD-ROM, there is no need to type the code if you want to use it for your own projects. We will illustrate how to copy the files from the companion CD-ROM to your hard drive for the code and the utilities that are supplied on this disc.

There are two ways to copy files on the PC platform: DOS and Windows. Pick the environment you are most comfortable in, and follow the steps below.

DOS

If you are in DOS or using Windows' DOS Prompt, follow these steps:

1. Move to the drive that you want to copy the files to. If you want to copy the files onto the C: drive, type

```
C:
CD\
```

and press ENTER after each line.

2. Create the directory you would like to store your files in. If you want to store the files in the html3ht directory, type

```
MD HTML3HT
```

and press ENTER.

3. Move to that directory. If you created a directory called HTML3HT, move to that directory by typing

```
CD HTML3HT
```

and press ENTER.

4. If you want to copy individual subdirectories from the CD-ROM to your hard drive, skip to step 5. If you want to copy the entire CD-ROM to your hard drive in this directory, type

```
XCOPYD:\*.*/V/S
```

assuming that d: is the drive letter of your CD-ROM drive. Notice there are some switches after the **XCOPY** command. These switches are required to successfully copy the contents of the CD-ROM to your hard drive; **/V** tells **XCOPY** to verify the files, and **/S** tells **XCOPY** to copy the subdirectories.

5. To copy individual subdirectories from the CD-ROM to your hard drive, you must create the chapter directories before you copy the contents. For example, if you wanted to copy the code for Chapters 2, 5, and 7, you would type

```
MDCHAP02
MDCHAP05
MDCHAP07
```

and press (ENTER) after each line. Then you would type

```
CD\HTML3HT\CHAP02
XCOPYD:\CHAP02/V/S

CD\HTML3HT\CHAP05
XCOPYD:\CHAP05/V/S

CD\HTML3HT\CHAP07
XCOPYD:\CHAP07/V/S
```

and press (ENTER) after each line. We are assuming that D: is the drive letter of your CD-ROM drive.

Windows

If you are using Windows 3.x or Windows 95, please follow these steps:

1. Open the File Manager in Windows 3.x or the Explorer in Windows 95.

2. In both File Manager or Explorer, locate the drive you want to copy to and click on it.

3. Select the location to copy the files to or create a new directory. In File Manager, select File, Create Directory; in Explorer, select File, New, Folder. Type in the directory name you want to copy your files to and select OK.

4. In both File Manager and Explorer, select the directory you want to copy files to.

5. In the File Manager, select the drive letter of your CD-ROM drive. In Explorer, open up a new copy of Explorer with the drive letter of your CD-ROM drive.

6. If you are copying individual directories from the CD-ROM to the hard drive, skip to step 7. Using both programs, drag the contents of the CD-ROM to the destination drive. Depending on the speed of your computer and the options set for it, the copying process may take a few moments or a few minutes.

7. Select each directory you want to copy to the destination drive by holding down (CTRL) and clicking on the directory with the mouse. When you are finished selecting directories, drag your selection over to the destination.

NOTE

Some of the software included on the bundled CD is shareware, provided for your evaluation. If you find any of the shareware products useful, you are requested to register it as discussed in its documentation and/or in the About screen of the application. Waite Group Press has not paid the registration fee for this shareware.

PART I
INTRODUCTION

CHAPTER 1
WEB BASICS

1

WEB BASICS

How do I...

The World Wide Web, or simply the Web, has been called the "killer app" of the Internet. Certainly its ability to display text and graphics and provide access to other pages and information resources has made it *the* fast-growing component of the Internet. You may already know how to explore the universe of information on the Web. But you may not know how to use the Web to display your own information to the world– information about you, your personal interests, or your business.

This chapter introduces you to the World Wide Web and guides you in getting onto the Web, ready to create your own HTML documents. This chapter is not intended to be a thorough introduction to the Web; there are other resources, both on the Web and in books, that can provide more detailed explanations of the Web and how to use it. This chapter simply explains the basics of the Web, including how to find an access provider, how to find and use a browser, and how to find space for the Web pages you create. Once you understand these basics, you can learn in future chapters how to create your own Web pages using HTML.

1.1   Get on the Web from America Online

Major online services—America Online, CompuServe, and Prodigy—now provide access to the World Wide Web. This How-To discusses how America Online's Internet service works and how you can use it to access the Web.

1.2   Establish a Connection to the Internet

Another way to access the Web is to get an account with an Internet service provider, or ISP. These accounts usually include access to the World Wide Web and other Internet resources, and often they provide space to store the Web pages you will be creating. This How-To explains how to find a local provider and get the kind of Internet access you need to explore the Web.

1.3   Find a Web Browser

As the Web has exploded, the number of browser programs—the programs you use to explore the Web—has increased. Now there are browsers for nearly every conceivable type of computer. These programs have also grown more sophisticated to the point where they will support advanced HTML features and extensions. This How-To explains how to find an appropriate Web browser for your computer.

1.4   Navigate via Browser Features

Once you have Web access and a working browser, you need to be able to move around on the Web. The easiest way to navigate on the Web is to use the features incorporated into your browser to move between pages. This How-To shows how to use these basic features to start moving around the Web.

1.5   Follow a Link

One very helpful feature the World Wide Web offers you is the ability to move from page to page by selecting specific highlighted words, phrases, or images, which are called links. This How-To explains what links are and how you can use them to explore the Web.

1.6   Open a Location

Another way to move around in the Web is to go directly to a specific page using its address, or URL (universal resource locator). This How-To explains how to go directly to a specific location on the Web using basic features found in Web browsers.

1.7 Find a Web Authoring Tool

Seeing the variety of pages already on the Web may inspire you to create your own. One of the easiest ways to do this is to find an authoring tool, or HTML editor, that will allow you to create your own pages much as you would using a word processor, without worrying about the right HTML tags to use. This How-To explains how authoring tools work and how to find them on the Internet.

1.8 Find a Home for My Web Pages

Once you've created your pages, you need a place to store them so they can be accessed by other people on the Web. This usually involves finding an ISP that provides Web space for its customers. This How-To discusses how to look for a home for your Web pages.

1.9 Get Information About the Evolution of HTML

Your initial forays into the World Wide Web and page creation may pique your interest in the language of the Web, HTML, and its evolution. There are resources on HTML and its development available on the Web (in addition to what's in this book). This How-To shows you how to find information on the evolution and future of HTML.

1.10 Design Effective Web Pages

Even if you don't know anything about HTML yet, you can still learn how to design effective pages. Many of the attributes of an effective page—its layout, design, and ease of use—can be mastered before learning HTML. This How-To offers helpful tips for designing effective Web pages yourself.

COMPLEXITY
BEGINNING

1.1 How do I...
Get on the Web from America Online?

COMPATIBILITY: NOT APPLICABLE

Problem

I plan to join America Online. How can I get on the World Wide Web using this service?

Technique

To use the World Wide Web from America Online, you need version 3+ of the America Online software, along with a modem.

Steps

The following steps show how to get onto the World Wide Web from America Online:

1. If you don't have version 3 of the America Online software on your hard disk, install it. The installation process is very easy and straightforward. Just follow the onscreen prompts. Be aware, however, that the AOL modem setting defaults to a Hayes modem configuration. If you have another brand of modem, make sure you change the AOL modem setting to match it.

2. Once America Online 3 is installed, start it up by double-clicking on the America Online icon. Sign on to America Online. This brings you to the Main Menu.

3. Select Internet Connection from the Main Menu. This brings you to the Internet Connection Menu that contains a series of Internet-related topics. Figure 1-1 shows this menu.

4. Select the World Wide Web icon.

5. The America Online browser will load. Your screen will then resemble Figure 1-2.

How It Works

America Online makes getting on the World Wide Web surprisingly easy. Loading the 3 software and browser gives you all the tools you need.

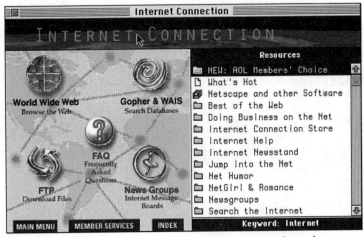

Figure 1-1 The Internet Connection menu on America Online

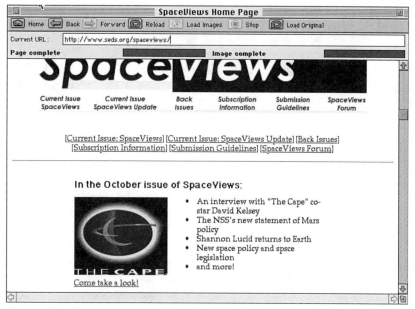

Figure 1-2 The America Online Web browser

Comments

If you have an older version of the America Online software, you will find the upgrade software in the Internet Connection section.

The faster the modem you have, the better.

COMPLEXITY
BEGINNING

1.2 How do I...
Establish a connection to the Internet?

COMPATIBILITY: ALL

Problem

Instead of using one of the online service providers, I'd like to get an account with a company that will provide me with direct Internet access. How can I get an Internet account, and what kind of connection do I need to be able to access the Web?

Technique

The number of companies that provide direct Internet access is rapidly increasing. These companies are usually called Internet service providers, or ISPs; they offer an account on their systems and access to the Internet. To take advantage of the graphics on the Web, though, you will likely need to look into special connections, such as SLIP and PPP, that can turn your computer into a temporary site on the Internet.

A shell account is the most basic type of Internet access. You dial into the Internet provider's computer and use a command-line interface (like UNIX or DOS) or a text-based menu. The provider's computer has all the software for e-mail, news, and other utilities. Your computer serves as a "dumb" terminal for the connection.

A Serial Line Internet Protocol (SLIP) or Point-to-Point Protocol (PPP) connection turns your computer into a temporary site on the Internet. You dial into the provider's computer as you would if you had a shell account, but instead of using that computer's software, you use programs on your own computer for e-mail, news, and other applications. The provider simply provides Internet access for your computer.

The Integrated Services Digital Network (ISDN) line is a new technology becoming available in many urban areas. These special phone lines provide connections that are much faster than those possible over ordinary phone lines. ISDN lines also feature two channels, so you can send a fax or talk on the phone while using your modem on the other channel. The speed can be expensive, though; it may cost several hundred dollars to install an ISDN line in your home or office.

Steps

In establishing an Internet connection, first determine the level of access you require. This is covered in step 1. Steps 2 and 3 offer tips for finding providers in your area and determining which one best suits your needs.

1. First, determine the level of Internet access you need. Since a shell account limits you to the provider's text-based applications, you can only use a text-based browser like Lynx. You can install software like The Internet Adapter (TIA) in your shell account that allows it to mimic a SLIP/PPP connection, but this is not as efficient as using a real SLIP or PPP connection.

If you plan on using a browser that displays graphics, like Netscape or Mosaic (see How-To 1.3), your best choice is a SLIP/PPP account so you can use the browser software on your own machine to explore the Web. You should get at least a 14.4K (14,400 baud) modem, and preferably a 28.8K modem, so that large files will transfer quickly to and from your computer.

If you plan on doing some heavy-duty Web surfing and need more speed than a SLIP/PPP connection, consider an ISDN line. The setup cost can be steep; however, you can save money by being able to transfer large files very quickly, saving on access charges.

2. Next, you need to identify the ISPs in your area. You can do this in a number of ways. Ask friends or colleagues who have Internet access about the providers they use or know about. If you have access to Usenet through another account (or know someone who does), locate the newsgroup `alt.internet.access.wanted` for current information on Internet providers. There are also resources on the Web if you or someone you know can access them. For example, the site `http://thelist.com/` provides a detailed list of hundreds of ISPs, broken down by area code in the U.S. and Canada and country code outside North America.

Once you're armed with a list of local ISPs, contact each of them and ask for information about the services they provide. Ask them about

- The type of Internet services they provide (shell accounts, SLIP/PPP, ISDN)

- The monthly fee for their services

- Whether they have an access number (or POP, Point of Presence) in your local calling area

- Whether they add any per-hour charges for premium services or special types of connections

- The highest modem speed they support (it should be at least 14.4K bps, and preferably 28.8K)

- The amount of disk space they provide for each user and what the surcharge is if you need additional space

Costs will vary from provider to provider and from area to area, depending on the local competition. As a rule of thumb, though, for a standard shell or SLIP/PPP connection, you will probably pay about as much per month as you would for cable TV. Of course, you are likely to find the Internet much more informative and educational than cable TV!

How It Works

Internet service providers usually buy access to fast 57.6K, T1, and T3 lines from larger network providers. ISPs then combine this network access with their own computers, along with banks of modems to handle incoming calls from customers like you, and sell you packages of Internet access based on this system.

Comments

If you live in a small city or rural area, there may not be any local ISPs in your area. In that case, you may want to investigate using one of the major online services or look into other services that provide long-distance Internet access (often through 800 numbers) for $5-10 an hour.

COMPLEXITY
INTERMEDIATE

1.3   How do I...
Find a Web browser?

COMPATIBILITY: ALL

Problem

I now have access to the Internet and the World Wide Web. Before I can start exploring, however, I need some kind of browser program to access the Web. How can I find one that best fits my needs?

Technique

There are many Web browsers now available, covering nearly all computer systems. Your system may already have a browser set up for your use; if not, there are plenty of options to choose from. Here are some of the more popular browsers:

- Netscape Navigator (see Figure 1-3) is far and away the most popular browser. Roughly 75 percent of all Web browsers now in use are Windows, Macintosh, and UNIX versions of Netscape. Netscape has taken the lead by providing its browser software at little or no cost and by developing HTML extensions that improve the graphics quality of Web pages.

- Microsoft provides Netscape with its strongest competition, Internet Explorer (see Figure 1-4). Versions of Internet Explorer for Windows and Macintosh machines are available free from the Microsoft Web site. The most recent versions of Internet Explorer have most of the same features as Netscape Navigator.

- Mosaic, the browser that started the Web explosion, is still around (see Figure 1-5), although it is no longer as popular because of the development of Netscape. New versions of Mosaic are still being developed at the National Center for Supercomputer Applications (NCSA) at the University of Illinois, which offers Macintosh, UNIX, and Windows versions of the browser at no cost. Mosaic has also been licensed to a number of companies that are creating their own enhanced versions of the browser.

- For people limited to text-only access, either through a shell account or with DOS, the best option for Web access is still Lynx, a text-based browser. While you cannot see the graphics used in Web pages with this browser, you can download these images for later viewing offline.

Figure 1-3 Netscape Navigator

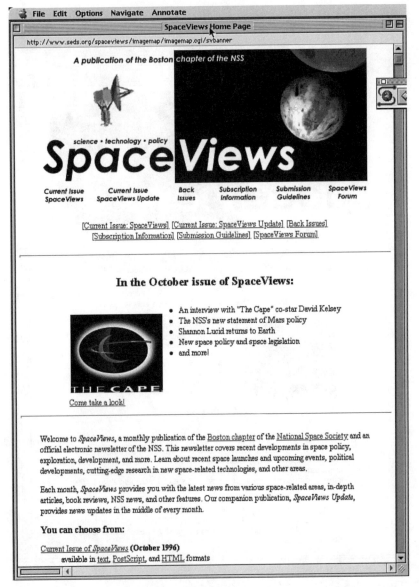

Figure 1-4 Microsoft Internet Explorer

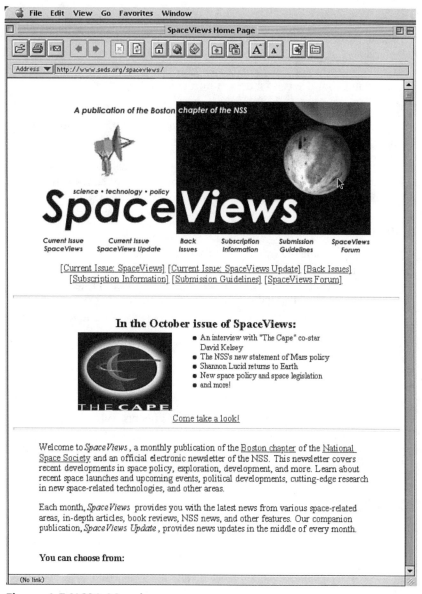

Figure 1-5 NCSA Mosaic

Steps

The type of browser you should use depends on the type of Internet access you have and what software, if any, is already configured on your system. Although Netscape is currently the most popular, there are a number of other browsers out there that may better suit your needs, so it doesn't hurt to look around.

1. If you have an account through your school or employer, there's a very good chance that you already have one or more Web browsers available. Check with your local system administrator, or ask fellow users what browsers they use.

2. If you're using a dialup shell account without any adapter software, you'll be limited to using a text-based browser like Lynx. Your ISP may already have Lynx installed; check with the provider's support staff to see if this is the case.

3. If you're accessing the Internet from a SLIP/PPP or ISDN connection, you'll need to get your own browser software. Fortunately, there are many browsers to choose from. In addition to the popular ones listed here, you can find a detailed list of browsers for most computer systems in Appendix B, WWW Resources. Once you've installed the software, you're ready to explore the Web.

How It Works

Web browsers serve as the interface with the World Wide Web. They send out requests over the Internet for particular Web pages and documents. When they receive the files, they turn the HTML files into the formatted versions displayed on your screen. Web browsers are also equipped to handle requests for information by using FTP, Gopher, and other methods.

Comments

The availability of Web browsers changes frequently as new browsers are released and current ones are upgraded. While Netscape is the current king of the browsers, a new browser may take its place at any time. This is an important point to keep in mind when you begin to design Web pages: Netscape uses a number of extensions to HTML that are not part of the standard HTML specification and are not supported by other browsers. If people stop using Netscape (or any other browser having its own extensions to HTML), the extensions in your page will no longer be usable.

COMPLEXITY
BEGINNING

1.4 How do I...
Navigate via browser features?

COMPATIBILITY: ALL

Problem

I've got my browser program running and I'm starting to explore the Web. I want to be able to easily move around from page to page and return to my home page. How can I navigate on the Web using my browser's features?

Technique

Nearly all browsers offer a set of basic navigational features that allow you to go from page to page with a single mouse-click or keypress. Browsers also allow you to go at any time to a "home page" that you can predefine.

Steps

Start up your browser. You will notice, either in the browser window or in one of the browser's menus, a number of commands like Home, Forward, and Back. These commands allow you to move back and forth among the Web sites you've visited.

1. Most browsers feature a Home button or menu option. When this option is selected, the browser returns the user to its home page, or the page that was automatically loaded when the browser started up. This is usually the home page of your Internet service provider or the home page of the company that created the browser. Many browsers do give you the option, however, of changing the default home page, usually by entering the appropriate address, or URL, of the page you desire in the appropriate field of the Preferences dialog box (or by using another similar option).

2. To go from the current page to the previous page you viewed, use the Back button or menu option on most browsers. You can use the Back option to go all the way back to the home page of the browser.

3. Similarly, you can use the Forward option to go forward in the sequence of Web pages visited (called a history), all the way up to the most recent page you loaded. (You can only use the Forward option if you previously used the Back option to back up from the last page loaded.)

4. While not strictly a navigational feature, the Reload option offered on most browsers allows you to reload a Web page you previously viewed from the server. This is important if you've been using the Back and Forward commands but want to make sure that a page you loaded some time ago is the most recent version of the page. Reload is also useful if the page updates itself periodically or did not load properly the first time you accessed it.

How It Works

Web browsers store pages in memory. When a Forward or Back button is selected, the required page loads from memory. Because the page contents may have changed since you last loaded it, the Reload command allows you to bring up the page from the server and get any additions or corrections.

Comments

If you back up several pages in your Web browser and then select a different link to follow, any pages that are listed forward of the new page that you are viewing will be removed from your history of pages. That is, you can only keep going backward and forward through your history of pages until you choose a new page somewhere in the list. When you choose a new page, all the pages forward of that new page will be removed from memory.

COMPLEXITY
BEGINNING

1.5   How do I...
Follow a link?

COMPATIBILITY: ALL

Problem

I've noticed that a number of words and phrases, and even some pictures, are highlighted on Web pages. I understand that these are called "links" and that they can take me to other places on the Web. How do I use a link to go from page to page?

Technique

Links use selected words or graphics (called anchors) to provide a gateway to another Web page, FTP site, Gopher menu, or other Internet resource. When you select the link, you are automatically taken to the new location.

Steps

1. If you're using a graphical browser like Mosaic or Netscape, links appear as words that are highlighted and/or underlined. Graphics that serve as links have highlighted borders the same color as the highlighted text. To select a link, move the mouse cursor over the highlighted text or graphic and press the mouse button. The browser will automatically follow the link.

2. If you're using a text-based browser, links usually appear as either bold or underlined text or with numbers beside them. To select a link, either enter the number of the link or use the arrow keys to move the cursor to the link, and then press the appropriate key.

How It Works

The document stores the location of the link along with the text or graphic that serves as the anchor for the link. When a user selects a particular link, the browser loads the Web page or other file associated with that link.

Comments

Many browsers let the user display the destination of the link at the bottom of the screen when the cursor passes over the link. This is a useful feature that lets you know exactly where the link goes and helps you decide whether to choose the link.

COMPLEXITY
BEGINNING

1.6 How do I...
Open a location?

COMPATIBILITY: ALL

Problem

A friend has told me about a great page on the Web. I don't know how I would find it using links, but my friend gave me something called a URL. How can I use this URL to open the page?

Technique

Another method of locating pages is to go directly to them using the page's universal resource locator (URL), which is nothing more than the address of the page. You type this URL into your browser to go directly to the page.

Steps

Before you can open a location, you need to have the URL of the location. A typical Web URL looks something like this:

```
http://www.fake.com/homepage.html
```

The URL consists of the name of the protocol (HTTP for Web pages), the name of the computer on which the file is located, and the name of the file. Chapter 8, Establishing Links, discusses URLs in greater detail.

Once you have the URL for the page, choose the Open or Open Location command on most browsers, and then enter the URL in the appropriate dialog box. The browser goes directly to that page, loading the contents into the browser for you to view.

How It Works

When a user enters a URL into the Open Location command of a browser, the browser loads the page associated with that URL. This works just as if a link to that page had been selected because links use URLs to define their destinations.

Comments

URLs can be used to describe more than just Web pages. They can be used for FTP sites, Gopher menus, Usenet newsgroups, electronic mail, and Telnet sites as well. All these types of URLs are discussed in greater detail in Chapter 8.

COMPLEXITY
BEGINNING

1.7 How do I...
Find a Web authoring tool?

COMPATIBILITY: ALL

Problem

I'd like to get started creating Web pages, but for now I'd like to avoid learning about all the markup tags needed to create an HTML document. I understand there's a way around this by using an HTML editor, or authoring tool, that will allow me to create HTML documents in much the same way as I already use a word processor. How do I find one of these programs?

Technique

HTML editors, or authoring tools, are programs that allow people to create HTML documents for their Web pages without getting into the nuts and bolts of HTML. These programs use a format similar to a word processor or page layout program that allows people to enter text and graphics onto a page. In addition, a number of the newer word processors, including WordPerfect and Microsoft Word, have HTML editing features. While you still need to know some basic HTML to use these programs, they do make it easier for beginners to create Web pages.

Steps

In selecting a Web authoring tool, you'll need to know how much memory and hard disk space you have available on your system so you can make sure the software will work.

1. Just as you did when looking for a Web browser, you may find that your Internet provider already has HTML authoring tools available for you to use. Ask your provider's support staff.

2. If your provider doesn't offer any authoring tools, you can search the Web, where you will find any number of authoring tools for Macintosh, UNIX, Windows, and other systems. A good place to start is `http://www.w3.org/hypertext/WWW/Tools/`. This page, provided by the World Wide Web Consortium, lists a number of editors, converters, and other tools to help you create HTML documents. It also offers links to more information and the locations from which you can download the software.

How It Works

A converter is a program that reads a file in one format (such as a standard word processor format) and converts it into an HTML document, with all the tags already added. An HTML editor is a program that works like a word processor and allows you to create HTML files by inserting HTML tags from menu items, instead of having to type them in.

Comments

Some editors claim to give you WYSIWYG (What You See Is What You Get). But remember, not all browsers display documents in the same way, and some browsers support HTML extensions that others do not. Thus, some browsers may be able to display documents the same way they appear to you while you're editing them, but others may not be able to do so. This is important to keep in mind when creating Web pages.

COMPLEXITY
BEGINNING

1.8 How do I...
Find a home for my Web pages?

COMPATIBILITY: ALL

Problem

I've created some pages that I'd like to put on the Web for everyone to see. However, I need to put the pages somewhere accessible to anyone on the Web. How do I find a home for these pages?

Technique

Most Internet service providers give users space to put their Web pages, sometimes for an additional charge. If your provider doesn't offer Web space, there are some other options.

Steps

When you look for a place to store your Web pages, decide beforehand how much space you need for your pages and what other special options, such as CGI scripts, you'll need to have. You can then more intelligently choose a home for your pages.

1. The first place to check for Web storage space is with your Internet service provider. ISPs often give a certain amount of Web space to their customers for little or no additional charge. Special services, such as scripts for forms in Web pages, may also be provided for an additional charge.

2. If you already have an account with your school or employer but don't have Web space, or if you are a subscriber to an online service that doesn't offer Web space to its customers, many ISPs will offer Web-only accounts at a special rate. Although you won't have a full account with the provider, you will have space for your Web pages and a method (often e-mail or FTP) to send new and updated versions of Web pages. The provider may also include other services, such as scripts, for an additional charge.

3. When looking for Web space with a provider, be sure to ask

- How much space is available per user, and how much is charged for extra space

- How easy it is to edit current pages and insert new pages (and whether this can be done online or via FTP or e-mail)

- How much "traffic" is included, and what the charges are for extra traffic (traffic referring to the number of times your pages are accessed, usually measured in megabytes, where a 10 kilobyte page that is accessed 5,000 times would come to 50 megabytes of traffic)

- What special services are available, like script creation or graphic design, and how much they charge for these services

How It Works

ISPs usually provide some space for users to place Web pages. This space might be in a special directory, or it might be linked to the home directory of the user. Providers may also allow users to include special scripts, or programs, in specific directories on the server for interactive Web pages.

Comments

While many providers offer special assistance in creating Web pages, this usually comes at a steep cost: often upwards of $25 an hour. A small investment of time learning HTML, like you're doing right now, can save you a lot of money in the long run when you create your own pages.

COMPLEXITY
BEGINNING

1.9   How do I...
Get information about the evolution of HTML?

COMPATIBILITY: ALL

Problem

Now that I'm starting to use HTML, I'd like to learn more about how HTML has developed and what its future directions are. Where can I find this information on the Web?

Technique

Information on the current state and future plans of HTML is available on the Web, particularly from the World Wide Web Consortium (W3C).

Steps

1. To get information on the current level of standard HTML, known as HTML 2, check the URL `http://www.w3.org/hypertext/WWW/MarkUp/html-spec/index.html`. This document provides links to other documents describing the features of HTML 2, which has been approved as an Internet standard and is currently supported by all browsers.

2. The next version of HTML, known as HTML 3.2 (code-named "Wilbur"), is in final review and will have been approved by the time you read this. HTML 3.2 incorporates many of the HTML extensions that had already been developed by Netscape and Microsoft. The HTML 3.2 proposal replaces the HTML 3 proposal, which was allowed to expire without being approved. HTML 3.2 information can be found on the Web at `http://www.w3.org/pub/WWW/MarkUp/Wilbur/`.

3. The next update to HTML, code-named "Cougar," is currently in the planning stages. Cougar will include more multimedia and other extensions to HTML. Look at `http://www.w3.org/pub/WWW/MarkUp/` for the latest information.

4. For a detailed description of universal resource locators, check the URL `http://www.w3.org/hypertext/WWW/Addressing/Addressing.html`. It explains all the various types of URLs and how they can be used in Web documents.

5. If you are interested in including some of the HTML extensions developed by Netscape, check the Netscape Extensions page at `http://home.netscape.com/assist/net_sites/index.html`. This page gives information about the extensions Netscape has provided for HTML, along with examples of advanced features such as tables, backgrounds, and dynamic documents.

How It Works

These links provide access to updated documents on the status of the current HTML draft (HTML 2.0), future HTML development (HTML 3.2), and about how URLs work.

Comments

The Netscape and Microsoft extensions to HTML are not currently part of either version of HTML, although some of the tags may be included in a later draft of HTML 3.x. Although a page that contains Netscape extensions can be read by other browsers, it will not be formatted in the same way as it is in Netscape.

COMPLEXITY
BEGINNING

1.10 How do I...
Design effective Web pages?

COMPATIBILITY: ALL

Problem

I want to make sure that the pages I create stand out (in a good way, of course), even though I'm just beginning to learn HTML. What are some of the basic techniques I need to know in order to create effective Web pages?

Technique

There are several fundamental aspects of designing a home page that transcend HTML. These include layout, design, and ease of use. Here are some helpful tips you can use to create any kind of Web page, from the simplest page to advanced pages with forms and graphics.

Steps

Before you begin to design your Web pages, review the following pointers. They will help you sharpen the design of your pages and avoid embarrassing mistakes.

1. First, decide what you're going to say. It sounds obvious, but there are many Web pages (not to mention other types of publications) that fail because they lack focus. The key points you want to present to the readers need to be clear. If people become confused about what you're trying to say, they probably won't come back to other pages you create and will steer others clear of them as well. (Word-of-mouth is especially powerful on the Internet.)

2. Once you've decided on the goals of your Web page, you need to plan what to include on the page. Now is a good time to start subdividing your material by content. The material can either be put on separate pages or combined on one page, depending on your mode of presentation.

3. Unless your page is going to be very short, it helps to have an introductory page briefly describing the purpose of your Web site, what information is available, and how to get to it. This serves as both an introduction and a table of contents, allowing the reader to quickly decide if the contents of the page are interesting enough to continue reading. Other pages, with more information about your topic, can be included as links on the introductory page. (See Chapter 7, Managing Document Spacing, for more information on links.)

4. If possible, make each page you design relatively short. There should be no more than one or two screens of text and graphics per page. If the page is longer, readers will have to scroll repeatedly to read the whole page, which can disrupt the flow of the document. If you have to make longer pages, include a table of contents and links to specific places within the document to make it easier for people to find information.

5. Don't overload a page with graphics. Graphics files can be very large, which means it takes much longer for a browser to load a page that includes them. The neat graphics you included on your page may take minutes for others to load. While you may have a fast network connection, other people may have relatively slow access over a modem.

6. When creating your pages, keep in mind that they will be viewed by people using a wide variety of browsers, from text-only browsers to the latest versions of Mosaic and Netscape. Thus, be sure to conform to the HTML standards when composing your document so that it is usable by the largest possible number of readers. Also, do not make your page overly reliant on graphics. Some people use text-only browsers or turn off image loading (an option provided by many browsers to enable documents to load faster). This doesn't mean you shouldn't take advantage of graphics and HTML extensions, but in the process, be careful that you don't make the document unusable to many readers.

7. Before you announce your pages to the world, carefully check them over to make sure they are free of errors and bad HTML. Look at the pages with different browsers (or ask friends who use different browsers to look at the pages) and make sure everything looks right. Putting an error-laden, poorly designed set of pages on the Web can be very embarrassing.

How It Works

The proper design of Web pages is not that different from the proper design of printed materials. You want to put your point across to your readers as succinctly as you can and with as few errors as possible.

Comments

Good style is largely in the eye of the beholder. What may appear stylish and hip to one person may appear ugly and boring to another. However, these pointers should help to improve any Web pages you design because they transcend the content of the pages and focus on the basics of presentation.

PART II
AUTHORING

CHAPTER 2
HTML BASICS

2

HTML BASICS

How do I...

The World Wide Web is an ever growing online information space filled with a myriad of commercial, educational, and entertaining materials. These materials, in the form of hypermedia documents accessed through the Internet, can be located anywhere in the world. No matter where it originates, every Web document is created using HyperText Markup Language (HTML).

HTML authoring is the process of creating and defining such documents. HTML version 3.2 is the most recent version of this powerful authoring language; unless otherwise indicated, the term HTML refers to the language as a general entity, while HTML 3.2, HTML 3, and HTML 2 refer to specific versions of the language. This chapter begins to explore how you can use HTML to publish hypermedia documents on the World Wide Web.

HTML elements are used to define document structure and format. An HTML element is the inclusive region defined by either a single tag or a pair of tags. (Tags are described more completely in How-To 2.5.) A tag is a string in the language surrounded by a less than (<) and a greater than (>) sign. An opening tag is any tag in which the string does not begin with a slash (/); also, with these you may see a list of allowable attribute/value pairs within an opening tag. An ending or closing tag is a string that does begin with a slash (/). Appendix A, HTML Quick Reference, provides a quick reference to those elements supported by HTML 3.2.

The material in this chapter covers the recognition and creation of simple HTML documents. The detailed usage of individual editors and converters is beyond the scope of this book, although several How-To's provide a brief introduction to them. You are also led through the processes for developing and viewing a simple home page.

The topics covered in this chapter introduce the essential basics of HTML authoring. Later chapters will provide you with insights and examples. The information in this chapter will jump-start you into the publication of your own HTML documents.

2.1   Recognize an HTML Document

You can present information in a variety of forms: GIF images, WAV sound, or PostScript text. HTML documents format textual information with embedded markup tags that provide style and structure information. In this How-To, you will learn the structure of HTML documents and how to identify a document as an HTML document.

2.2   Convert Word-Processed Documents to HTML

You have been developing documents using word processors for a long time. Some of these documents are exactly the ones that you wish to publish on the World Wide Web. Is there any easy way to transform these documents into HTML? In this How-To, you will learn how to automatically convert word-processed documents to HTML pages.

2.3   Convert Other Types of Files to HTML

You have been developing documents using a variety of text formatting languages. You have documents that you have developed in TeX and Scribe. You need to alter the markup tags to conform to HTML rather than the native formatting commands. Are there automatic tools to help with this task? In this How-To, you will learn how to convert text formatted documents to HTML pages.

2.4   Create HTML Documents with an Authoring Tool

If you want to jump straight into authoring but have no wish to become enmeshed in the details of HTML formatting, then this How-To may be your answer. It answers the question, "Is there a way to generate an HTML document without having to manually insert the formatting tags?" In this How-To, you will learn how to find and use HTML authorware.

2.5   Insert an HTML Element

Markup tags are the glue holding HTML documents together. These tags determine the various elements that are contained within your document. To a large extent, these elements define how the information in your document is treated and rendered. In this How-To, you will learn the process for placing this structural and formatting information into your HTML document.

2.6   Build a Simple HTML Document

HTML documents are the basis upon which the World Wide Web is built. Any attempt to author hypermedia objects for the World Wide Web will require the development of a suitable HTML document. This How-To provides step-by-step instructions for developing a simple HTML document. This simple example can serve not only as your first HTML document but also as your guide for developing well-structured HTML documents. In this How-To, you will learn how to build your first HTML page.

2.7   Include a Comment

Comments provide a mechanism for documenting the reasons you have developed a document in the way that you have. You don't want this information presented to the viewer, but it should be available to those interested in the design and development process. In this How-To, you will learn how to format comments in HTML.

2.8   Add Body Text

The body is the meat of an HTML document. The body element represents the information content of a document. In this How-To, you will learn how to author the body of HTML pages.

2.9   Set the Background Color of My Web Page

Graphical browsers such as Navigator and Internet Explorer use a default background color when displaying Web pages. HTML allows you to pick a more appropriate color. In this How-To, you will learn how to specify a Web page's background color.

2.10 Set the Color of the Text in My Web Page

HTML allows you to override a browser's default color for displaying text. In this How-To, you will learn how to indicate your choice of text color.

2.11 Set the Colors for the Hypertext Links in My Web Page

Browsers usually display the links from your Web page to other pages in a different color from the surrounding text. HTML allows you to specify the particular color for browsers to use. You can use aspects of this capability to have links that your viewer has already visited seem to either blend into the surrounding text or completely vanish from the page. In this How-To, you will learn how to select the colors that a browser should use to display the links in your Web page.

2.12 Use an Image as the Background for My Web Page

Going beyond changing the background color of a Web page, you can select an image for browsers to use as wallpaper forming the background for your Web page. Just as in applying real wallpaper to a room, the browser paints the background of your Web page using as many copies of the specified image as necessary to provide complete coverage. In this How-To, you will learn how to modify your Web page to include a background image.

2.13 Insert Special Characters into a Document

A variety of symbols beyond the standard alphanumeric characters may be required in your HTML documents. In this How-To, you will learn how to include such characters so that they appear correctly in a viewing environment such as Mosaic or Netscape.

2.14 Create a Home Page

You have created a few simple pages; now you are ready to create a page of your own where people can find information about you. This How-To walks you through the creation of a simple home page that can be expanded as your skill in HTML increases. In this How-To, you will learn how to create a basic home page.

2.15 View My Home Page

You have created an HTML document, but you have no idea what it will look like in Netscape or some other browser application. You need to view the documents that you create to determine how they will appear when viewed, not only in your current browser, but also in other browsers. In this How-To, you will learn how to view and test an HTML page.

2.1   How do I...
Recognize an HTML document?

COMPATIBILITY: HTML

Problem

What is an HTML document? How do I create one? How can I tell that a document has been formatted using HTML? What are the telltale signs?

Technique

Formatted textual information can be stored in a variety of ways:

- Word-processed documents
- PostScript documents
- HTML documents
- DVI documents

HTML documents serve as the basis for information published on the World Wide Web.

To determine whether a text file is an HTML document, you can check its document structure and look for the presence of HTML elements. These are the characteristics that identify an HTML document.

First, attempt to display the document using an HTML browser. If the text file is displayed properly within a browser's viewing window, then most likely the file is an HTML document.

Follow this by looking at the document with a text editor. Examine the file for HTML tags. A tag is a string in the language surrounded by a less than (<) and a greater than (>) sign. An opening tag is any tag in which the string does not begin with a slash (/). An ending or closing tag is a string that does begin with a slash (/). The region between an opening tag and a closing tag with the same string is referred to as an element.

Steps

This procedure determines whether a document is an HTML document. If at any particular step you determine that the file in question is or is not an HTML document, you are done and need not continue with the remainder of the steps.

1. Use your favorite browser to attempt to view the document in question.
You can do this with most browsers either via a menu option or a command

line argument. For example, with Mosaic you execute an Open Local from
the File menu. With Lynx you would open the local file `/amihtm.htm` by
issuing the following command. Be sure that you have named the local file
with the `.html` (or `.htm` for PC) filename extension. This indicates to most
browsers that the local file is to be accessed as an HTML document.

```
lynx /amihtm.htm
```

If the document does not appear in the browser's display, then more than
likely the file is not an HTML document. This is not a definitive test, however, because there are several possible conditions that could potentially
cause an HTML document not to appear.

2. Open the file in question using your favorite text editor. If the document
fails to open due to an error indicating that the document is a binary document of unknown format, then you can conclude that the file is not an
HTML document. All HTML documents are ASCII text documents. If you
receive an error message indicating that the file contains lines that are too
long, you should attempt to open the file using another editor with a
greater line length limit.

3. Examine the text file in the editor window. HTML 3.2 documents should
begin with a document type tag identifying it as an HTML 3.2 document.
Documents conforming to earlier versions of HTML may begin with just an
`<HTML>` tag. Tags are used to delimit structural or formatting elements in
HTML. An opening and a closing `<HTML>` tag should surround the entire
document. You should also find opening and closing tags for `<HEAD>` and
`<BODY>` elements. An HTML document should appear as shown in the following code:

```
<!DOCTYPE HTML PUBLIC "-//W3C//DTD HTML 3.2//EN">
<HTML>
<HEAD>
......
</HEAD>
<BODY>
......
</BODY>
</HTML>
```

4. If you find these statements in your document, you are looking at an HTML
document. However, older HTML documents may not have these structural
elements. Further, the additional information in the document type tag will
vary depending on the version of HTML and the language. This document
type tag indicates HTML 3.2 with an English language flavor.

5. At this point, you are looking at either an old-style HTML document or
some other ASCII text-based document, PostScript for instance. You should
scan through the document looking for any of the HTML elements specified
in Appendix A, HTML Quick Reference. If no tags can be found, the file is
not an HTML document. If tags are present, then the file is likely an HTML

document that was developed using a loose HTML specification. For example, the following code might represent an old-style HTML document.

```
<TITLE>Old Style Document</TITLE>
. . . .
```

How It Works

As you begin authoring HTML documents, you may wish to examine other authors' HTML documents and styles. Having a knowledge of the common architecture of HTML documents will allow you to analyze and adapt existing documents to suit your goals.

The first step in the identification process is to examine the document in question with an HTML browser such as Chameleon's WebSurfer. If the document fails to display, then it is likely that the document is not in HTML. However, this is not certain. A few possible explanations for such a failure are

- A filename extension used for the file you are viewing that is inappropriate for an HTML document

- The remapping of the `.html` (or `.htm`) filename extension to indicate a type other than HTML

- An error in the HTML code of the document

Most browsers will not render a file as an HTML document, even though it is, unless the file is appropriately named. Without the suitable filename extension (usually `.html` or `.htm`), the browser may treat the document as simple plain text (or as whatever the configured default type is). If the document fails to display for this reason, make sure you add the appropriate extension to your file before trying to view it with your browser.

To correct the second situation, either remap the `.html` (or `.htm`) extension to indicate an HTML document, or rename the file with the appropriate extension. If you plan to examine a number of local files, you may wish to perform the latter operation through your browser's menus or through its configuration files.

Next, all HTML documents are text-based. In other words, you should be able to examine them with a standard text editor, such as EDIT on a PC or SimpleText on a Mac. If the document is a binary file, then, by default, it is not an HTML document.

In addition, all well-constructed HTML 3.2 documents conform to a common document structure. By examining the text of the file for architectural features, you should be able to make an initial judgment concerning a document. Figure 2-1 illustrates this common architecture.

In some cases, this architectural information may not be sufficient to make an absolute determination, particularly for documents built upon an earlier HTML standard. (See the Comments section.) In this case, you need to examine the document for HTML elements. These elements may be of any type specified in Appendix A.

Figure 2-1 Structure of
an HTML document

Comments

This procedure will work for any HTML document. Certain caveats should be kept in mind, however.

PC, UNIX, and Mac platforms use slightly different combinations of carriage returns and line feeds to designate the end of a line; therefore, if the text file you are attempting to view was developed on a platform different from the one you are currently using, strange characters may appear at the end of text lines, or the file may appear as a single long string of text. This latter situation may cause difficulties with text editors that have fixed line-length limits.

With respect to structural features, certain browsers such as Mosaic can scan and display less well-constructed HTML documents. These capabilities permit the display of HTML documents that conform to a looser standard.

Browser applications perform a two-step procedure for determining whether a file is an HTML document or some other data object. First, the browser examines the server response header sent with the data object. If a `Content-type: text/html` line is present, then the browser assumes that the document is HTML. If the browser cannot determine the object type from the server, either because the object did not come from a server (a local file) or because a server did not supply a complete response header, it examines the file's filename extension. By default, if the extension is `.html` (`.htm` for PC), the browser attempts to display the object as an HTML document. You can often configure the specific filename extensions used by a particular browser through menu options or configuration files.

Servers determine that a file is an HTML document based solely on the filename extension. For HTML, the usual filename extension is `.html` (`.htm` for PC-based servers). As is true with browsers, you can usually configure the filename extensions for a server. (See Chapter 12, Server Basics, and Chapter 13, Handling Server Security.)

COMPLEXITY
BEGINNING

2.2   How do I...
Convert word-processed documents to HTML?

COMPATIBILITY: HTML

Problem

I don't want to start authoring documents from scratch. I have already developed a whole bank of documents suitable for use on the World Wide Web using my word processor. Is there any way I can use these preexisting documents without having to re-create them using HTML?

Technique

Converters exist for a number of popular word processing packages. These converters accept word processor documents and generate appropriate HTML documents as output. This How-To provides step-by-step instructions for acquiring and applying an appropriate converter.

The process requires familiarity with the use of anonymous FTP or FTP URLs. Your first task is to identify an appropriate converter. Next, acquire the converter. Then, apply the converter to your existing documents. Finally, fine-tune your document in an HTML editing environment.

Steps

This procedure provides the necessary steps to acquire and use word processor document converters.

1. Determine the word processing application you used to develop your documents.

2. Find the converter you will need to use. The following table lists examples of some of these environments by software package and provides pointers to information concerning them. If you cannot find your particular word processor in the following table, you may wish to use a Web search application to find an applicable converter.

Table 2-1 Common word processor conversion applications

WORD PROCESSOR	CONVERTERS	AVAILABILITY
Word for Windows	rtftohtml	`ftp://ftp.cray.com/src/WWWstuff/RTF`
	rtftohtm	`ftp://oak.oakland.edu/SimTel/msdos/`
		`windows3/html1060.zip`
Internet Assistant		`http://www.microsoft.com/pages/deskapps/`
		`word/ia/support.htm`
		(also on the CD-ROM)
WordPerfect	wptohtml	`ftp://oak.oakland.edu/SimTel/msdos/`
		`wordperf/wpt60d10.zip`
	Wp2x	`http://journal.biology.carleton.ca/`
		`pub/software/`
FrameMaker	WebMaker	`http://www.cern.ch/WebMaker/miftrans`
		`ftp://ftp.alumni.caltech.edu/pub/mcbeath/`
		`web/miftran/`
	frame2html	`ftp://bang.nta.no/pub/`

3. Use anonymous FTP or an FTP URL to acquire an appropriate converter package. Uncompress, unarchive, and install the converter application as appropriate for your platform.

■ On a UNIX platform, use the **uncompress** and **tar** commands to uncompress and unarchive the converter.

■ On a PC platform, the most common compression/archival program is ZIP. Use the unzip application to uncompress and unarchive the acquired converter.

■ On a Mac platform, the common compression/archival program is StuffIt. Use the StuffIt program to uncompress and unarchive the converter.

4. Apply the converter to your word-processed documents.

5. Use the process described in How-To 2.4 to fine-tune the converted documents.

How It Works

Many preexisting word processor documents may be suitable for use in the World Wide Web environment. Therefore, converter applications have been developed to take word-processed documents and generate equivalent HTML documents from them. The first step in converting these documents is acquiring a suitable converter.

Several converters have been developed for this purpose. Table 2-1 provides references to several of them. Many commercial applications are also available.

Once the converter is installed, converting existing documents into HTML is just a matter of judiciously applying the converter application. This will lead to HTML documents that look the way they did within the word processing environment.

The final step of this procedure is to use an editing environment to fine-tune the converted document. This fine-tuning includes two parts: corrections and additions.

Corrections are sometimes necessary when the converter does not know how to deal with a particular type of formatting in the word-processed file. These corrections may be performed using any of the authoring environment methods discussed in How-To 2.4.

Additions are also likely because most word processors do not support hypertext linking. Links provide associative connections between HTML documents. These connections link a location in one document to a location within another document; HTML designates these locations using the anchor tags `<A...>...</A>`. Therefore, the addition of anchors to word-processed documents is common. (See Chapter 8, Establishing Links, for detailed information on the use of the anchor element.)

Further, you may also add logical elements (in contrast to purely physical elements) at your discretion. Word processors usually support the conversion of physical elements, such as bold and italics (see How-To's 3.1 and 3.2); however, they do not support logical HTML elements, such as strong and emphasis (see How-To 4.2). Hence, desired logical elements need to be added after document conversion.

Finally, converters currently available do not support HTML level 3.2 elements. Inclusion of such elements involves editing the converted document using the methods described in How-To 2.4.

Converters are by no means perfect; therefore, remembering to perform this final step in the procedure is important. Simply taking the results of a conversion and asking your Web site administrator to install the documents may lead to disappointing results. Check your documents thoroughly in both Web browsers such as NCSA Mosaic, Microsoft's Internet Explorer, and Netscape Navigator, and HTML editing environments (as described in How-To 2.4).

Comments

The converters mentioned in this How-To do not comprise a complete list. They do represent a sampling of converters for many popular word processors. For converting documents developed in a word processor not mentioned in Table 2-1, you may wish to use any of the available Web search pages, such as Lycos (`http://lycos.cs.cmu.edu`) or Infoseek (`http://www.infoseek.com`).

Finally, not all converters are equal. The names of some commercially available products and contact information are provided in the following table.

PRODUCT	FORMATS	CONTACT
Cyberleaf	FrameMaker, Interleaf, Word, WordPerfect	Interleaf, Inc.
FasTag	FrameMaker, Interleaf, Word, WordPerfect	Avalanche Development
TagWrite	FrameMaker, Interleaf, Word, Ventura Publisher, WordPerfect	Zandar Corp

COMPLEXITY
BEGINNING

2.3 How do I...
Convert other types of files to HTML?

COMPATIBILITY: HTML

Problem

I have developed my documents using a document formatting language. I want to use these documents on my Web site. How can I use these documents with minimal additional effort? I've already inserted my formatting information through my development language. All that I need is a way to transform that information into HTML.

Technique

Many documents have been developed through formatting languages such as PostScript, TeX, and troff. This How-To provides step-by-step instructions for acquiring and applying converters to such documents. These packages will accept documents developed in common formatting languages and generate appropriate HTML documents as output.

The process requires familiarity with the use of anonymous FTP or FTP URLs. First, identify an appropriate converter. Next, acquire the converter. Then, apply the converter to your existing documents. Finally, fine-tune your document in an HTML editing environment.

Steps

The following steps are necessary to acquire and use document converters.

1. Determine the formatting language you used to develop your documents.

2. The following table shows examples of some of the available converters, listed by document formatting language, and provides pointers to information concerning them. Find the converter that you will need to use. You may wish to use a Web search page such as Lycos (`http://lycos.cs.cmu.edu`) to find an applicable converter if you need one for a document processing language not listed in Table 2-2.

Table 2-2 Common formatting language conversion applications

FORMATTING LANGUAGE	CONVERTERS	AVAILABILITY
TeX/LaTeX/Texinfo	latex2html	`http://cbl.leeds.ac.uk/nikos/`
		`tex2html/doc/latex2html/`
		`latext2html.html`
	tex2rtf	`ftp://skye.aiai.ed.ac.uk/`
		`pub/tex2rtf`
	texi2html	`ftp://src.doc.ic.ac.uk/`
		`computing/informationsystems/`
		`www/tools/translator`
troff	ms2html	`http://cui_www.unige.ch/`
		`ftp/PUBLIC/oscar/scripts/`
	mm2html	`ftp://bells.s.ucl.ac.uk/`
		`darpa/`
PostScript	ps2html	`http://stasi.bradley.edu/`
		`ftp/pub/ps2html/`
		`ps2html-v2.html`
Scribe	Scribe2html	`ftp://gatekeeper.dec.com/pub/`
		`DEC/NSL/www/`

3. Use anonymous FTP or an FTP URL to acquire an appropriate converter package. Uncompress, unarchive, and install the converter application as appropriate for your platform.

▪ On a UNIX platform, use the **uncompress** and **tar** commands to uncompress and unarchive the desired converter.

▪ On a PC platform, the most common compression/archival program is ZIP. Use the unzip application to uncompress and unarchive the acquired converter.

▪ On a Mac platform, the common compression/archival program is StuffIt. Use the StuffIt program to uncompress and unarchive the converter.

4. Apply the converter to your formatted documents.

5. Use the process described in How-To 2.4 to fine-tune the converted documents.

How It Works

Many preexisting documents may be suitable for use in the World Wide Web environment. Therefore, applications have been developed to convert such formatted documents to equivalent HTML documents. The first step in this process is acquiring a suitable converter. Table 2-2 names and references several of them.

Most document formatting languages support a similar suite of formatting commands. The primary difference is in the syntax of the language. Once the converter has been installed, it will map documents in the source formatting language to HTML documents.

The final step of this procedure is to fine-tune the converted document using the editing facilities described in How-To 2.4. This fine-tuning includes both additions and corrections.

Most converters will not insert hypermedia links into your document. Since most document formatting languages such as PostScript and troff do not support hypertext links, links do not appear in documents of this type; consequently, direct translation of such documents will not include links. Any desired hypertext links need to be added by the author after conversion. Chapter 8, Establishing Links, provides comprehensive information on link creation.

Despite their similarities, not all document formatting languages provide the same structuring and formatting elements. You may wish to add HTML elements to enhance the converted documents. For example, HTML supports logical elements as well as purely physical ones. The markup for a bolded statement (How-To 3.1) might carry over with no problem; however, if you wish to specify emphasis elements (How-To 4.2) that will connote semantic as well as physical characteristics, you will have to add these by hand.

Corrections will sometimes be necessary when the converter does not know how to deal with a particular type of formatting element in the source document. The converter may generate either no element or an erroneous element in the HTML document. In either case, the document needs correction to maintain the desired formatting.

Comments

The list of converters mentioned in this How-To is not necessarily comprehensive. It does contain a sampling of converters for many popular document formatting languages. For converting documents developed with a formatting language not mentioned in Table 2-2, you may wish to use any of the available Web search engines.

As with word processor conversion programs, different converters support different inputs and outputs. Furthermore, converters have varying degrees of success in maintaining formatting integrity. Prior to installing a converter on your server, you should view a document converted by it using several browsing packages to guarantee that your document looks the way you want it to look. For consistency, you may wish to compare this view to the appearance of the document in its original form.

Finally, basic elements can be automatically added to standard ASCII text files. One such program is asc2html. This application (reference `ftp://src.doc.ic.ac.uk/computing/information-systems/www/tools/translators`) will take a plain text file and generate an HTML document with a simple body containing the file's data within a `<PRE>` element. (See How-To 7.6 for information on the `<PRE>` element.) A title is inserted based on the filename, and URLs in the data are converted into hypertext links.

COMPLEXITY
BEGINNING

2.4 How do I...
Create HTML documents with an authoring tool?

COMPATIBILITY: HTML 2+

Problem

I want to start creating HTML documents, but I do not feel the need to learn every little HTML element. Some tools must exist that allow me to create a document without having to manually insert each and every tag. I see the relationship between text formatting languages such as PostScript and word processors. Why not a similar editor for HTML?

Technique

The editors used to create HTML documents tend to fall into three categories:

- Text editors—Manual insertion of HTML tags.

- Text editors with macros/pull-down menu tag selection—Creation of HTML elements through application of macros/menu items on selected areas of text.

- WYSIWYG (What You See Is What You Get) style—Tags inserted as with macro/menu-based approach; however, formatting displays as it will ultimately be rendered. (See the Comments section concerning HTML WYSIWYG limitation.)

This How-To examines these three classes of applications and gives a general means of acquiring them so you can use them to develop your documents.

Steps

The following procedures are broken down by these three categories. Each category provides the steps necessary to acquire an editor of this type for your platform, followed by a generic walk-through of the creation of a simple document.

The acquisition phase of each process is broken down by development platform. Further, the use of anonymous FTP or FTP URLs is required to retrieve most of the HTML editors described.

Text Editors

1. Determine the development platform you wish to use.

2. Find a text editor that you wish to use. The following table lists examples of typical text editors by platform.

EDITOR/ENVIRONMENT	PLATFORM(S)	AVAILABILITY
BBEdit-Lite	MAC	`ftp://ftp.std.com/pub/bbedit/`
		`freeare/bbedit-lite-30.hqx`
TeachText	MAC	Standard
EDIT	PC	Standard
Notepad	PC (Windows)	Standard
emacs	PC, UNIX	GNU archive sites
vi	PC, UNIX	PC archive sites, standard

3. Manually enter tags. Follow the procedure developed for creation of simple HTML documents defined in How-To 2.6.

Macro Packages and Editors with Pull-Down Menu Tag Selection

1. Determine the development platform you wish to use.

2. Find an editor that you wish to use. The following table lists examples of some of these editors by platform and provides pointers to information concerning them.

EDITOR/ENVIRONMENT	PLATFORM(S)	AVAILABILITY
Alpha	MAC	`ftp://cs.rice.edu/pub/Alpha`
BBEdit Ext. 1	MAC	`http://www.york.ac.uk/~ld11/`
		`BBEditTools.html`
BBEdit Ext. 2	MAC	`http://www.uji.es/bbedit-html-`
		`extensions.html`
HTML Assistant Pro	PC	Freeware version on the CD
HTMLed	PC (Windows)	`ftp://ftp.std.com/src/pc/`
		`www/htmled12.zip`
emacs HTML helper	PC, UNIX	`http://www.santafe.edu/~nelson/`
		`tools/`
tkHTML	UNIX	`http://www.infosystems.com/`
		`tkHTML/tkHTML.html`

Review the materials suggested in the this table before making your final decision.

3. Retrieve the desired editor from the location(s) suggested in the table.

4. Uncompress, unarchive, and install the software as and where necessary.

- On a UNIX platform, use the `uncompress` and `tar` commands to uncompress and unarchive the desired editor.

- On a PC platform, the most common compression/archival program is ZIP. Use the unzip application to uncompress and unarchive the desired editor.

- On a Mac platform, the common compression/archival program is StuffIt. Use the StuffIt program to uncompress and unarchive the desired editor.

You are now ready to begin.

5. Open the editor to start creating the document.

6. Type the text that is to appear in your document. Include all information content at this time.

7. Use the pull-down menus or the macros to insert appropriate HTML tags to create the desired document elements.

8. Save the document in a file with the filename extension indicating that the file content is an HTML document. This extension is usually `.html` (or `.htm`).

WYSIWYG Style

1. Determine the development platform you wish to use.

2. Find the HTML editor that you wish to use. The following table lists examples of some of these environments by platform and pointers to information concerning them.

EDITOR/ENVIRONMENT	PLATFORM(S)	AVAILABILITY
HTML Editor	MAC	`http://dragon.acadian.ca:1667/`
		`~giles/HTML_Editor/`
		`Documentation.html`
GT_HTML.DOT	PC (Word for Windows)	`http://www.gatech.edu/`
		`word_html/release.htm`
Internet Assistant	PC (Word for Windows)	`http://www.microsoft.com/`
		`pages/deskapps/word/ia/`
		`support.htm` (also on the CD)
Netscape Navigator Gold	PC, MAC, UNIX	`http://home.netscape.com`
tkWWW	UNIX	`http://tk-www.mit.edu:8001/`
		`tk-www/help/`

Review the materials suggested in the table before making your final decision.

3. Retrieve the desired HTML editor from the location(s) suggested in the table.

4. Uncompress, unarchive, and install the software as and where necessary.

■ On a UNIX platform, use the **uncompress** and **tar** commands to respectively uncompress and unarchive the converter. These applications are provided with the operating system.

■ On a PC platform, the most common compression/archival program is ZIP. Use the unzip application to uncompress and unarchive the acquired converter. Several ZIP applications are available through PC FTP sites, BBSs, and users' groups.

■ On a Mac platform, the common compression/archival program is StuffIt. Use the StuffIt program to uncompress and unarchive the converter. The StuffIt program is available through a variety of Mac FTP sites, BBSs, and users' groups.

You are now ready to begin.

5. Open the HTML editor to start creating the document.

6. Use the menus and macros to format your document. Commands have an immediate impact upon the way the information looks. Insert the desired information. Select formatting and linking tags from the available pull-down menus, hotkeys, and macros.

7. Save the file with an appropriate filename extension indicating that the file is an HTML document.

How It Works

These procedures explain the three types of editing environments used in developing HTML documents. Deciding which type to use is a question of weighing priorities.

Due to its availability and familiarity, a text editor may be the easiest and quickest to use in developing documents; however, most text editors do not provide suitable support for HTML authors. This type of authoring requires the author to have a good working knowledge of HTML tags and syntax. The other two types of editing environments will require some HTML knowledge for fine-tuning, but the bulk of development and tag insertion can be handled by the environment; on the other hand, these tools are more difficult or more expensive to obtain. Figure 2-2 displays an example of a text editor editing environment.

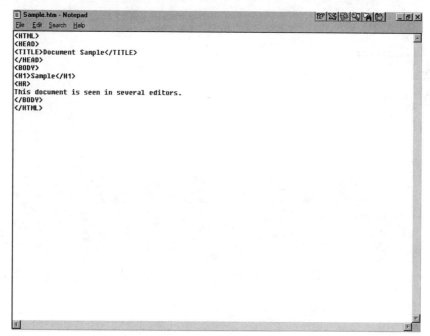

Figure 2-2 HTML document creation with a text editor

With a pull-down menu/macro type environment, you mark blocks of text and provide formatting information. The way you format each block of text varies by editor. On the surface, this type of environment might seem ideal since it requires minimal knowledge of HTML syntax, while making it easy to insert appropriate formatting tags and rendering information. However, knowledge gained in this type of environment may not be transferable. If you learn the macros and menu systems of a particular editor, that information may not apply in another authoring environment. Figure 2-3 shows an example of an environment of this type.

Finally, a WYSIWYG editor is useful because the document looks the same in development as it will when you are finished. However, unless the users accessing your documents are restricted to a particular browser application, the visible aspects of a document under development will not stand out as well. Figure 2-4 shows such an environment. The file SAMPLE.HTM on the CD contains the complete HTML source for the document appearing in Figures 2-2, 2-3, and 2-4.

For additional information about a particular editor or editing environment, refer to the documentation for the package in question. Table 2-3 lists the various applications and the location of available documentation.

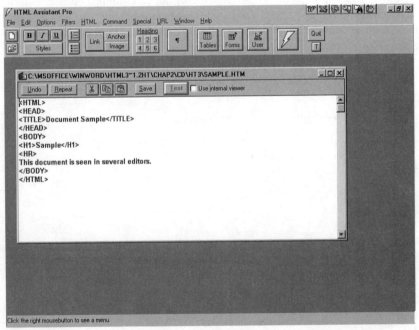

Figure 2-3 HTML document creation with a macro/menu editor

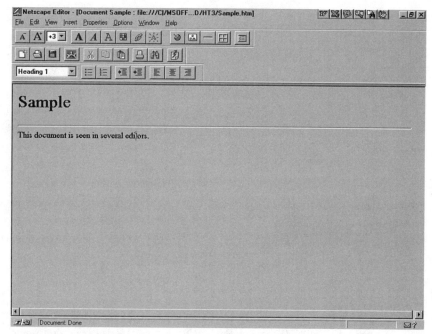

Figure 2-4 HTML document creation with a WYSIWYG editor

Table 2-3 Editor documentation

EDITING PACKAGE	PLATFORM(S)	DOCUMENTATION
Alpha	MAC	http://ww.cs.umd.edu/~keleher/
		alpha.html
BBEdit-Lite	MAC	ftp://ftp.std.com/pub/bbedit/
		freeware/bbedit-lite-30.hqx
BBEdit Ext. 1	MAC	http://www.york.ac.uk/~ld11/
		BBEditTools.html
BBEdit Ext. 2	MAC	http://www.uji.es/bbedit-html-
		extensions.html
HTML Editor	MAC	http://dragon.acadian.ca:1667/
		~giles/HTML_Editor/
		Documentation.html
GT_HTML.DOT	PC (Word for Windows)	http://www.gatech.edu/word_html/
		release.htm

continued on next page

continued from previous page

EDITING PACKAGE	PLATFORM(S)	DOCUMENTATION
HTMLed	PC (Windows)	`http://info.cern.ch/hypertext/WWW/` `Tools/HTMLed.html`
Internet Assistant	PC (Word for Windows)	`http://www.microsoft.com/pages/` `deskapps/word/ia/support.htm`
emacs	UNIX, PC	within emacs, GNU archive sites
emacs HTML helper	UNIX, PC	`http://www.santafe.edu/~nelson/` `tools/`
vi	UNIX, PC	UNIX man pages and external references
tkHTML	UNIX	`http://www.infosystems.com/tkHTML/` `tkHTML.html`
tkWWW	UNIX	`http://tk-www.mit.edu:8001/tk-www/` `help/`

Comments

The term WYSIWYG (What You See Is What You Get) is definitely a misnomer when applied to any particular HTML editor. What you see as an author may be significantly different from what a user gets when he or she accesses your document. So any claim that an HTML editor is WYSIWYG should be viewed with caution. WYSIWYG features should not be discounted, but you should still actively test your documents in a variety of browsers to guarantee that your document design carries through to most, if not all, viewing environments.

Furthermore, even though you use a "higher level" editor to abstract the lower level HTML syntax, a general knowledge of HTML is still useful for fine-tuning documents. Many editor-generated documents could be improved through the judicious use of manual alterations made in a text editor.

Finally, many HTML 3.2 features have not been incorporated in many of the editors currently available. To include these features at this time, you must use a text editor. So while you can create a document in any of the environments, in many editors placement of level 3.2 elements is only possible if you manually insert them.

COMPLEXITY
BEGINNING

2.5 How do I...
Insert an HTML element?

COMPATIBILITY: HTML

Problem

I want to build documents that will be used and usable. How do I structure my documents? How do I specify logical grouping within the information? How can I get browsers to render my documents with the appropriate formatting?

Technique

HTML uses elements to define document formatting and structuring. Document elements are created via tags. Elements are defined by an opening tag and, if necessary, a closing tag.

An opening tag is composed of an element name followed by an appropriate series of attribute/value pairs between a less than sign (**<**) and a greater than sign (**>**). Closing tags are similar to opening tags in that they mark one end of an element; however, they differ in terms of syntax. A closing tag will consist of an element name preceded by a slash (**/**). In addition, closing tags will not contain attribute/value lists.

Tagged elements follow four basic patterns:

- Empty element

```
<TAG>
```

- Empty element with attributes

```
<TAG ATTRIBUTE1="VALUE" ATTRIBUTE2="VALUE">
```

- Element with content

```
<TAG>
Enclosed Text
</TAG>
```

- Element with content and attributes

```
<TAG ATTRIBUTE1="VALUE" ATTRIBUTE2="VALUE">
Enclosed Text
</TAG>
```

Use an editing environment to add tags. The types of editing environments and the ways to acquire them for your development platform are described in How-To 2.4. The steps that follow indicate procedures for inserting tagged elements into your HTML documents through your editing environment. The insertion procedure is the same for all HTML elements.

Steps

The way you insert tagged elements into HTML documents depends upon the editing environment used to create the document. In a strictly text-based development environment, you insert all tags manually. With other editing environments, you add the tags through macros and/or menu selections provided by the software.

Either way, the resultant HTML document will have the appropriate elements included, demarcated by the appropriate tags.

1. Open the HTML document that you wish to edit in your favorite editing environment. (See How-To 2.4 on editing environments.)

2. Locate the position where you wish to add the desired element. If the element that you wish to add does not require any enclosed information (such as a horizontal rule, as described in How-To 7.1), go to step 3. Insert the text that will be enclosed between the opening and closing tags. An example of such a textual message is included in this code:

```
This text should appear in bold.
```

3. If the desired tags cannot be inserted with macro or menu options, skip to step 5. To insert an empty element, proceed to step 4. Select the body text you wish to include in the element.

4. If the macros work through inserting opening and closing tags, follow the instructions in steps 5 and 6; however, when you are instructed to insert a tag manually, you should use the appropriate macro. Otherwise, use the appropriate macro or menu option to format the selected text as desired. So for the example text, the sentence would be highlighted, and the macro or menu option for bold would be selected. You are now ready to proceed to step 7.

5. Move your insertion point to where you wish the element to begin. Insert an opening tag at this location. The following code illustrates the insertion of an opening bold tag. (How-To 3.1 provides detailed information on the use of the bold tag.)

```
<B>This text should appear in bold.
```

To insert an empty element, just insert the opening tag and proceed to step 7.

6. Move your insertion point to the end of the enclosed text and insert a closing tag at this location. The following code illustrates the insertion of a closing bold tag.

```
<B>This text should appear in bold.</B>
```

7. Save your document and continue adding elements by returning to step 2.

How It Works

The final product of this process is an HTML document with appropriate elements added. HTML documents are based on ASCII text; therefore, you should be able to view them as simple text, independent of how they appear in your editing environment. Each element should appear as an opening and a closing tag surrounding appropriate content information.

The following examples show a variety of possible opening tags.

`<B>`

This tag simply indicates the beginning of a bold element. The content information appearing between the opening and closing tags appears as bold text when displayed by a browsing package such as Mosaic. (See How-To 3.1 for information on bold elements.)

`<HR>`

This tag indicates the placement of a horizontal rule (line). Elements such as this one that do not require a closing tag are often referred to as empty elements since no content information is necessary. (See How-To 7.1 for information on the horizontal rule element.)

`<META NAME="GENERATOR" CONTENT="Internet Assistant for Word ">`

Finally, this HTML code represents another type of empty element: the meta-information element. This element provides supportive information about the document rather than a specific indication of how the document is presented. This element does not have content information in between opening and closing tags; however, information content is represented as attribute/value pairs contained within the opening tag itself. (See How-To 2.6 for information on the `<META>` element.)

Elements that are not empty are concluded with a closing tag. So for example, to close the bolding element `<B>`, the closing tag would appear as `</B>`.

In a text-based editing environment, all HTML tags must be inserted manually. When you want to include a particular element, you enclose the desired text with appropriate opening and closing tags.

In a macro/menu-based editing environment, tags, and consequently elements, are added to HTML documents through available macros and menu options. If elements are not supported by a particular editing environment, they may be added manually, as described for purely text-based editors.

WYSIWYG editors handle tag insertion in a manner similar to that used in a macro/menu-based environment; however, the tags for the elements may not be visible. Most character-level elements will be rendered as appropriate for the element. Bold elements appear in bold, as shown in Figure 2-5, rather than between `<B>...</B>` tags.

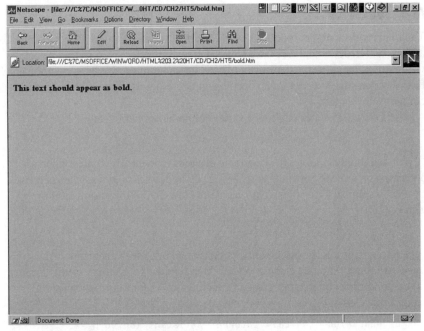

Figure 2-5 Document with bold tags inserted

The addition of various elements may also be performed automatically by your editing environment. For example, a sample document developed using Microsoft's Internet Assistant will automatically have the **<HTML>**, **<HEAD>**, **<BODY>**, and several **<META>** elements included automatically. The code for the HTML document seen in Figure 2-5 was developed in this editing environment and appears as follows. (The file BOLD.HTM on the CD also contains this HTML document.)

```
<HTML>
<HEAD>
<META NAME="GENERATOR" CONTENT="Internet Assistant for Word ">
<META NAME="BUILD" CONTENT="Feb 10 1995">
<META NAME="AUTHOR" CONTENT="">
<META NAME="CREATIM" CONTENT="1995:5:12:22:22:">
<META NAME="VERSION" CONTENT="1">
</HEAD>
<BODY>
<B>This text should appear as bold.</B>
</BODY>
</HTML>
```

NOTE

Later versions of Internet Assistant may insert the proper document type tag (e.g., `<!DOCTYPE HTML PUBLIC "-//W3C//DTD HTML 3.2//EN">`).

Comments

Most WYSIWYG and macro/menu editing environments currently support HTML level 2 elements. Level 3.2 elements and extensions usually require the use of a text editor and manual insertion. This situation will change as additional HTML editors are developed.

A reference to HTML 3.2 standard elements appears in Appendix A, HTML Quick Reference. The elements discussed in this How-To are delineated in the table that follows. The location field indicates the scope in which the element may appear.

ELEMENT	LOCATION	PURPOSE
`<HTML>...</HTML>`	file	Defines the scope of an HTML document (see How-To 2.1)
`<HEAD>...</HEAD>`	HTML	Defines the head of an HTML document (see How-To 2.1)
`<META...>`	HEAD	Supplies meta-information (see How-To 2.6)
`<TITLE>...</TITLE>`	HEAD	Defines the title of an HTML document (see How-To 2.6)
`<BODY>...</BODY>`	HTML	Defines the body of an HTML document (see How-To 2.8)
`<B>...</B>`	BODY	Defines a bolded element (see How-To 3.1)
`<HR>`	BODY	Places a horizontal rule when displayed (see How-To 7.1)

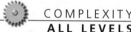

COMPLEXITY
ALL LEVELS

2.6 How do I...
Build a simple HTML document?

COMPATIBILITY: HTML 2+, INTERNET EXPLORER, NETSCAPE

Problem

I know how to browse the World Wide Web to find information. Now I want to take the next step and add information of my own. Where do I start?

Technique

The following procedure creates a simple HTML document. This document illustrates the components you'll need to include to create your own meaningful, well-structured HTML 3.2 documents.

The steps lead you through the definition of the overall HTML document and the construction of the head and body components. Several HTML elements and their use are introduced in the document development process.

Steps

The following guide you through the creation of a single HTML document titled "My First Page." This document contains the single statement "Hello World!"

You can follow these steps and alter the aforementioned strings to begin generating documents of your own.

1. Change directories to the location in which you wish to develop your HTML documents. Create a new file in your favorite text editor. Be sure to choose a filename with an extension that indicates an HTML document to your browser.

```
edit first.htm
```

2. Begin with a document type tag and an **<HTML>** opening tag. Enter the following lines in your document.

```
<!DOCTYPE HTML PUBLIC "-//W3C//DTD HTML 3.2//EN">
<HTML>
```

3. Indicate that you are beginning the **<HEAD>** element of the document by issuing a **<HEAD>** opening tag. If a **<HEAD>** element is included, it must appear within an **<HTML>** element. The following line should appear next in your document.

```
<HEAD>
```

A complete list of elements that you may include within your **<HEAD>** element is provided in the How It Works section.

4. The **<TITLE>** element is used to indicate the title of an HTML document. **<TITLE>** tags are placed within the head component of a document. The title of the document is placed between the opening and closing **<TITLE>** tags. Add this **<TITLE>** element to your document.

```
<TITLE>My First Page</TITLE>
```

Use of this element is required in all HTML 3.2 documents. This element usually will not have any visible effect within a browser's viewing window; however, the enclosed title may appear in the window title and/or the history list for the browser.

5. To end the head area, issue a **<HEAD>** closing tag.

```
</HEAD>
```

Thus, the **<HEAD>** element is nested within the **<HTML>** element.

6. At this point, the body of the document needs to be developed. A **<BODY>** opening tag indicates that this point has been reached. Enter the following line:

```
<BODY>
```

7. In this case, the body of the document is simply a text statement. More complex elements that can appear within the body component will be covered in other How-To's. For now, add the following statement to your file:

```
Hello World!
```

8. A **</BODY>** closing tag marks the end of the **<BODY>** element. Similar to the **<HEAD>** element, the **<BODY>** element is also completely nested within the **<HTML>** element. To end the **<BODY>** element, issue the closing tag in your document.

```
</BODY>
```

9. Finally, terminate the **<HTML>** element with an **</HTML>** closing tag. Add this to your document to complete your first HTML document.

```
</HTML>
```

10. Save the file. Remember to use the **.html** or **.htm** filename extension to indicate an HTML document.

How It Works

An HTML document consists of nested elements. An element is a document component enclosed between opening and closing tags. (Closing tags are not required for all elements.) The first tag indicates the type, version, and language of the particular document using a document type tag (e.g., **<!DOCTYPE HTML PUBLIC "-//W3C//DTD HTML 3.2//EN">**). The outermost element is an **<HTML>** element, beginning with an **<HTML>** opening tag and ending with an **</HTML>** closing tag. The remainder of the document is nested within this element.

The two primary subcomponents nested within the **<HTML>** element are a **<HEAD>** and a **<BODY>** element. Both of these elements appear within an **<HTML>** element, but neither appears nested within the other.

The **<HEAD>** element of a document contains meta-information about the information contained in the **<BODY>** element. This meta-information usually does not have a direct visible effect within a browser's viewing window, but the browser does have access to this meta-information. The following elements may appear within the scope of a **<HEAD>** element:

<BASE>
How-To 8.3 describes the use of this element in detail.

<ISINDEX>
How-To 14.5 details the use of this element.

<LINK>
How-To 8.4 fully describes the usage of this element.

■ **<META...>**
This element is used to specify additional meta-information not supported by another **<HEAD>** element or to specify additional information that should be sent by a server as part of a response header when the document is generated. (See Appendix G, The Hypertext Transfer Protocol (HTTP)). Netscape's **Client Pull** (See How-To 15.9) is one example using this element:

ATTRIBUTE	VALUE
CONTENT	Data associated with the name or http-equiv
HTTP-EQUIV	HTTP response header field to generate with the value specified in the content
NAME	Name of the meta-information in content

■ **<NEXTID...>** (an HTML 3 element not maintained in HTML 3.2)
This element contains a single attribute/value pair within the tag. The **N** attribute takes a value of the form **z123** where **z** indicates an alphabetic character and **123** represents a three-digit number. Several HTML editing environments use this element to generate unique identifiers. You should not use this element when manually creating HTML documents.

■ **<RANGE...>** (an HTML 3 element not maintained in HTML 3.2)
This element allows you to define and name regions within the body of the document. This element uses several attribute/value pairs. These pairs are specified in the following table:

ATTRIBUTE	VALUE
CLASS	Class of the region being defined
FROM	Name of the location within the body marking the beginning of the region
ID	Name that you wish associated with the defined region
UNTIL	Name of the location within the body marking the end of the region

■ **<STYLE...>...</STYLE>**
This element allows you to specify additional style and format information associated with both particular elements in the document as well as the document as a whole. The desired style information is enclosed between the tags. The actual specification of style elements is still under development. Chapter 16, Cascading Style Sheets, provides additional information on the use of the cascading style sheet type as supported in Microsoft's Internet Explorer. The **<TYPE>** attribute of this element specifies the format of the style information provided. For example, the following style element specifies in **text/css** notation that the left margin for the **<BODY>** element is 1 inch.

```
<STYLE TYPE="text/css">
                                BODY { margin-left: 1in }
</STYLE>
```

■ **<TITLE>...</TITLE>**
This is a required element in HTML 3.2. You should use this element to specify the title of the document defined in the **<BODY>** element.

How-To 2.8 describes the creation of the **<BODY>** element in greater detail.

■ Creating an HTML document is thus a process of nesting appropriate elements. The architecture of the sample HTML document (also on the CD in the FIRST.HTM file) is seen in Figure 2-6. Extending this, it can be seen that complex documents require deep levels of nesting. This is the code:

```
<!DOCTYPE HTML PUBLIC "-//W3C//DTD HTML 3.2//EN">
<HTML>
<HEAD>
<TITLE>My First Page</TITLE>
</HEAD>
<BODY>
Hello World!
</BODY>
</HTML>
```

■ The resultant rendering of this document appears in Figure 2-7. For the Mosaic browser, the **<TITLE>** element generates a document title that appears in the Title area of the user interface. The body appears as normal text in the display area.

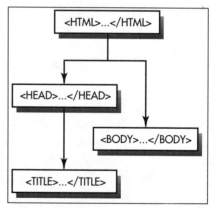

Figure 2-6 Architecture of a simple HTML document

Figure 2-7 Rendering of sample HTML document

Comments

A reference to the tags specified in the HTML 3 standard appears in Appendix A, HTML Quick Reference. The table that follows shows the elements discussed in this How-To.

ELEMENT	LOCATION	PURPOSE
`<HTML>...</HTML>`	file	Defines the scope of an HTML document (see How-To 2.1)
`<HEAD>...</HEAD>`	HTML	Defines the head of an HTML document (see How-To 2.1)
`<META...>`	HEAD	Includes other meta-information about the document
`<NEXTID...>`	HEAD	Used by HTML editors to generate unique ids
`<RANGE...>`	HEAD	Names a region within the document body
`<STYLE...>...</STYLE>`	HEAD	Specifies style information for use in the document
`<TITLE>...</TITLE>`	HEAD	Defines the title of an HTML document
`<BODY>...</BODY>`	HTML	Defines the body of an HTML document (see How-To 2.8)

When authoring HTML documents, remember that the way the final document appears will depend on the browser application. Each application will process HTML elements in its own way. For example, the Lynx browser renders the sample document slightly differently than Mosaic, as shown in Figure 2-8.

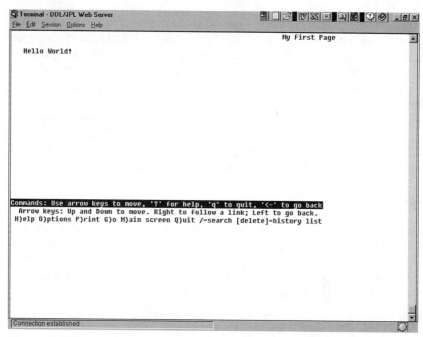

Figure 2-8 Rendering of sample HTML document in Lynx

Notice that, even for this very simple document, significant differences exist in the rendering. You need to keep this fact in mind while authoring, since your documents could potentially be viewed by any browser application. Thus, authoring to maximize appearance quality in a particular browser may result in poor appearance in other applications. With this in mind, you may wish to select a set of common browser applications, such as Mosaic and Netscape, and attempt to maximize appearance quality in the common browsers, while providing at least a minimal usability with other browsers.

COMPLEXITY
BEGINNING

2.7 How do I...
Include a comment?

COMPATIBILITY: HTML

Problem

I want information about my documents to be available to me or to future authors. I wish this information to be included in my HTML document, but I don't want it displayed to every casual viewer of the document.

Technique

HTML allows authors to include comments that reside in the document yet do not appear when the document is rendered. The process involves the use of a construct similar to an opening tag. A comment can be viewed as a very specific type of logical element that is just not visible to the common user.

The following procedure takes you through the process of creating comments within your HTML documents. Comments have two primary uses. First, they serve as a means for documenting design decisions you make while creating a document. Comments of this type become quite useful in the future for maintenance and modification. Second, certain applications will use "comments" to include additional application-specific information within an HTML document.

Steps

Comment element insertion is similar in many respects to the insertion of other logical elements. The following process steps you through the insertion of comment elements using a typical editing environment that does not support comment inclusion via a macro or menu mechanism. If yours does, you should refer to the documentation for your particular editing environment.

1. Open the HTML document you wish to edit in your favorite editing environment. (See How-To 2.4 on editing environments.)

2. Locate the position where you wish to add your comment element.

3. Move your insertion point to this location.

4. Begin the comment tag by typing <.

```
<
```

5. The code for a comment continues with an exclamation point immediately following the < sign. The code for your comment should now appear as follows:

```
<!
```

6. The exclamation point is followed by two dashes. Insert these two dashes into your HTML document. No spaces should be placed between any of these characters.

```
<!--
```

7. Type the remainder of your comment. Do not include a > sign within the body of your comment since this would be interpreted as the termination of your comment.

```
<!-- THIS IS A SAMPLE COMMENT
```

8. Your comment will be ended by a greater than sign preceded by two dashes. Spaces may appear between these two dashes and the closing **>**.

```
<!-- THIS IS A SAMPLE COMMENT -->
```

9. The comment has now been added to your document. You are now ready to save your HTML document and/or continue developing the document. If you wish to add further comments to this document, return to step 2 and proceed as before.

> **NOTE**
>
> Comments cannot be nested. Also, comments can span multiple lines, although it is not recommended in practice due to lack of support in many browsers. Here is an example of a multiline comment.

```
<!--

            This is a multi-line comment. By definition it is valid
     HTML 3.2; however, in practice, many viewers will misinterpret
                                                                  it.
-->
```

How It Works

The addition of comments to documents that you are developing is generally considered a good practice. For simple, self-explanatory documents, comments may not be necessary but for more complex documents, comments are not only desirable, but necessary.

HTML provides for comments by specifying an appropriate construct for their inclusion. Comments appear similar to standard HTML tags. In this way, applications scanning HTML documents can easily identify comments and treat them appropriately.

Comments are similar in structure to HTML opening tags. (For additional information on opening tags, see How-To 2.5.) The comment is enclosed in **<** and **>** signs. The first character after the less than sign is an exclamation point (**!**). Two dashes immediately follow the exclamation point. This string indicates the beginning of a comment.

A comment is terminated by two dashes followed by the greater than sign. Spaces may appear between the dashes and the terminating **>**. You may place the text of your comment within these stated bounds. Here are some example comments and explanations.

```
<!-- This is a sample of a valid comment. -- >
```

This is a standard comment style. You should note that the space after the final pair of dashes does not alter the comment status.

```
<!--

            This is a multiline comment. By definition it is valid
       HTML 3; however, in practice, many viewers will misinterpret
                                                                 it.

-->
```

The preceding example HTML segment represents a multiline comment. Many viewers do not handle this type of comment appropriately. A good practice would be to use the following HTML segment.

```
<!-- This is a multiline comment. By definition it is valid -->
<!-- HTML 3.2; however, in practice, many viewers will misinterpret -->
<!-- it. -->
```

This version will work with any viewer that supports comments, while the first one may fail with some browsing programs.

```
<!-- Commented HTML tags are often <B>misinterpreted</B> -->
```

Finally, you should not attempt using comment syntax to surround existing HTML elements. The preceding example code will be misinterpreted by most browser applications and yield undesirable effects. A better approach to making the desired text a comment appears in the following HTML segment.

```
<!-- Commented HTML tags are often --><!-- B --><!-- misinterpreted --><!--
/B-->
```

This comment will be handled appropriately. To comment existing HTML tags, you must carefully examine the code being commented in each case.

Figure 2-9 shows how the comments that appear in the following HTML code might be rendered; the COMMENT.HTM file on the CD also contains this document. Note that this browsing and editing environment handles the multiline comment. However, it interprets that "commented" tag for a bold element as the termination of the comment.

```
<!DOCTYPE HTML PUBLIC "-//W3C//DTD HTML 3.2//EN">
<HTML>
<HEAD>
<TITLE>Comments, Comments, and More Comments</TITLE>
</HEAD>
<BODY>
<!-- This is a sample of a valid comment. -- >
<!--

            This is a multiline comment. By definition it is valid
       HTML 3; however, in practice, many viewers will misinterpret
                                                                 it.

-->
<!-- Commented HTML tags are often <B>misinterpreted</B> -->
</BODY>
</HTML>
```

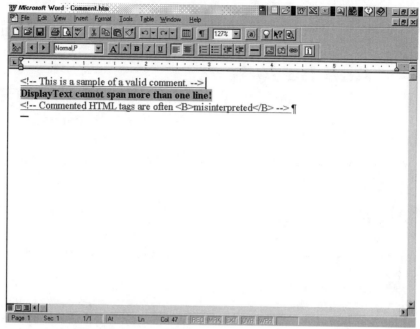

Figure 2-9 Appearance of comments document in a browser without multiline comment support

Comments

Comments are not treated equally by various application programs. Some browsers ignore comments completely. Others treat them as potential directives or even as document content, depending on how the comment was entered. Some browsers may have a particularly difficult time with multiline comments.

Several applications use specially tailored comments for application-specific tasks. NCSA server side includes (discussed in How-To 13.4) are an example of one such usage. Another example is the internal tracking of documents by Microsoft's Internet Assistant. This application automatically inserts specially tailored comments to track documents created within its environment.

A reference to HTML 3.2 standard elements appears in Appendix A, HTML Quick Reference. The elements discussed in this How-To are delineated in the table that follows. The location field indicates the scope in which the element may appear.

ELEMENT	LOCATION	PURPOSE
`<HTML>...</HTML>`	file	Defines the scope of an HTML document (see How-To 2.1)
`<!--...-->`	HTML	Represents an HTML comment element (see How-To 2.7)
`<HEAD>...</HEAD>`	HTML	Defines the head of an HTML document (see How-To 2.1)
`<TITLE>...</TITLE>`	HEAD	Defines the title of an HTML document (see How-To 2.6)
`<BODY>...</BODY>`	HTML	Defines the body of an HTML document (see How-To 2.8)
`<B>...</B>`	BODY	Represents a bolded element (see How-To 3.1)

2.8 How do I...
Add body text?

COMPATIBILITY: HTML 2+, INTERNET EXPLORER, NETSCAPE

Problem

I want to add content to my HTML document. Where do I put this information? What limitations are there on the information I can add?

Technique

The **<BODY>** element represents the information content of an HTML document. This element defines the portion of your document that includes information that will be rendered in a browser's display area.

Such content can be composed of any valid nested elements, plus any pure text you wish to include. This following procedure provides a step-by-step description for creating the meat of your HTML document.

Steps

Here are the basic tasks involved in beginning development of HTML document information content. This procedure assumes that you are using a simple text-based editor to author your HTML document.If that is not the case, you can tailor the procedure by ignoring steps that are handled implicitly by your environment. For example, if your environment automatically creates the **<BODY>** element, you can skip the step involving insertion of the **<BODY>** tag. You will need to reference the documentation for your particular editing environment to make such judgments.

1. Open the HTML document you wish to edit in your favorite editing environment. (See How-To 2.4 on editing environments.)

2. Locate the position where you wish to begin adding content. This location will vary depending upon your editing environment. In a text editor, this location is inside the scope of the **<HTML>** element and after the **<HEAD>** element.

3. Move your insertion point to this location.

4. If your document already contains a **<BODY>** element, proceed to step 5. Begin the content portion by inserting a **<BODY>** opening tag. You will begin your comment with the following code.

```
<BODY>
```

This opening tag may have several attribute/value pairs associated with it. These pairs are described in the How It Works section.

5. You are now ready to write the body of your HTML document. Enter any desired text and legal elements in the locations desired within the **<BODY>** element. Make any necessary corrections or additions. In Figure 2-10, the highlighted information represents the content added at this step in a text editor (Notepad). If you are creating this **<BODY>** element for the first time in this document, proceed with step 6; otherwise, continue with step 7.

6. End the body components of your HTML document with a **<BODY>** closing tag. This will end your **<BODY>** element.

`</BODY>`

> **NOTE**
>
> Keep in mind while editing that carriage returns in an HTML document do not necessarily imply a carriage return in the rendered document. Spaces and carriage returns in the text of the <BODY> element are largely ignored when displayed by browsers. Therefore, if spaces or carriage returns are desired, you will need to use appropriate HTML elements to force them. (See Chapter 7, Managing Document Spacing.)

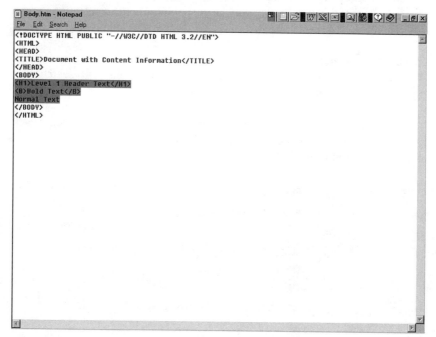

Figure 2-10 Content information example

7. You have now successfully added the **<BODY>** element of your HTML document. Save your document.

How It Works

The HTML **<BODY>** element represents the information content of your document. When you add or modify content, you alter this element.

A **<BODY>** opening tag may contain a list of attribute/value pairs associated with the **<BODY>** element. The following list describes the valid attributes and their potential values.

■ **ID=*"string"***

The **ID** attribute associates an identifier with the **<BODY>** element. Style effects and hypertext links may use this value for addressing purposes. The value must be unique within the scope of the HTML document. HTML 3.2 does not include this attribute, but use of HTML style sheets (as described in Chapter 16, Cascading Style Sheets) may require its presence.

■ **LANG=*"aa.bb"*** (HTML 3, not maintained in HTML 3.2)

The **LANG** attribute defines the language standard used within the context of the **<BODY>** element. The value is composed of two period-separated components: the two-letter abbreviation for the language and the two-letter abbreviation for the country variation. For example, **LANG="en.uk"** would indicate that the **<BODY>** element content should use the conventions associated with the English language as used in the United Kingdom.

■ **CLASS=*"string"***

This attribute associates a class name with the **<BODY>** element. Searches and styles may make use of this class information.

HTML 3.2 provides several additional attributes for specifying a Web page's background, text color, and link colors. Separate How-To's address these attributes, as outlined in the following table.

ATTRIBUTE	FEATURE	HOW-TO
BGCOLOR	Page's background color	2.9
TEXT	Page's text color	2.10
LINK	Color of link text	2.11
ALINK	Color of text for activated link	2.11
VLINK	Color of text for previously visited links	2.11
BACKGROUND	Image to wallpaper a page's background	2.12

A **\<BODY\>** element can contain any desired textual information, as well as any element allowed within the scope of a **\<BODY\>** element. When you add text and elements to HTML documents, you are assumed to be in fill mode. The effect of this is that all text and many elements you enter will appear contiguously in the rendered document. Some nested elements cause a carriage return in the rendered document, while others do not. Issues of spacing in document presentation are covered more deeply in Chapter 7, Managing Document Spacing.

Each HTML document can have at most one **\<BODY\>** element. If all the information can be contained within a document's **\<HEAD\>** element, then the **\<BODY\>** component is not required. For example, Figure 2-11 shows a document containing several nested elements as well as a single line of straight text. (See How-To's 4.1 and 3.1 for information on the heading **\<H1\>** and bold **\<B\>** elements, respectively.)

Here is the full HTML code for this document, which appears on the CD in the BODY.HTM file.

```
<!DOCTYPE HTML PUBLIC "-//W3C//DTD HTML 3.2//EN">
<HTML>
<HEAD>
<TITLE>Document with Content Information</TITLE>
</HEAD>
<BODY>
<H1>Level 1 Header Text</H1>
<B>Bold Text</B>
Normal Text
</BODY>
</HTML>
```

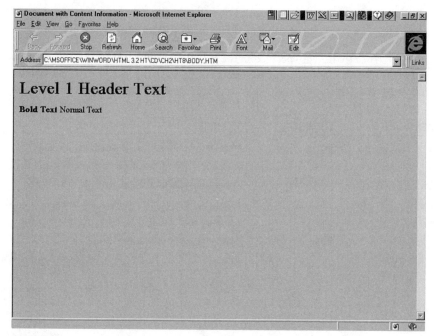

Figure 2-11 Document with content information

Compare this with Figure 2-11. Note that the carriage returns in the HTML code and the rendered document do not match. This is due to the way the browser interprets the level 1 heading element and the bold element. According to the viewer in Figure 2-11, a heading 1 element implies a carriage return in the rendered output, while a bold element does not.

Comments

This section introduces the basics of creating information content. Methods of including links, images, tables, lists, and other elements are clearly described in other portions of this book. The following table provides a quick reference to these locations.

INFORMATION TYPE	REFERENCE
Aligned text	Chapter 7, Managing Document Spacing
Physical character effects	Chapter 3, Adding HTML Physical Character Effects
Logical character effects	Chapter 4, Adding HTML Logical Character Effects
Comments	How-To 2.7
Images	Chapter 9, Using Images in Your Documents
Links	Chapter 8, Establishing Links
Lists	Chapter 6, Lists
Math symbols and effects	How-To's 20.11 and 20.12
Multimedia objects	Chapter 10, Adding Externally Linked Multimedia Objects
Special characters	How-To 2.13
Tables	Chapter 5, Tables

A reference to the tags specified in the HTML 3.2 standard appears in Appendix A, HTML Quick Reference. The elements discussed in this How-To are listed in the following table. The location field indicates the scope in which the element may appear.

ELEMENT	LOCATION	PURPOSE
<HTML>...</HTML>	file	Defines the scope of an HTML document (see How-To 2.1)
<!--...-->	HTML	Represents an HTML comment element (see How-To 2.7)
<HEAD>...</HEAD>	HTML	Defines the head of an HTML document (see How-To 2.1)
<TITLE>...</TITLE>	HEAD	Defines the title of an HTML document (see How-To 2.6)
<BODY>...</BODY>	HTML	Defines the body of an HTML document (see How-To 2.1)
<B>...</B>	BODY	Represents a bolded element (see How-To 3.1)
<H1>...</H1>		Represents the <BODY> level 1 heading element (see How-To 4.1)

COMPLEXITY
BEGINNING

2.9   How do I...
Set the background color of my Web page?

COMPATIBILITY: HTML 2+, INTERNET EXPLORER, NETSCAPE

Problem

I am tired of looking at the solid light gray background of my home page. I want to add some life by changing its background color.

Technique

You can use two methods to alter the background color of your Web page. The first method involves the use of HTML style sheets; How-To 16.4 details this method. The more common method requires the addition of an attribute to the opening tag of a page's body element. HTML 3.2 provides the `BGCOLOR` attribute contained within the `<BODY>` opening tag for this purpose.

The value that you assign to this attribute instructs browsers to use a particular color as the background for your page. The following procedure walks you through the process of altering the background color of your Web page.

Steps

These steps guide you through the process of setting the background color of a Web page using the `BGCOLOR` attribute of the body element.

1. Open your Web page in a text editor. (A variety of HTML editors provide additional support for specifying background colors; see the Comments section for an example of this.)

2. Locate the opening tag of the body element for your page. This tag should appear as follows:

```
<BODY>
```

Your body element may include other attributes; if this is the case, simply add the new ones according to the next steps.

3. Move your insertion point after the `Y` in the tag. Enter the attribute name `BGCOLOR` and the equal sign. The tag displays how your body tag should look at this point:

```
<BODY BGCOLOR=>
```

4. After the equal sign, indicate the color that you wish to use for the background of your Web page. You should place quotation marks around your color selection. Table 2-4 provides a list of commonly supported colors.

Table 2-4 HTML 3.2's sixteen defined colors (from the Original Windows Palette)

COLOR	HEXADECIMAL TRIPLET	COLOR	HEXADECIMAL TRIPLET
Black	#000000	Green	#008000
Silver	#C0C0C0	Lime	#00FF00
Gray	#808080	Olive	#808000
White	#FFFFFF	Yellow	#FFFF00
Maroon	#800000	Navy	#000080
Red	#FF0000	Blue	#0000FF
Purple	#800080	Teal	#008080
Fuchsia	#FF00FF	Aqua	#00FFFF

The How It Works section explains the use of the hexadecimal triplets in this table. For example, if you wanted a yellow background color for your page, you would use the following opening tag:

```
<BODY BGCOLOR="yellow">
```

> **NOTE**
>
> HTML 3.2 allows you to select colors other than the predefined ones indicated in Table 2-4. The How It Works section explains this process. In addition, Appendix H, Color Table, provides a listing of other common colors and the appropriate values to use with the BGCOLOR attribute.

5. Save your Web page.

6. Test your Web page by loading it into a browser.

How It Works

HTML 3.2 allows authors to select a background color for Web pages. The specification of a background color attribute (**BGCOLOR**) in the body element opening tag is the most common method of accomplishing this task.

When a background color-capable browser interprets this attribute, it locates the color closest to the one requested among those colors it has available. It uses this closest match to paint the background color of the page. Commonly, browsers specify a set of predefined colors for use in Web pages, including those listed in Table 2-4.

HTML 3.2 also supports another method of specifying a color based upon the red, green, and blue (RGB) components of the desired color. Using this method, a six digit hexadecimal number represents the relative intensity of each component of the color. A two digit hexadecimal number, ranging from **00** to **FF** (**0–255** in decimal), represents the intensity level for each component color. A low value, say **00** or **01**, indicates a dark RGB component, whereas a high value, say **FE** or **FF**, indicates a very bright RGB component.

Under this encoding, the value **000000** would indicate the color black, and the value **FFFFFF** would indicate the color white. Any value in between, where the three components are the same, will produce a shade of gray.

Once you have determined the appropriate RGB value for the desired color, you include that RGB value preceded by a pound sign (**#**) as the value for the **BGCOLOR** attribute. For example, the following tag could be used to create a slightly off-white background:

```
<BODY BGCOLOR="#FDFDFD">
```

NOTE

Microsoft's Internet Explorer does not require the leading pound sign (#), but for cross-browser support, you should include it.

Microsoft's Internet Explorer supports a three digit approach, where each digit has a value between **0** and **F** (**0–15** in decimal), indicating the intensity of the particular RGB component. For example, the following tag could be used to specify a medium gray background:

```
<BODY BGCOLOR="#888">
```

NOTE

Netscape's Navigator browser does not support the three digit hexadecimal format, only the six digit one. So, for cross-browser support, you should use either named colors or six digit hexadecimal representations.

Appendix H, Color Table, provides a convenient list associating traditional color names with their respective RGB values. The CD contains sample pages using these body elements—with a yellow background (from step 4), a slightly off-white background, and a medium gray background. These examples appear in the files YELLOW.HTM, GRAY.HTM, and WHITE.HTM, respectively. An example of a page without a specified background color appears in the file NORMAL.HTM.

Comments

The final step in the procedure can be crucial. First, using a particular background color may lead to difficulties in reading your page. For example, black text may be difficult to see on top of a dark background color, or an image included on the page may not appear properly against the new background. The latter situation is particularly relevant when dealing with transparent and translucent images. (See How-To's 9.5 and 9.17.)

Second, the appearance of colors varies depending on both the hardware and the software used by the viewer of your page. When adding a background color, you need to remember that browsers use a closest match to select the color, and your color selection is thus at the mercy of this matching routine.

Finally, since HTML 3.2 allows you to alter the color of various components of your Web page, you need to actually view your page to ensure that your entire color scheme creates a page that is not only visually appealing, but also legible.

Many HTML editors provide additional support for selecting background colors. For example, HTML Assistant Pro 3 for Windows (available on the CD) allows you to choose the color by selecting from a customizable palette. Figure 2-12 shows an example of this selection process. You access this feature by selecting the Special | Background Assistant menu option.

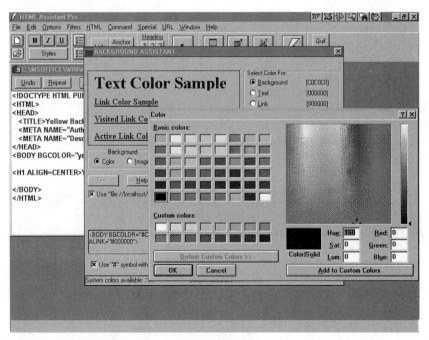

Figure 2-12 Altering a Web page's background color with HTML Assistant

COMPLEXITY
BEGINNING

2.10 How do I...
Set the color of the text in my Web page?

COMPATIBILITY: HTML 3+, INTERNET EXPLORER, NETSCAPE

Problem

Black text on a gray background looks dull on a Web page. I want to jazz up my page by changing the color of the text.

Technique

You can use several methods to alter the color of text on your Web page. The first method allows you to change the color of text in different areas of your documents; How-To 3.5 discusses this method. The next method involves the use of HTML style sheets; How-To 16.3 details this method. The last method is the easiest. This method requires the addition of an attribute to the opening tag of a page's body element. HTML 3.2 provides the **TEXT** attribute contained within the **<BODY>** opening tag for this purpose.

The value that you assign to this attribute instructs browsers to use a particular color to display the text in your page. The following procedure walks you through the process to alter the text color of your Web page.

Steps

These steps guide you through the process of setting the text color of a Web page using the **TEXT** attribute of the body element.

1. Open your Web page in a text editor. (See the Comments section for an example using an HTML editor.)

2. Locate the opening tag of the body element for your page. This tag should appear as follows:

```
<BODY>
```

Your body element may include other attributes; if this is the case, simply add the new ones described in the next steps.

3. Move your insertion point after the **Y** in the tag. Enter the attribute name **TEXT** and the equal sign. The following tag displays how your body tag should look at this point.

```
<BODY TEXT=>
```

4. After the equal sign, indicate the color that you wish to use for the text of your Web page. You should place quotation marks around your color selection. Table 2-4 in How-To 2.9 provides a list of HTML 3.2 supported, named colors; particular browsers may support additional named colors. For example, if you wanted purple text in your page, you would use the following opening tag:

```
<BODY TEXT="purple">
```

You can find a sample document using this body element on the CD located in the file PURPLE.HTM.

> **NOTE**
>
> HTML 3.2 allows you to select colors other than the predefined ones. The How It Works section explains this process; in addition, Appendix H, Color Table, provides a listing of other common colors and the appropriate values to use with the TEXT attribute.

5. Save your Web page.

6. Test your Web page by loading it into a browser.

How It Works

HTML 3.2 allows authors to select a background color for Web pages. The specification of a text color attribute (**TEXT**) in the body element opening tag is one means of accomplishing this task.

When a browser interprets this attribute, it locates the color closest to the one requested among those colors it has available. It uses this closest match to display the text of the page. Commonly, HTML 3.2 supports a set of predefined colors for use in Web pages, as indicated in Table 2-4 in How-To 2.9.

HTML 3.2 also supports another method of specifying a color based upon the red, green, and blue (RGB) components of the desired color. Using this method, a six digit hexadecimal number represents the relative intensity of each component of the color. A two digit hexadecimal number, ranging from **00** to **FF** (**0-255** in decimal), represents the intensity level for each component color. A low value, say **00** or **01**, indicates a very dark RGB component, whereas a high value, say **FE** or **FF**, indicates a very bright RGB component.

Under this encoding, the value **000000** would indicate the color black, and the value **FFFFFF** would indicate the color white. Any value in between where the three components are the same will lead to a shade of gray.

Once you have determined the appropriate RGB value for the desired color, you include the RGB value preceded by a pound sign (**#**) as the value for the **BGCOLOR** attribute. For example, the file RED.HTM on the CD contains the following tag to specify bright red text on a standard background:

```
<BODY TEXT="#FF0000">
```

> **NOTE**
>
> Microsoft's Internet Explorer does not require the leading pound sign (#); however, for cross-browser support you should include it.

Microsoft's Internet Explorer supports a three digit approach, where each digit ranges from **0–F** (**0–15** in decimal) indicating the intensity of the particular RGB component. For example, the following tag would specify white text on the standard background.

```
<BODY TEXT="#FFF">
```

Figure 2-13 shows a page using this body element to set a white text color. The source for this page appears on the CD in the WHITE.HTM file.

> **NOTE**
>
> Netscape's Navigator browser does not support the three digit hexadecimal format, only the six digit. So, for cross-browser support, you should use either named colors or six digit hexadecimal representations.

Appendix H, provides a convenient table associating traditional color names with their respective RGB values. In addition to the particular color examples, the CD provides the file NORMAL.HTM as an example of a page with standard text color.

Comments

The final step in the procedure can be crucial. First, the appearance of colors varies depending on both the hardware and the software of the viewer of your page. When selecting a text color, you need to remember that browsers use a closest match to select the color and that your color selection is at the whim of this matching routine. Second, when altering both the text color and a document background using a specific color (see How-To 2.9) or a tiled image (see How-To 2.12), you need to check that the text in your chosen color is still legible viewed against the background chosen.

The method discussed in this How-To describes the process for modifying your Web page using a text editor. Several WYSIWYG HTML editors are available that provide a more automated process for altering the color of your text. For example, with the Netscape Navigator Gold editor, you modify the color of your text by selecting a color from a customizable palette. Figure 2-14 shows an example of this selection process. You access this palette through the Properties | Document… menu option.

Figure 2-13 Using white text on a standard color background

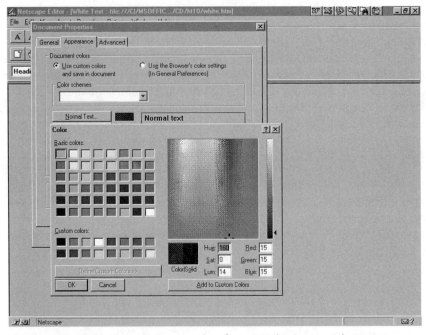

Figure 2-14 Selecting the text color for a Web page with Netscape Navigator Gold

COMPLEXITY
BEGINNING

2.11 How do I...
Set the colors for the hypertext links in my Web page?

COMPATIBILITY: HTML 3+, INTERNET EXPLORER, NETSCAPE

Problem

I've changed my text color and background color and my links no longer stand out to the viewer. How do I change the color of these links?

I want my links to fade into the remainder of the text once a reader has visited the link, or better yet, I want my links to disappear after a user has visited them.

Technique

HTML 3.2 allows you to select the color of your links, activated links, and previously visited links. The most common method of accomplishing this involves the addition of attributes to the opening tag of a page's body element. HTML 3.2 provides the `LINK`, `ALINK`, and `VLINK` attributes contained within the `<BODY>` opening tag for changing link color, activated link color, and visited link color, respectively.

The values that you assign to these attributes instruct browsers to use a particular color to display the links in your page. The next procedure walks you through the process to alter the link colors of your Web page.

Steps

These steps guide you through the process of setting the link colors of a Web page using the link color attributes of the body element.

1. Open your Web page in a text editor. (See the Comments section for an example using an HTML editor.)

2. Locate the opening tag of the body element for your page. This tag should appear as follows:

`<BODY>`

Your body element may include other attributes; if this is the case, simply add the new ones as described in the following steps.

3. Move your insertion point to after the **Y** in the tag. Enter the attribute name for the link types that you want to change and an equal sign after each. The following tag displays how your body tag should look at this point if you wanted to modify the color of all links (normal, visited, and activated).

```
<BODY LINK= ALINK= VLINK=>
```

> **NOTE**
>
> Microsoft's Internet Explorer does not support the activated link attribute (ALINK). It ignores this attribute, so feel free to set it for cross-browser support purposes.

If you only wanted to change the color of normal links and visited links, your tag should appear as

```
<BODY LINK= VLINK=>
```

4. After the equal sign, indicate the color that you wish to use for the links on your Web page. You should place quotation marks around your color selection. Table 2-4 in How-To 2.9 provides a list of HTML 3.2 supported, named colors. For example, if you wanted purple links in your page, yellow activated links, and black visited links, you would use the following opening tag:

```
<BODY LINK="purple" ALINK="yellow" VLINK="black">
```

A sample document using this **<BODY>** opening tag appears on the CD in the file PYB.HTM. If you only wanted to change the color of normal links to blue and visited links to green, your tag should appear as

```
<BODY LINK="blue" VLINK="green">
```

You can access an example document using this tag by following the link contained in the file PYB.HTM. This link triggers the access of the BG.HTM file, also on the CD.

> **NOTE**
>
> HTML 3.2 allows you to select colors other than the predefined ones. The How It Works section explains this process; in addition, Appendix H, Color Table, provides a listing of other common colors and the appropriate values to use with the link color attributes.

5. Save your Web page.

6. Test your Web page by loading it into a browser.

How It Works

HTML 3.2 allows authors to select a background color for Web pages. The specification of link color attributes (LINK, ALINK, VLINK) in the body element opening tag is the common means of accomplishing this task.

When a browser interprets these attributes, it locates the colors closest to the ones requested among those colors it has available. It uses these closest matches to display the links of the page. HTML 3.2 directly supports the use of the named colors in Table 2-4 in How-To 2.9.

HTML 3.2 also supports another method of specifying a color based upon the red, green, and blue (RGB) components of the desired color. Using this method, a six digit hexadecimal number represents the relative intensity of each component of the color. A two digit hexadecimal number, ranging from 00 to FF (0–255 in decimal), represents the intensity level for each component color. A low value, say 00 or 01, indicates a very dark RGB component, whereas a high value, say FE or FF, indicates a very bright RGB component.

Under this encoding, the value 000000 would indicate the color black and the value FFFFFF would indicate the color white. Any value in between, where the three components are the same, will lead to a shade of gray.

Once you have determined the appropriate RGB value for the desired color, you include the RGB value preceded by a pound sign (#) as the value for the BGCOLOR attribute. For example, the document red.htm, found on the CD, uses the following tag to create a bright red link:

```
<BODY LINK="#FF0000">
```

> **NOTE**
>
> Microsoft's Internet Explorer does not require the leading pound sign (#), but for cross-browser support, you should include it.

Microsoft's Internet Explorer supports a three digit approach, where each digit ranges from 0–F (0–15 in decimal), indicating the intensity of the particular RGB component. For example, the file YELLOW.HTM, included on the CD, contains the following tag to specify the use of yellow links:

```
<BODY LINK="#FF0">
```

> **NOTE**
>
> Netscape's Navigator browser does not support the three digit hexadecimal format, only the six digit. So, for cross-browser support, you should use either named colors or six digit hexadecimal representations.

Appendix H, Color Table, provides a convenient list associating traditional color names with their respective RGB values.

These features provide two useful tricks for HTML page designers with respect to previously visited links. First, by designating the visited link color attribute (**VLINK**) to the same value as the text color attribute for a Web page, links will seem to fade into the surrounding text once a readers visits the target of that link. This trick is more effective where links are not indicated in another manner, such as through underlining. In some cases, you as a Web page author can impact these additional indicators; for example, How-To 16.5 explains how you can remove the underlining of visited links using HTML style sheets. Figure 2-15 displays the use of this trick: Previously visited links simply blend into the surrounding text.

This particular example uses style sheet tricks to also remove the underlining from previously visited links. File BLEND.HTM on the CD contains the complete HTML source for this document. The body element opening tag for this document appears as

```
<BODY BGCOLOR="white" TEXT="black" LINK="green" VLINK="black">
```

This tag instructs the browser to display standard text in black, link anchor text in green, and previously visited links in black. Thus, once a viewer has followed a link, the browser displays this link in the same color as the rest of the text on all subsequent visits to this page.

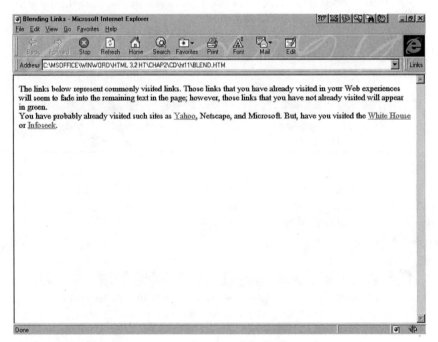

Figure 2-15 Blending previously visited links into the surrounding text

The second neat trick involving visited links allows you to make links seem to vanish once they have been visited. As with the blending of links, this trick works best when browsers do not supply additional link indicators, such as underlining and changing cursors. You make links seem to disappear once visited by selecting the same color for both visited links and the background of the page. For example, the file VANISH.HTM from the CD, pictured in Figure 2-16, uses the following body element opening tag:

```
<BODY BGCOLOR="white" TEXT="black" LINK="green" VLINK="white">
```

Unvisited links in the document appear green while previously visited links disappear into the document background color. Thus, by specifying the same color for both the **BGCOLOR** and **VLINK** attributes, previously visited links disappear in whichever documents you use this trick.

Comments

The final step in this procedure can be crucial. First, the appearance of colors varies depending on both the hardware and the software being used by the viewer of your page. When selecting link colors, you need to remember that browsers use a

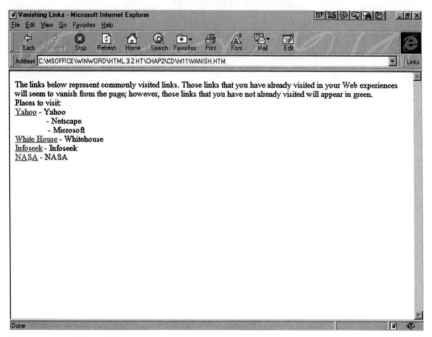

Figure 2-16 Vanishing previously visited links

closest match to select the color and that your color selection is at the whim of this matching routine. Second, when altering both link colors and a document background using a specific color (see How-To 2.9) or a tiled image (see How-To 2.12), you need to check that the links in your chosen color are still legible when viewed against your chosen background. Remember to check all three link states for appropriateness of the colors chosen.

The method discussed in this How-To describes the process for modifying your Web page using a text editor. Several HTML editors are available that provide a more automated process for altering the color of your links. For example, with HTML Assistant (available on the CD), you modify the color of your links by selecting a color from a customizable palette. Figure 2-17 shows an example of this selection process. You access this palette through the Special | Background Assistant... menu option.

This method alters the color of links throughout your document. An alternative method allows you to change link colors in different areas of your documents; How-To 16.3 discusses how you can accomplish this using HTML style sheets. In addition, How-To 16.5 shows you how to remove link underlining.

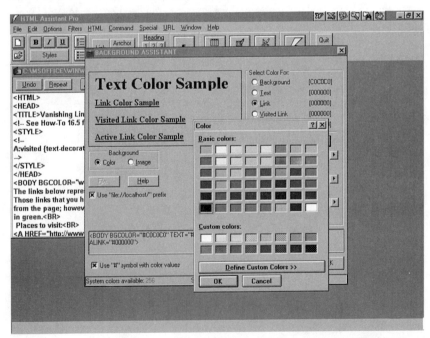

Figure 2-17 Selecting the link colors for a Web page with HTML Assistant

COMPLEXITY
BEGINNING

2.12 How do I...
Use an image as the background for my Web page?

COMPATIBILITY: HTML 3+, INTERNET EXPLORER, NETSCAPE

Problem

I want something more interesting than a simple solid color background. I want to personalize my Web page by applying some wallpaper.

Technique

HTML 3.2 supports the specification of an image that browsers should use as the background for a Web page. The browser uses as many copies of the specified image as are required to cover the width and height of the page.

First, you will need to either find or create an image to use as a background. You then set the **BACKGROUND** attribute of your document's body element opening tag to specify this image file. You identify this image with an appropriate URL reference. You can also indicate whether you want the background to scroll with your page's text or to remain fixed with respect to the motion of the text. Internet Explorer is currently the only browser that supports fixed backgrounds, referred to as watermarks.

Steps

The following steps guide you through the process of setting the background of a Web page using the **BACKGROUND** attribute of the body element.

1. Locate a background image, or create one yourself. Several Web sites provide images suitable for use as Web page backgrounds. Table 2-5 displays the names and URLs of several of these sites. Also, refer to Yahoo!'s list of background-related sites:
`http://www.yahoo.com/Computers_and_Internet/Internet/World_Wide_Web/Page_Design_and_Layout/Backgrounds/`.

Table 2-5 Background image Web sites

SITE	URL
The Background Archive	`http://www.public.iastate.edu/~haley/bgnds.html`
Ender's Realm	`http://www.ender-design.com/rg/backidx.html`

continued on next page

continued from previous page

SITE	URL
Homepage Designs	`http://www.geocities.com/WallStreet/1679/backgrounds.html`
KPT Background Archive	`http://the-tech.mit.edu/KPT/bgs.html`
My Background Farm	`http://www.missouri.edu/~c691759/Backgrounds.html`
Paul's Backgrounds	`http://funnelweb.utcc.utk.edu/~wallace/textures/`
	`textures.html`
Wallpaper Zone	`http://www.nitespots.com/wallpaper_zone/`
WebDesigns	`http://www.execpc.com/~jeffo/webdes/bckgrnd2.html`

For more information on the creation and modification of background images, see Chapter 9, Using Images in Your Documents.

2. Open your Web page in a text editor. (See the Comments section for an example using an HTML editor.)

3. Locate the opening tag of the body element for your page. This tag should appear as follows:

`<BODY>`

Your body element may include other attributes; if this is the case, simply add the new ones as described next.

4. Move your insertion point to after the Y in the tag. Enter the attribute name **BACKGROUND** and the equal sign. The following tag displays how your body tag should look at this point.

`<BODY BACKGROUND=>`

5. After the equal sign, indicate the URL of the image that you want to use for the background of your Web page. You should place quotation marks around this URL. For example, if you wanted to use the image having the URL, `http://www.mysite.edu/bg/marble.gif` as the background for your page, you would use the following opening tag:

`<BODY BACKGROUND="http://www.mysite.edu/bg/marble.gif">`

6. Decide whether or not you want the background to remain fixed with respect to the motion of your page's text when viewed with Internet Explorer. If you do want to turn on this feature, add the following attribute and value to your body element.

`<BODY BACKGROUND="http://www.mysite.edu/bg/marble.gif" BGPROPERTIES=FIXED>`

Browsers that do not support this attribute will generally ignore it.

7. Save your Web page.

8. Test your Web page by loading it into a browser.

How It Works

HTML 3.2 allows authors to select a background image for Web pages. Specifying a background image attribute (**BACKGROUND**) in the body element opening tag is one means of accomplishing this task.

When a browser interprets this attribute, it retrieves the indicated image file. It uses this image file to paint the background of the page. You will find that many images suitable for use as Web page backgrounds are freely available over the Web. Explore the sites provided in Table 2-5 and the sites listed in the Yahoo! Backgrounds category. Make sure to carefully read the instructions on each site where you download an image file: The site may require you to properly credit the creator of the image when you use it.

For example, Figure 2-18 shows the use of a background downloaded from the Ender's Realm background archive reference in Table 2-5. The body element for this page also contains a mixture of attributes described in How-To's 2.9, 2.10, and 2.11.

Here is the opening tag of the body element for this page:

```
<BODY TEXT="#FFFF00" BACKGROUND="tex6.jpg" LINK="red" VLINK="#FF0"
ALINK="silver">
```

Figure 2-18 Applying a marble wallpaper to a Web page

This particular open tag specifies that browsers should wallpaper the background of this page with the image `tex6.jpg`. In addition, the browser should display text in yellow, links in red, active links in silver, and previously visited links in yellow. The HTML source for this page appears in the file MARBLE.HTM on the CD; the file TEX6.JPG stores the background image.

An additional feature, currently supported by Microsoft Internet Explorer, allows you to keep the background fixed with respect to the motion of text when you scroll. The use of the `BGPROPERTIES` attribute with a value of `FIXED` turns on this feature. Most other browsers will simply ignore this attribute and treat the background in the standard fashion.

One neat trick with this feature allows you to choreograph your page content and background. Using this trick, you first create or retrieve an image larger than the visible portion of your page content, which does not necessarily imply a large image in terms of file size. You will want an image this large because browsers will still tile the image if the image is smaller than the visible area in the browser. You can use this method to include a standard letter head or border that will appear in all of your Web pages. Unlike a letterhead that scrolls off the screen as the viewer reads your page, the text of the page flows over the letterhead while the letterhead remains constant.

For example, Figure 2-19 displays the top of a page with a sign indicating that more information is further down. Figure 2-20 displays the same page at a point further down. You should notice that the `"more"` indicator has not moved from its position, despite the scrolling of the page's content. This page's body element opening tag appears as follows:

```
<BODY TEXT="red" BGCOLOR="#FFFFFF" LINK="fuchsia" VLINK="#FFFF00"⇐
ALINK="#FF0000" BACKGROUND="more.gif" BGPROPERTIES=FIXED>
```

The CD contains the complete HTML code for this document in the file WTR-MARK.HTM; you will also find the background image `more.gif`. The image used in this page was created using Paint Shop Pro (included on the CD). You should note that, despite the fact that the image has a height and width of 1024 pixels, the file size is only 3K bytes. The body element opening tag specifies the use of the image `more.gif` as a watermark background image. It also sets the colors for various aspects of this Web page.

Comments

The final step in this procedure can be crucial. Using background images requires you to closely examine the readability of the page's content. You may need to modify the color of your text and links (see How-To's 2.10 and 2.11) so that they are readable against your chosen background image. In addition, if your background image is transparent or translucent, you may want to test several background colors to determine which work best with your background image (see How-To 2.9).

Figure 2-19 Using a watermark background—top of the page

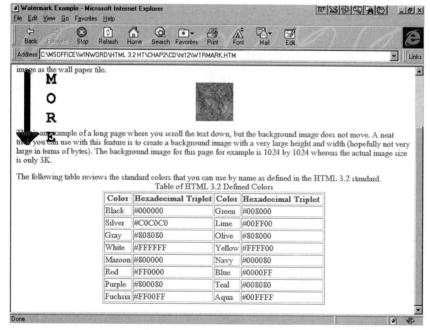

Figure 2-20 Using a watermark background—middle of the page

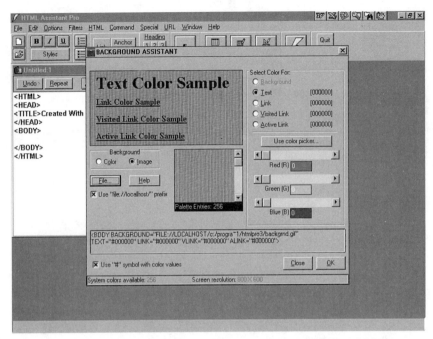

Figure 2-21 Selecting a background image using HTML Assistant

Some HTML editors provide automatic generation of an appropriate body element opening tag with background image support. For example, Figure 2-21 shows the use of HTML Assistant's background assistant to select a background image. You access this dialog through the Special | Background Assistant... menu option.

How-To 16.4 discusses a more advanced method for specifying background images, either for the entire document or for particular HTML elements. This alternative relies on the use of HTML style sheets.

COMPLEXITY
INTERMEDIATE

2.13 How do I...
Insert special characters into a document?

COMPATIBILITY: HTML, INTERNET EXPLORER, NETSCAPE

Problem

I would like to use characters in my documents that are interpreted as HTML code. Not only that, but I would like to include some words from a variety of languages. HTML supports the ISO Latin 1 character set, but my editing environment does not. How do I include these characters?

Technique

Any ISO Latin 1 character can be specified in an HTML document. HTML provides two reference types for including characters.

▪ Character references—Any character can be included through the use of its ISO Latin 1 character code.

▪ Entity references—Some frequently used characters have been assigned mnemonics. These characters can be included by specifying the appropriate mnemonic.

Steps

The following steps will allow you to insert special characters into your HTML documents. For character codes and entity references of specific special characters, refer to Table 2-6.

1. Open the HTML document you wish to edit using your favorite text editor. (See How-To 2.4 on HTML editing environments.)

2. Locate the position where you wish to insert a special character in the text. This location varies depending upon your editor. In a text editor, this location is usually within the document's **<BODY>** element.

3. Move your insertion point to this location.

4. Enter an ampersand (**&**) at this point in the code.

&

5. Follow the ampersand with either a character reference or an entity reference. (Refer to Table 2-6.) If you use a character reference, the ampersand is followed by a pound symbol (**#**), followed by the decimal code for the desired character. If you use an entity reference, the ampersand is followed by the mnemonic for the character that you wish to insert.

&#38
&amp

6. Finally, end the reference with a semicolon. The following sample code indicates the inclusion of two ampersands in the rendered HTML document.

&

7. Save your document or continue editing.

How It Works

By using either a character or entity reference, you can enter any ISO Latin 1 character into an HTML document. Many platforms do not support the full ISO Latin character set; therefore, HTML provides these two methods for including unsupported characters. Table 2-6 provides a list of ISO Latin characters beyond U.S. ASCII, as well as those characters that hold particular significance in HTML.

Table 2-6 ISO Latin 1 character set—special characters and beyond ASCII

CHARACTER	CODE	ENTITY REFERENCE	COMMENT
"	34	&quot;	HTML code
&	38	&amp;	HTML code
<	60		HTML code
>	62	&gt;	HTML code
¡	161		
¢	162		
£	163		
¤	164		
¥	165		
¦	166		
§	167		
¨	168		
©	169	&copy;	Netscape support
ª	170		
«	171		
¬	172		
-	173		
®	174	&reg;	Netscape support
¯	175		
°	176		
±	177		
2	178		
3	179		
´	180		
µ	181		
¶	182		
·	183		
¸	184		
1	185		

CHARACTER	CODE	ENTITY REFERENCE	COMMENT
º	186		
»	187		
¼	188		
½	189		
¾	190		
¿	191		
À	192	&Agrave;	
Á	193	&Aacute;	
Â	194	&Acirc;	
Ã	195	&Atilde;	
Ä	196	&Auml;	
Å	197	&Aring;	
Æ	198	&AElig;	
Ç	199	&Ccedil;	
È	200	&Egrave;	
É	201	&Eacute;	
Ê	202	&Ecirc;	
Ë	203	&Euml;	
Ì	204	&Igrave;	
Í	205	&Iacute;	
Î	206	&Icirc;	
Ï	207	&Iuml;	
Ð	208		
Ñ	209	&Ntilde;	
Ò	210	&Ograve;	
Ó	211	&Oacute;	
Ô	212	&Ocirc;	
Õ	213	&Otilde;	
Ö	214	&Ouml;	
x	215		
Ø	216	&Oslash;	
Ù	217	&Ugrave;	
Ú	218	&Uacute;	
Û	219	&Ucirc;	
Ü	220	&Uuml;	

continued on next page

continued from previous page

CHARACTER	CODE	ENTITY REFERENCE	COMMENT
Ý	221	Ý	
Þ	222	Þ	
ß	223	ß	
à	224	à	
á	225	á	
â	226	â	
ã	227	ã	
ä	228	ä	
å	229	å	
æ	230	æ	
ç	231	ç	
è	232	è	
é	233	é	
ê	234	ê	
ë	235	ë	
ì	236	ì	
í	237	í	
î	238	î	
ï	239	ï	
∂	240	ð	
ñ	241	ñ	
ò	242	ò	
ó	243	ó	
ô	244	ô	
õ	245	õ	
ö	246	ö	
÷	247		
ø	248	ø	
ù	249	ù	
ú	250	&uacute	
û	251	û	
ü	252	ü	
ý	253	ý	
þ	254	þ	
ÿ	255	ÿ	

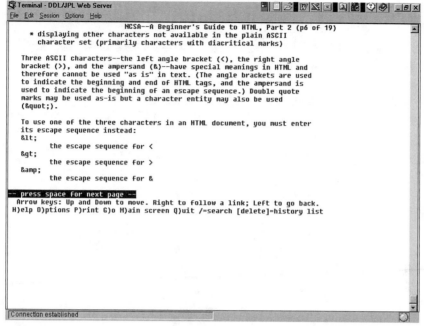

Figure 2-22 Special ASCII characters

Figure 2-22 shows the special ASCII characters—quotes, ampersand, greater than, and less than—that hold a particular significance in HTML. The quotes symbol is used to delimit attribute values. The ampersand is used to indicate a character or entity reference, and the greater than and less than signs are used to delimit HTML tags. A special entity is required for a nonbreaking space to differentiate it from a normal space. Both types of space are character code **32**, but a nonbreaking space implies that the text around the space should not be broken between lines.

HTML 3.2 also provides entity references for several non–ISO Latin 1 characters, such as the nonbreaking space. Table 2-7 outlines these entities.

Table 2-7 Entity references for non–ISO Latin 1 characters

CHARACTER	ENTITY REFERENCE	COMMENTS
Baseline dots	&ldots;	Three dots on the baseline
Center dots	&cdots;	Three dots on same level as a minus sign
Diagonal dots	&ddots;	Diagonal dots (top left to bottom right)
Dot fill	&dotfill;	Center dots filling column in an array
Em dash	&emdash;	Dash length of an em space
Em space		Space size of point size of current spot

continued on next page

continued from previous page

CHARACTER	ENTITY REFERENCE	COMMENTS
En dash	&endash;	Dash the length of an en space
En space		Space size of half the point size
Large space	&quad;	Huge space
Medium space	&sp;	Medium space
Nonbreaking space		ASCII 32, but with nonbreaking caveat
Thin space		Thin space
Vertical dots	&vdots;	Three vertical dots
Alpha	α	alpha
Beta	β	beta
Gamma	γ	gamma
Delta	δ	delta
Epsilon	ε	epsilon
Var Epsilon	&vepsilon;	var epsilon
Zeta	ζ	zeta
Eta	η	eta
Theta	θ	theta
Iota	ι	iota
Kappa	κ	kappa
Lambda	λ	lambda
Mu	μ	mu
Nu	ν	nu
Xi	ξ	xi
Omicron	ο	omicron
Pi	π	pi
Var Pi	ϖ	var pi
Rho	ρ	rho
Var Rho	ϱ	var rho
Sigma	σ	sigma
Var Sigma	&vsigma;	var sigma
Tau	τ	tau
Upsilon	υ	upsilon
Phi	φ	phi
Var Phi	ϕ	var phi
Chi	χ	chi
Psi	ψ	psi
Omega	ω	omega

Thus, special characters and non-ASCII characters can be included in HTML documents through the use of either character or entity references. When a browser detects an ampersand in your HTML code, it interprets the semicolon-terminated value that follows as a reference. If the first character beyond the ampersand (**&**) is a pound symbol (**#**), the value is taken as a character reference so when the document is rendered, the character indicated by the code is drawn. Otherwise, the value is taken to be an entity reference. The browser maps this reference to the appropriate character.

Comments

Some browsers may understand entity references differently than others. Further, some browsers may limit which references are supported. For example, certain text-based browsers may not support non-ASCII characters of any kind.

COMPLEXITY
BEGINNING

2.14 How do I...
Create a home page?

COMPATIBILITY: HTML

Problem

I know some of the HTML basics, and I want to create a home page to provide information about myself to the World Wide Web community. I don't need anything very fancy just yet, but I would like to create and install a functional home page.

Technique

The home page creation process is very similar to the creation process defined in How-To 2.6. Use the same document structure as you would develop for any other HTML 3.2 document, with a few additional elements included to mark the various sections.

Create the document with several sections. Create a contact information area, a biography area, and a modification date area. These areas will be separated by horizontal rules.

Steps

The following leads you through the creation of a single HTML document entitled "Home Page of John Q. Public." This document will serve as your business card in the World Wide Web community.

This process assumes that you are using a normal text editor to create your document. If you use a different editor, some of the steps outlined may not be necessary;

be sure to check the documentation for your particular editor to determine which steps apply.

1. Change directories to the location where you wish to develop your HTML document. Open a file in your editor. (See How-To 2.4 on editing environments.) Be sure to choose a filename with an extension indicating an HTML document to your browser.

```
edit homepage.htm
```

2. Begin with a document type tag and an **<HTML>** opening tag. Enter the following lines in your document.

```
<!DOCTYPE HTML PUBLIC "-//W3C//DTD HTML 3.2//EN">
<HTML>
```

3. Indicate that you are beginning the header area of the document by issuing a **<HEAD>** opening tag. The following line should appear next in your document. The **<HEAD>** element must appear within the scope of an **<HTML>** tag.

```
<HEAD>
```

4. The **<TITLE>** element indicates the title of an HTML document. Place **<TITLE>** tags in the header component of a document. Place the document title between the opening and closing **<TITLE>** tags. Add this title element to your document. Substitute your own name for John's.

```
<TITLE>Home Page of John Q. Public</TITLE>
```

This element is required. Many browsers use this information to generate and display the title of the document. If you omit this element, browsers that require strict HTML adherence may not display your document.

5. To end the head area, issue a **<HEAD>** closing tag.

```
</HEAD>
```

6. At this point, the body of the document needs to be developed. A **<BODY>** opening tag is used to indicate that this point has been reached. Enter the following line of code.

```
<BODY>
```

7. The body of your document consists of three components. The first part includes your contact information. You may wish to provide more or less information than the sample code, as determined by your needs.

```
<!-- Mark the beginning of this portion with a horizontal rule. -->
<HR>
<!-- Center your name as a level 1 header. -->
<H1 ALIGN="center">John Q. Public</H1>
<!-- Provide any desirable contact information. -->
999 Peachtree St.<BR>
Atlanta, GA 30314<BR>
USA<BR>
E-Mail: my_id@mysite.edu
```

8. The second portion of your document content includes your biographical statement.

```
<!-- Mark the beginning of this portion with a horizontal rule. -->
<HR>
<!-- Choose the heading text that you feel appropriate. -->
<H1>About Me</H1>
<!-- The formatting & information should be developed to suit your needs. -->
This is the first paragraph in this section about myself.
I have been at MY BUSINESS for the past X years.
<P>
I am currently working on several projects.
These projects include...
```

As you learn more about HTML, you will likely enhance this portion with other HTML 3.2 elements such as links, externally viewable objects, and inline images.

9. End your document by specifying the date and identifying the individual who last modified this document.

```
<!-- Mark the beginning of this portion with a horizontal rule. -->
<HR>
<!-- Substitute the appropriate information in your document. The date -->
<!--should appear in a long format with the month name written out since -->
<!--the order conventions for date abbreviations vary. -->
Last modified on CURRENT_DATE by YOUR_NAME (YOUR_E-MAIL)
```

10. Use a `<BODY>` closing tag to mark the end of the `<BODY>` element. Similar to the `<HEAD>` element, the `<BODY>` element is also completely nested within the `<HTML>` element. To end the `<BODY>` element, issue the closing tag in your document.

```
</BODY>
```

11. Finally, end the `<HTML>` element with an `<HTML>` closing tag. Add this to your document to complete your first HTML document.

```
</HTML>
```

12. Save the file. Remember to use a filename extension that indicates an HTML document.

13. Attempt to view your home page using as many different browsing applications as you can.

14. If there are problems with the way items display, modify the document as appropriate.

15. When you feel that your home page is ready for the rest of the world, ask your site administrator to install your document on your Web site. Follow his or her instructions to install the document in your home directory.

How It Works

Use this procedure to develop an initial home page that will serve as your introduction to the World Wide Web community. This first attempt at a home page provides information about you and your interests to network browsers around the world.

The procedure described takes you through the development of a basic HTML document composed of an **<HTML>** element and the two nested **<HEAD>** and **<BODY>** elements. The **<BODY>** element described contains three discrete components:

- Contact information—This section provides information on how people viewing the page can get in touch with you.

- Biographical information—This section gives you the opportunity to tell people about yourself. You can include information on what you have done, what you are doing, and what you are interested in doing.

- Creation/modification information—This final component should be included as a general practice in most HTML documents. Considering the fluidity of electronic information, the area provides your viewer with an idea of how current your information content is.

Figure 2-23 displays how the home page developed in this procedure would appear in a browser.

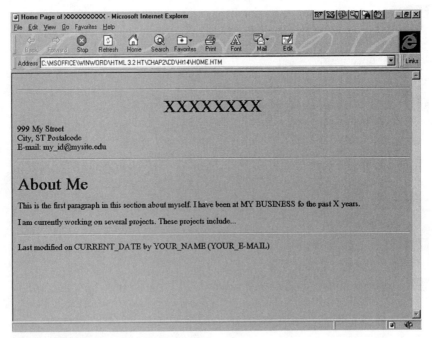

Figure 2-23 Home page example

Here is the complete HTML definition of this document.

```
<!DOCTYPE HTML PUBLIC "-//W3C//DTD HTML 3.2//EN">
<HTML>
<HEAD>
<TITLE>Home Page of John Q. Public</TITLE>
</HEAD>
<BODY>

<!-- Mark the beginning of this portion with a horizontal rule. -->
<HR>
<!-- Center your name as a level 1 header. -->
<H1 ALIGN="center">John Q. Public</H1>
<!-- Provide any desirable contact information. -->
999 Peachtree St.<BR>
Atlanta, GA 30314<BR>
USA<BR>
E-Mail: my_id@mysite.edu

<!-- Mark the beginning of this portion with a horizontal rule. -->
<HR>
<!-- Choose the heading text that you feel appropriate. -->
<H1>About Me</H1>
<!-- The formatting and information should be developed to suit your needs. -->
<TAB INDENT=5>This is the first paragraph in this section about myself.
I have been at MY BUSINESS for the past X years.
<P>
<TAB INDENT=5>I am currently working on several projects.
These projects include...

<!-- Mark the beginning of this portion with a horizontal rule. -->
<HR>
<!-- Substitute the appropriate information in your document. The date -->
<!--should appear in a long format with the month name written out since -->
<!--the order conventions for date abbreviations vary. -->
Last modified on CURRENT_DATE by YOUR_NAME (YOUR_E-MAIL)

</BODY>
</HTML>
```

As you become more experienced with HTML, you can enhance this basic home page with a large assortment of elements. You will be able to include lists (see Chapter 6, Lists), multimedia objects (see Chapter 10, Adding Externally Linked Multimedia Objects), links to other pages (see Chapter 8, Establishing Links), and a variety of other advanced features.

Comments

When adding elements of your own, remember that the document you are creating may be viewed by thousands if not millions of people. During your document development, you should take into consideration the variety of browsing environments in use, each with differing presentation capabilities.

A reference to the HTML 3.2 standard elements appears in Appendix A, HTML Quick Reference. The elements discussed in this How-To are listed in the next table.

ELEMENT	LOCATION	PURPOSE
<HTML>...</HTML>	file	Defines the scope of an HTML document (see How-To 2.1)
<!--...-->	HTML	Represents an HTML comment element (see How-To 2.7)
<HEAD>...</HEAD>	HTML	Defines the head of an HTML document (see How-To 2.1)
<TITLE>...</TITLE>	HEAD	Defines the title of an HTML document (see How-To 2.6)
<BODY>...</BODY>	HTML	Defines the body of an HTML document (see How-To 2.1)
<B>...</B>	BODY	Represents a bolded element (see How-To 3.1)
 	BODY	Represents a line break (see How-To 7.4)
<H1>...</H1>	BODY	Represents a Level 1 heading element (see How-To 4.1)
<HR>	BODY	Places a horizontal rule when displayed (see How-To 7.1)
<P...>	BODY	Represents a paragraph break (see How-To 7.4)

COMPLEXITY
BEGINNING

2.15 How do I...
View my home page?

COMPATIBILITY: BROWSER-SPECIFIC

Problem

I have created my home page using an editor. I don't know how the document will appear in a browser until I actually view it. I'd like to take a look at the page in a few different editors so that I get a feel for what other people will see when they view my page.

Technique

Use a browser to view the home page, or any other page that you create. Browsers typically provide mechanisms for examining local HTML documents. There are three common interfaces used to perform this task.

- Command line—The path to the file that you wish to open is passed to the browser application as a command-line argument.

- Open file—The browser application offers a menu option that accesses a local file.

▣ Open URL—The browser application has a menu option that allows you to open a URL. The protocol for a local file is simply `file`.

Procedures for opening local documents through these three interface types are provided in Steps.

Steps

The following methods open locally created documents for viewing within browser applications. Step-by-step instructions are provided for the three common interface types for specifying local files.

Consult the documentation for your particular browser application to determine which interfaces are appropriate. In all cases, your browser is assumed to be able to interpret the document that you are opening as HTML rather than plain text.

Command Line

1. Be sure that you name the local file with the `.html` (or `.htm` for PC) filename extension. This indicates to most browsers that the local file is to be accessed as an HTML document whether it truly is or not.

2. Invoke your browser application, with the file you wish to open as a command-line argument. For example, to attempt to open the file `myhome.htm` in the current directory using the Lynx browser, you would issue the following command:

```
lynx myhome.htm
```

Open File

1. Name the local file with the `.html` (or `.htm` for PC) filename extension. This indicates to most browsers that the local file is to be accessed as an HTML document whether the document truly is HTML or not.

2. Load your browser application.

3. Select the menu option or hotkey for opening a local file.

4. The interface for entering the file information varies among browsers. Consult the browser documentation to determine how to complete this operation successfully. In Netscape Navigator and Microsoft Internet Explorer, a file selection dialog is presented; you can browse the local directory hierarchy until you find the desired file.

Open URL

1. Be sure that you named the local file with the `.html` (or `.htm` for PC) filename extension. This indicates to most browsers that the local file is to be accessed as an HTML document, whether the document truly is or not.

2. Load your browser application from the command line or an appropriate icon.

3. Select the menu option or hotkey for opening a URL.

4. The interface for entering the file information will vary depending upon your particular browser. You should consult the browser documentation to determine how to successfully complete this operation. In Lynx, you press G, and the system prompts you to enter the URL you wish to open. If you want to open the local file `myhome.htm` in the `path_info` directory, you enter this URL:

```
file://localhost/path_info/myhome.htm
```

How It Works

When opening a local file, your browser application determines how to treat the contents of a file based upon the extension on the filename. The browser maps filename extensions to particular content types and will render the file as it deems appropriate. Your HTML files should have the `.html` extension (`.htm` on PC platforms).

The three methods examined for opening a local file accomplish the same task. The goal of the interface is to provide the browser with a path to the file that you wish to open. The command-line interface method takes this information directly when the application is started.

Many browsers support an open local file function. Since most HTML documents require viewing prior to installation on a Web site, the ability to view a local file is extremely useful in the authoring process. Many individuals track private information through personal webs stored locally that are not accessible to the world. Figure 2-24 exhibits this interface method. The desired file can be selected from a file selection dialog window.

Local files can also be accessed via a standard Open URL facility. Specifying a `file` protocol type tells the browser that the desired files can be found in the local file system. The Go feature of the Lynx browser is displayed in Figure 2-25.

Once the browser receives sufficient information to find the requested file, it attempts to open it according to the information provided. The browser determines the display type of this file by mapping the filename extension to a suitable content type. The browser reads the content and then displays it according to the type determined. HTML 3.2 files display as HTML documents.

Comments

Different browser applications support different subsets of these interfaces for opening local documents. The documentation for your particular browser contains the information on how this task is performed.

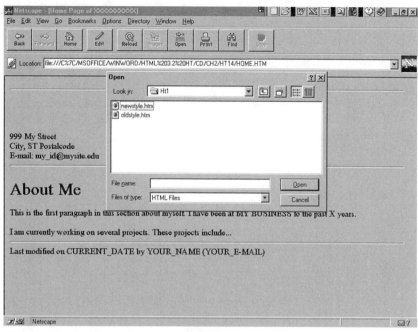

Figure 2-24 Netscape's Open Local facility

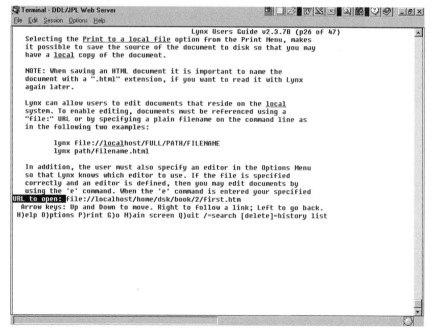

Figure 2-25 Lynx Go interface

If your HTML documents are being opened as plain text documents, the most likely reason is that your browser is not properly configured to treat these files as HTML documents. The browser determines whether a file contains an HTML document based upon the filename extension of the file being accessed. The most commonly used extension to indicate an HTML file is `.html` (or `.htm` on PC platform). If your files have this extension and are still not opening properly, check the configuration of your browser application. You may need to configure this extension to indicate an HTML document. For more information on this process, consult the documentation for your browser application.

CHAPTER 3

ADDING HTML PHYSICAL CHARACTER EFFECTS

3

ADDING HTML PHYSICAL CHARACTER EFFECTS

How do I...

When creating an HTML page, there will be times when you want to emphasize or otherwise set apart a word or phrase from the rest of the text. Just as word processors provide a number of styles—such as bold and italic—that can be used to alter the appearance of text, HTML offers a similar set of character effects. One sort, physical effects, is designed to alter the appearance of the text displayed. The styles include bold, italic, and underline, as well as alterations in the size and color of the text. This chapter provides an overview of the physical character effects available in HTML 3.2.

111

3.1   Use Bold Font

When you create a document on a word processor, there are often specific words and phrases you want to emphasize to bring them to the attention of the reader. This is frequently done by making the characters bold. HTML lets you do the same thing. This simple How-To explains how to add bold text to your page.

3.2   Use Italic Font

Certain names and other text elements—names of books and movies, for instance—require formatting in italics for proper style. You may also want to emphasize certain words in the text this way. This simple How-To explains how to place words and phrases in your page in italics.

3.3   Use a Fixed-Width Font

Samples of computer input and output, as well as other text items that require precise alignment, are often displayed in a fixed-width (or typewriter-style) font. This simple How-To explains how to add fixed-width text to your page.

3.4   Change Font Size

HTML 3.2 allows you to change the font size of the text in a document, making it larger or smaller to fit the needs of the document. This How-To explains how to use sets of tags to change the font size of text.

3.5   Change Font Color

A new addition to HTML 3.2 is the ability to change the color of the text displayed in a document. This How-To explains how to change the font color in a document, either by using an exact color description or by specifying a basic color name.

3.6   Underline Text

Another way to emphasize text is to underline it. This is often done when italics and bold aren't available or do not fit the style of the document. This simple How-To explains how to underline words and phrases in your page.

3.7   Specify Strikethrough Formatting

Strikethrough formatting is often used to show examples of incorrect text, such as the incorrect input for a computer program. This How-To explains how to include strikethrough formatting in your pages.

3.8   Include Superscripts and Subscripts

Superscripts and subscripts are used to move text elements above or below the rest of the line. These are often used in footnotes and in mathematical and scientific formulas. This How-To explains how to add superscripts and subscripts to your page using the new features of HTML 3.2.

COMPLEXITY
BEGINNING

3.1 How do I...
Use bold font?

COMPATIBILITY: HTML 2+

Problem

I have some text I would like to emphasize by making it bold. How do I make text bold in HTML?

Technique

It is very easy to make text bold in HTML. Simply by using the **<B>** tag, you can make any amount of text, from one letter to entire paragraphs, appear bold.

Steps

To make text bold, place the **<B>** tag at the beginning of the text and the **</B>** tag at the end:

```
This is normal text and <B>this is bold text.</B>

I only want to make the first letter of this <B>w</B>ord bold.
```

An example of bold and other physical styles as they are displayed in Netscape Navigator is shown in Figure 3-1. The same example as displayed in Microsoft Internet Explorer is shown in Figure 3-2. The code is also available on the CD-ROM as file 3-1.HTML.

How It Works

When a browser encounters a **<B>** tag, it displays the text contained between the **<B>** and the **</B>** tags as bold text. The browser does no other processing on the text.

Comments

Some browsers do not permit you to mix **<B>** with other tags, such as italics (**<I>**, see How-To 3.2). The **<STRONG>** tag (see How-To 4.2) often formats text in the same manner as the **<B>**. Which one to use is up to you. See How-To 4.9 for a discussion about using styles effectively.

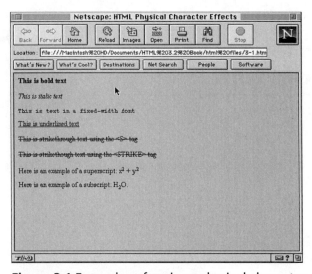

Figure 3-1 Examples of various physical character effects (Netscape Navigator)

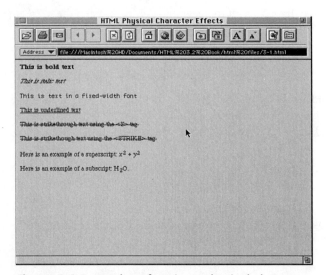

Figure 3-2 Examples of various physical character effects (Microsoft Internet Explorer)

COMPLEXITY
BEGINNING

3.2 How do I...
Use italic font?

COMPATIBILITY: HTML 2+

Problem

I have some text, including the titles of some books, that I need to show in italics. How do I display text in italics in HTML?

Technique

It is very easy to italicize text in HTML. The **<I>** and **</I>** tags will italicize any amount of text contained between them.

Steps

To italicize text, place the **<I>** tag at the beginning of the text and the **</I>** tag at the end:

```
This is normal text and <I>this is italicized text.</I>
```

```
I only want to put the first letter of this <I>w</I>ord in italics.
```

Examples of italics and other physical styles are shown in Figures 3-1 and 3-2. This code is also available on the CD as file 3-1.HTML.

How It Works

When a browser encounters an **<I>** tag, it displays the text contained between the **<I>** and the **</I>** tags in italics. The browser does no other processing on the text.

Comments

Some browsers do not permit you to mix **<I>** with other text style tags, such as **<B>**. The **<EM>** tag (see How-To 4.2) often formats text in the same manner as the **<I>**. Which one you use is up to you.

COMPLEXITY
BEGINNING

3.3   How do I...
Use a fixed-width font?

COMPATIBILITY: HTML 2+

Problem

I have some text that I would like to place in a fixed-width font to maintain the exact alignment of the words. How do I put words in a fixed-width font in HTML?

Technique

It is very simple to put text into a fixed-width font. Any text placed between the **<TT>** and **</TT>** tags (for TeleType or Typewritten Text) will be rendered in a fixed-width font.

Steps

To place text in a fixed-width font, put **<TT>** at the beginning of the text and **</TT>** at the end of the text:

```
This is normal text and <TT>this is text in fixed-width font.</TT>

I only want to put the first letter of this <TT>w</TT>ord in fixed-width
font.
```

Examples of fixed-width font and other physical styles are shown in Figures 3-1 and 3-2. The code is also available on the CD in file 3-1.HTML.

How It Works

When a browser encounters a **<TT>** tag, it renders the text between the **<TT>** and the **</TT>** tags in a fixed-width font. The actual fixed-width font used (such as Courier, Monaco, and so on) depends on the browser, and it can often be modified by the user. No other formatting of the text is done by the **<TT>** tag.

Comments

Some browsers don't allow you to combine **<TT>** with other text style tags, such as **<B>** and **<I>**, to format the same text. Since many browsers allow users to choose which fixed-width font to use in displaying text marked by **<TT>**, the displayed text may not appear to some users as it appears in your original.

COMPLEXITY
BEGINNING

3.4   How do I...
Change font size?

COMPATIBILITY: HTML 3.2

Problem

I need to include different-sized fonts in my documents. Most of the users accessing my documents will have browsers capable of rendering these fonts. How can I make the font size larger or smaller?

Technique

Font changes are accomplished by using elements that specify that the enclosed text should be rendered using a different font size.

Here are two methods of accomplishing this task. The first describes the use of the **<BIG>** and **<SMALL>** tags that are part of HTML 3.2. The second describes the use of the **<FONT>** and **<BASEFONT>** tags, also part of HMTL 3.2 providing greater flexibility in font size changes.

Steps

Open the HTML document that contains the text size you want to change.

1. To make the font size smaller by an arbitrary amount, place the **<SMALL>** tag at the beginning of the text and the **</SMALL>** tag at the end:

```
This is normal text and <SMALL>small text.</SMALL>

I only want to decrease the font size of the first letter of this
<SMALL>w</SMALL>ord.
```

2. Similarly, to increase the font size by an arbitrary amount, place the **<BIG>** tag at the beginning of the text and the **</BIG>** tag at the end of the text:

```
This is normal text and <BIG>big text.</BIG>

I only want to increase the font size of the first letter of this
<BIG>w</BIG>ord.
```

3. You can use the **SIZE** attribute of the **<FONT>** tag to provide finer control over the size of the font used in the document. **SIZE** can be specified by any integer between 1 and 7, with 3 as the usual default. For example, to place text in a very large font, use

```
<FONT SIZE=7>This text is very large</FONT>
```

4. You can change the font size of the entire document with the **<BASEFONT>** element at the beginning of the document. Use the **SIZE** attribute to change the default font size. For example, to create a document whose default font size is 2, you would enter

```
<BASEFONT SIZE=2>
```

5. You can also use the **SIZE** attribute to change the font size relative to the default font size by using a **+** or **−** sign to indicate the change from the default size. For example, to place text in a font two sizes larger than the default size, use

```
<FONT SIZE=+2>This text is two sizes larger than the default</FONT>
```

Examples of changes to font size and color are shown in Figures 3-3 and 3-4. This code is also available on the CD as file 3-2.HTML.

How It Works

When a browser encounters a **<BIG>** or **<SMALL>** element, it will render the text contained between the **<BIG>** and **</BIG>** (or **<SMALL>** and **</SMALL>**) tags by changing the font size by a predetermined amount. When a browser identifies the **<FONT>** tag, it reads the attributes and makes the required changes in the size or color of the font. When the browser reads the **<BASEFONT>** element, it adjusts all the text on the page to the font size specified by the **SIZE** attribute.

Figure 3-3 Examples of font size and color changes (Netscape Navigator)

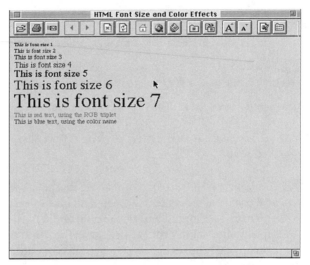

Figure 3-4 Examples of font size and color changes (Microsoft Internet Explorer)

Comments

Older browsers do not support any of the font tags, so they will not change the font size as specified by the tags. If you're looking to emphasize or otherwise call attention to certain passages of text, you'll want to consider using character effects like bold and italics to make your point.

COMPLEXITY
BEGINNING

3.5   How do I...
Change font color?

COMPATIBILITY: HTML 3.2

Problem

I would like to change the color of the text on my page. Most of the users accessing my documents will have browsers capable of changing the color of text. How can I make the font different colors?

Technique

HTML 3.2 provides a new way to change the color of text in a document. You can change the font color of selected portions of the text by using the **COLOR** attribute of the **<FONT>** tag.

Steps

Open the HTML document that contains the text color you want to change.

1. To change the color of the text, place the `<FONT COLOR>` tag at the beginning of the text and `</FONT>` at the end of the text

```
This is normal text and <FONT COLOR>this is colored text.</FONT>

I only want to change the color of the first letter of this <FONT
COLOR>w</FONT>ord.
```

2. To specify a specific color, you can use that color's RGB triplet, the hexadecimal combination of the red, green, and blue values of the color. This system uses `FF` for full intensity and `00` for no intensity. To use the RGB triplet values, set the `COLOR` attribute in the `<FONT>` tag equal to these values and place the pound (`#`) sign between the equal sign and the RGB triplet:

```
This is normal text and <FONT COLOR="#FF0000">this is red text.</FONT>

I only want to make the first letter of this <FONT
COLOR="#FFFFFF">w</FONT>ord white.
```

3. An alternative to using the RGB triplets is to use one of a set of predefined color names that are part of HTML 3.2. A list of these colors can be found in Appendix H, Color Tables.

To use these names, set the `COLOR` attribute in the `<FONT>` tag to equal them:

```
This is normal text and <FONT COLOR="red">this is red text.</FONT>

I only want to make the first letter of this <FONT
COLOR="white">w</FONT>ord white.
```

Examples of changes to font size and color are shown in Figures 3-3 and 3-4. This code is also available on the CD as file 3-2.HTML.

How It Works

When a browser encounters a `<FONT>` tag that has defined a value for the `COLOR` attribute, it colors the text between the `<FONT>` and `</FONT>` tags using the color defined by the attribute.

Comments

The **COLOR** attribute to **<FONT>** is only supported by more recent browsers, such as versions 2 and later of Netscape and Internet Explorer. Using the names of colors instead of RGB triplets was only added to Netscape in version 3. Also note that, while the RGB triplets allow you to define millions of colors, many monitors are only set up to display hundreds or thousands of colors. If the color requested isn't supported by the computer, the browser will pick the next closest color it can display.

COMPLEXITY
BEGINNING

3.6   How do I...
Underline text?

COMPATIBILITY: HTML 2+

Problem

I have some text in my document that I would like to underline. How can I underline text in HTML?

Technique

Underlining text is a simple process in HTML. The **<U>** and **</U>** tags will underline any amount of text contained between them.

Steps

To underline text, place the **<U>** tag at the beginning of the text and the **</U>** tag at the end of the text:

```
This is normal text and <U>this is underlined text.</U>

I only want to underline the first letter of this <U>w</U>ord.
```

Examples of underlines and other physical styles are shown in Figures 3-1 and 3-2. This code is also available on the CD as file 3-1.HTML.

How It Works

When a browser encounters a **<U>** tag, it underlines the text contained between the **<U>** and the **</U>** tags. The browser does no other formatting on the text.

Comments

Some browsers do not permit you to mix **<U>** tags with other tags, such as bold and italic, when trying to format the same word or phrase. Some browsers, like versions of Netscape before 3, do not support underlined text.

COMPLEXITY
BEGINNING

3.7 How do I...
Specify strikethrough formatting?

COMPATIBILITY: HTML 3.2

Problem

As an example of what text should not be entered into a program, I would like to show the text in a strikethrough style, that is, with a horizontal line running through it. How can I use strikethrough style in HTML?

Technique

HTML 3.2 supports the use of the **<S>** tag, which converts any text placed between it and the corresponding **</S>** tag into strikethrough style.

Steps

1. To place text in strikethrough style, put the **<S>** tag at the beginning of the text and the **</S>** tag at the end of the text:

```
This is normal text and <S>this is strikethrough style text.</S>

I only want to strikethrough the first letter of this <S>w</S>ord.
```

2. An alternative method supported by some browsers is the **<STRIKE>** tag, which works in the same way as the **<S>** tag:

```
This is normal text and <STRIKE>this is strikethrough style text.</STRIKE>

I only want to strikethrough the first letter of this <STRIKE>w</STRIKE>ord.
```

Examples of strikethrough style are shown in Figures 3-1 and 3-2. The code is also available on the CD as file 3-1.HTML.

How It Works

When a browser encounters an **<S>** or a **<STRIKE>** tag, it places the text between the **<S>** and **</S>** (or **<STRIKE>** and **</STRIKE>**) tags in strikethrough style by replacing the text with an identical font that has a horizontal line running through it.

Comments

Some browsers do not have access to a strikethrough font. If so, the browser may choose to use an alternative method for displaying the text. Since some browsers support only **<S>** or **<STRIKE>**, you should use both **<S>** and **<STRIKE>** around the text you want to place in strikethrough style:

```
Most browsers should display <STRIKE><S>this text</S></STRIKE> in
strikethrough style.
```

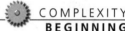
COMPLEXITY
BEGINNING

3.8   How do I...
Include superscripts and subscripts?

COMPATIBILITY: HTML 3.2

Problem

I have a paper I want to convert to HTML that includes mathematical equations, chemical formulas, and numbered footnotes. These all require numbers to be placed in superscripts or subscripts. How do I create superscripted and subscripted text in HTML?

Technique

HTML 3.2 provides support for superscripts (text shifted above the normal level of the line) and subscripts (text shifted below the normal level of the line). The **_{** and **}** tags place any text between them below the level of the line, and in a smaller font when possible. The **^{** and **}** tags place any text between them above the level of the line, also in a smaller font when possible.

Steps

Go to your document and identify the sections of the document to be displayed as subscript or superscript text.

1. To create a subscript, place the `<SUB>` tag at the beginning of the text to be subscripted and the `</SUB>` tag at the end of the text to be subscripted:

```
The chemical formula of water is H<SUB>2</SUB>0.
```

2. To create a superscript, place the `<SUP>` tag at the beginning of the text to be superscripted and the `</SUP>` tag at the end of the text to be superscripted:

```
A simple formula for a parabola is y = x<SUP>2</SUP>.
```

Examples of subscripts and superscripts are shown in Figures 3-1 and 3-2. The code is also available on the CD as file 3-1.HTML.

How It Works

When a browser encounters a `<SUB>` tag, it shifts all the text between the `<SUB>` and `</SUB>` tags below the level of the rest of the line and, depending on the browser, renders the text in a smaller size. When a browser encounters a `<SUP>` tag, it shifts all the text between the `<SUP>` and `</SUP>` tags above the level of the rest of the line and, again depending on the browser, renders the text in a smaller size.

Comments

Since `<SUB>` and `<SUP>` have only now been introduced with HTML 3.2, people using older, pre-HTML 3.2 browsers will not be able to see the subscripts or superscripts. To accommodate these users, an alternative for creating subscripts and superscripts in chemical formulas and mathematical equations is to create a graphic of the formula or equation in another program and to include the graphic in the page as an inline graphic. (See How-To 9.2.)

ADDING HTML LOGICAL CHARACTER EFFECTS

4.

ADDING HTML LOGICAL CHARACTER EFFECTS

How do I...

When creating an HTML page, there will be times when you want to emphasize or otherwise set apart a word or phrase from the rest of the text. HTML offers a set of tags called logical character effects that can be used not only to specify a particular formatting effect on the document text but to identify the meaning of the text as well. This chapter examines these logical character styles that are available in HTML 3.2, including headings, and shows you how to use character effects to improve the quality of a document.

4.1 Use Heading Styles

You often want to give your page a bold, distinct title to help readers identify it. Also, it's useful to add subheadings to a document to identify different areas of interest to readers. This simple How-To explains how to add headings of various styles to your page.

4.2 Place Emphasis and Strong Emphasis

There may be words or phrases in your pages that you want to emphasize, or strongly emphasize, where it doesn't matter whether the text is bold, italicized, or underlined. This simple How-To explains how to emphasize and strongly emphasize key words and phrases in your pages, allowing different browsers to render those passages in their different ways.

4.3 Specify a Citation

If you are placing an essay or journal paper on the Web, you will want to include citations to other papers and documents. Rather than developing your own style for including citations, it is useful to mark a section of text as a citation and let the reader's browser do the specifying. This How-To explains how to mark text as a citation for this purpose.

4.4 Emphasize a Defined Term

Your page may include a number of terms that are defined in the text. This simple How-To explains how to use the new `<DFN>` feature in HTML 3.2 to emphasize these words and phrases in your page.

4.5 Include Small Segments of Code and Variables

Often Web pages include references to computer code, and specifically the names of variables used in programs. These text elements are often best rendered in a format different from the rest of the text. This How-To explains how to use HTML tags to easily format text that includes computer code and variables.

4.6 Provide a Sample of Literal Characters

There are cases when you want to include literal, otherwise unformatted characters in your page. This How-To explains how to include samples of literal characters in your page.

4.7 Indicate Text as Keyboard Input

In the course of writing your page, you may want to insert brief sections of keyboard input, computer commands, or arguments. This How-To explains how you can format these text elements in HTML.

4.8 Specify an Address

There are many cases when you want to specify the owner of a document and how to reach that person. This simple How-To shows how to specify the address of a person in an HTML document.

4.9   Spruce Up My Home Page with Character Effects

The character effects described in this chapter and the previous chapter can be used to make a more impressive, interesting, and effective document. They can also be used to make a document ugly and difficult to read. This How-To suggests how you might best use these character effects to improve the look of your pages.

COMPLEXITY
BEGINNING

4.1   How do I...
Use heading styles?

COMPATIBILITY: HTML 2+

Problem

I would like to include a title on my page. I would also like to include subheadings for various parts of my page, but I don't want these subheadings to be as large as the title. How do I include titles and headings of various sizes in my page?

Technique

HTML allows users to identify headings and subheadings in a document through the `<Hn>` tag, where *n* is a number from 1 to 6. The largest heading is `<H1>` and the smallest is `<H6>`. You can also use attributes with these tags to align the headings with various parts of the page, or even to include images within the heading.

Steps

Go to your document and identify the words and phrases that will serve as titles and headings in the document.

1. To identify a section of text as a heading, place `<Hn>` at the beginning of the text and `</Hn>` at the end of the text, where *n* is replaced by an integer between 1 and 6:

```
<H1>This is an example of a level 1 heading</H1>
<H6>This is an example of a level 6 heading</H6>
```

2. To align a heading to the left, center, or right of the window using HTML 3.2, add the `ALIGN` attribute at the beginning of the heading. The default alignment is to the left.

```
<H1 ALIGN=LEFT>This is a level 1 heading aligned to the left of the⇐
window</H1>
<H1 ALIGN=CENTER>This is a level 1 heading aligned to the center of the⇐
window</H1>
<H1 ALIGN=RIGHT>This is a level 1 heading aligned to the right of the⇐
window</H1>
```

An example of how headings appear in Netscape Navigator is shown in Figure 4-1. An example of how headings appear in Microsoft Internet Explorer is shown in Figure 4-2. The code for both examples is available on the CD-ROM as file 4-1.HTML.

How It Works

When a browser encounters a heading tag, it automatically formats the text contained in the title according to its programming. This often includes changing the size of the text, making the text bold, and including carriage returns and line spacing. The exact way headings are formatted differs from browser to browser.

Comments

Since headings are rendered differently from browser to browser, take care when referring to them by their appearance within a document. Also note that, as a rule, headings below level 3 are the same size as normal text, if not smaller, so their use as titles may not be very effective.

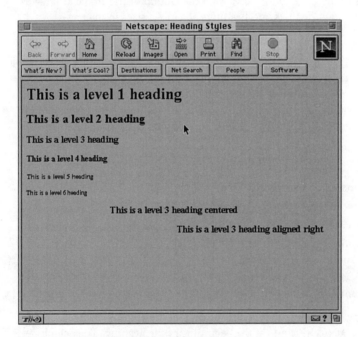

Figure 4-1 Various styles of headings
(Netscape Navigator)

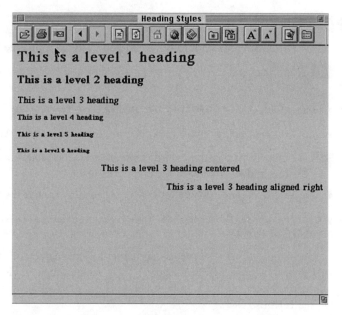

Figure 4-2 Various styles of headings
(Microsoft Internet Explorer)

COMPLEXITY
BEGINNING

4.2 How do I...
Place emphasis and strong emphasis?

COMPATIBILITY: HTML 2+

Problem

I would like to emphasize certain words and phrases on my page. However, I don't
need a specific style applied to them, like bold or italic. How can I emphasize generically or strongly emphasize text in HTML?

Technique

HTML supports the content-style tags **<EM>** and **<STRONG>**, for generic emphasis and
strong emphasis respectively. These tags highlight specific areas of text without requiring the browser to use a specific physical style for them.

Steps

Open your document and locate the text you wish to emphasize.

1. To emphasize a word or phrase, place `<EM>` at the beginning of the text and `</EM>` at the end of the text:

```
This is normal text and <EM>this is emphasized text.</EM>
```

```
I only want to emphasize the first letter of this <EM>w</EM>ord.
```

2. To strongly emphasize a word or phrase, place `<STRONG>` at the beginning of the text and `</STRONG>` at the end of the text:

```
This is normal text and <STRONG>this is strongly emphasized text.</STRONG>
```

```
I only want to strongly emphasize the first letter of this⇐
<STRONG>w</STRONG>ord.
```

An example of `<EM>`, `<STRONG>`, and other logical character effects, as displayed in Netscape Navigator, is given in Figure 4-3. The same example, as displayed in Microsoft Internet Explorer, is shown in Figure 4-4. The code is also available on the CD as file 4-2.HTML.

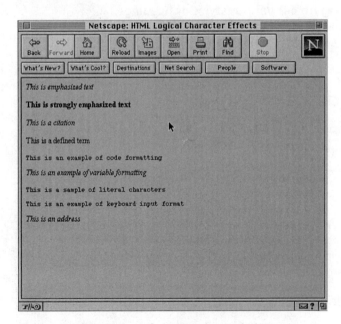

Figure 4-3 Examples of various logical character effects (Netscape Navigator)

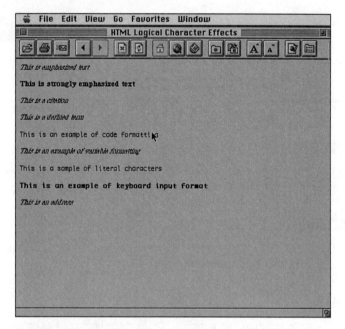

Figure 4-4 Examples of various logical character effects (Microsoft Internet Explorer)

How It Works

When a browser encounters an `<EM>` tag, it emphasizes the text contained between the `<EM>` and `</EM>` tags using the browser's specific instructions for emphasized text. When a browser encounters a `<STRONG>` tag, it emphasizes the text contained between the `<STRONG>` and `</STRONG>` tags, once again using its specific instructions for strongly emphasized text.

Comments

Most browsers interpret `<EM>` the same as `<I>` (that is, they use italics), and `<STRONG>` the same as `<B>` (that is, they use bold). However, some browsers interpret these tags in different ways or allow the user to define the interpretation of `<EM>` and `<STRONG>`. How and where to use `<EM>`, `<STRONG>`, `<B>`, and `<I>` is discussed in How-To 4.9.

COMPLEXITY
BEGINNING

4.3　How do I...
Specify a citation?

COMPATIBILITY: HTML 2+

Problem

I am putting an essay on the Web, and I would like a simple way to format on the page the references to other papers.. How can I format citations in HTML?

Technique

HTML makes it easy to format citations. The `<CITE>` tag will format a citation using a style built into each browser.

Steps

To format a citation, place the `<CITE>` tag at the beginning of the citation and `</CITE>` at the end of the citation:

```
Jane Doe's work showed how this could be accomplished <CITE>(Doe,⇐
1998).</CITE>
```

Examples of citations and other content styles are shown in Figures 4-3 and 4-4. The code is also available on the CD as file 4-2.HTML.

Technique

When a browser encounters the `<CITE>` tag, it formats the text between the `<CITE>` and `</CITE>` tags according to the style for indicating citations built into the browser.

Comments

Most browsers render the text marked by `<CITE>` in italics. However, since `<CITE>` is a content style, not a physical style, some browsers may be set to render such text differently. Keep this in mind when referencing a citation (or some part of a citation) using style tags.

COMPLEXITY
BEGINNING

4.4   How do I...
Emphasize a defined term?

COMPATIBILITY: HTML 2+

Problem

I have a number of words and phrases that are defined in my pages. I would like to call attention to those words, but I don't specifically want to use bold, italic, or another style. How can I emphasize these words in HTML?

Technique

HTML supports the **<DFN>** tag, which is designed specifically for words and phrases that are defined in the text. The physical method of emphasizing the words is left up to the browser.

Steps

To mark a word or phrase that has been defined, place the **<DFN>** tag at the beginning of the text and **</DFN>** at the end of the text.

```
A batter has a <DFN>full count</DFN> when he has three balls and two strikes.
```

Examples of definitions and other content styles are shown in Figures 4-3 and 4-4. The code is also available on the CD as file 4-2.HTML.

How It Works

When a browser encounters a **<DFN>** tag, it changes the style of the text contained between the **<DFN>** and **</DFN>** tags. The style used is dependent on the browser, but is usually either bold or italic.

Comments

Since the style is chosen by the browser and not by you, the defined terms may appear in a different style than you might anticipate. Thus, be careful when referring to defined words based on their style.

COMPLEXITY
BEGINNING

4.5 How do I...
Include small segments of code and variables?

COMPATIBILITY: HTML 2+

Problem

I have some samples of code from a program and some variables that I want to include in my page. I would like to format these to set them off from the rest of the text, but I don't want to go through a lot of work choosing a physical style. Is there an easy way to format code examples and variables in HTML?

Technique

HTML offers the `<CODE>` tag, which can be used to display sections of code from a program, usually in a fixed-width font, and `<VAR>`, which can be used to show variables from programs or other applications, often in italics.

Steps

Go to your document and locate the text you want to display as a variable or in code format.

1. To place a section of text in code format, place the `<CODE>` tag at the beginning of the text and the `</CODE>` tag at the end of the text:

```
The <CODE>goto 20</CODE> statement in the program should be replaced to⇐
improve the programming style.
```

2. To display a word as a variable, place the `<VAR>` tag at the beginning of the text and the `</VAR>` tag at the end of the text:

```
The <VAR>count</VAR> variable keeps track of the number ofiterations of the⇐
loop.
```

Examples of the code and variable styles as well as other content styles are shown in Figures 4-3 and 4-4. The code is also available on the CD as file 4-2.HTML.

How It Works

When a browser encounters a `<CODE>` tag, it places the text contained between the `<CODE>` and `</CODE>` tags in a style used by the browser for rendering code. This is usually a fixed-width font. When a browser encounters a `<VAR>` tag, it places the text contained between the `<VAR>` and `</VAR>` tags in the style used by the browser for variables. This is often italic.

Comments

Since **<CODE>** and **<VAR>** are not physical styles, the way they are presented depends on the browser. Thus, as with other content styles, take care when referring to specific items based on their style.

COMPLEXITY
BEGINNING

4.6 How do I...
Provide a sample of literal characters?

COMPATIBILITY: HTML 2+

Problem

I have some characters that I would like to show as a sample of literal, unformatted characters. How can I do this in HTML?

Technique

HTML offers the **<SAMP>** tag, which will display any text contained within the **<SAMP>** and **</SAMP>** tags as a sample of literal characters. This tag works in much the same way as **<CODE>** and **<TT>**, discussed previously.

Steps

To display text as a sample of literal characters, place the **<SAMP>** tag at the beginning of the text and **</SAMP>** at the end of the text:

```
This is an example of <SAMP>a sample of literal characters</SAMP>

In this case I only want to place <SAMP>o</SAMP>ne character in the sample.
```

Examples of sample text and other content styles are shown in Figures 4-3 and 4-4. The code is also available on the CD as file 4-2.HTML.

How It Works

When a browser encounters the **<SAMP>** tag, it formats the text contained between the **<SAMP>** and **</SAMP>** tags according to the rules built into the browser. Usually this means rendering the text in a fixed-width font, identical to the fonts used for **<CODE>** and **<TT>**, explained earlier, and **<KBD>**, explained in How-To 3.14.

Comments

Although text tagged with **<SAMP>** usually looks the same when rendered as text tagged with a number of other styles, it is still best to use **<SAMP>** when referring to a specific sample, if for no other reason than to allow an indexing program to properly identify the tagged item.

COMPLEXITY
BEGINNING

4.7 How do I...
Indicate text as keyboard input?

COMPATIBILITY: HTML 2+

Problem

On my page I would like to include some samples of input to a computer program. I would like to format these samples differently than the standard text is formatted. How can I do this in HTML?

Technique

The HTML keyboard style tag **<KBD>** allows you to mark text to be typed by the user. You can also use it to display computer commands and arguments, especially those to be entered by the user. The text tagged by **<KBD>** is usually shown in a fixed-width font.

Steps

To specify text that is to be keyboarded by the user, place the **<KBD>** tag at the beginning of the text and the **</KBD>** tag at the end of the text:

```
At the prompt enter the command <KBD>lpr output.txt</KBD>

Using the <KBD>-l</KBD> flag causes a long form of the directory to be⇐
listed.
```

Examples of keyboard style and other content styles are shown in Figures 4-3 and 4-4. The code is also available on the CD as file 4-2.HTML.

How It Works

When a browser encounters a **<KBD>** tag, it places everything between the **<KBD>** and **</KBD>** tags in keyboard style. Such text is usually rendered in a fixed-width font, but font style can vary among browsers.

Comments

Since `<KBD>` is a content style, its appearance may vary among browsers. The `<KBD>` style is also very similar to other styles, such as `<CODE>` and `<SAMP>`, so it can be used interchangeably with those styles. This was discussed in more detail in How-To 3.18.

COMPLEXITY
BEGINNING

4.8 How do I...
Specify an address?

COMPATIBILITY: HTML 2+

Problem

I want to include information about the author of a Web page. How can I specify an address of the author on a Web page?

Technique

The `<ADDRESS>` character effect is used to specify information about the creator or maintainer of a Web page. This information can include the name, e-mail address, phone number, mailing address, or other relevant information.

Steps

To specify text that is considered part of the address, place the `<ADDRESS>` tag at the beginning of the text and the `</ADDRESS>` tag at the end of the text:

```
This page was written by <ADDRESS>Jane Done</ADDRESS>.

<ADDRESS>Jane Doe / jane.doe@mycompany.com</ADDRESS>
```

Examples of the address effect and other logical character effects are shown in Figures 4-3 and 4-4. The code is also available on the CD as file 4-2.HTML.

How It Works

When a browser encounters an `<ADDRESS>` tag, it places everything between the `<ADDRESS>` and `</ADDRESS>` tags in address style. Such text is usually rendered in italics, but font style can vary among browsers.

Comments

The `<ADDRESS>` tag is usually used at the bottom of the document to identify the author of the page. Since the `<ADDRESS>` tag doesn't allow any control over the formatting of its appearance, authors often find it preferable to use other styles in "signing" their pages in their own manner.

COMPLEXITY
INTERMEDIATE

4.9   How do I...
Spruce up my home page with character effects?

COMPATIBILITY: HTML 2+

Problem

Now that I've learned about all these different styles, how can I use them most effectively to make my page more readable?

Technique

This problem is similar to the one encountered using fonts and type styles in word processors and page layout programs. With all the different styles available, there is a strong temptation to try them all. (After all, that's why they exist, right?) However, this can lead to pages that are aesthetically unpleasing and even difficult to read. This How-To contains some tips to help you use these styles effectively to spruce up your home page.

Steps

The following points will help you make the best use of physical or content styles in your Web pages.

1. Styles most effectively emphasize a point when used sparingly. If you make every other word bold or place large sections of text in italics, it becomes much harder to bring an important point to the attention of the reader.

2. In addition to diluting emphasis, frequent changing of styles, from normal to bold to italics and so on, makes it harder to read a document because your eyes have to stop and adjust to the new type style before you can continue to read. Keep style changes to a minimum to avoid this problem.

3. There has been considerable discussion among WWW users and document creators about the appropriate use of `<B>` versus `<STRONG>` and `<I>` versus `<EM>`. On most browsers (but not necessarily all!), the tags do the same thing and are interchangeable. There is no single right way to use these tags. As a general rule, though, consider the following: Whenever you want to emphasize a word or phrase, use **<EM>** or **<STRONG>**. When the particular word or phrase requires a specific formatting, like the title of a book or a specific name, use **<I>** or **<B>** instead. When in doubt, say out loud the sentence that contains the word or phrase in question. If you want to format the document to bring out the emphasis on the word or phrase as you would say it, use **<EM>** or **<STRONG>**.

4. HTML features another set of tags that are indistinguishable from one another when rendered on most browsers: **<TT>**, **<CODE>**, **<SAMP>**, and **<KBD>** all place text in a fixed-width format. Unlike the case described in step 3, things here are a bit more clear-cut. When you want to insert some code from a program, use the **<CODE>** tag. When you want to display the user input into a program, use the **<KBD>** tag. Use the **<SAMP>** tag when you want to display a sample of literal characters. Any other cases where you need to display text in a fixed-width font can be handled by the **<TT>** tag. This division not only allows individual browsers to choose the best method for displaying information, but it allows indexing programs that scan Web pages to identify any examples of code, input, and so on, through the tags used. If nothing but **<TT>** were used for all fixed-width type purposes, the output would probably look the same on most browsers, but the indexing program would have a much harder time finding code and input examples on Web pages.

5. When using tags to change the font size and color, keep in mind that some older browsers do not support these tags and won't change the text. Use these tags when other physical or logical effects won't emphasize the text in an acceptable way.

6. Due to differences in monitor resolution among different computer systems, text will not always appear the same size on different computers. As a rule of thumb, for a given font size specified with a **<FONT>** or **<BASEFONT>** tag (see How-To 3.4), the text will look bigger on Windows machines than on Macintosh computers. Keep this in mind before you change the font size to a very large or very small value.

Comments

With the judicious use of styles, you can easily spruce up your new home page and make it more interesting to read. Physical styles can improve the appearance of a page if care is taken with their use and it is understood that not all browsers will render physical styles in precisely the same way. The proper use of content styles will enable users to find the information of interest to them, and will allow indexing programs to better catalog the contents of your pages.

CHAPTER 5
TABLES

5

TABLES

How do I...

There are some powerful new techniques in HTML 3.2 that improve your ability to display the information on your page. Among them are the new mathematical symbols that allow you to display simple and complex mathematical and scientific equations. There are also new table formatting commands in HTML 3.2 that let you create tables and give you control over the size and alignment of the table contents. The How-To's in this chapter will show you how to effectively include math and tables in your Web pages.

5.1   Include a Table

The `<TABLE>` element in HTML 3.2 gives you the power to control the format and alignment of your information. You can place information into tables and be sure it will be properly aligned with the other information in the table, a great advantage when you're trying to display related information on a topic. This How-To gives the basics on including a table in your page.

5.2   Place a Caption in a Table

Captions are titles of tables, usually centered above the top of the table. This simple How-To explains how to add a caption to your table.

5.3   Insert a Table Heading

Table headings are the top row of the table and usually define what is in each column of the table. This How-To explains how to set up a table heading so you can easily identify the data in your table.

5.4   Define Data for a Cell or Table Element

Once you've set up a table, you need to be able to put data into it. In a table, data is stored in table elements, or cells. This How-To explains how to create cells and put your information into them.

5.5   Insert a Blank Data Cell

There are times when you may need to insert a blank cell into a table. This How-To explains two methods for doing this.

5.6   Create a New Row of Data

Once you've started creating table elements, you will want to put different items in different rows of the table. This How-To explains how to end one row of data and start a new row.

5.7   Define the Width of a Table Relative to the Browser Window

Sometimes you may wish to base the size of your table on the size of the user's browser window. This How-To shows how to make the width of a table relative to the browser window.

5.8   Specify the Distance Between Cells

Occasionally you may need extra control over the placement of cells in your table. This How-To explains how to specify a distance between cells.

5.9   Set the Distance from the Cell Edge to the Cell Data

There are times when you may want to control the distance from a cell's edge to the cell's data. This How-To explains how to accomplish this.

5.10   Put a Table in My Home Page

When you've mastered the basics of creating tables, you'll no doubt be eager to include them in your pages. This How-To covers some tips and tricks for effective use of tables, including some things you may not have thought of as tables.

COMPLEXITY
BEGINNING

5.1   How do I...
Include a table?

COMPATIBILITY: HTML 3

Problem

I have a collection of data that I would like to display as a table in my page. How do I define a table in HTML?

Technique

HTML 3.2 supports tables, which allow you to control the row and column placement of information on your page. This How-To explains how to define a table in HTML by using the **\<TABLE>** and **\</TABLE>** tags. How to format the data to include in the table will be covered later in the chapter.

Steps

Open your document. Identify where in the document you want to include a table. You may want to enter the table data into your document now, to serve as a guide when you add HTML **\<TABLE>** tags later.

1. To specify data presented as a table, place the **\<TABLE>** tag at the beginning of the data and **\</TABLE>** at the end of the data:

```
<TABLE>
    <!-- Here's where the table information goes... -->
</TABLE>
```

2. HTML does not include, as a default, borders around the cells of the table. If you want to display the borders using the lines programmed into the browser, add the **BORDER** attribute to the **<TABLE>** tag:

```
<TABLE BORDER>
    <!-- Here's where the table information goes... -->
</TABLE>
```

3. As with other HTML elements such as headings, you can use the **ALIGN** attribute to control the horizontal location of the table on the page. The **ALIGN** attribute can take on the following values:

Alignment options for tables

OPTION	DESCRIPTION
bleedleft	Flush with the left edge of the browser window
left	Flush with the left margin of the text
center	Centered between the left and right text margins
right	Flush with the right margin of the text
bleedright	Flush with the right edge of the browser window
justify	Fits the space between the left and right margins

For example, to center a table with a border, enter

```
<TABLE BORDER ALIGN=CENTER>
    <!-- Here's the data for the table... -->
</TABLE>
```

Or to place a borderless table flush against the left edge of the window, enter

```
<TABLE ALIGN=BLEEDLEFT>
    <!-- Here's the data for the table... -->
</TABLE>
```

4. When formatting a table, the browser automatically chooses a size for each column based on the text contained in each column. However, if you want to set a fixed size for each column, you can do so with the **COLSPEC** attribute in the **<TABLE>** tag. The **COLSPEC** attribute is followed by a series of letters and numbers; for example, **"L50 R30 C10"**. Here the letter stands for alignment of the text in the column: **L** for left, **C** for center, and **R** for right. The number is the width of the column. The units are set by the **UNITS** attribute, with the following choices:

Options for the UNITS attribute

OPTION	DESCRIPTION
en	En units (1 en = 1/2 point = 1/144 inch). This is the default.
relative	Relative units: The browser sums the units to determine the relative width of each column.
pixels	Pixels on the browser display.

For example, to define three columns, each left-aligned and each $1/2$ inch wide, enter

```
<TABLE COLSPEC="L72 L72 L72">
    <!-- Table data goes here... -->
</TABLE>
```

To create a four-column table with the first three columns left-aligned and the fourth right-aligned and half as wide as the others, enter

```
<TABLE UNITS=RELATIVE COLSPEC="L2 L2 L2 R1">
    <!-- Table data goes here... -->
</TABLE>
```

To create a table that has three columns, one left-aligned, one centered, and one right-aligned, each with a width of 100 pixels, enter

```
<TABLE UNITS=PIXELS COLSPEC="L100 C100 R100">
    <!-- Table data goes here... -->
</TABLE>
```

5. Similarly, you can control the width of the entire table by using the **WIDTH** attribute in the **<TABLE>** tag. Using the units defined by the **UNITS** attribute, the **WIDTH** attribute fixes the width of the table. If the **UNITS** attribute is set to **RELATIVE**, **WIDTH** interprets the number as the fraction of the distance between the left and right margins. For example, to set the width of a table to 4 inches (= 4×144 = 576 en), enter

```
<TABLE WIDTH=576>
    <!-- Table data goes here... -->
</TABLE>
```

To create a table that is centered on the screen and covers three-fourths of the distance between the left and right margins, enter

```
<TABLE ALIGN=CENTER UNITS=RELATIVE WIDTH=0.75>
    <!-- Table data goes here... -->
</TABLE>
```

How It Works

When a browser encounters a **<TABLE>** tag, it sets up the formatting to handle the data contained between the **<TABLE>** and **</TABLE>** tags. By reading the attributes contained between them, it knows where to override its default settings for creating tables, including the size and placement of the table.

Comments

The **BORDER** attribute tells the browser to use the lines defined within the browser; it is not currently possible to tell a browser to use a certain style of line, or to use lines only on specific cells. If you use the pixel unit for **COLSPEC** and **WIDTH**, note that not all pixels are the same size, so something that formats one way on your browser may look different on another browser. It's probably better to stick to en and relative units to help ensure that formatting works the way you want it to.

COMPLEXITY
BEGINNING

5.2   How do I...
Place a caption in a table?

COMPATIBILITY: HTML 3

Problem

I would like to add a title to the table in my page. I can do this with a heading, but is there a way to include a title as part of the table itself?

Technique

You can add a title, or caption, to the top or bottom of your table by using the **<CAPTION>** tag. Any text contained between the **<CAPTION>** and **</CAPTION>** tags is aligned with the table and, depending on the browser, may also be specially formatted in bold or italic.

Steps

Open your document. Decide on an appropriate caption for your table. It can be a title or a brief description of the table.

1. Enter the text for your caption in the table between the **<TABLE>** and **</TABLE>** tags.

2. To add a caption to a table, place a `<CAPTION>` tag at the beginning of the caption text and a `</CAPTION>` tag at the end of the text. If you want the caption to appear above the table, place the caption above the data in the table:

```
<TABLE>
    <CAPTION>This is the table caption</CAPTION>
    <!-- Here's the table data... -->
</TABLE>
```

To place a caption below the table, put the caption text and tags below the table data but before the `</TABLE>` tag:

```
<TABLE>
    <!-- Here's the table data... -->
    <CAPTION>This is the table caption</CAPTION>
</TABLE>
```

3. You can format the text within the `<CAPTION>` tags just as you would any other text, using the markup tags described in Chapter 3, Adding HTML Physical Character Effects. For example, to emphasize the caption of a table, enter

```
<TABLE>
    <CAPTION><EM>This is an emphasized caption!</EM></CAPTION>
    <!-- Here's the table data... -->
</TABLE>
```

You can also insert line breaks (as explained in Chapter 4, Adding HTML Logical Character Effects) to control the layout of the caption:

```
<TABLE>
    <CAPTION>This is the top line of the caption<BR>
    and this is the bottom line of the caption</CAPTION>
    <!-- Here's the table data... -->
</TABLE>
```

How It Works

When a browser encounters the `<CAPTION>` tag inside a table, it places the text contained between the `<CAPTION>` and `</CAPTION>` tags either above or below the table, depending on where it encounters the caption. The caption is usually aligned with the table. Some browsers may also format the caption with bold or italics.

Comments

Because some browsers may format the caption, be careful when using text formatting tags like `<B>` and `<I>` in the caption. These tags may be ignored by the browser, override the default setting, or be combined with the browser's format for the caption.

For example, if a browser is programmed to render captions in bold text, placing <I> and </I> around your caption text might mean the caption appears in italics, remains in bold, or appears as bold italics.

COMPLEXITY
INTERMEDIATE

5.3   How do I...
Insert a table heading?

COMPATIBILITY: HTML 3

Problem

In my table, I would like to have the top row consist of headings describing the contents of each column. I would like to easily set these headings off from the rest of the text. How can I accomplish this in HTML?

Technique

You can specify special heading cells in the table by using the **<TH>** tag. The text listed after the **<TH>** tag is considered to be part of the heading cell. You can use this tag anywhere in the table; the headings do not necessarily have to be at the top of a column. HTML also includes a number of sophisticated attributes that allow you to precisely format your table headings.

Steps

Open your document. Choose names for the heading cells. Heading cells can go across the columns or down the rows of your table, although for this example we will consider heading cells across the columns of a table.

1. Enter the word or phrase for each column heading in the table, between the **<TABLE>** and **</TABLE>** tags.

2. For each column in your table, place a **<TH>** tag, followed by the text for that column. For example, for a three-column table, enter

```
<TABLE>
    <CAPTION>Here's my table</CAPTION>
    <TH>Column 1<TH>Column 2<TH>Column 3
    <!-- Here's the data for the rest of the table... -->
</TABLE>
```

3. Although most browsers format the contents of heading cells differently from the rest of the text, you can still use normal text markup tags to alter the style of the heading. For instance, to place the heading for the second column of this example in italics, enter

```
<TABLE>
    <CAPTION>Here's my table</CAPTION>
    <TH>Column 1<TH><I>Column 2</I><TH>Column 3
    <!-- Here's the data for the rest of the table... -->
</TABLE>
```

4. You can make a heading extend across more than one row or more than one column by using the ROWSPAN and COLSPAN attributes, respectively, in the <TH> tag. For these attributes, you state how many rows down or columns across you would like the heading cell to extend. For example, to make the heading for the second column extend over to the third column as well, enter

```
<TABLE>
    <CAPTION>Here's my table</CAPTION>
    <TH>Column 1<TH COLSPAN=2>Column 2
    <!-- Here's the data for the rest of the table... -->
</TABLE>
```

Similarly, to make the heading for column 1 extend down two rows, enter

```
<TABLE>
    <CAPTION>Here's my table</CAPTION>
    <TH ROWSPAN=2>Column 1<TH>Column 2<TH>Column 3
    <!-- Here's the data for the rest of the table... -->
</TABLE>
```

The uses of the ROWSPAN and COLSPAN attributes will be discussed in greater detail in How-To 5.7.

5. You can use the ALIGN attribute inside the <TH> tag to define the alignment of the text within the header cell. The standard options of LEFT, CENTER, RIGHT, and JUSTIFY are available. To center the heading for the second column in this example, enter

```
<TABLE>
    <CAPTION>Here's my table</CAPTION>
    <TH ROWSPAN=2>Column 1<TH ALIGN=CENTER>Column 2<TH>Column 3
    <!-- Here's the data for the rest of the table... -->
</TABLE>
```

In addition to the standard alignment options, a fifth option, decimal, is also available. This is used to align the decimal points on each line of the cell if, for example, your cell has several lines of numbers (such as dollar amounts). If a line doesn't have a decimal point, the line is centered. You can use the DP attribute in the <TH> tag to define a decimal point if you want to use a character other than the default decimal point (.) symbol. An example of this would be using a colon like a decimal point to align a table of times, such as 1:15, 2:45, 3:30, and so on.

6. In addition to the horizontal alignment just described, you can align text vertically within a cell by using the **VALIGN** attribute. There are four options for **VALIGN**:

Vertical alignment options for table cells

OPTION	DESCRIPTION
TOP	Aligns text at the top of the cell
MIDDLE	Aligns text in the middle of the cell
BOTTOM	Aligns text at the bottom of the cell
BASELINE	Aligns all the text in a row with this alignment attribute set on a common baseline

For example, to have the heading for the third column line up along the top of the cell, enter

```
<TABLE>
    <CAPTION>Here's my table</CAPTION>
    <TH>Column 1<TH>Column 2<TH VALIGN=TOP>Column 3
    <!-- Here's the data for the rest of the table... -->
</TABLE>
```

To have the first and third columns aligned on the same baseline while the second column is aligned in the middle of its cell, enter

```
<TABLE>
    <CAPTION>Here's my table</CAPTION>
    <TH VALIGN=BASELINE>Column 1<TH VALIGN=MIDDLE>Column 2<TH
VALIGN=BASELINE>Column 3
    <!-- Here's the data for the rest of the table... -->
</TABLE>
```

How It Works

The **<TH>** tag tells the browser that the text after that tag and before the next **<TH>** tag (or **<TD>** or **<TR>** tag, discussed next) is part of a cell that has been designated as a heading cell. Most browsers will format the text in a bold or emphasized style, although some will treat a heading cell the same as a data cell (see How-To 5.5).

Comments

When using the **ROWSPAN** and **COLSPAN** attributes to specify the size of rows, be careful you don't end up with overlapping cells. This could cause a table to be rendered in a way you didn't plan, or to not even display at all, depending on the browser.

HTML 3.2 adds two more attributes that you can include in table heads and table cells:

- **WIDTH** Allows the user to specify the width of a cell in pixels

- **HEIGHT** Allows the user to specify the height of cell in pixels

COMPLEXITY
INTERMEDIATE

5.4   How do I...
Define data for a cell or table element?

COMPATIBILITY: HTML 3

Problem

Now that I've defined a table, added a caption, and set up headings for each column, I want to add my data to the table. How do I place data into table cells in HTML?

Technique

The process of adding data cells, or table elements, to your table is very similar to the technique used for adding table headings described in How-To 5.3. The **<TD>** tag indicates that the text after it and before the next table-related tag is to be placed into a cell. As with **<TH>**, there are a number of sophisticated attributes that can be used to control the placement and appearance of table cells.

Steps

Open your document. If you haven't done so already, enter the data you want to display in the table.

1. To place text in a data cell, put the **<TD>** tag in front of the text. The cell includes all the text that follows the data tag until it reaches another table-specific tag, such as **<TD>**, **<TH>**, **<TR>**, and so on. Here is an example for the first row of a three-column table:

```
<TABLE>
    <CAPTION>The table caption</CAPTION>
    <TH>Column 1<TH>Column 2<TH>Column 3
    <TR><TD>Data 1<TD>Data 2<TD>Data 3
</TABLE>
```

(Don't worry about the **<TR>** tag right now as it is explained in detail in How-To 5.6. Basically, it creates a new row in the table.)

2. As with heading cells in a table, you can use formatting tags like `<B>`, `<I>`, `<EM>`, and so on, to format the contents of a cell. Since data cells usually do not receive special formatting, unlike heading cells, this is a useful way to draw attention to a specific cell. For example, to highlight the data in the second column of this table, enter

```
<TABLE>
    <CAPTION>The table caption</CAPTION>
    <TH>Column 1<TH>Column 2<TH>Column 3
    <TR><TD>Data 1<TD><B>Data 2<B><TD>Data 3
</TABLE>
```

3. As described in How-To 5.3, you can use the `ROWSPAN` and `COLSPAN` attributes to identify data cells that have extended rows and columns. For example, to make the first data cell in the table extend over an extra column to the right, enter

```
<TABLE>
    <CAPTION>The table caption</CAPTION>
    <TH>Column 1<TH>Column 2<TH>Column 3
    <TR><TD COLSPAN=2>Data 1<TD>Data 3
</TABLE>
```

4. You can use the `ALIGN` attribute in `<TD>` to horizontally align the contents of the cell. As with `<TH>`, you can set `ALIGN` to `LEFT`, `CENTER`, `RIGHT`, `JUSTIFY`, and `decimal`, the last one being used to align the contents of the cell by using the decimal point (or another character specified using the `DP` attribute, as discussed in How-To 5.3). For example, to center the contents of the third data cell in the table, enter

```
<TABLE>
    <CAPTION>The table caption</CAPTION>
    <TH>Column 1<TH>Column 2<TH>Column 3
    <TR><TD>Data 1<TD>Data 2<TD ALIGN=CENTER>Data 3
</TABLE>
```

5. You can also use the `VALIGN` attribute to vertically align the contents of a cell. As with heading cells, the options for `VALIGN` are `TOP`, `MIDDLE`, `BOTTOM`, and `BASELINE`. To set the contents of the first data cell along the top of the cell, enter

```
<TABLE>
    <CAPTION>The table caption</CAPTION>
    <TH>Column 1<TH>Column 2<TH>Column 3
    <TR><TD VALIGN=TOP>Data 1<TD>Data 2<TD>Data 3
</TABLE>
```

How It Works

When a browser encounters a `<TD>` tag in a table, it creates a new data cell in the table, placing all the text from the `<TD>` tag to the next table-related tag (`<TH>`, `<TR>`, `<CAPTION>`, `</TABLE>`) in the cell. Any formatting for the contents of the cell depends on the attributes set for the cell, as well as on any formatting tags contained within the cell.

Comments

As with the `<TH>` tag, you should take care when using ROWSPAN and COLSPAN with `<TD>` in your table. If you create overlapping cells by misusing the tags, your table will not be rendered correctly, and it may not even display at all, depending on the browser's settings.

COMPLEXITY
INTERMEDIATE

5.5 How do I...
Insert a blank data cell?

COMPATIBILITY: HTML 3

Problem

There are times when I would like to insert a blank cell into a table. How do I do that?

Technique

You add a blank cell by literally defining a cell that either has nothing or simply a `<BR>` in it.

Steps

Open your document.

1. If you haven't done so already, create the table you wish to include the blank cell in.

2. Enter your blank cell by typing either one of the following two lines:

```
<TD></TD>
<TD><BR></TD>
```

Either method will give you a blank cell, but if you do not include the `<BR>` tag, the cell will not have any borders.

3. Check your table to make sure it looks like you want it to.

How It Works

When the browser finds a cell with nothing in it, that is exactly what it renders.

Comments

Figure 5-1 shows the difference between using the **
** tag and not using it.

COMPLEXITY
INTERMEDIATE

5.6 How do I...
Create a new row of data?

COMPATIBILITY: HTML 3

Problem

Now that I can add data cells to my table, I would like to split the cells up into rows. How can I divide the cells of my table into rows in HTML?

Technique

The **<TR>** tag creates a new row of cells in a table. You can use attributes with this tag to define the horizontal and vertical alignment of the contents of the row as well.

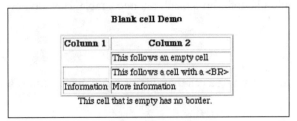

Figure 5-1 Using and not using the

 tag

Steps

Open your document. If you have not already done so, enter the rest of the data for your table, using the `<TH>` and `<TD>` tags described in How-To's 5.4 and 5.5.

1. To help you decide the number and length of your rows (and to make it easier to correct errors in code later), enter carriage returns at the end of each row of data.

```
<TABLE>
    <CAPTION>The table caption</CAPTION>
    <TH>Column 1<TH>Column 2<TH>Column 3
    <TD>Data 1<TD>Data 2<TD>Data 3
    <TD>Data 4<TD>Data 5<TD>Data 6
</TABLE>
```

2. To specify the end of one row and the beginning of another, add the `<TR>` tag at the beginning of the new row:

```
<TABLE>
    <CAPTION>The table caption</CAPTION>
    <TR><TH>Column 1<TH>Column 2<TH>Column 3
    <TR><TD>Data 1<TD>Data 2<TD>Data 3
    <TR><TD>Data 4<TD>Data 5<TD>Data 6
</TABLE>
```

The `<TR>` tag at the beginning of the first row of the table is optional, but it helps ensure parallelism in the HTML code describing the table and does not upset the formatting of the table.

3. To set the horizontal alignment of all the cells of the row to the same value, use the `ALIGN` attribute in the `<TR>` tag. `ALIGN` in this context can take on the same values it can with the `<TD>` and `<TH>` tags: `LEFT`, `CENTER`, `RIGHT`, `JUSTIFY`, and `decimal`. To center the cells in the second row of data in the example, you can do the following:

```
<TABLE>
    <CAPTION>The table caption</CAPTION>
    <TR><TH>Column 1<TH>Column 2<TH>Column 3
    <TR><TD>Data 1<TD>Data 2<TD>Data 3
    <TR ALIGN=CENTER><TD>Data 4<TD>Data 5<TD>Data 6
</TABLE>
```

You can override the formatting for any cell in that row by setting the `ALIGN` attribute within the particular cell. For example, if you wanted the cell in the second column of the second data row aligned to the right side of the cell, and not centered like the rest of the text, you could do the following:

```
<TABLE>
    <CAPTION>The table caption</CAPTION>
    <TR><TH>Column 1<TH>Column 2<TH>Column 3
    <TR><TD>Data 1<TD>Data 2<TD>Data 3
    <TR ALIGN=CENTER><TD>Data 4<TD ALIGN=RIGHT>Data 5<TD>Data 6
</TABLE>
```

The alignment specified in the COLSPEC attribute in the table overrides any formatting you set with the <TR> tag, although you can override the COLSPEC alignment in individual cells.

4. You can set the vertical alignment of all cells in the row by using the VALIGN attribute in the <TR> tag. In heading and data cells, VALIGN takes on the values TOP, MIDDLE, BOTTOM, and BASELINE. For example, to set the vertical alignment of the second data row in the example to the middle of the cell, enter

```
<TABLE>
    <CAPTION>The table caption</CAPTION>
    <TR><TH>Column 1<TH>Column 2<TH>Column 3
    <TR><TD>Data 1<TD>Data 2<TD>Data 3
    <TR VALIGN=MIDDLE><TD>Data 4<TD>Data 5<TD>Data 6
</TABLE>
```

To override the vertical alignment for a row in a given cell, set the alignment within that particular cell. To set the middle cell of the second data row to a bottom alignment, you can use the following code:

```
<TABLE>
    <CAPTION>The table caption</CAPTION>
    <TR><TH>Column 1<TH>Column 2<TH>Column 3
    <TR><TD>Data 1<TD>Data 2<TD>Data 3
    <TR VALIGN=MIDDLE><TD>Data 4<TD VALIGN=BOTTOM>Data 5<TD>Data 6
</TABLE>
```

How It Works

When a browser encounters the <TR> tag, it creates a new row in the table and places the cells located between the <TR> and the next <TR> or the end of the table in that row. If alignment attributes are specified, they are applied to all the cells in that row unless individual cells (or the COLSPEC attribute in <TABLE>) contain information that overrides the alignment specified in <TR>.

Comments

If you set the column alignments using the COLSPEC attribute in the <TABLE> tag, then any horizontal alignment placed in the <TR> tags will be ignored. The order of precedence for defining cell alignments is

- <TH> and <TD>
- COLSPEC in <TABLE>
- <TR>

COMPLEXITY
INTERMEDIATE

5.7 How do I...
Define the width of a table relative to the browser window?

COMPATIBILITY: HTML 3

Problem

I would like to have my table occupy a certain percentage of the browser's window. How do I accomplish this?

Technique

You add a **WIDTH** attribute to the **<TABLE>** tag to specify the width of the table. You may set the width to either a percentage of the window or to a number of actual pixels.

Steps

Open your document.

1. If you haven't done so already, create the table you would like to use.

2. Enter the **WIDTH** attribute into the **<TABLE>** tag. Set the width to the desired size. For example:

```
<TABLE WIDTH="50%">
 OTHER TEXT AND TAGS
</TABLE>
```

This tag will produce a table that occupies 50 percent of the browser.

3. View your document to make sure it looks like you think it should.

How It Works

The browser encounters the **WIDTH** attribute and renders the table according to the size given.

Comments

You may enter the width as a percentage, in which case it should be enclosed in quotes and include a % sign, or you may simply enter a number, in which case the browser will set the table width in actual pixels. Figure 5-2 shows a couple of different tables using the WIDTH attribute.

More examples may be found at `http://www.psnw.com/~jmz5/waite/tables.html`.

COMPLEXITY
INTERMEDIATE

5.8 How do I...
Specify the distance between cells?

COMPATIBILITY: HTML 3

Problem

I would like to have finer control over the distance between the cells of my table. How do I do this?

Technique

By adding the CELLSPACING attribute to the <TABLE> tag, you can control the space the browser shows between cells.

Steps

Open your document.

1. If you haven't done so already, create your table.

2. Modify the <TABLE> tag by adding the CELLSPACING attribute and a numeric value. The greater the value, the greater the distance between cells. For instance:

```
<TABLE CELLSPACING=5>
...OTHER TEXT AND TAGS
</TABLE>
```

3. View your document to make sure it looks like you think it should.

How It Works

The browser creates the table with space between each cell depending on the value of CELLSPACING.

Figure 5-2 The WIDTH attribute

Comments

CELLSPACING's default value is 2.

Figure 5-3 shows some examples of tables using cell spacing. You may see other examples at http://www.psnw.com/~jmz5/waite/tables.html.

Figure 5-3 Tables using cell spacing

5.9 How do I...
Set the distance from the cell edge to the cell data?

COMPATIBILITY: HTML 3

Problem

I would like to have finer control over the distance between the cell edges and the information inside them. How do I do this?

Technique

By adding the **CELLPADDING** attribute to the **<TABLE>** tag, you can control the space the browser shows between the cell edges and the cell's content.

Steps

Open your document.

1. If you haven't already done so, create your table.

2. Modify the **<TABLE>** tag by adding the **CELLPADDING** attribute and a numeric value. The greater the value, the greater the distance between the cells and the data. For instance:

```
<TABLE   CELLPADDING=5>
 OTHER TEXT AND TAGS
</TABLE>
```

3. View your document to make sure it looks like you think it should.

How It Works

The browser creates the table with the space between each cell edge and the information in that cell depending on the value of **CELLPADDING**.

Comments

CELLPADDING's default value is **1**.

Figure 5-4 shows some examples of tables using cell padding. You may see other examples at **http://www.psnw.com/~jmz5/waite/tables.html**.

Figure 5-4 Tables using cell padding

COMPLEXITY
INTERMEDIATE

5.10 How do I...
Put a table in my home page?

COMPATIBILITY: HTML 3

Problem

Now that I know all the elements of a table in HTML, I would like to start adding tables to my pages. How can I use these tables to effectively display my information? What sort of tips and tricks can I use to make my tables look better?

Technique

Tables are a good way to control the layout and format of information on a Web page. A good way to learn how to create effective tables is to go through a few examples of them step by step to see how they are constructed.

Steps

These examples will give you an idea of how to create tables and use them to display different types of information.

1. First, let's look at a simple table that might be used by someone listing a number of products for sale and their prices. It might look like this:

Widget price list (September 1997)

ITEM	COST
Mini Widget	$19.95
Widget	$29.95
Super Widget	$39.95
Widget Royale (with cheese)	$79.95

To produce this table, begin by setting up the <TABLE> tags at the beginning and end of the list. Let the browser choose the size of the cells, and put a border around the table:

```
<TABLE BORDER>

</TABLE>
```

Now add a title as a caption at the top of the list. Again, let the browser choose the style for the caption; don't include any style tags here. For the sake of clarity, indent the contents of the <CAPTION> tag, as well as anything else contained between the <TABLE> tags, to help set it off from the rest of the code for the page:

```
<TABLE BORDER>
    <CAPTION>Widget Price List (September 1997)</CAPTION>

</TABLE>
```

Now add the heading cells for the table. There are two columns in this table, so create two heading cells using the <TH> tag. You can start off the row with the <TR> tag, although it is not explicitly required.

```
<TABLE BORDER>
    <CAPTION>Widget Price List (September 1997)</CAPTION>
    <TR><TH>Item<TH>Cost

</TABLE>
```

Now add the rows of items and their prices. Start each row with the **<TR>** tag and put the **<TD>** tag in front of each item. Use italics (**<I>**) here to emphasize the phrase **with cheese**.

```
<TABLE BORDER>
    <CAPTION>Widget Price List (September 1997)</CAPTION>
    <TR><TH>Item<TH>Cost
    <TR><TD>Mini Widget<TD>$19.95
    <TR><TD>Widget<TD>$29.95
    <TR><TD>Super Widget<TD>$39.95
    <TR><TD>Widget Royale <I>(with cheese)</I><TD>$79.95
</TABLE>
```

You've now made a full-fledged, complete table, although you could still tweak it a little bit to improve its appearance if you wished. For example, if you included another item in the table with a price of more than $100.00, the formatting of the price column (which defaults to flush left) would be unattractive unless you set the alignment for the price cells to be flush right, as follows:

```
<TABLE BORDER>
    <CAPTION>Widget Price List (September 1997)</CAPTION>
    <TR><TH>Item<TH>Cost
    <TR><TD>Mini Widget<TD ALIGN=RIGHT>$19.95
    <TR><TD>Widget<TD ALIGN=RIGHT>$29.95
    <TR><TD>Super Widget<TD ALIGN=RIGHT>$39.95
    <TR><TD>Widget Royale <I>(with cheese)</I><TD ALIGN=RIGHT>$79.95
    <TR><TD>Mega Deluxe Widget<TD ALIGN=RIGHT>$109.95
</TABLE>
```

You could also use the **COLSPEC** attribute in the heading if you wanted to specify the size of the columns as well. Try this, using relative units and making the left column three times as wide as the right column, as follows:

```
<TABLE BORDER UNITS=RELATIVE COLSPEC="L3 R1">
    <CAPTION>Widget Price List (September 1997)</CAPTION>
    <TR><TH>Item<TH>Cost
    <TR><TD>Mini Widget<TD>$19.95
    <TR><TD>Widget<TD>$29.95
    <TR><TD>Super Widget<TD>$39.95
    <TR><TD>Widget Royale <I>(with cheese)</I><TD>$79.95
    <TR><TD>Mega Deluxe Widget<TD>$109.95
</TABLE>
```

The output of this table is shown in Figure 5-5. The code is also available on the CD as file 5-5.HTML.

A Price List as an HTML Table

Widget Price List (September 1997)

Item	Cost
Mini Widget	$19.95
Widget	$29.95
Super Widget	$39.95
Widget Royale *(with cheese!)*	$79.95

A Price List using Table Alignments

Widget Price List (September 1997)

Item	Cost
Mini Widget	$19.95
Widget	$29.95
Super Widget	$39.95
Widget Royale *(with cheese!)*	$79.95
Mega Deluxe Widget	$109.95

Figure 5-5 A price
list table in HTML

2. Now try another type of table, which will show an effective way of using
COLSPAN and ROWSPAN. Say you want to include the score from a baseball
game in a Web page as a table. An example of a score is shown here.

Today's Game

TEAM	SCORE		
	R	H	E
Red Sox	8	11	0
Yankees	0	3	1

As you did in the first example, start with the <TABLE> tags and include the title
of the table as the caption. For this example, do not include a border; all you
want to do here is format the text the right way.

```
<TABLE>
    <CAPTION>Today's Game</CAPTION>

</TITLE>
```

Before you proceed any further, sketch out how the rows and columns will be
set up. It's clear that this table will have four columns: one for the name of the
team and three for the various score categories (R, H, and E, which stand for
Runs, Hits, and Errors). In this table, unlike the one in the previous example,
there won't be an item for every cell. One way to deal with this would be to
just skip cells by including cell tags in the table but not putting any text in them.

To do that, you immediately follow one table-related tag with another. Apply this to the first row of the table, where only two of the four columns contain any text, as follows:

```
<TABLE>
    <CAPTION>Today's Game</CAPTION>
    <TR><TH>Team<TH><TH>Score<TH>

</TABLE>
```

The second row is similar, but only missing one cell:

```
<TABLE>
    <CAPTION>Today's Game</CAPTION>
    <TR><TH>Team<TH><TH>Score<TH>
    <TR><TH><TH>R<TH>H<TH>E

</TABLE>
```

Finish the rest of the table using data cells for the team names and scores:

```
<TABLE>
    <CAPTION>Today's Game</CAPTION>
    <TR><TH>Team<TH><TH>Score<TH>
    <TR><TH><TH>R<TH>H<TH>E
    <TR><TD>Red Sox<TD>8<TD>11<TD>0
    <TR><TD>Yankees<TD>0<TD>3<TD>1
</TABLE>
```

The output of this table is shown in Figure 5-6. The code is also available on the CD as file 5-5.HTML.

This layout succeeds in skipping cells, but the result is less than aesthetically pleasing. The third column, which contains the number of hits, also includes the word Score. Since this word is much larger than the numbers or the letter H, the column is automatically sized wide enough to fit Score, which ends up disrupting the flow of the layout for the scores shown here. A solution to this problem is to use COLSPAN: You can define the top row to have only two columns, but have the second column of the row be three columns wide:

Figure 5-6 A box score table made by skipping cells

```
<TABLE>
     <CAPTION>Today's Game</CAPTION>
     <TR><TH>Team<TH COLSPAN=3>Score
     <TR><TH><TH>R<TH>H<TH>E
     <TR><TD>Red Sox<TD>8<TD>11<TD>0
     <TR><TD>Yankees<TD>0<TD>3<TD>1
</TABLE>
```

Note that, when you added the COLSPAN attribute, you must delete the extra <TH> tags; if you don't, the table will include the extra columns and its flow will be disrupted. While you're at it, use the ROWSPAN attribute on the first cell in the first row (Team) to make it two rows deep:

```
<TABLE>
     <CAPTION>Today's Game</CAPTION>
     <TR><TH ROWSPAN=2>Team<TH COLSPAN=3>Score
     <TR><TH>R<TH>H<TH>E
     <TR><TD>Red Sox<TD>8<TD>11<TD>0
     <TR><TD>Yankees<TD>0<TD>3<TD>1
</TABLE>
```

Note that, when you add the ROWSPAN attribute, you must delete the extra <TH> tag in the second row, which is no longer needed and would otherwise disrupt the layout of the table. While this doesn't affect the layout as much as the COLSPAN attribute did, it makes it easier to change the alignment of the text in the cell. For example, if you wanted the word Team in that cell placed on the bottom of the cell instead of the top, you could write

```
<TABLE>
     <CAPTION>Today's Game</CAPTION>
     <TR><TH ROWSPAN=2 VALIGN=BOTTOM>Team<TH COLSPAN=3>Score
     <TR><TH>R<TH>H<TH>E
     <TR><TD>Red Sox<TD>8<TD>11<TD>0
     <TR><TD>Yankees<TD>0<TD>3<TD>1
</TABLE>
```

Figure 5-7 A box score table made with ROWSPAN and COLSPAN

This is easier, and it is also better form than making empty cells and moving text among the cells when you want to change the layout. The output of this table is shown as Figure 5-7 and is also available on the CD as file 5-7.HTML.

3. The examples shown here and elsewhere in the chapter have assumed you have short, one-line entries for the tables. However, there is no reason the tables need to have only short entries for each cell. You can use tables to format larger pieces of text, and control their layout better than if you used line breaks, paragraphs, or other HTML features discussed in Chapter 4, Adding HTML Logical Character Elements. For example, you want to format a troubleshooting guide for a product that will consist of a series of stated problems and a set of solutions for them. Here's how you can format this using a table.

First, create the `<TABLE>` tags and include the title of the table:

```
<TABLE BORDER>
    <CAPTION>Widget Troubleshooting Guide</CAPTION>

</TABLE>
```

The best way to format this would be to use two columns: one column with problems and the other with the corresponding solutions. Place heading cells into the table based on this:

```
<TABLE BORDER>
    <CAPTION>Widget Troubleshooting Guide</CAPTION>
    <TR><TH>Problem<TH>Solution

</TABLE>
```

Now add the problems and the solutions. Add the text just as you would for any other table. Since HTML considers all text placed between the `<TD>` tag and the next table-specific tag as part of a single cell, you can easily put multiple lines of text into a single cell. For example:

```
<TABLE BORDER>
    <CAPTION>Widget Troubleshooting Guide</CAPTION>
    <TR><TH>Problem<TH>Solution
    <TR>
        <TD>Widget won't turn on
            <TD>Make sure the widget is plugged in. Also make sure the power
switch is in the on position. If the widget still will not turn on, take
your widget to the nearest repair shop for servicing.
    <TR>
        <TD>Widget behaving erratically
            <TD>Press the reset button on the underside of the widget. If the
widget still behaves erratically, turn the power off and then back on. If
this does not work, take your widget to the nearest repair shop for
servicing.
</TABLE>
```

You can continue to do this, making table cells many lines long, if necessary. The only limit is the amount of your data (although style may play a part too).

Widget Troubleshooting Guide	
Problem	**Solution**
Widget won't turn on	Make sure the widget is plugged in. Also make sure the power switch is in the on position. If the widget still will not turn on, take your widget to the nearest repair shop for servicing.
Widget behaving erratically	Press the reset button on the underside of the widget. If the widget still behaves erratically, turn the power off and then back on. If this does not work, take your widget to the nearest repair shop for servicing.

Figure 5-8 A troubleshooting list as a table in HTML

The output of this code is shown in Figure 5-8. The code is also available on the CD as file 5-8.HTML.

How It Works

Browsers format tables based on their own predefined settings, plus any specific commands contained in the table. These commands give you considerable power to control the layout of the table.

Comments

As you have seen, tables are a powerful way to format text in your pages. Tables are versatile: Not only can they be shaped to best display your information, but they are not just limited to plain text. Tables can be used to display graphics (Chapter 9, Using Images in Your Documents) or forms (Chapter 11, HTML Interactive Forms), or to format lists of links to other documents (Chapter 7, Managing Document Spacing). Tables can include essentially any HTML element, including line breaks and paragraphs, and even lists (Chapter 6, Lists). Tables take a little time to understand completely, but your effort will be rewarded by a better ability to control the layout and present your information. Adding colors to tables will be discussed in Chapter 15, Navigator and Internet Explorer HTML Extensions.

For an example of how changing different table attributes affects the table, check out the accompanying Web page at `http://www.psnw.com/~jmz5/waite/tables.html`.

CHAPTER 6
LISTS

6

LISTS

How do I...

A lot of information is best displayed in lists: ingredients for a recipe, your top ten favorite albums, the outline for a presentation, or the definitions for a set of terms. You can use tags like <P> and
 (see Chapter 7, Managing Document Spacing) to manage the placement of items in a document and create lists, but these tags are cumbersome and provide you with little flexibility to create the types of lists that best fit your information. Fortunately, HTML has other tags that permit you to create lists that include numbers, bullets, indentations, and other features. Moreover, HTML 3.2 includes new attributes that give you even greater ability to create the best lists for your data. This chapter covers the various types of lists that can be generated in HTML and shows you how they can be used to create a more effective home page.

6.1   Create a Numbered List

Some information is ideally suited to be displayed in a numbered list: rankings, "top ten" lists, step-by-step procedures, and so on. This simple How-To shows how you can create a numbered, or ordered, list that appears in a document, with the ranking automatically included.

6.2   Specify the Style and Sequence of My Numbering

There are many cases where the standard style of numerical lists isn't the best way to present the information. A different style of numbering is needed sometimes, as in outlines, and in other cases a numbered list should begin with a number other than one. This How-To explores the ways you can alter the style and sequence of numbering used in an ordered list.

6.3   Create a Bulleted List

Some information is better suited to a point-by-point list: outlines, menus, and so on. Each item on such a list is usually marked with a point, or bullet, to set it apart from other elements of the list. This simple How-To shows you how to create a bulleted list.

6.4   Modify the Appearance of My Bullets

Sometimes the standard style of bullets isn't the way you want to present your data. HTML 3.2 provides alternatives to the standard bulleted list that give the writer some control over the bullets used. This How-To shows how to use those attributes to modify the appearance of bullets in these lists.

6.5   Create an Unmarked List

In some cases, neither a numbered list nor a bulleted list is appropriate for the information you want to include in a document. Sometimes the best type of list is one without any sort of number or mark in front of each item. This How-To explains how to create an unmarked list.

6.6   Create a Menu List

Lists, when combined with links to other documents or other locations in the same document, are often the best way to present the reader of a document with a menu of choices. This How-To explains how to use the menu feature to create menus in HTML versions predating HTML 3.2.

6.7   Create a Directory List

Some information takes the form of a list of entries from a directory: a list of files, a list of people, and so forth. This How-To explains how to use the directory feature in HTML versions predating HTML 3.2 to create a directory of that information.

6.8   Create a Glossary List

Creating a glossary—a list of words and their definitions—requires special formatting to achieve the best results. This How-To explains how to use features in HTML to easily create a glossary.

6.9   Nest Lists Together

Some elements of a list may, in fact, be lists themselves, such as entries in an outline. This How-To shows how to nest lists within lists, as well as mix different types of lists together.

6.10   Use Lists to Jazz Up My Home Page

With the knowledge of how to use lists, it is now possible to create a better-structured home page that gives readers easier access to the information they need. This How-To provides some tips on style and explains how to effectively add lists to a page.

 COMPLEXITY
BEGINNING

6.1   How do I...
Create a numbered list?

COMPATIBILITY: HTML 2+

Problem

I have a set of data I would like to display as a list. I want each item in the list to be preceded by a number. However, since the order of the list items may change from time to time, I would like to have the numbers generated automatically so I don't have to spend time manually editing the number for each item. How can I create a numbered list in HTML?

Technique

HTML allows you to create a numbered, or ordered, list that will automatically generate numbers in front of each item in the list. The number placed in front of an item depends on the location of the item in the list: The first item gets the numeral 1, the second 2, and so on. You can do this by using the `<OL>` and `<LI>` tags, described in the Steps section.

Steps

Open your document. Identify the locations in your document where you want to include a list.

1. First, place the items to be included in the list in your document. For clarity, separate each item with a carriage return. For example:

```
<H2>My Five Favorite Baseball Teams</H2>
Red Sox
Cubs
Royals
Dodgers
Indians
```

2. At the beginning of the list, place the `<OL>` (for ordered list) tag. At the end of the list, place the `</OL>` tag:

```
<H2>My Five Favorite Baseball Teams</H2>
<OL>
Red Sox
Cubs
Royals
Dodgers
Indians
</OL>
```

3. In front of each item in the list, place the `<LI>` (list item) tag:

```
<H2>My Five Favorite Baseball Teams</H2>
<OL>
<LI>Red Sox
<LI>Cubs
<LI>Royals
<LI>Dodgers
<LI>Indians
</OL>
```

4. Some browsers permit you to conserve space in a document by making a list more compact. A compacted list usually has less space between list entries and may use a smaller, more compressed font. To specify a compacted list, replace the `<OL>` at the beginning of the list with `<OL COMPACT>`:

```
<H2>My Five Favorite Baseball Teams (compact form)</H2>
<OL COMPACT>
<LI>Red Sox
<LI>Cubs
<LI>Royals
```

```
<LI>Dodgers
<LI>Indians
</OL>
```

Examples of numbered lists are shown in Figures 6-1 and 6-2. The code is also available on the CD-ROM as file 6-1.HTML.

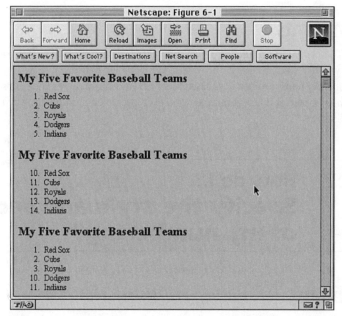

Figure 6-1 Examples of numbered lists

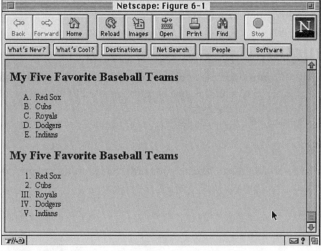

Figure 6-2 More examples of numbered lists

How It Works

When an HTML browser, such as Mosaic or Netscape, loads a numbered list such as the one just shown, it converts each **<LI>** it finds between the **<OL>** and the **</OL>** into a number; the first **<LI>** becomes the number 1, the second becomes 2, and so on. The browser also puts a carriage return just before the number to better format the text.

Comments

The **COMPACT** attribute is not well supported, so it may not give the results one expects when viewed in popular browsers. With the list markup just described, all lists will start with the number 1 and increment upwards from there. The next section describes how to start at different numbers and even use different numbering systems for ordered lists.

COMPLEXITY
BEGINNING

6.2 How do I...
Specify the style and sequence of my numbering?

COMPATIBILITY: HTML 3.2

Problem

I have a list that I don't want numbered in the conventional way. I'd like to be able to adjust the style of numbers used to create a table, and I would also like to start my lists at a number other than 1. How can I adjust the style and sequence of numbers in my numbered lists?

Technique

HTML 3.2 introduces several attributes that can be used with numbered lists. One allows you to alter the style of numbers used in the lists, while another sets the starting number of the lists.

Steps

Open your document. Create your ordered list in the manner described in How-To 6.1.

1. To start an ordered list at a number other than 1, place the **START** attribute on the **<OL>** tag at the beginning of the list. Set the attribute equal to the value of the first number in your list. For example, to create a list that starts with number 10, enter

```
<H2>My Five Favorite Baseball Teams</H2>
<OL START=10>
<LI>Red Sox
<LI>Cubs
<LI>Royals
<LI>Dodgers
<LI>Indians
</OL>
```

2. You can also use the **VALUE** attribute within the **<LI>** tag to change the numbering sequence within a list. For example, to start numbering a list at 1 but change to a higher value later in the list, enter

```
<H2>My Five Favorite Baseball Teams</H2>
<OL>
<LI>Red Sox
<LI>Cubs
<LI>Royals
<LI VALUE=10>Dodgers
<LI>Indians
</OL>
```

3. You can select the type of numbering system to be used with the **TYPE** attribute. The following table lists the possible values of the **TYPE** attribute.

ATTRIBUTE VALUE	DEFINITION
A	Use uppercase letters (A, B, C, etc.)
a	Use lowercase letters (a, b, c, etc.)
I	Use uppercase Roman numerals (I, II, III, etc.)
i	Use lowercase Roman numerals (i, ii, iii, etc.)
1	Use standard numbers, the default (1, 2, 3, etc.)

Values for the **TYPE** attribute

For example, to use uppercase letters in a list, enter

```
<H2>My Five Favorite Baseball Teams</H2>
<OL TYPE=A>
<LI>Red Sox
<LI>Cubs
<LI>Royals
<LI>Dodgers
<LI>Indians
</OL>
```

4. You can also use the **TYPE** attribute within the **<LI>** tag to change the numbering scheme within a list. For example, to change from standard numerals to uppercase Roman numerals, enter

```
<H2>My Five Favorite Baseball Teams</H2>
<OL>
<LI>Red Sox
<LI>Cubs
<LI TYPE=I>Royals
<LI>Dodgers
<LI>Indians
</OL>
```

Examples of numbered lists are shown in Figures 6-1 and 6-2. The code is also available on the CD as file 6-1.HTML.

How It Works

When an HTML browser encounters an ordered list with the **START** attribute set equal to some value, it starts the numbered list with that value. Similarly, when it encounters the **TYPE** attribute equal to some value, it matches the value with a predefined list of numbering types, and uses the appropriate type to number the list. When the browser encounters a **<TYPE>** or **<VALUE>** tag in a list element, it changes the list numbering scheme according to the value set in the tag.

Comments

Since **TYPE**, **START**, and **VALUE** are all additions to HTML 3.2, they may not be supported by older browsers. There is currently no way in HTML to alter the rate of numbering, that is, to create lists that use only even or odd numbers, or go down instead of up. Should you need to create such a list, you will be best off to manually enter the numbers in an unmarked list (see How-To 6.5).

COMPLEXITY
BEGINNING

6.3 How do I...
Create a bulleted list?

COMPATIBILITY: HTML 2+

Problem

I have a set of data that I would like to display as a list. I want to call attention to each item on the list by placing a bullet in front of it, and I would like to have the bullet created automatically so I don't have to design a special graphic. How can I create a bulleted list in HTML?

Technique

HTML allows you to create a bulleted, or unordered, list with the bullets automatically created and placed in front of each list item. The technique is very similar to the numbered list technique; the only difference is in the tags that are used at the beginning and the end of the list.

Steps

Open your document. Identify the locations in your document where you want to include a list.

1. First, place the items to be included in the list in your document. For clarity, separate each item with a carriage return. For example:

```
<H2>My Five Favorite Baseball Teams</H2>
Red Sox
Cubs
Royals
Dodgers
Indians
```

2. At the beginning of the list, place the **<UL>** (for unordered list) tag. At the end of the list, place the **</UL>** tag:

```
<H2>My Five Favorite Baseball Teams</H2>
<UL>
Red Sox
Cubs
Royals
Dodgers
Indians
</UL>
```

3. In front of each item in the list, place the **<LI>** tag:

```
<H2>My Five Favorite Baseball Teams</H2>
<UL>
<LI>Red Sox
<LI>Cubs
<LI>Royals
<LI>Dodgers
<LI>Indians
</UL>
```

4. Some browsers permit you to conserve space in your document by making your list more compact. A compacted list usually has less space between list entries and may use a smaller, more compressed font. To create a compacted list, replace the **<UL>** tag at the beginning of the list with **<UL COMPACT>**:

```
<H2>My Five Favorite Baseball Teams (compact form)</H2>
<UL COMPACT>
<LI>Red Sox
<LI>Cubs
<LI>Royals
<LI>Dodgers
<LI>Indians
</UL>
```

Examples of bulleted lists are shown in Figure 6-3. The code is also available on the CD as file 6-2.HTML.

How It Works

Just as it does for a numbered list, a browser converts each **<LI>** it finds between the **<UL>** and **</UL>** tags, in this case into a bullet. It also inserts a carriage return immediately before the bullet to format the text.

Comments

The actual shape and size of the bullet is determined by the browser; different browsers use different shapes for bullets. HTML 3.2 does allow for some choice in selecting the type of bullets used (see How-To 6.4). When bullets are used in nested lists (see How-To 6.9), different bullet shapes may be used at different levels of nesting; again, this depends on the browser. If you want to use a bullet with a specific shape, or another special graphic, you should consider creating an inline image of the desired bullet (see How-To 9.2) and placing this in front of each item, using an unmarked list, as described in How-To 6.5.

Figure 6-3 Examples of bulleted lists

COMPLEXITY
BEGINNING

6.4   How do I...
Modify the appearance of my bullets?

COMPATIBILITY: HTML 3.2

Problem

I would like to be able to replace the standard bullets used in my bulleted lists with another style. How can I alter the appearance of the bullets in HTML lists?

Technique

New attributes in HTML 3.2 allow you to alter the type of bullet used in an unordered list. You can easily select from a number of different styles of bullets with this feature.

Steps

Open your document. Create a bulleted list in the manner described in How-To 6.3.

1. To change the type of bullet used throughout the list, place the **TYPE** attribute in the **<UL>** tag at the beginning of the list. **TYPE** can have one of three values: **DISC**, **SQUARE**, and **CIRCLE**. For example, to create a bulleted list that uses squares as bullets, enter

```
<H2>My Five Favorite Baseball Teams</H2>
<OL TYPE=SQUARE>
<LI>Red Sox
<LI>Cubs
<LI>Royals
<LI>Dodgers
<LI>Indians
</OL>
```

2. You can change the type of bullet in the middle of the list by placing the **TYPE** attribute in the **<LI>** tag at the appropriate location in the list. To start with the disc style of bullets and then switch over to circles, use

```
<H2>My Five Favorite Baseball Teams</H2>
<OL TYPE=DISC>
<LI>Red Sox
<LI>Cubs
<LI>Royals
<LI TYPE=CIRCLE>Dodgers
<LI>Indians
</OL>
```

Examples of bulleted lists are shown in Figure 6-3. The code is also available on the CD as file 6-2.HTML.

How It Works

When an HTML browser encounters an unordered list with the **TYPE** attribute set equal to some value, it matches the value with a predefined list of bullet types and uses the appropriate bullet to mark the list. When the browser encounters a **<TYPE>** tag in a list element, it changes the list bulleting scheme according to the value set in the tag.

Comments

Since **TYPE** is an addition to HTML 3.2, these features may not be supported by older browsers. Currently only circle, disc, and square bullets are available.

 COMPLEXITY
BEGINNING

6.5 How do I...
Create an unmarked list?

COMPATIBILITY: HTML 2+

Problem

I have a set of data that I would like to display as a list. I want to display this simply as a list of items separated by carriage returns, without numbers or bullets. How can I do this in HTML?

Technique

There are several ways to do this in HTML. Perhaps the simplest way is to insert line breaks, **
**, after each list element. There are other techniques, though, that allow you to create unmarked lists and even set them off from the rest of the text. These methods are described next.

Steps

Open your document. Identify the locations in your document where you want to include a list.

1. To separate list items using line breaks, place **
** tags after each list element:

```
<H2>My Five Favorite Baseball Teams, using &lt;BR &rt;</H2>
Red Sox<BR>
Cubs<BR>
Royals<BR>
Dodgers<BR>
Indians<BR>
```

(The **<** and **&rt;** are special key sequences that will print the **<** and **>** characters, respectively. They are used here because **<** and **>** are reserved for HTML commands.)

2. In HTML 2.0, you can create an identical list using the `<DL>` and `<DT>` tags:

■ Place a `<DL>` (for descriptive list) at the beginning of the list and a `</DL>` at the end of the list:

```
<H2>My Five Favorite Baseball Teams</H2>
<DL>
Red Sox
Cubs
Royals
Dodgers
Indians
</DL>
```

■ Place the `<DT>` tag in front of each item of the list:

```
<H2>My Five Favorite Baseball Teams, using &lt;DT &rt;</H2>
<DL>
<DT>Red Sox
<DT>Cubs
<DT>Royals
<DT>Dodgers
<DT>Indians
</DL>
```

3. To create a list that is indented from normal text, use the `<DL>` and `</DL>` tags at the beginning and end of the list, but use `<DD>` instead of `<DT>` before each list item:

```
<H2>My Five Favorite Baseball Teams, using &lt;DT &rt;</H2>
<DL>
<DD>Red Sox
<DD>Cubs
<DD>Royals
<DD>Dodgers
<DD>Indians
</DL>
```

The output generated by these different kinds of unmarked lists is shown in Figure 6-4. The code is also available on the CD as file 6-3.HTML.

How It Works

For the first kind of unmarked list, your browser simply replaces all the `<BR>` tags it finds with carriage returns. For the second kind of unmarked list, the browser replaces all the `<DT>` tags between the `<DL>` and `</DL>` tags with carriage

Figure 6-4 Examples of unmarked lists

returns. The browser does the same with the **<DD>** tags in the third kind of list, only it also includes a tab before the list item. The length of the indentation is set by the browser and can't be controlled within the document.

Comments

While the **<DT>** and **<DD>** tags should be used together in glossary lists (see How-To 6.8), most browsers will render lists using only **<DT>** or **<DD>** without problems.

COMPLEXITY
BEGINNING

6.6 How do I...
Create a menu list?

COMPATIBILITY: HTML 2

Problem

I have a set of data that I wish to display as a list. I want to show the items specifically as a menu of options for users to choose from. How do I do this in HTML?

Technique

HTML versions 2.0 and earlier support a tag called **<MENU>**, which allows list items to be displayed as a menu. **<MENU>** is not included in HTML 3.2, but if you are working in an environment that uses older browsers, the **<MENU>** tag may still be useful.

Steps

Open your document. Identify the locations in your document where you want to include a list. If you haven't done so already, enter the list items in the document, separated by carriage returns.

1. Place the **<MENU>** tag at the beginning of the list and the **</MENU>** tag at the end of the list:

```
<H2>My Five Favorite Baseball Teams</H2>
<MENU>
Red Sox
Cubs
Royals
Dodgers
Indians
</MENU>
```

2. In front of each item of the list, place an **<LI>** tag:

```
<H2>My Five Favorite Baseball Teams</H2>
<MENU>
<LI>Red Sox
<LI>Cubs
<LI>Royals
<LI>Dodgers
<LI>Indians
</MENU>
```

Figure 6-5 shows the output of this list. The code is also available on the CD in file 6-4.HTML.

How It Works

As with other lists, a browser replaces all the **<LI>** tags between **<MENU>** and **</MENU>** with its predefined symbol or spacing. Often this is a bullet, so a list using the **<MENU>** tag frequently looks just the same as the bulleted list described in How-To 6.2.

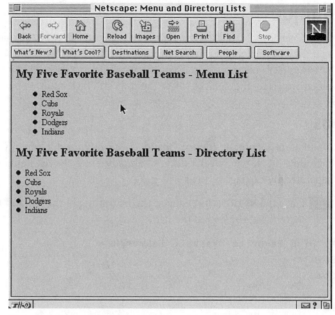

Figure 6-5 Examples of menu and directory lists

Comments

<MENU> is not supported in HTML 3.2. Thus, any documents that include a <MENU> list may not format correctly when displayed on an HTML 3.2-compliant browser. However, if you are designing pages for a closed environment using older browsers, the <MENU> tag will continue to work and might be the best way to format your information.

 COMPLEXITY
BEGINNING

6.7   How do I...
Create a directory list?

COMPATIBILITY: HTML 2

Problem

I have a set of data that I want to display as a directory of related items. How can I create a directory list in HTML?

Technique

HTML versions 2.0 and earlier support a tag called **<DIRECTORY>** that lists the items as if they were filenames in a computer directory. HTML 3.2 does not support the **<DIRECTORY>** tag; however, if you are working in a specific environment that uses older browsers, the **<DIRECTORY>** tag may still be useful.

Steps

Open your document. Identify the locations in your document where you want to include a list. If you haven't done so already, enter the list items in the document, separated by carriage returns.

1. Place the **<DIRECTORY>** tag at the beginning of the list and the **</DIRECT-ORY>** tag at the end of the list:

```
<H2>My Five Favorite Baseball Teams</H2>
<DIRECTORY>
Red Sox
Cubs
Royals
Dodgers
Indians
</DIRECTORY>
```

2. In front of each item, place an **<LI>** tag:

```
<H2>My Five Favorite Baseball Teams</H2>
<DIRECTORY>
<LI>Red Sox
<LI>Cubs
<LI>Royals
<LI>Dodgers
<LI>Indians
</DIRECTORY>
```

Figure 6-5 shows the output of this list. The code is also available on the CD in file 6-4.HTML.

How It Works

As with other lists, a browser turns each **<LI>** tag into a predefined symbol or spacing. Most browsers interpret **<DIRECTORY>** lists by turning **<LI>** tags into carriage returns, making the lists another form of unmarked list (see How-To 6.5). Some browsers, such as Netscape, add a bullet in front of each item, turning directory lists into bulleted lists.

Comments

Since HTML 3.2 does not support the **<DIRECTORY>** tag, any use of these tags in a document read by an HTML 3.2-compliant browser means the document may not format properly. Older browsers can still read and interpret these lists, though, so if you are designing pages for a closed environment using older browsers, this may still be a useful way to display information.

 COMPLEXITY
BEGINNING

6.8 How do I...
Create a glossary list?

COMPATIBILITY: HTML 2+

Problem

I have a set of data that I would like to display as a list of terms and their definitions. I would like to emphasize the terms and set them apart from their definitions. How can I create such a glossary in HTML?

Technique

How-To 6.5 discusses the use of the **<DL>**, **<DT>**, and **<DD>** tags in HTML 2.0 as a way to format an unmarked list. For the unmarked list, the **<DT>** and **<DD>** are used separately, but they can be combined to create a glossary that emphasizes words and their definitions.

Steps

Open your document. Decide what information you would like to present as a glossary list.

1. Compile a list of terms and their definitions, separating them by carriage returns and tabs for clarity:

```
<H2>Some terms and definitions</H2>
Term 1
        This is the definition for term 1
Term 2
        This is the definition for term 2
```

2. Place the **<DL>** tag at the beginning of the list and the **</DL>** tag at the end of the list:

```
<H2>Some terms and definitions</H2>
<DL>
Term 1
        This is the definition for term 1
Term 2
        This is the definition for term 2
</DL>
```

3. Place the `<DT>` tag in front of each word to be defined:

```
<H2>Some terms and definitions</H2>
<DL>
<DT>Term 1
        This is the definition for term 1
<DT>Term 2
        This is the definition for term 2
</DL>
```

4. Place the `<DD>` tag in front of each definition:

```
<H2>Some terms and definitions</H2>
<DL>
<DT>Term 1
        <DD>This is the definition for term 1
<DT>Term 2
        <DD>This is the definition for term 2
</DL>
```

5. Some browsers permit you to conserve space in your document by making your list more compact. A compacted list usually has less space between list entries and may use a smaller, more compressed font. To create a compacted list, replace the `<DL>` tag with the `<DL COMPACT>` tag:

```
<H2>Some terms and definitions (compact form)</H2>
<DL COMPACT>
<DT>Term 1
        <DD>This is the definition for term 1
<DT>Term 2
        <DD>This is the definition for term 2
</DL>
```

Figure 6-6 shows the output of these lists. The code is also available on the CD as file 6-5.HTML.

Figure 6-6 Example of a glossary list

How It Works

The browser software converts each **<DT>** found between the **<DL>** and **</DL>** tags into a carriage return. The browser converts the **<DD>** tags into a carriage return and an indentation.

Comments

HTML 3.2 requires that, whenever you use the **<DL>** and **</DL>** tags, you also use both the **<DD>** and **<DT>** tags in the list. While this makes it more difficult to create unmarked lists (see How-To 6.5), it has no impact here, since glossary lists need both types of tags to provide the best formatting. Note that the **COMPACT** attribute is not widely supported among the major browsers, so it may not produce the results expected.

COMPLEXITY

BEGINNING

INTERMEDIATE

6.9 How do I...
Nest lists together?

COMPATIBILITY: HTML 2+

Problem

I have a set of data that I would like to display as an outline so that each main heading has subheadings and so forth. Can I use nested lists to create a formatted outline in HTML?

Technique

HTML makes it easy to nest lists. Lists can be inserted within lists and then be interpreted by a browser as sublists and set off from the main list. Examples of different kinds of nested lists are provided in the Steps section.

Steps

Open your document. Identify the lists in your document you would like to nest, decide what type of list you would like to create, and follow the steps for the given type of list.

Numbered List

1. For a numbered list, enter the items for each list level, using carriage returns to set them apart and tabs to better show the level of nesting of each item in the outline:

```
<H2>An Example of Nested Lists</H2>
Point 1
        Subpoint 1
                Subsubpoint 1
                Subsubpoint 2
                Subsubpoint 3
        Subpoint 2
        Subpoint 3
Point 2
        Subpoint 1
        Subpoint 2
Point 3
```

2. For the top-level list, place an **<OL>** at the beginning of the list, an **</OL>** at the end of the list, and an **<LI>** in front of only the top-level points:

```
<H2>An Example of Nested Lists</H2>
<OL>
<LI>Point 1
          Subpoint 1
                  Subsubpoint 1
                  Subsubpoint 2
                  Subsubpoint 3
          Subpoint 2
          Subpoint 3
<LI>Point 2
          Subpoint 1
          Subpoint 2
<LI>Point 3
</OL>
```

3. For each sublist, place an **<OL>** at the beginning of the sublist, an **</OL>** at the end of the sublist, and an **<LI>** in front of each list item for that particular sublist. Continue this process for all the sublists:

```
<H2>An Example of Nested Numbered Lists</H2>
<OL>
<LI>Point 1
          <OL>
          <LI>Subpoint 1
                  <OL>
                  <LI>Subsubpoint 1
                  <LI>Subsubpoint 2
                  <LI>Subsubpoint 3
                  </OL>
          <LI>Subpoint 2
          <LI>Subpoint 3
          </OL>
<LI>Point 2
          <OL>
          <LI>Subpoint 1
          <LI>Subpoint 2
          </OL>
<LI>Point 3
</OL>
```

The output of this list is shown in Figure 6-7. The code is available on the CD in file 6-6.HTML.

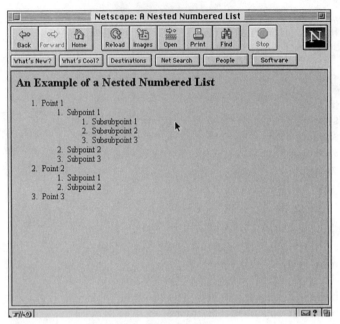

Figure 6-7 A nested numbered list

Bulleted List

For bulleted lists, the technique is exactly the same as that for a numbered list, except that the **<OL>** and **</OL>** tags are replaced with **<UL>** and **</UL>**:

```
<H2>An Example of Nested Bulleted Lists</H2>
<UL>
<LI>Point 1
            <UL>
            <LI>Subpoint 1
                    <UL>
                    <LI>Subsubpoint 1
                    <LI>Subsubpoint 2
                    <LI>Subsubpoint 3
                    </UL>
            <LI>Subpoint 2
            <LI>Subpoint 3
            </UL>
<LI>Point 2
            <UL>
            <LI>Subpoint 1
            <LI>Subpoint 2
            </UL>
<LI>Point 3
</UL>
```

Figure 6-8 shows the output of a nested bulleted list. The code is available on the CD in file 6-7.HTML.

Figure 6-8 A nested bulleted list

Menu List

For menu lists, follow the steps as shown for a nested bulleted list, and use **<MENU>** and **</MENU>**:

```
<H2>An Example of Nested Menu Lists</H2>
<MENU>
<LI>Point 1
          <MENU>
          <LI>Subpoint 1
                 <MENU>
                 <LI>Subsubpoint 1
                 <LI>Subsubpoint 2
                 <LI>Subsubpoint 3
                 </MENU>
          <LI>Subpoint 2
          <LI>Subpoint 3
          </MENU>
<LI>Point 2
          <MENU>
          <LI>Subpoint 1
          <LI>Subpoint 2
          </MENU>
<LI>Point 3
</MENU>
```

Figure 6-9 shows the output of this list, which usually appears just the same as a nested bulleted list. The code is available on the CD in file 6-8.HTML. Note that **<MENU>** is not part of HTML 3.2.

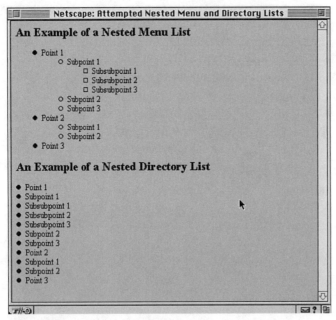

Figure 6-9 Attempts at nested menu and directory lists

Directory List

Most browsers, such as Netscape, do not support nested directory lists. Each item in a directory list is shown together with the other items, regardless of the level of nesting indicated for that item.

For a directory list, follow the steps as shown for nested menu lists, and use `<DIRECTORY>` and `</DIRECTORY>`:

```
<H2>An Example of Nested Directory Lists</H2>
<DIRECTORY>
<LI>Point 1
          <DIRECTORY>
          <LI>Subpoint 1
                  <DIRECTORY>
                  <LI>Subsubpoint 1
                  <LI>Subsubpoint 2
                  <LI>Subsubpoint 3
                  </DIRECTORY>
          <LI>Subpoint 2
          <LI>Subpoint 3
          </DIRECTORY>
<LI>Point 2
          <DIRECTORY>
          <LI>Subpoint 1
          <LI>Subpoint 2
          </DIRECTORY>
<LI>Point 3
</DIRECTORY>
```

The output of this list is shown in Figure 6-9. The code is available on the CD in file 6-8.HTML. Note that **<DIRECTORY>** is not part of HTML 3.2.

Unmarked List

You cannot create nested unmarked lists using the **
** tag, because there is no way for the browser to know what list level each item belongs to. However, by using the **<DL>** and **</DL>** list tags, and either the **<DT>** or **<DD>** tags for each list item, you can create a nested unmarked list.

For a simple nested unmarked list, use **<DL>** and **</DL>** at the beginning and end of each list and sublist and **<DT>** in front of each list item:

```
<H2>A Nested Unmarked List Using &lt; DT &rt;</H2>
<DL>
<DT>Point 1
          <DL>
          <DT>Subpoint 1
                 <DL>
                 <DT>Subsubpoint 1
                 <DT>Subsubpoint 2
                 <DT>Subsubpoint 3
                 </DL>
          <DT>Subpoint 2
          <DT>Subpoint 3
          </DL>
<DT>Point 2
          <DL>
          <DT>Subpoint 1
          <DT>Subpoint 2
          </DL>
<DT>Point 3
</DL>
```

Figure 6-10 shows the output of this nested unmarked list. The code is available on the CD in file 6-9.HTML.

For a nested unmarked list that is indented from the rest of the text, use **<DD>** in place of **<DT>** in the preceding example:

```
<H2>A Nested Unmarked List Using &lt; DD &rt;</H2>
<DL>
<DD>Point 1
        <DL>
        <DD>Subpoint 1
               <DL>
               <DD>Subsubpoint 1
               <DD>Subsubpoint 2
               <DD>Subsubpoint 3
               </DL>
        <DD>Subpoint 2
        <DD>Subpoint 3
        </DL>
<DD>Point 2
        <DL>
        <DD>Subpoint 1
```

continued on next page

continued from previous page

```
            <DD>Subpoint 2
            </DL>
<DD>Point 3
</DL>
```

Figure 6-10 shows the output of this unmarked nested list. The code is available on the CD in file 6-9.HTML. You can also mix the **<DT>** and **<DD>** tags to create nested glossary lists.

Combining Lists

You can combine and nest different kinds of lists. The following example shows how to nest a bulleted list within a numbered list, which in turn is nested within an unmarked list:

```
<H2>A Nested List Using Unmarked, Numbered, and Bulleted Elements</H2>
<DL>
<DT>Point 1
            <OL>
            <LI>Subpoint 1
                    <UL>
                    <LI>Subsubpoint 1
                    <LI>Subsubpoint 2
                    <LI>Subsubpoint 3
                    </UL>
            <LI>Subpoint 2
            <LI>Subpoint 3
            </OL>
<DT>Point 2
            <OL>
            <LI>Subpoint 1
            <LI>Subpoint 2
            </OL>
<DT>Point 3
</DL>
```

Figure 6-11 shows the output of this combined nested list. The code is available on the CD in file 6-10.HTML.

Take care when mixing nested unmarked lists inside other types of lists. In some browsers, if you use the **<DT>** tag to mark list items in the unmarked list, the items may appear on the next higher list level. If you were to replace the bulleted sublist in this example with an unmarked list using **<DT>** in front of each list item, you might get an aesthetically unpleasing result. By using **<DD>** in place of **<DT>**, you get a better result.

How It Works

When a browser encounters a tag that marks the start of a new list before it encounters a tag that marks the end of the current list, it considers the contents of the new list to be a sublist nested inside the current list. The browser then formats the sublist accordingly. The format of the sublist may vary from browser to browser.

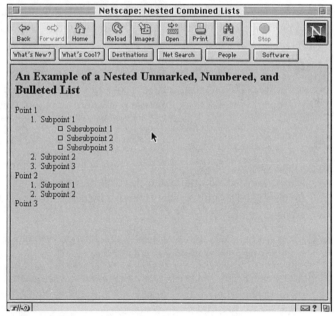

Figure 6-10 Examples of nested unmarked lists

Figure 6-11 Examples of nested combined lists

Comments

Different browsers use different styles to format nested lists. Some browsers may mix letters and numbers in different levels of nested numbered lists, and some browsers may use bullets of different shapes and sizes for different levels of nested bulleted lists. Thus, when designing your pages, be careful when referring to specific list items by number or bullet, because the reader may not see the same number or bullet that you do. Also note that, when mixing lists, some browsers will use the bullet or number style appropriate to that level, even if this is the first list of that type being used. Be cautious about making references to specific numbers or bullets.

COMPLEXITY

BEGINNING

INTERMEDIATE

6.10 How do I...
Use lists to jazz up my home page?

COMPATIBILITY: HTML 2+

Problem

I would like to add lists to my home page so that I can better present my information. How can I effectively use lists to jazz up my home page?

Technique

Like any aspect of HTML, lists can be used—and abused. The right way to use lists varies, depending on what information you want to put into a list.

Steps

1. Avoid very long lists. Long lists are boring and difficult to read, and it's hard for the user to find a particular piece of information in them. Instead, break up any long lists into smaller lists, subdivided by topic. This is where nested lists can be useful.

2. Maintain parallelism in your lists. Don't change verb tenses or make other style changes in the middle of a list.

3. Along those lines, keep each list item about the same length. Lists can be made of short, one-word elements or long, paragraph-length statements, but the two shouldn't be combined.

How It Works

These tips help make your lists more effective by allowing a user to quickly find the information of interest to him or her. By grouping list items into related groups and by using parallel structure, it becomes easier for a user to sort through the information provided.

Comments

Proper use of lists and good list style help set the good Web pages apart from the rest. With a little practice, you'll soon be able to create all sorts of useful lists for your pages.

CHAPTER 7

MANAGING DOCUMENT SPACING

7

MANAGING DOCUMENT SPACING

How do I...

How you lay out or space your page is important in making a Web page that is tight and readable. Spacing is often initially overlooked when planning a Web page, which can be a mistake. A page that is properly spaced is easier to read and, therefore, visited more often by readers. A poorly spaced page might cause readers to miss information that is either too far off a page or too clumped together with other information to be noticed. This chapter will help you create an easy-to-read home page.

7.1   Add a Horizontal Line to an HTML Document

Horizontal lines separate distinct sections of documents. This How-To shows you how to add horizontal lines to your documents.

7.2   Align Text on a Line Using Tables

Tables can align text to go along the top or the bottom of a table row, a useful feature in formatting text. This How-To explains how to set the table formatting in HTML 3.2.

7.3   Center Text

An important aspect of document spacing and layout is the ability to center text on a page. This How-To shows the various ways to center text in HTML 3.2.

7.4   Manage Vertical Spacing: Paragraphs Versus Line Breaks

Two of the simplest tags in HTML are the paragraph `<P>` and line break `<BR>` tags. This How-To shows you the difference between the two tags and when you might want to use each one.

7.5   Stop a Browser from Breaking a Line at a Critical Point

Because of the differences in user preferences in browsers and among browsers themselves, text may be broken at different places in a Web page for different viewers, which may create unintended formatting problems. This How-To shows how to tell a browser not to break a line at an important place in a document.

7.6   Include Preformatted Text in My Web Page

All text delimited by `<PRE>` tags is displayed by a browser in a fixed-width font, including any white space within that text. This simple How-To shows you how to make the best use of the `<PRE>` tag.

7.7   Insert a Block Quotation

A block quotation is a long quotation from a book, speech, or other source that is set off from the rest of the document with different spacing and margins. This simple How-To shows how to format a section of text in a document as a block quotation.

7.8 Create Divisions in My Web Page

Divisions allow the Web page designer to group together blocks of text and other objects in a Web page and give that section, or division, special formatting. This How-To explains how to include these divisions in your Web page.

7.9 Exploit Tables to Arrange Images, Embedded Objects, and Text

One of the most powerful tools to control the layout of a Web page is the use of tables. Different objects, such as text, images, and other multimedia features, can be arranged on the page in the manner chosen by the designer. This How-To shows how to use tables to create these advanced layout effects.

7.10 Use Transparent Images to Manage Layout Control

A special trick for controlling layout in a Web page is the use of transparent images that, while remaining invisible, force the page layout to shift. This How-To shows how to use transparent images to create a desired layout for a page.

7.11 Create Columnar Text Spanning a Table

Another feature of tables is the ability to place text in separate columns to give a Web page the feel of a magazine or newspaper. This How-To explains how to use tables to place text in multiple columns.

7.12 Space My Home Page

At first, spacing of a page might seem trivial. However, proper spacing can lead to a page that is easier to read and is thus read more often. Improper spacing can cause a reader to either intentionally or unintentionally skip over important information. This How-To helps you space your page in a user-friendly manner.

COMPLEXITY
BEGINNING

7.1 How do I...
Add a horizontal line to an HTML document?

COMPATIBILITY: HTML 2+

Problem

I want to separate the credits for my page from the other information on my page. I see other pages that use horizontal lines to do this. How can I add a horizontal rule or line to my document?

Technique

Add horizontal lines to documents by using the **<HR>** (horizontal rule) tag. HTML 3.2 includes several attributes for **<HR>** that allow the user to change the width, thickness, and appearance of horizontal lines.

Steps

Open the HTML document in which you want to include horizontal lines.

1. Decide where you want to add a horizontal rule. In the example shown next there is a horizontal rule separating the page's body from its footer. This is a common use for horizontal rules.

2. Enter an **<HR>** tag wherever you want to place a horizontal rule. For example:

```
<Html>
<HEAD><TITLE>My Example</TITLE></HEAD>
<Body>
<H2>How to add a horizontal rule to a document</H2>
Horizontal lines or rules are added to documents through the use of the HR
tag. They are very easy to use and can make a document look quite profes-
sional. Horizontal Rules are so easy to add that some people may get carried
away with their use. This is something you should be careful with. Still,
<b>experiment</b>!  Have fun!
<P>
<P>
<HR>
This page was created by John Smith on 1/1/95. It was last modified on
6/1/95.
</Body>
</Html>
```

3. You can change the thickness of the line in HTML 3.2 with the **SIZE** attribute. Set the **SIZE** attribute to an integer equal to the desired thickness of the line in pixels. The default thickness is typically 2. For example, to include a line with thickness 5 in this document, you would replace the **<HR>** with

```
<HR SIZE=5>
```

4. You can alter the width of the line by adding the **WIDTH** attribute to **<HR>**. **WIDTH** can be set to either the number of pixels wide the line should be or the percentage of the browser window's width the line should span. For example, to create a line 100 pixels wide, you would enter

```
<HR WIDTH-100>
```

If instead you wanted a line that went across 60 percent of the screen, you would enter

```
<HR WIDTH="60%">
```

Note that you put quote marks around **60%** to be sure you didn't confuse the browser by putting in a symbol that is neither a number nor a letter.

5. Most popular browsers show a horizontal line generated by **<HR>** as a type of shaded 3D line. However, if you would prefer to have your line appear as a simple black line, you can add the **NOSHADE** attribute to the **<HR>** tag. To create a line of size 5 that is 100 pixels across and appears only as a black line, you would enter

```
<HR SIZE=5 WIDTH=100 NOSHADE>
```

An example of the various types of horizontal lines is shown in Figure 7-1. The code for this figure is available on the CD-ROM as file 7-1.HTML.

Figure 7-1 Examples of horizontal rules in HTML

How It Works

When a browser encounters an `<HR>` element, it generates a line on the page using the size, thickness, and color specified by the attributes in the tag.

Comments

The real trick here is not adding the line but deciding where the line should go and, for that matter, how many lines you should have on a page. The latter is largely a matter of taste. Some people believe you should use no more than two horizontal lines per page. Others believe the more the merrier. There are some standard places where horizontal lines are often used in documents:

- Around forms, to separate the form from the rest of the document

- At the end of a document, to separate information about the document (date created, author, and so on) from actual information contained in the document

It is possible to get carried away with horizontal lines, making your document harder to read and bigger than it should be. Be yourself, but use caution.

COMPLEXITY
INTERMEDIATE

7.2 How do I...
Align text on a line using tables?

COMPATIBILITY: HTML 3.2

Problem

I have some text in a table that I would like to align with the top or bottom of the table. How can I do this in HTML?

Technique

HTML 3.2 includes the `VALIGN` attributes to HTML, which allows you to specify how you want text aligned in a table. This is particularly useful with tables that have multiple cells of varying heights per row.

Steps

Open the HTML document with the table cells you want to align with the top or bottom of the row.

1. To align the text to the top of the row, place the **VALIGN=TOP** attribute in each table cell in that row. For example, in a three-cell row:

```
<TABLE>
<TR>
<TD VALIGN=TOP>
This is the text for the first cell of the table.
</TD>
<TD VALIGN=TOP >
This is the text for the second cell of the table. This cell
has more text that the first cell so that it takes more space
in the table.
</TD>
<TD VALIGN=TOP >
This is the text for the third cell of the table., which isn't as long as
the second cell.
</TD>
</TR>
</TABLE>
```

2. A similar effect can be obtained from the **VALIGN=BASELINE** attribute. For example, in a three-cell row:

```
<TABLE>
<TR>
<TD VALIGN=BASELINE>
This is the text for the first cell of the table.
</TD>
<TD VALIGN=BASELINE >
This is the text for the second cell of the table. This cell
has more text that the first cell so that it takes more space
in the table.
</TD>
<TD VALIGN=BASELINE >
This is the text for the third cell of the table., which isn't as long as
the second cell.
</TD>
</TR>
</TABLE>
```

3. To align text to the bottom of the row, replace the **VALIGN=TOP** in the preceding example with **VALIGN=BOTTOM**:

```
<TABLE>
<TR>
<TD VALIGN=BOTTOM>
This is the text for the first cell of the table.
</TD>
<TD VALIGN=BOTTOM >
This is the text for the second cell of the table. This cell
has more text that the first cell so that it takes more space
in the table.
```

continued on next page

continued from previous page

```
</TD>
<TD VALIGN=BOTTOM >
This is the text for the third cell of the table., which isn't as long as
the second cell.
</TD>
</TR>
</TABLE>
```

An example of type of text alignment in tables is shown in Figure 7-2. The code for this figure is available as file 7-2.HTML.

How It Works

When a browser encounters the **<VALIGN>** tag in a table cell, it will align the contents of the table cell with the top or bottom of the cell. The size of the cell is determined by the contents of all the cells in the row.

Comments

In addition to the **TOP**, **BASELINE**, and **BOTTOM** values, **VALIGN** can also be set to **MIDDLE**. This would center the contents of the cell. For the task of aligning text with a line, this attribute is less useful. Note that **BASELINE** is not officially part of HTML 3.2 but is widely supported by major browsers.

Figure 7-2 Vertical text alignment in tables

COMPLEXITY
BEGINNING

7.3 How do I...
Center text?

COMPATIBILITY: HTML 3.2

Problem

I want to draw attention to a section of text by centering it in the browser window. How can I do this in HTML?

Technique

There are several methods to center text using HTML 3.2. The `<CENTER>` and `<DIV ALIGN=CENTER>` tags enable you to center whole blocks of text and other Web page elements. Other text tags, like `<H>` and `<P>`, now support the `ALIGN` attribute, which can be used to center the text contained within those tags.

Steps

Open the HTML document that contains the text you want to center.

1. One method of centering text is the `<CENTER>` tag. To use this, place the `<CENTER>` tag at the beginning of the text and the `</CENTER>` tag at the end of the text. An example of centered text using `<CENTER>` is

```
<CENTER>This line is centered.</CENTER>
```

2. You can achieve identical results with the `<DIV ALIGN=CENTER>` tag. Place the `<DIV ALIGN=CENTER>` tag at the beginning of the text to be centered and the `</DIV>` tag at the end of the text. Here is an example of centered text using `<DIV ALIGN=CENTER>`.

```
<DIV ALIGN=CENTER>This line is centered.</DIV>
```

Further uses of the `<DIV>` element will be explained in How-To 7.8.

3. The `ALIGN` attribute can be used to center headings (see How-To 4.1). To do this, insert the `ALIGN=CENTER` attribute to the beginning of the header tag:

```
<H1 ALIGN=CENTER>This heading is centered</H1>
```

4. The **ALIGN** attribute can also be used to center individual paragraphs (see How-To 7.4). To do this, insert the **ALIGN=CENTER** attribute at the beginning of the paragraph tag:

```
<P ALIGN=CENTER>This paragraph is centered</P>
```

An example of the various types of centered text is shown in Figure 7-3. The code for this figure is available as file 7-3.HTML.

How It Works

The **<CENTER>** and **<DIV ALIGN=CENTER>** work in the same way: They tell the browser to center all the text, as well as any other page elements, located between the opening and closing centering tags. Likewise, the **ALIGN=CENTER** attribute instructs the browser to center the contents of the heading or paragraph.

Comments

Why does HTML 3.2 have both **<CENTER>** and **<DIV ALIGN=CENTER>** tags, when they both do the same thing? The **<CENTER>** element was introduced by Netscape in an earlier version of their browser, even though the tag was not included in any draft version of HTML 3 or 3.2. Since **<CENTER>** gained widespread acceptance by Web page designers looking for ways to center parts of documents, **<CENTER>** was included in HTML 3.2 as a synonym for **<DIV ALIGN=CENTER>**.

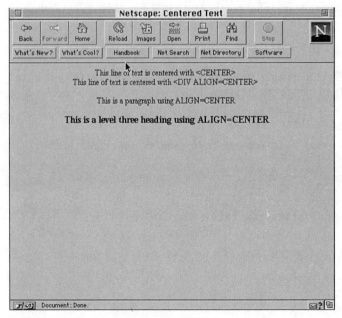

Figure 7-3 Centered text in HTML

COMPLEXITY
BEGINNING

7.4   How do I...
Manage vertical spacing: paragraphs versus line breaks?

COMPATIBILITY: HTML 2+

Problem

How can I tell when I should use a new paragraph tag **<P>** and when I should use a line break tag **
**?

Technique

Normally, a browser displays text across the available area of your text window. Text starts on a new line only when a complete word cannot be displayed on the current line. You have two methods of controlling where text breaks: the paragraph **<P>** and the line break **
** tags. Which one you use is sometimes determined by personal taste and sometimes by the situation. Use a **<P>** tag to start a new paragraph, to which you may assign new attributes if you wish. Most browsers also place extra space after a **<P>**. A **
** causes the browser to maintain the current paragraph attributes but to start placing text on a new line. The **
** element is useful for such things as separating items in a list and breaking up lines of a song or a poem.

Steps

Create an HTML document with the text editor of your choice.

1. In the document, decide where you wish to use new paragraphs and where you wish to use simple line breaks. Usually it is pretty clear where to use each. A **<P>** tag is used wherever you would start a new paragraph if you were using a word processor. Use a line break **
** if you wish to keep information grouped together within the same paragraph, but on separate lines. For instance, you would not want a name and address to be in separate paragraphs, but you would want them to be on separate lines.

The format of the new paragraph tag can be as simple as

```
<P>text
```

since this tag does not need to be closed.

2. While the simple tag is fine in most cases, the new paragraph tag has been expanded in HTML 3.2 to include alignment of the paragraph. This format is

```
<P ALIGN=RIGHT | LEFT | CENTER> text </P>
```

The text and images between the `<P>...</P>` tags are aligned to either the right, left, or center of the window depending on the option you select. Which format you choose is determined by personal taste and by the browser you are using.

3. The format of the break tag is also simple:

```
<BR>
```

However, this tag has been expanded on for use when you are working with images and text that are aligned. See Chapter 9, Using Images in Your Documents, for more details.

The following code was used to create the sample document in Figure 7-4, which illustrates some of the differences between `<BR>` and `<P>`.

```
<HTML>
<HEAD>
<TITLE>Demo of Paragraph <P> vs. Line
Breaks<BR></TITLE>
</HEAD>
<BODY>
This is the first line. A simple paragraph tag.&lt;P&gt;<P>
Second line. Line break &lt;BR&gt;<BR>
This is the third line.
<P align=center>
Remember a browser normally does not break a sentence until it no longer has
room to display the current word in the window. A new paragraph tag causes a
new paragraph to begin, to which new attributes can be assigned. A line
break tag causes a line break, giving you a little more control of
things.</P>
<P ALIGN=left>
Here is a paragraph aligned to the left. The text flows until it comes to
the end of the window, or a new paragraph tag or line break. This line is
followed by a line break.&lt;BR&gt;<BR>
Notice the difference between that line and this one ended by a new para-
graph &lt;P&gt;.<P>
This is the next line.
Unordered list with paragraphs between items:
<UL>
<LI>One&lt;P&gt;<p>
<LI>Two&lt;P&gt;<p>
</UL>
<P>
Unordered list with line breaks:
<UL>
<LI>One&lt;BR&gt;<br>
<LI>Two&lt;BR&gt;<br>
</UL>
</BODY>
</HTML>
```

An example of the uses of **
** and **<P>** is shown in Figure 7-4. The code for this figure is available as file 7-4.HTML.

How It Works

A browser displays text across the current line of the window until one of the following things happens:

- There isn't enough room on the current line to display the current word.

- A **
** tag is encountered, in which case the browser starts a new line in the same paragraph.

- A **<P>** tag is encountered, in which case the browser not only begins a new paragraph but also allows the document creator to assign new paragraph attributes to the text that follows.

Comments

With the new structure of the **<P>** tag, some people think it is a nice touch to close paragraphs with a **</P>**. While this may be a good practice, it is not needed because the browser assumes that a **</P>** tag precedes a **<P>** tag.

Also, remember that the exact way a paragraph is displayed is governed by a combination of factors, such as the browser used, the style sheet setup, and various other tags.

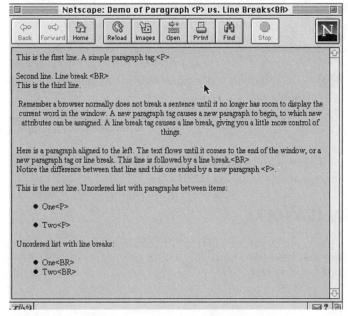

Figure 7-4 Various uses of <BR> and <P>

7.5 How do I...
Stop a browser from breaking a line at a critical point?

COMPATIBILITY: NETSCAPE NAVIGATOR, INTERNET EXPLORER

Problem

I have a section of text that must remain together and not have a line break put in the middle of it. Is there a way I can keep a line from breaking in HTML?

Technique

The `<NOBR>` can be used to specify that a line *should* break at a particular point, which ensures that a section of text that follows will remain together on a single line.

Steps

Open the HTML document with the text you want to keep from breaking.

1. Just before the text in question (that is, at the point where you *do* want the line to break), place the `<NOBR>` tag. For example, to make sure the phrase that begins `looks like it is getting very long` is not broken, you can enter

```
While this line  <NOBR> looks like it is getting very long, we can use HTML
to make sure a section of text stays all on one line.
```

2. At the end of the text segment that should remain unbroken, place the `</NOBR>` tag:

```
While this line  <NOBR> looks like it is getting very long, we can use HTML
to make sure a section of text stays </NOBR> all on one line.
```

An example of a nonbreaking line is shown in Figure 7-5. The code for this figure is available as file 7-5.HTML.

How It Works

When a browser encounters the `<NOBR>` tag, it places the text that follows it on a new line regardless of how much more room in the browser window is available to include more text.

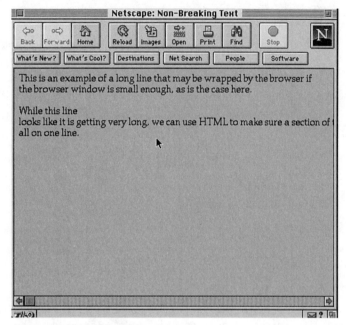

Figure 7-5 Nonbreaking lines

Comments

The `<NOBR>` tag is not widely supported by older browsers, so they may not ensure lines will remain unbroken, as in this example.

COMPLEXITY
BEGINNING

7.6   How do I...
Include preformatted text in my Web page?

COMPATIBILITY: HTML 2+

Problem

I see a lot of pages in which the author includes rows of text evenly displayed in a monospace font, in which all the letters are the same width. How do I do this?

Technique

You can use the **<PRE>...</PRE>** tags to display preformatted blocks of text with a fixed-space font. When they appear inside **<PRE>** tags, white space, line breaks, and tabs are also displayed. Placing text between the **<PRE>** tags allows you to set up a sort of poor man's table, and it is also useful for simulating program listings.

Steps

Open the HTML document that contains the text which should retain its original formatting.

Place a **<PRE>** tag at the beginning of the preformatted text and a **</PRE>** tag at the end of the preformatted text. For example:

```
<PRE>
                <B>Gross sales</B>
Salesman                    Sales Ranking
Tim                         $10,000                    2
Tom                         $ 5,000                    3
Tammy                       $20,000                    1
<P><P><P>
These figures reflect the last quarter of 95. The first column of numbers was
created with spaces, the second with tabs. There are also carriage returns in
this paragraph within the sentences that would continue past the screen.
</PRE>
```

In the chart, the first set of numbers is separated by spaces and the second set by tabs, since tabs are not ignored in text that appears between the preformatted text tags.

Notice after each salesman's sale figures how the carriage returns work. Also notice how the bold **<B>** tags still work inside the **<PRE>** tags, but the new paragraph tags **<P>** are ignored.

An example of preformatted text is shown in Figure 7-6. The code for this figure is available as file 7-6.HTML.

How It Works

The browser displays all text between the **<PRE>...</PRE>** tags in a fixed-width font without ignoring carriage returns and tabs. The next example shows the difference between how the same information is displayed when it appears between **<PRE>...</PRE>** tags and when it does not appear between **<PRE>...</PRE>** tags. The results can be seen in Figure 7-6.

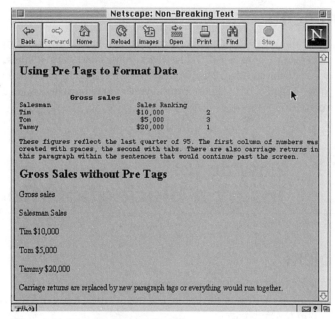

Figure 7-6 Preformatted text

```
<HTML>
<HEAD>
<TITLE>Preformatted text example</TITLE>
<BODY>
</HEAD>
<H2>Gross Sales By Sales People</H2>
<HR>
<PRE>
            Gross sales                   <BR>
Salesman                    Sales<BR>
Tim                         $10,000<BR>
Tom                          $5,000<BR>
Tammy                       $20,000<BR>
Each line has a carriage return after it. Also notice what happens to this
line.
</PRE>
<HR>
<H2>Gross Sales without Pre Tags</H2>
<HR>
            Gross sales                   <P>
Salesman                    Sales<P>
Tim                         $10,000<P>
Tom                          $5,000<P>
Tammy                       $20,000<P>
</HR>
Carriage returns are replaced by new paragraph tags or everything would run
together.
</BODY>
</HTML>
```

Comments

While the **<PRE>...</PRE>** tags may be useful for quick-and-dirty tables, the advent of **<TABLE>** tags in HTML 3.2 has made doing tables with **<PRE>** somewhat less desirable. Probably the biggest use for **<PRE>** now is displaying program listings in documents. **<PRE>** can also be useful in forms if you wish to have fields line up underneath one another.

COMPLEXITY
BEGINNING

7.7   How do I...
Insert a block quotation?

COMPATIBILITY: HTML 2+

Problem

I have a long quotation that I want to include in my Web page. I would like to set it off from the rest of the text of the document. How can I include a block quotation in my Web page?

Technique

HTML supports the **<BLOCKQUOTE>** tag, which allows the user to specify that a specific block of text be formatted like a block quotation in a book: usually with indented margins on both the left and right sides.

Steps

Open the HTML document that contains the text that will be formatted as a block quotation.

Place a **<BLOCKQUOTE>** tag at the beginning of the pertinent text and a **</BLOCKQUOTE>** tag at the end of the text. For example:

```
Here is the documentation on the tag from the W3C:
<BLOCKQUOTE>
insert text here
</BLOCKQUOTE>
```

An example of a block quotation is shown in Figure 7-7. The code for this figure is available as file 7-7.HTML.

How It Works

When a browser encounters the **<BLOCKQUOTE>** tag, it formats the text contained between the **<BLOCKQUOTE>** and the **</BLOCKQUOTE>** tags using its rules for block quotations. Usually this means indenting the text at both the left and right margins to give an appearance similar to block quotations in books.

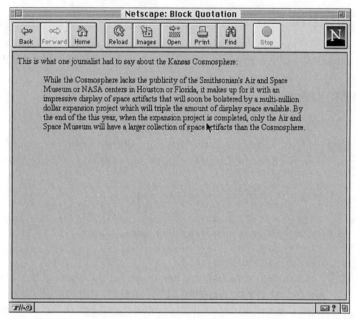

Figure 7-7 Example of a block quotation

Comments

Many Web page authors use `<BLOCKQUOTE>` to give the text on their pages more white space between the margins and the edge of the browser window. Since this trick can also be done with tables, it is not of as great utility as it once was. Also, many older browsers may not simply indent the text, but will use a different formatting technique.

COMPLEXITY
BEGINNING

7.8   How do I...
Create divisions in my Web page?

COMPATIBILITY: HTML 3.2

Problem

I would like to divide my Web page into a number of different sections that each has its own formatting rules. How can I do this in HTML 3.2?

Technique

HTML 3.2 includes the new `<DIV>` element for creating divisions in Web pages. These divisions can be used to set the alignment for a whole section of a Web page.

Steps

Open the HTML document that you want to add sections to.

1. Place the `<DIV>` tag at the beginning of the section you want to create in your document. Place the `</DIV>` tag at the end of the section:

```
<DIV>
This is the first section of my Web page.
</DIV>
<DIV>
This is the second section of my Web page
</DIV>
```

2. You can use the `ALIGN` attribute to set the alignment of the text within the section. `ALIGN` can be set to `LEFT`, `CENTER`, or `RIGHT`. For example, to left-align the first section of the page and right-align the second section, enter

```
<DIV ALIGN=LEFT>
This is the first section of my Web page.
</DIV>
<DIV ALIGN=RIGHT>
```

This is the second section of my Web page.

```
</DIV>
```

Examples of the various alignments of divisions are shown in Figure 7-8. The code for this figure is available as file 7-8.HRML.

How It Works

When a browser encounters the `<DIV>` tag, it will take all of the text located between the `<DIV>` and `</DIV>` tags and format it according to the instructions contained in the attributes of the `<DIV>` tag, such as alignment.

Comments

The `<DIV>` tags provide the default alignment for the text contained within them. That alignment can be overridden by specifying the alignment of a header or paragraph within the division. You can still center a heading in a division even if the division is set to align right.

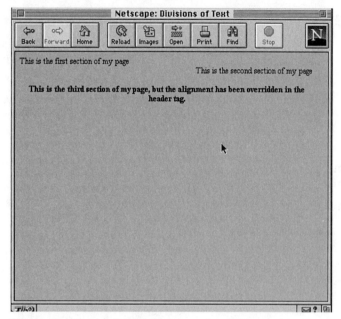

Figure 7-8 Examples of divisions in HTML

COMPLEXITY
BEGINNING

7.9 How do I...
Exploit tables to arrange images, embedded objects, and text?

COMPATIBILITY: HTML 3.2

Problem

I would like to have more control over the location of the images, text, and other objects that make up my Web page. How can I do this using tables?

Technique

Tables provide a powerful way to control the layout of a Web page. You can insert sections of text, images, and other objects in table cells and control exactly where the items will appear on the browser window.

Steps

Open the HTML document that contains the text, images, and other objects that you will format. Since there is a wide variety of possible ways to use tables to control format, we will show just one example here: placing text around an image.

1. Decide how you want to lay out the display. In this case we want to have text around an image, so we need table cells containing text above, below, and to the left and right of an image. This will require three rows of table cells, so set up the table like this:

```
<TABLE>
<TR>
<!-- table row 1 -->
</TR>
<TR>
<!-- table row 2 -->
</TR>
<TR>
<!-- table row 3 -->
</TR>
</TABLE>
```

2. With the rows laid out, you can now decide how many table cells you need. We described putting text on four sides of an image, so we will need four table cells, plus a cell for the image. We'll place a single cell each in the top and bottom rows, then span the table, and place three cells in the middle row of the table:

```
<TABLE>
<TR>
<TD COLSPAN=3>
<!-- table row 1, top cell -->
</TD>
</TR>
<TR>
<TD>
<!-- table cell for left text -->
</TD>
<TD>
<!-- table cell for image -->
</TD>
<TD>
<!-- table cell for right text -->
</TD>
</TR>
<TR>
<TD COLSPAN=3>
<!-- table row 3, bottom cell -->
</TD>
</TR>
</TABLE>
```

3. With the table cells laid out, we can now go in and place the images and text in the appropriate cells:

```
<TABLE>
<TR>
<TD COLSPAN=3>
This is the text for the top row of the table. This text will span across the
entire width of the cell because of the COLSPAN attribute in the table cell
tag.
</TD>
</TR>
<TR>
<TD>
This is text for the left side of the image. This text is below the top row text and
above the bottom row text.
</TD>
<TD>
<IMG SRC="myimage.gif" ALT="My Image" WIDTH=100 HEIGHT=100>
</TD>
<TD>
This is text for the right side of the image. This text is below the top row text and
above the bottom row text.
</TD>
</TR>
<TR>
<TD COLSPAN=3>
This is the text for the bottom row of the table. This text will span across the
entire width of the cell because of the COLSPAN attribute in the table cell
tag.
</TD>
</TR>
</TABLE>
```

4. Once you have the basic layout set up, you can tweak the layout by setting the **VALIGN** and **WIDTH** attributes of the table cells.

An example of the table-based layout described here is shown in Figure 7-9. The code for this figure is available as file 7-9.HTML.

How It Works

When a browser encounters a table, it sets up the table according to the values set in the attributes (if any), the numbers of rows and columns, and the contents of the table cells themselves. Table cells do not have to contain merely words: Images and other objects are valid in cells.

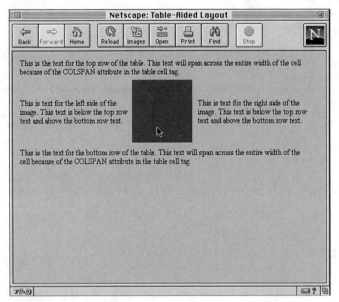

Figure 7-9 An example of a table-based layout

Comments

In this example, we have not included a table border. For layouts like these, the table borders are not useful and can even be distracting to the layout of the page. Note that the detailed formatting in use here will go to waste on older browsers that don't support tables.

COMPLEXITY
INTERMEDIATE

7.10 How do I...
Use transparent images to manage layout control?

COMPATIBILITY: HTML 3.2

Problem

I've heard that it's possible to use transparent images to control the layout of a Web page. How do I do this?

Technique

It's possible to use a transparent image (an image that takes up space on the browser screen but cannot be seen by the user) to shift the location of text and other page elements in the browser window. While the use of images in Web pages in general will be discussed in Chapter 9, Using Images in Your Documents, this How-To will show how to include transparent images for layout control.

Steps

Open the HTML document whose layout you want to alter.

1. Before you make any changes to the document, you first need a transparent image that you will use in the layout. One example, a 1 pixel by 1 pixel transparent GIF file, is included on the CD as file CLEARPIX.GIF. Place this image in the same folder or directory as the HTML file you plan to edit.

2. Immediately in front of the text you want to move, inset the HTML tag `<IMG SRC="clearpix.gif" ALT="">`. This is the HTML code for inserting an image in the document. For example:

```
This is a normal line of text in this document.<BR>
<IMG SRC="clearpix.gif" ALT="">This is an indented line of text.<BR>
```

The syntax of the `<IMG>` tag will be discussed in complete detail in Chapter 9.

3. In this example, if you wanted to indent the second line by a number of pixels, you could use the `HEIGHT` and `WIDTH` attributes to `<IMG>` to expand the size of the image to the desired width. For example, to move the second line in 100 pixels, set the `WIDTH` attribute to **100** while setting `HEIGHT` to **1**:

```
This is a normal line of text in this document.<BR>
<IMG SRC="clearpix.gif" ALT="" WIDTH=100 HEIGHT=1>This is an indented line of
text.<BR>
```

4. Another method of doing the same thing would be to use the `HSPACE` (horizontal space) and `VSPACE` (vertical space) attributes. They do not resize the image but create a blank border of the specified size around the image. Thus, if the attribute were set to **n**, the image would become $2n+1$ pixels tall or wide. You could indent the line in the preceding example 101 pixels by replacing the `<WIDTH>` and `<HEIGHT>` tags with `HSPACE=50` and `VSPACE=1`:

```
This is a normal line of text in this document.<BR>
<IMG SRC="clearpix.gif" ALT="" HSPACE=50 VSPACE=1>This is an indented line of
text.<BR>
```

5. Similarly, you could use transparent images to alter the vertical layout of a page by adjusting `HEIGHT` and `VSPACE` instead of `WIDTH` and `HSPACE`. In the following example, a second line of text is placed far below the first line.

```
This is a normal line of text in this document.<BR>
<IMG SRC="clearpix.gif" ALT="" WIDTH=1 HEIGHT=100><BR>
This is a line of text far below the first.<BR>

This is a normal line of text in this document.<BR>
<IMG SRC="clearpix.gif" ALT="" HSPACE=1 VSPACE=50> <BR>
This is a line of text far below the first.<BR>
```

Examples of the use of transparent images are shown in Figure 7-10. The code for this figure is available as file 7-10.HTML.

How It Works

When a browser encounters the `<IMG>` tag, it loads the named image. It scales the image according to the `HEIGHT` and `WIDTH` attributes found in the tag, and adds a clear border around the document using the `<VSPACE>` and `<HSPACE>` tags. This graphic then alters the location of the remaining text in the document, even though this transparent image cannot be seen.

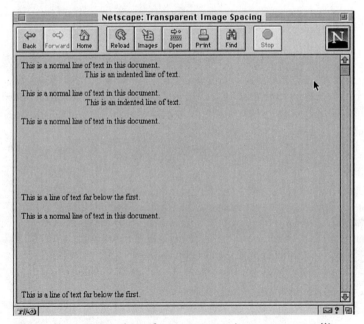

Figure 7-10 Examples of transparent images controlling layout in HTML

Comments

For this "trick" to work, the browser must be loading images. If the browser has the auto-loading of images turned off, the space on the page may still be reserved (because of the **HEIGHT** and **WIDTH** tags), but an icon that represents an image will appear. This technique will also not work for text-only browsers, such as Lynx.

COMPLEXITY
INTERMEDIATE

7.11 How do I...
Create columnar text spanning a table?

COMPATIBILITY: HTML 3.2

Problem

I would like to format the text on my Web page like a newspaper or magazine: by splitting it into a number of columns that appear side by side on the screen. Is there a way to do this in HTML?

Technique

You can use a table (see Chapter 5, Tables) to split the layout of a page into several columns and place text in each column to create a multicolumn layout.

Steps

Open the HTML document with the text you want to place in multiple columns.

1. Create the table by entering a **<TABLE>** tag at the beginning of the text and a **</TABLE>** at the end of the text:

```
<TABLE>
<!-- this is where your text goes -->
</TABLE>
```

2. Since we are concerned with splitting the text into a number of columns and don't have any concern over rows, we'll only create a single row. Place a **<TR>** tag just after the **<TABLE>** tag and a **</TR>** tag just before the **</TABLE>** tag:

```
<TABLE>
<TR>
<!-- this is where your text goes -->
</TR>
</TABLE>
```

3. Now we need to add the `<TD>...</TD>` tags that define the columns. You will need a table cell for each column. For the case of a two-column layout, you would need two sets of `<TD>...</TD>` tags, with the split between columns about halfway through the text. You would use something like the following:

```
<TABLE>
<TR>
<TD>
<!-- this is where the first half of your text goes -->
</TD>
<TD>
<!-- this is where the second half of your text goes -->
</TD>
</TR>
</TABLE>
```

You would use similar setups for other multiple column layouts: For a three-column layout, for example, you would use three sets of `<TD>...</TD>` tags.

4. To make sure all the text is aligned at the top of the table, insert the `VALIGN=TOP` attribute in each `<TD>` statement:

```
<TABLE>
<TR>
<TD VALIGN=TOP>
<!-- this is where the first half of your text goes -->
</TD>
<TD VALIGN=TOP>
<!-- this is where the second half of your text goes -->
</TD>
</TR>
</TABLE>
```

5. You can also use the `WIDTH` attribute of `<TD>` to control the width of the cell. In this example, if you wanted the first cell to occupy 40 percent of the width of the browser window and the second to take the remaining 60 percent, you would enter

```
<TABLE>
<TR>
<TD VALIGN=TOP WIDTH="40%">
<!-- this is where the first half of your text goes -->
</TD>
<TD VALIGN=TOP WIDTH="60%">
<!-- this is where the second half of your text goes -->
</TD>
</TR>
</TABLE>
```

An example of a two-column format is shown in Figure 7-11. The code for this figure is available as file 7-11.HTML.

Figure 7-11 A two-column layout using tables

How It Works

This is another application of tables, which are discussed in greater detail in Chapter 5, Tables. The content of each table cell is a block of text, which can span many paragraphs. The table cells are placed in a single row, and the `VALIGN=TOP` attribute makes sure the text is aligned at the top, a precaution in case the cells are of different lengths.

Comments

One precaution when creating tables is to keep the number of columns used to a minimum. If the person viewing a page with many columns only has a small screen, either each browser will be very narrow, making it hard to read, or the table will extend past the right end of the browser window, requiring the user to scroll horizontally as well as vertically.

COMPLEXITY
BEGINNING

7.12 How do I...
Space my home page?

COMPATIBILITY: NOT APPLICABLE

Problem

How can I make a home page so that it is easily readable, yet still compact enough that readers don't have to scroll a lot?

Technique

The technique used here is a mixture of good judgment, common sense, and personal taste. Spacing is often a matter of personal taste. Bad spacing is easy to identify: If you can't read your page, nobody else can either. Good spacing is a bit harder to identify. You wrote your page, so you can tell where everything is, but that doesn't mean that another reader will be able to. Have a few people read your page and give you feedback on it. There are also a few pointers to follow that will help make your page flow smoothly and be easy to read.

- Be consistent with your spacing.

- Be consistent with how you use horizontal lines.

- Feel free to ignore these points. After all, it is your page. Just remember, though, that if things are run together or spaced too far apart, readers may miss something you want them to read.

Steps

The following steps give general instructions on how to space your page. Feel free to follow or ignore any suggestions given.

1. Decide which type of spacing and horizontal line rules you wish to use, if any.

2. Incorporate these rules into your pages. The following document is a very simple home page about poetry. It uses an **<HR>** to separate the two poems and another **<HR>** to separate the footer from the main text body of the page. It also uses **
** tags to cause each verse of the poem to appear on a separate line.

```
<HTML>
<HEAD>
<TITLE>My Page of Poems</TITLE>
<BODY>
</HEAD>
<H2>My Poetry Page</H2>
Here are a couple of my favorite poems:<P>
This one from my childhood:
<P ALIGN=CENTER>
Mary had a little lamb<BR>
Its fleece was white as snow<BR>
Everywhere that Mary went the lamb was sure to go!<BR>
</P>
<HR>
This one from my adulthood:
<P ALIGN=CENTER>
Roses are Red<BR>
Violets are Blue<BR>
I love you<BR>
<HR>
<CITE>
This page is maintained by: J. Smith.
</CITE>
</BODY>
</HTML>
```

3. Experiment to see what you think works best.

How It Works

You blend elements, tags such as **<P>**, **
, and **<HR>, and different levels of headers to create a page that is pleasing to the eye, informative, and yet not too long. It is helpful to have a set of rules that govern the use of certain tags. For example:

- Use an **<HR>** after a level heading.

- Use an **<HR>** before any footer or trailer information.

- Use an **<HR>** to separate distinct items.

- Use two **<P>** elements to separate new sections.

- Use **
** between lines of addresses.

- Always start a page with a title displayed as a level 2 header.

Comments

For the most part, pages can be broken down into three sections:

- Heading information that could include a snappy logo or information about who and where you are

- Body content that includes information or links to information you find important

- Footer information such as where to reach you, when the document was last updated, links to sites that are directly related to your page, and an e-mail address

CHAPTER 8
ESTABLISHING LINKS

8

ESTABLISHING LINKS

How do I...

8.15   Create links to pages in other users' home directories?

8.16   Add links to lists and tables?

8.17   Add links to my home page?

With only a small amount of markup, you can format text files for effective presentation on the World Wide Web. This alone makes HTML and WWW a good way to publish documents over the Internet. But it only captures a small fraction of the potential of the World Wide Web. Imagine being able to give the reader of your document the ability, with a single keypress or mouse click, to move to another part of your document, another document on your computer, or Internet resources around the world. HTML provides the ability to add links to other documents and resources. You'll learn about links in this chapter, starting with some background about how links work and progressing through a series of methods to connect other documents to your own.

8.1   Interpret a URL

Universal Resource Locators, or URLs, are what World Wide Web browsers use to locate files on the Internet. This How-To explains the various parts of a URL and shows how to construct URLs to point to various kinds of documents.

8.2   Understand a Relative URL

If you have a number of pages located on your computer, but placed in various directories, relative URLs let you identify their location without typing the entire pathname of the file. This How-To explains how relative URLs work and how you can create relative URLs for your own needs.

8.3   Add a Base for Relative URLs Within the Body of a Document

If a page contains relative URLs and is transferred from one location to another, the relative URLs will no longer work in the new location. This How-To explains how to get around this problem by specifying a base for these URLs within the body of your page.

8.4   Specify a Relationship Between This Document and Other Resources

A page you're developing may be one of a set of related pages, and you would like to be able to show how a particular page fits in with the other pages. This How-To explains how to specify relationships between a page and other pages and resources.

8.5   Create a Link to a Local Page

The simplest type of link is linking a page you've created with other pages and files on your computer. This simple How-To shows how to link together the pages you've created on your computer.

8.6   Create a Link to Other Pages

The World Wide Web connects thousands of pages around the world. This How-To shows how to connect your page to any number of pages around the world.

8.7   Send Data to an HTTP Server via a URL

When using forms or key word searches, there are instances when you want to pass some information on to an application on a specific computer. This How-To explains how to attach key word information to a URL to be passed on to an application.

8.8   Create a Link to a Specific Part of a Page

When creating a page, especially a very long page, it may be useful to provide links to other parts of the page to make it easy for readers to move around the document. This How-To explains how to create links to a specific part of a page.

8.9   Create a Link to an FTP Site

File Transfer Protocol (FTP) is a popular method of transferring files across the Internet. There are FTP servers located around the world, with information on a wide range of topics including, no doubt, information useful for your pages. This How-To explains how to link an FTP site to your page.

8.10   Create a Link to a Gopher Site

Gopher provides an easy-to-use, menu-based interface to information resources on the Internet. This How-To explains how to link a Gopher site, and specific items at the site, to your page.

8.11   Create a Link to a Telnet Site

Some sites on the Internet provide information by Telnet, requiring a user to log on to the computer to access information. This How-To explains how to link a Telnet site to your page.

8.12   Create a Link to a WAIS Site

The Wide Area Information Servers (WAIS) technology is a method of providing searchable databases on the Internet, making them useful for finding specific items of information. This How-To explains how to link a WAIS site to your page.

8.13   Create a Link to a Usenet Newsgroup

There are thousands of Usenet newsgroups that cover seemingly every conceivable topic under the sun, as well as a number of inconceivable topics. This How-To explains how to link a Usenet newsgroup to your page.

8.14   Create a Link to Electronic Mail

It's often useful for people to easily contact you or other people concerning the contents of your page. One way to do this is to make it possible for readers to automatically e-mail people. This How-To explains how to link electronic mail to your page.

8.15 Create Links to Pages in Other Users' Home Directories

You may want to include links to pages located in the directories of other users on a multiuser machine. Rather than specifying the full pathname for the page, you can use a shortcut to create a link to that page. This How-To explains how to create a simple link to a page in another user's directories.

8.16 Add Links to Lists and Tables

Lists and tables provide ways to efficiently organize information. They can be combined with links to create easy-to-use menus of options. This How-To explains how to add links to the lists and tables in your page.

8.17 Add Links to My Home Page

Links can be simple and fun to add to your pages, but if done incorrectly, they can make your page difficult to understand or use. This How-To explains how to add links to your page that will increase the information content of your page and make it more fun to read.

COMPLEXITY
INTERMEDIATE

8.1 How do I...
Interpret a URL?

COMPATIBILITY: HTML 2+

Problem

I want to include links in my page, so I understand that I'll need to use URLs. However, I'm unfamiliar with the structure and composition of URLs—what goes into them, and where. How do I interpret a URL?

Technique

HTML uses Universal Resource Locators, or URLs, to provide a simple, consistent way of accessing information using a wide variety of protocols. A URL consists of three main items: a protocol code, the address of the computer with the desired file (or an e-mail address or newsgroup name), and the location and filename of the file containing the information.

Steps

The following steps illustrate how to interpret a URL.

1. The first part of a URL is the protocol. The protocol indicates what method should be used to obtain the requested information. There are seven main protocols, listed in Table 8-1, which will be discussed in greater detail later in the chapter.

Table 8-1 URL protocols

PROTOCOL	DESCRIPTION
ftp	File Transfer Protocol (FTP)
gopher	Gopher
http	HyperText Transfer Protocol (HTTP)
mailto	Electronic Mail
news	Usenet News
telnet	Telnet
wais	Wide Area Information Servers (WAIS)

2. For five of the seven protocols (ftp, gopher, http, telnet, and wais), the protocol is followed by a colon and two forward slashes (//). Immediately following the slashes is the address of the computer that is host to the relevant information. Some examples are

```
http://www.stateu.edu
ftp://ftp.widgets.com
gopher://info.stateu.edu
```

For the mailto protocol, the protocol is followed by a single colon and an e-mail address.

```
mailto:john@stateu.edu
mailto:help@widgets.com
```

For the news protocol, the protocol is followed by a single colon and the name of a Usenet newsgroup.

```
news:alt.widgets
news:comp.infosystems.www.users
```

3. For protocols other than mailto and news, the address of the computer is followed by the path to the desired file or directory. Some examples are

```
http://www.stateu.edu/pub/teams/yankees.html
ftp://ftp.widgets.com/etc/images/widget1.gif
gopher://info.stateu.edu/00/pubinfo/good%20restaurants
```

How It Works

When a browser encounters a URL, it first checks the protocol to determine what method the program must use to get the information. The browser then gets the address of the computer (or newsgroup name or e-mail address), accesses the site, and uses the path information in the URL to find the file and bring a copy back to the browser's computer.

Comments

Some browsers don't support some URL protocols like `news` and `mailto`; such browsers require additional software or connections to work properly. A browser must be configured to use a communications program in order to use any Telnet URLs, and it must have access to a WAIS server or be able to use a WAIS server elsewhere as a proxy in order to use any WAIS URLs.

To better understand the structure of URLs, you may want to look at the URLs contained in a variety of Web pages. Those URLs will provide additional examples of how URLs are constructed.

COMPLEXITY
INTERMEDIATE

8.2   How do I...
Understand a relative URL?

COMPATIBILITY: HTML 2+

Problem

When I've looked at some World Wide Web pages, I've seen URLs that don't have a protocol of any kind. Instead, it's just a filename or some kind of path. How do these kinds of URLs work?

Technique

When a URL does not begin with a protocol, that means it is referencing a file local to that computer (or possibly a file based on another computer; see How-To 8.3). Pathnames can be used to find files in directories other than the base directory.

Steps

To better understand the following examples, refer to Figure 8-1. This figure is a graphical representation of the directory structure used in the examples.

1. To access a file located in the same directory the current page is in, use only the name of the file as the URL. For example, if you are in `page1.html` and you want to go to `page2.html`, simply enter

```
page2.html
```

If you are in `page6.html` and you want to access `info.txt`, enter

```
info.txt
```

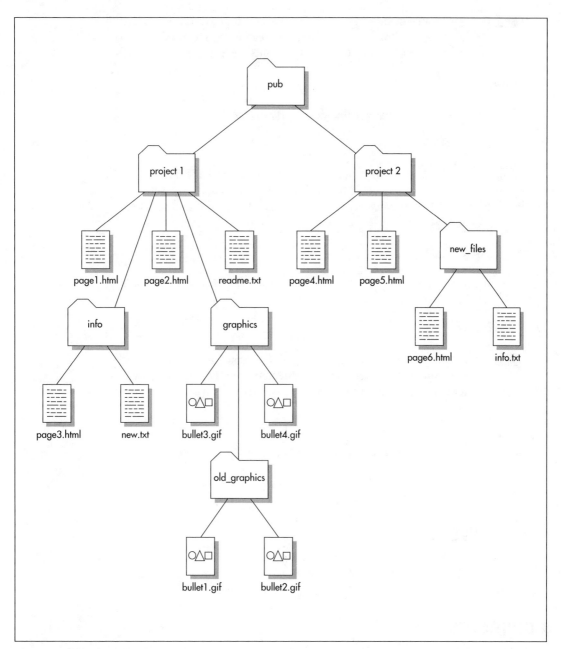

Figure 8-1 A sample directory structure

2. For files located in subdirectories of the current page's directory, include the subdirectory name(s), separated from the filename by a forward slash (/). For example, to get from `page1.html` to `page3.html`, enter

`info/page3.html`

To get from `page2.html` to the file `bullet2.gif`, enter

`graphics/old_graphics/bullet2.gif`

3. For files located in parent directories (directories above the directory of the current page), use a double period (`..`) separated from the filename by a forward slash for each level up. For example, if you want to get back to `page4.html` from `page6.html`, enter

`./page4.html`

If you are in `bullet2.gif` and you want to access `readme.txt`, you will need to enter

`././../readme.txt`

4. You can combine steps 2 and 3 to access files located in directory branches separate from the branch the current directory is in. For example, if you are in `page4.html` and you want to go to `page2.html`, enter

`./project1/page2.html`

If you are in `page6.html` and you want to open `new.txt`, enter

`././../files/project1/info/new.txt`

How It Works

When a protocol is omitted from a URL, a Web browser assumes that the location given is relative to the location of the current page. It uses the path information to move up or down directories to locate and retrieve the file.

Comments

Relative URLs are a great way to specify the location of pages and other files without having to write out a full pathname. However, if the page with the relative URLs is moved to another directory, then the URLs will no longer work because they will point the way to files and directories that are not in the same relative location they originally were (unless, of course, all the files and directories are moved along with the page). You can solve this problem by using the <BASE> element described in How-To 8.3.

COMPLEXITY
INTERMEDIATE

8.3 How do I...
Add a base for relative URLs within the body of a document?

COMPATIBILITY: HTML 2+

Problem

I need to move a page with a number of relative URLs in it. However, I can't move the files along with the page, and I don't want to spend the time editing the page to insert the new, longer pathnames for these files. How can I define a base for URLs in my document?

Technique

HTML has an element called <BASE> that can be included in the heading of a document to specify the base for all the relative URLs in the document. This allows you to move your page around without breaking the relative URLs, or permits you to use shortcuts in your URLs if you need to reference a number of files from the same location.

Steps

Open your document and go to the heading section (between the <HEAD> and </HEAD> tags; see Chapter 2, HTML Basics, for background information about headings in HTML documents).

1. Inside your page heading, insert the <BASE> tag. Inside the <BASE> tag, include the attribute HREF and set it equal to the full path for the desired directory, assuming that directory is located on the same computer as the page. For example, if you want to set the base for relative URLs to the directory /pub/projects/data/, enter

```
<HEAD>
<TITLE>My Page</TITLE>
<BASE HREF="/pub/projects/data/">
</HEAD>
```

2. If the desired base for your URLs is located on another computer, include the full-fledged URL, including the protocol and name of the computer. If, for example, the base is on a Web server at `www.stateu.edu` in the directory `pub/images`, you would enter

```
<HEAD>
<TITLE>My Page</TITLE>
<BASE HREF="http://www.stateu.edu/pub/images/">
</HEAD>
```

3. Or if the base is located on the FTP server `ftp.stateu.edu` in the directory `/pub/images`, the code would be

```
<HEAD>
<TITLE>My Page</TITLE>
<BASE HREF="ftp://ftp.stateu.edu/pub/images/">
</HEAD>
```

How It Works

The `<BASE>` element tells the browser to append the URL contained in it to any relative URLs located in the document. The contents of the `<BASE>` element are ignored for any URLs in the document that are fully formed, that is, that have protocols specified.

Comments

You can set the `<BASE>` element only once in a document, in the header. The `<BASE>` element does not work outside of the header. Thus, if you have two sets of relative URLs for which you want to specify separate bases, you can use the `<BASE>` element for only one set. You must edit the other set to include the full pathnames and protocols.

COMPLEXITY
INTERMEDIATE

8.4   How do I...
Specify a relationship between this document and other resources?

COMPATIBILITY: HTML 2+

Problem

I'm creating a number of Web pages that are all related to one another. I would like to be able to specify the relationship of each page to other pages for possible use by Web browsers. How can I specify a relationship between pages in HTML?

Technique

Use the `<LINK>` element in the header of an HTML document to identify relationships between documents and other resources. These relationships include preceding and following documents, tables of contents, indexes, and other document parts. The `<LINK>` element can also identify the author of a document.

Steps

Open your document and go to the heading section (between the `<HEAD>` and `</HEAD>` tags).

1. Place the `<LINK>` element in the header of a page.

```
<HEAD>
<TITLE>My Page</TITLE>
<LINK>
</HEAD>
```

2. The `<LINK>` element supports two kinds of attributes, `REL` and `REV`. `REL` indicates a relationship between the current document and a document listed in the element using the `HREF` attribute (as in How-To 8.3). The `REL` attribute can take on a number of different values. The most common ones, which have been reserved in HTML, are listed in Table 8-2.

Table 8-2 Values for the `REL` attribute in `<LINK>`

VALUE	DESCRIPTION
Bookmark	A specific section of a document
Copyright	A document with copyright information
Glossary	A glossary document
Help	A help document
Home	The home page or top of a hierarchy
Index	An index document
Next	The next document in a series
Previous	The previous document in a series
TOC	A table of contents document
Up	The parent document to the current one

A common use for these attributes is to identify the previous and next pages in a sequence of documents. For example, if your current page is the document `page4.html`, and you want to identify the previous document (`page3.html`) and the next document (`page5.html`), you could use

```
<HEAD>
<TITLE>Page 4</TITLE>
<LINK REL=Previous HREF="page3.html">
<LINK REL=Next HREF="page5.html">
</HEAD>
```

Note that each reference is contained in a separate `<LINK>` element in the header.

3. The `REV` attribute is the opposite of `REL`. Instead of specifying another document's relationship to the current page, it specifies the current page's relationships to other pages. Applying this to the example results in the following:

```
<HEAD>
<TITLE>Page 4</TITLE>
<LINK REV=Next HREF="page3.html">
<LINK REV=Previous HREF="page5.html">
</HEAD>
```

You are now saying that this document (`page4.html`) is `page3.html`'s next document and `page5.html`'s previous document, instead of saying that `page4.html`'s previous document was `page3.html` and `page4.html`'s next document was `page5.html`. Confusing? This kind of confusion can be avoided by using only one of the two attributes to specify relationships. `REL` is the attribute of choice for most people.

4. `REV` has found another use as a way to identify the author of the page. This can be done by placing the e-mail address of the author in a `mailto` URL (see How-To's 8.1 and 8.14 for more information about `mailto` URLs) and setting it equal to `REV`.

```
<HEAD>
<TITLE>Page 4</TITLE>
<LINK REV="mailto:jfoust@mit.edu">
</HEAD>
```

How It Works

The browser reads and stores the information contained in the `<LINK>` elements regarding the location of related files. Some browsers provide users with the ability to select those documents, using a toolbar or other techniques.

Comments

`<LINK>` elements are a good way to indicate relationships among documents, but many Web browsers ignore the information contained in them. If you want to be sure that all readers have the ability to go to the files you've referenced in the `<LINK>` elements, you should include the links in the body of your page. Techniques for including these links are discussed starting in the next How-To.

COMPLEXITY
BEGINNING

8.5 How do I...
Create a link to a local page?

COMPATIBILITY: HTML 2+

Problem

I would like to link one page I've created with another page, which is also located on my computer. How can I create a link in one of my pages that references a local page in HTML?

Technique

HTML uses the **<A>** and **</A>** tags to identify areas of the text that serve as anchors for links to other files. The **HREF** attribute in the **<A>** tag lists the location of the page or other resource.

Steps

Open your document. Decide what documents you would like to link to the current document.

1. Identify the word or phrase in your page that you want to use as an anchor for the link. Place the **<A>** tag at the beginning of the anchor and the **</A>** tag at the end of the anchor.

```
I enjoy watching <A>baseball</A>, but I'm not a good player.

I've visited <A>New York</A> a few times.
```

2. Inside the **<A>** tag, place the **HREF** attribute, and set it equal to the filename of the other page, provided the destination page is located in the same directory as the page you're working on. The filename should be enclosed in double quotation marks.

```
I enjoy watching <A HREF="baseball.html">baseball</A>, but I'm not a good player.

I've visited <A HREF="newyork.html">New York</A> a few times.
```

3. If the destination page is located in a subdirectory of the directory that contains your current page, you can indicate the path by including the subdirectory name(s) in the **HREF** attribute, separating the subdirectory names from each other and the filename with a forward slash (**/**), as shown in How-To 8.2:

```
I enjoy watching <A HREF="sports/baseball.html">baseball</A>, but I'm not a
good player.
```

```
I've visited <A HREF="usa/cities/east-coast/newyork.html">New York</A> a few
times.
```

4. If the destination page is located in a directory above the directory of your current page, you can go up the directory structure by using (..), two periods without any spacing between them, as shown in How-To 8.2.

```
I enjoy watching <A HREF="../baseball.html">baseball</A>, but I'm not a good
player.
```

```
I've visited <A HREF="../../newyork.html">New York</A> a few times.
```

5. Links can retrieve more than just other pages. You can include sounds, graphics, text files, even compressed binary files in a link. For example, to include a link to a text file, enter

```
I have some <A HREF="info.txt">older information</A> about this subject.
```

or to include a link to an image, enter

```
I took a <A HREF="gcanyon.gif">picture</A> of the Grand Canyon from the South
Rim.
```

Figure 8-2 shows some examples of links. The code is included on the CD-ROM as file 8-2.HTML.

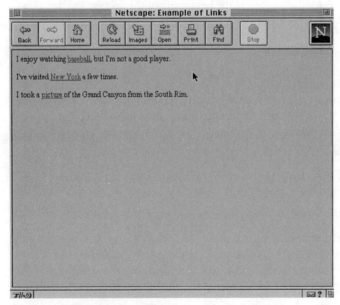

Figure 8-2 Examples of links

How It Works

The <A> and </A> tags tell the browser to identify the text contained between them as a link, which is usually done by highlighting or underlining the text. The HREF attribute provides the location of the file the browser should load if the link is selected. If the location of the file includes directory information, the browser assumes the location is given relative to the location of the current page. The <BASE> element (How-To 8.3) can be used to set that location to another path, or even to another computer.

Comments

When a browser encounters a link to a file other than another WWW page, the browser decides how to deal with the file. Most browsers display a text file the same as an HTML file (although with no formatting) and launch an external application for other files: a graphics program for an image, an audio program for a sound file, and so on. This depends on the availability of a compatible external application. If no application exists on the reader's computer to handle a file, the file cannot be viewed or heard. Thus, when including links to images, sounds, and animations, try to use common formats for these files whenever possible.

COMPLEXITY
BEGINNING

8.6   How do I...
Create a link to other pages?

COMPATIBILITY: HTML 2+

Problem

I would like to include a link to a great page that has a lot of information relevant to my page. However, the page is located on another computer, so I can't use a link to a local page. How can I create a link to a page on another computer?

Technique

Using the HyperText Transfer Protocol (HTTP), you can connect to one computer and transfer a copy of a document on that computer to a browser running on another computer by placing the URL of the document in the anchor of a link, using the HREF attribute.

Steps

Open your document. Locate the words or phrases to be used for the links.

1. Identify the text you want to use as a link by placing the **<A>** tag at the beginning of the anchor text and the **</A>** tag at the end of the anchor text.

```
I enjoy watching <A>baseball</A>, but I'm not a good player.

I've visited <A>New York</A> a few times.
```

2. Place the HREF attribute in the **<A>** tag and set it equal to the URL of the page. (See How-To 8.1 for more information about URLs.) Enclose the URL in double quotation marks.

```
I enjoy watching <A HREF="http://www.stateu.edu/sports/baseball.html">
baseball</A>, but I'm not a good player.

I've visited <A HREF="http://www.stateu.edu/cities/newyork.html">New York⇐
</A> a few times.
```

3. This technique can transfer other types of files, such as text files and images. For example, to transfer a text file, simply use that file's pathname in the URL

```
I have some <A HREF="http://www.stateu.edu/info/info.txt">older⇐
information</A> about this subject.
```

or to transfer an image, use the image file's pathname.

```
I took a <A HREF="http://www.stateu.edu/images/scenic/gcanyon.gif">picture</A>
of the Grand Canyon from the South Rim.
```

4. You can use an http URL without a filename at the end for some special cases. Doing this displays the default page in the directory (usually named index.html or default.html, depending on how the HTTP server on that computer is configured), if it exists. Otherwise, it displays the contents of the directory, with the filenames linked to the files. For example, to load the default file on a subdirectory of www.stateu.edu, enter

```
I've created a new <A HREF="http://www.stateu.edu/pub/users/john/">home
page</A> in my user's directory.
```

How It Works

The http in the URL tells a browser to use the HyperText Transfer Protocol to locate and transfer the file listed in the URL. The browser displays the page just like a local file. For text files, images, and other files, the browser uses the URL to locate the file and then transfers a copy using HTTP. The browser then displays the contents of the file or transfers the file to the appropriate external application.

Comments

Web servers often use different filenames for the default file. For example, CERN HTTPD uses `default.html` while NCSA HTTPD uses `index.html`. Some browsers may be configured to use a specific name instead of either of these two; check the server documentation or ask the Webmaster of the site for specific information.

COMPLEXITY
INTERMEDIATE

8.7 How do I...
Send data to an HTTP server via a URL?

COMPATIBILITY: HTML 2+

Problem

I'm developing a form to include in a page using a search key word, and I want to be able to send the results to a server to be processed by a program there. Is there a way to include that response or other information in a URL to send to a server?

Technique

It is possible to include key words or other basic pieces of information in a URL. A question mark is placed at the end of the URL for an application, followed by the data. Browsers usually do this automatically when they submit data.

Steps

Open your document. Locate the words or phrases for the links to the HTTP server.

1. If you want to include a key word or other data in a link, first create an anchor in the text appropriate to the data you want to send. For example, to create a pair of links that will send the answers yes or no to a question, enter

```
<H3>Do you want to subscribe to our magazine?</H3>?
<UL>
<LI><A>Yes!</A>
<LI><A>No thanks</A>
</UL>
```

2. Now, use the HREF attribute to add a link to a program on an HTTP server that will receive the data. (For now, don't worry about the specifics of the program. Forms and CGI applications are covered in Chapter 11, "HTML

Interactive Forms," and Chapter 14, "The Common Gateway Interface (CGI)," respectively.) If, for example, the program is called "response" and is located on the `http` server at `www.stateu.edu`, your code would look like this:

```
<H3>Do you want to subscribe to our magazine?</H3>?
<UL>
<LI><A HREF="http://www.stateu.edu/applications/response">Yes!</A>
<LI><A HREF="http://www.stateu.edu/applications/response">No thanks</A>
</UL>
```

3. Now add to the end of the URL a question mark and the key word you want sent to the application. For this example, let the responses be yes and no.

```
<H3>Do you want to subscribe to our magazine?</H3>?
<UL>
<LI><A HREF="http://www.stateu.edu/applications/response?yes">Yes!</A>
<LI><A HREF="http://www.stateu.edu/applications/response?no">No thanks</A>
</UL>
```

How It Works

The browser interprets anything in a URL after a question mark to be data that is sent to a URL. The application referenced in the URL then receives the key word as input and processes it accordingly.

Comments

The example shown here can actually be done better with forms. See Chapter 11 to find out how to create forms for your pages, and Chapter 14, to see how to write applications to process the data. When key word searching is enabled (using the `<ISINDEX>` tag in the header, as shown in Chapter 14), the question mark and key word are added automatically and don't need to be manually included in the URL.

COMPLEXITY
INTERMEDIATE

8.8 How do I...
Create a link to a specific part of a page?

COMPATIBILITY: HTML 2+

Problem

I have a long document I am converting into a WWW page using HTML. I want to use a table of contents to refer to the various sections of a document so the reader can quickly refer to those sections. I would also like to be able to refer to different sections of the document from other pages. How can I create a link to a specific part of a page in HTML?

Technique

The **NAME** attribute used in the anchor tag identifies a section of a page. Users can then access this section via a link from within the document or from other documents.

Steps

Open your document. Identify the words or phrases that will serve as links. Also, decide what sections of the document you want links to lead to.

1. To identify a section of a document, place the **<A>** and **</A>** tags at the beginning of the section. Include the **NAME** attribute in the **<A>** tag and set it to the name you want to give the section. Enclose the name in double quotation marks. Unlike the **<LINK>** tags, there is no need to include any text between the **<A>** and **</A>** tags.

```
<A NAME="section1"></A>
<H1>Section 1</H1>
<!-- text of section 1 -->
```

2. To include a link to the named section elsewhere in your page, create a link as described in How-To 8.5 and set HREF equal to the name of the section as defined by the NAME attribute. Enclose the name in double quotation marks and precede it with a pound symbol (#) to differentiate it from the name of another document.

```
You will find the relevant background information in <A
HREF="#section1">section 1</A>.
```

3. To include a link to the named section from another local document, create a local link as described in How-To 8.5 and include the name of the section, preceded by the pound symbol (#), in the location of the link defined by the HREF attribute.

```
You will find the relevant background information in <A
HREF="report.html#section1">section 1</A>.
```

4. For documents located on other computers, the process is similar. Attach the name of the section, preceded by the pound symbol (#), to the end of the URL for the document.

```
You will find the relevant background information in <A
HREF="http://www.stateu.edu/documents/report.html#section1">section 1</A>.
```

How It Works

When a browser loads a URL with a # symbol, it looks for the section of the document with an anchor tag matching the name after the # symbol. The browser then displays the loaded page, with the beginning of the named section at the top of the screen.

Comments

When used to create links, the <A> tag must include text. When <A> tags are used merely to identify a section of a document, text is not necessary. This is because the tag is being used only to mark a section of a document for later use in a link, not to function itself as a link to another document. There is no need to include text between the tags, since this text is not highlighted and cannot be used to jump to another document or section of a document.

8.9 How do I...
Create a link to an FTP site?

COMPATIBILITY: HTML 2+

Problem

I've found a file that I would like to include as a link in my page. However, the file is not accessible on the World Wide Web, only by anonymous FTP. How can I add a link to a file on an FTP site?

Technique

You can construct a URL for the file located on the FTP site and include that in a standard HTML link. The link will function like a link to a page or other document accessible via HTTP.

Steps

Open the document and find the words or phrases you want to use as links.

1. To construct the URL, you need to know the name of the site where the file is located and the path for the file (that is, the directory where the file is located). For example, to access a file named `contents.txt` located on the server `ftp.stateu.edu` in the directory `pub/info`, you would use this URL:

```
ftp://ftp.stateu.edu/pub/info/contents.txt
```

To access the image file `gcanyon.gif` from `ftp.stateu.edu` in the directory `pub/photos/arizona`, you would use this URL:

```
ftp://ftp.stateu.edu/pub/photos/arizona/gcanyon.gif
```

2. You can now include either of these URLs in a link by setting the `HREF` attribute of the link equal to the URL.

```
The <A HREF="ftp://ftp.stateu.edu/pub/info/contents.txt">contents</A> of the
directory can be easily viewed.

I took an incredible <A
HREF="ftp://ftp.stateu.edu/pub/photos/arizona/gcanyon.gif">photo</A> of the
Grand Canyon during my last trip there!
```

3. You can use FTP URLs to access entire directories and display their contents in the browser window. To do this, include the pathname to the directory in the URL, but do not add a filename to the end of the URL.

```
My <a HREF="ftp://ftp.stateu.edu/pub/photos/">photos directory</A> contains⇐
a lot of pictures I took while on vacation in Arizona.
```

Figure 8-3 shows an example of an FTP directory accessed in HTML.

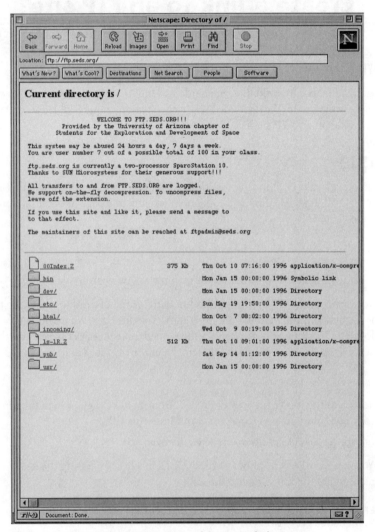

Figure 8-3 An FTP site as viewed in a Web browser

4. By default, the FTP URL uses anonymous FTP. However, you can create an FTP URL that uses nonanonymous FTP. To do so, include the username and password, separated by a colon, in front of the address of the FTP site. Include the @ symbol between the password and the computer address. To access the FTP server at `ftp.stateu.edu` as user `weather`, using the password `stormy`, you would use the following code:

```
There is an archive of <A
HREF="ftp://weather:stormy@ftp.stateu.edu/pub/weather/">weather data</A> that
includes satellite photos and updated forecasts.
```

How It Works

When a link with an FTP URL is selected, the browser opens an FTP connection with the specified computer. It goes to the appropriate directory and copies the file. The file then appears in the browser window or in an external application, depending on the type of file retrieved.

Comments

Unlike manually FTPing files, there is no need to specify whether to transfer a file as a binary, or ASCII, file. The browser checks the suffix of the file. If it matches with a suffix associated with binary files, the file is transferred as a binary file. Otherwise, it is transferred as a text file. Also, unless a username and password are specified, most browsers automatically log in to the FTP site as anonymous and transfer a string, usually your e-mail address, as the password. If you do include a nonanonymous FTP URL in your page, remember that the password is available for anyone to view, so don't put the password to your account there. This should only be used for special, limited-use accounts whose passwords can be distributed freely.

COMPLEXITY
INTERMEDIATE

8.10 How do I...
Create a link to a Gopher site?

COMPATIBILITY: HTML 2+

Problem

I would like to reference a file stored on a Gopher server for my page. How can I add a link to a Gopher server? Can I go directly to the file or do I have to go through the directory structure of the Gopher server?

Technique

A few years ago, Gopher servers were a popular method of making information easily available to Internet users. Even with the rapid growth of the World Wide Web, many Gopher servers are still in use and contain information you may want to reference on your page. This can be done with a Gopher URL, either to the top-level directory or directly to the file.

Steps

Open the document and find the words or phrases you want to use as links.

1. First, define the anchor text in your page using the `<A>` tag.

```
There is a <A>Gopher site</A> with more information on baseball.
```

2. To construct a URL for the top-level directory of a Gopher server, take the address of the Gopher site and attach `gopher://` to the front of it, such as `gopher://gopher.stateu.edu`. You can then set the `HREF` attribute in the link tag equal to this URL.

```
There is a <A HREF="gopher://gopher.stateu.edu">Gopher site</A> with more
information on baseball.
```

3. To construct a URL for a specific file or directory on a Gopher server, you need to know the full path to it. To get this information, you will need to check the Gopher server and find the URL for it (usually available by selecting the "Display technical information about this item" option in most Gopher programs). As a rule, files have a `/00/` in their URL after the name of the server, directories have a `/11/` after the name of the server, and spaces in file or directory names are represented in the URL by the code `%20`. For example, to reference a file on a Gopher server, enter

```
There is a <A HREF="gopher://gopher.stateu.edu/00/teams/yankees.txt">file</A>
with more information on the New York Yankee.
```

To reference a directory on a Gopher server, enter

```
There is a <A HREF="gopher://gopher.stateu.edu/11/teams">directory</A> with
information on all the major league baseball teams.
```

To reference a file with a space in its name, enter

```
There is a <A REF="gopher://gopher.stateu.edu/00/teams/the%20yankees">file</A>
with information on the New York Ynkees.
```

How It Works

When a Gopher link is selected, the browser contacts the site given in the URL using the Gopher protocol and returns the information requested, either a file or a directory. The browser displays the file based on its rules for file types; text files usually display in the window, but image and sound files retrieved by Gopher are sent to the appropriate external application. If a directory is retrieved, it appears in the window, with each directory item serving as a link to another Gopher item.

Comments

Before including a link to a specific directory or file on a Gopher server, be sure to check the exact URL for the file. Different servers use different methods of defining paths to files and directories, and the name of the file or directory given in the Gopher menu may be entirely different from the real name and location of the resource.

COMPLEXITY
INTERMEDIATE

8.11 How do I...
Create a link to a Telnet site?

COMPATIBILITY: HTML 2+

Problem

I would like to create a link to an Internet resource accessible only by Telnet. I don't know how to include all the information, with the username and port number as well, in the URL. How do I create a link to a Telnet site in HTML?

Technique

A Telnet URL is similar to those used for FTP and Gopher sites. You can specify the port number, the username, and the password for logging in to the site.

Steps

Open the document and find the words or phrases you want to use as links.

1. As with other links, first specify the anchor text for the link in your document. Place the **<A>** tag at the beginning of the anchor and the **</A>** tag at the end of the anchor.

```
The State University<A>weather server </A> provides updated forecasts and
weather conditions.
```

2. To create a standard Telnet login, using the standard port and not specifying the username or password, place `telnet://` in front of the address of the site, such as `telnet://suvax.stateu.edu`. You can now set the `HREF` attribute in the anchor tag equal to this URL.

```
The State University<A HREF="telnet://suvax.stateu.edu">weather server </A>
provides updated forecasts and weather conditions.
```

3. Many special services offered by Telnet operate from a nonstandard port. To specify the port to Telnet to, place a colon after the address of the site and add the port number after the colon.

```
The State University<A HREF="telnet://suvax.stateu.edu:3000">weather server
</A> provides updated forecasts and weather conditions.
```

4. To specify the username to be used when logging in to the Telnet site, place the username in front of the site address and separate the two with the @ symbol.

```
The State University<A HREF="telnet://weather@suvax.stateu.edu">weather server
</A> provides updated forecasts and weather conditions.
```

5. To provide a password as well as a username, place a colon after the username and insert the password between the colon and @ symbol.

```
The State University<A HREF="telnet://weather:stormy@suvax.stateu.edu">weather
server </A> provides updated forecasts and weather conditions.
```

How It Works

When a Telnet link is selected, the browser starts up a Telnet session using the Telnet program set by the browser. The port number, username, and password, if provided, are used to establish the connection.

Comments

To be able to use a Telnet link, a browser must be able to access a Telnet program on the browser's computer; otherwise, the link cannot be used. The Telnet program that the browser uses is defined by the browser and can usually be changed by the reader. Since URLs are freely available and not encrypted, placing the password for an account in a URL creates a serious security hazard to that computer, unless the account is especially designed to be used solely for special applications. When in doubt, do not place the password to a computer account in a URL.

COMPLEXITY
INTERMEDIATE

8.12 How do I...
Create a link to a WAIS site?

COMPATIBILITY: HTML 2+

Problem

I would like to access a WAIS database of information relevant to a topic on my page. How can I include a link to a WAIS server on my page?

Technique

WAIS provides the ability to conduct key word searches on a variety of databases. You can include a link to a WAIS URL in your document that allows users to search a specific database on a topic or topics.

Steps

Open the document and find the words or phrases you want to use as links.

1. First, identify the anchor for the link. Place the `<A>` tag at the beginning of the link and `</A>` at the end of the link.

```
You can also search a <A>database</A> of reports and other information on
this topic.
```

2. Create the URL for the WAIS database by adding the protocol tag `wais://` in front of the name of the server. Include information on the location of the database after the name of the server. If the WAIS server is running on a port other than the standard port (210), include the port number after the address of the computer and separate the two items with a colon. Set the `HREF` attribute in the anchor tag equal to this URL.

```
You can also search a <A HREF="wais://server.stateu.edu/report-
database.src">database</A> of reports and other information on this topic.
```

```
You can also search a <A HREF="wais://server.stateu.edu:8001/report-
database.src">database</A> of reports and other information on this topic.
```

3. To specify a key word for a WAIS search, include the key word at the end of the URL and separate it from the name of the database with the question mark symbol. To search for all documents that contain the key word "baseball," enter

```
You can also search a <A HREF="wais://server.stateu.edu/report-
database.src?baseball">database</A> of reports and other information on this
topic.
```

How It Works

The WAIS protocol tag in a URL informs the browser to start a WAIS search on the given database using the key word, if provided. The browser then returns the results of the search in the window, often listing the filenames of the documents that have the given key word and providing links to the files.

Comments

Many browsers either do not support WAIS searches or require special software be installed to run the searches. Fortunately, there are not many WAIS databases available, and few people include links to WAIS databases in their pages. There has been some development of software that allows users to conduct WAIS searches using forms. (See Chapter 11, HTML Interactive Forms, for more information on how forms work.) This method will probably supersede the WAIS protocol tag in HTML.

COMPLEXITY
BEGINNING

8.13 How do I...
Create a link to a Usenet newsgroup?

COMPATIBILITY: HTML 2+

Problem

I want to reference a Usenet newsgroup that is relevant to the subject of my page. How do I create a link to a Usenet newsgroup in HTML? Does the reader need special newsreading software to access the newsgroup?

Technique

Usenet newsgroups, forums for discussion on a wide range of topics, can be accessed from a page. No special software is needed, and the titles of the articles usually appear as a list of links to the articles themselves within the Web browser once the user specifies the address of a news server.

Steps

Open the document and find the words or phrases you want to use as links.

1. As with other links, mark the anchor text for the link. Place the `<A>` tag at the beginning of the anchor text and the `</A>` tag at the end of the anchor text.

```
A number of <A>discussions</A> about the Big Bang are in progress.
```

2. You can create the URL for the newsgroup by appending the name of the newsgroup to the protocol tag `news:`. You can then set the `HREF` attribute equal to this URL.

```
A number of <A HREF="news:sci.astro">discussions</A> about the Big Bang are⇐
in progress.
```

3. In some cases, you can refer to a specific server for newsgroup articles. The URL in this case is constructed much like the URL for Web or FTP sites, with the name of the server followed by the name of the newsgroup.

```
A number of <A HREF="news://news.state-u.edu/sci.astro">discussions</A>⇐
about the Big Bang are in progress.
```

This is not a feature of HTML 3.2, but is supported by Microsoft Internet Explorer and Netscape Navigator.

How It Works

When a news URL is selected, the browser accesses the newsgroup from its news-feed. The titles of the unread articles (articles you have not yet read) appear in the window, serving as links to the full text of the articles.

Comments

To successfully use a news link, the reader's browser must have access to a news-feed, and unless the server is specified in the URL, the newsgroup in question must be carried by the browser's newsfeed. Keep this in mind when creating links to local, limited-distribution newsgroups. If you include links to Seattle-area newsgroups, for example, it's unlikely that a reader in Boston has a newsfeed that carries these newsgroups and hence won't be able to access them.

COMPLEXITY
BEGINNING

8.14   How do I...
Create a link to electronic mail?

COMPATIBILITY: HTML 2+

Problem

I would like to include a link that will allow readers to send e-mail to me with their comments about my page. I want to keep this simple, and not take the time and trouble of creating a form and software to parse the form. How can I include a link to electronic mail in HTML?

Technique

HTML includes a URL tag called `mailto`, which identifies the address to which e-mail should be sent. If the link is selected, the browser will start a mail program to send a message to the recipient listed in the URL.

Steps

Open the document and find the words or phrases you want to use as links.

1. Identify the anchor text to be used for the link by placing the `<A>` tag at the beginning of the anchor and the `</A>` tag at the end of the anchor.

```
Send me <A>e-mail</A> with your comments about my page.
```

2. Create the URL for the link by placing the protocol tag `mailto:` in front of the e-mail address to which mail should be sent. Set the `HREF` attribute in `<A>` equal to this URL.

```
Send me <A HREF="mailto:nobody@stateu.edu">e-mail</A> with your comments ⇐
about my page.
```

3. Netscape versions 2 and later allow you to specify the subject of the message in the `mailto` tag. This information will appear in the Subject: line of the mail message when the mail window appears. To include this, enter a question mark (`?`) after the e-mail address, then the word `subject`, an equal sign, and the desired subject line for the message. For example, to include a subject line called "My Comments" in the example, we would enter

```
Send me <A HREF="mailto:nobody@stateu.edu?subject=My Comments">e-mail</A> with
your comments about my page.
```

How It Works

When a `mailto` link is selected, the browser starts up its electronic mail program (as defined by the browser), setting the To: line in the message to the address given in the URL.

Comments

The `mailto` URL works successfully only if the browser has access to an electronic mail program. The program used can usually be set by the user. Using forms (see Chapter 11, HTML Interactive Forms) is often a better way to get feedback on a page because it doesn't require the use of an external program. The subject line addition to the `mailto` URL that works in Netscape will not work in most other browsers, and it may even make the link useless for the user. Take care when using it in an open environment.

COMPLEXITY
BEGINNING

8.15 How do I...
Create links to pages in other users' home directories?

COMPATIBILITY: HTML 2+

Problem

I'd like to access some pages located in another user's directory. However, I would like to be able to shorten the length of the URL and not type the full path to the page. Is there a way I can easily create links to pages in other users' home directories?

Technique

On UNIX file systems, it is possible to abbreviate the path to a user's home directory by using the username preceded by the tilde (˜) symbol. This can be used on local and remote systems to shorten the length of the URL of a page.

Steps

Open the document and find the words or phrases you want to use as links.

1. Specify the anchored text in your document. Place the **<A>** tag at the beginning of the anchor and **</A>** at the end of the anchor.

```
There's more information on the topic on <A>John's page</A>.
```

2. If the page is located in another user's directory on the same computer as your page, you can reach that user's home directory by using the username preceded by a tilde. For example, to access a page in user John's home directory, enter

```
There's more information on the topic on <A HREF="˜john/info.html>John's
page</A>.
```

You can also access another user's subdirectories by including them in the URL. For example, if the page listed here was located in the subdirectory **pub**, you would enter

```
There's more information on the topic on <A HREF="˜john/pub/info.html>John's
page</A>.
```

3. This technique also works for pages in users' directories on other computers. If John's page was located on the computer `www.stateu.edu` in his home directory, you could create the following link to it.

```
There's more information on the topic on <A
HREF="http://www.stateu.edu/~john/info.html>John's page</A>.
```

If the page was located in a subdirectory, it could be accessed by including the directory path in the URL.

```
There's more information on the topic on <A
HREF="http://www.stateu.edu/~john/pub/info.html>John's page</A>.
```

How It Works

The ˜ symbol in the URL tells the browser to go to the home directory or to the listed subdirectory of the specified user and retrieve the document.

Comments

The ˜ notation only works for those computer systems that support multiple users and use UNIX or a variation of UNIX. Also, for a document to be retrievable in this way, its author must have given permission by making the contents of the directory readable by all users.

COMPLEXITY
BEGINNING

8.16 How do I...
Add links to lists and tables?

COMPATIBILITY: HTML 2+ (LISTS), HTML 3 (TABLES)

Problem

I would like to create a menu for the reader by organizing a set of links to different pages. It seems that the best way to do this is with a list or a table. How can I add links to lists and tables in HTML?

Technique

You can add links to lists and tables just as you would to ordinary text on a page. Each list item or table entry can serve as a link to a different page, FTP site, and so on.

Steps

Open the document and decide what information you would like to display in lists or tables, and what resources you would like to link to a different page, FTP site, and the like.

1. First, create the list or table, including all the list items and table entries, just as you would with an ordinary list or table. For example, a list might look like this:

```
<UL>
    <LI>Boston Red Sox
    <LI>New York Yankees
    <LI>Toronto Blue Jays
</UL>
```

A similar table might be formatted as follows:

```
<TABLE BORDER>
    <CAPTION>Three American League Teams</CAPTION>
    <TR><TH>Team<TH>Wins<TH>Losses
    <TR><TD>Boston Red Sox<TD>90<TD>72
    <TR><TD>New York Yankees<TD>88<TD>74
    <TR><TD>Toronto Blue Jays<TD>77<TD>85
</TABLE>
```

2. Now add the links where appropriate in the list or table, just as you would in the text of a document.

```
<UL>
    <LI><A HREF="redsox.html">Boston Red Sox</A>
    <LI><A HREF="yankees.html">New York Yankees</A>
    <LI><A HREF="bluejays.html">Toronto Blue Jays</A>
</UL>

<TABLE BORDER>
    <CAPTION>Three American League Teams</CAPTION>
    <TR><TH>Team<TH>Wins<TH>Losses
    <TR><TD><A HREF="redsox.html">Boston Red Sox</A><TD>90<TD>72
    <TR><TD><A HREF="yankees.html">New York Yankees</A><TD>88<TD>74
    <TR><TD><A HREF="bluejays.html">Toronto Blue Jays</A><TD>77<TD>85
</TABLE>
```

Figure 8-4 shows the output of this list and table. The code is also available on the CD as file 8-4.HTML.

How It Works

Links in lists and tables are treated the same as links elsewhere in a document. You can add links of all types that function exactly the same as links in other parts of a document.

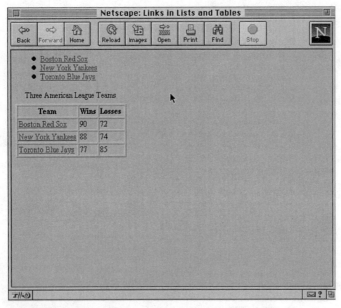

Figure 8-4 Examples of lists and tables with links

Comments

A good way to use links in lists and tables is to create a table of contents or a menu of choices for the reader. This works best if each link is given one line of the list or one entry in the table. Links can extend over multiple list or table entries, but they become less useful that way.

COMPLEXITY
INTERMEDIATE

8.17 How do I...
Add links to my home page?

COMPATIBILITY: HTML 2, HTML 3

Problem

I now know all about creating links in a page. However, I'm not sure how to put them into my document—that is, where they should go, how they should relate to the text of my document, and so on. How can I effectively add links to my home page?

Technique

There are many ways links can be used in a page. Consequently, there are many ways links can be misused as well. Some common problems with the use of links are described next, along with solutions to those problems.

Steps

These steps assume you know the basics of constructing links. These tips will help you use that knowledge to create effective ones.

1. First and foremost, a link must have some text or graphics (see How-To 9.12) that a reader can select. The following link might be to the best resource on the World Wide Web

```
<A HREF="http://www.stateu.edu/cool.html"></A>
```

but it will be useless for the reader of the document because, with no text between the anchor elements, there is no way to select the link. Always make sure there is some relevant text between the anchor elements to permit readers to select the link.

An exception to this is when the **NAME** attribute is used in the anchor. Since the **NAME** attribute only identifies a specific location in a document and is not itself a link to another resource, the following usage is valid.

```
<A NAME="section1"></A>
```

In fact, this is often the best way to identify sections of a page without including additional text.

2. One of the most common problems with links, and one of the most annoying, is what is often called the "click here" syndrome. An example of code with this problem might look like this:

```
<A HREF="coolpic.gif">Click here</A> for a cool picture I took!
```

There are several problems with this statement. First, it disrupts the flow of a document. To understand this better, look at the following example:

```
The St. Louis Browns were one of baseball's most infamous teams. <A
HREF="badteams.html">Click here</A> for information on other bad teams in
baseball history. They appeared in only one World Series, in 1944, when most
of baseball's stars were in the armed forces during World War II. For more
information on the World Series, click <A HREF="series.html">here</A>. Their
Series opponents were their hometown rivals, the St. Louis Cardinals. All the
games in that series were played in one stadium, Sportsman's Park, the home
stadium for both teams. <A HREF="sportsman.gif">Click here</A> for a picture
of Sportsman's Park.
```

(This paragraph is shown in Figure 8-5. The code is available on the CD as file 8-5.HTML.)

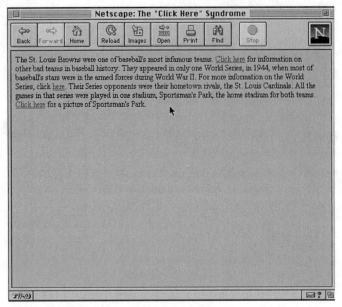

Figure 8-5 The "click here" syndrome

Imagine reading this without being able to access the links. All the `click here` statements disrupt the flow of the paragraph. While it's thoughtful of the writer to explain what all the links are, the extra sentences make it harder to understand the main points of the paragraph. A solution to this problem is to use relevant words and phrases in the paragraph as anchors for the links. This will be discussed in more detail shortly.

Another problem with the `click here` statement is that it assumes that all readers of the page are using a graphical Web browser. Many people access the Web using a text-based browser such as Lynx. For these users, links are usually selected by a number, not by using a mouse, so the "`click here`" terminology is not useful for them, and it could even be confusing.

3. Another problem with links, at an extreme from the "`click here`" problem, are poorly labeled links. Ideally, the anchor phrase and the context of that phrase within the document should indicate where, in general, the link will lead. However, it's not uncommon for links to refer to resources that don't clearly follow from the anchor text. For example:

```
The St. Louis Browns were one of baseball's most infamous <A
HREF="badteams.html">teams</A>. They <A HREF="series.html">appeared</A> in
only one World Series, in 1944, when most of baseball's stars were in the⇐
armed forces during World War II. Their Series opponents were their⇐
hometown rivals, the St. Louis Cardinals. All the games in that series were⇐
played in one <A HREF="sportsman.gif">stadium</A>, Sportsman's Park, the⇐
home stadium for both teams.
```

(This paragraph is shown in Figure 8-6. The code is available on the CD as file 8-6.HTML.)

The problem here is not a profusion of `click here` statements but of vague links. If a user reads this and sees the word `teams` in the top line linked, he or she may not know where that link leads: a list of bad teams, a list of all the teams in baseball, or general information about teams.

There is a middle ground between these two problems, a way to smoothly incorporate links into a document and still make it clear from the context of the document what the function of each link is. The sample paragraph, reworked, illustrates the solution.

```
The St. Louis Browns were one of baseball's most <A
HREF="badteams.html">infamous teams</A>. They appeared in only one <A
HREF="series.html">World Series</A>, in 1944, when most of baseball's stars
were in the armed forces during World War II. Their Series opponents were⇐
their hometown rivals, the St. Louis Cardinals. All the games in that⇐
series were played in one stadium, <A HREF="sportsman.gif">Sportsman's⇐
Park</A>, the home stadium for both teams.
```

(This paragraph is shown in Figure 8-7. The code is available on the CD as file 8-7.HTML.)

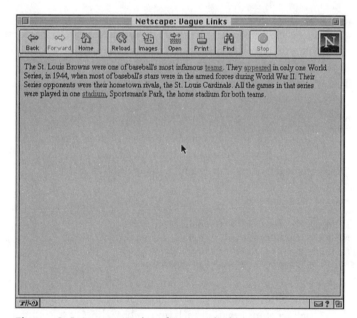

Figure 8-6 An example of vague links

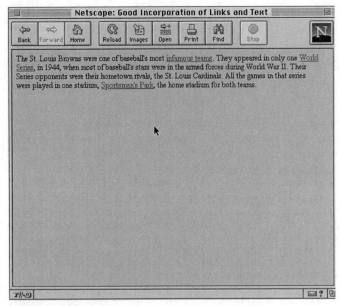

Figure 8-7 Good incorporation of links in text

The `click here` statements have been eliminated and the function of the links is clearer. Seeing `infamous teams` linked, for example, suggests to the reader that the link probably leads to some specific information on bad teams. In some cases you may need to rewrite the text slightly to use this technique, but it is best if links can derive their meaning from the context of the document.

4. Similarly, it is often useful to add explanatory information when using links in lists. Using short link names in a list of links may make it easy to create the list, but it may make it harder for a reader to decipher what each option specifically offers. For example, consider this list of links:

```
<H3>Menu of Options</H3>
<UL>
<LI><A HREF="intro.html">Introduction</A>
<LI><A HREF="techdata.html">Technical Data</A>
<LI><A HREF="prices.html">Price List</A>
<LI><A HREF="comments.html">Comments</A>
</UL>
```

Reading this, you can get some idea of what each link leads to, but it's hard to tell what information each option has, short of selecting it. Adding a bit of description can help a user better understand the contents of each list option. A good way to do this is with a glossary list (see Chapter 6, Lists). Applying a glossary list to this example would create the following:

```
<H3>Menu of Options</H3>
<DL>
<DT><A HREF="intro.html">Introduction</A>
<DD>A welcome message from the President and some background material about⇐
widgets.
<DT><A HREF="techdata.html">Technical Data</A>
<DD>Technical specifications for all 13 types of widgets we sell
<DT><A HREF="prices.html">Price List</A>
<DD>A complete list of prices for all widgets and information on special⇐
sales
<DT><A HREF="comments.html">Comments</A>
<DD>How to send us your comments and suggestions
</DL>
```

This list gives the reader a much clearer idea of the functionality of each link. These two lists are shown in Figure 8-8. This code is available on the CD as file 8-8.HTML.

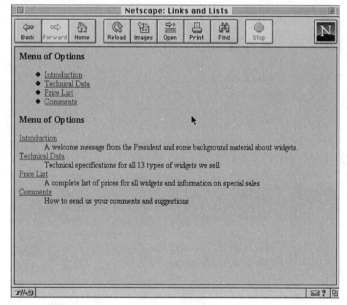

Figure 8-8 Bad and good ways of including links in lists

How It Works

The key to using links is to incorporate them into the text of your document as smoothly as possible, but also without obscuring their meaning. The examples given show that, with some practice, this can be done.

Comments

Links make the World Wide Web just that: a web of information spanning the globe. By incorporating links to other documents in your pages (and, invariably, having your pages included as links in other people's documents), you can spin your own little section of the World Wide Web.

CHAPTER 9

USING IMAGES IN YOUR DOCUMENTS

9

USING IMAGES IN YOUR DOCUMENTS

How do I...

9.15 Use a small or low-resolution image while a larger one loads?

9.16 Speed image transmission?

9.17 Create an animated GIF?

One of the key features that distinguishes the World Wide Web from other parts of the Internet is images. Images, when used correctly, can liven up a Web page. This chapter shows numerous ways in which you can add images to make your HTML documents more interesting to read and to look at.

9.1 Build an Icon to Use in an HTML Document

Icons liven up an HTML document and help make a page more concise and compact by replacing a lot of words with one picture. This How-To shows how you can create icons for your documents.

9.2 Add an Inline Image

Now that you know how to create an icon, you need to include it in your HTML documents. This How-To shows how easy it is to add images to your documents.

9.3 Align Images and Text Using the Advanced Tags

This How-To shows you a number of options you may use when aligning text and images in your documents.

9.4 Use the <ALT> Tag for Nongraphical Browsers

Sometimes a reader looking at your document is either using a browser that can't view images or that has image loading turned off. This How-To shows how to use the <ALT> tag to put up a text description in place of an image.

9.5 Include an Image with a Transparent Background

Standard inline images display on a browser with white space around the edges. While this is sometimes acceptable, it can at times look unprofessional. This How-To shows how to make an image's background transparent so it will blend in with the document.

9.6 Create an Interlaced Inline Image on My Page

Standard GIF images load from top to bottom. This is fine, but somewhat bland. Interlacing allows an entire image to load in a complete, but low-resolution form, then build up to higher and higher resolution. This How-To shows how to make GIF images into interlaced images and suggests strategies for using them.

9.7 Create a Thumbnail Version of an Image

Thumbnail versions of images are not as large and as time-consuming to load as full-fledged versions of images. Therefore, there are times when it is beneficial to display a thumbnail copy of an image on a page. This How-To shows a number of ways to create thumbnail images.

9.8　Use an Image as a Link

It can be a nice touch to either replace or augment a text link with an image that links to another document. This How-To shows how to use images as links.

9.9　Create a Background Pattern for My Page

HTML 3 on up has added the feature of being able to change your background color. This How-To demonstrates how to change the background on your pages to be virtually anything you find pleasing.

9.10　Create a Server-Side Clickable Imagemap

Clickable images or imagemaps are often used in place of text menus or as interactive maps. They are images that link a user to certain spots, depending on where the user clicks on that image. They add a nice graphical touch to your user interface. This How-To shows how to add imagemaps to documents.

9.11　Include Client-Side Imagemaps

Client-side clickable images are alternatives to server-side clickable images. They function the same way as server-side imagemaps, only they have the advantage of not needing a CGI script to execute them as the browser handles the processing. This How-To shows how to add these types of imagemaps to documents.

9.12　Color Reduce an Image

Lots of times you will find that an image has more colors (or has allocated space for more colors) than needed. This makes your image larger than it has to be and slows down the transmission of your pages. This How-To explores ways of reducing the number of colors in images.

9.13　Use `WIDTH` and `HEIGHT` Attributes with an Image

By using `WIDTH` and `HEIGHT` attributes with an image, you can speed up the image's transmission to a browser. This will make your pages load faster. This simple How-To shows how to use these attributes.

9.14　Scale an Image on My Page

By changing the original `WIDTH` and `HEIGHT` attributes with an image you can effectively scale the image. This simple How-To shows how to use these attributes.

9.15　Use a Small or Low-Resolution Image While a Larger One Loads

Often it is nice to have a smaller image load before a larger image loads. This not only gives readers something to look at while the larger image loads, but it allows your page to load any text that may be around the image, thus allowing readers a nice look at your page while they wait for the larger image to load. This simple How-To shows how to use this technique.

9.16   Speed Image Transmission

For the most part, the faster a Web page loads the better. This How-To will explore techniques you can use to speed transmission of your Web pages.

9.17   Create an Animated GIF

Animated GIFs bring life to a Web page without using any CGI scripting or Java. This How-To shows how to create and use animated GIFs in Web pages.

COMPLEXITY
BEGINNING

9.1   How do I...
Build an icon to use in an HTML document?

COMPATIBILITY: HTML

Problem

My documents work fine, but I would like to make them look snappier by adding icons. How can I create one or more icons that I can use later in my documents?

Technique

Icons are small graphical images saved in GIF format. Icons are usually small—either 64 by 64 or 32 by 32 pixels—but there is no set rule on this. They are created much as you would any other image for your computer, using a graphics program. You create and save the image in GIF format, or you create the image in another format and then convert it to GIF format. Finally, you transfer the GIF image to your server.

Steps

The following procedure shows you how to create icons. The actual process will vary depending on the software you use and the machine you are on, but the concepts remain the same.

1. Lay out your image on paper. Decide what you want to show and how you want it to look. Unless you are a talented artist, it is best to start simply. Something like the little balloon (a circle with a line) shown in Figure 9-1 is good for learning purposes.

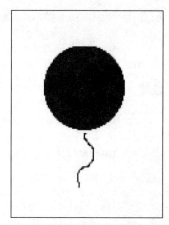

Figure 9-1 A simple
image to use for an icon

2. Decide which graphics program you would like to use. Practically any graphics package available can be made to work. There are also a number of programs whose sole purpose is to facilitate the creation of images on the Web. The decision of which to use is usually a matter of availability and personal preference. There are a number of features, though, that do come in handy when creating images for the Web: being able to easily control the pixel size of an image or the number of colors the image may have, for example, and the ability to save in GIF format. You may want to take these factors into account before choosing your program. One popular program available for the Macintosh that meets all these standards is GraphicConverter. One popular program for the UNIX and PC worlds is GIFTOOL.

3. Open a new image. It is best to set the pixel size and the number of colors at the beginning. Pixel size is the number of horizontal and vertical squares that you use to create the image. The unwritten standard seems to be either 64 by 64 or 32 by 32, but like most other things on the Web, there are no set rules, only conventions or suggestions. If your image fits in a 1 inch by 1 inch square, you should be in pretty good shape. When choosing colors, keep the number as low as possible because the more colors you use, the bigger the image will be and the longer it will take to load. Use four or five colors to create an image that looks nice and is fairly colorful, but is not very large.

4. Use whatever tools your application offers to draw your image. This is where no book in the world can help you. If you have artistic ability, go crazy! Still, even if you have no artistic ability, creating something like the balloon used in this example should be fairly simple.

5. Once you are satisfied with your icon, save the image. If your program allows you to pick the format to save in, choose GIF. If GIF is not available, then TIFF and PICT make good alternatives as they are easy to convert to GIF. It is best to save the image with a short, descriptive name. For our example, something like `balloon.GIF` works well.

6. If your graphics program does not have a GIF option to save in, find one of the many available GIF converter programs and convert the image to GIF. Some possible choices for converting images to GIF are GIFConverter for the Macintosh, GIFTOOL for UNIX and PC machines, or the PBMPLUS library available for a number of UNIX environments. All these programs work in the same way: You open up `balloon.tiff` (for example), then save it in GIF format as `balloon.GIF`.

7. If your finished GIF icon is on a different machine than your server, transfer the icon to the appropriate machine. You will then be ready to go.

How It Works

There is no trick at all to this. Icons are just like any other graphic you create with your computer. The only difference between an icon you create for your Web pages and an icon you see on your computer's windows is that your icon is saved in GIF format.

Comments

Even if you have absolutely no artistic ability at all, you can still create nice-looking images for icons by using graphical text. Figure 9-2 shows an example of using graphical text as an icon.

GIF stands for Graphic Interchange Format, which loosely translates to: This format is readable by a wide number of different machines. That is what makes GIF so convenient to use on the Web. Currently, GIF is the only graphical format that most browsers can show without the aid of a helper application, but it should be noted that JPEG format is also easily displayed by a wide number of browsers.

It should also be pointed out that there is no one right way to convert an image to GIF format. While all the tools mentioned in steps 2 and 6 may work a little differently, they all do work. The **PBMPLUS** library may not be as easy to use as the other choices, but it offers greater control and a larger number of options. The downside to the **PBMPLUS** library is that you must write scripts in order to perform conversions. The following Perl script is included as an example of how the **PBMPLUS** library is used. This program not only converts a TIFF image to GIF, but it also rotates the GIF 90 degrees. This example illustrates both the power and complexity of the library.

Figure 9-2 Graphical text icon

```perl
#!/usr/bin/perl

$netpbm = '/home/netpbm.bin';

# Get a list of all .tif files in the current directory.

opendir(DIR, ".");
@TIFFS = grep(/\.TIF$/, readdir(DIR));
closedir(DIR);

# Add the NetPBM tool directory to our path.

$ENV{'PATH'} = "$netpbm:$ENV{'PATH'}";

# Convert all the files

foreach $TIFF (@TIFFS) {
  $GIF = $TIFF; $GIF =~ s/\.TIF$/\.GIF/;
  print "Translating $TIFF to $GIF\n";
#   system("tifftopnm $TIFF | pnmflip -rotate90 | ppmtoGIF >$GIF");
  system("tifftopnm $TIFF | ppmtoGIF >$GIF");
  unlink $TIFF || print "Couldn't delete $TIFF: $!\n";
  print "\n";
}

exit 0;
```

COMPLEXITY
BEGINNING

9.2 How do I...
Add an inline image?

COMPATIBILITY: HTML

Problem

I have an HTML document and I have an image that's saved as a GIF. Now, how do I include this image in my document?

Technique

Adding an image to an HTML document is surprisingly easy. You must either create the image with a graphics program or by scanning an existing image. Once you have the image, save it in GIF format. Then use the `<IMG SRC>` tag to include the image in your document.

Steps

The following procedure shows you how to add images to your documents.

1. Create the GIF image you wish to include in your document. For learning purposes, it is best to keep the image simple, such as the `balloon.GIF` used in the previous How-To. If you are unsure how to create this image, refer to How-To 8.1.

2. Create the HTML document that will eventually hold the image. Again, for learning purposes, it is best to keep this document simple. For instance:

```
<HTML>
<HEAD><TITLE>My First Image</TITLE></HEAD>
<BODY>
<H1>My First Image</H1>
This is a picture of a balloon:
</BODY>
</HTML>
```

3. Add the image to your document with the `<IMG SRC>` tag. This tag is an empty tag with the basic format:

```
<IMG SRC="URL">
```

Other optional attributes that can be added to this tag will be discussed later in this chapter.

After adding the tag, the document will resemble the following:

```
<HTML>
<HEAD><TITLE>My First Image</TITLE></HEAD>
<BODY>
<H1>My First Image</H1>
This is a picture of a balloon:
<IMG SRC ="BALLOON.GIF">
</BODY>
</HTML>
```

4. Save your HTML document as a text document, giving it a meaningful name such as `balloon.html`.

5. Make sure everything looks the way you think it should by viewing the document with either the `Open Local` or `Open File` command in your browser. If all went well, your document should resemble Figure 9-3.

Figure 9-3 The balloon, now in a document

6. Transfer the completed HTML document and the GIF file to the server where they will reside, and inform your system administrator about the presence of the new document.

How It Works

Whenever a browser encounters the `<IMG SRC ="URL">` tag, it attempts to display the image addressed by the URL. If the image is in GIF format, the browser displays it on the screen without using a helper application. This creates the effect of the image being "inline" in your document.

Comments

For this example, the URL of the image was a very simple relative address since the image resides in the same directory as the document. This is not always the case. You may use any image at any URL, even if it doesn't reside on your server.

The image tag has grown and expanded more than probably any other tag in HTML. The following list shows other attributes and options you may include inside the tag. The less obvious of these will be dealt with in greater detail in later sections.

▨ **alt** Alternative text to display for nongraphic browsers

▨ **align** Aligns graphic with the surrounding text, where values include left, right, and center

▨ **vwidth** The amount of spacing above and below an image and surrounding text

▨ **hwidth** The amount of spacing between an image and surrounding text

- ▩ `border` Sets a border around a graphic, where the greater the number, the thicker the border

- ▩ `width` Sets the width of the image

- ▩ `height` Sets the height of the image

- ▩ `lowsrc` Specifies a low-resolution version of the image to load first

COMPLEXITY
BEGINNING

9.3   How do I...
Align images and text using the advanced tags?

COMPATIBILITY: HTML 3.2

Problem

I have an HTML document with an inline image. I would like to wrap some text to the left of one image and to the right of another. How do I accomplish this?

Technique

HTML 2 allows for simple aligning of text and images by adding the **ALIGN** attribute to the **<IMG SRC>** tag. HTML 3 expanded this attribute by adding **left** and **right** options. When you use these options, text flows down the right or left side of an image aligned to them. The text flow continues until either the text passes the image, the text ends, or the browser encounters a **<BR CLEAR="left|right|all">** tag.

Steps

The following steps show you how to use the advanced text and picture alignment capabilities in your documents and what effect each of these alignment options has on images and text.

1. Create a GIF image you wish to include in your document. The `balloon.GIF` image used earlier in this chapter can serve as an example.

2. Create the HTML document that will eventually hold the image. To help illustrate the point, this example contains two versions of the image:

```
<HTML>
<HEAD><TITLE>Practicing with Align</TITLE>
<BODY>
<H1>My First Image</H1>
```

```
Here is a picture:
<! picture goes here ->
Here is another picture:
<! another goes here ->
</BODY>
</HTML>
```

3. Replace the comments with `<IMG SRC>` tags.

```
<IMG SRC ="BALLOON.GIF">
```

4. Add the `ALIGN` option to the `<IMG SRC>` tag. The basic format of this tag with the `ALIGN` option is

```
<IMG ALIGN=TOP|MIDDLE|BOTTOM SRC"URL">
```

Netscape and HTML 3 add `left` and `right` to these. The `left` option puts the image on the left side of the browser and then aligns any adjacent text to this image. The `right` option does the opposite. The two image tags look like this:

```
<IMG ALIGN=LEFT   SRC="BALLOON.GIF">
<IMG ALIGN=RIGHT  SRC="BALLOON.GIF">
```

5. Place any descriptive text around the first image.

6. Insert the `<BR CLEAR="left">` command at the spot in the descriptive text where you want the text to stop flowing around the image.

7. Place any descriptive text around the second image.

8. Insert the `<BR CLEAR="right">` command at the spot in the text where you wish the text to stop flowing around the second image. When you are done, the document should resemble the following:

```
<HTML>
<HEAD><TITLE>Practicing with Align</TITLE>
<BODY>
<H1>Netscape align</H1>
Here is a picture aligned left:<P>
<IMG ALIGN=LEFT SRC="BALLOON.GIF">
This is a balloon. Balloons float in the air. Balloons come in many colors
and sizes. Balloons can now even be given as GIFts for birthdays and such.
Balloons are
cool.
<P>
Just put in a new paragraph so you could see the results.
<BR CLEAR=LEFT>
Here is the same picture aligned right:
<!-- No new paragraph marker so you can see the difference -- if any -->
<IMG ALIGN=RIGHT SRC="BALLOON.GIF">
This is a second balloon. It is identical to the first except for its posi-
tion on the screen. Text flow can look very good, especially when using
better images than smiley faces.
<BR CLEAR=RIGHT>
```

continued on next page

continued from previous page

```
This text should no longer flow around the image.
</BODY>
</HTML>
```

9. Make sure everything looks the way you think it should by viewing the document locally with your browser. If all went well, your document should resemble Figure 9-4.

10. After you decide which ALIGN option you prefer, save your HTML document as a text document.

11. If necessary, transfer the completed HTML document and the GIF file to the server where they will reside and inform your system administrator or Webmaster about the presence of the new document and file.

How It Works

Wherever a browser comes across an <IMG SRC> tag, the browser displays that image on the screen without a helper application if the image is in GIF format. If there is no ALIGN option included in the tag, the image is not associated with any text. If there is an ALIGN left or right option, any text in the same paragraph as the <IMG SRC> tag will flow into that image until either the text surpasses the image, the text runs out, or the browser encounters a corresponding <BR CLEAR = "left|right|all"> tag.

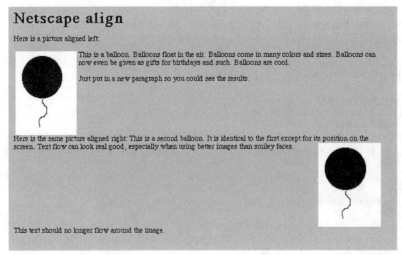

Figure 9-4 The aligned document

Comments

These extensions to this attribute add a great deal of power to the **<IMG SRC>** tag. When combined with the new **<TABLE>** tags, these expressions can even make an HTML 3 document appear much like a multiple column document such as you might create with a desktop publishing package.

It is also possible to get the same effects as these extensions provide by adding the **ALIGN** attribute to the **<P>** tag in HTML 3. See Chapter 4, Adding HTML Logical Character Effects, for more information on this.

COMPLEXITY
BEGINNING

9.4 How do I...
Use the <ALT> tag for nongraphical browsers?

COMPATIBILITY: HTML

Problem

I have an HTML document with an image in it. How can I show people with non-graphical browsers that there is an image in my document?

Technique

Images are added to documents with the **<IMG SRC>** tag. To inform nongraphical browsers (or a browser with image loading turned off) that there is an image in your document, include the **ALT** option in the tag, setting the **ALT** attribute to a text message that tells users what they are missing.

Steps

The following procedure shows you how to use the **ALT** attribute in your documents.

1. Create a GIF image you wish to include in your document. For now, let's stick with the balloon, **balloon.GIF**.

2. Create the HTML document that will eventually hold the image. At first, keep this document simple, like the document used in the previous section.

3. Add the image to your document with the **<IMG SRC>** tag. The document should resemble the following:

```
<HTML>
<HEAD><TITLE>An Alt Example</TITLE></HEAD>
<BODY>
<H1>An Alt Example</H1>
```

continued on next page

continued from previous page
```
This is a picture of a balloon:
<IMG SRC ="BALLOON.GIF">
</BODY>
</HTML>
```

4. Add the `ALT` option to the `<IMG SRC>` tag. The format of the `<IMG>` tag with the `ALT` option is

```
<IMG ALT="some text" SRC = "URL">
```

which in the sample document becomes

```
<IMG ALT="a picture of a balloon goes here" SRC ="BALLOON.GIF">
```

The result is something like Figure 9-5 when viewed through a nongraphical browser.

5. Save your HTML document as a text document.

6. Make sure everything looks the way you think it should by viewing the document with either the `Open Local` or `Open File` command in your browser.

7. If necessary, transfer the completed HTML document and the GIF file to the server where they will reside, and inform your system administrator about the presence of the new document.

How It Works

Whenever a browser comes across an `<IMG SRC>` tag, the browser attempts to display the image if it is in GIF format. If the browser is unable to display the image, it replaces it with any text found in the `ALT="text"` attribute.

Comments

It is considered good net manners to use the `ALT` attribute whenever possible. This way, people using nongraphical browsers, such as Lynx, will still get the general idea of how a page is meant to be laid out. It is also a good idea to test how your `<IMG ALT SRC>` tags work by turning off automatic image loading in your browser, then checking out your documents.

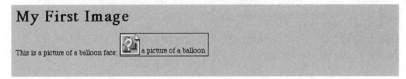

Figure 9-5 Use of the `ALT` attribute

COMPLEXITY
BEGINNING

9.5   How do I...
Include an image with a transparent background?

COMPATIBILITY: HTML

Problem

Now I have an inline image in my HTML document, but there is a lot of white space around it. How do I remove this white space so my image will have a transparent background that blends in better with my page?

Technique

With the right tools, creating an image with a transparent background is only slightly more complicated than creating an image without one. You still follow the same process to create the image, but you need to add an extra step or two. Once you create the image, you must fill in the areas that you want to be transparent with a color that is not used anywhere else in the image. Then set that fill color to be the transparent GIF color and save the image in GIF89a format.

Steps

The following procedure gives you a general overview of what you must do to create a transparent image. How you create the image depends on the machine you are working on and the tools you are using, but the basic procedure remains the same.

1. Lay out your image on paper. Decide what you want to show and how you want it to look. For learning purposes, it is best to start with something simple like the balloon (`balloon.GIF`) used throughout this chapter.

2. Decide which graphics program to use. Your choices are almost endless because almost any available graphics program will work. There are also a number of utility programs around whose sole purpose is the creation of transparent images on the Web. The decision of which to use is usually a matter of availability and personal preference. There are a number of features that come in handy when creating images for the Web. Some of these are listed below:

■ The ability to easily control the pixel size of an image

■ The number of colors the image may have

■ The ability to select a transparent color

■ The ability to save in GIF89a format

You may want to take these into account before deciding on the package you want to use. Programs such as GraphicConverter for the Macintosh and GIFTOOL for UNIX and PCs are good choices.

3. Open up a new image. It is best to set the pixel size and the number of colors at the outset. Pixel size is the number of horizontal and vertical squares that you use to create the image. When choosing colors, keep the number as low as possible. The more colors you use, the bigger the image will be and the longer it will take to load. Use four or five colors to create an image that looks nice and is fairly colorful, but is not very large.

4. Draw your image. The file `balloon.GIF` should be very simple to create. It is simply a circle with a line attached.

5. Fill in the area you wish to make transparent with a color not used in the image. It does not matter what the color is as long as it is not used elsewhere in the image.

6. Set the transparent GIF color to the color you filled with. This is done slightly differently depending on the application you are using. For example, with GraphicConverter for the Macintosh, this setting can be found at the bottom of the Colors item found in the Picture menu.

7. Save your image in the GIF89a format. For this example, the new image is named `balloont.GIF`. In practice you do not need to use an altered name to differentiate between transparent and nontransparent images.

8. If your finished image is on a different machine than your server, transfer the icon to the appropriate machine.

How It Works

The color you use as the transparent color is automatically set to whatever a browser looking at that image happens to have as its background, the effect being that your image blends in perfectly with the background.

Comments

The only difference between a transparent GIF and a nontransparent GIF is the format the two are saved in. The HTML tags are identical. For example:

```
<HTML>
<HEAD><TITLE>Transparent Demo</TITLE>
<BODY>
```

```
<H1>Transparent Demo</H1>
This is a balloon:
<IMG SRC="BALLOON.GIF">
This is a transparent balloon:
<IMG SRC="BALLOONT.GIF">
</BODY>
</HTML>
```

The tags are identical except for the URL, but the results are quite different, as shown by Figure 9-6.

It is easy to turn an existing image into a transparent GIF. Open the image and then perform steps 5 and 6.

People often use transparent GIFs to add unique horizontal rules in a document. For example, if you wish to have a red, white, and blue horizontal rule in one of your pages instead of using the `<HR>` command (which doesn't allow for color), you can use the following procedure:

1. Use a graphics program to create a red, white, and blue line.

2. Save the line as a transparent GIF, naming it something like `cline.GIF`.

3. Insert the following `<IMG SRC>` tag into the document where you want to place the line:

```
<IMG SRC="CLINE.GIF">
```

This causes the browser to insert the red, white, and blue line wherever it finds this tag. It should be noted, though, that some people consider using images for horizontal lines to be a waste of server time since it takes longer to load a graphical image than a line drawn with the horizontal rule tag `<HR>`. Still, this is a personal call. If you want a colorful line on your page, go ahead and make one. It is, after all, your page.

Finally note that, due to the number of choices you have when converting an image to a transparent GIF, this chapter has only touched the surface. The following are other options you might want to consider.

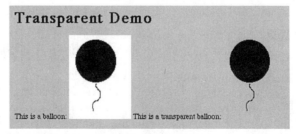

Figure 9-6 A comparison between a transparent GIF and a nontransparent GIF

■ GIFTOOL Available for UNIX and DOS machines

■ The PBMPLUS library Available for UNIX machines

■ GraphicConverter or Transparency Available for the Macintosh

COMPLEXITY
BEGINNING

9.6 How do I...
Create an interlaced inline image on my page?

COMPATIBILITY: NETSCAPE, INTERNET EXPLORER

Problem

I have a document with an inline image that works fine, but my image loads from top to bottom. I occasionally see other people's images loading progressively: First a complete rough image appears, and then this image becomes finer and finer. How can I get my images to appear like this?

Technique

The technique used to cause an image to appear gradually is called *interlacing*. With the right tools, it is a simple step to convert a normal image to an interlaced GIF image. GIFConverter on the Macintosh and GIFTOOL for UNIX and PC machines can convert a graphic from any number of formats to an interlaced GIF.

Steps

The following procedure gives you a general overview of what you must do to create an interlaced image. Some of the details for doing this depend on the machine and the tools you are using. Still, the basic procedure remains the same.

1. Find or create an image you wish to turn into an interlaced GIF. The `bal-loon.GIF` file from the previous section would work well as an example.

2. Decide which program you would like to use to convert the image to an interlaced GIF. There are many available options across the three major platforms. Some of the major choices are GIFConverter for the Macintosh, GIFTOOL for UNIX machines and PCs, and the PBMPLUS tools for UNIX machines.

3. Open the image.

4. Save the image as an interlaced GIF. This procedure differs depending on the application you are using, but it is usually very easy to figure out. In GIFConverter, for example, you click the interlaced box that appears in the Save As dialog box.

5. View the image locally with your browser to make sure it looks the way you think it should.

6. If necessary, transport the image to your server.

How It Works

There really isn't much work for you to do here. The tool performs the conversion. Now when a browser loads the new interlaced image, the entire image appears gradually, going from a low resolution outline to the finished image. You really don't need to know more than that.

Comments

The steps shown in this How-To vary depending on what graphics program you use and what system you are on; still, the technique is the same. Interlacing is so easy to accomplish that it is possible to get carried away and have too many interlaced images on a page. The main advantage to interlacing comes when displaying larger images on the screen. An interlaced image will display a low resolution "preview" of the image while the larger image loads. This allows a reader to view the rest of the page as the image finishes loading. Smaller images should probably not be interlaced, as they load pretty quickly. You should never interlace a background image as nobody wants to see your background load four times. So feel free to experiment, but just try not to go overboard.

COMPLEXITY

BEGINNING

9.7 How do I...
Create a thumbnail version of an image?

COMPATIBILITY: HTML

Problem

I have a large image that some people may be interested in seeing, while others may not. How can I make a thumbnail version of this image?

Technique

Thumbnail images are no different from any other images you see on the Web. They just happen to be smaller. You can make one by using any graphics program that has scaling ability to shrink the image to thumbnail size. You can then make the thumbnail image work like a button your viewer clicks on to load the original image. This technique is shown in How-To 9.9.

Steps

The following procedure gives you a general overview of what you must do to create a thumbnail image. How you create the image depends on the machine and the tools you are using. Still, the basic procedure remains the same.

1. Find or create an image you wish to turn into a thumbnail. For this example, use `balloon.GIF` from the previous section.

2. Decide which program you would like to use to scale (or resize) the image to thumbnail size. Almost any graphics program has the ability to scale images. Choose a graphics program that both scales images and saves them in GIF format.

3. Open the image with the graphics program of your choice.

4. Find and select the scale option.

5. Set the new, smaller size of your image. How this works may differ slightly from application to application, but it always involves changing the percentage of the object's size. In this case the object is being shrunk to 30 percent of its original size.

6. Save the smaller image as a GIF, or in some format that you can easily translate to GIF. Make sure you give the new image a distinct but related name such as `ballon_s.GIF`. The name `ballon_s.GIF` is less likely to be confused with the original than `balloons.GIF`, but readers using Macintoshes, Windows 95, or UNIX should feel free to use a longer, more distinctive name.

The following document will resemble Figure 9-7 when viewed through a browser:

```
<HTML>
<HEAD><TITLE>Thumbnails</TITLE></HEAD>
<BODY>
<H1>Thumbnails</H1>
This is the original: <IMG SRC="BALLOON.GIF">
This is the resized thumbnail: <IMG SRC="BALLON_S.GIF">
</BODY>
</HTML>
```

7. If necessary, transfer the finished image to your server machine.

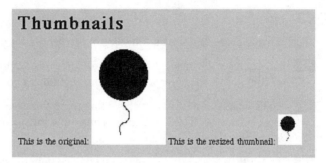

Figure 9-7 The thumbnail version of `balloon.gif`

How It Works

There isn't anything tricky at all here. The thumbnail version of the image is nothing more than a scaled-down version of the original. The most difficult task in this How-To is choosing which software package to do the work in.

Comments

One of the best uses for thumbnails is as clickable images that lead to the full-sized image. How-To 9.8 shows how to make them work that way.

Many programs, such as Adobe Photoshop and GraphicConverter, automatically create thumbnails of images when you save them. You can copy these thumbnails and paste them into your own documents. Consult your system's documentation for instructions on how to do this.

COMPLEXITY
BEGINNING

9.8 How do I...
Use an image as a link?

COMPATIBILITY: HTML

Problem

I have noticed Web authors often use images for links, either in place of text or along with text. How can I do this?

Technique

Using an image as a link to another image or document is very simple. Image links are no different from regular hypertext links. To create an image link, place the **<IMG SRC>** tag with the URL of the image between **<A HREF = "URL">...</A>** tags.

Steps

The following procedure shows you step by step how to use an image as a link.

1. Find or create the image you wish to use. For this example, the `ballon_s.GIF` image from the previous section is a good choice.

2. Decide what you want the image to link to. In this case, the small balloon image links to an HTML document containing the full-sized balloon image and a description of balloons.

3. Create the base HTML document that will contain the link. The document, kept small, would look something like this:

```
<HTML>
<HEAD><TITLE>My First Image Link</TITLE>
<BODY>
<H1>My first image link</H1>
This is a small balloon:
<IMG SRC="BALLON_S.GIF"> click on it to go to a page with a larger
balloon.<p>
</BODY>
</HTML>
```

4. Add the link. If the document you want to link to is called `bal_info.html`, then the link would be

```
<A HREF="BAL_INFO.HTML"><IMG SRC="BALLON_S.GIF"></A>
```

This is fairly straightforward. If you understand hypertext links, you should have no trouble at all with this structure. The hypertext that is normally placed between the `<A HREF>...</A>` tags is in this case replaced by an `<IMG SRC>` tag. The document now looks like this:

```
<HTML>
<HEAD><TITLE>My First Image Link</TITLE>
<BODY>
<H1>My first image link</H1>
This is a small balloon:
<A HREF="BAL_INFO.HTML"><IMG SRC="BALLON_S.GIF"></A>click on it to go to a
page with a larger balloon<p>
</BODY>
</HTML>
```

When viewed through a browser, the page looks much like Figure 9-8. As you can see, the small balloon image is highlighted, which means it is a link. Selecting that image sends the browser off to whatever URL is specified in the `<A HREF="URL">` tag.

5. Save your document as a text file. Give it any name that is simple, yet descriptive and unique. In this case, `ball_lnk.html` seems acceptable.

6. View the document locally with your browser.

Figure 9-8 A small image being used as a link

7. Make any fine-tuning changes that may be needed, then save the document.

8. If necessary, transfer the finished document and image to your server and inform your system administrator about the presence of the new document and image.

How It Works

When a browser comes across the `<A HREF="URL">...</A>` tags, it uses any text or valid URL of an image as the anchor for that tag, thus making text and images interchangeable for links. When a reader selects the hyperimage, he or she will be brought to the URL set with the `<A HREF="URL">` tag.

Comments

It is also possible to combine text and images between the `<A HREF="URL">...</A>` tags.

Note that people using Macintoshes, Windows 95, and UNIX systems should feel free to use variable and document names that contain more than eight characters, plus a three-letter tag.

COMPLEXITY
BEGINNING

9.9   How do I...
Create a background pattern for my page?

COMPATIBILITY: NETSCAPE, INTERNET EXPLORER

Problem

I see a lot of pages on the Web that appear in Netscape with different backgrounds than the standard Netscape gray. How can I change the background on my page?

Technique

Change backgrounds by using the **BACKGROUND** attribute. The **BACKGROUND** attribute is an HTML 3 extension to the **<BODY>** tag. You can use the **BACKGROUND** attribute to set the URL of a GIF that will be used as the document's background.

Steps

The following eight steps show how you can add a unique background to your documents.

1. Decide what kind of background you would like to use. Remember, you will place text on top of this background, so it is best to keep it light and simple.

2. Select the graphics program of your choice. You can use any graphics program, but it saves a conversion step if you use a program that can save images in GIF format.

3. Open a new image.

4. Set the document size to something relatively small. A 1-inch by 1-inch square works well.

5. Select a small color palette. It is best to stick with 4 or 16 colors.

6. Create a new image. Here artistic skill helps, but it is possible to do a fairly nice job with very little ability. Remember, keep the colors light. Also, remember that this color box is repeatedly juxtaposed on the background, so strive for something that will flow smoothly. Experiment until you come up with something you like.

7. Once you have something you like, save it as GIF, for example, `backgr.GIF`.

8. Add the **BACKGROUND** attribute to any **<BODY>** tag in any document where you wish to have `backgr.GIF` be the background color. The format of this is

```
<BODY BACKGROUND="BACKGR.GIF"> Document here!</BODY>
```

How It Works

When Netscape 1.1 or higher encounters a **BACKGROUND** attribute, it sets the screen's background to the GIF file specified by that background.

Comments

Backgrounds look nice, but do have a cost—speed. Loading a background image increases the amount of time your page takes to load. The speed factor is the reason it is best to keep the background simple.

To check out possible background colors, go to `http://www.infi.net/wwwimages/colorindex.html`.

COMPLEXITY
INTERMEDIATE

9.10 How do I...
Create a server-side clickable imagemap?

COMPATIBILITY: HTML 2+

Problem

There are places on the Web that use clickable pictures for menu bars and navigational tools. How can I add such clickable images to my own documents?

Technique

Clickable images or imagemaps are not really all that much different from regular inline GIF images. The only real difference is that imagemaps have had hot spots assigned to them. Hot spots are areas of the image that link to certain URLs when you click in them. The hot spots are often assigned through a utility imagemap program whose sole function is to assist you in setting the coordinates for hot spots. You inform a browser that an image is a clickable imagemap by appending the ISMAP attribute to an `<IMG SRC>` tag. This tag appears between `<A HREF="URL">...</A>` tags that contain the URL of the text file that contains the imagemap coordinates. The browser then uses a Common Gateway Interface to parse the results and figure out where to establish the link.

Steps

The following procedure gives you a general overview of what you must do to create an imagemap. How you create it depends on the machine you are using, the tools you have available, and the type of server your system is on. Still, the basic procedure remains the same.

1. Find or create a suitable image for your imagemap. This image can be as big and as complicated as you would like it to be. However, the less complicated it is, the easier it will be for the user to figure out what he or she can or can't click on, and the less time-consuming it will be to load. Imagemaps place a significant burden on the server and do have a delay time while the server processes your click, so frequent "mis-clicks" can be frustrating. For this example, the simple word W E B ! is a good choice. It should be easy to create with any graphics program, plus it has four distinct parts—each character—that are easily differentiated from one another. Call this image `web.GIF`.

2. Now that you have the image, you need to map out the location of the hot spots. You need some way of telling the server that the pixels of the image between these points lead to this URL. The area of the hot spot may be square, round, or a polygon. You need to compute the boundaries of each hot spot. For each area you wish to make a hot spot, you must find the coordinates, and then define the URL these coordinates will link to. Figure 9-9 depicts some sample coordinates for the `web.GIF` image.

While you can do all this by hand, it is usually preferable to use a utility program to map out areas for you. There are many tools to choose from, depending on what platform you are using. On the Macintosh, WebMap is a good public domain choice. On Windows and X Windows systems, MapEdit is a popular choice. All these utilities work in the same way: They present you with a series of familiar tools that let you capture the coordinates of the parts of the image you wish to use as hot spots. Figure 9-10 shows WebMap in action.

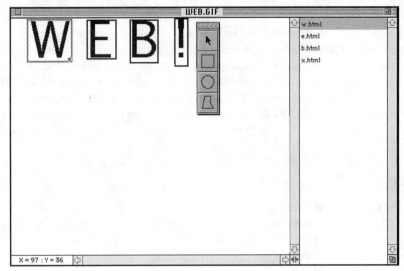

Figure 9-9 Coordinates for the `web.GIF` image

Figure 9-10 WebMap capturing the W's of the word W E B's coordinates

3. After you have mapped out the boundaries of your imagemap, save these boundaries as a text file, naming it `web.map`. The `web.map` file for the above example making each letter selectable will look like this:

```
default DEFALT.HTM
rect W.HTML 27,1 99,66
rect E.HTML 121,2 168,62
rect B.HTML 188,2 233,68
rect X.HTML 257,0 279,73
```

4. Transfer the `web.map` text file to the server.

5. Create the HTML base document that will contain the imagemap.

6. Now that you have the document, enter the `<IMG SRC>` tag inside of an `<A HREF>` tag:

```
<A HREF="/cgi-bin/imagemap/WEB.MAP"><IMG SRC="WEB.GIF" ISMAP></A>
```

The ISMAP attribute at the end of the `<IMG SRC>` tag is the key here. That tells the browser that this GIF file is a clickable imagemap and that the text file named at the end of the `<A HREF>` tag should be the file fed to the imagemap CGI gateway to interrupt clicks. The complete document would look like this:

```
<HTML>
<HEAD>
<TITLE>Sample Image Map</TITLE>
<BODY>
<H1>This is a sample imagemap!</H1>
Clicking on any letter will bring you to a description of that letter:
<A HREF="/cgi-bin/imagemap/WEB.MAP"><IMG SRC="WEB.GIF" ISMAP></A>
</BODY>
</HTML>
```

7. Create any of the linked-to documents that you might need. This example would need five more documents: one for each letter, one for the exclamation point, and one default document that gets returned when the user clicks on a spot that is not a hot spot. The document names should match the ones used in the map file. A sample document might look like this:

```
<HTML>
<HEAD>
<TITLE> W!!</TILE>
</HEAD>
<BODY>
<-- This document is W.HTML -->
You selected the W -- the 23rd letter of the alphabet.<P>
</BODY>
</HTML>
```

8. If necessary, transfer the HTML document(s) to your server.

9. Ask your system administrator to activate your new imagemap document.

How It Works

An imagemap is really nothing more than a GIF file that is related to a text file through your server's CGI imagemap interface. The CGI interface can be a bit tricky if you had to write it—luckily, all the major servers come with this interface already written for you, so all you have to do is access it. When the browser encounters the `<ISMAP>` tag, it relates the GIF file in the tag to the text document pointed to by the URL in the `<A HREF="URL">` tag.

Comments

Because of the overhead involved, some systems don't allow their users to have imagemaps in their documents. It is a good idea to check with your system administrator before starting an imagemap.

Imagemaps vary slightly from server to server. NCSA deals with the coordinates of hot spots a little differently than CERN. If you use the proper tools, these differences will be largely handled for you. Still, it is always a good idea to consult with your server system's documentation or with your system's Webmaster before starting an imagemap.

COMPLEXITY
INTERMEDIATE

9.11 How do I...
Include client-side imagemaps?

COMPATIBILITY: NETSCAPE, INTERNET EXPLORER

Problem

I want to develop an imagemap, but I don't have the time or the know-how to write a CGI application that will read an imagemap and return the appropriate page. How can I include a simple imagemap on my page?

Technique

Netscape and Microsoft's Internet Explorer support client-side imagemaps where the different regions of the image are specified within the document or in another HTML document. The syntax is similar to that for the proposed **SHAPE** attribute in HTML 3. No CGI applications are required to read client-side imagemaps. Therefore, they even work while not connected to the Internet, which is handy for examining local Web pages.

Steps

Open your document. Then load an image with a viewer such as Photoshop that allows you to get the pixel locations from the image so you can specify image locations in the links.

1. First, identify areas on the image that you want to have serve as links. As of this writing, the only shape supported is a rectangle. Note the pixel locations of the upper-left and lower-right corners of the rectangle.

2. In the HTML document, insert the **<MAP>** and **</MAP>** tags. Use the **NAME** attribute for **<MAP>** to give a unique name for the imagemap. For example, to create an imagemap named **mymap**, you would enter

```
<MAP NAME="mymap">
</MAP>
```

3. Between the **<MAP>** and **</MAP>** tags, insert an **<AREA>** tag. There should be one **<AREA>** tag for each link on the map. If your imagemap has three areas, enter

```
<MAP NAME="mymap">
<AREA>
<AREA>
<AREA>
</MAP>
```

4. The SHAPE attribute of <AREA> identifies the shape of the area in the imagemap. Since rectangles are the only currently supported shape, SHAPE can have only one value, "RECT".

```
<MAP NAME="mymap">
<AREA SHAPE="RECT">
<AREA SHAPE="RECT">
<AREA SHAPE="RECT">
</MAP>
```

5. The COORD attribute identifies the boundaries of the area on the imagemap. For "RECT", COORD has four values, separated by commas: the x coordinate of the upper-left corner, the y coordinate of the upper-left corner, the x coordinate of the lower-right corner, and the y coordinate of the lower-right corner. For example, for three rectangles in different areas of the image:

```
<MAP NAME="mymap">
<AREA SHAPE="RECT" COORD="10,10,30,50">
<AREA SHAPE="RECT" COORD="50,50,70,70">
<AREA SHAPE="RECT" COORD="90,90,120,95">
</MAP>
```

6. For each area, the HREF attribute identifies the URL of the document that should be loaded if that area is selected by the user. The document can be a local file or a document on another server. Adding HREF attributes to the above example gives us

```
<MAP NAME="mymap">
<AREA SHAPE="RECT" COORD="10,10,30,50" HREF="info.html">
<AREA SHAPE="RECT" COORD="50,50,70,70" HREF="projects/info/data.html">
<AREA SHAPE="RECT" COORD="90,90,120,95" HREF="http://www.widgets.com/">
</MAP>
```

7. The imagemap information can be referenced to an image on the page by adding the USEMAP attribute to the <IMG> element. USEMAP is set equal to the name of map information from the NAME attribute of <MAP>. For example, if the file imagemap.GIF serves as the imagemap, using the information from the last step, you would enter

```
<IMG SRC="imagemap.GIF" ALT="An imagemap" USEMAP="#mymap">
```

The map description does not have to be in the same document as the imagemap itself. If the map description is stored in the file maps.html in the same directory as the file with the imagemap, you can use

```
<IMG SRC="imagemap.GIF" ALT="An imagemap" USEMAP="maps.html#mymap">
```

How It Works

When a user clicks on an image that includes the USEMAP attribute, Netscape reads the corresponding imagemap description contained within the <MAP> element. If the user selects an area described by one of the <AREA> tags, the browser loads the document identified by the HREF attribute.

Comments

Not all browsers support client-side imagemaps, so people using some browsers cannot access those imagemaps. Since the **USEMAP** attribute takes precedence over ordinary links, there are two ways to work around this. One way is to enclose the image in a link that references a standard imagemap routine:

```
<A HREF="/cgi-bin/imagemap.cgi"><IMG SRC="imagemap.GIF" ALT="An imagemap"
USEMAP="#mymap"></A>
```

This method requires that you have configured an imagemap CGI application and have set up the appropriate description files for that application. Another approach is to include a link to a document that gives an error message and informs the user that the imagemap can only be accessed by those browsers that support client-side imagemaps:

```
<A HREF="error.html"><IMG SRC="imagemap.GIF" ALT="An imagemap"
USEMAP="#mymap"></A>
```

You can find updated information about client-side imagemaps in Netscape at `http://www.netscape.com/assist/net_sites/html_extensions_3.html`.

COMPLEXITY
INTERMEDIATE

9.12 How do I...
Color reduce an image?

COMPATIBILITY: HTML

Problem

My images are quite big and my page takes longer to load than I would like. I understand I might be able to use color reduction to make my images smaller. How do I do this?

Technique

This is an interesting problem, and there really is more than one solution to it. None of the solutions involve HTML, however, but rather involve planning how many actual colors to use when creating your image, then deciding on the type of format to use for your images. The latter choice will be based on, and is sometimes governed by, the first. The fewer the colors you can use to create your image, the smaller that image will be.

Steps

The following steps show how you can choose a format for your image that will allow for the maximum reduction in the number of colors used, while still keeping your image looking good.

1. Create your image, either by hand or with a scanner.

2. Decide on the format you wish to save the image in. Your two main choices are GIF and JPEG. Each has its own strengths. It is a general rule of thumb that you use GIF for images that are small and do not need a lot of colors to look good. This is because graphics programs such as Photoshop allow you to index the colors of a GIF file, in effect permitting the image to only store the colors it needs, thus making the image smaller. JPEG is considered best for photographs, as the compression method it uses usually loses very little in quality with photographs, while it still creates an image that is smaller than the comparable image as a GIF.

3. Add the image to a HTML document with the `<SRC>` tag.

How It Works

You will need to experiment. Some images will look better in GIF format, others in JPEG format. You will also need to experiment with the number of colors. If the image is a GIF, you can use Photoshop or another graphics program of your choice to optimize the image by indexing the colors. If the image is a JPEG, you may find that medium compression may still yield an acceptable image.

Comments

The goal here should be to get the best image that takes up the least possible space. Sometime the choice of what format to use is easy. If you want to display over 256 colors, then you must use JPEG, as GIF only allows up to 256 colors. If you are dealing with an image that only needs a few colors, such as an icon, GIF will usually give you better quality and can be optimized so the image is actually smaller than its JPEG counterpart. The really tricky part is choosing a format for an image that uses up to 256 colors. Generally speaking, the GIF version will look better, but will be bigger, though this doesn't always hold true. Many times, which format you use and how you reduce the colors will depend on personal preferences.

Remember you can not optimize a file through the use of HTML tags; you must rely on a graphics program to do such things as indexing and compression.

For online examples of these concepts, feel free to check out `http://www.psnw.com/~jmz5/waite/graphics.html`.

COMPLEXITY
BEGINNING

9.13 How do I...
Use WIDTH and HEIGHT attributes with an image?

COMPATIBILITY: NETSCAPE, INTERNET EXPLORER

Problem

My images take longer to load than I would like. I understand I can speed this process up if I use the WIDTH and HEIGHT attributes when I load the image. How do I do this?

Technique

You use the WIDTH and HEIGHT attribute in the <IMG> tag to automatically control the width and height of the image that will load.

Steps

The following simple procedure shows how to load images with the WIDTH and HEIGHT attributes.

1. Create or find the image you wish to include in an HTML document.

2. Use a graphics program to determine the height and width of the image. This information is readily available with most software packages.

3. Add the <IMG> tag, and include the proper WIDTH and HEIGHT attributes. For example:

```
<IMG  WIDTH=256 HEIGHT=269 SRC="slow.GIF">
```

4. View the document to make sure the image loads correctly.

How It Works

If the WIDTH and HEIGHT attributes are not included, the browser will calculate the size of all images it loads "on the fly". If you include these attributes in an <IMG> tag, the browser then uses the values given to define the size of the object. The browser can then load the image faster.

Comments

When you have a lot of images on a page, using these attributes can make a noticeable difference in speeding up the loading of a page.

An online example may be found at `http://www.psnw.com/~jmz5/waite/demoall.html`.

COMPLEXITY
BEGINNING

9.14 How do I...
Scale an image on my page?

COMPATIBILITY: NETSCAPE, INTERNET EXPLORER

Problem

I would like to present different sized versions of the same image on a page without having to save the image multiple times. How do I do this?

Technique

To scale an image, you use the `WIDTH` and `HEIGHT` attribute in the `<IMG>` tag. But instead of using the image's original size, you change the values to reflect the new size.

Steps

The following simple procedure shows how to load images with the `WIDTH` and `HEIGHT` attributes.

1. Create or find the image you wish to scale in an HTML document.

2. Decide what size you would like to make the object; then do the math. For instance, if you want to scale the object down 50 percent, cut the object's original `WIDTH` and `HEIGHT` attributes in half.

3. Add the `<IMG>` tag and include the scaled `WIDTH` and `HEIGHT` attributes. For example, here's how to scale the image used in How-To 9.13:

```
<IMG  WIDTH=128 HEIGHT=135 SRC="slow.GIF">
```

4. View the document to make sure the image loads correctly. Figure 9-11 shows one example of using scaling.

How It Works

If the `WIDTH` and `HEIGHT` attributes given with the `<IMG>` tag do not match the image's actual size, the browser scales the image to match the attributes before it renders the image.

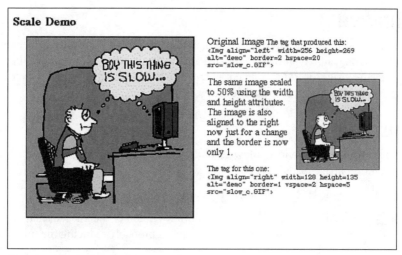

Figure 9-11 A scaling example

Comments

Netscape and Microsoft's Internet Explorer do a nice job of scaling images as long as you keep the ratios consistent.

An online example may be found at `http://www.psnw.com/~jmz5/waite/demoall.html`.

COMPLEXITY
BEGINNING

9.15 How do I...
Use a small or low-resolution image while a larger one loads?

COMPATIBILITY: NETSCAPE

Problem

I have a big image that takes a while to load. I would like readers to be able to see a smaller version of this image while they wait for the large version to load. How do I do this?

Technique

You may load a smaller, lower resolution image by placing a `<LOWSRC>` element inside of an `<IMG>` tag. The browser will load any image the `<LOWSRC>` points to before it loads the image the `<SRC>` element points to. This image will load in the same place the larger image will eventually occupy.

Steps

Follow these steps to load a low-resolution version of an image before the higher resolution image loads.

1. Create the HTML document that will hold the image.

2. Create the image and a lower resolution version of the image. There are many ways to do this. The most simple is probably reducing the number of colors in the image.

3. Add the image to the document by using the `<IMG>` tag and including a `<LOWSRC>` element and URL besides the normal `<SRC>` element and URL. For example:

```
<IMG LOWSRC="slow.GIF SRC="slwo.GIF">
```

4. View your document to make sure everything works correctly and that the `<LOWSRC>` images load before the one named in the `<SRC>` element.

How It Works

When the browser spots the `<LOWSRC>` element, it loads the image associated with that element. This allows other items on your page to load. Once those are loaded, the regular image will load.

Comments

The image pointed to by `<LOWSRC>` does not have to actually be smaller than the normal image. The browser does not check this. `<LOWSRC>` can make a nice alternative to interlacing. `<LOWSRC>` can really make a difference if you have an especially large image to load.

Samples of this tag in use may be found at `http://www.psnw.com/~jmz5/waite/demoall.html`.

9.16 How do I...
Speed image transmission?

COMPATIBILITY: HTML

Problem

My page has a lot of images and can take a long time to load. How can I speed image transmission?

Technique

There are many different methods you can use to make sure your page loads as fast as possible. These methods have all been mentioned in the preceding sections, including color reduction, using **WIDTH** and **HEIGHT** attributes, and using interlacing or **<LOWSRC>**.

Steps

The following steps will give some possible ways you can speed the transmission of your page.

1. Optimize your images so they use the fewest colors, or the greatest compression, and still look good. Often you can successfully use far fewer colors than you might believe.

2. Use **WIDTH** and **HEIGHT** attributes in **<IMG>** tags in order to speed up the loading process.

3. Avoid large background images that slow down the loading process. Backgrounds images should for the most part be small and subtle. Also, remember to never interlace a background image.

4. If you would like your readers to get an overview of your page while the larger images load, consider using interlacing or **<LOWSRC>**.

5. Experiment to find what works best for you.

How It Works

The process is actually based on a simple given: the smaller the images, the faster they will load. And if you supply **WIDTH** and **HEIGHT** attributes, you save the browser from having to compute these; thus, the page will load faster. Interlacing and **<LOWSRC>** don't actually make your page load faster, but since they allow the user to view the layout of the page quicker than if these options were not used, the page seems to load faster.

Comments

What methods you use depends greatly on your personal preference and your target audience. If your target audience consists mostly of people using 28.8 or even 14.4 modems (and remember, due to system loads and other factors, these modems will often not even be effectively producing these speeds), you will want to be considerate with bandwidth and not put a lot of high-resolution images on your page. Also, remember that a lot of little images can also take time to load. One good way to anticipate how fast your page will load is to assume 1 second for every K of text and graphics a page has. A general rule of thumb often heard is that the sum total of all the images on your page should not exceed 40–50k, though many of the most popular sites on the Web use far more bandwidth than this. So this rule, like most other Web design rules is very flexible and left up to the designer's personal taste.

COMPLEXITY
INTERMEDIATE

9.17 How do I...
Create an animated GIF?

COMPATIBILITY: NETSCAPE, INTERNET EXPLORER

Problem

I want to add some life to my Web page, but I don't have time to learn Java or CGI scripting. I've noticed a lot of pages have cool animated icons. How can I add these types of icons to my pages?

Technique

One GIF file is actually able to hold many different images. By slightly varying each of these images you can in effect perform animation by simply putting a GIF on the screen with an `<IMG>` tag. The process works much like an animation flip book changing from one image to another, thus giving the illusion of motion.

Steps

The following steps show you a general way to create animated GIFs.

1. Create the different versions of image you wish to animate. To keep it simple, each image should be the same size and use the same colors. Label each of these images in sequence. For example, `image01.GIF`, `image02.GIF`, `image03.GIF`. Figure 9-12 shows one possible series. This example will produce an animated count up from 1 to 3.

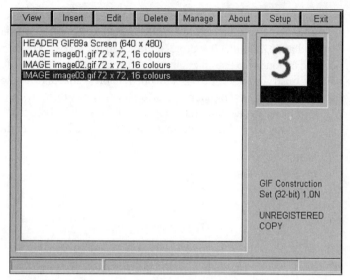

Figure 9-12 The sequence for animation

2. Open a new file with whatever animated GIF tool you are using.

3. Load each image of the sequence, in order, into the new file.

4. For each image, set the number of 1/100 of a second for it to delay or stay on the screen.

5. Decide how many times you wish the image to loop and set that.

6. Set any other attribute you may want to change from the default.

7. Save the new image as a GIF. It is best to use a name that corresponds to the sequence names that make up the file.

8. Use the GIF in an HTML document with a simple `<IMG>` tag. For example:

```
<img src="image,gif">
```

How It Works

When Netscape sees a GIF that contains more than one image, it cycles through those images at a speed set by the user for the number of loops set by the user.

Comments

Too many animated GIFs on a page can be annoying and can cause cache problems.

This is a generalized way to create an animated GIF. The process will differ a bit, depending on what tools you use. GIF Construction set is a popular choice in the PC world and GifBuilder is a popular choice in the Mac world. They can be found by going to your web search engine of choice and searching for their names.

GIF Construction set 3.2 (the current version available from the Web site as of this writing) makes creating animated GIFs extremely easy through the use of Animation Wizard, which can be found in the File menu. This Wizard prompts you along each step of the way needed to create an animated GIF, making the entire process quite painless.

ADDING EXTERNALLY LINKED MULTIMEDIA OBJECTS

10

ADDING EXTERNALLY LINKED MULTIMEDIA OBJECTS

How do I...

10.14   Spin a VRML object?

10.15   Include animated textures on VRML objects?

Multimedia information is generally more intuitive and more informative than plain textual information. However, HTML 3.2 only provides limited means for including multimedia objects in your documents. This chapter explores the use of links to indirectly include this type of information in your document. Some of this information is also relevant to the development of multimedia for direct inclusion using nonstandard methods discussed in Chapter 18, Direct Inclusion of Multimedia Objects.

Many types of information cannot be represented directly in HTML 3.2. For example, while most browsers support images within HTML documents using **<IMG>** elements (see Chapter 9, Using Images in Your Documents), only a limited number of types, usually GIF and JPEG, are directly supported. Further, HTML does not provide any direct support for the inclusion of other media types, such as audio or animation.

Processed data, such as PostScript or DVI files, cannot be included directly in HTML documents either. If a converter is available, you can translate this data to HTML. (See How-To 2.7.) However, converters generally create a single HTML document rather than a component suitable for inclusion in an HTML document.

Links provide a means for indirectly including both multimedia information and processed data. When a reader triggers a link to such information, the requested item is retrieved as any other file would be. However, when the browser receives an object that is not HTML, or some other type that it directly interprets, it uses a helper application to render the object in an appropriate manner. If the user's hardware or software does not support the particular media type retrieved, then the object is not displayed.

This chapter explains the use of links that allow you to include a variety of information objects not directly supported by HTML. The procedures for including these objects, along with pointers to helper applications for displaying these objects, are provided. Table 10-1 summarizes the location of the relevant How-To's corresponding to various types of multimedia files and processed data files. How-To 10.1 provides a general approach to, as well as a complete example of, incorporating external objects into an HTML document.

Table 10-1 Multimedia objects covered in this chapter

INFORMATION TYPE	STORAGE FORMAT	HOW-TO'S	FILENAME EXTENSION
application	DVI	10.9	`.dvi`
application	PostScript	10.8	`.ps`
audio	AIFF	10.6 and 10.7	`.aiff (.aif)`
audio	AU	10.6	`.au`
audio	WAV	10.6 and 10.7	`.wav`
image	GIF	Chapter 9 and 10.2	`.gif`
image	JPEG	Chapter 9 and 10.2	`.jpeg (.jpg)`
image	PNM	10.2	`.ppm .pnm .pbm .pgm`

INFORMATION TYPE	STORAGE FORMAT	HOW-TO'S	FILENAME EXTENSION
image	PICT	10.2	.PICT
image	RGB	10.2	.rgb
image	TIFF	10.2	.tiff(.tif)
video	AVI	10.4 and 10.5	.avi
video	MPEG	10.4 and 10.5	.mpeg(.mpg)
video	QUICKTIME	10.4 and 10.5	.mov
x-world	VRML	10.10 - 10.15	.wrl

10.1   Add Links to Multimedia in My Home Page

You have a variety of multimedia objects and you want to include these objects in your home page. You want your place on the World Wide Web to be more dynamic and exciting. In this How-To, you will learn how to build a home page with linked multimedia.

10.2   Add an External Image

HTML supports inline images, and browsers implement this support for a limited number of image formats. You want to be able to include images in other formats in your HTML documents. In this How-To, you will learn how to incorporate external images in your HTML pages.

10.3   Convert Among Image Formats

You want to make your documents with large inline images more efficient. You have added images that can be viewed through an external viewer, but you want to include some of these as inline images. What do you need to do to show the images on your HTML page? In this How-To, you will learn how to convert among image formats.

10.4   Insert a Video

You want to include video clips in your HTML pages. How do you include them in your documents? What kind of support do readers need so they can view this information? In this How-To, you will learn how to add digital video to your pages.

10.5   Convert Among Video File Formats

What types of video file formats are there? How do you convert a file from one to another? Readers can view your video clips with a helper application, but you need the clip in another format so that you can edit it with your current hardware and software. In this How-To, you will learn how to convert among video formats.

10.6   Insert a Sound File

You want to include a voice description of the current document. The text and pictures do not totally convey the point you are trying to make with the current document. How do you include this sound file? And how do you tell your readers how to access this information? In this How-To, you will learn how to place sound files in your HTML pages.

10.7   Convert Among Audio File Formats

A variety of audio file formats has been developed on several different platforms. You need to easily convert from one format to another so that you can efficiently edit and tailor the audio that you include in your documents. In this How-To, you will learn how to convert among sound file formats.

10.8   Include a PostScript Document

Much of your documentation is in the PostScript format. You want to build HTML documents that provide Web-based access to these PostScript files. How do you include PostScript documents in your HTML documents? In this How-To, you will learn how to access PostScript files from your HTML pages.

10.9   Include a Device-Independent (DVI) File

You have written documents using the TeX formatting language. You know you can convert these documents to HTML, but they are more useful to you as either TeX or DVI files. How do you provide access to your DVI files from HTML documents? In this How-To, you will learn how to provide access to DVI files from your HTML pages.

10.10   Find a VRML Browser

The Virtual Reality Modeling Language (VRML), like HTML, serves as a basis for network-based documents. As with HTML Web pages, you need a suitable browser to view these documents. In this How-To, you will learn how to locate a browser, or plug-in, suitable for use on your platform.

10.11   Create a VRML Document

The intricacies of VRML are beyond the scope of this book. However, an introduction to the recognition and creation of such documents will provide you with a glimpse into this growing area of Web documents. In this How-To, you will learn how to create a basic VRML document and how to recognize such a document if you retrieve one.

10.12   Locate Prebuilt VRML Objects

Authors around the Internet have developed a wide variety of VRML objects. A large number of such objects are freely (or not so freely) available for your use in your own worlds. In this How-To, you will learn about several repositories containing reusable VRML objects.

10.13   Make My VRML World More Realistic

VRML worlds often do not create a realistic environment. Several methods exist to improve the realism in your VRML worlds. In this How-To, you will learn how to use level of detail (LOD) and textures to improve the realism of your creation.

10.14   Spin a VRML Object

The current VRML standard does not provide support for any independent motion within worlds, but many new VRML browsers and plug-ins support independent object motion. In this How-To, you will learn how to include simple moving objects within your VRML world.

10.15   Include Animated Textures on VRML Objects

Textures applied to VRML objects enhance the realism of objects; however, textures can also convey additional, mobile information. By using an animated GIF image as a texture, you can project this animation onto the surface of any VRML object. In this How-To, you will learn how to apply an animated GIF image to a VRML object.

COMPLEXITY

INTERMEDIATE

10.1   How do I...
Add links to multimedia in my home page?

COMPATIBILITY: HTML

Problem

I would like to introduce myself to the world. Can I include a voice welcome and introduction on my home page? Better yet, can I include a small video segment of myself stating who I am and what I do? How do I add multimedia elements to my home page?

Technique

You can incorporate multimedia objects into a home page. The use of tailored anchor elements to access helper applications for specified file types is the key to this process. Each multimedia file or processed data file added to an HTML 3.2 document, with the exception of inline images or active Java applets, is added in this manner.

Steps

The following steps lead you through the creation or modification of a single HTML document titled "Home Page of Me." This document will serve as your business card in the World Wide Web community.

This process assumes that you are using a normal text editor for your document creation. If you use a different kind of editor, some of the steps outlined may not be necessary; be sure to check the documentation for your editor to determine which steps apply.

Step-by-step instructions are provided here to modify a home page, or any page, to include multimedia objects of all sorts.

1. Change directories to the location where you wish to develop your HTML documents. Open the file containing your HTML home page in your favorite text editor.

```
edit homepage.htm
```

2. If you have not created a home page for yourself, review How-To 2.14 to help you create a home page.

3. Follow the procedure identified in Table 10-1 that is appropriate for the media type you want to include. For example, you might want to include a voice introduction to yourself or your Web pages in a home page constructed through the procedure in How-To 2.14

```
USA<BR>
E-Mail: my_id@mysite.edu
<A HREF="http://www.mysite.edu/~me/audio/intro.au">
<IMG SRC="/icons/sound.xbm" ALT="[Audio Icon]">
Welcome Message</A> (1.2 MB AU Audio)<BR>
```

or include an image of your project group that can be viewed with a helper application.

```
I am currently working on several projects with
<A HREF="http://www.mysite.edu/~me/group.jpg">group gold</A> (1.4 MB JPEG).
These projects include...
```

4. Save the file. Remember to use the `.html` or `.htm` filename extension to indicate an HTML document.

5. Attempt to view your home page using as many different browsers as you have access to.

6. If there are problems with the way items display, modify the document as appropriate.

7. When you feel that your home page is ready for the rest of the world, ask your site administrator to install your document on your Web site, or follow his or her instructions to install the document in your home directory.

How It Works

Multimedia elements other than inline images are added to HTML documents by specifying links that refer to the required files. HTML does not support direct inclusion of such files. So to develop your multimedia home page, you must create or acquire appropriate multimedia or processed data files, install them on your Web server, and provide access to them via links from your home page.

If your software and hardware permit it, you might want to include a small video or audio segment introducing yourself. Or you might include a reference to a photo of your project team. Your imagination is the only limit to what you can accomplish.

Once you have created or acquired suitable multimedia and processed data files, test them extensively to make sure they work exactly as you want; then install them on the server. Chapter 12, Server Basics, discusses installation of documents on a server.

Use the procedures in this chapter to develop a multimedia home page that will serve as your introduction to the World Wide Web community. You should feel free to experiment with including other elements to create a home page suited to your interests and goals. However, for ease of understanding, the following example extends the home page developed in How-To 2.14.

```
<!DOCTYPE HTML PUBLIC "-//W3C//DTD HTML 3.2//EN">
<HTML>
<HEAD>
<TITLE>Home Page of John Q. Public</TITLE>
</HEAD>
<BODY>

<!-- Mark the beginning of this portion with a horizontal rule. -->
<HR>
<!-- Center your name as a level 1 header. -->
<H1 ALIGN="center">John Q. Public</H1>
<!-- Provide any desirable contact information. -->
999 Peachtree St.<BR>
Atlanta, GA 30314<BR>
USA<BR>
E-Mail: my_id@mysite.edu<BR>
<A HREF="http://www.mysite.edu/~me/audio/intro.au">
<IMG SRC="/icons/sound.xbm" ALT="[Audio Icon]">
Welcome Message</A> (1.2 MB AU Audio)

<!-- Mark the beginning of this portion with a horizontal rule. -->
<HR>
<!-- Choose the heading text that you feel appropriate. -->
<H1>About Me</H1>
<!-- The formatting and information should be developed to suit your needs.
-->
This is the first paragraph in this section about myself.
I have been at MY BUSINESS for the past X years.
<P>
I am currently working on several projects with
<A HREF="http://www.mysite.edu/~me/group.jpg">group gold</A> (1.4 MB JPEG).
These projects include...

<!-- Mark the beginning of this portion with a horizontal rule. -->
<HR>
<!-- Substitute the appropriate information in your document. The date should
-->
<!-- appear in a long format with the month name written out since the order
-->
<!-- conventions for date abbreviations vary. -->
Last modified on CURRENT_DATE by YOUR_NAME (YOUR-E-MAIL)

</BODY>
</HTML>
```

You can now add links to your own multimedia and processed data files. Standard HTML 3.2 anchor elements can be used to specify these hypermedia links. (See Chapter 8, Establishing Links.) The above document contains two such example links. Figure 10-1 shows how this document would appear with one of these links activated.

The selection of the link triggers a request for the file specified in the anchor element. If the request is successful, this server generates a response that includes both the type of the requested file and its contents.

Servers maintain a database that maps filename extensions to information types in order to generate type information sent to browsers. Therefore, take care to ensure that the proper filename extensions are used. Chapter 12, Server Basics, and Appendix C, Multipurpose Internet Mail Extensions (MIME), provide further information on document installation and document types.

When a browser receives a file from the server, it determines how to present the data based upon the type of information provided by the server. Most browsers will only directly render text and HTML documents in their display window. Helper applications display information of other types. This process is illustrated in Figure 10-2.

Comments

When adding elements of your own, remember that the document you are creating may be viewed by thousands, if not millions, of people. You should take into consideration the variety of browsers with differing presentation capabilities during your multimedia document development.

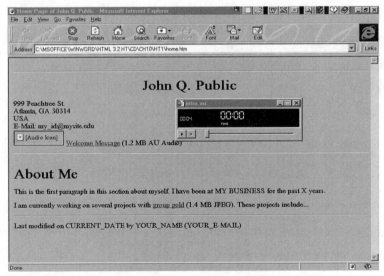

Figure 10-1 Rendering of a multimedia home page

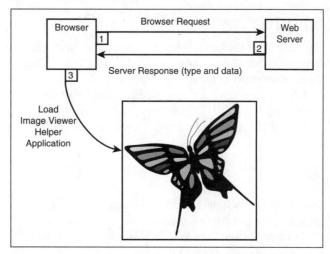

Figure 10-2 Retrieval and rendering process of external objects

Additional object types and suitable viewers can be added in the same way you would add the file types discussed in this chapter. For example, you can include virtual reality files by configuring the browser to launch an appropriate external viewer when it encounters a virtual reality file, creating links to appropriate objects, and installing a helper application capable of displaying the file. For more information on virtual reality files, see How-To's 10.10 through 10.15.

Several popular browsers support additional, nonstandard mechanisms for including multimedia objects within a Web page. See Chapter 17, Web Programming with Java and JavaScript, and Chapter 18, Direct Inclusion of Multimedia Objects, for additional information on these methods.

COMPLEXITY
BEGINNING

10.2   How do I...
Add an external image?

COMPATIBILITY: HTML

Problem

With inline images (Chapter 9, Using Images in Your Documents), I am limited to GIF format images, X bitmap files, and sometimes JPEG images. I would like to include images in other formats. I know that I cannot include them directly because HTML does not support other image formats. However, I need to make these image objects available.

Technique

You can provide access to images not supported through the inline `<IMG>` HTML element by establishing a link to the desired image. When a reader selects a link, the browser retrieves the linked file from the server where it is stored and displays it. If the browser does not support direct display of the file, it uses a helper application.

The following procedure shows how to include links to external images in your HTML documents.

Steps

The method for including an external image in your HTML document depends upon the editor used to create the document. In a strictly text-based editor, you manually insert an anchor. With WYSIWYG or macro/menu-based editors, you might add the anchor through macros or menus.

Either way, your HTML document will include the appropriate anchor element, specified by opening and closing anchor tags. The following procedure assumes you create your anchor element in a text editor. If you are not using a text editor, you should consult your editor's documentation to determine whether modifications of the procedure are necessary.

1. Open the HTML document you want to edit in your HTML editor. (See How-To 2.4 on HTML editing environments.)

2. Locate the position where you want to include your image. Place the cursor at this location.

3. Insert the text that you want to enclose between the opening and closing anchor tags. If the image file is large, let the reader know. An example of such a message is

```
owl image (1.2 MB JPEG)
```

4. Place the insertion point where you want the anchor to begin. Insert an opening anchor tag at this location. Minimally, this should include the target of the link and the URL of the image you want to include. You include this URL as the value of an `HREF` attribute. The following code shows an opening anchor tag.

```
<A HREF="http://www.mysite.edu/images/owl.jpeg">owl image (1.2 MB JPEG)
```

5. Place the insertion point after the enclosed text. Insert a closing anchor tag. The following code shows a complete anchor element for the example image.

```
<A HREF="http://www.mysite.edu/images/owl.jpeg">owl image</A> (1.2 MB JPEG)
```

6. Save your document, or continue adding elements by returning to step 2.

How It Works

Most browsers support GIF and X bitmap images within a document using the HTML `<IMG>` element. When this element was added to HTML, GIF was one of the most widely used image formats. Recently, support for direct inclusion of JPEG images has been suggested and has become standard in several popular browsers.

Since many images are available in a variety of other file formats, you can use an external image viewer to access images in these formats in HTML documents, as shown in Figure 10-3.

Many different image formats exist, and you must have a suitable viewer if you want to view images of a particular type. Generic viewers can recognize and display images in a variety of formats. Consequently, it is easier to use image viewers of this type than to require a separate viewer for each image format.

You access an external image by activating an HTML anchor that links to such an image. This anchor provides no information to the reader about the size and format of the linked image. Therefore, a useful practice is to specify both the format and size of the image in the text of the document. The format information allows the reader to decide whether he or she has an image viewer that can display the linked image. The size information allows the reader to decide whether he or she wants to wait the amount of time the image will take to download.

A common practice is to provide a smaller inline version of the image as part of the anchor for the linked image. This thumbnail image gives the user a preview of the larger external image. See How-To 9.7 for detailed information on the proper use of thumbnail images.

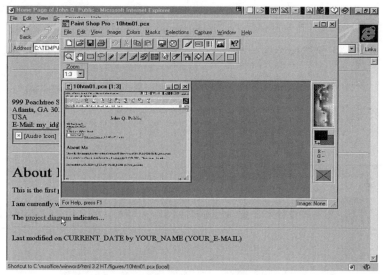

Figure 10-3 Browser and image viewer helper application

When a browser receives an image file from a server, it determines how to display the image based upon the format of the image data. Most browsers directly display plain text and HTML documents. Other types of information, such as images, are shown by helper applications.

Comments

The anchor elements in this How-To make use of only the **HREF** attribute. Chapter 8 provides additional information to HTML 3.2 anchor elements, including information on other available attributes. Appendix A, HTML Quick Reference, provides a quick reference on HTML 3.2 anchor elements. See How-To 10.1 for a complete example of incorporating external images into HTML documents.

To properly display external images, both the browser accessing the image and the server providing the image must be configured properly. Your Web site administrator is responsible for properly configuring your server. Instructions for configuring server support for external images are provided in How-To 12.6.

Configuring a browser to support external images requires either the modification of its configuration files or the alteration of a helper program list from the program's menu. You need to examine your browser documentation to determine the procedure to configure support for external images.

The following table lists some suitable image viewers. You need the proper application for your computer system to view non-inline images. This is not a comprehensive list. If a suggested application does not meet your needs, use a Web search engine such as Infoseek (`http://www.infoseek.com`) to find a more suitable application.

PLATFORM	APPLICATION	LOCATION
Mac	JPEGView	`ftp://ftp.ncsa.uiuc.edu/Mosaic/Mac/Helpers/`
PC	Lview	
PC	PaintShop Pro	`http://www.jasc.com` (also on the CD-ROM)
UNIX	xv	`ftp://ftp.cis.upenn.edu/pub/xv`

COMPLEXITY
INTERMEDIATE

10.3 How do I...
Convert among image formats?

COMPATIBILITY: HTML

Technique

Many images are created and stored in a format that is not the best for your desired use. Fortunately, converters exist for a number of popular image formats.

The conversion process requires a familiarity with the use of anonymous FTP or FTP URLs. First, identify an appropriate converter. Next, acquire the converter. Use it to convert your images. Finally, view your converted image using an image viewer to determine whether the image's integrity was maintained through the conversion process.

Steps

The following step-by-step procedure shows how to acquire and use an image converter. The listed converters accept images stored in particular file formats and generate appropriate image files as output.

1. Determine the original image file format as well as the format that you want to use for your converted image.

2. Find the converter you want. Table 10-2 lists some common converter applications. If you cannot find a suitable converter among them, you may want to use a Web search application to find an appropriate converter.

Table 10-2 Common image formatting conversion applications

PLATFORM	CONVERTERS	LOCATION
PC, Mac, UNIX	Adobe Photoshop	Adobe Systems, Inc.
		`http://www.adobe.com/prodindex/photoshop`
		`/main.html`
PC	PaintShop Pro	JASC, Inc., `http://www.jasc.com/`, also on the CD-ROM
UNIX	PBMPLUS	`ftp://wuarchive.wustl.edu/graphics/graphics/`
		`packages/NetPBM/`
UNIX (X-Window)	xv	`ftp://ftp.cis.upenn.edu/pub/xv/`

3. Use anonymous FTP or an FTP URL to acquire an appropriate converter. Uncompress, unarchive, and install the converter application as appropriate for your computer platform.

On a UNIX platform, use the **uncompress** and **tar** commands to uncompress and unarchive.

On a PC platform, the most common compression/archival program is ZIP. Use the unzip application to uncompress and unarchive.

On a Mac platform, the most common compression/archival program is StuffIt. Use the StuffIt program to uncompress and unarchive.

4. Convert your image file.

5. Examine the results of your image conversion in a suitable viewer. Edit the converted image if necessary.

6. Use the process described in How-To 10.2 to include external images in your HTML document. Use the procedures in Chapter 9, Using Images in Your Documents, to use inline images.

How It Works

Image objects are created with a variety of applications and stored in many image formats. Many applications save in a single format. This format may not be suitable for use on your World Wide Web pages.

Most image formats provide essentially the same information. Therefore, converting the different formats is only a matter of translating the information from the source format to the target format. Depending on the conversion being performed, however, the converter may perform a more complex transformation where information from the source image must be used to calculate or modify data to generate the target.

You may want images in different formats for several reasons. First, if you wish to include an inline image, the image must be stored in GIF or JPEG format. Therefore, the first reason you might need an image converter is to generate a GIF or JPEG image from an image in some other format. Once you have converted the image to GIF or JPEG, you can include the image inline using the `<IMG>` element, as described in Chapter 9, or as an external image, by including a reference to the image using an anchor, as specified in How-To 10.2.

Further, you may want to use a converter program to generate thumbnail images to provide a preview of images that can be seen with a viewer. To do this, use the editing capabilities of the converter to shrink the entire image or to clip a relevant portion. Save the new image or image portion as a GIF or JPEG image. Include the new thumbnail as an inline image in an anchor element. For example, if you have a 2MB JPEG image of an owl, and you create a 15KB GIF thumbnail version of the same image, you could include the following code as a link to the original image:

```
<A HREF="http://www.mysite.edu/images/owl.jpeg">
<IMG SRC="http://www.mysite.edu/images/owl.gif" ALT="Owl Image" ALIGN=bottom>
(2 MB JPEG)
</A>
```

Finally, you may want to remove inline images and provide access to them via an external viewer. The GIF format might not be the most compact of formats for the particular image. You can use a converter to store the image in a variety of formats and determine which will be the most efficient external image. The time it takes to download a particular page has an impact upon the usability of that page by a reader. If your page takes an excessively long time to retrieve, the reader is less likely to wait for the download to complete and is very unlikely to visit the page again.

Comments

Several of the packages mentioned in Table 10-2 allow you to edit and modify the images you convert. You can use these features to fine-tune the image and to generate an altered version of the image. You may want to generate thumbnail images for use as links to other media types such as movie segments or audio.

When you convert an image file, make sure that you provide the correct filename extension on the newly generated image file. The filename extension is used by servers and browsers to determine the type of data being accessed. Table 10-3 lists the common filename extensions for a variety of image types. The final column displays the Multipurpose Internet Mail Extensions (MIME) types that browsers and servers use to send information on image types.

Table 10-3 Image file formats and common filename extensions

IMAGE FORMAT	FILENAME EXTENSION	MIME TYPE
GIF	.gif	image/gif
Image exchange format	.ief	image/ief
JPEG	.jpeg, .jpg, .jpe	image/jpeg
PICT	.pict, .pct	image/pict
TIFF	.tiff, .tif	image/tiff
Portable Image	.pnm	image/x-portable-anymap
Portable Bitmap	.pbm	image/x-portable-bitmap
Portable Graymap	.pgm	image/x-portable-graymap
Portable Pixmap	.ppm	image/x-portable-pixmap
RGB	.rgb	image/x-rgb
X Window-Dump	.xwd	image/x-xwindowdump
X Bitmap	.xbm	image/x-xbitmap
X Pixelmap	.xpm	image/x-xpixmap

Appendix C, Multipurpose Internet Mail Extensions (MIME), provides more complete information about the use of MIME types in the World Wide Web environment.

COMPLEXITY

INTERMEDIATE

10.4 How do I...
Insert a video?

COMPATIBILITY: HTML

Problem

I want to include movie segments in my HTML 3.2 documents. However, HTML does not directly support the inclusion of video. Is there a way to provide access to my video object from my HTML 3.2 documents?

Technique

You cannot insert video segments directly into standard HTML 3.2 documents, but you can include links to video files. The movie object is retrieved and displayed by a helper application.

You can acquire a video object in one of three ways:

- Download an existing clip
- Copy royalty-free clip video (much like clip art packages)
- Create video clips yourself

The first two approaches are easiest; archives and CD-ROM clip libraries are widespread. The last option requires access to more specialized hardware and software. If you have access to such equipment, familiarize yourself thoroughly with the documentation provided with your hardware and software before you begin.

Steps

The following procedure lets you create links to video files. Depending on your editor, you can either insert the appropriate tags manually or use the macro or menu features of your editor. In either case, the HTML document will contain the appropriate anchor element. These directions assume you are using a text editor to add the element.

1. Open the HTML document you want to edit.

2. Locate the position where you want to place the link to the desired video object. Move the cursor to this location.

3. Insert the anchor text between the opening and closing anchor tags. An example is

```
The flight (10MB MPEG Video) of the owl is quite graceful.
```

4. Place the insertion point where you want the anchor to begin. Insert an opening anchor tag at this location. Minimally, this should include the URL where the image file is located, using the **HREF** attribute. The following example shows an opening anchor tag.

```
The <A HREF="http://www.mysite.edu/images/flight.mpeg">flight (10MB MPEG
Video) of the owl is quite graceful.
```

5. Move your insertion point to the end of the enclosed text. Insert a closing tag. The following example shows the full anchor element and surrounding text.

```
The <A HREF="http://www.mysite.edu/images/flight.mpeg">flight</A> (10MB MPEG
Video) of the owl is quite graceful.
```

6. Save your document, or return to step 2 to continue adding elements.

How It Works

HTML 3.2 does not directly support the inclusion of digital video. The digital video category includes both animations and movie clips. You can include video objects in an HTML document through links to the desired video file. The browser uses an external viewer to display the movie segment. Figure 10-4 shows a browser and the helper application used to display a video object.

When you create a link to a video clip, include the size and type specifications for the video clip referenced in or near the anchor text. The reader uses this information to determine whether he or she wants to download and view the referenced video clip.

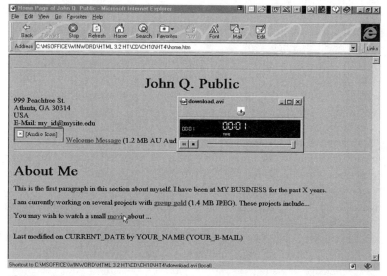

Figure 10-4 Browser and movie viewer helper application

You may also use a thumbnail image to indicate the content of the video. You could even convert the first frame of the video clip to a GIF image file and reduce it; then you could include it in your document as a link to the video clip. This may not be easy with some MPEG files due to compression. MPEG file compression works by storing the difference between two frames rather than storing the identical portions of the frames twice; therefore, extracting a single frame may require the processing of all preceding frames. For example, if you have a movie clip of an owl in flight, you could use a thumbnail of an owl to provide visual information describing the content of the movie. One example of how this could be done in HTML is

```
<A HREF="http://www.mysite.edu/images/owl.mpeg">
<IMG SRC="http://www.mysite.edu/images/owl.gif" ALT="Owl Image" ALIGN=bottom>
(10 MB MPEG)
</A>
```

When a user activates a link to a video file, the browser requests the specified file. The server responds with both type and data information from the requested movie file. When a browser receives this information, it displays the movie with the helper application appropriate for the movie type.

Therefore, you must install video files on your Web site or have your Web administrator install them. When these files are properly installed, you can create links to them using the standard HTML 3.2 anchor element. Install video objects in either MPEG or QuickTime format. These formats are the most widely supported by browsers in any computer platform.

Comments

Chapter 8, Establishing Links, provides a detailed discussion of the use of the HTML 3.2 anchor element. Appendix A, HTML Quick Reference, provides a handy reference to this element and a list of valid attributes. You should see How-To 10.1 for a general discussion of including external objects, as well as an example within a complete HTML document.

Both the browser accessing the video file and the server providing the files must be configured properly. Your Web site administrator is responsible for the proper server configuration. Instructions for configuring server support for video clips are provided in How-To 12.6.

In addition, browsers that are intended to access video files must have a video helper application installed and configured. The way you configure your browser to support helper applications differs from browser to browser. You might need to edit a configuration file used by the browser, or you might need to enter the proper information by selecting a Preferences (or similar) option from one of your browser menus. Read your browser's documentation to determine the procedure for configuring your browser to use helper applications for movie files.

The following table lists some video players you can use. You need suitable hardware, a viewer, and a properly configured browser to view video files. This list is not comprehensive. If a suggested application does not meet your needs, you should use a Web search engine to attempt to find a more suitable helper application.

PLATFORM	APPLICATION (FORMATS)	LOCATION
Mac	Sparkle (MPEG)	ftp://sumex-aim.stanford.edu/
		info-mac/gst/mov/sparkle-*.hqx
Mac	SimplePlayer	ftp://ftp.ncsa.uiuc.edu/Mosaic/
		Mac/Helpers/Simple_Player.hqx
PC	Mpegplay (MPEG)	http://www.winsite.com/info/pc/
		win3/desktop/mpegw32g.zip
PC	Qtw (QuickTime)	ftp://winftp.cica.indiana.edu/
		pub/pc/win3/desktop/qtw*.zip
UNIX	xanim (MPEG, QuickTime)	ftp://crl.dec.com/pub/X11/
		contrib/applications/
UNIX	mpeg_play (MPEG)	ftp://tr-ftp.cs.berkeley.edu/
		pub/multimedia/mpeg/mpeg-play*.tar.Z

Several browsers support nonstandard means for directly including video files within a Web page. Chapter 18, Direct Inclusion of Multimedia Objects, introduces you to the use of these inclusion mechanisms.

COMPLEXITY
ADVANCED

10.5 How do I...
Convert among video file formats?

COMPATIBILITY: HTML

Problem

My video files are not as generically useful across computer platforms as I want them to be. I need to convert my movie files to a more useful format.

Technique

MPEG and QuickTime are the most common video formats on the World Wide Web. If you have Windows AVI format movies or Macintosh-specific QuickTime clips, you must convert them to either MPEG or "flattened" QuickTime. Macintosh-specific QuickTime movies exploit certain features of the Macintosh hardware and software; "flattening" a QuickTime movie removes these dependencies so that the movie supports cross-platform viewing.

Steps

The next procedure outlines the process for acquiring converters and using them to convert video files. These converters accept video files in a particular format and save them in a different video file format.

The process requires a familiarity with the use of anonymous FTP or FTP URLs. Your first task is to identify an appropriate converter. Next, you must acquire the converter and apply it to your existing documents. Finally, you should examine the result of the conversion process prior to installing the converter.

1. Determine the format of your video files and the format to which you want to convert.

2. Find a suitable converter. Table 10-4 lists some software packages and points to their location on the Internet. If you cannot find a converter that meets your needs in the table, use a Web search engine to find a suitable converter.

Table 10-4 Common video format conversion applications

VIDEO FORMAT	CONVERTERS	LOCATION
MPEG to QuickTime	Sparkle (Mac)	ftp://sumex-aim.stanford.edu/
		info-mac/gst/mov/sparkle-*.hqx
QuickTime to MPEG	Qt2Mpeg (Mac)	http://www.prism.uvsq.fr/public/wos/
		multimedia/files/qt2mpeg.sit.hqx
AVI, QuickTime	Mac Video for	http://www.prism.uvsq.fr/public/
	Windows (MAC)	wos/multimedia/files/vfw11.sit
QuickTime "flattener"	Flatten MooV (Mac)	ftp://sumex-aim.stanford.edu/
		info-mac/gst/mov/flatmoov.hqx
AVI to MPEG	XingCD (PC)	Xing Technology
QuickTime, AVI	SoundCap (PC)	ftp://ftp.intel.com/pub/IAL/
		Indeo_video/indeo/utilities/smartv.exe
QuickTime "flattener"	QFlat (PC)	ftp://venice.tcp.com/pub/anime-manga/
		software/viewers/qtfat.zip
QuickTime to MPEG	Qt2Mpeg (UNIX)	http://www.prism.uvsq.fr/public/wos/
		multimedia/files/qt2mpeg.zip

3. Acquire an appropriate converter package from an FTP site or software store. Install the converter application, as appropriate for your platform.

4. Convert your video files.

5. Use a viewer to examine the video files. The displayed video should be very close to the original. If there are notable flaws, edit or convert the original to create a suitable video file in the correct format.

6. Use the process described in How-To 10.4 to include videos in HTML 3.2 documents.

How It Works

The video clips that you find or create come in different formats, but for generic use on the World Wide Web, you want these objects in either QuickTime ("flattened") or MPEG format. Currently, viewers for these formats are available across multiple platforms.

If your clips are in another format, you should acquire an appropriate converter and convert them to a suitable format. Then view these files using a suitable helper application to assure that information was not lost or significantly altered in the conversion process.

If you have access to a video editing application, you may wish to adjust your videos. For MPEG video, you can use the MpegUtil program available for the UNIX platform (`http://www.comp.lancs.ac.uk/computing/users/phillip/mpegUtil.html`). The Adobe Premiere program serves as an editor for QuickTime movies on both the Macintosh and PC/Windows platforms (`http://www.adobe.com/prodindex/premiere/main.html`). Also, a shareware application called QuickEditor for QuickTime editing is available for the Macintosh (`http://www.umich.edu/~archive/mac/powermac/` or `ftp://sumex-aim.stanford.edu/info-mac/gst/mov/`).

Once you are satisfied with the results of the conversion or editing, you are ready to install the documents on your Web site. You now should be able to make your video files accessible by referencing them in anchor elements, as described in How-To 10.4.

Comments

Even if your files are in a suitable format, you must decide whether you want to provide video, and if so, in which format(s). The biggest limitation for MPEG video is that, although the MPEG format does support an audio track, most players do not. Until recently, the QuickTime standard was viewed primarily as a Macintosh-specific format, which limited the availability of viewers for other platforms. Further, the requirement that QuickTime movies be "flattened" for cross-platform use adds an additional step in the development process. Weigh these factors when deciding on the format that you ultimately use.

When you convert a video file, make sure you provide the correct filename extension for the newly generated video file. The filename extension is used by servers and browsers to determine the format of the file. Table 10-5 lists the common filename extensions for a variety of video file types. Browsers and servers communicate data type information using Multipurpose Internet Mail Extension (MIME) types; the MIME types for several video file formats appear as well.

Table 10-5 Video file formats and common filename extensions

IMAGE FORMAT	FILENAME EXTENSION	MIME TYPE
Microsoft Video Format	`.avi`	`video/msvideo`
MPEG Format Video	`.mpeg, .mpg, .mpe`	`video/mpeg`
QuickTime Format Video	`.qt, .mov`	`video/quicktime`

Appendix C, Multipurpose Internet Mail Extensions (MIME), provides more complete information on the use of MIME types on the World Wide Web.

COMPLEXITY
BEGINNING

10.6 How do I...
Insert a sound file?

COMPATIBILITY: HTML

Problem

I would like to include sound clips in my home page. How can I provide links to sound files?

Technique

HTML does not allow you to include audio files in your pages. However, you can create a link to an application that will play a specified sound file.

The most commonly used audio file type on the World Wide Web is SUN's AU audio file format. The AU standard supports several types of encoding for sound samples. The most prevalent sample encoding is 8-bit μ-law. The sound quality derived from this encoding is not as high as with other formats, but use of other formats such as AIFF, IFF, WAV, or MPEG audio yields audio segments that are not as portable. As multiplatform support grows for these other sound formats, the usage of the formats that provide higher quality audio will also increase.

Steps

The following instructions let you create links to sound files in your HTML documents. This procedure assumes that you use a text editor to edit your page. If this is not the case, consult your editor's documentation to determine any necessary changes in the procedure.

1. Open the HTML document you want to edit in your favorite text editor.

2. Place the insert cursor at the position where you want to create a link to the desired sound file.

3. Insert the text that you want to enclose in the anchor element. When transferring large files, you should specify the file size to warn the reader. An example of such a message is

```
Hoot of an Owl (2 MB AU Audio)
```

4. Position the insertion point where you want the anchor element to begin. Insert an opening anchor tag at this point. Minimally, this tag should include the URL where the sound file is located. Use the **HREF** attribute to specify this value. The following example shows the insertion of an opening anchor tag.

```
<A HREF=http://www.mysite.edu/sounds/owl.au>Hoot of an Owl (2 MB AU Audio)
```

5. Move the insertion point to the end of the enclosed text. Insert a closing anchor tag. The next example shows a complete anchor element linking to a sound file.

```
<A HREF=http://www.mysite.edu/sounds/owl.au>Hoot of an Owl</A> (2 MB AU ⇐
Audio)
```

6. You can also use a thumbnail image to indicate the nature of the audio file. For example, if you have an audio clip of an owl hooting, you could use a thumbnail image of an owl to provide a visual cue to what the audio file contains, as in the following example.

```
<A HREF="http://www.mysite.edu/sounds/owl.au">
<IMG SRC="http://www.mysite.edu/images/owl.gif" ALT="Owl Image" ALIGN=bottom>
(2 MB AU Audio)
</A>
```

7. You can also use an icon to indicate the type of object rather than its content. The following code might be used to include an icon for the same audio file.

```
<A HREF=http://www.mysite.edu/sounds/owl.au>
<IMG SRC="http://www.mysite.edu/icons/sound.bmp" ALT="Sound Icon" ⇐
ALIGN=bottom>Hoot</A>  of an Owl (2 MB AU Audio)
```

8. Save your document, or continue adding elements by returning to step 2.

How It Works

When you create a link to a large file, such as an audio clip, you should include in the text near the anchor, or as part of it, the size and type of the file. The reader can use this information to decide whether the file is a suitable size and format to retrieve.

When the reader selects a link, it triggers the retrieval of the object specified in the anchor element. If the request is successful, the server sends a response containing both the type of the requested file (audio/*) and the file itself (audio data).

To perform this task, the server maintains a database that maps filename extensions to information types. If you use audio files on your Web site, make sure you use the proper filename extensions. Chapter 12, Server Basics, provides information on configuring your server to properly transmit sound files.

When a browser receives a file from the server, the browser determines how to display the object based on the type of the file. Most browsers only process pure text and HTML documents in their display window. Other types of information are presented to the reader by prespecified helper applications.

Comments

Chapter 7, Managing Document Spacing, provides a detailed discussion of the various attributes that might be used with the anchor element.

To be served and rendered correctly, both the browser accessing the object and the server providing the audio object must be configured properly. Your Web site administrator will be responsible for the proper configuration of your server. Instructions for configuring server support for audio are provided in How-To 12.6.

Configuring a browser to support audio usually requires either modifying configuration files or changing a list of helper programs in the browser's menu. Consult your browser's documentation to determine how to configure helper applications for playing audio files. Several browsers support nonstandard means for directly including video files within a Web page. Chapter 18, Direct Inclusion of Multimedia Objects, introduces you to the use of these inclusion mechanisms.

Table 10-6 lists some audio players suitable for use as helper applications. You will need suitable hardware such as a sound card and speakers or headphones, a program that plays sound files, and a browser that is configured to support audio.

Table 10-6 Common audio player helper applications

PLATFORM	APPLICATION	LOCATION
Mac	SoundMachine (AU, AIFF, AIF)	`ftp://ftp.ncsa.uiuc.edu/Mosaic/Mac/`
		`HelpersSoundMachine.sit.hqx`
PC	WHAM (AU, WAV, AIFF, IFF)	`ftp://ftp.ncsa.uiuc.edu/Mosaic/Windows/`
		`viewers/wham*.zip`
UNIX	showaudio (Metamail)	`ftp://thumper.bellcore.com/pub/nsb/`
	(AU, AIFF, AIF)	

This is not a comprehensive list. Should a suggested application not meet your needs, use a Web search engine such as Lycos (`http://lycos.cs.cmu.edu`) to find a more suitable helper application.

COMPLEXITY
ADVANCED

10.7 How do I...
Convert among audio file formats?

COMPATIBILITY: HTML

Problem

I want to save my homemade audio files in a format that most Web users can access. How do I do this?

Technique

You can acquire audio files in several ways:

- You can digitally record voice data through a microphone connected to many multimedia computer systems.

- You can use royalty-free audio clips from purchased packages.

- You can download audio files from bulletin boards or the Internet.

- With appropriate hardware and software, you can digitally record sound directly from a CD-ROM reader.

Audio files come in several formats. The most popular audio format used in the World Wide Web environment is SUN's AU. If you have audio in other formats, you may want to convert them to AU.

If AU sound quality is sufficient for your task, you should convert your sound file to the AU format. If you require higher quality, the two standards most commonly used, other than the AU format files, are the AIFF and WAV formats. Audio files stored in these formats are likely to have better sound quality than AU files.

The price of using WAV or AIFF formats rather than AU is reduced portability. If a browser supports audio, it most likely supports the AU format. In addition, the higher quality audio usually requires more storage, resulting in a longer transmission time. This is a particular disadvantage for people with slow Internet connections.

Once you decide on the format you want to use, acquire the appropriate converter and convert your audio files. You should then play these audio files using a suitable helper application to assure that information was not lost or significantly altered in the conversion process.

Once you are satisfied with the results of the conversion, you are ready to install the documents on your Web site. You now should be able to access these audio information objects through appropriately constructed anchor elements, as described in How-To 10.4.

The process requires a familiarity with the use of anonymous FTP or FTP URLs. You must first identify an appropriate converter. Next, acquire the converter and apply it to your existing documents. Finally, you should examine the result of the conversion process prior to installing the converter.

Steps

The following shows you how to acquire converters and use them to convert audio files.

1. Determine the source and target file format of your audio information object.

2. Find the converter that you will need to use. Table 10-7 gives examples of some of these environments by software package and pointers to information concerning them. If you cannot find the file formats and/or platforms that you require in Table 10-7, you may want to use a Web search application to find an appropriate converter.

Table 10-7 Common audio format conversion applications

AUDIO FILE FORMAT	CONVERTERS	LOCATION
WAV, SND, AIFF	SoundApp (Mac)	ftp://sumex-aim.stanford.edu/
		info-mac/snd/util/
SND to AU	μ-law (Mac)	ftp://sumex-aim.stanford.edu/
		info-mac/snd/util/
AU, WAV, AIFF, SND	SOX (UNIX/PC)	ftp://ftp.cs.ruu.nl/pub/MIDI/PROGRAMS/

3. Use anonymous FTP or an FTP URL to acquire an appropriate converter package. Uncompress, unarchive, and install the converter application as appropriate for your platform.

4. Apply the converter to your source audio files.

5. Use the process described in How-To 10.6 to include audio objects.

How It Works

The file formats available store sound as digital samples of the sound rather than the original analog signal—that is, like a CD rather than a record—and the size of the sample stored in part determines its quality.

Oftentimes audio file conversions are lossy; when converting from a higher quality format to a lower one, loss of information occurs, particularly if the source uses 16-bit encoding and the target uses 8-bit, or the source is stereo and the target is mono. In these cases, you can only convert the file in one direction. Attempting to reverse the process will lead to audio segments in the original file format, but with significantly reduced sound quality.

Sound editors will allow you to modify sound files. Use such tools to tailor sounds or to mask out distortions. The WHAM application specified in Table 10-6 provides extensive sound editing capabilities for the PC platform. PlayerPro allows the same kind of audio editing on the Macintosh platform.

Comments

After generating a new audio file, make sure you save the file with the correct filename extension. The filename extension specifies the type of file being accessed. Table 10-8 lists the common filename extensions for a variety of video information object types. Servers and browsers use Multipurpose Internet Mail Extension (MIME) types to pass information concerning transmitted files.

Table 10-8 Audio file formats and common filename extensions

AUDIO FORMAT	FILENAME EXTENSION	MIME TYPE
AU 8-bit, μ-law	.au, .snd	audio/basic
AIFF	.aiff, .aif	audio/x-aiff
Microsoft Audio	.wav	audio/x-wav
RealAudio	.ra, .ram	audio/x-pn-realaudio
RealAudio plug-in	.rpm	audio/x-pn-realaudio-plugin

Appendix C, Multipurpose Internet Mail Extensions (MIME), provides more complete information on the use of MIME types in the World Wide Web environment.

COMPLEXITY
INTERMEDIATE

10.8 How do I...
Include a PostScript document?

COMPATIBILITY: HTML

Problem

I have a document archive consisting of a set of PostScript files. I need to keep these documents in this format so I can print them when required. Converting all of them to HTML 3.2 would mean that I would have to maintain the integrity of both sets of documents when changes are made. Can I provide access to my existing archive through HTML documents?

Technique

PostScript is one of the most commonly used printer languages. You can develop and maintain PostScript documents using many different applications. To avoid converting PostScript documents to HTML and maintaining two independent document sets containing the same information, you can use only the original PostScript files.

The disadvantage of this approach is that PostScript documents do not support hypermedia links. The advantages are that the documents are ready to print and that only one set of documents needs to be updated. You will need to decide whether to store your documents as PostScript, HTML, or both.

You can create a link to a PostScript file in an HTML document rather than converting the PostScript file to an HTML document. (See How-To 2.3 for information about document conversion.) When a reader selects the link, the browser retrieves the PostScript file and displays it in a suitable viewer. You need not convert your PostScript documents to HTML to allow World Wide Web access, thus obviating the need to have two sets of the same documents.

When creating a link to a PostScript document, you should indicate in or near the text of the anchor element that the object referenced is a PostScript document. If a reader's browsing environment will not render PostScript documents, then he or she does not need to bother trying to trigger the link. Further, you should specify the approximate length of the document referenced. This allows individuals with a slow network connection to make an informed decision about whether or not to trigger the link.

Steps

The following procedure shows how to link a PostScript file to your HTML documents. If you are creating HTML pages using an editor other than a text editor, consult your documentation to determine the correct procedure for adding an anchor element.

1. Open the HTML document you want to edit in your favorite text editor.

2. Move the cursor to the position where you want to add a link to a PostScript file.

3. Insert the text that you want enclosed between the opening and closing anchor tags.

4. Move your insertion point to where you want the anchor to begin, and then insert an opening anchor tag. The **HREF** attribute of this tag should specify the URL of the PostScript file. The following example shows an opening tag for such an anchor element.

```
Printer ready version of this document is
<A HREF="http://www.mysite.edu/papers/owl.ps">available. (1.2 MB)
```

5. Insert a closing anchor tag after the enclosed text. The next example shows a complete anchor element of this type.

```
Printer ready version of this document is
<A HREF="http://www.mysite.edu/papers/owl.ps">available</A>. (1.2 MB)
```

6. You can use an icon in the anchor to indicate the type of the linked file. The following code might be used to include an icon for the same PostScript file.

```
Printer ready version of this document is
<A HREF="http://www.mysite.edu/papers/owl.ps">available
<IMG SRC="http://www.mysite.edu/icons/psdoc.gif" ALT="PostScript Icon"
ALIGN=bottom>
</A>. (1.2 MB)
```

7. Save your document, or continue adding elements. Add additional links to PostScript files by returning to step 2.

How It Works

Select a link to request the file specified in the anchor element. If the request is successful, the server sends a response containing both the file's Multipurpose Internet Mail Extension (MIME) type (application/PostScript) and the file itself.

To perform this task, the server maintains a database that maps filename extensions to MIME types. Therefore, if you use PostScript files on your Web site, make sure you use the proper filename extensions. Chapter 12, Server Basics, provides more information on configuring servers to support PostScript documents.

When a browser receives a PostScript file from the server, it determines how to display the file based upon the MIME type sent by the server. Most browsers only directly display pure text and HTML documents. Helper applications display other information types, such as PostScript documents. Figure 10-5 shows the results of triggering a link to a PostScript document.

Comments

Chapter 8, Establishing Links, provides a detailed discussion of HTML hypertext links. This How-To only uses the **HREF** attribute of the anchor element, but you may want to include others as you see fit.

To provide access to PostScript documents on a server, you must properly configure the server to transmit PostScript files. Your Web site administrator is responsible for the proper configuration of your server; instructions for configuring a server to support PostScript documents are provided in How-To 12.6.

In addition, any browser that wants to access the PostScript documents must also be configured for direct rendering, or more likely for using a helper application, to display the file. Consult your browser's documentation to determine the procedure for configuring helper applications for PostScript files.

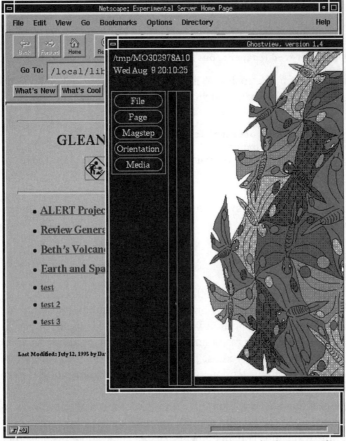

Figure 10-5 Browser and PostScript viewer helper application

The next table lists some PostScript viewers for several platforms. To view PostScript files, you will need suitable hardware, a helper application, and a browser configured to view PostScript documents.

PLATFORM	APPLICATION	LOCATION
Mac	mac-ghost	`ftp://sumex-aim.stanford.edu/info-mac/gst/grf/`
PC	gsview	`ftp://ftp.ncsa.uiuc.edu/Web/Mosaic/Windows/`
		`viewers/gsview` and `gs*exe`(both required)
UNIX	ghostview	`ftp://ftp.cs.wisc.edu/pub/ghost/gnu/ghostview*.gz`
	ghostscript	`ghostscript*.gz`
	ghostscript fonts	`ghostscript-fonts*.gz`

This is not a comprehensive list. If a suggested application does not meet your needs, you can use a Web search engine to find a more suitable helper application.

COMPLEXITY
INTERMEDIATE

10.9 How do I...
Include a device-independent (DVI) file?

COMPATIBILITY: HTML

Problem

Most of my previous documents have been developed using the TeX formatting language. DVI files are generated by processing TeX documents. I have an archive of all my DVI files ready to print, and I would like to use HTML documents to provide online access to this archive. I don't want to have to maintain both the HTML and DVI documents. Is there a way I can use the DVI files without converting the entire archive to HTML?

Technique

TeX files can be converted to HTML documents. (See How-To 2.3 for information about converting documents.) However, two separate sets of documents would require twice as much maintenance. You can maintain a single set of TeX documents with their associated DVI files ready. These DVI files then can be accessed from HTML documents.

To accomplish this, create a link that, when selected, causes the browser to retrieve the DVI file and present it to the reader via a suitable viewer.

Steps

The way you include an external object, such as a DVI file, in your HTML page depends on the editing environment used to create the document. These steps assume that you manually insert the anchor element with a text editor. For other editor types, consult your editor's documentation on how to add anchor elements.

The following step-by-step procedure shows how to create a link to a DVI file.

1. Open the HTML document you wish to edit in your text editor.

2. Position the cursor where you want to add the DVI file.

3. Insert the text that you want enclosed in the anchor element.

4. Move the cursor to where you want the anchor element to begin, and insert an opening anchor tag. Set the **HREF** attribute in this tag to the URL of the DVI file that you want to include. The following example shows such an opening tag.

```
Device Independent (DVI) version of this document is
<A HREF="http://www.mysite.edu/papers/owl.dvi">available. (2 MB)
```

5. Move the insertion point to the end of the anchor text. Insert a closing anchor tag. The following code shows a complete anchor element linking to a DVI file.

```
Device Independent (DVI) version of this document is
<A HREF="http://www.mysite.edu/papers/owl.dvi">available</A>. (2 MB)
```

6. You can use an icon in the anchor to indicate the type of the linked file. The following code might be used to include an icon for the same DVI file.

```
Printer ready version of this document is
<A HREF="http://www.mysite.edu/papers/owl.dvi">available
<IMG SRC="http://www.mysite.edu/icons/dvidoc.gif" ALT="DVI Icon" ALIGN=bottom>
</A>. (2 MB)
```

7. Save your document, or continue adding elements by returning to step 2.

How It Works

Prior to WYSIWYG style editors, formatted documents were developed using tags to mark the various formatted elements in the documents. Various document formatting languages were developed for this purpose: troff, runoff, and TeX. The TeX formatting language provided such features as incorporation of mathematical expressions, tabular formatting, font changes, and a host of additional features.

The TeX application creates DVI files when it processes source files. You can use the DVI files to display or print the formatted document in any number of environments. In most cases, the DVI file needs to be translated to the display device's particular formatting language.

For those who wish to provide access to their TeX documents on the World Wide Web, there are two options.

The first option is to convert the TeX documents to HTML. This approach leads to two sets of documents, each of which requires maintenance when one document is altered. In addition, HTML does not support all the capabilities of TeX.

The second approach is to maintain the original TeX documents and generate new DVI files as the TeX documents are updated. In this way, the documents are maintained only once and the DVI files are available to be shown on any display capable of processing a DVI file, as well as being accessible via links in HTML documents.

Selecting the link initiates a server request for the DVI file specified in the anchor element. If the request is successful, the server issues a response containing both the data type and the data itself.

To do so, the server maintains a database that maps filename extensions to information types. Therefore, if DVI files are installed on your Web site, be sure you use the proper filename extensions. Chapter 12, Server Basics, provides information on configuring a server to support DVI files.

When a browser receives a DVI file from the server, it determines how to display the file based on the type of information provided by the server. Most browsers only directly support pure text and HTML documents in their display windows. Information of other types is displayed by prespecified helper applications. Figure 10-6 shows the result of activating a link to a DVI file.

Figure 10-6 Browser and DVI viewer helper application

Comments

HTML 3.2 anchor elements support a variety of attributes, though this How-To only makes use of the HREF attribute. For your purposes, you may need to use other attributes. Chapter 8, Establishing Links, provides detailed information on HTML 3 anchor elements.

While not as common as the other media types described in this chapter, DVI files require both server and browser configuration. Your Web site administrator is responsible for the proper configuration of your server. How-To 12.6 provides instructions for configuring server support for DVI files.

In addition to having your Web site administrator configure the server, you need to configure browsers to support DVI files. Consult the documentation for your browser to determine the procedure for configuring helper applications such as a DVI viewer.

The following table lists some suitable DVI viewers for use as helper applications. You must have suitable hardware, a DVI viewer, and a browser that is configured properly.

PLATFORM	APPLICATION	LOCATION
Mac	dvi-preview	http://www.tex.ac.uk/
		tex-archive/systems/mac/cmactex/
PC	TrueTex (Commercial)	http://styx.ios.com/
		~kinch/truetex.html
UNIX	xdvi	ftp://export.lcs.mit.edu/
		contrib/applications/

This list is not comprehensive. If a suggested application does not meet your needs, use a Web search engine to find a more suitable helper application.

COMPLEXITY
BEGINNING

10.10 How do I...
Find a VRML browser?

COMPATIBILITY: VRML

Problem

While surfing the Web, I have found sites providing 3D information. I need a viewer to explore and examine these 3D models and virtual worlds. How can I find a VRML browser?

Technique

The Virtual Reality Modeling Language (VRML, pronounced "vermel") provides a platform-independent means of specifying three-dimensional models and constructs. Servers can easily distribute such models across the World Wide Web. In fact, specific constructs in the language provide the ability to create links to other worlds or Web pages.

VRML documents are becoming increasingly more abundant on the World Wide Web. Consequently, a need for VRML viewers has developed, driving the creation of numerous products running on a variety of hardware and software platforms.

Figure 10-7 shows a world rendered using a VRML viewer integrated into a browser. Figure 10-8 displays a world using a standalone VRML viewer.

Steps

The following procedure shows how to acquire a VRML browser and configure your Web browser to recognize VRML worlds.

1. Examine Table 10-9 to find a VRML viewer to meet your hardware and software requirements.

2. Download or purchase the VRML viewer you have selected.

Figure 10-7 VRML world using plug-in

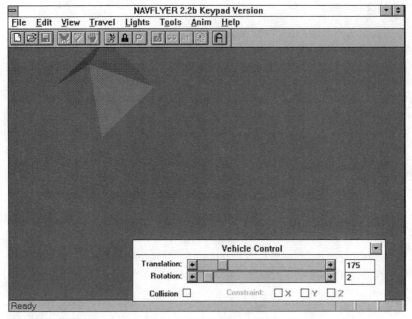

Figure 10-8 VMRL World using standalone viewer

3. Follow the applicable installation instruction for your VRML viewer.

4. If the VRML viewer's installation process does not automatically configure your Web browser, configure your browser to launch this viewer when it receives a document with the MIME type x-world/x-vrml. (For more information on MIME types, see Appendix C, Multipurpose Internet Mail Extensions [MIME].) This configuration process is browser-specific.

How It Works

Web servers transmit VRML worlds in the same way that they transmit any other objects, such as audio files. The server signals the browser that it is sending a VRML world. The browser recognizes this signal and runs an appropriate VRML viewer.

A large variety of VRML browsers have been developed recently. Table 10-9 lists several available VRML viewers by software and hardware type.

Table 10-9 VRML browsers

PLATFORM	VRML BROWSER	URL
cross-platform	VRweb	http://www.iicm.tu-graz.ac.at/Cvrweb
cross-platform	WebSpace	http://www.sgi.com/Products/
		WebFORCE/WebSpace/

PLATFORM	VRML BROWSER	URL
Mac/PowerMac	Virtus Voyager	`http://www.virtus.com/voyager.html`
Mac/PowerMac	VRML Equinox	`http://www.northplains.com/`
		`equiinfo.html`
Mac/QD3D	Whirlwind 3D	
	Browser	`http://www.info.apple.com/`
		`qd3d/Viewer.HTML`
PC/Windows 3.1, 95	Fountain	`http://www.caligari.com/`
PC/Windows 3.1, NT, 95	NAVFlyer 2.2b	`ftp://yoda.fdt.net/pub/users/m/micgreen`
PC/Windows 3.1, NT, 95	VR Scout	`http://www.chaco.com/vrscout/`
PC/Windows 3.1, NT, 95	WorldView	`http://www.webmaster.com/vrml`
PC/Windows NT, 95	GLView	`http://www.snafu.de/~hg/`
PC/Windows NT, 95	VRealm	`http://www.idsnet.com/ids/vrealm.html`
SGI/IRIX 5.2	i3D	`http://www.crs4.it/~3diadm/`
		`i3d-announce.html`
SGI/X-Window	WebView	`http://www.sdsc.edu/projects/`
		`vrml/tools/webview/`
		`help/webview_building_v1.0b1.html`
SGI,SUN/X-Window	WebOOGL	`http://www.geom.umn.edu/software/`
		`weboogl/`

Comments

VRML worlds and associated image files may be large, so do not be too surprised at experiencing delays if you are accessing the Web over a 14.4K modem. For additional information on viewers and VRML software, see URL `http://rosebud.sdsc.edu/vrml`.

COMPLEXITY
INTERMEDIATE

10.11 How do I...
Create a VRML document?

COMPATIBILITY: VRML

Problem

I want to create three-dimensional spaces for the World Wide Web community to visit. How does the Virtual Reality Modeling Language (VRML) provide this capability? How do I author VRML documents?

Technique

You author VRML documents using either a text editor or a three-dimensional modeling application. The VRML language allows you to specify three-dimensional objects in an ASCII text file. Using a text editor, you can create a VRML document by stringing together appropriate VRML constructs. Alternatively, you can graphically create three-dimensional spaces using suitable software that saves in VRML format.

Steps

You can create VRML documents in one of two ways. You can use a VRML editing environment to graphically create three-dimensional spaces, or you can directly create a VRML document by inserting VRML constructs in a text file.

Three-Dimensional Editing Environment

Recently, a large number of three-dimensional modeling packages have been developed for the creation of VRML documents. The following procedure outlines the steps for acquiring and installing a modeler suitable for your hardware and software platform.

1. Find a modeler suitable for your software and hardware platform. Table 10-10 summarizes several available modeler packages.

Table 10-10 VRML modelers

PLATFORM	MODELER	URL
Mac	STRATA StudioPro Blitz	`http://www.strata3d.com:80/tools/`
		`studiopro/index.html`
Mac/PC	Virtus WalkThrough Pro	`http://www.virtus.com/vwtpro.html`
PC	Fountain/Caligari	`http://www.caligari.com/`
PC	Spinner	`http://www.3dweb.com/`
PC	TriSpectives	`http://www.eye.com/subhomes/freehm.htm`
PC	World Builder	`http://www.caligari.com/`
PC	Home Space Builder	`http://www.us.paragraph.com/vhsb`
SGI	Ez3d Modeler	`http://www.webcom.com/~radiance/`
SGI	WebSpace Author	`http://webspace.sgi.com/WebSpaceAuthor/`
		`index.html`

2. Download or purchase the selected software.

3. Follow the instructions provided to install your modeler software.

4. Configure your Web browser to launch this application if your modeler will also serve as your default VRML viewer.

5. Open your modeler application and create your three-dimensional model.

6. Save your model to a file with the `.wrl` filename extension. If your modeler supports a variety of formats, select VRML.

Text Editor Creation

VRML documents contain standard ASCII text. This text represents the various constructs available through VRML. The following steps lead you through the VRML document creation process using a text editor.

1. Open a new document in your text editor.

2. Insert the following line. This line indicates that the file contains ASCII-based VRML constructs.

```
#VRML V1.0 ascii
```

3. Add desired VRML elements until you have created your desired scene. A variety of commonly used elements appears in the How It Works section.

4. Save the document. Use the `.wrl` filename extension when you save to indicate that the file is a VRML document.

In either case, add a link to your created world from a portion of a relevant Web page, or use the nonstandard methods for direct inclusion discussed in Chapter 18, Direct Inclusion of Multimedia Objects.

How It Works

Using a modeler is the easier of the two construction methods. A modeler allows you to visually create your three-dimensional information space. You can see on the screen what your model will look like when rendered. For example, Figure 10-9 shows a scene composed of three visible objects: a cylinder, a torus, and a cube. This scene was built using the Fountain modeler. (See reference in Table 10-10.) The VRML file for this scene is available on the accompanying CD in the COMPLEX.WRL file.

The challenge you face when creating a VRML document with a 3D modeling package is learning how to draw in a three-dimensional space. If you are familiar with CAD packages or other 3D environments, the transition is fairly easy. The user interfaces of these VRML environments vary significantly. The primary source of information on these products is documentation provided online either with the package or via the Web, and your own experience with the product. As you become more comfortable with the package, your productivity and accuracy will improve.

Ultimately, when you finish building your 3D scene, you save it to a VRML file. Many modelers support a variety of output formats. For access over the World Wide Web, you should save your scene in VRML. The standard filename extension used to indicate a VRML scene is `.wrl`. Use this extension when saving each of your scenes.

You can create or modify a VRML document using a text editor. The VRML format saves 3D information in standard ASCII text and stores 3D scenes in a hierarchy

Figure 10-9 Scene created with a 3D modeler

of nodes referred to as a scene graph. The scene graph specifies both the objects in the scene and the order in which those objects are evaluated. Nodes earlier in the scene graph can affect nodes later in the scene.

Each VRML node has several general characteristics:

- *Name*: Each node can have a unique name associated with it.

- *Type*: Each node has a particular type, such as `cube` or `translation`.

- *Parameters*: Each node has a set of parameters specifying the specific characteristics of the individual node. For example, a sphere node would have a radius parameter.

- *Child nodes*: Nodes may contain other nodes, thereby creating the hierarchical structure of a scene graph.

The standard format for specifying a node in a VRML scene graph is ObjectName ObjectType { Parameters Children }. For example, the following nodes specify a scene containing a pinkish cone, a purple cube, and a perspective camera. Figure 10-10 displays this scene in a VRML browser. A pound sign (#) indicates that the remainder of a line is a comment.

```
#VRML V1.0 ascii

Separator { # 1st Grouping
    PerspectiveCamera { # Establish Perspective
        position    160 -200 430
    }

    Separator { # position, color, and place cube
```

```
    Transform { # set position
        translation 160 -200 -2
    }
    Material { # set color
        diffuseColor .3 .1 .3
    }
  Cube { # create a cube using established color at specified position
        width 100
        height 100
        depth 100
    }
}

Separator { # position, color, and place cone
    Transform { # set position
        translation 120 -80 50
    }
    Material { # set color
        diffuseColor 1 .5 .5
    }
  Cone { # create a cone using established color at specified position
        bottomRadius 50
        height 80
    }
}
}
```

This VRML source code also appears on the CD in the SIMPLE.WRL file.

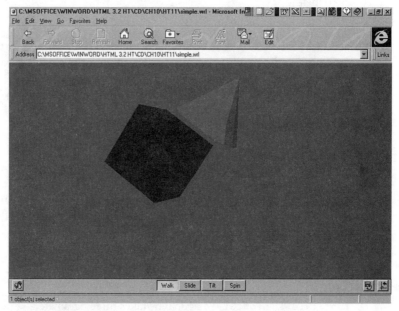

Figure 10-10 Small scene created by a text editor

A `Separator` node represents the root of the hierarchy. This node has a `PerspectiveCamera` child and two `Separator` children. The camera object indicates to the VRML browser the initial perspective of the scene. Each of the two `Separator` children contains three children: a `Transform`, specifying the base location objects, a `Material`, specifying the material used to draw objects (purple and pink, respectively), and a visible object (e.g., `Cube` and `Cone`).

VRML nodes fall into four broad categories: shapes, properties, groups, and WWW. The following list details several of the more widely used node types. For a complete description of VRML version 1, see URL `http://rosebud.sdsc.edu/vrml`, or check out *VRML Construction Kit* (Waite Group Press). Lengths and distances in VRML are measured in scaled meters.

Shapes

- `AsciiText`: This object type defines a string of characters. The commonly used parameters of this type are `string` and `justification`. The `justification` property has three possible values: `LEFT`, `CENTER`, or `RIGHT`. For example, to create a centered string object displaying `"I love VRML"`, you could use the following object.

```
AsciiText { string "I love VRML" justification CENTER }
```

- `Cone`: This creates a cone object in the scene graph. The `height` and `bottomRadius` properties set the cone's parameters. For example, the following node describes a cone that is 20 meters high and has a base with a radius of 10 meters.

```
Cone { height 20 bottomRCadius 10 }
```

- `Cube`: Use this node type to create a cubic object. The `height`, `width`, and `depth` properties of this node need not have the same value. For example, the specification of a 40x20x20 box in VRML would appear as

```
Cube { height 40 width 20 depth 20 }
```

- `Cylinder`: A node of this type creates a cylinder in the scene graph. This shape has a `height` and a `radius` property. The following line creates a cylinder with a base radius of 5 and a height of 25.

```
Cylinder { radius 5 height 25 }
```

- `Sphere`: You can create a sphere object with this node type. The only required property of this node type is a `radius`. For example, use the following line to create a sphere of radius 75.

```
Sphere { radius 75 }
```

Properties

- `FontStyle`: The `FontStyle` node type takes three parameters: `size`, `style`, and `family`. A `FontStyle` node affects all text in objects appearing after and below it in the scene graph hierarchy until another `FontStyle` node supersedes it. The possible values of the `style` property are `NONE`, `BOLD`, and `ITALICS`. The values of `family` are `SERIF`, `SANS`, and `TYPEWRITER`. The following node sets the font to serif, bold, 10 point.

```
FontStyle { size 10 style BOLD family SERIF }
```

■ **Material**: This node describes the material used to render all shapes after and below it in the scene graph. The most commonly used property is `diffuseColor` which, specified as an RGB triplet, sets the color used to draw shapes. Each value in the color triplet ranges from `0` to `1`, indicating the intensity of the color component. For example, to color shapes red, use the following `Material` node.

```
Material { diffuseColor 1 0 0 }
```

■ **Transform**: This node establishes the relative location used to place shapes appearing below or after the `Transform` node in the scene graph. Two useful properties of this node type are `translation` and `scaleFactor`. The following node sets the translation to four meters in the positive x direction and scaling of two in the y direction only. (In scaling, `x` and `z` values are set to one to indicate no scaling.)

```
Transform { translation 4 0 0 scaleFactor 1 2 1 }
```

■ **PerspectiveCamera**: A `PerspectiveCamera` node establishes a viewpoint for the scene. If only one such camera is specified, browsers often take this as the initial view of the scene. The most commonly set property of this node type is `position`, specifying the location of the camera. The following camera is positioned at x, y, z coordinates 25, 72, -200.

```
PerspectiveCamera { position 25 72 -200 }
```

Group

■ **Group**: This node contains an ordered list of other VRML nodes. The property nodes accumulate as they are traversed in the order. This accumulated information is passed back to the parent of the group node in the scene graph.

```
Group {
    ...          # object 1
    ...          # object 2
}
```

■ **Separator**: A separator node is like a group node. It contains an ordered list of child nodes. The difference between a separator and a group is that the accumulated property information in a separator is discarded at the end of the separator. The parent node continues with the accumulated transformations, in effect, prior to the separator.

```
Separator {
    ...           # object 1
    ...           # object 2
}
```

WWW

- WWWAnchor: This node type works exactly like a separator object, except that it supports several additional properties. These properties are name, description, and map. The value of the name property indicates the URL to load when a child of this grouping node is selected. The value of the description property may be used by a VRML browser to display a description of the URL linked through the name property. The map property can have one of two values: NONE or POINT. A POINT value indicates that the coordinate selected in the scene should be appended to the URL specified by the name property. This capability gives rise to the possibility of a 3D "image" map.

```
WWWAnchor {
    name "http://rosebud.sdsc.edu/vrml"
    description "Link to VRML Repository"
    ...           # object 1
    ...           # object 2
}
```

- WWWInline: This node allows a VRML document to incorporate another VRML document located at a specified URL. Use the name property to assign this URL value. For example, to include the world located at http://www.mysite.edu/myworld.wrl, you would use the following node in the scene graph.

```
WWWInline { name "http://www.mysite.edu/myworld.wrl" }
```

Using these nodes, you can successfully create and edit VRML worlds. This list serves as a brief introduction to the nodes and node properties available in VRML. For a complete specification of VRML 1, examine URL http://rosebud.sdsc.edu/vrml.

Comments

VRML 1 is still experimental in nature. Consequently, many browsers and modelers speak slightly different dialects of VRML. Several also provide additional proprietary constructs.

When authoring, keep in mind that VRML documents can rapidly become very large. The larger the file, the longer a Web browser takes to download and present it. Consequently, users with a low bandwidth network connection, such as a 14.4K modem, will experience significant delays in viewing your VRML documents.

In addition, the complexity of your VRML document and the processing power of the viewer's machine impact the speed of rendering. A VRML document that renders and updates quickly on an SGI Reality Engine might take considerably longer to display and update on a 486 machine.

COMPLEXITY
BEGINNING

10.12 How do I...
Locate prebuilt VRML objects?

COMPATIBILITY: VRML

Problem

I don't want to create my worlds from scratch. How do I find VRML objects that I can use in the worlds that I create?

Technique

A variety of 3D objects are available through a number of sites on the Internet. These sites offer free, or not-so-free, 3D objects that you can use in constructing VRML worlds.

So, you can use prebuilt objects to jump-start your world-building process. Start by connecting to one of the following sites. Select and download a desired object. Then incorporate that object into your VRML world.

Steps

The following procedure walks you through the identification, retrieval, and use of prebuilt VRML objects available over the Internet.

1. Connect to a VRML object repository site. Table 10-11 lists several as potential starting points, or you can use one of the many Web search tools to pinpoint repositories on your own.

Table 10-11 **Sampling of VRML object repository sites**

SITE NAME	URL
New College vrmLab	`http://www.newcollege.edu/vrmLab`
Grafman's VRML Gallery	`http://www.graphcomp.com/vrml`
UK-VR SIG	`http://www.dcs.ed.ac.uk/~mxr/objects.html`

2. Select and download the object(s) you want.

3. Either reference the downloaded object as a `WWWInline` node or insert the contents of the downloaded object directly into your VRML world.

4. Save the VRML world.

How It Works

Just as image, audio, and video clip archives have developed over the years, VRML object repositories are beginning to appear. Table 10-11 lists several of these sites.

Reuse of existing objects will save you considerable time in the world development process. The files that you download contain the developed objects. You can incorporate the object into your world in one of two ways:

◻ `WWWInline`: This node allows you to incorporate another VRML document located at a specified URL. Use the `name` property to assign this URL value. For example, to include the VRML object `dnld_object.wrl`, you would use the following node in the scene graph.

```
WWWInline { name "dnld_object.wrl" }
```

◻ Textual Copying: Within your VRML page, directly insert the VRML code from the downloaded file that describes the object which you want to use. You should use this method when the downloaded file contains multiple objects of which you want to use only one.

See the information in How-To 10.12 to further flesh out the world you are creating. You may also want to consult the remainder of the How-To's in this chapter for more advanced VRML effects.

Comments

You should carefully read the rights and restrictions notice of the site from which you obtain 3D objects. Most sites allow free use of objects for noncommercial purposes, but some sites may apply further restrictions. If in doubt, contact the site administrator or the object author for further guidance.

As with any VRML space, you can include the world in a Web page using a link as described in How-To 10.1, or use the nonstandard methods of multimedia object incorporation discussed in Chapter 18, Direct Inclusion of Multimedia Objects.

COMPLEXITY
INTERMEDIATE

10.13 How do I...
Make my VRML world more realistic?

COMPATIBILITY: VRML

Problem

My VRML worlds seems to lack realism. Are there any ways that I can make my world appear more realistic to people wandering through it?

Technique

This How-To describes two methods of improving the realism of VRML worlds:

- *Level of Detail Nodes*: Level of Detail (**LOD**) nodes allow you to specify alternate representation of groups of objects in your world. When a viewer enters your world, the version of this group of objects that he sees is dependent upon his relative distance to that group of objects.

- *Texture Nodes*: Material nodes provide a basic means for specifying the appearance of different objects in your world. These materials do not provide the variety and randomness encountered in the real world. Texture nodes allow you to specify an image to use as wrapping paper over the surface of an object.

You can use the following two procedures to add these features to your VRML worlds.

Steps

The following two procedures provide step-by-step instruction for adding more realism to your worlds by adding levels of detail nodes and texture nodes.

Levels of Detail

1. Open your VRML document in a text editor.

2. Move the insertion point to just prior to the group of objects for which you want to add alternate levels of detail representation.

3. Start an **LOD** node by typing the following:

```
LOD {
```

4. Determine the distance at which you want the alternate representations to switch. For example, you might want the most detailed representation seen when a viewer is within 25 meters of the group, the next most detailed when the user is between 25 and 75 meters, and the least detailed when the viewer is beyond 75 meters.

5. Translate this into a **range** attribute of the **LOD** node by determining the switch points. Insert the appropriate **range** attribute. For the example in step 3, the switch points are **25** and **75**, so you would enter the following **range** attribute:

```
range [25,75]
```

6. Place the current representation of your chosen group into a new **separator** group.

```
Separator {
    # Your Chosen Group of Objects
}
```

7. Create a representation for each distance range specified; you will need the number of switch points in the **range** attribute, plus one. Select the position of the current representation among these alternates, and create the remaining representations, each in its own **separator** group.

8. Arrange the alternate representations from the representation seen at the closest range to the representation seen at the farthest range.

9. End the **LOD** node with a closing curly brace.

```
}
```

10. Save your VRML document.

11. Test your VRML document.

Texture Mapping

1. Find or create a texture map image that you want to wrap around a VRML object. See How-To 10.12 for information on finding existing texture images. See Chapter 9, Using Images in Your Documents, for more information on images in general. The How-To's dealing with background images may be particularly useful.

2. Open your VRML document in a text editor.

3. Place each VRML object upon which you want to apply the texture within a **Separator** node of its own.

```
Separator {
    # Your Chosen Object(s)
}
```

4. Add a `Texture2` node to the node prior to which you want to apply the texture. The `filename` attribute of the texture node should contain the URL of the chosen texture. For example, to select the `wood.gif` image as the texture for the remaining objects within the `separator` group, you might use the following:

```
Separator {
    Texture2 {
        # Specify the URL of the texture
        filename "wood.gif"
    }
    # Your Chosen Object(s)
}
```

5. Save your document.

6. Test your document.

How It Works

Two areas where VRML worlds fall short of reality are the lack of shifting perspectives as a viewer approaches an object and the lack of irregularities in VRML object surfaces. The two node types discussed in this How-To improve the realism in these areas.

Level of detail (`LOD`) nodes allow you to selectively alter the representation of a group of VRML objects based upon the distance of the viewer from that group of objects. As a viewer approaches the group of objects, the representation alters in the specified manner. This effect gives the impression that the details of the particular portion of the scene are clarifying as the viewer approaches. Obviously, a finite number of alternate representations is not a substitute for the smooth clarification of detail in the real world, but the use of `LOD` nodes provides an improvement.

Texture (`Texture2`) nodes provide a simulation of the irregularities found in real world surfaces. Simply using `Material` nodes to define the composition of object surfaces leads to objects with seemingly smooth, perfect exteriors. Using an appropriate image to wrap the object gives the object a more natural or realistic appearance. As with `LOD` nodes, texture nodes are not perfect, but they do improve realism. Using textures does require a measure of tradeoff. Objects with texture maps take marginally longer to draw. Further, each additional texture used within a world requires the browser to download a separate image file.

Comments

An added benefit of the use of `LOD` nodes is the speed of rendering distant objects. Since objects further away from the viewer require less detail, the VRML representation will be simpler, requiring fewer, less detailed objects. The net effect of this is that the VRML browser, or plug-in, requires less time to render those distant objects while reserving computational resources for positioning and drawing detailed nearer objects.

As with any VRML space, you can include the world in a Web page using a link as described in How-To 10.1, or use the nonstandard methods of multimedia object incorporation discussed in Chapter 18, Direct Inclusion of Multimedia Objects.

COMPLEXITY
INTERMEDIATE

10.14 How do I...
Spin a VRML object?

COMPATIBILITY: VRML 2

Problem

I want to add some motion to the worlds that I am creating. A static world just doesn't reflect the world I want to put on display. How do I add at least some motion to my world?

Technique

VRML 2 provides the new **SpinGroup** node. The **SpinGroup** node allows you to specify a group of VRML objects to be set in continuous motion.

Items that you wish to spin in a particular manner will be grouped within a **SpinGroup** node. Use multiple **SpinGroup** nodes within a single world to set objects in motion subject to different constraints.

Steps

The following steps walk you through the process of adding a **SpinGroup** node to your VRML world.

1. Open your VRML world in a text editor.

2. Move your insertion point to the location just prior to the objects that you wish to set in motion subject to the same rotational constraints.

3. Insert a **SpinGroup** node around this group of objects.

```
SpinGroup {
    # Objects to Set in Motion
}
```

4. Insert a **rotation** attribute at the beginning of your **SpinGroup** node.

```
SpinGroup {
    rotation 0 1 1 .2
```

```
# Objects to Set in Motion
}
```

5. Save your document.

6. Test your document.

How It Works

The `SpinGroup` node places its contents in motion according to the parameters specified in the node's rotation attribute. This `SpinGroup` acts much like a `Separator` in terms of grouping objects in the VRML scene. The fact that the visible objects within the group are in motions makes the visual effect of this grouping significantly different.

The `rotation` attribute of the `SpinGroup` node actually controls the axes of rotation and the speed at which the objects within the group move. The `rotation` attribute requires four value parameters. The first three values represent the X, Y, and Z axes of the object, where a **1** value indicates that the object will rotate about that axis, while a **0** value indicates no rotation about that axis. The fourth value is a decimal value representing the rotational speed of the spin. The greater the absolute value of this number, the faster the spin. The positivity or negativity of this value determines whether the group spins towards the positive or negative ends of the axes selected for rotation.

For example, Figure 10-11 shows the following `SpinGroup` node:

```
SpinGroup {
    rotation 0 1 1 .2

    Separator {
            Translation {
                    translation 160 -200 -2
        }
        Material {
            diffuseColor .3 .1 .3
        }
            Cube {
            width 100
            height 100
            depth 100
        }
        }
    }
```

The `SpinGroup` adapts the cube created in the simple demonstration world created in How-To 10.11. Loading this VRML world into an appropriate viewer, you will notice that the cube is now in motion, spinning on its Y and Z axes.

The complete source for the VRML world shown in Figure 10-11 appears on the CD in the SPINNING.WRL file. The file TWOSPIN.WRL sets both the cone and the cube in motion in opposite directions.

Figure 10-11 Spinning cube with stationary cone

Comments

Spin groups may not work with older VRML browsers or plug-ins. The `SpinGroup` node is part of the VRML 2 specification. If you have neither an enhanced VRML 1 browser nor a VRML 2 browser, you may want to pick one up. Both Netscape Navigator and Microsoft Internet Explorer, through appropriate plug-ins or active X controls, support this feature.

As with any VRML space, you can include the world in a Web page using a link as described in How-To 10.1, or use the nonstandard methods of multimedia object incorporation discussed in Chapter 18, Direct Inclusion of Multimedia Objects.

COMPLEXITY
ADVANCED

10.15 How do I...
Include animated textures on VRML objects?

COMPATIBILITY: VRML

Problem

I would like the surface of a VRML object to shift and move as the viewer watches. How can I project an animation onto the surface of a VRML object?

Technique

This technique is very similar to the one described in How-To 10.13 for standard texture images. The primary difference lies at the front end in the construction of the texture image.

VRML browsers that support animated textures expect the GIF files specified in a particular format. This How-To walks you through the process required to create a multiple image GIF file suitable for use as an animated surface texture. You will need an appropriate image manipulation program that supports the GIF file format to construct the proper image. See Chapter 9, Using Images in Your Documents, and How-To's 10.2 and 10.3 for additional information on image editors.

You will first create an appropriate image. Then, you will use the procedure in How-To 10.13, defining the use of texture nodes to insert the new texture into your VRML document.

Steps

The following procedure walks you through the creation of a multiple-image GIF file suitable for use as an animated texture. The last instruction has you insert this image as a texture in your VRML document using the procedure described for this purpose in How-To 10.13.

1. Plan out the animation that you want to project onto a VRML object surface. Define the size and number of frames. You should use single size, square frames. For example, each of the frames in the animation developed in Figure 10-12 is 128x128 pixels.

2. Create each frame as a separate image of your chosen size.

3. Merge the frames into a single image with a width equal to the width of a frame and a height equal to the height of a frame times the number of frames. For example, the combined image in Figure 10-12 is 128 pixels in width and 512 pixels in height.

4. Set the background color of the combined image to the desired color of the VRML object onto which you will project the animation.

5. Save the combined image as a GIF89a format image.

6. Specify this image within a texture node by using the proper procedure defined in How-To 10.14.

How It Works

VRML browsers support the use of multiple image GIF files as textures. Therefore, you must construct or locate a suitable multiple image GIF file. Following this procedure, PaintShop Pro was used to create the four separate GIF files, found on the CD: HTM8.GIF, HTM9.GIF, HTM10.GIF, and HTM11.GIF. These four GIF files were combined into the `htmani.gif` file as seen in Figure 10-12.

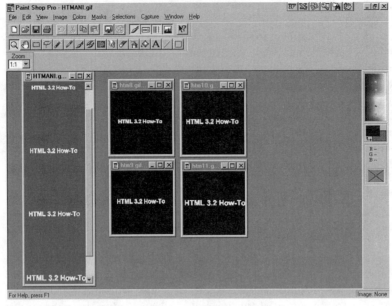

Figure 10-12 Animated texture construction

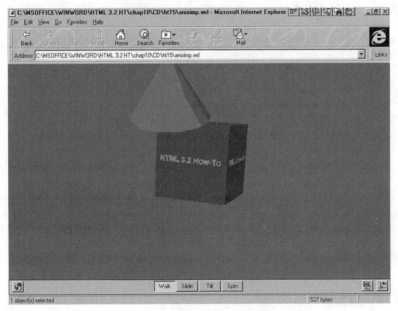

Figure 10-13 Spinning cube with animated texture

You should note that the background of the combined image was altered from the original four. This was required to maintain the purple color of the cube in the world displayed in Figure 10-13. The VRML world displayed in Figure 10-13 uses the multiple image GIF file seen in Figure 10-12 as the texture for the spinning cube seen in Figure 10-11 in How-To 10.14. Without this background modification, the black background of the multiple image GIF file might override the material node within the VRML world.

The ANISPIN.HTM file on the CD contains the complete source code for the animation seen in Figure 10-13.

Comments

The latest VRML specification contemplates significantly greater flexibility in the type of moving imagery projectable onto visible object surfaces. For example, you might project an MPEG or QuickTime movie onto the surface of a VRML cone, or any other visible VRML object.

As with any VRML space, you can include the world in a Web page using a link as described in How-To 10.1, or use the nonstandard methods of multimedia object incorporation discussed in Chapter 18, Direct Inclusion of Multimedia Objects.

CHAPTER 11

HTML INTERACTIVE FORMS

11

HTML INTERACTIVE FORMS

How do I...

You've come this far with HTML and are proceeding along just fine. You know how to create a nice-looking home page that has links to lots of other pages all over the WWW. The thing is, so far the information has been flowing in only one direction. You have been able to show people who read your pages whatever is on your mind, but your readers have had no way of giving you feedback. They can't let you know how they like your page or what they would like you to do differently. That is where forms come into play. You can include forms in your HTML document that allow your readers to send you input in a variety of different ways.

The form creation process is actually twofold. The first part of the process is to include the HTML tags in your document that create the form. This first part is often referred to as the front end. The second part of the process involves creating a script in a language such as Perl or C that processes the information contained in the form. This part of the process is called the back end. This chapter deals mainly with the first part, or front end, of the form creation process.

11.1   Create a Basic Form

Before you can let a user interact with your documents, you need to create a basic form. This How-To shows you how to add the tags needed to create a startup form that lets a user enter lines of text.

11.2   Add a Text Box to a Form

There are instances when a user is going to want to enter more than one line of text at a time. This How-To shows you how to add scrollable text boxes of any size to your forms.

11.3   Add Check Boxes to a Form

Sometimes you want to let a user check off various options or choices. This How-To shows how to add check boxes to a form.

11.4   Add Radio Buttons to a Form

Sometimes you would like to let a user choose only one option among many from a list, like pushing the buttons on a radio where selecting one item unselects any other item that had been selected. This simple How-To shows how to add radio buttons to your forms.

11.5   Add Password Fields to a Form

There are times when you want a user to enter sensitive information into a field, but you want to disguise this input so a passerby or onlooker cannot read it. This How-To shows the process used to create password fields in which user-supplied information is replaced by asterisks.

11.6   Add Pulldown Menus to a Form

Sometimes you may wish to let a user select from a number of options or choices, but only show the currently selected choice on the form. This simple How-To lets you add pulldown menus to your forms.

11.7   Add a File Selector Dialog Box to a Form

There are times when you would like a user to select a file from among a group of files. This How-To shows you how to add a file selector dialog to a form.

11.8   Add a Single Line Text Field to a Form

Often you may wish the user to input only a single line of code. This simple How-To shows you how to add single line prompts to your forms.

11.9   Use a Clickable Image as a Submit Button

At times you may want to spruce up your forms by using an image for the Submit button. This simple How-To shows you how to use an image for your Submit button.

11.10   Pass Information Between Forms

When creating dynamic documents, you may want to pass information from a current form to another form that you will build based partly on information from the current form. This How-To shows how to add hidden fields that can be used to store information to pass from one form to another.

11.11   Choose a Request Method to Send Data to the HTTP Server

Now that you have a complete form, you need a way for a reader to say, "I'm finished," and then to deliver the information contained in the form to the HTTP server. This How-To will show you how to submit a form and how to pick the submission method that is right for you.

11.12   Process a Form

Now that you have a complete form all ready to go, you need a way to bridge the gap between the HTML document that contains the form and the HTTP server that will process the form. This How-To gives you a basic rundown on how to create a Common Gateway Interface (CGI) script that will send and process a form.

COMPLEXITY
INTERMEDIATE

11.1   How do I...
Create a basic form?

COMPATIBILITY: HTML 2+

Problem

I would like to add forms to my documents so I can receive user feedback and create more dynamic documents. How do I do this?

Technique

Creating a form isn't all that difficult. Forms are created as part of an HTML document by including the <FORM> tag, along with its associated tags that create

- Text fields
- Check boxes
- Radio buttons
- Pop-up menus

The form is later submitted to the HTTP server by using either the get or the post method. The form can then be processed by a script.

Steps

The following procedure shows you how to create a form and include it in a document.

1. Open a new file with any editor or word processor you choose. Make sure that whatever tool you use is able to save documents as text or ASCII, depending on the environment you are in.

2. Create a base HTML document. This document consists of the items needed to make an HTML document. This base document should include

- <HTML>...</HTML> tags
- <HEAD>...</HEAD> tags
- <TITLE>...</TITLE> tags
- <BODY>...</BODY> tags

Your document should resemble the following:

```
<HTML> <HEAD>
<TITLE>Input Form</TITLE>
</HEAD>
<BODY>
</BODY>
</Html>
```

3. Put two horizontal rule <HR> tags in the body of your document. Your form will go between these two tags. This step is entirely optional, but it helps the form stand out more. Your document should now look something like this:

```
<HTML> <HEAD>
<TITLE>Input Form</TITLE>
</HEAD>
<BODY>
<HR>
My form will go here!
<HR>
</BODY>
</Html>
```

4. Add the `<FORM>...</FORM>` tags to your document. The basic tag syntax is

```
<FORM METHOD="Get or Post" ACTION="URL" ENCTYPE="type">
Field definitions
</FORM>
```

The `<FORM>` tag tells a browser that there is a fill-in-the-blank form in this HTML document.

The `METHOD` attribute states the method to be used when you send the form to the server. The two acceptable methods are `get` and `post`. `Get` sends the information entered in the form to the server at the end of the URL. `Post` sends the information entered in the form to the server as a data body. `Get` is the default method, but `post` is the method preferred by many HTML designers.

The `ACTION` attribute gives the address of the script that will process the form. This script may be written in almost any language, but Perl and C are the two dominant choices.

The `ENCTYPE` attribute specifies how the data is to be encoded. This attribute only applies if you use the `post` method, and even then, there is only one possible value, the default value "`application/w-www-form-urlencoded`". The `ENCTYPE` attribute is included here only so that you recognize it if you see it.

The `METHOD`, `ACTION`, and `ENCTYPE` attributes are all optional; however, for the sake of clarity, it is best if you always include the `METHOD` and `ACTION` attributes.

Now your document and form will look like this:

```
<HTML> <HEAD>
<TITLE>Input Form</TITLE>
</HEAD>
<BODY>
<HR>
<FORM METHOD=POST ACTION="/cgi-bin/MY_SCRIPT">
My form will go here!
</FORM>
<HR>
</BODY>
</Html>
```

My form will go here!

Figure 11-1 The starting point

Figure 11-1 shows how this document will look when viewed with a browser. It doesn't look like much yet, but you have built a strong base on which to construct the rest of your form.

5. Add an `<INPUT>` tag so you can accept some input from a reader. The `<INPUT>` tag is a standalone tag. The syntax for this is

```
<INPUT TYPE="type" NAME="NAME" SIZE="number" VALUE="value">
```

There are many kinds of `<INPUT>` types available, but you are going to start with the most basic kind, a text entry field. To create a text entry field in a document, you include the following between the `<FORM>`...`</FORM>` tags:

```
<INPUT TYPE="text" NAME="NAME" SIZE=30 VALUE="John Smith">
```

6. Put some text around the `<INPUT>` tag to give readers an idea of what you expect them to enter in the space provided. The document should now look like this:

```
<HTML> <HEAD>
<TITLE>Input Form</TITLE>
</HEAD>
<BODY>
<HR>
<FORM METHOD=POST ACTION="/cgi-bin/MY_SCRIPT">
Enter your name here :
<INPUT TYPE="text" NAME="NAME" SIZE=30 VALUE="John Smith">
</FORM>
<HR>
</BODY>
</Html>
```

Now you're getting somewhere. You have a form on the screen that a reader can enter information into.

7. Finish off this first form by giving the user a chance to either submit this information, or to reset the information and enter something else. This is done by using the `<INPUT>` tag and setting the `TYPE` to either `"SUBMIT"` or `"RESET"`. For example:

```
<INPUT TYPE="SUBMIT" NAME="SUBMIT_BUTTON" VALUE="Submit">
<INPUT TYPE="RESET" NAME="RESET_BUTTON" VALUE="Oops">
```

Here, the **TYPE** attribute tells the browser what kind of button you are dealing with. The **NAME** is a variable that you can access later when referring to this information. The value is what is written in the button. Adding these lines to your document, you will have

```
<HTML> <HEAD>
<TITLE>Input Form</TITLE>
</HEAD>
<BODY>
<HR>
<FORM METHOD=POST ACTION="/cgi-bin/MY_SCRIPT">
Enter your name here:
<INPUT TYPE="TEXT" NAME="NAME" SIZE=30 VALUE="John Smith">
<INPUT TYPE="SUBMIT" NAME="SUBMIT_BUTTON" VALUE="Submit">
<INPUT TYPE="RESET" NAME="RESET_BUTTON" VALUE="OOPS">
</FORM>
<HR>
</BODY>
</Html>
```

8. Save the document as a text or ASCII file. It is a good idea to give the document a reasonable name such as **sampform** along with an **.htm** or an **.html** extension. By saving the document in this manner you can view it through either the **Open Local** or **Open File** commands in your browser. When viewed in this manner, the document should then look very much like Figure 11-2.

How It Works

The **<FORM>...</FORM>** tags tell the browser to expect various **<INPUT>** tags between these two tags. These tags, along with other HTML tags and anything else that's valid in an HTML document, all make up a fill-in-the-blanks form (from now on referred to as simply a form). When the reader presses the Submit button, the contents of the form are sent to the HTTP server in a data stream in the form of

```
action?name=value&name=value
```

Comments

What has been created so far is a framework to gather information—the front end of the form. This allows you to interact with a reader, but you still need a script to

Figure 11-2 An actual form!

process this information. The script is dealt with briefly later in this chapter and in greater detail later in the book.

11.2   How do I...
Add a text box to a form?

COMPATIBILITY: HTML 2+

Problem

Once I have a form in my HTML document, I would like to let readers enter more than one line of text at a time. How do I do this?

Technique

Once you are familiar with setting up a basic form, adding parts to this form is quite easy. To make a text box that creates a scrollable text field on the screen, insert the **<TEXTAREA>...</TEXTAREA>** tags somewhere between the **<FORM>...</FORM>** tags. You may have as many **<TEXTAREA>** tags as needed, and you may include other HTML tags between these tags.

Steps

The following steps show how to add **<TEXTAREA>** tags to your forms.

1. Decide on the number of text boxes you need and how you are going to lay them out on the form. The number of text boxes used on a form is normally quite easy and straightforward to determine: one or two is usually sufficient. Add a text box every place you think a reader needs a lot of room to write something. The layout is a matter of personal taste and preference. Don't be surprised if the actual layout you end up with is different from the one you first envisioned.

2. Open the HTML document that contains the form you wish to add the text box to. You may open the document in any text editor or word processor you feel comfortable using. In this case, you will expand on the document used in How-To 11.1.

3. Add the **<TEXTAREA>...</TEXTAREA>** tags between the **<FORM>...</FORM>** tags. The basic syntax is

```
<TEXTAREA NAME="NAME" ROWS="number of rows" COLS="number of columns"> any
default text </TEXTAREA>
```

The variable in the **NAME** attribute is what you will use to refer to this **<TEXTAREA>** when you later reference it in a script. The **ROWS** attribute is set to an integer for the number of rows the text box has. The **COLS** attribute is set to an integer for the number of columns the text box will have. The text between the **<TEXTAREA>...</TEXTAREA>** tags is the text that initially appears in the text box.

For this example, you will create a text box called **"COMMENTS"**. It is 5 rows long and 60 columns wide. This should give the reader sufficient area to voice an opinion. If the reader needs more space, the box will scroll. Use this command sequence:

```
<TEXTAREA NAME="COMMENTS" ROWS=5 COLS=60>Your comments go here</TEXTAREA>
```

4. Put some text near the **<TEXTAREA>** tag to give the reader a better idea of what to enter.

The document should now resemble this:

```
<HTML> <HEAD>
<TITLE>Input Form</TITLE>
</HEAD>
<BODY>
<HR>
<FORM METHOD=POST ACTION="/cgi-bin/MY_SCRIPT">
Enter your name here: <INPUT TYPE="text" NAME="NAME" SIZE=30 VALUE="???">
<TEXTAREA NAME="COMMENTS" ROWS=5 COLS=60>Your comments go here</TEXTAREA>
<INPUT TYPE="submit" NAME="SUBMIT_BUTTON" VALUE="SEND ME">
<INPUT TYPE="reset" NAME="RESET_BUTTON" VALUE="OOPS">
</FORM>
<HR>
</BODY>
</Html>
```

5. Enter any other text or HTML tags to help clarify the document and make it easier to read. For this document, use a level two heading tag (**<H2>**) to let people know what to expect, plus a couple of new paragraph tags (**<P>**) to space things out a little more.

```
<HTML> <HEAD>
<TITLE>Input Form</TITLE>
</HEAD>
<BODY>
<H2>INPUT FORM -- Textarea</H2>
<HR>
<FORM METHOD=POST ACTION="/cgi-bin/MY_SCRIPT">
Enter your name here: <INPUT TYPE="text" NAME="NAME" SIZE=30 VALUE="???">
<P>
What do you think:<TEXTAREA NAME="comments" ROWS=5 COLS=60>Your comments go
here</TEXTAREA>
<P>
<INPUT TYPE="SUBMIT" NAME="SUBMIT_BUTTON" VALUE="Submit">
<INPUT TYPE="RESET" NAME="RESET_BUTTON" VALUE="OOPS">
</FORM>
<HR>
</BODY>
</Html>
```

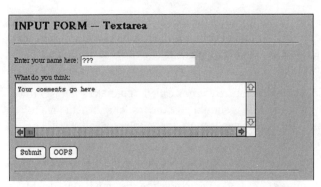

Figure 11-3 The form complete with a text field

6. Save the document as text. Remember to give it a reasonable, clear name such as `sampform.html`.

7. Use `Open File` or `Open Local` on your browser to make sure your form looks the way you expect it to. If all went well, it will look much like Figure 11-3.

How It Works

The `<FORM>...</FORM>` tags tell the browser to expect form `<INPUT>` tags between these two tags. The `<TEXTAREA>...</TEXTAREA>` tags create a space where a user may enter data within this form. Once the Submit button is pushed, the information contained in the text area will be sent to the HTTP server. The information can later be accessed by referring to the name assigned to the text area with the `NAME` attribute.

Comments

The appearance of forms is certainly not carved in stone and is largely a matter of personal taste. Some people like to wrap their forms in `<PRE>...</PRE>` tags. This gives them more control over where they place items in the form. If you don't like how your text box looks, experiment with it. Try changing the values for `ROWS` and `COLS` in the `<TEXTAREA>` tag. You may also want to try moving the text box around the form some. The look of a form is very much a matter of individual taste.

COMPLEXITY

INTERMEDIATE

11.3 How do I...
Add check boxes to a form?

COMPATIBILITY: HTML 2+

Problem

Now that I have a form in my HTML document, I would like to be able to let users make choices while using it. How do I do this?

Technique

Check boxes allow a user to click on any number of choices from a list. They are added to forms in much the same manner as text boxes. To create a check box, insert an <INPUT> tag between the <FORM>...</FORM> tags. Inside the <INPUT> tag, set the TYPE to "checkbox". You may have as many check boxes as needed.

Steps

The following steps show how to add check boxes to forms.

1. Decide how many check boxes you are going to need and how you are going to lay them out on the form. The number of check boxes you need is usually pretty straightforward, since you should have a pretty good idea of how many lists of choices you wish to give a reader. The layout is more of a matter of personal taste and preferences. Don't be surprised if the actual layout you end up with is different from the one you first envisioned. In this example, you will have two groups of check boxes: one so readers can select colors they like from a list, and another so readers can pick foods they like. Just for fun, lay out one group horizontally and the other vertically.

2. Open the HTML document that contains the form you wish to add the check boxes to. You will be expanding on the document used in How-To 11.1.

3. Add the <INPUT> tag for the first check box between the <FORM>... </FORM> tags. In the <INPUT> tag, set the TYPE to "checkbox". The basic syntax for this is

```
<INPUT TYPE="checkbox" NAME="NAME" VALUE="value" [CHECKED] > "Text"
```

The TYPE attribute declares that this field is a check box. The variable in the NAME attribute is what you will refer to this check box with when you later reference it with a script. The VALUE attribute is what this check box is set to when it is checked. The CHECKED attribute is optional and tells the browser to show this check box as checked when it is first viewed. "Text" is for whatever text you wish to associate with each particular check box.

The tags for the color check boxes look like this:

```
<INPUT TYPE="checkbox" NAME="COLOR_CHECK1" VALUE=0>Red
<INPUT TYPE="checkbox" NAME="COLOR_CHECK2" VALUE=0>Blue
<INPUT TYPE="checkbox" NAME="COLOR_CHECK3" VALUE=0>Yellow
<INPUT TYPE="checkbox" NAME="COLOR_CHECK4" VALUE=1 CHECKED>Green
```

The tags for food check boxes look like this:

```
<INPUT TYPE="checkbox" NAME="FOOD_CHECK1" VALUE=0>Lobster <P>
<INPUT TYPE="checkbox" NAME="FOOD_CHECK2" VALUE=0>Spam<P>
<INPUT TYPE="checkbox" NAME="FOOD_CHECK3" VALUE=1 CHECKED>Chocolate<P>
```

4. Put some header text near the check boxes so readers have a good idea of what you want them to do.

5. Enter any other text or HTML tags to help clarify the document and make it easier to read. The document should now resemble this:

```
<HTML> <HEAD>
<TITLE>Input Form -- Check Boxes</TITLE>
</Head>
<BODY>
<H2>INPUT FORM check boxes</H2>
<HR>
<FORM METHOD=POST ACTION="/cgi-bin/MY_SCRIPT">
Enter your name here: <INPUT TYPE="text" NAME="NAME" SIZE=30 VALUE="???"><p>
What colors do you like:
<INPUT TYPE="checkbox" NAME="COLOR_CHECK1" VALUE="yes">Red
<INPUT TYPE="checkbox" NAME="COLOR_CHECK2" VALUE="yes">Blue
<INPUT TYPE="checkbox" NAME="COLOR_CHECK3" VALUE="yes">Yellow
<INPUT TYPE="checkbox" NAME="COLOR_CHECK4" VALUE="yes" CHECKED>Green
<P>
What foods do you like:
<P>
<INPUT TYPE="checkbox" NAME="FOOD_CHECK1" VALUE="yes">Lobster <P>
<INPUT TYPE="checkbox" NAME="FOOD_CHECK2" VALUE="yes">Spam<P>
<INPUT TYPE="checkbox" NAME="FOOD_CHECK3" VALUE="yes" CHECKED>Chocolate<P>

<INPUT TYPE="submit" NAME="SUBMIT_BUTTON" VALUE="Submit">
<INPUT TYPE="reset" NAME="RESET_BUTTON" VALUE="OOPS">
</FORM>
<HR>
</BODY>
</HTML>
```

6. Save the document as text or ASCII.

Figure 11-4 The form complete with check boxes

7. Use **Open File** or **Open Local** on your browser to make sure your form looks the way you expect it to. If all goes well, it will look very much like Figure 11-4.

How It Works

The **<FORM>...</FORM>** tags tell the browser to expect form **<INPUT>** tags between these two tags. The **<INPUT>** tag, when the **TYPE** is set to **"checkbox"**, creates a check box for the user to click on to select that particular item. The check box toggles between on and off as the user clicks on it. If a particular check box is selected, then the variable name that refers to that check box will be set to value. Once the Submit button is pushed, the information contained in the form will be sent to the HTTP server. To see what check boxes were selected and not selected, you can use the names assigned with the **NAME** attribute and check their values.

Comments

Though check boxes may be physically grouped together on the page or form, it is usually not a good idea to logically group them together under one variable name. It is possible to have more than one check box checked at any given time, so it is a good idea to give each check box its own unique variable name. It is also best to keep the value assigned to the box when it is checked something simple. I usually choose **"yes"**. The example shows one group of check boxes running across the page, and the other group running down the page. This is done purely to illustrate the number of ways you can present check boxes. Experiment to find the presentation you prefer.

COMPLEXITY
INTERMEDIATE

11.4   How do I...
Add radio buttons to a form?

COMPATIBILITY: HTML 2+

Problem

Now that I have a form in my HTML document, I would like to use radio buttons in it so I can let a user pick just one item out of a list. How do I do this?

Technique

Radio buttons are added to forms in much the same manner as check boxes. To create a radio button that allows a user to click on only one of a number of choices from a list, insert an **<INPUT>** tag between the **<FORM>...</FORM>** tags. Inside the **<INPUT>** tag, set the **TYPE** to **"radio"**. You may have as many radio buttons as needed, and you may include other HTML tags between these tags.

Steps

The following steps show how to add radio buttons to forms.

1. Decide how many radio buttons you need and how you are going to lay them out on the form. The number is usually quite easy and straightforward to determine. The layout is a matter of personal taste and preferences. In this example, you will use one group of radio buttons for a reader to pick a favorite color and another for the reader to pick a favorite food.

2. Open the HTML document that contains the form you wish to add the radio buttons to. For this example, start with the document used in How-To 11.1.

3. Add the **<INPUT>** tag for the first radio button between the **<FORM>...</FORM>**tags. In the **<INPUT>** tag, set the **TYPE** to **"radio"**. The basic syntax for this is

```
<INPUT TYPE="radio" NAME="NAME" VALUE=value [CHECKED] > "Text"
```

The **TYPE** attribute declares this field a radio button. The variable in the **NAME** attribute is what you will refer to this group of radio buttons as when you later reference them in a script. The **VALUE** attribute is what this radio button is set to when it is checked. The **CHECKED** attribute is optional and tells the browser to show this radio button as checked when it is first displayed. **"Text"** is for whatever text you wish to associate with each particular button.

The tags for the favorite color radio buttons look like this:

```
<INPUT TYPE="radio" NAME="COLOR_RADIO" VALUE=1>Red
<INPUT TYPE="radio" NAME="COLOR_RADIO" VALUE=2>Blue
<INPUT TYPE="radio" NAME="COLOR_RADIO" VALUE=3>Yellow
<INPUT TYPE="radio" NAME="COLOR_RADIO" VALUE=4 CHECKED>Green
```

The tags for the favorite food radio buttons look like this:

```
<INPUT TYPE="radio" NAME="FOOD_RADIO" VALUE=1>Lobster <P>
<INPUT TYPE="radio" NAME="FOOD_RADIO" VALUE=2>Spam<P>
<INPUT TYPE="radio" NAME="FOOD_RADIO" VALUE=3 CHECKED>Chocolate<P>
```

4. Put some heading text near the radio buttons so readers have a good idea of what you want them to do.

5. Enter any other text or HTML tags to help clarify the document and make it easier to read. The document should now resemble this:

```
<HTML> <HEAD>
<TITLE>Input Form</TITLE>
</HEAD>
<BODY>
<H2>INPUT FORM radio buttons</H2>
<HR>
<FORM METHOD=POST ACTION="/cgi-bin/MY_SCRIPT">
Enter your name here: <INPUT TYPE="text" NAME="NAME" SIZE=30 VALUE="???"><p>
What is your favorite color:
<P>
<INPUT TYPE="radio" NAME="COLOR_RADIO" VALUE=1>Red
<INPUT TYPE="radio" NAME="COLOR_RADIO" VALUE=2>Blue
<INPUT TYPE="radio" NAME="COLOR_RADIO" VALUE=3>Yellow
<INPUT TYPE="radio" NAME="COLOR_RADIO" VALUE=4 CHECKED>Green
What is your favorite food:
<P>
<INPUT TYPE="radio" NAME="FOOD_RADIO" VALUE=1>Lobster
<INPUT TYPE="radio" NAME="FOOD_RADIO" VALUE=2>Spam
<INPUT TYPE="radio" NAME="FOOD_RADIO" VALUE=3 CHECKED>Chocolate

<INPUT TYPE="submit" NAME="SUBMIT_BUTTON" VALUE="Submit">
<INPUT TYPE="reset" NAME="RESET_BUTTON" VALUE="OOPS">
</FORM>
<HR>
</BODY>
</HTML>
```

6. Save the document as text or ASCII.

7. Use the `Open File` command or the `Open Local` command on your browser to make sure your form looks like Figure 11-5.

How It Works

The `<FORM>...</FORM>` tags tell the browser to expect form `<INPUT>` tags between these two tags. The `<INPUT>` tag, when the `TYPE` attribute is set to `"radio"`, creates

INPUT FORM radio buttons

Enter your name here: ???

What is your favorite color:

○ Red ○ Blue ○ Yellow ◉ Green What is your favorite food:

○ Lobster ○ Spam ◉ Chocolate [Submit] [OOPS]

Figure 11-5 The form complete with radio buttons

a radio button for the user to click on to select that choice. You can only select one radio button at a time from among any group of buttons associated with the same **NAME**. If a particular radio button is clicked on, the variable **NAME** that refers to that group of radio buttons is set to that button's particular value. Once the Submit button is pushed, the information contained in the form is sent to the HTTP server. To see what radio button was selected, check the **NAME** variable's value with a CGI script.

Comments

Though radio buttons may greatly resemble check boxes, there is one big difference: Only one radio button from any group of radio buttons may be selected at a time. Therefore, only one name is assigned to the entire group of buttons.

COMPLEXITY
INTERMEDIATE

11.5 How do I...
Add password fields to a form?

COMPATIBILITY: HTML 2+

Problem

I would like users to enter their password so I can verify that they are who they say they are. How can I let them type their password so a nosy onlooker will not be able to read it?

Technique

Password fields in forms are displayed as text fields in which the entered text is shown as asterisks. To create a password field, insert an **<INPUT>** tag between the **<FORM>** **...</FORM>** tags. Inside the **<INPUT>** tag, set the **TYPE** to **"password"**. You may have as many password fields as you wish, but you usually only need one.

Steps

The following steps show how to add password fields to forms.

1. Decide how you would like to lay out your form. You will probably want to use only the name and password fields until you can verify that the user is actually who he or she claims to be.

2. Open the HTML document that contains the form you wish to add the password field to. Once again, use the basic document created in How-To 11.1.

3. Add the **<INPUT>** tag for the password field between the **<FORM>...** **</FORM>** tags. In the **<INPUT>** tag, set the **TYPE** to **"password"**. The basic syntax for this is

```
<INPUT TYPE="password" NAME="VARIABLE_NAME" SIZE="number" VALUE="initial
value">
```

The **TYPE** attribute declares this field as a passworded text box. The variable in the **NAME** attribute is what you will refer to when you later want to check what's been entered here. **SIZE** is the length of the passworded text field. The **VALUE** attribute is what this field is initially set to. For example:

```
<INPUT TYPE="password" NAME="PASSWRD" VALUE=secret>
```

4. Put some descriptive text near the field so the reader has a good idea of what you expect him or her to enter.

5. Enter any other text or HTML tags to help clarify the document and make it easier to read. The document should now resemble the following:

```
<HTML> <HEAD>
<TITLE>Input Form</TITLE>
</HEAD>
<BODY>
<H2>INPUT FORM passwords</H2>
<HR>
<FORM METHOD=POST ACTION="/cgi-bin/MY_SCRIPT">
Enter your name here: <INPUT TYPE="text" NAME="NAME" SIZE=30 VALUE="???"><p>
What is your password:
<INPUT TYPE="password" NAME="PASSWRD" VALUE=secret>
<P>
<INPUT TYPE="submit" NAME="SUBMIT_BUTTON" VALUE="Submit">
<INPUT TYPE="reset" NAME="RESET_BUTTON" VALUE="OOPS">
</FORM>
<HR>
</BODY>
</HTML>
```

6. Save the document as text or ASCII.

7. Use the **Open File** command or **Open Local** command on your browser to make sure your form looks like Figure 11-6.

INPUT FORM passwords

Enter your name here: ???

What is your password: ●●●●●●

[Submit] [OOPS]

Figure 11-6 The form complete with a password field

How It Works

The `<FORM>...</FORM>` tags tell the browser to expect form `<INPUT>` tags between these two tags. The `<INPUT>` tag, when the `TYPE` is set to `"password"`, is a text field with text displayed as asterisks. Once the Submit button is pushed, the information contained in the form is sent to the HTTP server. To see what was entered in the field, use the name assigned with the `NAME` attribute.

Comments

Password fields are, for all intents and purposes, text fields. Instead of displaying what the user typed, however, the text displays as asterisks. You will still need a CGI script to analyze this password. For information about creating a CGI script, see How-To 11.12.

COMPLEXITY
INTERMEDIATE

11.6 How do I...
Add pulldown menus to a form?

COMPATIBILITY: HTML 2+

Problem

I would like to allow a reader to select one item from a list of items, while showing only the currently selected item on the form. How can I do this?

Technique

Use the `<SELECT>...</SELECT>` tags to create a pulldown menu inside a form. To create a pulldown menu, insert the `<SELECT>` tags between the `<FORM>` tags. Label each option that can be selected separately with an `<OPTION>` tag. The form may include other HTML tags and elements.

Steps

The following steps show how to add pulldown menus to forms.

1. Decide which items you wish to place in pulldown menus and how you wish to place these items in your form. Sticking with the food motif, you will create one menu that lets a reader pick a food.

2. Open the HTML document that contains the form you wish to add the pulldown menu to. For now, expand on the document used in How-To 11.1.

3. Add the **<SELECT>...</SELECT>** tags between the **<FORM>...</FORM>** tags. Then add each **<OPTION>** tag between the **<SELECT>** tags:

```
<SELECT NAME="NAME">
<OPTION> An option
.....</SELECT>
```

The variable in the **NAME** attribute is what you will refer to when you later want to reference this menu. You have one **<OPTION>** tag for every item in the menu. You may not use any HTML markup tags between these options.

```
<SELECT NAME="MY_PULL_DOWN">
<OPTION>Lobster
<OPTION>Spam
<OPTION>Chocolate
</SELECT>
```

4. Put some descriptive text near the menu so the reader has a good idea of what you want him or her to do.

5. Enter any other text or HTML tags to help clarify the document and make it easier to read. The document should now resemble this:

```
<HTML> <HEAD>
<TITLE>Input Form </TITLE>
</HEAD>
<BODY>
<H2>INPUT FORM pulldown menus</H2>
<HR>
<FORM METHOD=POST ACTION="/cgi-bin/MY_SCRIPT">
Enter your name here: <INPUT TYPE="text" NAME="NAME" SIZE=30 VALUE="???"><p>
Pick a food:
<SELECT NAME="MY_PULL_DOWN">
<OPTION>Lobster
<OPTION>Spam
<OPTION>Chocolate
</SELECT>
<P>
<INPUT TYPE="submit" NAME="SUBMIT_BUTTON" VALUE="Submit">
<INPUT TYPE="reset" NAME="RESET_BUTTON" VALUE="OOPS">
</FORM>
<HR>
</BODY>
</HTML>
```

Figure 11-7 The form complete with a pulldown menu

6. Save the document in text or ASCII format.

7. Use the `Open File` command or `Open Local` command on your browser to make sure your form looks something like Figure 11-7.

How It Works

The `<FORM>...</FORM>` tags tell the browser to expect associate form tags between these two tags. The `<SELECT>...</SELECT>` tags tell the browser to display the text next to each `<OPTION>` tag as a choice in a pulldown menu. Once the Submit button is clicked, the information contained in the form is sent to the HTTP server. To see what was entered in the field, use the name that was assigned with the `NAME` attribute. In a pulldown menu, the variable used with the `NAME` attribute is actually assigned the value in the selected `<OPTION>` tag.

Comments

Pulldown menus are a kind of cross between check boxes and radio buttons because they are usually associated with one value. However, it is possible to have more than one option selected at a time. Many people like pulldown menus because they do not use as much space on the screen as check boxes or radio buttons.

COMPLEXITY
INTERMEDIATE

11.7 How do I...
Add a file selector dialog box to a form?

COMPATIBILITY: HTML 2+

Problem

Now that I have a form in my HTML document, I would like to be able to give users a way to choose a document to be attached to the file's contents that will be sent to the server. How do I do this?

Technique

File selector dialog boxes are added with the **<INPUT>** tag. To create a file selector dialog box that allows a user to select a file from a list of files in a directory, insert an **<INPUT>** tag between the **<FORM>...</FORM>** tags. Inside the **<INPUT>** tag, set the **TYPE** to **"file"**.

Steps

The following steps show how to add file selector dialog boxes to forms.

1. Decide the layout of your form on paper. In this simple example, you will use one text field and one file selector field.

2. Open the HTML document that contains the form you wish to add the radio buttons to. For this example, start with the document used in How-To 11.1.

3. Add the **<INPUT>** tag for the first radio button between the **<FORM>...</FORM>**tags. In the **<INPUT>** tag, set the **TYPE** to **"file"**. The basic syntax for this is

```
Text<INPUT TYPE="file" NAME="NAME" SIZE="width of field" VALUE="value"
ACCEPTt="MIME contents types"  >
```

The **TYPE** attribute declares this field will hold a filename selected from a dialog box button. The variable in the **NAME** attribute is what you will refer to this file as when you later reference it in a script. The **VALUE** attribute is the default value of this field. The **SIZE** attribute sets the width of the field that will hold the filename. The **ACCEPT** attribute allows the user to limit the types of files that can be attached.

The tags for use in this example look like this:

```
<INPUT TYPE="file" NAME="FILEATH" VALUE="Cool File">
```

4. Put some heading text near the field that will contain the name of the file selected so readers have a good idea of what you want them to do.

5. Enter any other text or HTML tags that might help clarify the document and make it easier to read. The document should now resemble the following:

```
<HTML> <HEAD>
<TITLE>Input Form</TITLE>
</HEAD>
<BODY>
<H2>INPUT FORM File Dialog Box</H2>
<HR>
<FORM METHOD=POST ACTION="/cgi-bin/MY_SCRIPT">
Choose the file you wish to attach: <INPUT TYPE="file" NAME="FILEAT" SIZE=30
VALUE="COOL FILE"><p>
<P>
<INPUT TYPE="submit" NAME="submit_button" VALUE="Submit">
<INPUT TYPE="reset" NAME="reset_button" VALUE="Oops">
</FORM>
<HR>
</BODY>
</HTML>
```

6. Save the document as text or ASCII.

7. Use the `Open File` command or the `Open Local` command on your browser to make sure your form looks like Figure 11-8.

How It Works

The `<FORM>...</FORM>` tags tell the browser to expect form `<INPUT>` tags between these two tags. The `<INPUT>` tag, when the `TYPE` attribute is set to `"file"`, creates a field to hold a value, and a button for the user to click on to call up a dialog box that will, in turn, let him or her select a file for a directory. Once the Submit button is pushed, the information contained in the form is sent to the HTTP server.

Figure 11-8 The form complete with a file selector dialog box

Comments

As of this writing, we have not seen any sites that use this feature. Still, it is a nice addition to HTML that will no doubt be utilized in the future. It should also be noted that the ACCEPT attribute is not supported by all browsers.

COMPLEXITY
INTERMEDIATE

11.8 How do I...
Add a single line text field to a form?

COMPATIBILITY: HTML 2+

Problem

Now that I have a form in my HTML document, I would like to let the user enter just one line of text. How do I do this?

Technique

Single line text fields are added to forms by use of the `<INPUT>` tag. To create a single line text field that allows a user to enter a single line of text, insert an `<INPUT>` tag between the `<FORM>`...`</FORM>` tags. Inside the `<INPUT>` tag, set the TYPE to `"text"`. You may have as many single line text fields as needed, and you may include other HTML tags between these tags.

Steps

The following steps show how to add single line text fields to forms.

1. Decide how many you need and how you are going to lay them out on the form. The number is usually quite easy and straightforward to determine. The layout is a matter of personal taste and preference. In this example, you will use just one single line text field.

2. Open the HTML document that contains the form you wish to add the single line text field to. For this example, start with the document used in How-To 11.1.

3. Add the `<INPUT>` tag for the first radio button between the `<FORM>`... `</FORM>`tags. In the `<INPUT>` tag, set the TYPE to `"text"`. The basic syntax for this is

```
<INPUT TYPE="text" NAME="NAME" VALUE=value SIZE="length of the field">
```

The TYPE attribute declares that this field is a simple text field. The variable in the NAME attribute is what you will refer to this single line text field by when you later reference it in a script. The VALUE attribute is what this field is initially set to. The SIZE attribute is used to set the width of the field.

4. Put some heading text near the single line text field so readers have a good idea of what you want them to do.

5. Enter any other text or HTML tags that might help clarify the document and make it easier to read. The document should now resemble the following:

```
<HTML> <HEAD>
<TITLE>Input Form</TITLE>
</HEAD>
<BODY>
<H2>INPUT FORM SINGLE LINE TEXT FIELD</H2>
<HR>
<FORM METHOD=POST ACTION="/cgi-bin/MY_SCRIPT">
Enter your name here: <INPUT TYPE="text" NAME="NAME" SIZE=30 VALUE="???"><p>
<P>
<INPUT TYPE="submit" NAME="submit_button" VALUE="Submit">
<INPUT TYPE="reset" NAME="reset_button" VALUE="Oops">
</FORM>
<HR>
</BODY>
</HTML>
```

6. Save the document as text or ASCII.

7. Use the Open File command or the Open Local command on your browser to make sure your form looks like Figure 11-9.

How It Works

The <FORM>...</FORM> tags tell the browser to expect form <INPUT> tags between these two tags. The <INPUT> tag, when the TYPE attribute is set to "text", creates a field to hold a line of text. Once the Submit button is pushed, the information contained in the form is sent to the HTTP server. To access that information, use the NAME variable's value with a CGI script.

INPUT FORM -- Single line text prompt

Enter your name here: ???

Submit   OOPS

Figure 11-9 The form complete with a single text line

Comments

`Text` is the default value type of the `<INPUT>` tag.

COMPLEXITY
INTERMEDIATE

11.9 How do I...
Use a clickable image as a Submit button?

COMPATIBILITY: HTML 2+

Problem

Those text Submit buttons on forms are boring looking. I would like to liven my form up by using an image as my Submit button. How do I do this?

Technique

Using an image as your Submit button is surprisingly easy. To create a graphical Submit button, insert an `<INPUT>` tag between the `<FORM>...</FORM>` tags. Inside the `<INPUT>` tag, set the `TYPE` to `"image"`.

Steps

The following steps show how to use images as Submit buttons in forms.

1. Decide what type of image you would like to use as your Submit button, and then create it with your favorite graphics program. Remember, for capability it is best to use a GIF file.

2. Open the HTML document that contains the form you wish to add the radio buttons to. For this example, start with the document used in How-To 11.1.

3. Add the `<INPUT>` tag for the graphical Submit button between the `<FORM>...</FORM>` tags. In the `<INPUT>` tag, set the `TYPE` to `"image"`. The basic syntax for this is

```
<INPUT TYPE="image" SRC="url of the graphio" NAME="SUBMIT" VALUE="Go for⇐
it" >
```

The `TYPE` attribute declares that the image pointed to by `SRC` is to be used as the Submit button. The `NAME` and `VALUE` attributes will be used by non-graphical browsers to render a Submit button.

4. Enter any other text or HTML tags to create the form that will hold the information to be submitted.

```
<HTML> <HEAD>
<TITLE>Input Form </TITLE>
</HEAD>
<BODY>
<H2>INPUT FORM CLICKABLE IMAGES FOR SUBMIT</H2>
<HR>
<FORM METHOD=POST ACTION="/cgi-bin/MY_SCRIPT">
Enter your name here: <INPUT TYPE="text" NAME="NAME" SIZE=30 VALUE="???"><p>
<INPUT TYPE="image" SRC="button.gif"> NAME="SUBMIT_BUTTON" VALUE="Go for
it!">
<INPUT TYPE="reset" NAME="RESET_BUTTON" VALUE="OOPS">
</FORM>
<HR>
</BODY>
</HTML>
```

5. Save the document as text or ASCII.

6. Use the `Open File` command or the `Open Local` command on your browser to make sure your form looks like Figure 11-10.

How It Works

The `<FORM>...</FORM>` tags tell the browser to expect form `<INPUT>` tags between these two tags. When the `TYPE` attribute is set to `"image"`, a button is created on the form that will contain the image pointed to by the `SRC` attribute. The image will function as the Submit button for the form. Once the user selects this button, it acts as if the user had just pressed a standard Submit button as it sends the information to the method named in the action attribute in the `<FORM>...</FORM>` tag.

Comments

This feature is a nice addition to HTML because it can help liven up forms some. Remember to include the `NAME` and `VALUE` attributes for nongraphical browers.

Figure 11-10 The form with an image Submit button

11.10 How do I...
Pass information between forms?

COMPATIBILITY: HTML 2+

Problem

I want to build two forms and have something in the second form be contingent on something entered in the first form. Since a form is not accessible again once it is submitted, how can I do this?

Technique

It is possible to pass information between forms with hidden fields. These fields can be accessed by a CGI program or script even after the form has been submitted to determine what course of action to take in building a second form.

Steps

The following steps give a general description of how you can pass information from one form to another. For more complete information on this topic, see Chapter 13, Handling Server Security.

1. Create an HTML document. For this example, use the one from How-To 11.1.

2. Enter the holder for the hidden field. A hidden field is created with the `<INPUT>` tag much like a text field.

```
<INPUT TYPE="hidden" NAME="HIDDEN_FIELD"  VALUE="info">
```

Here the **TYPE** attribute is set to **"hidden"** so a reader cannot see the field. The **NAME** attribute is set to whatever name you wish to use to access this field with later. The **VALUE** attribute is any state information you wish to carry in this field.

```
<HTML> <HEAD>
<TITLE>Input Form</TITLE>
</HEAD>
<BODY>
<HR>
<FORM METHOD=POST ACTION="/cgi-bin/my_script">
```

continued on next page

continued from previous page

```
Enter your name here: <INPUT TYPE="text" NAME="NAME" SIZE=30 VALUE="John
Smith">
<INPUT TYPE="hidden" NAME="HIDDEN_FIELD"  VALUE="info">
<INPUT TYPE="submit" NAME="SUBMIT_BUTTON" VALUE="Submit">
<INPUT TYPE="reset" NAME="RESET_BUTTON" VALUE="OOPS">
</FORM>
<HR>
</BODY>
</Html>
```

This form looks identical to the form created in How-To 11.1, when displayed by a browser.

3. After the form is submitted to the server, use a CGI script to refer to the field.

How It Works

When you place a hidden field inside the `<FORM>...</FORM>` tags, you create space to hold information. The reader will not see or use this space, but a CGI script can utilize it. You can access this field as you would any other field.

Comments

This is just a very general introduction to this topic, with just enough information to let you recognize it when you see it later. It is very easy to create the hidden field on the form. To utilize this field, though, requires a CGI script written in Perl or C, or some other language. There is an example of this technique and more information on hidden fields in Chapter 14, The Common Gateway Interface (CGI).

COMPLEXITY

INTERMEDIATE +

11.11 How do I...
Choose a request method to send data to the HTTP server?

COMPATIBILITY: HTML 2+

Problem

Now that my form is all ready to go, what method should I use to send the information to the HTTP server, and how do I tell the form to send this information?

Technique

First, decide if you are going to use the **get** or **post** method. This is largely a matter of personal preference, but the consensus seems to be that you should use **post**. Use the **<INPUT>** tag to create a Submit button. When the user selects this button, the information in the form is sent to the HTTP server.

Steps

The following steps give a general overview of the procedure used to decide which method you wish to use when submitting information from a form to a server.

1. Decide what you want to include in your form and how you wish your form to be laid out. For this example, use a simple form that asks a reader for his or her name and comments.

2. Decide which method you wish to use to post your information. You have two choices: **get** or **post**. Sometimes this choice is dictated by the type of server your system is using, in which case it is a good idea to call your system administrator and see if he or she recommends either of the two methods. If not, then the choice is a matter of your preference. The **post** method seems to be the most common choice.

The **get** method passes the contents of the form as a string in a query URL. The server places this string into the environment variable **query_string**.

The **post** method sends the contents as a data block through the standard input stream of the CGI script named in **ACTION**. The length of this string is stored in the environment variable **content_length**.

No matter which method you choose, the data will still be encoded the same: **field1=content&field2=content&.**

3. Create your HTML document, complete with a form.

```
<HTML><HEAD><TITLE>A Simple Sample Form</TITLE></HEAD>
<BODY>
<HR>
<FORM METHOD=POST ACTION="$ME/post">
Name: <INPUT TYPE="text" NAME="INPUT_NAME" SIZE=30
VALUE="???">
<P>Comment:<TEXTAREA NAME="TEXT_COMMENTS" ROWS=5 COLS=50>
</TEXTAREA>
<P><INPUT TYPE="submit" NAME="SUBMIT_BUTTON" VALUE="SEND">
<HR>
</FORM>
</BODY>
</HTML>
```

4. Save your document in text or ASCII format.

5. Read the next section to see how you can process this and other forms.

How It Works

Selecting the Submit button passes the information in the form to the server. For this example, if a user entered "John Smith" for `input_name` and "Nice WWW site!" for `text_comments`, these would be sent to the server as

```
input_name=John+Smith&text_comments=Nice+WWW+site!
```

It is then up to the CGI script processing the form to parse out the data.

Comments

There is much information online that addresses choosing between the `get` and `post` methods. To see what NCSA has to say, access the following URL: `http://hoohoo.ncsa.uiuc.edu/docs/setup/admin/NCSAScripts.html`.

COMPLEXITY
INTERMEDIATE+

11.12 How do I...
Process a form?

COMPATIBILITY: HTML 2+

Problem

Now that I have created this great form, how can I let somebody actually use it over my Web server? Then, how can I process the information they send me?

Technique

Information stored in a form is sent to the HTTP server as part of a data stream, either as part of a URL or as a data block. It is possible to use environment variables to extract the user input from this data stream. Processing a form requires a CGI script to act as a go-between among the HTML, the HTTP server, and the information sent in the form. This script may be written in any high-level language your site supports. Favorite choices are Perl and C. This very simple sample script is broken into three parts:

▪ The first part looks at the arguments sent to the server in the URL and determines what actions to take.

▪ The second part displays the form for a user to interact with.

■ The third part extracts and decodes the form's information, after which it processes that information.

Steps

The following procedure uses a form created from techniques used in previous sections of this chapter to show one method of capturing and then utilizing information from forms.

1. Develop a form that you wish to use. For this example, we will use a very simple three-item form:

```
<HTML><HEAD><TITLE>A Simple Sample Form</TITLE></HEAD>
<BODY>
<HR>
<FORM METHOD=POST ACTION="$ME/post">
Name: <INPUT TYPE="text" NAME="INPUT_NAME" SIZE=30
VALUE="???">
<P>Comment:<TEXTAREA NAME="TEXT_COMMENTS" ROWS=5 COLS=50>
</TEXTAREA>
<P><INPUT TYPE="submit" NAME="SUBMIT_BUTTON" VALUE="Submit">
<HR>
</FORM>
</BODY>
</HTML>
```

2. Create a CGI script in the editor or word processor of your choice. The CGI script in this example is broken up into three parts. The first part, or main program, sets up the routine and decides if the server should send the reader a form to fill out or if the reader has sent the server a form to process. The Perl code for this script immediately follows.

The first part of the script is actually broken up into two sections. The first section takes care of the overhead:

```
#!/usr/bin/perl
$ME = "HTTP://MY_SERVER/cgi-bin/SAMPFORM.CGI";
$PATHINFO = $ENV{PATH_INFO};

print <<EOF;
Content-type: text/HTML

EOF
```

The first line tells the Perl compiler that this is a Perl script. The next line sets up the address given in the **<FORM>** tag's **ACTION** attribute. You should of course replace the **MY SERVER** with your server's URL. The third line grabs the path information from the environment variable **path_info**. This information is used in the next section of the script to determine if the program should send the user a form to fill out, or if the user has sent information from the form. The next four lines initialize the server to expect an HTML document.

```
if ($PATHINFO eq "") {
   &send_form;
} elsif ($PATHINFO =~ m|^/post|){
   &post_form;
}
exit 0;
```

These lines use the path information to determine what course of action the script is to take. If the path information is blank (""), that means to send the user a form to fill out. If the information contains a string that contains the word **post**, that means the user has seen the form and pressed the Submit button on the form, and now it is time to process the information in the form.

3. The next part of the script is the **send_form** subroutine. This part outputs to the HTTP server the form you wish the reader to see.

```
sub send_form
{
   print <<EOF ;
<HTML><HEAD><TITLE>A Simple Sample Form</TITLE></HEAD>
<BODY>
<HR>
<FORM METHOD=POST ACTION="$ME/post">
Name: <INPUT TYPE="text" NAME="INPUT_NAME" SIZE=30 VALUE="???">
<P>Comment:<TEXTAREA NAME="TEXT_COMMENTS" ROWS=5 COLS=50> </TEXTAREA>
<P><INPUT TYPE="submit" NAME="SUBMIT_BUTTON" VALUE="Submit">
<HR>
</FORM>
</BODY>
</HTML>
EOF
}
```

This is straightforward. The HTML document prints to the server, allowing a user to interact with the form.

4. The final part of the script is the **post_form** subroutine. This is put into action after the user has submitted the form. This subroutine reads the form's input from the standard input stream, splits the input into appropriate fields and values, and then removes any strange characters the server may have added when it encoded the input. You are now free to access the information contained in the form via the names assigned to each field.

```
sub post_form
{
# Get the input.
   read(STDIN, $BUFFER, $ENV{'CONTENT_LENGTH'});
   # Split the name-value pairs.
   @pairs = split(/&/, $buffer);
   foreach $PAIR (@pairs)
   {
```

```
    ($NAME, $VALUE) = split(/=/, $pair);
# Un-Webify plus signs and %-encoding
    $VALUE =~ tr/+/ /;
    $VALUE =~ s/%([a-fA-F0-9][a-fA-F0-9])/pack("C", hex($1))/eg;
    $FORM{$NAME} = $VALUE;
  }
```

Without diving too much into Perl (there are other Waite Group Press books on that subject), it is sufficient to say here that this code reads the contents of the standard input into a variable called **$BUFFER**. The string in **$BUFFER** is a **content_length** bytes long string of continuous data sent like this:

INPUT_NAME=john+smith&text_comments=nice+web+server

The next few lines of code use the **split** command to separate variables and their values. The lines after that remove those **+** signs from the value and translate any encoded characters.

```
  print <<EOF ;
<HTML>
<HEAD><TITLE>Here's what was input</TITLE></HEAD>
<BODY>
The name entered was: $FORM{'INPUT_NAME'}. <P>Their comments are
$FORM{'TEXT_COMMENTS'}.
</BODY></HTML>
EOF
```

The final part of this routine outputs another HTML document that utilizes the information sent in the form. To use the person's name in the form, refer to it by **$FORM{'INPUT_NAME'}**. This **$FORM{'INPUT_NAME'}** is replaced in the outputted HTML document by **John Smith**.

5. The script is now complete. Save it with whatever name you think best describes it. For this example, simply call it **sampform.cgi**.

sampform.cgi

6. If you created your script with a word processor or editor on a system other than the system your server resides on, you will need to transfer the script to the appropriate spot on your server system. Check with your system administrator for information on how to do this for your particular system.

7. Once the script is on the server, change the access rights to the script. Most HTML documents do not need a user to execute them, but CGI scripts do. The mode should be changed to

chmod 755 sampform.cgi

8. A script that will not run on your server will not work. Compile the script to make sure there are no errors. To compile the script, type either

sampform.cgi

or

```
perl sampform.cgi
```

If all went well, this should output something that looks like this:

```
Content-type: text/HTML

<HTML><HEAD><TITLE>A Simple Sample Form</TITLE></HEAD>
<BODY>
<HR>
Send me your comments:<BR>
<FORM METHOD=POST ACTION="MY_SERVER/cgi-bin/SAMPFORM.CGI/post">
Name: <INPUT TYPE="text" NAME="INPUT_NAME" SIZE=30 VALUE="???">
<P>Comment:<TEXTAREA NAME="TEXT_COMMENTS" ROWS=5 COLS=50> </TEXTAREA>
<P><INPUT TYPE="submit" NAME="SUBMIT_BUTTON" VALUE="Submit">
<HR>
</FORM>
</BODY>
</HTML>
```

9. Access the CGI script over the Web by using the **Open Location** command in your browser's menu. Then enter the URL specified by the **METHOD** action. For example, to use the CGI script used in the sample, type

```
HTTP://MY_SERVER/cgi-bin/sampform.cgi
```

replacing **MY_SERVER** with your server's actual URL. When first accessed, the form should look much like Figure 11-11.

Once the form is submitted, the screen will look like Figure 11-12.

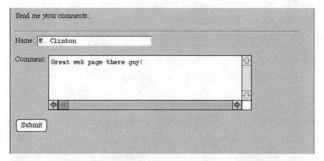

Figure 11-11 The form served by the sample script

Figure 11-12 The form's information after it is processed

How It Works

The first part of the script sets the table and checks the **path_info** environment variable to see if the server has sent anything to the script. If nothing was sent, the script sends an HTML document for the browser to display. If the path information contains **post**, the server has sent a form that must be processed. The fields are encoded, so they must first be separated, then stripped of all the characters the system adds. After this, the information in the fields may be accessed by referring to their variable names. An in-depth analysis of how CGI and forms interact goes beyond the scope of this chapter and will be covered later, in Chapter 13, Handling Server Security. Still, you do not need a total understanding of the form and CGI interaction to successfully use forms.

Comments

Not all system administrators allow users to have their own CGI scripts. It is a good idea to check with your system administrator before starting. Not only will he or she be able to tell you if you can place scripts on your server, but the administrator can probably also point you in the right direction. The script given here is a very bare-bones script. It doesn't have any error checking or safety precautions built into it. In addition, the form could have contained other types of form tags. Still, it should give you the basic idea of how CGI and forms interact with each other. Experiment by plugging in your own forms.

For more information on forms and CGI look in the Yahoo! directory at `http://www.yahoo.com/Computers_and_Internet/Internet/World_Wide_Web/Programming/Forms/`.

The complete final CGI script used at the end of this chapter looks like this:

```
#!/usr/bin/perl
#
# This is a CGI script which lets users interact with a form.
# If the CGI PATH_INFO passed to us is empty, then we just
# return an HTML document with a form allowing the user to post
# feedback. If the CGI PATH_INFO is set to post, the user's feedback
# is shown to them
#
#
# URL for this script (without arguments) on this server. Note: this
# server using WN this URL would look slightly different with NCSA
#    "http://address/cgi-bin/name"
#
# Note: the examples use variable names in upper case as per the WPG⇐
# standard only here variable names are in lower case as in the Perl⇐
# standard
#
# Note: I am using my server's actual URL in this example

$me = "http://zeb.nysaes.cornell.edu/cgi-bin/SAMPFORM.cgi";
```

continued on next page

continued from previous page

```perl
# side note: this example is written with NCSA server in mind, but if the WN
# server was used the /cgi-bin/ directory would not be needed as WN can
# recognize that a file is a cgi script by the .cgi suffix.

# Get the argument from the URL.

$pathinfo = $ENV{PATH_INFO};

# Start out by sending a content-type for the document we'll be returning.

print <<EOF;
Content-type: text/html

EOF

# See what we're supposed to be doing.

if ($pathinfo eq "") {
   &send_form;
} elsif ($pathinfo =~ m|^/post|){
   &post_form;
}
exit 0;

# &send_form; returns a menu of available options for this gateway
#script.

sub send_form
{
#
# The form for them to interact with -- you can plug your own in
# here...
#
   print <<EOF ;
<HTML><HEAD><TITLE>A Simple Sample Form</TITLE></HEAD>
<BODY>
Send me your comments:<BR>
<HR>
<FORM METHOD=POST ACTION="$me/post">
Name: <INPUT TYPE="text" NAME="input_name" SIZE=30 VALUE="???">
<P>Comment:<TEXTAREA NAME="text_comments" ROWS=5 COLS=50> </TEXTAREA>
<P><INPUT TYPE="submit" NAME="submit_button" VALUE="Submit">
<HR>
</FORM>
</BODY>
</HTML>
EOF

}
# post_form; show them what they entered

sub post_form
{
```

```
# Get the input.
  read(STDIN, $buffer, $ENV{'CONTENT_LENGTH'});
  # Split the name-value pairs.
  @pairs = split(/&/, $buffer);
  foreach $pair (@pairs)
  {
    ($name, $value) = split(/=/, $pair);
# Un-Webify plus signs and %-encoding
    $value =~ tr/+/ /;
    $value =~ s/%([a-fA-F0-9][a-fA-F0-9])/pack("C", hex($1))/eg;
    $form{$name} = $value;
  }
#
#The form we're outputting based on what the user gave us -- you
#can modify this to meet your requirements
#
  print <<EOF ;
<HTML>
<HEAD><TITLE>Here's what was input</TITLE></HEAD>
<BODY>
The name entered was: $form{'input_name'}. <P>Their comments are⇐
$form{'text_comments'}.
</BODY></HTML>
EOF
}
```

PART III
SERVING

CHAPTER 12
SERVER BASICS

12

SERVER BASICS

How do I...

A Web server is an application that listens to the Internet, awaiting connections and requests from Web browsers and other user agents such as search engines. The server examines a request and, if it is appropriate, supplies the requested services. For most casual users, this abridged description is enough. However, if you are developing your own Web site, you will find the How-To's in this chapter of great benefit.

Browsers use the HyperText Transfer Protocol (or HTTP) to communicate with servers. This is a generic protocol language developed specifically for the transmission of hypertext documents across the Internet. Whenever you specify a URL with the HTTP protocol prefix, you are requesting the use of this protocol to transmit the referenced document. Browsers send an appropriate HTTP request to the specified server.

Servers respond to user agent requests with a two-part response. The first component of the response, the response header, contains a variety of information about the server handling the request and the file or data being sent. For example, the type information is in the response header; this information is used by many browsers to determine whether a helper application or an appropriate plug-in is needed to process the object sent. The second part of the response is the message body. The content of this component is the actual data from the requested file, whether it is an HTML document, an AIFF audio segment, or data of some other type.

This chapter introduces information necessary for establishing and maintaining a Web site. This includes directions for server configuration, document installation, and addition of file types. The examples concentrate on the NCSA HTTPD server package, which serves as the basis for both other UNIX-based servers, such as Netscape's Commerce Server, and servers for other platforms, such as WinHTTPD for Windows 3.1 and Website for Windows NT. Several How-To's also examine the installation and configuration of Netscape's FastTrack server.

Chapters 13, "Handling Server Security," and 14, "The Common Gateway Interface (CGI)," discuss server security and gateway application development, respectively.

12.1   Choose Server Software

Once you decide that you are going to establish a server, you need to select and find the appropriate server software. What is appropriate depends upon several factors, such as hardware, operating system, and reliability. This How-To will help you make the right choice.

12.2   Install Server Software

Each server software package will have its own installation guide and requirements. The general installation tasks are similar; however, specific installation details are slightly different from server to server. This How-To examines in detail the installation process for the HTTPD server software developed by NCSA.

12.3   Install a Netscape FastTrack Server

Netscape's recent addition to the server software market provides an easy-to-use, entry level server for the Windows 95/NT and UNIX markets. This How-To examines in detail the installation process for the Netscape FastTrack server software.

12.4   Configure the Server

Each Web site has its own requirements and restrictions. Therefore, simply downloading and installing the software may not be enough to establish a working Web site. This How-To provides information concerning configuring an HTTP server for your site. The specifics of configuring an NCSA HTTPD server are discussed in detail.

12.5   Configure a Netscape FastTrack Server

Unlike NCSA type servers that require direct editing of configuration files, the FastTrack server uses a separate administration server to support configuring of the primary Web server. The administration server provides an HTML form-based interface for configuring the primary server. This How-To examines the use of the FastTrack Web interface to configure a server.

12.6   Register Additional MIME Types

Documents of various types can be stored on HTTP servers. Servers specify document types using Multipurpose Internet Mail Extension (MIME) types. The server must know the type of each document so that it can perform its tasks appropriately. If you add a document of a new type to the server, you must register this new type. This How-To describes how you register new types.

12.7   Install Documents

The primary purpose of the server is to respond to requests for documents. To do so, the server must know where documents are stored. This How-To provides directions for installing documents on an NCSA HTTPD server or on derivative servers such as WinHTTPD.

12.8   Start or Stop the Server

The server must be active to receive requests from clients. You activate the server by starting it and deactivate it by stopping it. These functions are performed as required for maintenance of the server. This How-To describes how you stop and start a UNIX server.

12.9   Register My Server

When your server site runs properly, you will want to let others know it exists. The instructions in this How-To outline a procedure for introducing your site to the World Wide Web community.

COMPLEXITY

INTERMEDIATE

12.1   How do I...
Choose server software?

COMPATIBILITY: ANY SERVER

Problem

How do I choose server software for my Web site? What are the issues involved? Why is one platform or server more efficient or reliable than another? I need to know what my options are and how I can evaluate them.

Technique

The purpose of server software is to appropriately respond to client requests. This involves listening for client requests (perhaps simultaneous requests), evaluating them, and generating suitable responses.

To choose the software that best suits your needs, you must first evaluate the capabilities of your hardware and operating system. Use the evaluation in steps 1–3 to determine whether your platform is adequate for your needs or if you should move to a different one.

Once you have determined your optimal hardware and operating system platform, consider the various server software packages. Select the package that best meets your needs according to the criteria that appear in step 4.

Finally, acquire your chosen server software, either from the manufacturer or by using FTP.

Steps

This How-To presents step-by-step instructions for evaluating and selecting an appropriate server software package to meet the needs of your Web site. To acquire a particular package, you need to be familiar with the use of anonymous FTP or FTP URLs (unless the chosen package is a commercial product, in which case you will need to contact the appropriate vendor). Appendix F, "Summary of Selected Server Software," provides a summary of several available server packages.

1. Identify your hardware platform. This list specifies several hardware platforms suitable to a Web server site.

   ▢ Apple Macintosh computer and compatibles

   ▢ IBM PCs, PC compatibles

   ▢ Sun systems

2. Identify the operating system(s) running on your hardware platform. You may need to consult your system's manuals to determine this information. Server software has been developed for the following operating systems:

   ▢ Mac OS

   ▢ UNIX

   ▢ MS Windows environment

   ▢ MS Windows 95 environment

   ▢ MS Windows NT environment

3. Your hardware and operating system greatly affect your choice of server software, since each HTTP server has been engineered for a single platform. If you have a choice of operating systems, the following list shows, in descending order, the optimal choices in operating systems for a server site. This order assumes similar processing and memory capabilities on the hardware. The How It Works section discusses the basis for this order.

UNIX

MS Windows 95 environment, Windows NT, Mac OS

Windows

4. Based upon your platform, you are now ready to select a server. You need to think about the features you wish to support on your server. Some of these key issues are described next.

Hardware and software platform support. This criterion places the first restriction upon your choice of server packages. Appendix F provides a brief summary of server software packages by operating system. Each description in this appendix ends with a URL that provides additional information on the specified server.

Security. Different server packages provide different levels and types of security. Levels of security range from restricting access to the entire server to restricting access to individual documents. Access may be restricted by machine address, user name and password, or both.

Gateway interface compliance. Many applications work in conjunction with HTTP server software. These applications serve as gateways between a Web server and resources available at the server site. A common interface specification for such applications is the Common Gateway Interface (CGI), which is explained in Chapter 14. (For current release information, see `http://hoohoo.ncsa.uiuc.edu/cgi/overview.html`.) However, different servers support this interface to varying degrees, ranging from full compliance to no gateway application support at all.

Firewall support. Firewalls are another type of security feature. A firewall limits Internet traffic between machines inside and outside the firewall. Running behind a firewall limits your selection of server packages.

Search capabilities. What kind and depth of search capability do you want built into the server software? Additional search capabilities can be built with gateway applications; however, certain server packages directly support searching.

File inclusion support. File inclusion allows your server to incorporate files from your server site into the HTML documents that it distributes. For instance, this feature could be used to include a standard business letterhead on all the HTML documents at your site.

Request types supported. HTTP supports many request types. The most common type is the GET request, supported by most servers. (Appendix G, "The Hypertext Transfer Protocol (HTTP)," provides detailed information on additional request types.) Requests for HTML documents are usually the result of GET requests from browsers.

5. Once you select a list of criteria, you are ready to choose among the various HTTP server software packages available for your platform. Consult Appendix F for a brief description of many commonly used servers.

6. Contact the server software manufacturer, or use FTP to acquire your chosen server software. The example demonstrates how you might use anonymous FTP to acquire the NCSA HTTPD server from a UNIX machine. Open an FTP connection to the `ftp.ncsa.uiuc.edu` site. Then enter

```
glean dsk 151 >ftp ftp.ncsa.uiuc.edu
Connected to ftp.ncsa.uiuc.edu.
220 curley FTP server (Version wu-2.4(25) Thu Aug 25 13:14:21 CDT 1994)⇐
ready.
```

7. When prompted, enter the name **anonymous**. For a password, enter your e-mail address.

```
Name (ftp.ncsa.uiuc.edu:dsk): anonymous
331 Guest login ok, send your complete e-mail address as password.
Password:
230 Guest login ok, access restrictions apply.
```

8. Change directories to the location of the current version of HTTPD by entering the following command.

```
ftp> cd Web/httpd/Unix/ncsa_httpd/current
```

9. Change the transfer mode to binary using the binary command.

```
ftp> binary
200 Type set to I.
```

10. Issue the appropriate `get` command to retrieve the server package appropriate for your UNIX platform.

```
ftp> get httpd_1.4.1_sunos4.1.3.tar.Z
200 PORT command successful.
150 Opening BINARY mode data connection for httpd_1.4.1_sunos4.1.3.tar.Z
(296970 bytes).
226 Transfer complete.
local: httpd_1.4.1_sunos4.1.3.tar.Z remote: httpd_1.4.1_sunos4.1.3.tar.Z
296970 bytes received in 72 seconds (4 Kbytes/s)
```

How It Works

If you are establishing a Web site for providing information to the World Wide Web community, consider several platform issues. First, your server site must run reliably 24 hours a day. You cannot know at what time or from what location accesses will be made; therefore, your hardware and operating system platform must run reliably on a constant basis (or as constantly as possible).

In addition, your server should be efficient. You want to be able to service many incoming requests as quickly as possible. Popular sites service over a thousand requests an hour. These requests could be spaced over the entire hour or within a single minute. In a perfect world, closely spaced or even simultaneous requests would be serviced as quickly as those made at wider intervals. Your hardware and software will have a significant impact upon this performance.

Finally, you should consider the maintenance of a server on your platform. A server should be easily maintained and updated. Keep in mind that, in some cases, ease of maintenance decreases as the number of supported features increases.

With these needs in mind, the available server platforms can be prioritized from most to least suitable as follows: UNIX; Windows NT, Windows 95, or MacOS; and Windows. The UNIX operating system features true multitasking, the ability to run many processes at the same time. This capability makes it possible for an HTTP server to answer many simultaneous requests. Further, the UNIX operating system provides a clear separation between user processes, such as an HTTP server, and operating system tasks, such as a printer manager. This capability improves the reliability of your server significantly. Your server will remain intact under high system loads and will have a reduced likelihood of system crashes. Finally, the UNIX platform was the first to be used for HTTP server development; consequently, many new features and capabilities are added to UNIX servers before they reach servers for other platforms.

Windows NT, Windows 95, and MacOS are about equally desirable. They support servers that, in general, are easier to configure, particularly if you are unfamiliar with UNIX. They also support both multitasking and task separation, although not as strongly as these features are supported in UNIX. Unless you are managing an excessively popular site with a large number of gateway applications running, server performance on these platforms competes nearly on a par with the UNIX servers.

Finally, DOS and Windows are the least favorable for establishing a stable Web site. Neither of these environments supports true multitasking, nor do they support task separation particularly well. Windows systems simulate a limited form of multitasking, but not to the same degree as UNIX. The lack of true multitasking leads to sluggish response time, which increases quickly with the number of requests. The lack of task separation leads to reduced reliability in general; user applications can cause system crashes that place your Web site out of commission until the system is rebooted. System crashes for a single user are annoying, but system crashes for your Web site mean that your site is dead to the world.

For some of the platforms mentioned above, server selection is limited; however, for several there is a significant selection available with varying capabilities. Therefore, consider the features you wish to support when choosing your platform and server.

Comments

Ultimately, the choice of hardware, operating system, and server platform hinges on personal choice. Many Web administrators agree that HTML documents are best distributed over the Web through the combination of a UNIX-based machine and either the NCSA or CERN HTTP servers. Both of these servers are freely available from URLs `http://hoohoo.ncsa.uiuc.edu/docs/Overview.html` and `http://www.w3.org/hypertext/WWW/Daemon/Status.html`, respectively.

Finding a UNIX machine is not as difficult a task as it might sound. The Linux operating system is a UNIX clone that has been developed for PC-compatible computers. This operating system is freely available, and information can be found at URL `http://sunsite.unc.edu/mdw/linux.html`. Seriously consider this option for establishing a reliable, low-cost Web site. Even though Linux will run on a 386 platform, you can greatly increase the reliability and efficiency of your Web site if you have a 486 or Pentium-based system, preferably one with more than 16 megabytes of RAM.

COMPLEXITY
INTERMEDIATE

12.2 How do I...
Install server software?

COMPATIBILITY: UNIX-BASED SERVER

Problem

I have selected and acquired my server software. Now I need to install it correctly on my system. NCSA HTTPD server software is one of the most commonly used UNIX-based server packages; it has been ported to a variety of other platforms and is the basis for several other popular servers. How do I install this package?

Technique

Server software is usually acquired in a compressed archive. This software must then be uncompressed and unarchived to an appropriate location on your hard disk. If a suitable executable copy of the server software has been acquired, the process is complete; otherwise, the server software package needs to be compiled prior to use.

This How-To explains how to install the NCSA HTTPD server. A similar process is required by most UNIX server packages; examine your documentation to learn how to install your server software.

Steps

The steps outline the procedure for installing the NCSA HTTPD server on a UNIX system; many of the instructions given for this server will also apply to other platforms. These instructions are also suitable for updating the server software.

1. If you have a compressed archive version of this program, you must first uncompress the archive file; if the file is not compressed, proceed to step 2. Use the following command to uncompress the server archive.

```
uncompress httpd_1.4.1_sunos4.1.3.tar.Z
```

2. Unarchive your server software archive. Install the software in an appropriate location on your hard disk. (If you have already unarchived and installed your server software in a suitable location, proceed to step 3.) This step varies by platform; however, in general, you should place your server software in a location that you can easily access and maintain. The following example shows the installation of the NCSA HTTPD software in the /usr/local directory.

```
glean# ls
adm      include
bin      lib
conf     man
etc      typescript
httpd_1.4.1_sunos4.1.3.tar
glean# tar xf httpd_1.4.1_sunos4.1.3.tar
glean# ls
adm      httpd_1.4.1_sunos4.1.3.tar
bin      include
conf     lib
etc      man
httpd_1.4.1     typescript
```

3. This step is optional, but it is recommended for platforms capable of creating aliases. Create an alias to the location where you installed your server software. This link can be referenced when starting your server rather than the installation directory created in step 2. Thus, when you update the server, your references to your server application need not change. When an update is made, install the new version as specified in steps 1 and 2, and link the update to the old alias. This process is shown in the example, which demonstrates the creation of an alias for a server installation under UNIX, followed by an update to point to a new server installation.

```
glean# ls -l
total 10
lrwxrwxrwx  1 root           10 Jun 15 15:36 httpd -> httpd_1.3R
drwxr-sr-x  2 root          512 Jun 15 15:36 httpd_1.3R
drwxr-sr-x  8 524           512 May 21 23:37 httpd_1.4.1
glean# rm httpd
rm: remove httpd? y
glean# ln -s httpd_1.4.1 httpd
glean# ls -l
total 10
lrwxrwxrwx  1 root           11 Jun 15 15:38 httpd -> httpd_1.4.1
drwxr-sr-x  2 root          512 Jun 15 15:38 httpd_1.3R
drwxr-sr-x  8 524           512 May 21 23:37 httpd_1.4.1
```

4. Finally, create the root directory of your data tree. The root directory is the base of your document hierarchy, the top-level directory where you place most of your Web documents. If you plan to run multiple servers providing access to multiple hierarchies, select several locations. Choose these locations based upon the goals for the particular data tree. For most situations, you'll need to choose a hard disk with adequate space for your documents. If your data tree will be relatively static and development has already been completed, you should already have a good idea how much disk space is required; however, if the document tree is dynamically changing and growing, you may need to link space from a large drive to your chosen location. The example demonstrates this task on a UNIX platform.

```
glean# df
Filesystem      kbytes     used      avail    capacity      Mounted on
/dev/sd3a       32791      4102      25410    14%       /
/dev/sd3d       281599     168051    99469    63%       /usr
/dev/sd3e       47185      6347      38479    14%       /var
/dev/sd3g       516811     484585    6386     99%       /export/tools/sparc.sunos.4
/dev/sd3h       807204     40134     726710   5%        /export/home/00
swap            281280     16        281264   0%        /tmp
schemer:/export/home/00/users/dsk
                1255494    546059    646661   46%       /tmp_mnt/home/dsk
schemer:/export/home/00/users/omonroe
                1255494    546059    646661   46%       /tmp_mnt/home/omonroe
glean# mkdir /export/home/00/htdocs
glean# ls -F /export/home/00
ht1/      htdocs/           lost+found/   shen@         users/
```

How It Works

Installing server software is usually a straightforward process. Configuring and administering the server is where the complexity increases. You can acquire server software through either anonymous FTP or via an FTP URL. How-To 12.1 provides an example of using anonymous FTP to acquire server software. Figure 12-1 shows how you could use Netscape and an FTP URL to acquire the same server package.

Software packages are often stored on archive sites in compressed and archived formats. In the UNIX world, compression and archival support often use two separate utilities. For PCs and Macintoshes, these functions are usually supported through the same application. For proper installation, the package needs to be uncompressed and unarchived.

Where you place the server software package is often determined by convenience; you will need to have access to the configuration files as well as the executable programs. The space required by the server software is fairly fixed; therefore, you won't need large amounts of extra disk space beyond the server software requirements. You may wish, however, to retain enough space to potentially install the next version of the software when it becomes available. Step 3 above showed you how to prepare for such an eventuality. Creating a link to the installation directory and specifying server-related files with respect to this link makes such upgrades easier to manage; all you'll need to do is replace the link to the old version with a link to the new version.

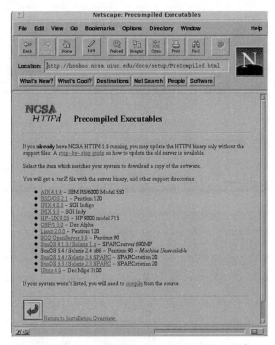

Figure 12-1 Acquiring NCSA HTTPD with an FTP URL

Finally, choose a location to serve as the root of your data tree. Most servers provide a way to address HTML documents and other Web objects outside this hierarchy. However, for security, most documents should reside in this location. The more documents outside this controlled area, the higher the security risk. If you plan on running multiple independent servers from your computer, choose several such locations. Figure 12-2 shows a diagram of a UNIX directory hierarchy and displays a potential choice for the root of a data tree.

This choice usually depends on the amount of free disk space in a particular partition. If you expect your Web site to grow, extra space is essential. If your document set is fixed, free disk space may not be as important.

Comments

Many servers—such as OS2HTTPD, WinHTTPD, Website, Apache, and others—are based upon the NCSA HTTPD server; consequently, the installation procedures given above for the UNIX HTTPD server apply to them as well. The specific methods of decompression and extraction vary, depending on platform, but decompression and extraction will generally be required. Still, be careful to read the specific installation instructions provided with your server software.

Keep in mind that server software development is an ongoing process; therefore, both software and documentation may change from one day to the next. You should pay attention to the developments and evolution of the server package you choose and make upgrades as new products become available and stable.

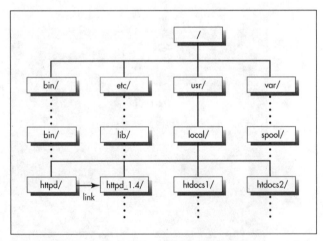

Figure 12-2 UNIX NCSA HTTPD directory hierarchy diagram

COMPLEXITY
INTERMEDIATE

12.3 How do I...
Install a Netscape FastTrack server?

COMPATIBILITY: NETSCAPE FASTTRACK SERVER

Problem

I've purchased a Netscape FastTrack server for my hardware and operating systems platform. I now need to install the products so that I can begin providing my HTML documents to the world.

Technique

The Windows installation process involves the self-extraction of the archive file provided by Netscape. Invoking this file begins the installation. Once the file extraction process is complete, the familiar Windows software Setup Wizard allows completion of the installation. This application requests the information necessary to minimally install the FastTrack server. The Setup Wizard will then automatically complete the installation.

Steps

These steps outline the procedure for installing the Netscape FastTrack server on a Windows 95 system. The process for installation on a UNIX system more closely resembles the process described in How-To 12.2.

1. Netscape distributes the FastTrack server by FTP as a self-extracting archive. By double-clicking on the file in Windows Explorer, you trigger the decompression and installation of the server software. The archive file unpacks itself and launches the setup program.

2. When the Netscape FastTrack Server Installation dialog box appears, select Yes to continue. The Welcome screen should appear.

3. Click Next from the Welcome screen to continue. The Software License Agreement should appear.

4. Click Accept to accept the agreement. If you choose not to accept, the installation process ends.

5. The setup program requests you to select the location to install the server. Choose the default location, enter another directory, or select the browse option to pick a directory.

6. Click Next to continue with the installation. The setup program copies the necessary files to the specified directory.

7. Click Next to continue with the installation. The Configure Netscape FastTrack Server screen should appear. The configuration information required in the next several steps provides FastTrack with the minimal configuration information necessary to complete installation. (How-To 12.5 describes how to modify and extend this minimal configuration information.)

8. The application requests the complete name of the server host. Enter the fully qualified domain name of your server machine, and click Next.

9. Enter the administration password. Also, select either the default administration user name, admin, or select one of your own. Click Next to continue.

10. Finally, at the prompt enter the location of your primary document directory. Select the default, enter a directory, or browse through the directories and make your selection. Click Next to continue.

11. At the Finish screen, click Finish to complete installation. The installation procedure completes itself by installing several items to the Windows 95 Start Menu as well as a new icon in the Windows Control Panel.

How It Works

The basic installation process on the Windows platforms conforms to standard installation of most Windows-based software. If you are installing Netscape FastTrack on a UNIX system, the installation process will more closely resemble the process described in How-To 12.2.

Netscape provides its server software as a self-extracting, self-installing archive file. The installation process begins when this archive file is executed from Windows Explorer, the software installer in the Control Panel, or from a command line. The file first extracts the necessary files into the system's temporary area. Once this is complete, the file invokes the standard Setup Wizard. The only information necessary to complete the first portion of the process is the name of the directory where the setup program should install the server software, as shown in Figure 12-3. You should select a location on your hard disk with at least 16 megabytes of free space to store the necessary server files.

Figure 12-3 Setup procedure requesting the destination directory

The setup program continues by placing the necessary server files in the specified directory. The setup program screen tracks the status of the installation process. Figure 12-4 displays an example tracking of an installation of the FastTrack server.

The Setup Wizard proceeds by requesting minimal configuration information necessary for proper installation. Installation requires three pieces of essential configuration information:

▪ **Server Name.** Installation requires the specification of the Internet name of the machine running the server. This must include both the host name and the domain name. Figure 12-5 displays the screen used to enter this information. Either confirm the default name provided or enter the proper name for the server host. Clicking Next confirms the choice currently specified.

▪ **Administrator User Name and Password.** The FastTrack server allows administration of the Web servers running on a host machine through the use of a special Web server running on the host machine. This administration Web server supports the creation and administration of information Web servers on the host machine. Access to the administration Web server is initially limited to individuals using the user name and password specified at this stage. Figure 12-6 shows the dialog window which requires this information. Initial configuration of the server requires the use of this user name and password. How-To 12.6 describes this configuration process using the administration server.

▪ **Document Directory Location.** The installation process requires the location of the document root directory. This directory is the location where the server locates documents that clients, usually Web browsers, request. Choosing this directory requires an analysis of current disk usage on your host machine and an estimate in bytes of the expected amount of information to be supplied by the server. Although it is possible to move the document directory and reconfigure the server, proper selection of a document root directory may reduce the need for this task. Figure 12-7 displays the dialog that configures the document directory location.

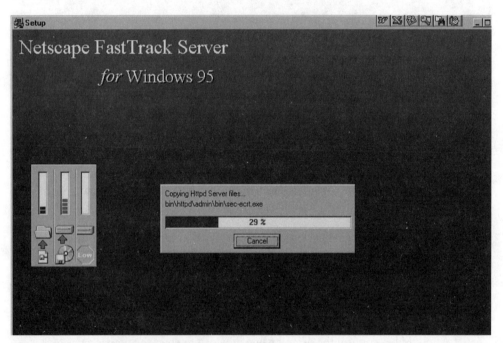

Figure 12-4 Setup installation tracking screen

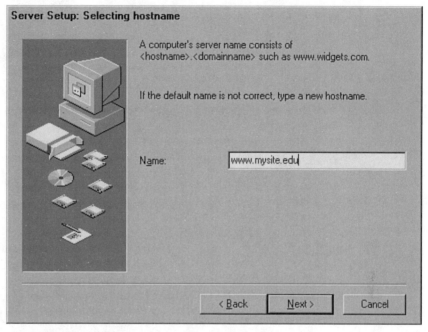

Figure 12-5 Specifying the server host name

Figure 12-6 Specifying the administrator's user name and password

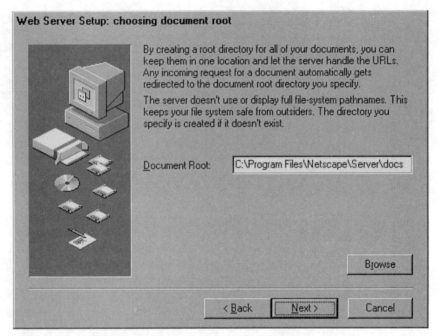

Figure 12-7 Specifying the document directory location

Once the setup program performs the minimal configuration, the installation completes itself with the creation of several menu and Control Panel items. The installation application creates menu items for running the administration server, accessing the FastTrack release notes, and uninstalling the FastTrack server. New Control Panel icons allow the control of all FastTrack servers running on the particular machine. For example, Figure 12-8 displays this server's control console.

Once installation is complete, the next task is server configuration (see How-To 12.5).

Comments

The operating system platform often determines the degree of automation involved in the installation of the server software. In the Windows world, automatic installation of software tends to be the norm, whereas in the UNIX world, a more controlled manual process dominates. The procedures found in this How-To and How-To 12.2 provide examples from both ends of this spectrum.

In the end, either method suffices to get the job done.

Figure 12-8 Access the Netscape Server Management Control Panel through the Windows Control Panel

COMPLEXITY
ADVANCED

12.4 How do I...
Configure the server?

COMPATIBILITY: HTTPD-BASED SERVERS

Problem

I need to tailor the server environment to my needs. What are the various attributes that I need to set? Where are they located, and what values do they take? Can I configure multiple servers to run on the same machine?

Technique

HTTPD servers require three general types of configuration:

◻ Server configuration

◻ Resource configuration

◻ Security configuration

These three configurations tell the server how it should run, what resources it has at its disposal and where they are, and who has access to which resources. The manner in which these configurations are performed may vary among servers; however, most servers require at least the first two to be done prior to startup.

The following procedure provides instructions for performing the first two of the three types of configurations for the NCSA HTTPD server. Initial security configuration is also described for this package. (Configuring and maintaining server security is covered in detail in Chapter 13.) For performing tasks specific to other software, read the documentation for your server software.

Steps

The following procedures provide instructions for configuring an NCSA HTTPD server. The individual steps walk you through tasks in the configuration process. For further information on configuring an NCSA HTTPD server, see NCSA's online documentation at URL `http://hoohoo.ncsa.uiuc.edu/docs/setup/Configure.html`. Configuration of the WinHTTPD server software is very similar, so hints for configuring this server are included in the steps as well. The configuration of these server packages entails including the correct commands in the correct configuration file. Configuration file commands are also referred to as directives.

Choosing a Directory

You need to provide a directory for each independent server running on your host machine. This directory contains the configuration files, log files, and possibly unique icons and gateway applications associated with the particular server.

Change directories to the location where you wish to configure the server. If this is your primary server, the configuration directory can be the same as your installation directory. To properly configure a second server, you need to copy the necessary configuration files to another location. The example demonstrates the creation of a new directory for configuring a second NCSA HTTPD server.

```
glean# cd /usr/local
glean# ls
adm     conf     httpd       include        man
bin     etc      httpd_1.4.1 lib
glean# mkdir httpd2
glean# cp -r httpd/conf httpd2
glean# ls httpd2/conf
access.conf-dist        mime.types
httpd.conf-dist         srm.conf-dist
glean# mkdir httpd2/log
```

Server Configuration

Once you have chosen or created a configuration directory, you must perform any necessary server configuration tasks. For NCSA HTTPD, this process involves editing the `httpd.conf` file. (For WinHTTPD, this is the `httpd.cnf` file.)

1. Open `httpd.conf` in your favorite text editor.

2. Configure (UNIX HTTPD only) the `ServerType` directive. This directive can take one of two values: `standalone` or `inetd`. `Standalone` configures the server to run by itself, while `inetd` specifies that the server be controlled by the inetd process, an application that monitors various network functions. Stand-alone servers tend to run more efficiently than inetd-controlled servers due to reduced overhead. To establish a stand-alone server, the following line should appear in the configuration file.

```
ServerType standalone
```

Servers using inetd require a slightly different configuration approach than a stand-alone server. Examine URL `http://hoohoo.ncsa.uiuc.edu/docs/setup/Configure.html` for more information on configuring an inetd server.

3. Assign a port number for the server. The default port for HTTP servers is port 80. To use this port, you must start the server as the privileged user, `root`. Port numbers less than 1023 are reserved for the various network services provided by the UNIX operating system. Some common port choices for servers are 1080 and 8080. To configure a server to listen at port 8080, issue the `Port` command:

```
Port 8080
```

4. UNIX allows you to start several server processes running at startup. Specify the initial number and the maximum number using the `StartServers` and `MaxServers` directives. The default values for these directives are, respectively, **5** and **20**. You can change these values depending on your hardware capabilities and the volume of traffic you expect. The following lines establish these default values.

```
StartServers 5
MaxServers 20
```

5. Assign (in a UNIX HTTPD configuration) the user and group names for the individual who runs the HTTPD process. For security, you may not wish the server to run with the privileges of the individual who is executing the HTTPD process; you probably do not want the server to run as the privileged user, root—even if root actually starts the server. To configure the server to run as if it were run by username me and group mygroup, issue the following directives in the configuration file.

```
User me
Group mygroup
```

You can specify the values for these directives by user or group names or by user or group numbers. If you use numbers, precede the specific number with the pound sign (#).

6. Next, set the name (e-mail address) of the individual administering this server with the ServerAdmin directive. The following line sets me@www.mysite.edu as the administrator for this server.

```
ServerAdmin me@www.mysite.edu
```

7. Add a line to specify the base address of the directory in the file system you will use to store the various server files. For example, the following line in your configuration file would establish /usr/local/http2 as the base location for your server files.

```
ServerRoot /usr/local/http2
```

8. Specify the location of the various log files used by the server. Specify where the error, transfer, agent, and referer logs are located. If the specified path does not begin with a slash (/), the path is relative based upon the path specified with the ServerRoot directive. Use the following lines to set these locations.

```
ErrorLog logs/error_log
TransferLog logs/access_log
AgentLog logs/agent_log
RefererLog logs/referer_log
```

9. Specify where the process ID for the primary server process will be stored. Use the PidFile directive to specify this information. As with the log files, this specification can be either relative to the server root directory, or absolute.

```
PidFile logs/httpd.pid
```

10. Specify how the server refers to itself by using the `ServerName` directive. Many Web sites use servers with names beginning with `www` as server names. However, simply placing this name in the configuration file will not make this file usable by the outside world. To accomplish this, you must contact your network administrator to set up the new name as an alias for your machine. The following line would establish `www.mysite.edu` as the name of a server.

```
ServerName www.mysite.edu
```

11. Once you have completed the configuration, save this file and configure the server resources.

Resource Configuration

Next, you must configure the resources available to the server. This involves telling the server where it can locate a variety of resources. You can configure this aspect of the NCSA HTTPD server by editing the `srm.conf` file (WinHTTPD: `srm.cnf`).

1. Open `srm.conf` in your favorite text editor.

2. Set the location of your data tree with the `DocumentRoot` directive. For example, the following line sets the document root to be located in the `/export/home/00/htdocs` directory.

```
DocumentRoot /export/home/00/htdocs
```

3. Specify the subdirectory of individual user directories visible to this server. This subdirectory is commonly called `public_html`. (This particular directive is not supported by WinHTTPD.) If you wish the subdirectory accessible by the server to be referred to as `www_docs`, you would issue the following directive:

```
UserDir www_docs
```

If someone wished to access a document called `doc.htm` from the home directory of `user` through your server, he or she would use the URL `http:// www.mysite.edu/~user/doc.htm`.

4. The `DirectoryIndex` directive specifies the name of the default file to open when none is given in a URL addressing the site. If an individual accesses your server without specifying a particular file (for example, `http://www.mysite.edu/`), the server responds with a predefined default file. The default name used by NCSA HTTPD is `index.html` (WinHTTPD: `index.htm`). If a directory does not have a prewritten index, a directory index may be generated dynamically. The following code specifies that the default directory index is in a file named `index.htm`.

```
DirectoryIndex index.htm
```

5. The access control information for each directory is stored in a single file. Configure the name of this file with the `AccessFileName` directive. The default specification appears as

```
AccessFileName .htaccess
```

See Chapter 13 for information on how to use directory-level access control files.

6. You may register additional document types provided by this server. Several methods for performing this task are described in detail in How-To 12.4.

7. If the server cannot determine the document type of a requested file, it provides a default type in the response to the request. Use the `DefaultType` directive to designate the default document type that the server uses. In most cases, the Multipurpose Internet Mail Extension (MIME) type `text/plain` is an appropriate value for this attribute. (See Appendix C, "Multipurpose Internet Mail Extensions (MIME)," for additional information on MIME types.) You could use the following line of code to designate this default type:

```
DefaultType text/plain
```

8. You may associate icons with particular document types. For example, a folder icon could be associated with a directory. HTTPD-based servers come with several specified default icons that you may optionally replace or extend with your own. When you issue the `AddIcon` directive, specify the filename extension with which you desire to associate an icon, as well as the location of the icon on the hard disk. Specify this location using any path aliases that you established for this server with `Alias` directives. So, for example, to establish an alias for the `icons` directory in the `/usr/local/http2` directory and then associate an icon with movie files, issue the following set of directives:

```
Alias /icons/ /usr/local/etc/httpd/icons/
AddIcon /icons/movie.xbm .mpg .qt
```

NCSA HTTPD allows you to establish up to 20 separate directory aliases for your server.

9. HTTPD-based servers provide a special alias for the directory containing CGI applications. (See Chapter 14 for a detailed description of CGI programs.) Specify this location with the `ScriptAlias` directive. For example, if you want to specify `/cgi-bin/` as the alias for this directory and the actual location of this directory is `/usr/local/httpd/cgi-bin`, use the following line of code in your configuration file.

```
ScriptAlias /cgi-bin/ /usr/local/httpd/cgi-bin/
```

10. Save this configuration file and proceed with the security configuration.

Security Configuration

Finally, you must configure security. The steps in this section provide a method for configuring an HTTPD-based server with limited security. This represents a bare-bones configuration that allows you to get your server up and running. For advanced security configuration and for security configuration of other servers, see Chapter 13 along with the documentation for your server software.

You can configure the security of an NCSA HTTPD server by editing the `access.conf` file (WinHTTPD: `access.cnf`).

1. Open `access.conf` in your favorite text editor.

2. Specify the location of the standard server script directory. The entry contained in the distribution file assumes a default location. The default entry appears in the following code:

```
<Directory /usr/local/etc/httpd/cgi-bin>
Options Indexes FollowSymLinks
</Directory>
```

To modify this entry, change the `/usr/local/etc/httpd/` portion of the directory path to wherever you placed the script directory. This is usually in the server root directory (`ServerRoot`) in a subdirectory called `cgi-bin`.

3. Modify the second directory element to point to the root of your data tree. The default entry appears as

```
<Directory /usr/local/etc/httpd/htdocs>
```

Modify this entry to point to the directory defined as the root of your document hierarchy (`DocumentRoot`).

4. Save this configuration file.

You have completed the configuration of your server and are now ready to start the server and begin serving HTML documents to the World Wide Web community.

How It Works

Server configuration entails establishing values required for the server to run properly. The server needs to know who should own the server process, where various server files are located, who the server administrator is, and a variety of other information. This information forms the constraints under which the server runs.

Resource configuration involves specifying information concerning the data tree. This task includes providing a reference to the root of the document hierarchy. It involves establishing mappings for additional document types. And many times, server-specific as well as general aliases can be established for directories and documents in the data tree. The steps above specify a bare minimum resource configuration. Additional modifications can be made to tune the server more extensively. For more detailed information on configuring the server resource map file for HTTPD-based servers, refer to the available online documentation.

If you have chosen a server that, by default, allows access to documents, you need not concern yourself too much with security configuration unless you wish to place restrictions upon some portion of your data tree. Information about security configuration for particular server packages is described in Chapter 13. If you have a server that denies access, such as WN (see Appendix F), you need to configure security prior to starting your server. In this case, examine your server documentation to properly establish your security.

When the server initially runs, it reads the commands from the configuration files. These directives establish the constraints under which the server runs. Each server on your system requires a full set of configuration files tailored to specify the constraints and capabilities that you want.

When you alter a configuration file, the server needs to be stopped and restarted for the configuration changes to take effect. Since the configuration files are only read when the server is initially run, the changes are not seen until the server restart causes the configuration files to be read anew.

Comments

The configuration files and formats for servers which are derived from NCSA HTTPD, such as WinHTTPD, Apache, and OS2HTTPD, are quite similar to those of their parent. Consequently, you can usually use the procedures defined above for configuring these servers.

Certain variations exist between platforms, however. You should examine the documentation for your package, keeping an eye out for these differences. Most server packages have considerable online documentation to help you with the configuration process.

The online documentation provides you with up-to-the-minute information on the current status of your server software. If you have waited even a few days to install the package you downloaded, a better version may have become available in the intervening time.

COMPLEXITY

ADVANCED

12.5 How do I...
Configure a Netscape FastTrack server?

COMPATIBILITY: NETSCAPE FASTTRACK SERVER

Problem

Installing the FastTrack server provided only minimal configuration information. I need to add an alias for additional directories on my server. I would like to create specific configuration styles applicable to selected portions of my server. And I need to create a server capable of listening to another Internet port.

Technique

Two methods exist to configure a FastTrack server. The first method involves the direct editing of the FastTrack configuration files, namely the `magnus.conf` file and the `obj.conf` file. Although the format and commands differ, this process closely resembles the configuration of an NCSA server just described in How-To 12.4. The online documentation provided with FastTrack explains the specific commands for use in these files.

The second method uses the administration server that provides menu-based access to the configuration of all FastTrack servers running on a host machine. When the administration server is invoked, the administrator selects a server to configure. Upon selection, the administration server displays the administration menu for the chosen server. From this menu, the administrator can configure all aspects of the chosen server.

Steps

The steps outline the procedure for configuring the Netscape FastTrack server on a Windows 95 system. Beyond the initial extraction of the distribution files, the Windows 95 installation process is similar to those for both Windows and UNIX. These instructions also provide directions for running additional servers on the same host machine.

1. Invoke the administration Web server in one of the following three ways:

- Enter the URL for the administration Web server using Netscape Navigator.

- Select the Netscape icon from the Windows Control Panel.

- Choose the Start | Programs | Netscape | Administer Netscape Server item from the Windows Start menu.

2. If you do not wish to create a new server on this host, proceed to step 5. Select the Install a New Netscape FastTrack Server button.

3. Enter the requested information:

- **Server Name.** This must include the complete Internet host name and domain name.

- **Port Number.** This specifies the port to which the new server should listen.

- **Server Identifier.** This name serves to identify the new server within the scope of the administration Web server.

- **Document Root.** This directory will serve as the root of primary document repository for the new server.

4. Select the OK button to complete the creation of the new server. At the success screen, select Configure Your New Server to configure the new server.

5. View the current settings of your server by selecting the View Server Settings option in the System Settings window, which examines the current configuration of the server.

6. Select the items from the displayed settings that require alteration. Some of the common items that you may wish to change:

- **Primary Document Directory.** This directory will serve as the root of primary document repository for the new server.

- **Additional Document Directories.** This allows the association of aliases for specific directories on the host machine.

- **Port Number.** This specifies the port to which the new server should listen.

- **Error Log.** This gives the location of the error log file for this server.

- **Default MIME type.** If the server cannot determine the type of a file, the server uses this type.

- **Access Log.** This gives the location of the access log file for this server.

- **Configuration Style Creation.** Configuration styles provide a method for reusing and reapplying a configuration to a particular subset of documents on the Web server.

> **NOTE**
> Each menu in the administrator provides access to help tailored to the specific configuration information under review.

7. Whenever configuration information changes, select OK to submit the specified changes.

8. Select Save to confirm the changes. Changes do not take effect until they are applied. If you are done changing the configuration, proceed to step 9; otherwise, return to step 6.

9. Once you have entered all desired configuration changes, click the Apply button at the top right corner of the administration Web server main directory. This will stop and restart the Web server, incorporating the changed configuration.

How It Works

The administration Web server provided with the Netscape FastTrack server is the primary means of configuring a server. You access the server locally either by invoking the Programs | Netscape | Administer Netscape Server options from the Windows Start menu or by selecting the Administer button on the Netscape Server Management Control Panel available from the Windows Control Panel. Figure 12-9 displays these two methods of starting the administration Web server. These two methods both result in the launching of Netscape Navigator Gold, which provides the access to the server. From remote sites, launch Netscape Navigator Gold and directly access the administration Web server using its URL; this URL is `http://server_name:5709`, by default.

Navigator prompts you for a user name and password to access the administration Web server. If the user name and password are accepted, the main administration page appears in the browser as shown in Figure 12-10. From this page, you may

- Create a new server on the current host machine

- Remove a server from the current host machine

- Configure the administration server

- Turn a server on or off

- Configure a server on the current host machine

Figure 12-9 Access the FastTrack administration server

Figure 12-10 Access administration functions through the administration server main access page

How-To 12.8 discusses the various methods of turning servers on and off. Further, Chapter 13 addresses those configuration issues specific to server security. Selecting the server removal provides a fill-out form through which any server, including the administration server, may be removed from the host machine; removal of the administration server is not advisable unless you plan to remove all FastTrack servers from the host machine.

A single host machine may run multiple instances of the FastTrack server. The Install a New Server option provides a form-based interface to this creation process, as displayed in Figure 12-11. This form provides the minimal configuration information necessary to establish the new server. Submission of this form triggers the installation of the new server; the confirmation screen seen in Figure 12-12 provides access to the new server's main configuration page.

Figure 12-13 displays a typical server administration page. The administration page provides access to all of the commonly configured aspects of the server. The top menu bar in this page delineates configurable areas. Initially, the page appears with system settings menu items set. The available system settings appear in the far left frame. The right frame contains the configurable information pertinent to the topic selected in the top menu and the subtopic selected from the left frame. A particularly useful subtopic under system settings is View Server Settings. Not only does this subtopic summarize the current server settings, but it also provides links to windows that allow modification of these current settings. Figure 12-14 displays an example of the View Server Settings frame within the context of the administration page.

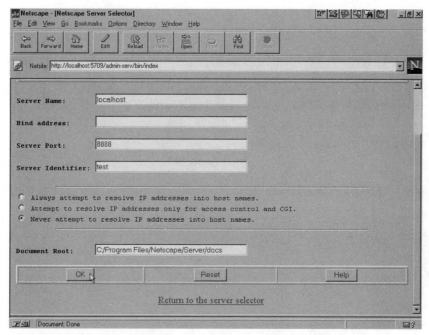

Figure 12-11 Provide minimal configuration information through the install new server page

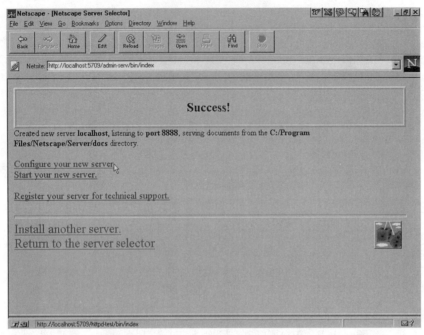

Figure 12-12 Complete configuration process accessible from the successful installation page

Figure 12-13 Configure a server through its administration page

Figure 12-14 Viewing server settings provides a handy means to access commonly configured server attributes

The other top frame menu items allow configuration of other essential areas of the server. The Access Control and Encryption items are discussed in How-To 13.9. The Programs item supports the configuration of various types of server-side application programs such as common gateway applications (discussed in Chapter 14), server-side Java applications, and other types of server-side applications. The Server Status item provides access and summarizes the various activity logs for the server. The Config Styles menu items allow the creation, deletion, and modification of configuration styles. A configuration style is a named set of configuration settings that can be attached to multiple portions of a particular server's document directories. Finally, the Content Management menu items support miscellaneous configuration options dealing with the document base of the server. These items permit the modification of the default types of documents in directories (subject to the constraints), the specification of forwarding URLs, and the creation of aliases to secondary document directories, to name several of the most commonly configured subtopics.

Modifications can either be applied immediately upon specification of each configuration item or saved for application at once after all modifications are complete. After each modification, a confirmation form appears in the configuration frame (bottom right). This form allows several options: go back to prior to requesting change, undo the requested change, save the requested change, and save and apply the requested change. Figure 12-15 shows a typical confirmation form. Once all configuration changes are complete, they must be applied using the Apply button in the top frame menu, if they have not already been applied individually.

Figure 12-15 Confirmation forms allow for immediate or delayed application of configuration changes

Selecting the Apply button places the Apply window in the bottom right frame. This frame provides buttons labeled: Apply Changes and Load Configuration Files. The second option applies if the configuration files (`magnus.conf` or `obj.conf`) were modified manually and required reloading to establish the correct current configuration information. Selecting the Apply button results in the application of all previously saved configuration changes. Figure 12-16 presents the results of submitting a series of saved changes. The FastTrack server, like the servers in How-To 12.4, requires a shutdown and restart process for changes to take effect. One nice aspect of FastTrack is that this process occurs automatically upon the application of configuration changes through the administration server.

Comments

The administration server system described in this How-To provides an easy interface to the Netscape FastTrack configuration files. Using a text editor also allows configuration. The FastTrack server uses two primary configuration files, named by default `magnus.conf` and `obj.conf`. Configuration information for a particular server can be entered manually. See the online documentation accompanying FastTrack for the formats of these configuration files.

Figure 12-16 Results of the application of configuration changes to the server

If the administration server suits your needs, you should use this server in preference to manual editing. Besides providing a user interface, the forms supporting administration place some constraints on how the configuration information may be changed. Manual modification of the configuration files does not impose such constraints. The trade-off in using these methods is the ease of modification using the administration server versus the flexibility achieved through complete control over configuration edits.

COMPLEXITY
INTERMEDIATE

12.6 How do I...
Register additional MIME types?

COMPATIBILITY: HTTPD-BASED SERVERS, NETSCAPE FASTTRACK

Problem

When I access some documents with a browser, the documents display as a strange mix of control characters because they are a type of file my server won't support. I would like to add documents of this type on my Web site and have them supported by my server. How do I configure the server to support this new document type?

Technique

Multipurpose Internet Mail Extension (MIME) types are used by Web servers and clients to specify the document type of files. This type information is provided to a client through a content type field sent in a server response. The server determines the file type by examining a document's filename extension. This filename extension maps into an internal table that associates filename extensions with document types.

You can modify this table of associations in three ways. This How-To takes you through each method.

Steps

You can use the following three methods to modify or extend the document types that your NCSA HTTPD server can serve properly. These three methods are

- Types file modification

- Resource map file modification

- Access file modification

Types File Modification

The types file is commonly located in the configuration subdirectory. The file supplied with the NCSA HTTPD and Netscape FastTrack distributions is called `mime.types`. The name of this file can be configured in an NCSA server configuration file (`httpd.conf`) using the `TypesConfig` directive.

1. Open the types configuration file in your favorite text editor. This file will either be named `mime.types` or whatever you have specified in the server configuration file using the `TypesConfig` directive.

2. The types configuration file lists the file types recognized, one per line. The MIME type (see Appendix C) is followed by the filename extension that will be associated with that type. Comments in this file appear following a pound sign (#) in the line.

3. If you wish to add a new document type, add a new line to this configuration file. For example, if you want to provide support for Excel spreadsheets using an NCSA server, add the following line:

```
application/excel              xls
```

or using a Netscape FastTrack server, add the following line:

```
type=application/excel         exts=xls,xl
```

4. If you wish to modify an existing entry, move to the type you wish to modify and edit the line. For example, to modify the `text/html` line to accept both `.html` and `.htm` as acceptable extensions, for an NCSA server change the following line:

```
text/html      html
```

to this:

```
text/html      html htm
```

or using a Netscape FastTrack server, change the following line:

```
type=text/html          exts=html
```

to this:

```
type=text/html          exts=html,htm
```

5. Once you have made the alterations that you desire, save this configuration file; then restart the server to realize the changes you have made.

Resource Map File Modification

You can add or modify types using an NCSA server resource map file. Issue `AddType` directives to extend or supersede the default types provided through the types configuration file. In a FastTrack server, you may add or modify types using the object configuration file (`obj.conf`) for the server: Issue the `ObjectType` directive to accomplish this task.

1. For an NCSA Web server, open the server resource map file in your text editor. This file is named `srm.conf`, or whatever you specified in the server configuration file using the `ResourceConfig` directive. For an NS FastTrack server, open the object configuration file; the default name for this file is `obj.conf`.

2. This file contains a series of directives defining the various resources available to the server. Each line is either a comment or a directive. Comments in this file follow a pound sign (#).

3. To add a new document type or to supersede any default types, add a new line to this file. For example, to provide support for Excel spreadsheets, add the following line to this file:

```
AddType        application/excel        .xls
```

or using a Netscape FastTrack server, add the following line:

```
ObjectType fn=type-by-exp exp=*.xls type=application/x-excel
```

4. To add server-wide support for CGI applications outside the specified script directory or server-side includes, issue the following `AddType` directives:

```
# Add support for CGI application through recognition of the cgi extension.
AddType          application/x-httpd-cgi          .cgi
# Add support for server side includes through use of the shtml extension.
AddType          text/x-server-parsed-html          .shtml
```

5. Once you have made the desired changes, save the file. Restart the server to realize the changes you have made.

Access File Modification

You can modify or extend the supported types by changing the access control files, either in the global access control file or at the individual directory level. The types defined in this manner are only available in the designated directories. Such types will supersede those defined in the types configuration file or the server resource map file.

1. Open the access control file in your text editor. The global access control file is named `access.conf` or whatever you specified in the server configuration file using the `AccessConfig` directive. The per-directory access control file is in the directory you wish to affect and is called either `.htaccess` or whatever filename you specified using the `AccessFileName` directive in the server resource map file.

2. To add a new document type or supersede any default types, add a new line to the file. For example, if you want to provide support for Excel spreadsheets, add the following line:

```
AddType          application/x-excel          .xls
```

If you are modifying the global access configuration file, make sure you are adding the type within the appropriate `<Directory>` element(s).

3. If you wish to add directory-level support for CGI applications outside the designated script directory or server-side includes, you can issue the following `AddType` directives:

```
# Add support for CGI application through recognition of the cgi extension.
AddType          application/x-httpd-cgi          .cgi
# Add support for server side includes through use of the shtml extension.
AddType          text/x-server-parsed-html          .shtml
```

4. Save the file and restart the server to realize the changes.

How It Works

The file specified in the server configuration file using the `TypesConfig` directive indicates the default MIME types an NCSA server uses (see Appendix C). A Netscape

FastTrack server locates this file using the load-types function of Init in the object configuration file. This file defines the base types that will be served. This set of types is usually left unaltered and may be used by several servers to define the supported base types. This approach impacts all servers that look to this file for types definitions.

The types added through the resource configuration file impact only the individual server using that configuration file. These added types extend the allowable types over the entire server. For example, you could use this method to make a single server capable of serving Excel spreadsheets while other servers running on the same computer could not.

Finally, you can use the access configuration file modification approach for more fine-tuned control than for an entire server. Modifications through this method have an impact only upon the directories specified. If the method is used in a directory level access control file, then the extensions or modifications are only available when accessing a document in that directory.

The object configuration file in an Netscape FastTrack server supports the finer granularity configuration of types.

Comments

In general, determine which method you will use to add types based upon how widely you wish to support the new type. Most types can be added at the resource configuration level, unless you are particularly worried about security, in which case global or directory-level access control may be the more suitable option. This is particularly true for types such as CGI applications; you, as the Web site administrator, may wish to limit the location of such files to either the script directory or several controlled locations.

In addition, all three methods require you to stop and restart the server for the changes to take effect.

COMPLEXITY
BEGINNING

12.7   How do I...
Install documents?

COMPATIBILITY: ANY SERVER

Problem

I have created Web pages and would like to make them accessible to the World Wide Web community. I already have access to a Web site (see How-To's 12.1–12.5). How do I install my HTML documents on this site?

Technique

The approach used to install documents on a server site will vary by hardware and software platform. In general, you install documents by placing copies of these documents in a predefined area of the file system allocated for this purpose. On operating systems that support file-level access control, the access protection of the documents needs to be set properly.

With many servers, documents can also be placed in preconfigured user directories. The following steps outline the installation of a document on an NCSA HTTPD server or a Mac server.

Steps

The steps define two procedures. The first describes the mechanism a Web site administrator could use for installing documents in the main document area of the server. The second instructs users in how to install documents in their home directories that are accessible by the server.

Document Root Installation

If you are a Web site administrator, you can use the following method for installing documents in the data tree. The location of this document hierarchy is specified in the NCSA server resource file using the `DocumentRoot` directive. In the Netscape FastTrack `obj.conf` file, use the `NameTrans` directive.

1. Examine the documents. Identify the type of each document. If the document type is not supported by your server, either reconfigure the server to support the desired type (see How-To 12.7) or let the author of the document know that the document type is not supported.

2. View each document that is to be placed upon your server in an appropriate viewing environment such as a browser or image viewer. Verify documents of all types before you install them on your server.

3. Once you have checked the documents, move them to an appropriate location in the document hierarchy. If you were to install the file `hello.htm` in the `welcome` subdirectory of the `DocumentRoot`, `/export/home/00/htdocs`, you could use the following UNIX command:

```
mv hello.htm /export/home/00/htdocs/welcome
```

4. Check the permissions settings for the document. You must set these permissions so that the user running the server has read and execute permission on the document. For example, the following command sets the protection of the `hello.htm` document to allow all users to read and execute the document.

```
chmod +rx hello.htm
```

For more information on the UNIX `chmod` command, consult a UNIX reference manual.

5. The document is now accessible through your HTTPD-based server. If you are running a server such as WN that, by default, denies access to documents, configure the access control to the document to provide the desired access level. This allows your server to service requests for this document.

User Directory Installation

The following process outlines the steps required to install documents in your home directory. Documents installed in this manner are subject to constraints established by your Web site administrator.

1. Contact your Web site administrator to determine if documents in your home directory can be supported through your server. If this option is not supported, you must have the site administrator install the documents that you develop. If documents can be served from your home directory, you need to know which subdirectory to use. Your site administrator can provide this information.

2. If you do not already have the designated subdirectory in your home directory, you will need to create it. The default subdirectory specified by the NCSA HTTPD server is the `public_html` directory. Under UNIX, the following command, issued in your home directory, creates such a directory.

```
mkdir public_html
```

The following statement would be placed on the Web site to explain to users of the system that there is a communications malfunction. In any case, the following lines would be added to the server's object configuration files.

```
NameTrans fn=document-root root="C:/Program Files/Netscape/Server/docs"
```

3. Examine the documents. Identify the type of each document. You may have to ask your site administrator which document types are supported by your server. If the document type is not supported, either ask your site administrator to reconfigure the server to support the desired type, or attempt to support the document type yourself using a per-directory access control file (see How-To 12.4). The latter option may not be available, depending on the configuration of the global access file. If you cannot support the type on your own, either attempt the former or redevelop the document using a supported type.

4. You should view each document that is to be placed on your server in an appropriate viewing environment such as a browser or an image viewer. Check that you are not putting incorrect or improper documents on your server.

5. Move the documents to the appropriate subdirectory of your home directory. For example, to install the file `hello.htm` from your home directory, use the following UNIX command.

```
mv hello.htm public_html
```

6. Check the permissions settings for the documents you install. These permissions must be set so that the user running the server has at least read and execute permission on the documents. For example, the following command sets the protection of the `hello.htm` document to allow all users to read and execute the document, while also giving the owner write privileges.

```
chmod 755 hello.htm
```

7. The document is now accessible through your NCSA HTTPD server. If your site is running a server that, by default, denies access to documents, configure the proper access control for the document. This step allows your server to service requests for the document.

How It Works

Servers provide the World Wide Web community with access to documents on your machine. For the server to find these documents, they need to be located in a limited number of predefined locations. The two most common locations are a specified document directory and a specific subdirectory of each user's home directory.

The root of the document hierarchy is specified in the server resource map file. The `DocumentRoot` directive specifies this location. Documents installed in this directory or its subdirectories are visible to the server and may be requested by appropriate clients. The documents in this hierarchy must have protections set so that the server has read and execute permission on the file.

Documents are also commonly installed in users' home directories. The `UserDir` directive can be used in the NCSA HTTPD server resource map file to designate the particular subdirectory in the home directory where the server looks for documents. Once you place documents in this subdirectory, they will be available for access over the World Wide Web. Set the permissions on these files so that the server can access them and provide them to requesting clients. The documents you place in this directory are subject to the limitations imposed by your Web site administrator.

Use caution when installing documents. Once the document has been made available, anyone with the proper access can request and view the file. You should review each document before installing it on your server. Check for both correctness of the document and suitability of the material. Documents that are improperly formatted or badly designed reflect upon your site as a whole. Further, be wary of installing published materials on the Web that may violate copyright laws.

Comments

If you are a Web site administrator, you should develop rules and procedures for developing and submitting documents for installation on your server. To help prevent future problems, these rules should be cleared through the appropriate publications and legal offices of your business. In addition, you should give your users a clear policy for publishing Web-based materials on your site.

If you are a document developer, you should ask your Web site administrator to provide you with a copy of your site's publication policies. This will give you some guidelines to follow when publishing information over your Web site.

Chapter 13 provides more information about document access control and security configuration.

COMPLEXITY
INTERMEDIATE

12.8 How do I...
Start or stop the server?

COMPATIBILITY: UNIX SERVERS, NETSCAPE FASTTRACK SERVERS
(COMMENTS)

Problem

I have installed my server software and am ready to begin making HTML documents available to the World Wide Web community. How do I start my server?

I need to perform some maintenance or reconfiguration of my server. How do I start and stop the server to accomplish my task?

Technique

Maintenance of a server requires you to start, stop, and restart a server. This is true for most servers. How you start the server depends upon the specific parameters that your server accepts and whether the server is run as a stand-alone server or by the Internet services manager process, inetd. Stopping the server entails determining the process ID for the server process and terminating it. To stop and restart the server, you can either do a manual stop and start of the server or use a command that will do both.

This How-To describes these three tasks in detail, with specific examples for the NCSA HTTPD server.

Steps

This section provides instructions for starting and stopping UNIX servers. The examples given use the NCSA HTTPD server as a typical UNIX server.

Starting the Stand-Alone Server

You can most often start a stand-alone server manually from a command prompt. If you are running the server through the inetd process, see Starting the inetd Server.

1. To start the server from a command prompt, run the server program with appropriate parameters for your configuration. Table 12-1 presents the arguments supported by the HTTPD application.

Table 12-1 Command line options for HTTPD

ARGUMENT	EXPLANATION
-d path	Specifies where the server looks for its configuration files. It should match the location specified using the ServerRoot directive in the server configuration file.
-f file	Tells the server which server configuration file to use.
-v	Prints the version number of the server you are running.

If you want to run an HTTPD server with the configuration information in the default directory and default files, issue the following command at a UNIX prompt:

```
/usr/local/etc/httpd/httpd
```

If you want to run another server with configuration files in the **conf** subdirectory of **/usr/local/httpd2**, issue the following command:

```
/usr/local/etc/httpd/httpd -d /usr/local/httpd2
```

2. If you want the server to run whenever the system reboots, you need to modify the system's automated startup files. You must access the system through a privileged user account to perform this task. Once you have logged in to the system as the superuser, open the appropriate startup file in your favorite text editor. This file is called **/etc/rc.local** on many versions of the UNIX operating system.

3. Add the following lines of code at the end of this file:

```
if [ -f /usr/local/etc/httpd/httpd ]; then
   /usr/local/etc/httpd/httpd -d /usr/local/httpd2
fi
```

Change the second line to reflect the command you would have used from a UNIX prompt.

4. Save this file. The next time the system reboots, the server will start automatically. If you are starting a server with the inetd process, you should proceed to the next set of steps; otherwise, you are done.

Starting the inetd Server

If you are starting an inetd-controlled server, you need to verify or modify several files to make sure they are configured properly.

1. The first file you must examine is the /etc/services file. This file lists many Internet services such as Telnet and FTP. Log in as superuser and open the file in your favorite text editor.

2. Add a line for your server. This line should consist of the service name http, followed by a specification of the port and protocol. The following line adds the HTTP service to port 8080 using TCP:

```
http          8080/tcp
```

3. Save the /etc/services file.

4. Open the /etc/inetd.conf file.

5. Add the following line:

```
http stream tcp nowait nobody /usr/local/etc/httpd httpd
```

6. Append to this line any arguments that are suitable for your configuration. For example, if the server root for this server is /usr/local/httpd2, use the following line:

```
http stream tcp nowait nobody /usr/local/etc/httpd httpd -d /usr/local/httpd2
```

See Table 12-1 for applicable command line options.

7. Save the file. You are now ready to start the server.

8. The server is controlled by the inetd process; therefore, to start the server, stop and restart the inetd process. Anytime the system reboots, furthermore, the server starts automatically when the inetd process starts.

Stopping the Server

The UNIX operating system assigns a process ID to each running process. You use the process ID to terminate a running process.

1. Identify the process ID for the server application. This process ID can be found in one of two ways. If your server provides this information, you can retrieve it from the server log files. For example, an NCSA HTTPD server logs its process ID in the file specified with the PidFile directive in the server configuration file. So if this file were specified as log/httpd.pid in the /usr/local/httpd2 directory, you would issue the following cat command to retrieve the process ID for the server.

```
cat /usr/local/httpd2/log/httpd.pid
```

The other approach is to list the running processes using the `ps` command and identify the process ID for the server from this list. Use a filtering program such as `grep` to narrow the list of potential processes. For example, to list all HTTPD processes, use the following command:

```
ps -aux | grep httpd
```

Then, choose the appropriate process ID from the list.

2. Once you have determined the process ID for the server process, you need to terminate the process using the `kill` command. For example, if you have determined that the process ID of the server is 4099, issue the following command at the UNIX prompt:

```
kill 4099
```

Stopping and Restarting the Server

Here you have two choices. You can either follow the procedures for stopping the server and then restarting it, or follow the instructions here for stopping and restarting the server in one step.

1. To stop the server and automatically restart it, follow the above directions for stopping the server through step 1.

2. Then instead of using the `kill` command by itself, add the option `-1` to it. For example, if you have determined that the process ID of the server is 4099, issue the following command at the UNIX prompt:

```
kill -1 4099
```

How It Works

Start your server after the initial installation. The server must also be started after your system has rebooted, which may occur for reasons ranging from a software upgrade to a power failure. The server can either be started manually or through an automatic start procedure, depending upon the server type.

Start a stand-alone server manually by executing the appropriate server command at the UNIX prompt. This starts the process. If you are running the server as a user other than yourself as you are specified in the server configuration file, run the server as `superuser`. If the server is run automatically, a suitable command needs to be added to the system startup files. This command tells the system to run the server whenever the system is started. In any case, the first time you run a stand-alone server, it will have to be from the command line, unless you wish to reboot your system.

If the server is controlled by the inetd process, you must register the server with this process. This involves modifying several static configuration files that the inetd process uses when starting. These files tell inetd about the processes it will control. Once you have modified these files appropriately, you can stop and restart inetd.

This causes the configuration files to be read and your server to be started. You will also have configured the server to start whenever the system starts since inetd is automatically run when the system starts.

You need to shut down the server when you wish to perform extended maintenance on your site or server configuration. You must also bring the server down when you wish to upgrade or change your server software. Shutting down involves identifying the server process ID and having the operating system terminate that process.

Finally, you will stop and restart the server when configuration changes are necessary. Stopping and restarting the server causes the server to initialize itself using the new values stored in the configuration files. Changes made to the configuration files will not take effect until the server has been restarted.

Comments

Configuration alterations in the `access.conf`, `httpd.conf`, `mime.types`, and `srm.conf` files necessitate a server stop and restart to apply the changes. You can modify these files while the server is running in its previous configuration, and then use the Stopping and Restarting the Server procedure described above to stop and immediately restart the server.

Starting and stopping a Netscape FastTrack server is a significantly more automated task. This software provides several means of starting and stopping the server.

▦ **Netscape Server Management Control Panel.** Selecting a server and then clicking the Start or Stop button manually starts and stops the selected server. This control panel also allows the configuration of a server to automatically start with Windows. Figure 12-17 displays this control panel.

▦ **Administration Server Main Access Page.** The administration server triggers the start or stop of a particular Web server running on the host machine when the switch next to the identifier for that server is flipped on the administration server main access page. In Figure 12-18, three servers run on the particular host machine. One of these servers is on, while the other two are off. Selecting the switch associated with a particular server toggles its current status.

▦ **Particular Server Administration Page.** A server's administration page allows the toggling of its on/off status. Figure 12-19 shows the initial appearance of a server's administration page; the page displays the current status, as well as providing buttons for starting and stopping the server.

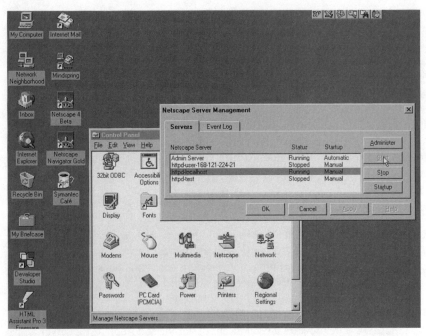

Figure 12-17 Starting/stopping the server through the server management control panel

Figure 12-18 Starting/stopping a server through the administration server main access page

Figure 12-19 Starting/stopping a server through its administration page

COMPLEXITY
BEGINNING

12.9   How do I...
Register my server?

COMPATIBILITY: ANY SERVER

Problem

My server is running, and I have installed several documents. However, I am finding that few people are connecting to my server. How do I let people know that my server is active and what type of information I am providing?

Technique

Once you have created your site, you can register it in appropriate locations to attract the interest of people likely to use your Web site. Do this by registering your site through other Web sites and newsgroups.

This How-To provides step-by-step instructions for publicizing your Web site throughout the world by making use of several available forums.

Steps

Three primary methods are used to announce your server to the world. The following instructions provide a stepwise guide to the registration procedure.

1. Register your server with appropriate Web sites. Registrations are often categorized by location of site or subject. The following list provides URL references to selected sites suitable for the registration of your site.

☐ `http://web.city.ac.uk/citylive/pages.html`

☐ `http://web.nexor.co.uk/aliweb/doc/aliweb.html`

☐ `http://www.ncsa.uiuc.edu/SDG/Software/Mosaic/Docs/whats-new-form.html`

☐ `http://www.w3.org/hypertext/DataSources/bySubject/Overview.html`

☐ `http://www.w3.org/hypertext/DataSources/WWW/Geographical_generation/new_servers.html`

☐ `http://www.yahoo.com/bin/add`

In addition to these Web sites, you should attempt to publicize your Web site through other Web sites at your facility or in your community by contacting the appropriate Web administrator.

2. Submit news of your server site to the Usenet newsgroup `comp.infosystems.www.announce`. You can access this group through the newsreader program with which you are most familiar. If your server is of particular interest to a particular domain, you may wish to announce its location in other suitable newsgroups. Before taking such an action, consider that you are likely to generate a considerable increase in access volume through such an announcement. Therefore, you should be sure that the information you provide is both interesting and relevant to the newsgroup where you advertise. Usenet News is an extremely large forum, and by selectively choosing the newsgroups to which you announce your Web site, you will attract only those individuals most likely to use and benefit from your site.

3. Finally, you may wish to announce your site through mailing lists. Send announcements to mailing lists related to the information at your site. Since mailing lists distribute to a limited number of subscribed members, this type of an announcement might serve as a test for your decision to announce your site to a general newsgroup. You may wish to announce to a relevant mailing list and wait for feedback from the list membership before placing an item in a newsgroup distributed worldwide. In addition, you will probably wish to send a message to a mailing list which is devoted to listing such announcements, such as `net-happenings@is.internic.net`.

How It Works

Unless you publicize the existence of your site, very few members of the World Wide Web community will access your server.

The methods described above publicize your site to users who may be interested in the information you are providing. You can announce your site's existence through appropriate newsgroups.

In addition, many existing sites will list new Web sites in a special area of their own site. This provides some additional publicity as well as providing users with access points to your server. When you first create your Web site, no other site links to information on your server. This situation will change when people know that your site exists. Registering your site at other locations provides people with initial access to your Web site, and once your site has been found, others will begin to provide links within their own information to relevant documents on your server.

Comments

Keep in mind that you can cross-list with other Web sites in your area or at your facility. Many site administrators will provide a link to your site if they feel it is appropriate. You may in turn provide a link back to their site.

CHAPTER 13
HANDLING SERVER SECURITY

13

HANDLING SERVER SECURITY

How do I...

Once you have announced the existence of your Web server, people—many people—will attempt to access your site. You have no control over who will try to view your material, so you will need to decide whether to establish security for your site. If you are distributing sensitive or restricted information, then security constraints are a necessity.

The two most commonly used forms of security provided by server software are domain restrictions and browser authentication. Domain restrictions allow you to specify which machines on the Internet may or may not access your Web site. Browser authentication restricts access by requiring a valid username and password. These two mechanisms can be combined for even stronger security.

The various server software packages provide a variety of security features and hazards. This chapter examines the security capabilities of the following server software packages.

- NCSA HTTPD (UNIX), also derivatives such as Apache
- WinHTTPD (Windows 3.1)
- CERN HTTP (UNIX, VMS)
- MacHTTP (Mac)
- Netscape FastTrack server (Windows 95)

13.1 Specify Allowable Features on an HTTPD Server

You may not wish to allow certain features to be used in particular portions of your document tree on your HTTPD server. This How-To shows how to specify the features you wish to support in each directory of your document tree.

13.2 Establish Domain and Address Security on an HTTPD Server

HTTPD domain-based security allows you to place restrictions on parts of your document tree based on the domain or machine making a request. This How-To describes how to use this feature on the HTTPD server.

13.3 Set Up User and Password Security on an HTTPD Server

HTTPD supports user authentication security, which requires the user to enter a username and password prior to accessing restricted information. In this How-To, you will learn how to configure password security on an HTTPD server.

13.4 Use HTTPD Server-Side Includes

HTTPD and Netscape's FastTrack support a feature known as server-side includes, which allows inclusion of server-generated, dynamic information in HTML documents. Since server resources are utilized, this feature represents a potential security hazard; however, with careful supervision, this risk can be minimized while still retaining the convenience and usefulness of this feature. In this How-To, you will learn how to use HTTPD server-side includes.

13.5   Establish Directory-Level Security on a CERN HTTP Server

You can set access restrictions on a CERN HTTP server to limit actions in specified directories of the document tree through a combination of host filtering and user authentication. These restrictions, unlike those in HTTPD, can only be set to selectively allow access; no means of selectively denying access is supported. This How-To describes how you can set up directory-level security on a CERN HTTP server.

13.6   Set Up File-Level Security on a CERN HTTP Server

In addition to directory-level security, as supported in HTTPD, the CERN package provides a way to specify access restrictions at the file level. With the CERN server, individual files within the same directory can be configured with different security constraints. In this How-To, you will learn how to configure file-level security on a CERN server.

13.7   Install a CERN Proxy Server

The CERN HTTP server software can be run as a proxy server allowing communication from behind an Internet firewall. The information in this How-To shows how you can configure your CERN server to act as such a proxy.

13.8   Establish Domain and Address Security and Password Authentication on a MacHTTP Server

This How-To describes the basic forms of server-level security available with the MacHTTP server. As the other major Web server packages do, MacHTTP allows domain name and machine name specification as well as user authentication. Methods are covered for securing a server and the individual documents and directories that it serves, along with the method for entering usernames and passwords.

13.9   Configure SSL Security on a FastTrack Server

The Netscape FastTrack server provides mechanisms for security at several levels. The first level of security involves the encryption level of the connection between Web browsers and the server. This How-To details how to configure this security measure through the FastTrack administration server.

13.10   Set Up User and Password Security on a FastTrack Server

The Netscape FastTrack server also supports user name/password and Internet domain security. This How-To walks you through the configuration of user name/password security and Internet domain restrictions.

13.11   Use Public Key Encryption

Web servers and browsers communicate in the open. Servers transmit Web pages in an unsecured fashion using standard HTTP. In this How-To, you will learn how Web servers and browsers can use public key encryption techniques to provide secure transmission of HTML documents.

COMPLEXITY
INTERMEDIATE

13.1   How do I...
Specify allowable features on an HTTPD server?

COMPATIBILITY: HTTPD-BASED SERVERS

Problem

The HTTPD server offers a wide range of features, which is what makes it so versatile. However, some of these features may cause security risks in certain areas. Furthermore, not all features are necessary in all areas of the document tree.

How can I selectively choose which features to allow in which areas of my document tree?

Technique

The HTTPD server software, and derivatives such as Apache and WinHTTPD, allow you to specify which server features to support in each directory of the document tree. The server finds these specifications in two locations:

- The global access configuration file

- Per-directory access control files

You can edit the appropriate files to specify the features you want to support in each directory. If you are not the site administrator, you will likely find it easier to create per-directory access control files in those directories for which you are responsible. The following steps walk you through this process. The available features are described in the "How It Works" section that follows.

Steps

These steps show how to specify the features to be supported in a given directory. You may specify this information in either the global access configuration file for the server or in a per-directory access control file located in the directory.

1. To edit a per-directory access control file, begin with step 4 below. Otherwise, change directories to the configuration directory for the server. Usually this is the `conf subdirectory` of the `ServerRoot`, for example, `/usr/local/etc/httpd/conf`.

2. Open the global access control file in your favorite text editor. By default, this file is called `access.conf` (`access.cnf in WinHTTPD`). If this file is not present, check the server resource map file (`srm.conf` or `srm.cnf`) and look for the `AccessConfig` directive, which should tell you the location and filename of the correct file.

3. At the end of the file, create a directory-sectioning directive to store your feature specifications. A directory-sectioning directive has an opening tag composed of the `<Directory>` label, followed by the path to the directory for which you are creating the sectioning directive. The closing tag is composed of the `</Directory>` label. For example, to create a directory-sectioning directive for the `/usr/local/mydocs` directory, insert the following lines in the file:

```
<Directory /usr/local/mydocs>

</Directory>
```

All feature directives for this directory should be contained between the opening and closing tags for this directory-sectioning directive. You should now proceed with step 5.

4. Change to the directory where you want to specify features. In this directory, edit (or create, if necessary) a per-directory access control file. The default name for such a file is `.htaccess` (`#haccess.ctl` in WinHTTPD). This name can be changed with the `AccessFileName` directive in the server resource map file, usually `srm.conf` or `srm.cnf`. Open the appropriate file in your text editor. Your insertion point should not be within the boundaries of an existing sectioning directive (unless you are editing the contents of that particular directive). The beginning or the end of the file is a good place to enter a new directive.

5. Insert the directive for the feature you want to support in this directory. Directives can either be sectioning or single-line directives. For example, to insert a directive that associates the description "My Family Picture" with the file `fam1999.gif`, insert the following directive:

```
AddDescription 'My Family Picture' fam1999.gif
```

The acceptable feature directives are listed in the "How It Works" section.

6. Save the file. If you have made changes to the global configuration files, you must stop and restart the server for your changes to take effect, as described in How-To 12.8.

How It Works

Each feature that you want to support in a directory is specified with a directive. HTTPD supports two types of directives in access files. The standard directive is specified in a single line. The first string in the line is the directive command; the remainder of the line may contain any necessary data associated with the particular command. The `AddDescription` directive, shown in step 5 above, is an example of this type of directive.

The second type of directive is the sectioning directive. A sectioning directive has similar syntax to an HTML element: It begins with an opening tag and ends with a closing tag. Directives may be specified within the scope of a sectioning directive. The `<Directory>` directive used in step 3 above is an example of a sectioning directive. This How-To and the following two cover the current comprehensive set of access file directives. The ones in this How-To determine features allowed in a particular directory or set of directories. The following is a list of these directives and their functions.

- `AddDescription`: Use this directive to associate a description with a particular file. This description is used when an automatic index of the directory is generated. A description is often much more helpful than a filename. This directive can be used in either the global access file or a per-directory access file. For example, to associate the phrase **"Hang 10"** with the file **surf.htm**, issue the following directive:

```
AddDescription 'Hang 10' surf.htm
```

Descriptions may also contain links; therefore, if a brief description is not sufficient, you can link a portion of the description to a Web document.

```
AddDescription 'My <A HREF="http://www.mysite.edu/~me/fam.htm">Family</A>
Picture' fam1999.gif
```

The above line associates the description **"My Family Picture"** with the file **fam1999.gif**; the word **"Family"** is a hypertext link to the document **http://www.mysite.edu/~me/fam.htm**.

- `AddEncoding`: Use this directive to associate a particular filename extension with an appropriate encoding mechanism. Browsers requesting encoded documents need to have local capability to decode that particular type of encoding, as well as to support the HTTP encoding header elements. For example, to specify that the **.gz** filename extension should indicate **gzip** compression, issue the following directive:

```
AddEncoding x-gzip gz
```

This directive may be used in either type of access file.

- **AddIcon**: You may use the **AddIcon** directive in both the global access configuration file and per-directory access control files. Use this directive to associate a particular icon with a particular file type. If the server performs automatic indexing, this icon is presented with any file meeting the established filename extension criteria. The arguments to this directive are the path to the icon along with a list of filenames, wildcards, filename extensions, or one of two special names: **^^DIRECTORY^^** or **^^BLANK_ICON^^**.

Several examples of this directive follow:

```
AddIcon /icons/image.gif .gif .jpeg .fif .xbm
```

When the server automatically generates an index for this directory and finds a file with the extension **.gif**, **.jpeg**, **.fif**, or **.xbm**, it references the **/icons/image.gif** image to display next to the filename.

```
AddIcon /icons/dir.xbm ^^DIRECTORY^^
```

If a subdirectory is found during automatic indexing, then the **/icons/dir.xbm** image displays with that index entry.

```
AddIcon (SND,/icons/sound.gif) *.au
```

This example specifies both an icon and an alternative textual message that may be used by browsers that do not support inline images. This directive causes the **/icons/sound.gif** image to display next to any AU sound file. If the browser does not support inline images, then the text message SND displays instead of the icon.

- **AddType**: The **AddType** directive provides MIME type information for special document types found in a particular directory. This directive contains three parts: the command, the MIME type, and a list of recognized filename extensions. Use this directive in either the global access file or a per-directory access file.

For example, if you want the server to run CGI executables outside the script directory, issue the following directive:

```
AddType application/x-httpd-cgi .cgi
```

- **AllowOverride**: Use of this directive is limited to the global access configuration file. The **AllowOverride** directive specifies which features may be overridden by a per-directory access control file. The directive is followed by a list of options that may be overridden by the local access control.

Table 13-1 summarizes the available arguments for this directive.

Table 13-1 AllowOverride arguments

ARGUMENT	FEATURE
ALL	Local access control may override any features.
AuthConfig	Accesses security information. (See How-To 13.2–13.3.)
FileInfo	AddType and AddEncoding directives.
Limit	Limit sectioning directive. (See How-To 13.2–13.3.)
None	Local access control may not override any global specified features.
Options	Options directives.

■ **DefaultIcon**: This directive specifies an icon for the server to use if a specific icon cannot be associated with the desired file. This directive may be used in either the per-directory or the global access control files. If you want to use the icon **unknown.xbm** when an icon is required but the actual icon is unknown, issue the following directive:

```
DefaultIcon /icon/unknown.xbm
```

A serverwide default icon is usually defined in the server resource map file. The access control directive overrides the server default for a specific directory.

■ **DefaultType**: This directive may be used in either the global access file or a per-directory access control file. The data supplied with the directive specifies the default MIME type for files in the directory. If the server is unable to determine the type of a file in the directory based on filename extension, it uses this default type.

A serverwide default type is specified in the server resource map file; however, you can override this default with an access file default type. The most commonly used default type specified in the server resource file is text/plain, which tells the server to treat a data object as a straight ASCII text file if the type of the object cannot be determined.

If you created a directory that contains only GIF files, you might want to issue the following directive:

```
DefaultType image/gif
```

This directive is required if any of the GIF files in the directory do not have the **.gif** filename extension.

■ **Directory>**: Use this directive only in the global access configuration file to specify the directory affected by the enclosed directives. For example, to create a directory-sectioning directive for the **/htdocs/private/mydocs** directory, use the directive shown below:

```
<Directory /htdocs/private/mydocs>

</Directory>
```

You can use the asterisk as a wildcard character to create a directory directive that affects multiple similarly named document directories. For example, to refer to all the document directories in user home directories (usually in a subdirectory called `public_html`), use the following directive:

```
<Directory /*/public_html*>

</Directory>
```

■ **IndexIgnore**: Use this directive in either access file to specify filename patterns that should be ignored by server automatic indexing. Follow the directive command with a list of the filenames (possibly using wildcards) to be ignored by indexing. For example, to ignore all files with the `.bak` extension, issue the following directive:

```
IndexIgnore *.bak
```

■ **Options**: Use the **Options** directive in either the global or a per-directory access file. This directive tells the server which server options are available in a particular directory. Follow the directive with a list of those options that you want to be available. Table 13-2 indicates the options available on the HTTPD server (with the final column indicating whether you can use the argument with WinHTTPD).

Table 13-2 Options arguments

ARGUMENT	FEATURE	WINHTTPD
All	Makes all options available	Yes
ExecCGI	Allows execution of CGI applications	No
FollowSymLinks	Allows following of symbolic links	No
Includes	Allows use of server-side includes	No
IncludesNoExec	Allows use of server-side includes, except exec	No
Indexes	Generates index file automatically	Yes
None	Makes no options available	Yes
SymLinksIfOwnerMatch	Allows symbolic links only if owner of link and source is the same	No

■ **ReadmeName**: Use this directive in either the global access configuration file or a per-directory access control file. A serverwide `readme` filename may be established in the server resource map file. The filename specified in this directive is used when automatic indexing occurs. This file is presented to the user at the top of the directory listing.

Comments

If you have modified the global access configuration file, you must stop and restart the server for the changes to take place.

For better security, the site administrator may want to use the following access practices:

- When possible, issue an `AllowOverride None` directive for directories in the global access configuration file.

- Do not allow server-side includes. At a minimum, restrict the use of the `exec` server-side command with the `Options` directive.

- Since the site administrator does not have complete control over the content of the directory trees, protect users' home directories. You can do this by inserting the following directory-sectioning directive into your global access configuration file.

```
<Directory /*/public_html*>
AllowOverride None
Options Indexes SymLinksIfOwnerMatch
</Directory>
```

Modify the argument in the opening tag to reflect the locations of your user document trees.

COMPLEXITY
INTERMEDIATE

13.2   How do I...
Establish domain and address security on an HTTPD server?

COMPATIBILITY: HTTPD-BASED SERVER

Problem

I do not want people outside my business to access some critical documents that I do want to make available to employees within the business. I have some even more sensitive documents that I want to make accessible only to people on a particular computer at my site. How can I attain this kind of security?

Technique

You can restrict access to portions of your server by either allowing or denying access to particular computers or domains on the Internet. This type of security is referred to as domain/address security or host filtering.

You can achieve this level of security by using a **<Limit>** sectioning directive to modify the access control files of your server either at the global level, in the server access configuration file, or the local level in the per-directory access control files.

Steps

The following instructions show you how to establish host filtering security for particular portions of your document tree.

1. To establish host filtering using a per-directory access control file, skip to step 4 below. Otherwise, log in as the Web site administrator and change directories to the configuration directory for the server. Usually this is the **conf subdirectory** of the **ServerRoot**.

2. Open the global access control file with your text editor. By default, this file is called **access.conf** (**access.cnf** in WinHTTPD). If this file is not present, check the server resource map file and look for the **AccessConfig** directive, which should tell you the location of the correct file.

3. Locate the directory-sectioning directive associated with the document tree that you want to protect. If a **<Directory>** directive does not exist, go to the end of the file and add it. (See How-To 13.1 for more information on creating a directory-sectioning directive.) Your insertion point should be between the opening and closing tags of this directive. Then skip to step 5.

4. Change to the directory where you want to specify features. In this directory, edit (or create, if necessary) a per-directory access control file. The default name for such a file is **.htaccess** (**#haccess.ctl** in WinHTTPD). This name can be changed with the **AccessFileName** directive in the server resource map file. Open the appropriate file in your text editor. Your insertion point should not be within the boundaries of an existing sectioning directive (unless you are editing the contents of that particular directive); the beginning or the end of the file is a good place to add it.

5. If a **<Limit>** sectioning directive already exists, modify this directive to suit your new security needs. If not, you can create such a directive by inserting the appropriate opening and closing tags in your access file. The **<Limit>** opening tag is composed of the command, followed by a list of HTTP methods that you want to restrict. Insert the following lines of code to create a directive to restrict **GET** method transactions:

```
<Limit GET>

</Limit>
```

The code within the **<Limit>** directive establishes the host filtering that occurs when a client requests a transaction of a specified method type in the protected directory.

6. Use a combination of three subdirectives to achieve this protection: `order`, `allow`, and `deny`. The `order` directive defines the order of evaluation for `allow` or `deny` directives. The `allow` and `deny` directives respectively permit or restrict access to the machines or domains specified as arguments for the directive. For example, to allow clients running on the machine `mysite.edu` access to the directory, you could use the following `<Limit>` sectioning directive:

```
<Limit GET>
order deny,allow
deny from all
allow from mysite.edu
</Limit>
```

More details on these subdirectives and further examples can be found in the "How It Works" section at the end of these steps.

7. Save the file. If you have made changes to the global configuration files, you must stop and restart the server for your changes to take effect, as described in How-To 12.8.

How It Works

You can support host filtering by the `<Limit>` sectioning directive in either a server's global access configuration file or a per-directory access control file. This directive begins with an opening tag containing the `<Limit>` command followed by a list of HTTP methods to which you want this directive to apply. The methods that are currently understood are `GET`, `PUT`, and `POST`; however, the `PUT` method is not currently implemented by HTTPD.

Specify the host restrictions you want to make, using one of the subdirectives listed below:

- `Order`: This subdirective specifies the order in which to evaluate `allow` and `deny` subdirectives in the `<Limit>` sectioning directive. The two possible values for the argument of this directive are `allow,deny` and `deny,allow`. Depending on which value you select, the server evaluates all `allow` subdirectives followed by all `deny` subdirectives, or all `deny` subdirectives followed by all `allow` subdirectives. The default order is `deny,allow`. Thus, the ordering determines whether `allow` will override `deny`, or vice versa.

- `allow from`: The `allow` subdirective specifies machines and domains that are allowed to access information in the protected directory. The arguments of this directive are those names, IP addresses, or partial names and addresses for which you want to allow access. Place a space between each such name or address.

▣ **deny from**: The **deny** subdirective specifies machines and domains that are not allowed to access information in the protected directory. The arguments of this directive are those names, IP addresses, or partial names and addresses for which you want to deny access. Place a space between each such name or address.

Figure 13-1 shows the results of an attempted access to a document in a directory protected with the following **<Limit>** directive.

```
<Limit GET>
order deny,allow
deny from all
allow from .ncsa.uiuc.edu
</Limit>
```

GET method access to the documents in this directory is denied to all browsers except those running on machines in the **.ncsa.uiuc.edu** domain. **GET** requests made from machines within this domain will receive the requested document.

NOTE

The special name **all** refers to requests from any site.

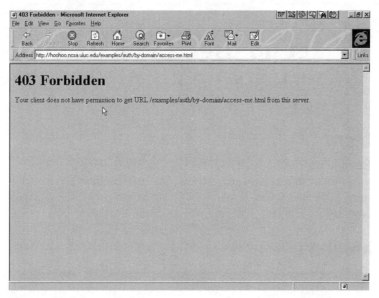

Figure 13-1 Attempting to access a domain-protected document

The `<Limit>` directive below would deny access to browsers run on the `mysite.edu` machine, but allow access from anywhere else.

```
<Limit GET>
order allow,deny
allow from all
deny from mysite.edu
</Limit>
```

Thus, host filtering supported by HTTPD allows you to place access restrictions by allowing or denying access to a portion of the document tree by Internet machine name or address or domain name or address.

Comments

`<Limit>` sectioning directives can be created for each specific HTTP method that may be used to access documents in the protected directory.

The require subdirective of the `<Limit>` directive is described fully in How-To 13.3, which describes user authentication protection. Furthermore, you can combine host filtering with user authentication to create multiple levels of security.

COMPLEXITY
INTERMEDIATE

13.3 How do I...
Set up user and password security on an HTTPD server?

COMPATIBILITY: HTTPD-BASED SERVERS

Problem

Host filtering will not suffice for my security needs; the people who need to access the sensitive information are at diverse locations and use a variety of machines in many different domains. Is there a way I can require user authentication with a password before allowing access to a private portion of my document tree?

Technique

The Basic authentication package is supported by a variety of server software packages, including HTTPD. This authentication package requires that a browser submit a username and password to authenticate itself. This information is checked against a list of acceptable users and passwords stored on the server. If the submitted username and password are authorized to access the requested document, the server provides the requested material; if not, access is denied.

HTTPD supports user authentication through the use of password files, group files, and access file directives. The instructions below lead you through the process of setting up user authentication-based security for specified portions of your document tree.

Steps

The following steps show how to configure the HTTPD server to provide password-based user authentication for access to portions of your document tree. Using these instructions, you can create password and group files and issue appropriate access file directives. These new access file directives are explained in greater detail in the "How It Works" section below.

1. Create a password file. HTTPD includes the **htpasswd** program to aid you in this task (**htpasswd.exe** in WinHTTPD). Locate this program in the **support** subdirectory of the server. You should change directories to the location where you want to store a password file. If a password file already exists in this directory, proceed to step 2. Otherwise, create a new password file with this program. For example, to create a new password file called **newpass** in the current directory and add an entry for the user **duke**, issue the command below:

```
htpasswd -c newpass duke
```

2. Use the **htpasswd** application to add password file entries for any users you want to create. Since the password file already exists, do not use the **-c** parameter. For example, to add an entry for a user **harpo** in the **newpass** password file, use the following command:

```
htpasswd newpass harpo
```

3. If you want to establish groups of users who will share similar access privileges, create or edit a group file. If you do not want to create user groups, skip to step 6. Otherwise, you should change directories to the location where you want to store the group file.

4. Create a group file or open an existing one in your text editor. Add, delete, or alter entries as appropriate. Each entry is contained on a single line. The line begins with a group name followed by a colon (**:**). The remainder of the entry is a list of users in the group. For example, the following line designates the **tv** group, composed of users **duke** and **harpo**:

```
tv: duke harpo
```

5. After you make your edits, save this group file.

6. If you want to establish user authentication protection using a per-directory access control file, proceed with step 9 below. Otherwise, log in to your machine as the Web site administrator and change directories to the configuration directory for the server. Usually this is the `conf subdirectory` of the `ServerRoot`.

7. Open the global access control file in your text editor. By default, this file is called `access.conf` (`access.cnf` in WinHTTPD). If this file is not present, check the server resource map file and look for the `AccessConfig` directive, which should tell you the location of the correct file.

8. Locate the directory-sectioning directive associated with the document tree you want to protect. If a `<Directory>` directive does not exist, go to the end of the file and add such a directive. (See How-To 13.1 for more information on creating a directory-sectioning directive.) Place your insertion point between the opening and closing tags of this directive, but not within another sectioning directive, such as a `<Limit>` directive. Proceed with step 10.

9. Change directories to where you want to specify features. In this directory, edit (or create, if necessary) a per-directory access control file. The default name for the file is `.htaccess` (`#haccess.ctl` in WinHTTPD). This name can be changed with the `AccessFileName` directive in the server resource map file. Open the appropriate file in your text editor. Do not place your insertion point within the boundaries of an existing `<Limit>` directive. The beginning or end of the file is a good location.

10. Issue an `AuthType` directive to let the server know the type of authentication scheme to use when access attempts are made. In general, you will use the Basic protection scheme. Insert the following line in the access file:

```
AuthType Basic
```

11. Give the server a name for the security setup. This information is sent to the browser making an access attempt. The `AuthName` directive assigns this information. For example, you could use the following directive to assign the name `ProtectionExample` to the setup used to protect the documents in the current directory tree.

```
AuthName ProtectionExample
```

This name may appear as the title of the pop-up window requesting authentication information.

12. Specify the location of the password file that contains the username and password pairs for users who have access to the documents in this document tree. Use the `AuthUserFile` directive to designate the location of this file. For example, to specify the `/usr/local/httpd/conf/newpass` as the password file, issue the following command in your access file:

```
AuthUserFile /usr/local/httpd/conf/newpass
```

13. Specify the location of a group file with the `AuthGroupFile` directive. For simple single-user security, specify a dummy file. If you use NCSA HTTPD, insert the following line in your access file:

```
AuthGroupFile /dev/null
```

If you use WinHTTPD, insert the following line in your access file:

```
AuthGroupFile c:/httpd/conf/empty.pwd
```

Or to specify an actual group file (such as `c:\httpd\conf\group.pwd`), use the following directive:

```
AuthGroupFile c:/httpd/conf/group.pwd
```

14. Finally, create or edit the `<Limit>` directive for this directory. If a `<Limit>` directive already exists, modify this directive to suit your new security needs. If not, create the directive by inserting the appropriate opening and closing tags in your access file. The `<Limit>` opening tag is composed of the command, followed by a list of HTTP methods that you want to restrict. Insert the following lines to create a directive to restrict `GET` method transactions:

```
<Limit GET>

</Limit>
```

15. Use the `require` subdirective to specify the users who have access to the document tree. For example, if you want to allow users **duke** and **milo** and members of the **tv** group access to the directory, use the following `<Limit>` sectioning directive:

```
<Limit GET>
require user duke
require user milo
require group tv
</Limit>
```

The specified users and groups must appear as entries in the password and group files, respectively.

16. Save this file. If you have made changes to the global configuration files, you must stop and restart the server for your changes to take effect, as described in How-To 12.8.

How It Works

HTTPD allows the restriction of access to protected material by requiring that a user supply a valid username and password. Three key elements are necessary for this to work with HTTPD.

1. First, files containing valid username and password pairs must be stored on the server in a read-accessible location.

2. Next, group files need to be created or modified as necessary.

3. Finally, access files, either global or local, must be configured to specify which users are eligible to access the protected files in a given manner.

Figure 13-2 shows the result of an attempt to access a document protected with user authentication. Many browsers remember the username and password that you have entered and supply this information the next time authentication is required. If a different username and password pair is required for other restricted documents, the browser prompts you for this new information.

Password Files

The `htpasswd` program (`htpasswd.exe` in WinHTTPD) is provided with the HTTPD software and is located in the `support` subdirectory. This application takes either two or three parameters. The format for such a command appears as follows:

```
htpasswd [-c] password_file user_name
```

You need to use three parameters when you create the first username and password pair in a given password file. The `-c` parameter specifies that a new password file is being created. The other two parameters, the password filename and the username, are the same whether you are creating a new file or adding an entry to an existing file. For example, the HTTPD procedure to create a new password file called `example.pwd` with two users, `bill` and `ted`, appears below:

```
glean dsk 151 >htpasswd -c example.pwd bill

Adding password for bill.
New password:
Re-type new password:
glean dsk 152 >htpasswd example.pwd ted
Adding user ted
New password:
Re-type new password:
```

The resultant password file might look like this:

```
bill:VCPfU..tx1IjY
ted:KAUrn7rvfOroM
```

Multiple password files may exist on a single server, with several stipulations. First, all password files must be stored in a location readable by the server application. Second, each directory may specify only a single password file; therefore, the password file must contain all users who need to access the directory that references that password file.

Figure 13-2 Attempting to access a document protected by basic authentication

Group Files

Specifying a list of individual users is often unwieldy. You might choose to create groups of users with similar access privileges. These groups are specified in a group file. The format of a group file is a series of entries, with each entry appearing on a single line.

Each line is composed of a group name and a user list. These two elements are separated by a colon (`:`). For example, the following group file defines two groups, `friends` and `relatives`.

```
friends: paul jess steve jeanne
relatives: jenny elliot mom
```

The `friends` group consists of users `paul`, `jess`, `steve`, and `jeanne`. The relatives group consists of users `jenny`, `elliot`, and `mom`.

Access Files

The HTTPD user authentication feature also requires the configuration of access files to establish the particular authentication required for designated portions of the document tree. Several access file directives are required to support this security mechanism. These directives may be used in either the global access configuration file or the local per-directory access control files.

- **AuthGroupFile**: The **AuthGroupFile** directive specifies the location of the group file to be used in the user authentication protection of the current directory. For group-based access restriction, this file must be readable by the HTTPD server. The directive command is immediately followed by the file specification of the group file. For example, the directive below designates the file `c:\httpd\conf\group.pwd` as the group file for authentication.

```
AuthGroupFile c:/httpd/conf/group.pwd
```

- **AuthName**: This directive indicates the name of the authentication setup being used by the server. This information is passed to a browser making a request so that the end user can determine which username and password he or she needs to use to access the desired material. This name can be arbitrarily chosen by the person configuring the authentication security. The string immediately following the directive command is the name associated with the authentication setup.

- **AuthType**: The most common authentication type is Basic. However, limited alternatives exist for certain browsers and servers. In general, use the following line in your access file to specify the Basic authentication method:

```
AuthType Basic
```

- Table 13-3 displays some other common authentication types. This table also provides pointers on where to find additional online information on these authentication types.

Table 13-3 Authentication types

TYPE(SERVER)	URL
Anonymous(Apache)	http://www.apache.org/docs/1.1/mod_auth_anon.html
DBM(HTTPD)	http://hoohoo.ncsa.uiuc.edu/docs/tutorials/howto/dbm_support.html
DBM(Apache)	http://www.apache.org/docs/auth_dbm.html
Berkeley DB(Apache)	http://www.apache.org/docs/mod_auth_db.html
Kerberos(HTTPD)	http://hoohoo.ncsa.uiuc.edu/docs/tutorials/howto/kerberos.html
MD5(HTTPD)	http://hoohoo.ncsa.uiuc.edu/docs/tutorials/howto/md5_auth.html
MD5(Apache)	http://www.apache.org/docs/mod_digest.html
mSQL(Apache)	http://www.apache.org/docs/1.1/mod_auth_msql.html

- **AuthUserFile**: This directive specifies the password file used in the authentication setup. The directive consists of the command, followed by the path of the password file to be used. Password files must be readable by the server software for user authentication protection to be handled properly. Furthermore, the specified password file should contain an entry for each user either directly specified in a **require** subdirective or indirectly included as a group member through a **require** subdirective. For example, the following directive indicates the use of **c:\httpd\conf\password.pwd** as the password file for the current authentication setup.

```
AuthUserFile c:/httpd/conf/password.pwd
```

- **require** (**<Limit>** subdirective): **Require** subdirectives must occur within a **<Limit>** sectioning directive. (Other aspects of the **<Limit>** directive are covered more completely in How-To 13.2.) The **require** subdirective consists of a directive command, **require**, followed by a type, either **user** or **group**, concluded by a username or group name, depending on the stated type. The server restricts transactions of the type specified by the **<Limit>** directive to only authenticated users specified with require subdirectives. For example, to restrict **GET** access of documents in a given directory to valid user "bill" and members of the **relatives** group, include the following **<Limit>** directive.

```
<Limit GET>
require user bill
require group relatives
</Limit>
```

Comments

<Limit> sectioning directives can be created for each specific HTTP method that may be used to access documents in the protected directory.

The **order**, **allow**, and **deny** subdirectives of the **<Limit>** directive are described fully in How-To 13.2. Further, user authentication can be combined with the host filtering methods described in How-To 13.2 to create multiple levels of security.

In addition, the usernames and passwords used to support user authentication may or may not have any correlation to the usernames and passwords with which individuals log in to their system.

> **NOTE**
>
> In general, HTTP requests using Basic Authentication send user names and passwords used as simple encoded text. Anyone with access to the packet transmissions between the browser and the server can easily retrieve this information. Use of either SSL or SHTTP provides a more secured method of transport. Check your particular server for this support. The SSLeay package is freely available for use with the NCSA HTTPD and Apache Web servers for the UNIX platform; see http://www.psy.uq.oz.au/~ftp/Crypto/ for more information on this package. Also, see How-To 13.9 for configuring SSL with a Netscape FastTrack server.

COMPLEXITY
ADVANCED

13.4   How do I...
Use HTTPD server-side includes?

COMPATIBILITY: HTTPD-BASED, NETSCAPE FASTTRACK

Problem

I need to include dynamic information in my HTML document, but I don't want to write a small gateway application for each of these tasks. How can I incorporate on-the-fly information in a convenient manner?

Technique

The NCSA HTTPD server and its derivatives provide a mechanism for placing dynamic information within HTML documents. This mechanism is referred to as server-side includes.

In an HTTP transaction, a user makes a request and the server responds with the requested item, with little regard for the actual content data. When an HTML document containing server-side includes is requested, the server reads the document, resolves server-side includes, and creates the resulting document.

The procedure below shows you how to use server-side includes.

Steps

Enabling server-side includes on your Web site involves two primary tasks. You need to make several system configuration modifications, and you need to add the server-side include commands to appropriate documents. An explanation of each of these tasks is presented below.

Configuration

HTTPD-Based Servers

This procedure describes the modifications you must make to your server configuration to allow the support of server-side includes.

1. If you wish to configure server-side includes with a per-directory access control file, skip to step 4. Otherwise, log in to your machine as the Web site administrator and change directories to the configuration directory for the server. Usually this is the `conf` subdirectory of the `ServerRoot`.

2. Open the global access control file in your text editor. By default, this file is called `access.conf`. If this file is not present, check the server resource map file and look for the `AccessConfig` directive, which should tell you the location of the correct file.

3. Locate the directory-sectioning directive associated with the document tree in which you want to use server-side includes. If a `<Directory>` directive does not exist, go to the end of the file and add such a directive; see How-To 13.1 for more information on creating a directory-sectioning directive. Your insertion point is between the opening and closing tags of this directive. Then skip to step 5.

4. Change directories to the directory where you want to allow HTML documents with server-side includes. In this directory, edit (or create, if necessary) a per-directory access control file. The default name for such a file is `.htaccess`. This name can be changed with the `AccessFileName` directive in the server resource map file. Open the appropriate file in your text editor. Your insertion point should not be within the boundaries of an existing sectioning directive; the beginning or the end of the file is a good location.

5. Insert the following `AddType` directive in this access file. The filename extension may be changed if you want to associate a different extension with documents that contain server-side includes. For example:

```
AddType text/x-server-parsed-html .shtml
```

6. Issue an `Options` directive to allow server-side includes. If no `Options` directive is present, the default value is `All`; in this case, you can either continue with step 7 or create an `Options` directive for this directory. The directive should, at a minimum, include the `Includes` or `IncludesNOEXEC` option. For example, the following directive specifies automatic indexing and server-side includes, with the exception of `exec`s in the configured directory.

```
Options Indexes IncludesNOEXEC
```

7. Save the file. If you have made changes to the global configuration files, you must restart the server for your changes to take effect, as described in How-To 12.8.

Netscape FastTrack

This procedure describes the modifications you must make to your Netscape FastTrack server configuration to allow the support of server-side includes.

1. Access the FastTrack administration server.

2. Select the server that you want to configure for server-side includes. The server's administration page should appear.

3. Select the Content Management option from the top frame menu.

4. Select the Parse HTML option from the left frame menu. The Parse HTML configuration form should appear to the right. See Figure 13-3.

5. Select the location(s) for which you want to configure server-side includes. You can select an existing pattern from the menu, browse the document directory, or specify a wildcard pattern.

6. Choose the level of parsed HTML desired. Selecting No turns off this feature. The other choices both allow includes; however, the `no exec` option, the equivalent of the HTTPD `IncludesNoEXEC` option, supports all server-side include directives except `exec`.

7. Select the types of HTML files that the server should parse. Selecting all HTML files instructs the server to parse all files with the `text/html` MIME type (see Appendix C, Multipurpose Internet Mail Extensions (MIME), for more information on MIME). Selecting files with the extension `.shtml` instructs the server to parse only those files ending with the `.shtml` file-name extension.

8. Save the file. If you have completed all changes to the server, you must apply the changes by selecting the Apply button from the top frame menu of the particular server's administration page.

Figure 13-3 Configuring server-side includes through the Parse HTML configuration form

NOTE

Direct modification of the particular FastTrack server's `obj.conf` file provides an alternative means of configuring this feature. See the online documentation for additional information on this process.

Inserting Directives

Once you have configured your server to allow server-side includes, you can begin using server-side include commands in your documents. The steps below walk you through the process of incorporating server-side include commands into your HTML documents.

1. Change directories to the location where the HTML documents in which you want to use server-side includes are stored.

2. Open the document in want you wish to include server-side information in your text editor. Move the insertion point to the location in the document where you want to insert the dynamic information.

3. Issue a server-side include command within the context of an HTML comment. The text of the comment should begin with a pound symbol (**#**). For example:

```
<!--#command tag1="..." tag2="..." ... -->
```

So if you wanted to include the text of the file `DocumentRoot/header.htm` in your document, you would issue the following directive in your document:

```
<!--#include virtual="/header.htm" -->
```

4. When your edits are complete, save your document. The filename extension of your document should indicate the presence of server-side includes.

5. Check the document in your browser.

How It Works

Several popular server software packages provide server-side includes as a mechanism for incorporating dynamic information into static HTML documents. The server accomplishes this by parsing embedded commands within the text of the document, then evaluating these commands to generate the final document sent to the client.

For the server to properly differentiate documents that have server-side includes from those that do not, the server needs to be configured to recognize objects of the `text/x-server-parsed-html` MIME type (`magnus-internal/parsed-html` with Netscape's FastTrack), created to support server-side includes. Add this type and associate it with an appropriate filename extension, usually `.shtml`. Unless you wish to allow server-side includes in documents serverwide, issue the appropriate

`AddType` directives in the HTTPD access files that control the specific directories in which you want to permit server-side includes. If you do want to globally support server-side includes, issue this directive in the HTTPD server resource map file. For FastTrack servers, establish directory restrictions through the Parse HTML configuration page.

In addition, for HTTPD-based servers, you must configure the options in the directories where you want to support server-side includes. By default, all options are available in all directories. However, if you need to restrict some options while supporting server-side includes, issue an `Options` directive with either the `Includes` or the `IncludesNOEXEC` argument. The `Includes` option allows use of all server-side commands; the `IncludesNOEXEC` argument allows use of all server-side commands except `exec`. With Netscape FastTrack Server, you perform these same configuration tasks by selecting items through the Parse HTML configuration form. Use of `exec` may constitute a security risk, hence the need for two separate options.

Below is a list of supported server-side include commands, as well as a summary of how they work and the arguments they take. This discussion is followed by Table 13-5, which describes the environment variables that are visible to server-side include documents.

- `config`: This command defines several characteristics of file parsing. Table 13-4 shows the tags supported by this command.

Table 13-4 Tags in a config server-side include commands

TAG	VALUE
errmsg	Specifies the error message that is sent to the client if an error occurs during the parsing process.
timefmt	Format to use when a date is requested. The string must conform to the specification of date format strings for the UNIX `strftime` library function.
sizefmt	Format to use when a file size is displayed. The two acceptable values for this tag are
	`bytes`: Represents the straight byte count of the file.
	`abbrev`: Shows an abbreviated file size (for example, 1.2MB).

For example, the command

```
<!--#config errmsg="Error in parsed HTML" timefmt="%D" sizefmt="abbrev">
```

would set the error message to `"Error in parsed HTML"`, the time format to `"%D"`, so a date might appear as 1/1/99, and the size format to `"abbreviated"`, so a file size of 9,876,543 displays as 9.9MB.

- `echo`: The `echo` command can display any of the environment variables specified in Table 13-5. The single valid tag for this command is `var`. The value associated with this tag is the variable to be displayed.

For example, to display the current date in your document, use the following server-side include.

```
<!--#echo var="DATE_LOCAL">
```

■ **exec**: This include puts the results of executing the command passed as a tag into the resultant document sent to the client. The valid tags for this command are **cmd** and **cgi**.

The value of the **cmd** tag must be a string. This string is passed to **/bin/sh** for execution. The variables specified in Table 13-5 may be used by this command.

The **cgi** tag is used to refer to a gateway application whose results will be included in the resultant document. The reference to the CGI program should be a standard virtual path to a valid gateway program.

The following include could be used if, for example, you wanted to include a listing of the people currently logged in to the server site within an HTML document.

```
<!--#exec cmd="/usr/ucb/finger">
```

■ **fsize**: The **fsize** command has the same valid tags as **include**: **file** and **virtual**. It displays the size of the file referenced in the tag. This data is shown in the format specified with the **sizefmt** tag of the **config** command.

If you wanted to track the size of a particular file, you might create an HTML document that displays this information whenever you access it. For example, the following include displays the size of the file **/export/home/OO/ht1/logs/error_log**.

```
<!--#fsize virtual="/logs/error_log">
```

■ **flastmod**: The **flastmod** command has the same valid tags as **include**: **file** and **virtual**. This command displays the date the target referenced by the tag was last modified. This date is printed in the format specified using the **timefmt** tag in the **config** command.

Use this command to keep track of when a particular file was last modified. For example, if you wish to always know when the last server error occurred, create an HTML document that dynamically determines when the server error log was last changed. Such a command might look like the following:

```
<!--#flastmod virtual="/logs/error_log">
```

■ **include**: This command places the text of one document within another. Documents to be included are subject to the standard access control restrictions. This command uses one of two valid tags.

The **file** tag specifies the location of the file to be included relative to the current directory. The target may be another parsed HTML document, but not a CGI application.

The `virtual` tag references a document by way of the virtual path from the `DocumentRoot`. As with the target of a file tag, this file may be another parsed document, but may not be a gateway application. You can find an example of this command in step 3 of Inserting Directives above.

Several environment variables are set when server-side includes are evaluated. These variables appear in Table 13-5.

Table 13-5 Environment variables set while server-side includes are evaluated

VARIABLE	VALUE
DOCUMENT_NAME	Current filename
DOCUMENT_URL	Virtual path to the current document
QUERY_STRING_UNESCAPED	Any search query the client sent
DATE_LOCAL	Current date, local time zone
DATE_GMT	Current date, Greenwich mean time
LAST_MODIFIED	Date current document was last modified

Comments

Server-side includes provide a means of including dynamic information within HTML documents, without resorting to gateway scripts, but there are significant drawbacks: inefficiency and lack of security.

Server-side includes decrease server efficiency. The server can no longer act strictly as a dispatcher since it must not only processes the requests, but also read and comprehend the content of the response to generate the appropriate resultant HTML document. This inefficiency can be minimized by using only server-side includes in directories that require them. In other words, place the configuration information in either per-directory access control files or within a directory-sectioning directive in the global access configuration file in an HTTPD-based server; for Netscape's FastTrack server, limit your choice of directories using the location specification portion of the parsed HTML configuration form. If potential inefficiency is not an issue, much of the configuration information can be declared serverwide in the server resource map file (HTTPD) or Entire Server location selection (FastTrack).

In addition, server-side includes represent a security risk. The most flagrant potential risk is the `exec` command, which allows an HTML document to include the results of the execution of an application. This command could allow unauthorized access to the server machine. You can reduce this risk by using the `Options` directive to restrict either all server-side include commands or only `exec` commands.

COMPLEXITY
INTERMEDIATE

13.5 How do I...
Establish directory-level security on a CERN HTTP server?

COMPATIBILITY: CERN HTTP

Problem

I have sensitive data in certain areas of my document tree that I need to distribute to a select audience via my CERN HTTP server software. How can I make sure that only the people I specify can access the protected documents?

Technique

The CERN server software uses a combination of host filtering and user authentication to provide directory-level server security. Establishing directory-level security entails the following tasks:

▪ Establishing the protection setup

▪ Associating these setups with portions of the document tree

▪ Generating any supporting password and group files

This How-To shows how to accomplish these tasks, letting you establish directory-level security for your CERN server.

Steps

The directory-level security configuration process can be broken down into three broad categories:

▪ Protection setup definition

▪ Directory association

▪ Auxiliary file maintenance

These tasks are handled individually in the procedures below. In each category, several alternative approaches are described.

Examples of several directory-level protection configurations are provided in the "How It Works" section.

Protection Setup Definition

The CERN server software provides three methods for specifying protection setups. You can

▪ Define named setups in the global configuration file

▪ Define setups as separate external security setup files

▪ Define setups through inline specification

The procedures below cover the first two approaches. Later in this How-To, the "Association of Directories to Protection Setups" section describes the third method.

Defining Named Setups

If you wish to define a setup in a separate file, use the procedure given under Defining Setup Files. Otherwise, log in to the server machine as the site administrator.

1. Change directories to the location of your global server configuration file. This file is usually located in the `config` subdirectory of the server software.

2. Open the configuration file in your text editor.

3. Move the insertion point to a new line. You should define your protection setup object before you attempt to associate it with a particular directory. If you are editing an existing setup, move your insertion point to within the setup object and skip to step 7.

4. Insert the following lines of code, substituting whatever you choose for the object name represented by `PROTNAME` in the code.

```
Protection PROTNAME {
}
```

5. Place your insertion point between the opening curly brace and the closing curly brace.

6. Insert a `UserId` directive to indicate the user ID that the server must assume to access the protected directory. For example, if the server needs to run as user `me` to access directories owned by this user, issue the following directive:

```
UserId me
```

The default user ID is `nobody`.

7. Insert a `GroupId` directive to indicate the group ID that the server must assume in order to access the protected directory. For example, if the server needs to run as a group called `users` to access the desired directories, use the following directive:

```
GroupId users
```

The default group ID is `nogroup`.

8. Insert the following directive to specify the authentication type:

```
AuthType Basic
```

9. Use a `ServerId` directive to specify a name for the setup. For example, to name the setup `MySetup`, use the following directive:

```
ServerId MySetup
```

10. Specify the password file to use with this setup using the `PasswordFile` directive. To use the password file `/home/htpass`, include the following line:

```
PasswordFile /home/htpass
```

11. Specify the group file to use with this setup using the `GroupFile` directive. To use the group file `/home/htgroups`, include the following line:

```
GroupFile /home/htgroup
```

12. Specify the masks for the setup to indicate the types of transactions and the limitations on them. You can specify this as either a generic mask or a series of transaction-specific masks. The syntax of a `mask` command is shown below:

```
mask_command group, user user@address, @address, ...
```

Table 13-6 specifies the valid `mask` commands.

Table 13-6 Mask directives

MASK COMMAND	TRANSACTIONS COVERED
delete-mask	Protects DELETE method requests
get-mask	Protects GET and HEAD method requests
mask	Use this mask when method-specific mask is unavailable
post-mask	Protects POST method requests
put-mask	Protects PUT method requests

The `mask` command itself is followed by a series of usernames, group names, and machine/domain addresses in any combination. Additional information on the syntax of this list can be found in the "How It Works" section below. This syntax is referred to as a group definition; it is the same as the one used in group files described in the "Auxiliary File Maintenance" section below. For example, to restrict **PUT** method requests to user `jenny`, use either of the following directives:

```
put-mask jenny
```

or

```
mask jenny
```

The second is more restrictive in that transactions of all methods are restricted to the user **jenny**. If a generic mask is defined, it serves as the default mask if a specific transaction mask is not defined.

13. You have now defined a protection setup. If you have no more protection setups to create at this time, save the current file.

14. Since you have modified the global configuration file, you must stop and restart the server process to put your configuration changes into effect.

Defining Setup Files

You can define security setups as external files. Except for limited exceptions, these files contain the same information as named setups. Files, however, contain neither the **UserId** nor the **GroupId** directives. This information is provided at the time the setup file is associated with a document tree.

1. Change directories to the location where you want to store the file that defines a protection setup. Each file defines a single protection setup.

2. Choose a name for your protection setup file and open this file in your text editor.

3. Insert the following directive to specify the authentication type:

```
AuthType Basic
```

4. Use a **ServerId** directive to specify a name for the setup. For example, to name the setup **MySetup**, use the following directive:

```
ServerId MySetup
```

5. Specify the password file to use with this setup using the **PasswordFile** directive. To use the password file **/home/htpass**, include the following line:

```
PasswordFile /home/htpass
```

6. Specify the group file to use with this setup using the **GroupFile** directive. To use the group file **/home/htgroups**, include the following line:

```
GroupFile /home/htgroup
```

7. Specify the masks for the setup to indicate the types of transactions and the limitations on them. You can specify this as either a generic mask or a series of transaction-specific masks. The syntax of a **mask** command is shown below:

```
mask_command group, user user@address, @address, ...
```

Table 13-5, in the Defining Named Setups section above, specifies the valid `mask` commands. The `mask` command itself is followed by a series of user-names, group names, and machine/domain addresses in any combination. Additional information on the syntax of this list can be found in the "How It Works" section below. This syntax is referred to as a group definition; it is the same as the one used in group files described in the "Auxiliary File Maintenance" section below. For example, to restrict **PUT** method requests to user `jenny`, use either of the following directives:

```
put-mask jenny
```

or

```
mask jenny
```

The second is more restrictive in that transactions of all methods are restricted to the user `jenny`. If a generic mask is defined, it serves as the default mask if a specific transaction mask is not defined.

8. You have now defined a protection setup. Save the current file.

Association of Directories to Protection Setups

Several methods exist for configuring a particular directory with a specific security setup. The steps outlined below lead you through several variations of the **Protect** directive in the server configuration file to create these associations. Instructions for using the **DefProt** directive for this task can be found in the documentation for the CERN server software.

1. Associate a protection setup with a directory in the server configuration file. Change directories to the location of your global server configuration file; this file is usually located in the **config** subdirectory of the server software.

2. Open the configuration file in your text editor. Move the insertion point to a new line. If you have defined protection setups within your configuration file, this insertion point should be farther down in the file than the protection setup objects you want to use. If you are editing an existing directory-level protection association, move your insertion point to the desired **Protect** directive.

3. Insert (or modify) a **Protect** directive to associate a protection setup with a directory. If you plan to use a protection setup only once, consider associating the directory to an inline specification of a setup, as shown in step 5. If you want to associate a directory with a previously declared setup object in the configuration file, proceed with step 4. Otherwise, associate a directory with an external protection setup file using the directive shown below:

```
Protect template path user.group
```

In this directive, the template is the path to the tree of documents to be protected. This path is an absolute path to the protection setup file that specifies the desired protection for the document tree. Finally, the `user.group` field specifies the identity the server needs to assume to gain access to the document tree. So, for example, to protect the `/horses/mysystem` directory using the `/WWW/config/prot.setup1` protection setup file with the server running as user `me` in group `users`, issue the following directive:

```
Protect /horses/mysystem/* /WWW/config/prot.setup1 me.users
```

You have now protected the specified directory. Proceed with step 6.

4. Using a previously defined protection setup object, insert a `Protect` directive with the following syntax:

```
Protect template prot_obj
```

The template is a wildcard-capable specification of the directory to be protected, and `prot_obj` is the name used as the second parameter to the `Protection` directive when creating the object. A wildcard-capable directory specification may include an asterisk (`*`) to match multiple paths; for example, `/horse/*` refers to all subdirectories of the `/horse` directory. Use the following directive to protect the `/horses/mysystem` directory using the PROTNAME protection setup object.

```
Protect /horses/mysystem PROTNAME
```

You have now protected the specified directory. Proceed with step 6.

5. Associate an inline protection setup with a directory. You should create an inline protection setup only for one-time use. Be careful with the syntax of this usage of the `Protect` only directive. It should appear as follows:

```
Protect template {
    setup
}
```

Make sure to place a space between the template and the opening brace, as well as to place the closing brace on a line by itself. In addition, comments are not permitted within the scope of an inline setup object. In the syntax above, `template` refers to the directory to be protected, while `setup` refers to a series of directives as defined in steps 6–12 of the Defining Named Setups section above. An example of this usage is shown below:

```
Protect /horses/mysystem {
    UserId me
    GroupId users
    AuthType Basic
    ServerId MySetup
    PasswordFile /home/htpass
```

```
GroupFile /home/htgroup
GetMask jenny elliot mom @(*.*.cau.edu)
}
```

This associates the inline setup provided with the specified directory.

6. When you are done, save the server configuration file. You must now restart the server before your changes can take effect.

Auxiliary File Maintenance

CERN security requires the maintenance of two types of auxiliary files: password files and group files. These files serve the same purpose as they do in the HTTPD server. The formats and maintenance utilities, however, differ. The steps below take you through the creation and maintenance of CERN password and group files.

The CERN server package provides the `htadm` application to help maintain server password files. The "How It Works" section below explains how to use this application. However, the first three of the following steps show how to create and add user/password pairs with this program.

1. Change directories to the location where you want to store a password file.

2. Create a new password file using the following `htadm` application syntax:

```
htadm -create filename
```

For example, use the following command to create a password file called `.htpass` in the current directory:

```
htadm -create .htpass
```

3. Add users to the password by calling this application with the syntax appearing below:

```
htadm -adduser filename username password realname
```

For example, the following command creates an entry in the `.htpass` password file for user `jenny` with password `math` and a real name of Jenny Helen:

```
htadm -adduser .htpass jenny math Jenny Helen
```

You may use this command to create as many users as required. Additional password maintenance functions are described in the "How It Works" section.

4. If you do not need to create a group file, you have completed setting up directory-level protection. Otherwise, change directories to the location where you want to store a group file. Either choose a name for this group file, or edit an existing group file. In either case, open your chosen group file in your text editor.

5. A group file is a series of lines, each of which defines a group. The line begins with a group name, followed by a colon (:), followed by a list of items. The syntax of an entry is shown below.

```
groupname: item, item, item, item, ...
```

6. An `item` can be a user, a group, a machine, a domain, or any combination of users or groups with machines or domains. The list defines the group. Create or edit any necessary groups.

7. Save the group file.

How It Works

Like HTTPD, the CERN HTTP server software supports security through host filtering and user authentication. Unlike HTTPD, the syntactic specification of both types of security is remarkably similar in the CERN package. The first component required to establish directory-level protection of a CERN server is the protection setup object or file. Once that is located, you need to know which directives to use. Table 13-7 summarizes the directives used in the specification of a protection setup.

Table 13-7 Protection directives

DIRECTIVE	PURPOSE	RESTRICTION
AuthType	Specifies authentication scheme to be used	None
GroupFile	Specifies full path of the group file for this setup	None
GroupId	Designates group server needs to run as mask commands (see Table 13-5)	Setup object
		None
PasswordFile	Specifies full path of the password file for this setup	None
ServerId	Name to differentiate among setups on a server	None
UserId	Designates user server needs to run as	Setup object

The `mask` command takes a group definition as a parameter. A group definition is a comma-separated list of users, groups, potentially wildcarded Internet address, and combinations of users or groups with an address or addresses. Parentheses are used for logical groupings of users/groups or address templates. For example, the following are all valid group file entries, each composed of a group name, a colon, and a group definition.

The group **us** consists of users **you** and **me**:

```
us: you, me
```

The group **them** consists of users **he** and **she**, and also the user **it**; however, **it** must be attempting to access the server from a machine in the **auc.edu** domain

(**144.125.*.*** is the **auc.edu** domain). This entry does not restrict users **he** and **she** to a particular machine or domain:

```
them: he, she, it@144.125.*.*
```

The group **us_and_them** consists of all users in the groups **us** and **them** plus users from the CERN domain (**128.141.*.*** is CERN):

```
us_and_them: us, them, @128.141.*.*
```

The group **some_of_them** consists of only those members of the group **them** accessing the server from machines in either the **auc.edu** or the **jpl.gov** domains (**128.149.*.*** is the **jpl.gov** domain):

```
some_of_them: them@(*.*.auc.edu, 128.149.*.*)
```

The group **we** consists of the users **me**, **myself**, and **i** when attempting to access the server from Internet address **144.125.96.233**:

```
we: (me, myself, i)@144.125.96.233
```

Two special predefined groups exist—**All** and **Anybody**. The **All** group consists of all valid users in the designated password file. The **Anybody** group represents protection without user authentication; this is the implied group when an item in a group definition is only an at sign (**@**), followed by a machine or domain address.

The **mask** commands specify those individuals who may have a particular type of access to the protected portion of the server. Thus, with the capabilities of the **mask** directives, you could create protections to support strict host filtering or user authentication. For example, the following setup object performs host filtering that only allows access from machines in the **jpl.gov** domain (**128.149**).

```
Protection jplFilter {
    UserId me
    GroupId users
    AuthType Basic
    ServerId HostFilter
    PasswordFile /dev/null
    GroupFile /dev/null
    getmask @128.149.*.*
}
```

Protection setups can also be defined to strictly perform user authentication. For example, the following object defines a protection allowing access for users **jenny** and **david**, regardless of what machine they use to access the server.

```
Protection authEx {
    UserId me
    GroupId users
    AuthType Basic
    ServerId UserAuthenticate
    PasswordFile /WWW/.htpass
    GroupFile /dev/null
    getmask jenny, david
}
```

Compared to NCSA HTTPD, the limitation of the protection setups is their inability to deny access to specified users, groups, or machines. However, the trade-off is the ability to combine specific users and groups with specific machines or domains.

Protection setups are the first stage in establishing directory-level security. The second stage of this process is the association of protection setups with particular portions of the document tree. Use the **Protect** directive to accomplish this task. Several syntactic forms of this command, along with relevant examples, are provided in steps 3–5 of the Association of Directories to Protection Setups portion of the Steps section above.

Finally, the users and groups specified in the protection setup masks need to be defined in the designated password and group files, respectively. CERN password files are maintained using the **htadm** package distributed with the CERN software. Use this application to create, edit, and check password files. Table 13-8 summarizes the parameters and usage of this application.

Table 13-8 htadm parameters

PARAMETERS	PURPOSE
-adduser password_file user password real_name	Adds the specified user to the designated file
-check password_file user password	Checks the specified user's password
-create password_file	Creates the designated password file
-deluser password_file user	Deletes the user from the designated file
-password password_file user password	Changes the specified user's password

Group files are maintained with a standard text editor. Groups are specified one per line. Each line is composed of a group name, a colon, and a group definition. The group definition uses the same syntax as described in step 12 of the "Defining Named Setups" section above.

Once protection setups have been defined and associated with relevant portions of the document tree, and necessary auxiliary files have been created, directory-level security is configured for the specified directories. When a client requests a document in a protected directory, the protection setup associated with the directory is examined. If the type of access is restricted and the requester does not fit the appropriate mask criteria, then access is denied.

Comments

Directory-level security can be used in combination with file-level access control (see How-To 13.6) to achieve two levels of security. If both file and directory-level restrictions are imposed, then the conditions defined by both the mask and file-level access control list must be met for access to be granted.

Use of the `DefProt` directive establishes a default protection setup; however, without an access control list or a `Protect` directive, no documents are actually protected. If the setup-file argument is missing from a `Protect` rule, this information is inherited from the most recently used `DefProt` directive. Further information on the `DefProt` directive can be found in the documentation for the CERN HTTP server at URL `http://www.w3.org/hypertext/WWW/Daemon/User/Config/Rules.html`.

COMPLEXITY
INTERMEDIATE

13.6 How do I...
Set up file-level security on a CERN HTTP server?

COMPATIBILITY: CERN HTTP

Problem

I need more finely tuned control than directory-level protection. Most of the documents in my protected document tree can be safely viewed by a large group of valid users; however, I want to restrict the access of several particular documents to only a few users out of that large group. Is there a way I can do that?

Technique

The CERN HTTP server lets you set up security on a file-by-file basis using access control list files that reside in directories in which file-level restrictions are desired. In the access control file, each individual file in the directory can be referenced with an allowable transaction method and associated with a group of valid users.

This access control list provides host filtering and user authentication requirements for the file in the protected directory. If directory-level protection is already in force, then the access control list serves as a second level of security.

Thus, the specification of file-level security involves the creation of an access control list file in the directory that is to be protected. The following steps show how to create a CERN access control list file.

Steps

You should be familiar with establishing directory-level security before configuring file-level protection. How-To 13.5 provides this information. You need not include a `mask` command if you do not want to require two levels of security.

Once you have established directory-level security for the directory in which you want to install file-level security, you can proceed with the steps below.

1. To allow the file-level access control list to supersede any masks in the protection setup, insert the following directive in the protection setup associated with the directory protected.

`ACLOverRide On`

2. Change to the directory where you want to install file-level security.

3. Create a file named `.www_acl` in your text editor. If it already exists, you may edit the previously defined security constraints in the existing file.

4. Each line of this file represents the security configuration for a particular file or set of files. The general syntax for the access control list file line appears below:

`file_specification: METHOD_LIST : group_definition`

To add protection for a file, add a line to the access control list file. The file specification is the name of a file in the current directory, or a wildcard specification matching a number of local files. The `METHOD_LIST` determines which types of HTTP transactions are permitted. Finally, the group definition is a list of items with the same syntax as either mask parameters or group definitions in group files. The following line allows `GET` method access to all files with the `.htm` file extension by group-list items `dsk` and `them`.

`*.htm: GET : dsk, them`

5. You may add additional lines to specify file-level security for additional files.

6. When you have completed your edits, save the file.

How It Works

CERN server file-level security is configured with access control files. These access control files are located within the directory where the protected files reside. The standard name used by the server package for these files is `.www_acl`.

This file is composed of entry lines, each of which is examined whenever a request is made for a document within the directory. Actually, unless an `ACLOverRide On` directive appears in the directory protection setup, the request transaction must meet the restriction specified with the `mask` directive, if such directives are present. If these directory-level restrictions have been met, the request is then checked against the file-level security in the access control file.

The entries in the access control file are composed of three colon-separated fields. The first field contains the specification of a file to be protected; this specification can potentially contain a wildcard to protect several similarly named files. The second field is a list of HTTP methods that are to be protected for the given file specification. Finally, the last field contains a group definition that has the same syntax as described for **mask** directives and group file entries, described in How-To 13.5.

Having passed the directory-level security, the file specification and request method are matched against entries in the access control list. Unlike the matching of rules in the configuration file, examination does not stop when a matching file specification and method are found, but continues until no more entries are found or until a valid entry is found.

For example, given the following access control list file:

```
ping*: GET, POST: jim, alex, @(*.*.auc.edu)
*.htm: GET, POST, PUT: jenny@(*.*.jpl.gov)
```

a **GET** method request by authenticated user **jenny** on a machine in the ***.*.jpl.gov** domain for the **pingpong.htm** file would succeed. This is so even though an earlier file specification and method match had been identified, but with a failure for invalid authentication.

For an access control list to be useful, the directory must already be configured in the global configuration file for directory-level security. This is required primarily to establish the password and group files to be used in evaluating group definitions in the access control list file.

Comments

File-level access control requires the definition of directory-level access control within the server's configuration file, either through a **Protect** or a **DefProt** directive for the directory in question. This directory-level specification is necessary to specify the password and group files that need to be referenced to verify valid users. If masks are defined in the directory access control, then both the masks as well as the restrictions in the access control list must be met to achieve access.

Inclusion of an **ACLOverRide On** directive in a protection setup for a directory allows a local access control list file to supersede the restriction specified in the setup. In effect, **mask** directives in the setup are ignored. Overriding the protection setup is a potential security risk and should be weighed by the site administrator before he or she includes the override directive in a protection setup.

13.7 How do I...
Install a CERN proxy server?

COMPATIBILITY: CERN HTTP

Problem

For security reasons, my site is running behind an Internet firewall, but behind the firewall we still need access to Internet-based information. Can a CERN HTTP server provide proxy service to the machines within the firewall?

Technique

The CERN HTTP server can act as a proxy server. In fact, the server software can function as both a proxy server and a standard HTTP server at the same time.

To provide proxy service, the server's global configuration file needs to be set properly. You can specify various aspects of your proxy: what methods are supported, which sites may use your proxy, whether caching occurs, and even whether your proxy server actually uses another proxy server to fulfill requests. Once your proxy is running on the firewall machine, requests from inside the firewall are filtered and serviced through the proxy server accessing information outside the confines of the firewall.

Clients also need to be properly configured to recognize and use the proxy server. Environment variables need to be set to designate a proxy server to use for the various supported Internet protocols. Many popular browsers support proxy access, including Lynx, Mosaic, and Netscape. Tips on configuring particular browsers are provided in the "How It Works" section below.

The following instructions provide an approach to configuring a CERN server to act as a proxy server.

Steps

Do not start the proxy configuration from scratch. The CERN server software comes with several example configuration files. If you cannot find these files, they are available in the CERN server documentation and can be found at URL `http://www.w3.org/hypertext/WWW/Daemon/User/Config/Examples.html`. You should select the proxy configuration file that does or does not configure caching, whichever you require.

The following steps show you several ways to modify the available example configurations.

1. Change directories to the location of your global server configuration file; this file is usually located in the `config` subdirectory of the server software.

2. Open the configuration file in your text editor. Move your insertion point to the first instance of the `Pass` directive. Modify proxy parameters from this point forward.

3. Oftentimes file and FTP protocols are used interchangeably. For your proxy to support this alias, insert or uncomment the following directive:

```
Map file:* ftp:*
```

4. Selectively comment or uncomment the `Pass` directives for the protocols you want your proxy to support. Comment lines in the configuration file begin with a pound sign (#). Configure a `Pass` directive for each protocol you want the proxy to service. For example, the following line supports HTTP protocol proxy support.

```
Pass http:*
```

5. By default, only `GET`, `POST`, and `HEAD` HTTP methods are enabled on your proxy server. To support other methods, issue an appropriate `Enable` directive in your configuration file. For example, to allow `PUT` method requests, add the following line:

```
Enable PUT
```

On the other hand, if you wanted to restrict already enabled methods, issue a suitable `Disable` directive. For example, the following line disables `POST` method requests on the proxy server:

```
Disable POST
```

6. Use host restrictions to designate particular domains and machines that may use your CERN server as a proxy. Define a protection to limit access according to the instructions in How-To 13.5. This definition must not contain a reference to any password or group files. Further, use the `mask` directive to specify a generic mask for this protection. Finally, do not include references to specific users or groups in the mask you set in the protection setup. Once you have created an appropriate protection setup, associate this setup with the particular proxy protocol you wish to protect. Use a standard `Protect` directive to configure your host restrictions. For example, the following directive associates the PROT1 setup with HTTP protocol proxy service:

```
Protect http:* PROT1
```

7. One of the features that a proxy server can provide is the caching of documents retrieved from external sites. This feature provides greater efficiency in situations where particular outside resources are accessed on a regular basis. Selected directives used to configure a caching proxy server are discussed in the "How It Works" section below. In the configuration of a caching proxy server, start with the caching proxy configuration file provided through either the CERN distribution directories or the URL `http://www.w3.org/hypertext/WWW/Daemon/User/Config/Examples .html`. If you intend for your server to act as a caching proxy, enable caching by specifying a directory to store cached documents. Use the `CacheRoot` directive for this task. For example, to enable caching with documents stored in the `/usr/local/cache` directory, issue the following directive:

```
CacheRoot /usr/local/cache
```

8. Skip to step 9 if you are not configuring your server to act as an inner proxy server accessing an outer proxy server that provides access to the Internet. To configure your CERN server as an inner proxy server, issue the following directives indicating the URL of the outer proxy server as the parameter of the directives.

```
ftp_proxy http://other.proxy.server.edu/
gopher_proxy http://other.proxy.server.edu/
http_proxy http://other.proxy.server.edu/
wais_proxy http://other.proxy.server.edu/
```

Choose only those directives appropriate to the protocols for which you want the outer proxy consulted.

9. Save these changes. Stop and restart the server to realize your changes.

How It Works

For security reasons, many businesses and institutions are placing firewall systems between their own internal networks and the rest of the Internet. This provides greater security against a variety of potential problems. However, the downside is that the firewall not only keeps people out, but it also keeps people in.

A proxy server acts as a bridge between those within the firewall and information residing on the Internet that can be accessed through several popular protocols. Figure 13-4 graphically demonstrates the job of a proxy server. Machines within the firewall, `in1`, `in2`, and `in3`, place HTTP requests with the proxy server running on the machine maintaining the firewall. The proxy server acts as the original requester's agent; it retrieves the desired information from sites outside the protected local network, `out1`, `out2`, `out3`, and `out4`. Then, the proxy passes the retrieved information to the requester.

Figure 13-4 Providing proxy service through a firewall

Many clients support the use of a file proxy, which works the same as an FTP proxy. To support this use of the file proxy, add the line shown in step 3 above. This line tells the server to treat all file requests as FTP requests.

The CERN server can act as a proxy server for a variety of Internet protocol requests. The CERN proxy server may support the following protocols:

■ FTP

■ Gopher

■ HTTP

■ News

■ WAIS

Use a **Pass** directive, as described in step 4 above, to allow proxy access to any of these services.

You can configure the CERN proxy server to restrict access to particular proxy services. These restrictions are limited to host filtering. To establish this type of protection for a particular type of service, issue a **Protect** directive to associate a previously defined protection setup with a particular service. Step 6 above includes an example of associating a protection setup with HTTP proxy service.

Caching allows a proxy server to retain documents retrieved beyond a single request. When caching is enabled, a proxy client requests a document from the proxy, and the proxy retrieves the file from the appropriate site as usual. Then, instead of just passing the document back to the requesting client, the proxy server also retains a copy of the document for possible future use.

You enable caching, either explicitly by issuing a `Caching` directive, or implicitly by specifying a cache directory using the `CacheRoot` directive. Since a cache directory is necessary for caching documents, use of this directive serves as sufficient indication to the software that caching is enabled. The list below summarizes some of the directives available for configuring caching.

- `Caching`: Use this directive to explicitly enable caching. The two valid parameters of this directive are `On` and `Off`. Add the following line to your configuration file to turn on caching:

```
Caching On
```

- `CacheRoot`: Designate the cache directory using this directive. The single parameter for this directive is the directory where you want cached documents stored. Step 7 above provides an example of this directive.

- `CacheSize`: Establish the maximum cache size in megabytes with this command. When the size of the cache reaches this limit, the proxy server begins deleting older and larger cached documents. The default size is 5 megabytes. For example, issue the following command to specify a 40-megabyte cache:

```
CacheSize 40 M
```

- `CacheUnused`: Use this directive to specify how long unused cached files stay in the cache. Multiple instances of this directive specify the time limit for different types of cached documents. If a document matches several of these directives, then the last `CacheUnused` directive appearing in the configuration file and matching the document applies. For example, if the following set of `CacheUnused` directives appears in the configuration file, the document `ftp://www.mysite.edu/README` remains in the cache seven days rather than four and a half days.

```
CacheUnused *                          4 days 12 hours
CacheUnused ftp:*                      5 days
CacheUnused ftp://www.mysite.edu/*     7 days
```

URL `http://www.w3.org/hypertext/WWW/Daemon/User/Config` provides information on additional directives for more fine-tuned control of proxy server caching.

A CERN proxy server may also act as client with reference to another proxy server. Step 8 above provides information on configuring this feature. This situation arises from a potential need to pass multiple levels of firewalls or to create multiple levels of document caches.

In the first case, security concerns lead to the creation of multiple levels of firewalls to better protect more sensitive areas of the local network. Examine Figure 13-4 again; picture `in1`, not as a machine, but as a subnet protected by a firewall, with an inner proxy used by the systems inside the subnet to access both the machines in the local network and the outer proxy, which in turn can access the rest of the Internet.

In the second case, efficiency concerns lead to the creation of multiple levels of caching proxies. By caching often-used documents, the proxy server obviates the need to retrieve the document at each usage; the proxy sends the previously retrieved copy to service new requests. Multiple levels of caches provide a storage hierarchy supporting the retention of the most frequently used documents at the closest location, and they provide a means of establishing priority of retained documents. The outer proxy has one set of criteria for retaining documents, while the inner proxy has a more specific set of criteria based upon the requirements of those clients serviced by the inner proxy. In this way, the outer proxy caches documents frequently accessed by all of its clients, while the inner proxy provides access to documents cached in its own cache as well as those in the outer proxy's cache.

Comments

The steps provided above do not attempt to describe the entire server configuration process. They deal solely with the configuration of the proxy server. You should consult the CERN server documentation for instructions on adding and/or modifying appropriate directives within the configuration file. Online information is available at URL `http://www.w3.org/hypertext/WWW/Daemon/User/Config/find_this_URL`.

When configuring a proxy server, you must not attempt to establish user authentication on proxy services. The only security that functions properly for proxy service is host filtering.

A CERN server may act as both proxy server and HTTP server at the same time. To configure your server to perform in this way, configure your server as you would for a standard HTTP server, then continue with the procedure defined in this How-To.

The latest release of the Apache Web server contains an experimental module that provides support for proxy service. See `http://www.apache.org/docs/1.1/mod_proxy.html` for additional information on installing and configuring an Apache server as a proxy server.

Browsers behind a firewall must also be configured for use with proxies. The Netscape Navigator browser provides a dialog box from the Preferences menu that allows you to perform this configuration task. Figure 13-5 displays this dialog.

Using this dialog, specify the host names for the machines that serve as proxies for the desired protocol. The No Proxy portion of the dialog allows the specification of Internet domains that are accessible directly without requiring a proxy.

Figure 13-5 Configuring proxy service with Netscape Navigator

Configuring other browsers to deal with proxies usually involves setting environment variables. Browsers such as Mosaic and Lynx use environment variables to set this information. In UNIX and VMS, the following environment variables configure the protocol-specific proxies:

- `ftp_proxy`
- `gopher_proxy`
- `http_proxy`
- `news_proxy`
- `wais_proxy`

For example, to configure UNIX Mosaic to access **proxy.mysite.edu** for HTTP requests, issue the following C shell command before running Mosaic:

```
setenv http_proxy "http://proxy.mysite.edu/"
```

Consult the relevant portions of your browser documentation for other browsers.

COMPLEXITY
INTERMEDIATE

13.8 How do I...
Establish domain and address security and password authentication on a MacHTTP server?

COMPATIBILITY: MACHTTP

Problem

I want to allow and deny access to my server MacHTTP based on the machine or network that a user is trying to access from. I would also like to require passwords for certain documents and directories on my server. How can I do this?

Technique

You can restrict access to your server based on the user's machine name, domain name, or IP address by editing the `MacHTTP.config` file for your server. Two command key words, `ALLOW` and `DENY`, enable you to limit the machines and networks that have access to your server.

User authentication handles file-level and directory-level security. User authentication is based on the notion of realms. A realm is a group of files or folders that contain a common substring in their names. A realm is specified in the `MacHTTP.config` file using the key word `REALM`. The `REALM` key word is followed by a name substring and a description. The specified substring is unique to all of the names of the protected files or of their parent directories. The description is effectively the name of the realm. No blank spaces are allowed in the realm name. (The entire description must be a contiguous string of characters.)

The following procedures show how to add serverwide host filtering and file-level and folder-level user authentication.

Steps

The first procedure below outlines the steps necessary to establish host filtering on your MacHTTP server. These instructions are immediately followed by the process for installing user authentication at the file and folder levels. In both cases, make the necessary modifications to the `MacHTTP.config` file.

Host Filtering

The following procedure describes the necessary steps for configuring host filtering on your server. Host filtering works across all documents on your server.

1. Open the `MacHTTP.config` file in your text editor.

2. For each machine or network domain that you want to allow on your server, issue an `ALLOW` directive. The parameters of the `ALLOW` command are either names or appropriate IP addresses. For example, to allow access to the server from machine `foo.bar.com`, add the following directive:

```
ALLOW foo.bar.com.
```

Or to allow access to the server from all machines in the `bozo.net` network, add the following directive.

```
ALLOW bozo.net.
```

3. For each machine or network domain that you want to prevent from accessing your server, issue a `DENY` directive. The parameters of the `DENY` commands are either names or appropriate IP addresses. For example, to deny access to the server from machine `foo.bar.com`, add the following directive:

```
DENY foo.bar.com.
```

Or to deny access to the server from all machines in the `bozo.net` network, add the following directive:

```
DENY bozo.net.
```

4. Save this file and restart your server.

User Authentication and Password Creation

User authentication provides file-level and directory-level security on MacHTTP servers. The process below describes the two components necessary to configure user authentication. The first component of configuration is the specification of files to be protected. The second is the specification of usernames and passwords that allow access to protected files.

1. Open the `MacHTTP.config` file in your text editor.

2. For each set of files or folders you want to protect, issue a `REALM` directive. The `REALM` command requires two parameters: a string that defines which files are in the realm and a description that serves as the name of the realm. For example, to create the realm `round` protecting files containing the string `cam` in their path, issue the following `REALM` directive:

```
REALM cam round
```

3. Save this file and restart your server.

4. Add users by selecting the Passwords interface found at the bottom of the Edit pull-down menu.

5. Select the realm you want this user to have access to in the pull-down menu found at the bottom of the Passwords interface. (All realms that have been declared in the `config` file should show up here.)

6. Enter a username and a password with which this user will access protected files in this realm.

7. If you want this user to have access to multiple realms, repeat steps 5 and 6 for every realm that you want to allow this user to access.

8. Exit this dialog.

How It Works

MacHTTP provides both host filtering and user authentication security. The host filtering facilities let machines and domains, specified by name or IP address, be allowed or denied access to the server as a whole. User authentication provides finer-tuned security by requiring a username and password to access any files or folders containing a specified string in their path.

Host filtering uses the **ALLOW** and **DENY** commands to specify access restrictions. The **ALLOW** and **DENY** key words are followed by an explicit machine name followed by a period, or a substring of the machine or domain name without a period, specifying that every access from a machine or network that contains that substring should be either allowed or denied access. You specify machines and domains by either name or IP address.

For example, to allow access to all machines whose IP addresses start with **128.122.1**, and to deny access to all machines in the **bar.com** domain, enter the following statements.

```
ALLOW 128.122.1
DENY bar.com.
```

Notice that the **bar.com** entry is followed by a period. All domain names are case-sensitive and must be followed by a period. Also notice that the IP address is not followed by a period. This allows machines with IP addresses starting with **128.122.1** to access the server; this specification includes machines such as **128.122.12.7**, **128.122.1.1**, and **128.122.193.74**. If you want to be specific, append a period to the end of the IP address. For example, to allow access from only the machine with IP address **128.122.1.1**, issue the following directive:

```
ALLOW 128.122.1.1.
```

MacHTTP assumes that you will specifically deny and allow all machines if you use the **DENY** or **ALLOW** statements. That is, there is an implicit **DENY** for all machines if you use the **ALLOW** command. This means that, if you want to allow access from all machines with the exception of a machine called, say **whoopy.fun.gov**, you would need to expressly allow all machines before denying this last one with the following statements:

```
ALLOW 1
ALLOW 2
ALLOW 3
ALLOW 4
ALLOW 5
ALLOW 6
ALLOW 7
ALLOW 8
ALLOW 9
```

```
DENY whoopy.fun.gov.
```

Notice that there are no periods following the numbers. This means that any machines whose IP addresses start with the numbers 1–9 will be allowed access, with the exception of **whoopy.fun.gov**, which is specifically denied access.

In a similar fashion, if you wanted to deny access from all machines except machines in the **spew.org** domain, but you also wanted to deny access from one machine within this domain called **pooky**, you could take advantage of the explicit **DENY** and use the following statements:

```
ALLOW spew.org.
DENY pooky.spew.org.
```

MacHTTP's user authentication facility supports security at the file and folder levels. Use the **REALM** directive to specify the protected files and folders. This command takes two parameters: a name substring and a description. The name substring determines which files are protected. The description serves as the name of the protected realm. (The description must not contain blank spaces.)

For example, to create a realm called **My_Friends** that controls all files and directories whose names contain the string **friend**, enter the following statement in your **config** file:

```
REALM friend My_Friends
```

Now, you could create a folder on your server called **friend**, **friends**, **my_friend23**, or any other legal filename that contains the string **friend**. Only users associated with the **My_Friends** realm can access the files in this folder. Likewise, if you had a file on your server called **cool_friends.html**, this file would also be governed by the **My_Friends** realm.

Similarly, if you wanted to create realms for `Trusted_Users`, `Officers`, `Presidents`, and `Riff_Raff`, you could declare the following realms.

```
REALM trust      Trusted_Users
REALM office     Officers
REALM pres       Presidents
REALM rifraf     Riff_Raff
```

Any files that contained `trust` somewhere in their URL would be governed by the `Trusted_Users` realm; likewise, any URL on this server containing `office` would fall under `Officers`, `pres` under `Presidents`, and so on.

Once you have set up your realms, you need to create usernames and passwords for people who will be able to access these documents. This is a relatively easy task that can be done using the Passwords interface found at the bottom of the Edit pull-down menu when your MacHTTP server is running. Figure 13-6 displays the dialog you see when selecting this option.

A user can be removed from a realm using this same interface. The interface lists the entries as *Username• Realm*, so delete the entry for the realm(s) that you no longer want this user to access.

Comments

MacHTTP's security features are similar to the features found in NCSA's HTTPD and the CERN server, if somewhat crude in comparison. MacHTTP doesn't let you allow and deny machines and networks on a per-directory level as the NCSA server does. But user authentication is easy to set up and administer, and it provides an adequate level of security for most installations.

Figure 13-6 MacHTTP passwords interface

COMPLEXITY
INTERMEDIATE

13.9 How do I...
Configure SSL security on a FastTrack server?

COMPATIBILITY: NETSCAPE FASTTRACK SERVER

Problem

Standard HTTP transmits information over the Internet in the clear. This method is vulnerable to interception by anyone with the proper know-how and access. I want to encrypt my HTTP transmissions. How do I configure this security using my Netscape FastTrack server?

Technique

The Netscape FastTrack server provides several levels of access security. The administration server provides the interface for configuring this security information.

The FastTrack server supports the following types of server security:

- SSL (Secure Sockets Layer): SSL provides encryption of the communications between the FastTrack server and SSL compatible browsers.

- User and Group Access Restrictions: User and group restrictions provide restricted access to specified users.

- Host Machine and Domain Restrictions: This security measure restricts or allows access to or from particular Internet machines or domains.

These three levels of security provide an effective means of limiting access to restricted documents on your FastTrack server. The SSL level applies to the server as a whole; user and group restrictions and host and domain restrictions apply on a per-directory or per-file basis. See How-To 13.10 for information on configure username/password or domain restrictions on your FastTrack server.

Steps

The following sets of steps lead you through the configuration of SSL security on a FastTrack server. This process only applies if you plan to register your server with a third-party certification authority, such as Verisign (`http://www.verisign.com`); this process entails paying a fee.

1. Access the FastTrack administration server.

2. Select the server that you want to configure for server-side includes. The server's administration page should appear.

3. Select the Encryption option from the top frame menu. If you have generated a key pair, proceed with step 6.

4. Access the Generate Key option of the left frame menu. Follow the procedure outlined in the Netscape Info window, as displayed in Figure 13-7.

5. Enter the relative path of the key pair generated in step 4 in the `Key File Path` field of the Generate a Key Pair. Select OK, and from the confirmation screen, select the Save and Apply button.

6. Select the Request Certificate option from the left frame menu. If you have already requested a certificate, proceed to step 8.

7. Fill out the form provided in the right frame. The information entered is sent to the e-mail address of the Certificate Authority (or CA), that you specified in the form. (See `http://www.verisign.com` for additional information on certificates.)

8. Install the certificate that you receive from your CA, using the Install Certificate option from the left frame menu.

9. Enable SSL from the Encryption On/Off form, using the On/Off option from the left frame menu. This form also allows the selection of port numbers for SSL communications. The default port for such communications is 443, just as the default port for standard Web servers is 80. Make your changes, and then click the OK button.

10. Select Save and Apply for your changes to take effect.

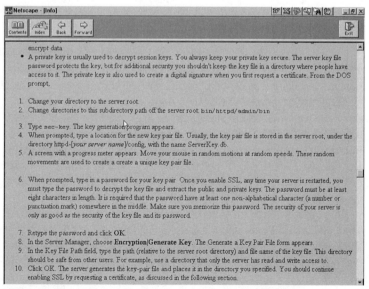

Figure 13-7 Netscape Info for generating a key pair

How It Works

FastTrack supports encrypted communications channels between browsers and servers. The server uses SSL as the mechanism for supporting this communication. To differentiate this protocol from standard HTTP, URLs requested via a secure channel to use the HTTPS protocol. (For more information on the standard HTTP communications process, see Appendix G, The Hypertext Transfer Protocol (HTTP).) When a browser requests a secure channel from the server, the following conversation occurs:

- Connection: The browser successfully connects to the server via the HTTPS protocol.

- Server Certificate Response: The server responds with its digital certificate.

- Server Certificate Verification: The browser confirms the certificate with a third-party certificate authority, the CA. If the certificate is not trustworthy, the browser can either reject the connection or warn the user about the situation.

- Master Key Generation and Transmission: The browser uses the server's public key and a random number to generate a master key. The browser sends this key to the server.

- Master Key Decryption: The server uses its private key to decrypt the master key.

- Session Key Generation: The server and browser generate session keys using the master key.

- Encrypted Transmissions: All further communications between the browser and server use the session key for encryption.

For this process to work, the server must have a digital certificate installed. Preferably, a recognized CA has signed this server certificate. FastTrack supports the acquisition and installation of signed digital certificates through the administration server.

The initial generation of a key pair occurs through a DOS window. The FastTrack distribution provides the sec-key program to generate the initial key pair. The process uses the motion of the mouse to generate a random number which gets incorporated into the key pair. The program stores the key pair in the file requested at the outset. This file name should be entered into the Generate a Key Pair configuration form of the server so that the server knows where the keys are installed, as seen in Figure 13-8.

Once you generate the key pair, you'll need to request a certificate from a CA. The FastTrack server provides a form to facilitate the certificate request process, as shown in Figure 13-9. Verisign (`http://www.verisign.com`) is currently one of the most popular CAs. You must enter the e-mail address for a CA so that the administration server knows where to send the request. The CA will return a certificate to you via e-mail. The CA will usually charge a renewable fee for supplying their service. To install the certificate, enter the appropriate information in the Certificate Installation form of the administration server, as displayed in Figure 13-10.

Figure 13-8 Generate a Key Pair configuration form

Figure 13-9 Requesting a certificate

Figure 13-10 Installing a certificate

Enable SSL communications by turning on this feature in the Encryption On/Off form, as seen in Figure 13-11. You may also wish to specify the port over which the server should listen for HTTPS requests; the default port is 443. Selecting any other port will require that users specify the port when requesting a document. Once you have enabled SSL, you need to Save and Apply the changes for them to take effect.

Comments

Configuring SSL does not require the configuration of user and group or host restrictions. (See How-To 13.10.) Using SSL alone provides secure communications channels between browsers and your server. Therefore, all transmissions over the secure channel will be encrypted. In this manner, you can protect the integrity of information sent from your server against prying eyes with access to the Internet packet communications. Viewers of information from your server know that the information originated from your server and that any attempt to insert substitute packets into the information stream will fail since an intruder will not have access to the proper session key.

In addition to the administration server interface, aspects of security configuration can be accomplished through direct editing of the proper server configuration file(s), usually **obj.conf**. See the online documentation for the FastTrack server for detailed information on this process. This method is not recommended for the novice or causal site administrator. Unless you have significant experience in the syntax for FastTrack server configuration files, or previous experience with configuring

Figure 13-11 Encryption On/Off form

HTTPD-based or CERN servers, the benefits gained over just using the administration server do not generally rise above the cost of the learning curve.

COMPLEXITY
INTERMEDIATE

13.10 How do I...
Set up user and password security on a FastTrack server?

COMPATIBILITY: NETSCAPE FASTTRACK SERVER

Problem

Certain areas of my server contain sensitive information that I want available through my server; however, I want some control over who accesses these documents. Different documents on my server require different levels of access security. How do I configure this security using my Netscape FastTrack server?

Technique

The Netscape FastTrack server provides several levels of access security. The administration server provides the interface for configuring this security information.

The FastTrack server supports the following types of server security:

▪ SSL (Secure Sockets Layer): SSL provides encryption of the communications between the FastTrack server and SSL compatible browsers. (See How-To 13.9.)

▪ User and Group Access Restrictions: User and group restrictions provide restricted access to specified users.

▪ Host Machine and Domain Restrictions: This security measure restricts or allows access to or from particular Internet machines or domains.

These three levels of security provide an effective means of limiting access to restricted documents on your FastTrack server. User and group restrictions and host and domain restrictions allow you to restrict access to your server on a per-directory or per-file basis.

Steps

The following sets of steps lead you through the configuration of username/password and domain security on a FastTrack server. This process steps you through the tasks of user management, group management, and restriction of particular documents based upon users or groups or based upon the Internet machine or domain.

User and Password Management

1. Access the FastTrack administration server.

2. Select the server that you want to configure for server-side includes. The server's administration page should appear.

3. Select the **Access Control** option from the top frame menu.

4. If you want to modify an existing user database, proceed to step 5. Otherwise, you will need to create a new database by selecting the **Manage User Databases** option from the left frame menu. The right frame that appears allows you to create or remove a user database.

5. Select the particular option from the left frame menu applicable to the task you wish to perform. FastTrack supports the following permissible tasks:

Create User: Create a new user with an associated password in a particular user database.

Remove User: Select an existing user to remove from a particular user database.

List Users: Display the users in a particular user database.

Edit User: Edit information concerning a specified user.

6. Fill out the forms associated with specific tasks, making sure to select the particular database(s) you want to affect.

7. Select OK to process the form information.

Group Management

1. Access the FastTrack administration server.

2. Select the server that you want to configure for server-side includes. The server's administration page should appear.

3. Select the Access Control option from the top frame menu.

4. If you want to modify an existing user database, proceed to step 5. Otherwise, you will need to create a new database by selecting the Manage User Databases option from the left frame menu. The right frame that appears allows you to create or remove a user database.

5. Select the particular option from the left frame menu applicable to the task you wish to perform. FastTrack supports the following permissible tasks:

Create Group: Create a new group in a particular user database.

Remove Group: Select an existing group to remove from a particular user database.

List Group: Display the groups in a particular user database.

Edit Group: Edit the users and groups contained within a specified group.

6. Fill out the forms associated with specific tasks, making sure to select the particular database(s) you want to affect.

7. Select OK to process the form information.

8. Depending upon the task accomplished, you may have to select Save and Apply to effect the changes that you have entered.

Application of Restrictions

1. Access the FastTrack administration server.

2. Select the server that you want to configure for server-side includes. The server's administration page should appear.

3. Select the Access Control option from the top frame menu.

4. Select the Restrict Access option from the left frame menu.

5. Select the directories or files for which you want to enable access controls. You can select an existing pattern from the menu, browse the document directory, or specify a wildcard pattern.

6. Click the Turn On Access Control button. Additional options will become available in the right frame configuration form.

7. Choose the default accessibility of the chosen location, directories or files. The defaults may be set for both reads and writes to the specified location. The default accessibilities are either `allow` or `deny`. Selecting `deny` denies all attempts to access the location; selecting `allow` allows all attempts to access the location.

8. Select the Edit Permissions button to restrict the defaults chosen.

9. Select the domain and host restrictions that you want established for the location.

10. If the default chosen is `deny`, select the user and groups allowed to access the location.

11. Select the Done button when you have finished entering information.

12. Upon return to the Restrict Access form, select the OK button.

13. Select the Save and Apply button to effect the changes that you have made. The administration server makes appropriate changes to the configuration files, then stops and restarts the server.

How It Works

User and Group Management

The first stage in establishing user or group restrictions for your server is creating the database of users who will be able to access the various parts of your server. How you organize these users will depend upon your particular needs. FastTrack provides several levels of user data organization. The highest level of organization is the user database. Within a particular database, groups serve as collection mechanism. Further, not only do groups organize users, but they may also organize other groups. These levels of organization are not necessary for the establishment of user restrictions; however, they ease the configuration of restrictions for blocks of users.

From an organizational standpoint, you may want to create distinct user databases for different divisions of users. All FastTrack servers running on the same host share access to all user databases created. Databases serve as the unit of user information, transportable to servers running on different host machines. If each division of a company runs its own internal server with a database of users, a company might incorporate each division's database to restrict access to the company's overall Web server. The server administration page of a particular server allows the creation of new databases through the Access Control | Manage User Databases options, as shown in Figure 13-12. User databases store both user and group information.

Figure 13-12 Managing user databases

Each user to whom you want to give access to a particular portion of the Web server requires an entry in a user database accessible to that server. The administration server provides several options for maintaining information in user databases:

■ Create User: This option allows the creation of a new user within a specified user database. Figure 13-13 shows the administration server interface to this function. The database stores the username, real name, and password for the user. The user enters the specified username and password whenever accessing documents on the server, subject to this user entry.

■ Remove User: This option removes a user from a specified database. The entry form requires the specification of the user name of the entry to remove and the menu selection of the database from which to make the removal.

■ List Users: Initially, this option displays the user names of all users in the currently selected database without any filtering of the usernames. Once the interface appears, however, you may select a different database and provide a wildcard pattern limiting the search of usernames. Pressing the Show Users button displays the users, subject to the entered specifications.

■ Edit User: The edit user option allows the alteration of the data associated with a particular username. So you accomplish real name and password changes for a particular username through the provided form.

Figure 13-13 Creating a new user

Group-organize users, also previously created groups, within the context of a particular database. Groups provide a convenient mechanism for specifying blocks of users with similar access privileges. As with the user management functions, the administration server provides several form interfaces for group creation and management:

■ Create Group:This option provides support for the creation of a new group. The interface provided by the administration server requires the selection of a database, the specification of a group name, and the selection of a parent group. If the new group is part of an existing group, you will need to select this existing group as the parent; otherwise, select NONE as the parent group. Figure 13-14 displays this interface.

■ Remove Group: This option allows you to remove an existing group from a particular database. You will need to select the database and select the group that you want to remove. Selecting OK processes this selection.

■ List Group: This option provides a list of all groups existing within the selected database. As with the List User option discussed under user management, the interface allows the selection of a database and the specification of a wildcard filter. This information constrains the search when you press the List Groups button.

■ Edit Group: Once a group exists, the Edit Group option supports the selection of users and groups that comprise the selected group. The interface provides a selection list of users and other groups in the selected database. The highlighted items in the group and user selection lists are those groups and users that are, or are intended to be, part of the selected group. Figure 13-15 displays an example of this screen.

Figure 13-14 Creating a new group

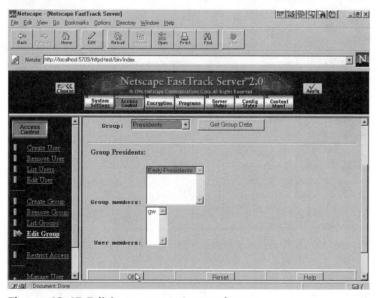

Figure 13-15 Editing a group's members

Group operations performed may require alter configuration information. Therefore, to effect such changes, the server may need to be stopped and restarted. If this is the case, the administration server will generally follow the configuration screen with a Save and Apply screen which automatically performs the requisite stop and restart. You can manually stop and restart the server using the procedures outlined in How-To 12.8.

Once the necessary databases, users, and groups are created, you establish access privileges for users or groups through the Access Control | Restrict Access option.

Application of Access Restrictions

The FastTrack server allows the specification of user or group restrictions and host or domain access restrictions. The administration server provides the means for enabling both of these security features. Figure 13-16 displays the Restrict Access form presented by the administration server. In this form, you enter the location(s) for which you want to enable access controls, and then you turn on or off the access controls as appropriate. If access controls are enabled, the form also allows you to specify the default access modes for read and write operations to the specified location(s). In addition, you can specify an alternate message for when an unauthorized user attempts to access a protected document.

Figure 13-16 Applying access restrictions

The Permissions button appears next to the default access mode for reading and writing. The selection of this button allows the configuration of exceptions to the default access mode indicated. The form that appears depends upon the default chosen. If the **allow** default is selected, the form appearing allows the specification of host machine and Internet domains that should be denied access; this configuration form appears in Figure 13-17. If the **deny** default is selected, the form appearing allows the specification of host machine and Internet domains that should be allowed access, as well as specific users and groups allowed access when making requests from specific machines; Figure 13-18 displays this configuration form. In either case, select the Done button once you enter all desired information.

Selecting the Done button returns you to the Restrict Access form. At this point, you are not completely finished: You will need to stop and restart the server to effect your changes. The easiest way to do this is to select the OK button at the bottom of the Restrict Access form. This triggers the appearance of the familiar Save and Apply form, seen in Figure 13-19. Selecting the Save and Apply button automatically performs all the necessary steps to effect the specified change. If you are making other changes, you can select the Save button; and then after all configuration changes are done, you will select the Apply button from the top menu frame of the administration server.

Figure 13-17 Editing allow permissions

Figure 13-18 Editing deny permissions

Figure 13-19 Saving and applying the changes

Comments

You can configure and use user and group or host restrictions regardless of whether you have enabled SSL. Without SSL, however, usernames and passwords get sent over an unencrypted communications channel. This is the common situation for most servers supporting the Basic authentication package. You derive the best security from use of both mechanisms; however, based on the sensitivity of information on your server and the cost, you may wish to just use the user name and group restriction mechanism.

In addition to the administration server interface, aspects of security configuration can be accomplished through direct editing of the proper server configuration file(s), usually `obj.conf`. See the online documentation of the FastTrack server for detailed information on this process. This method is not recommended for the novice, or causal, site administrator. Unless you have significant experience in the syntax for FastTrack server configuration files, or previous experience with configuring HTTPD-based or CERN servers, the benefits gained over use of the administration server do not generally rise above the cost of the learning curve.

COMPLEXITY
INTERMEDIATE

13.11 How do I...
Use public key encryption?

COMPATIBILITY: PUBLIC KEY ENCRYPTION-CAPABLE SERVER AND BROWSER

Problem

I have confidential documents that I want to provide to select users in a secure fashion. The Basic authentication scheme will not suffice because under this scheme, servers transmit documents and browsers send requests in the open. Consequently, unauthorized individuals monitoring the network traffic may view my confidential pages.

Technique

Servers and browsers use encryption on documents and requests prior to transmission over an open connection. The recipient decrypts the transmission prior to presenting the document or servicing the request. Thus, diverting or examining transmissions yields only an encrypted transmission.

Steps

For a browser or server that has built-in encryption capabilities, the actual encryption process should be transparent and not require any additional work on your part. The only exception to this may be a requirement to acquire a certification of authenticity transported by a secure means, such as Secure Sockets Layer (SSL) or SHTTP (Secure HTTP). (See `http://www.verisign.com/netscape/index.html` and How-To 13.9 for additional information on receiving and using a digital ID with a Netscape FastTrack server.)

For browsers and servers requiring plug-in components, installation and configuration will vary. The steps below provide a generic approach for finding the appropriate encryption software.

1. Determine the type of public key encryption software necessary for you to communicate. Table 13-9 specifies the common public key encryption software.

Table 13-9 Common public key encryption software

ENCRYPTION SOFTWARE	LOCATION
PGP	`http://www.efh.org/pgp/pgpwork.html`
RIPEM	`http://www.cs.indiana.edu/ripem/dir.html`

2. Download a software package suitable for your hardware and software platform. Source and executable code for these packages may be accessed through the references provided in Table 13-8.

3. Examine the manual for the software package to determine how to generate, maintain, and publish public keys.

4. Configure your browser and server to call the plug-in package when receiving an encrypted transmission.

Configuring an NCSA HTTPD Server with PGP/PEM Hooks

The following procedure provides a stepwise approach for configuring an HTTPD server to serve encrypted HTML pages and respond to encrypted requests.

1. If you did not compile your server with the **-DPEM_AUTH** flag set, you need to acquire such a server or recompile with this flag set. (This must be an export-controlled version of 1.5; only the export-controlled version contains the necessary hooks.)

2. Retrieve scripts that will call the encryption software to either decrypt requests or encrypt documents. (These scripts are available in distributions of HTTPD 1.3, and will likely be available through the export-controlled version of 1.5.)

3. Edit and install the scripts as necessary and described within the scripts.

4. Edit the server configuration file `httpd.conf`. Add the following directives to add pointers to the PGP and PEM scripts.

```
PGPEncryptCmd /usr/local/somewhere/pgp-enc
PGPDecryptCmd /usr/local/somewhere/pgp-dec
PEMEncryptCmd /usr/local/somewhere/ripem-enc
PEMDecryptCmd /usr/local/somewhere/ripem-dec
```

The paths should specify where these scripts are located on your server site.

5. Add the following two lines to indicate the name of the server entity used to identify the server's public key.

```
PGPServerEntity webmaster@mysite.edu
PEMServerEntity webmaster@mysite.edu
```

This entity should be the same one you place on the public/private keys that you generate for your server.

6. To protect desired HTML pages with encryption, open the local or global access file in an editor.

7. Within the file or within the proper **<DIRECTORY>** element in the global file, change or add an **AuthType** directive with a value of PEM or PGP as desired.

```
AuthType PEM
```

The remainder of the access file can be modified, as described in How-To's 13.1–13.3.

8. Close the file, or edit another **<DIRECTORY>** element.

Configuring an NCSA X-Mosaic Browser with PGP/PEM Hooks

The steps below guide you through configuring NCSA's X-Mosaic browser to use a plug-in PGP- or PEM-based package to encrypt or decrypt HTTP requests and responses.

1. If you did not compile your Mosaic browser with the **-DPEM_AUTH** flag set, you need to acquire such a browser or recompile with this flag set.

2. Open your **X** resources file and add the following resources. Modify the data values to correspond to appropriate information for your system.

```
Mosaic*pemEncrypt: /usr/local/somewhere/ripem-enc
Mosaic*pemDecrypt: /usr/local/somewhere/ripem-dec
Mosaic*pemEntity: me@mysite.edu
Mosaic*pgpEncrypt: /usr/local/somewhere/pgp-enc
Mosaic*pgpDecrypt: /usr/local/somewhere/pgp-dec
Mosaic*pgpEntity: me@mysite.edu
```

The entity value should correspond to the key name that you previously sent to the server administrator.

3. Save the resource file, and restart your **X** environment.

How It Works

Transferring encrypted transmissions over the Web requires the use of several HTTP header elements and compatible encryption/decryption software supported by both the browser and server. The actual encryption/decryption software may be supplied as part of the browser or server, as it is with Netscape's Navigator and Commerce Server, or as external plug-in components, as it is with NCSA's HTTPD and Mosaic. Once you add the plug-in components, or acquire a package with included software, the actual encryption/decryption process is transparent.

The benefit of plug-in encryption is that you are not limited to those encryption technologies supplied with your browser or server. The primary disadvantage is that you are required to acquire, install, and configure the plug-in encryption modules to meet your needs. On the other hand, the benefit of built-in encryption is that your use of it is transparent from the start. The disadvantage is that you are limited to the encryption technologies supplied with your browser or server.

The proposed public key protection differs slightly from the prototype scheme implemented by NCSA. The following discussion examines the proposed scheme. (See the Comments below for an examination of NCSA's prototype implementation.) If you are unfamiliar with HTTP, consult Appendix G as a reference.

First, the browser requests a file protected by encryption.

```
GET /protected/mydoc.htm HTTP/1.0
UserAgeny: MyBrowser/1.0
```

The server denies this initial request for the document unless the request includes required authentication information. This denial includes a copy of the server's public key in the WWW-Authenticate HTTP response header field. For example, such a response might look like the following:

```
HTTP/1.0 401 Unauthorized -- authentication failed
WWW-Authenticate: Pubkey realm="RealmName", key="EncodedServerPublicKey"
```

When the browser determines that the server denied an unauthorized request, the browser prompts the user for an authorized username and password. The browser concatenates this username and password with the IP address of your machine, a time stamp, and the browser's public key. A colon separates each of these fields. The browser encrypts this string using the server's public key and generates a new request.

```
GET /protected/mydoc.htm HTTP/1.0
UserAgeny: MyBrowser/1.0
Authorization: Pubkey EncodedEncryptedString
```

The server unencodes and decrypts the authorization data. The server checks the structure of the data to confirm that it contains five colon-separated fields. Next, the IP address contained in the string is matched against the IP address of the machine actually making the request. The server then compares the time stamp to the current server time. If any of these checks fails, authorization is denied. Once these checks succeed, a process similar to the Basic authentication scheme is used to check the validity of the specified username and password for the requested document.

Once the server completes these checks, it generates a response. This response uses the browser's public key to securely transfer the information necessary for the browser to decrypt the requested document. The server encrypts the document itself, using a single-key encryption method such as **DES** or **IDEA**; for large documents, public key encryption methods require significantly more time than single-key encryption systems. The response body contains this encrypted document. The response header includes fields that, in conjunction with the browser private key, allow decryption of the response body. These fields include **DEK-Info**, **Key-Info**, and **MIC-Info**. Such a response might appear as follows:

```
HTTP/1.0 200 OK
DEK-Info: DES-CBD,...
Key-Info: DES_ECB,...
MIC-Info: MD5,...
Content-Length: ...

Encrypted Document
```

The browser uses its private key and the information in the header to decrypt the transmitted document, which it presents to the user. (For more information on these additional header fields, see Request for Comments number 1421, available at URL `http://www.w3.org/hypertext/WWW/AccessAuthorization/rfc1421.html`.)

Comments

NCSA implemented a prototype of this scheme using either PGP or RIPEM for HTTPD 1.3 and Mosaic (X Window version); however, because of legal restrictions, they removed the hooks for this scheme. Current documentation indicates that encryption mechanisms may be added back to HTTPD in an export-controlled version of 1.5.

The SSLeay package is a free product that supports SSL for HTTPD and Apache servers. You should read the documentation carefully before installing this package with your server. Several legal issues exist concerning retaining proper software necessary licenses for SSL to work properly. These issues differ, depending on whether you are within or outside the United States. See `http://www.psy.uq.oz.au/~ftp/Crypto/` for a more detailed discussion of both how to configure an HTTPD or Apache server with SSLeay and the legal ramifications and requirements.

Netscape's Navigator and FastTrack Server make use of RSA encryption technology. This encryption software is built-in. Therefore, these packages will use this encryption software as necessary in a transparent manner.

The NCSA prototype implementation supports calls to external encryption software to encrypt/decrypt transmissions. An example transcript of the HTTP request process under this prototype appears as follows:

First, the browser requests a document:

```
GET /protected/mydoc.htm HTTP/1.0
UserAgent: Mosaic/X 2.2
```

The server denies access:

```
HTTP/1.0 401 Unauthorized
WWW-Authenticate: PEM entity="webmaster@mysite.edu"
Server: NCSA/1.3
```

The browser retrieves the public key for the specified entity, using the finger command, and sends an encrypted request as the body of an HTTP request using a proprietary content type. Table 13-10 shows the proprietary MIME types created to support this prototype.

Table 13-10 Proprietary MIME types to support encryption system prototype

MIME TYPE	PURPOSE
application/x-www-pem-request	Body contains a PEM-encrypted request.
application/x-www-pgp-request	Body contains a PGP-encrypted request.
application/x-www-pem-reply	Body contains a PEM-encrypted response.
application/x-www-pgp-reply	Body contains a PGP-encrypted response.

The browser generates an encrypted request by using the retrieved public key to encrypt the actual request. The browser places this encrypted request as the HTTP request body. The request header specifies both the browser's PEM or PGP entity and the content type, from among those mentioned in Table 13-10.

```
GET / HTTP/1.0
Authorization: PEM entity="me@mysite.edu"
Content-type: application/x-www-pem-request

--- BEGIN PRIVACY-ENHANCE MESSAGE ---
Encrypted request...
--- END PRIVACY-ENHANCE MESSAGE ---
```

The server generates a response in a similar fashion. The server retrieves the public key for the specified entity from a local key file and generates an encrypted response. This encrypted response becomes the body of the HTTP response sent. The header of the response uses one of the reply MIME types listed in Table 13-10.

```
HTTP/1.0 200 OK
Content-type: application/x-www-pem-reply

--- BEGIN PRIVACY-ENHANCE MESSAGE ---
Encrypted response...
--- END PRIVACY-ENHANCE MESSAGE ---
```

## CHAPTER 14

THE COMMON GATEWAY INTERFACE (CGI)

14

THE COMMON GATEWAY INTERFACE (CGI)

How do I...

Common Gateway Interface (CGI) applications are the source of dynamic, interactive HTML documents. They can present snapshots of current server information.

They can accept user-specified data, process it, and respond with ad hoc HTML 3.2 pages generated from the processed information.

CGI applications present changing data such as up-to-the-minute stock quotes. They can interpret and process input, such as sending an e-mail message, and they can provide a dynamic response to input data, such as presenting the results of a database query. This chapter discusses common gateway interface issues, from the interaction between the server, browser, and CGI program to interpreting data passed to CGI programs. Finally, this chapter describes the development of CGI programs by presenting and explaining how to allow people to send you e-mail.

CGI applications are often referred to as gateway applications, programs, or scripts. The name may vary, but the purpose of these programs remains the same, to generate dynamic World Wide Web documents.

The server executes gateway programs locally; therefore, these applications may access system resources beyond those commonly available through the server. Consequently, CGI applications represent a potential security risk for the server site, and the server administrator may restrict the development, installation, and maintenance of applications.

14.1 Pass Data to a CGI Application

When a user activates a link or a button triggering a CGI application, the server launches that program. First, the CGI application needs to acquire information. In this How-To, you will learn how the server receives information from an HTML page and sends it to CGI applications.

14.2 Send Information to a Browser from CGI Applications

Once a CGI program has performed its appointed task, it sends the result to the server, which passes it on to a browser. In this How-To, you will learn how to use the two most common methods for transmitting information to a browser from a gateway application.

14.3 Create a Simple CGI Application

You want people to access up-to-date data through an HTML document, but you don't want to make an employee modify the document every 10 minutes. In this How-To, you will learn how to develop a CGI application to generate an HTML page from raw data whenever the page is accessed.

14.4 Install a CGI Application

You have created a CGI application to generate dynamic HTML documents. Now you want people to link and send data to your program. In this How-To, you will learn how to make your gateway program accessible from your servers.

14.5 Create a Query Document Using the `<ISINDEX>` Element

The HTML `<ISINDEX>` element allows users to input a single piece of data. In this How-To, you will learn how to use this element to provide data to gateway programs.

14.6   Access Client Data in sh CGI Scripts

If you are running a UNIX-based server, or a server equipped with a Bourne shell script interpreter, your first CGI application is likely to be developed in this Bourne shell script language. In this How-To, you will learn how to access input data in a CGI Bourne shell script.

14.7   Parse Client Data in CGI Programs and scripts

You develop gateway programs in many different languages. Acquiring user data from HTML forms is a common task, independent of the CGI programming language chosen. In this How-To, you will learn how to acquire data from HTML forms.

14.8   Process FILE Type Input from an HTML Form

The common method of entering gateway application is through form input fields. HTML 3.2 adds a **FILE** input type to these existing input types. This addition requires the modification of the standard method of parsing and retrieving data sent to gateway applications. In this How-To, you will learn how to parse HTML form data in a manner consistent with **FILE** type submissions.

14.9   Write a CGI Application to Send Me E-Mail

In this How-To, you will learn how to combine all the necessary elements of CGI application development to build a CGI e-mail support package.

COMPLEXITY
ADVANCED

14.1   How do I...
Pass data to a CGI application?

COMPATIBILITY: HTML, HTTP, CGI/1.1

Problem

When I create dynamic documents, I need to send input data from my HTML page to the server. This data passes through many hands before my CGI application can process it and generate an HTML document. The HTML document that calls the CGI application directly affects how information is passed to my gateway program. What is this process? And how will the data eventually reach my application? How is the passing mechanism determined?

Technique

Your CGI application receives data from three sources: the server, a user, and the author of the HTML page triggering the application. Ultimately, all data passed to your gateway program is sent by the server. The data supplied by the server is available via special environment variables. This type of data is commonly available to gateway programs of all types. Details on these environment variables are documented in the Comments section.

Browsers transform user and author data, and then send it to the server. The server, in turn, sends it to your CGI application in a manner prescribed by the common gateway interface protocol. Both of these data types are sent in the form of attribute/value pairs. (For example, a pair might associate the value **red** with the attribute **color**.) User data is supplied by the reader, and author data is supplied by you or whomever is authoring the HTML page accessing your gateway program.

CGI provides several mechanisms for passing data to your applications. The way data is sent depends on the input and the HTTP request method used. There are three common methods:

■ **Command line arguments.** The server starts your application and passes the data on the command line.

■ **Environment variables.** The gateway program accesses data placed in specified environment variables. The server places this information in these locations before starting your application.

■ **Standard input data block.** The server launches the gateway program and places a data block in an area accessible to your program. The gateway application then reads and interprets this data.

Figure 14-1 graphically displays these three methods.

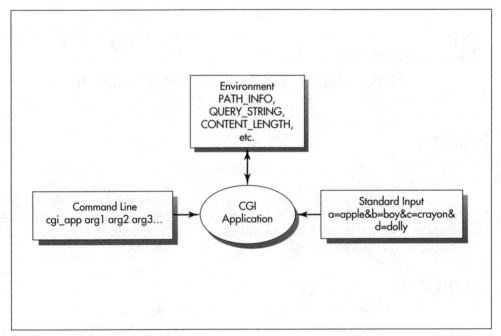

Figure 14-1 CGI provides three data-passing mechanisms

Steps

The way the server passes data to your application is based on the way you gather your input data and how you send it. In addition to user input, the server places specific information in the execution environment of your CGI application, independent of how user data is passed.

This How-To demonstrates how to pass user and author data to gateway programs from your HTML documents.

Sending Command Line Argument Input Data

<ISINDEX> user data generates command line arguments. This is the only way a server passes command line arguments to a gateway application. To generate CGI application input data as command line arguments, use an **<ISINDEX>** element to request user data.

1. Open the searchable document in a text editor.

2. Include an **<ISINDEX>** element in the **<HEAD>** element of the document.

3. Save this document.

> **NOTE**
>
> **<ISINDEX>** elements may only be used in searchable documents. If your server does not support all HTML documents as searchable documents, this element may only be used in dynamically searchable documents generated by gateway applications.

Sending Input Data Through the Environment

Two types of data can be made available through environment variables. Server-specified data is available when any gateway application is started. This commonly available data is described in the Comments section.

This section describes how to send user-entered and author-entered data via the **QUERY_STRING** environment variables. This data is entered via an HTML interactive form. The procedure describes how to create this embedded form:

1. Open the document from which data will be sent to your gateway application.

2. Move your insertion point to the location in the document where you want to request and specify data.

3. Insert a **<FORM>** element. This element should use the **"get"** method. Enclose in the **<FORM>** element any elements necessary to request the desired data. For example, the following element transmits the user data via an environment variable to the **cgi_app** CGI application.

```
<!-- Appropriate HTML elements for document -->
<FORM METHOD="GET" ACTION="http://www.mysite.edu/cgi-bin/cgi_app"⇐
ENCTYPE="application/x-www-form-urlencoded">
```

continued on next page

continued from previous page

```
...
<INPUT TYPE="submit" VALUE="Mail">
</FORM>
<!-- More HTML elements to conclude document -->
```

Chapter 11, HTML Interactive Forms, provides more information on the creation of HTML forms.

4. Save this document.

Sending Additional Author Input Data Through the Environment

This section describes how you can specify author data to be passed to a gateway application via the `PATH_INFO` environment variables. This data is included as additional path information in a URL referring to the target gateway application. Thus, you can send this type of information via either an `ACTION` attribute of a form when user input is also required, or via a standard link anchor when user input is not required. The following procedure describes how to send this type of author data.

1. Open the document from which additional author data will be sent to your gateway application.

2. Move your insertion point to the location in the document where you specify the URL of the gateway application.

3. If this is in a `<FORM>` element, include on the tail end of the form's `ACTION` URL the desired author data. Enclose in the `<FORM>` element any elements necessary to request the desired user input. (Chapter 11 provides more information on the creation of HTML forms.) For example, the following element transmits the user data via environment variable to the `cgi_app` CGI application. The `PATH_INFO` environment variable stores the author data `"author_data"`.

```
<!-- Appropriate HTML elements for document -->
<!-- The form's method may be either GET or POST -->
<FORM METHOD="GET" ACTION="http://www.mysite.edu/cgi-
bin/cgi_app/author_data" ENCTYPE="application/x-www-form-⇐
urlencoded">
...
<INPUT TYPE="submit" VALUE="Mail">
</FORM>
<!-- More HTML elements to conclude document -->
```

Or, if in an anchor, include on the tail end of the anchor's `HREF` URL the desired author data. For example, the following element transmits the author data via the `PATH_INFO` environment variable to the `cgi_app` CGI application.

```
<!-- Appropriate HTML elements for document -->
A standard link can be used to pass
<A HREF="http://www.mysite.edu/cgi-bin/cgi-app/author_data">author data</A>
to a gateway application.
<!-- More HTML elements to conclude document -->
```

4. Save this document.

Sending Input Data Through Standard Input

This is the most common method of passing input data. Unlike the other methods, this approach is not hindered by the size restriction of a command line or environment variables.

This section describes how you can send data to your CGI application as a data block on the standard input stream. This data is entered through an HTML document with a form specifying the **"post"** method. The procedure describes how to pass data to CGI applications through the application's standard input.

1. Open the document from which data will be sent to your gateway application.

2. Move your insertion point to the location in the document where you want to request and specify data.

3. Insert a **<FORM>** element. This element should use the "post" method. Enclose in the **<FORM>** element any elements necessary to request the desired data. For example, the following element transmits data by the standard input to the **cgi_app** CGI application.

```
<!-- Appropriate HTML elements for document -->
<FORM METHOD="POST" ACTION="http://www.mysite.edu/cgi-bin/cgi_app"
ENCTYPE="application/x-www-form-urlencoded">
...
<INPUT TYPE="submit" VALUE="Mail">
</FORM>
<!-- More HTML elements to conclude document -->
```

How It Works

Your CGI application receives information by three means:

- Command line arguments
- Environment variables
- Standard input

Sending Command Line Argument Input Data

The server generates command line inputs by interpreting the data entered into an **<ISINDEX>** element. For example, Figure 14-2 displays a sample document containing an **<ISINDEX>** element. The input field generated by the **<ISINDEX>** element prompts the user for information from an HTML document.

The reader enters data in the input field. Once the data is entered, the browser generates a **"get"** method HTTP request. The browser submits a query URL with the **"get"** request. This URL is composed of the current URL with the input data

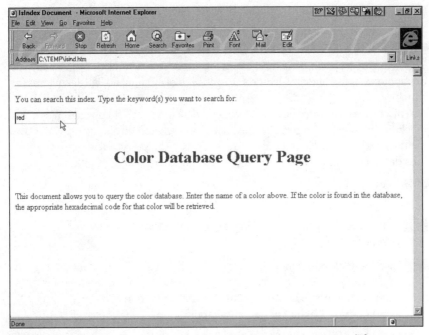

Figure 14-2 `<ISINDEX>` tag causes reader to be prompted for search terms

appended as a query string. Each word in the input field is separated by a plus sign in the query URL:

```
URL?arg1+arg2+arg3+arg4...
```

This query URL is passed to the server, which starts the gateway program in the URL with the arguments on the command line:

```
cgi_app arg1 arg2 arg3 arg4...
```

> **NOTE**
>
> You can also pass author data by simulating the results of an `<ISINDEX>` input request. The query URL in this form would take the place of a standard URL when specifying a link anchor. Generally, an appended query string that does not contain an equal sign (=) is considered an `<ISINDEX>` type request. For example:
>
> ```
> <A HREF="URL?arg1+arg2+arg3+arg4...">...</A>
> ```

Sending Input Data Through the Environment

`"GET"` method HTML forms generate user data sent via environment variables. For example, the following elements transmit one piece of user data and two pieces of author data via environment variable to the specified CGI program. (Chapter 11, HTML Interactive Forms, provides more information on the creation of HTML forms.)

```
<!-- Appropriate HTML elements for document -->
<FORM METHOD="GET" ACTION="http://www.mysite.edu/cgi-bin/cgi_app"
ENCTYPE="application/x-www-form-urlencoded">
Enter the Text of your message below:<BR>
<TEXTAREA NAME="arg1" ROWS=10 COLS=40></TEXTAREA>
<INPUT TYPE="hidden" NAME="arg2" VALUE="dsk@cau.auc.edu">
<INPUT TYPE="hidden" NAME="arg3" VALUE="Miscellaneous">
<INPUT TYPE="submit" VALUE="Mail">
</FORM>
<!-- More HTML elements to conclude document -->
```

The text area element in this form represents information entered by the reader that the gateway application accesses. The two hidden input elements contain information specified by the author of the HTML page calling the gateway application.

When the reader enters data in the input fields of the form and presses the Submit button, the browser generates a **"get"** method HTTP request. The **"get"** request includes a query URL composed of the gateway URL specified by the form's **ACTION** attribute, with the input data appended. Data is transformed to encode special characters and spaces prior to submission to the server. The appended query string contains attributes and values separated by equal (=) signs, with each attribute/value pair separated by the ampersand (**&**):

```
URL?arg1=val1&arg2=val2&arg3=val
```

This query URL is sent to the server, which runs the gateway program represented by the URL in the following environment.

```
QUERY_STRING="arg1=val1&arg2=val2&arg3=val3"
```

> **NOTE**
>
> A query URL in this format can replace a standard URL as the target of a link anchor in an HTML document. Use this method, as well as hidden form input fields, to send author data as attribute/value pair data to a gateway application. For example:
>
> ```
> <A HREF="URL?arg1=val1&arg2=val2&arg3=val3...">...</A>
> ```

Sending Additional Author Input Data Through the Environment

The **PATH_INFO** environment variable stores data that is appended to a URL. Whether the URL is the target of a link, the action of a **"get"** method form, or the action of a **"post"** method form, you can send author data through this variable. For example, the **ACTION** URL and the link target URL both specify author data sent to the **cgi-app** gateway application.

```
<!-- Appropriate HTML elements for document -->
<FORM METHOD="GET" ACTION="http://www.mysite.edu/cgi-bin/⇐
cgi-app/author_data"
ENCTYPE="application/x-www-form-urlencoded">
Enter the Text of your message below:<BR>
<TEXTAREA NAME="arg1" ROWS=10 COLS=40></TEXTAREA>
```

continued on next page

continued from previous page

```
<INPUT TYPE="submit" VALUE="Mail">
</FORM>
<!-- More HTML elements to conclude document -->
A standard link can be used to pass
<A HREF="http://www.mysite.edu/cgi-bin/cgi-app/author_data">author data</A>
to a gateway application.
<!-- More HTML elements to conclude document -->
```

When a link or button is pressed, the reader triggers an appropriate HTTP request. The **METHOD** attribute of the form specifies the method to use if the results of a form are submitted. A standard **"get"** method request is performed if a link is activated. The browser generates a URL to submit with the request. This URL is composed of the gateway application's URL, with the author-specified data appended. Table 14-1 displays the possible browser-generated URLs depending on the access method.

Table 14-1 URLs generated to send author data

ACCESS TYPE	URL GENERATED
Link	URL/author_data
"get" method form	URL/author_data?user_data
"post" method form	URL/author_data

This URL is passed to the server that runs the gateway program represented by the URL. The server places the author data in the **PATH_INFO** environment variable:

```
PATH_INFO="/author_data"
```

Sending Input Data Through Standard Input

Standard input passed data is generated through an HTML form with the **"post"** method specified. For example, the following **<FORM>** element sends data to the **cgi_app** application's standard input.

```
<!-- Appropriate HTML elements for document -->
<FORM METHOD="POST" ACTION="http://www.mysite.edu/cgi-bin/cgi_app"
ENCTYPE="application/x-www-form-urlencoded">
Enter the Text of your message below:<BR>
<TEXTAREA NAME="arg1" ROWS=10 COLS=40></TEXTAREA>
<INPUT TYPE="hidden" NAME="arg2" VALUE="dsk@cau.auc.edu">
<INPUT TYPE="hidden" NAME="arg3" VALUE="Miscellaneous">
<INPUT TYPE="submit" VALUE="Mail">
</FORM>
<!-- More HTML elements to conclude document -->
```

When this form is submitted, one piece of user data, **"arg1"**, and two pieces of **"author data"**, **"arg2"** and **"arg3"**, are sent to the standard input of the **cgi_app** application.

The reader enters data in the form's input fields. Once the Submit button is pressed, the browser generates a **"post"** method HTTP request containing a gateway URL specified by the form's **ACTION** attribute. The input data from the form is transformed and sent to the server in the request body. (See Appendix G, The Hypertext Transfer Protocol (HTTP), for information on the format of an HTTP request.)

The server runs the gateway application specified by the URL in the request. The server sends the input data to this program's standard input. The environment variable **CONTENT_LENGTH** stores the number of characters sent by the server.

The data sent on the standard input is formatted as a series of attribute/value pairs. The attributes and values are separated by equal signs (=), and each pair is separated by an ampersand (**&**):

```
arg1=val1&arg2=val2&arg3=val3
```

General Information on Data Passing

The data passing approach chosen is based upon the request type (**"get"** or **"post"**) and nature (**<ISINDEX>**, form, or link) of the input being sent. Table 14-2 summarizes these options. The Input Provider column specifies where the input to the gateway application originates. Readers generate **"user"** data when they input information into the HTML document calling the gateway application. Authors specify **"author"** information when they append information to a target URL or when they include hidden input fields in a form. The URL column shows the format of the URL generated by the browser and sent to the server as part of the HTTP request. The final column specifies the way the gateway application receives the input data.

Table 14-2 Data passing methods for various interaction types

ACCESS TYPE	INPUT PROVIDER	URL PASSING METHOD
<ISINDEX>	User: URL?arg1+arg2...	Command line
Link	Author: URL?arg1+arg2...	Command line
"get" form	User: URL?arg1=val1&arg2=val2...	Environment
Link	Author: URL?arg1=val1&arg2=val2...	Environment
"get" form	User and author: URL/author_data?arg1=val1...	Environment
"post" form	User and author: URL/author_data	Env./standard input
Link	Author: URL/author_data	Environment
"post" form	User: URL	Standard input

NOTE

When author data is passed through a query URL (**"get"** method form style or **<ISINDEX>** style), the HTML document author is responsible for encoding the special characters in the query string. (See Table 14-3.)

When a client sends information from an HTML form, special characters in the data are transformed prior to transmission to the server. This is done so that the meanings of special characters are not misinterpreted. Table 14-3 shows the special characters and how they are transformed in a data block or a query string.

Table 14-3 Permuted characters and escaped values

CHARACTER NAME	CHARACTER	INPUT VALUE
Tab	\ t	%09
Carriage return	\ n	%0A
Exclamation point	!	%21
Double quote	"	%22
Pound	#	%23
Dollar sign	$	%24
Percent sign	%	%25
Single quote	'	%27
Open parenthesis	(	%28
Close parenthesis	)	%29
Plus sign	+	%2B
Comma	,	%2C
Slash	/	%2F
Colon	:	%3A
Semicolon	;	%3B
Less than	<	%3C
Greater than	>	%3E
Question mark	?	%3F
Open bracket	[	%5B
Back slash	\	%5C
Close bracket	]	%5D
Caret	^	%5E
Back quote	`	%60
Open brace	{	%7B
Pipe			%7C
Close brace	}	%7D
Tilde	~	%7E

How-To's 14.6, 14.7, and 14.8 discuss procedures for accessing the input data and transforming it into a usable format.

Comments

Information is placed in the environment by the server and is made available when a gateway application is launched. Table 14-4 explains commonly accessed environment variables and the values they hold. This information will help you develop your own CGI applications.

Table 14-4 Commonly accessed environment variables

ENVIRONMENT VARIABLE	VALUE
CONTENT_LENGTH	Length of data block on standard input for "post" or "put" method requests.
CONTENT_TYPE	MIME type of the information being sent via the "post" or "put" method.
PATH_INFO	String containing the additional information appended to the application path.
QUERY_STRING	Contains the information appended to the URL passed to the server. This information follows the question mark. <ISINDEX> data is available both through command line arguments and through this variable.
REMOTE_ADDR	IP address of the remote machine accessing the server.
REMOTE_HOST	Name corresponding to the remote machine accessing the server. If this information is unavailable, this entry is left blank.
REMOTE_IDENT	Contains the unauthenticated ID of the user requesting the CGI application.
REQUEST_METHOD	Specifies the HTTP method sent to the server by the client ("get", "post", etc.).
SCRIPT_NAME	Contains the name of the script being called as it would appear in a URL.
SERVER_NAME	Specifies the name of the server being accessed.
SERVER_SOFTWARE	String contains the name and version of the server software being run.

A full specification of environment variables available to CGI applications can be found via the CGI specification at `http://hoohoo.ncsa.uiuc.edu/cgi/overview.html`. Further, additional environment variable information is usually available. These variables have the `HTTP_` prefix. The information contained in these variables is directly incorporated from the client's HTTP request header (as described in Appendix G). So for example, `HTTP_USER_AGENT` would contain the data passed to the server in the User-Agent field of the HTTP request header.

COMPLEXITY
ADVANCED

14.2 How do I...
Send information to a browser from CGI applications?

COMPATIBILITY: HTML, HTTP, CGI/1.1

Problem

I want to send my results from a gateway application to the server and then to a browser. How does the server get the information, and what does it do with it? I need to know the details of this process to properly build my CGI programs.

Technique

The browser receives gateway-generated information via the server in two ways:

▪ **Parsed header.** Gateway application results are placed on its standard output. The server takes this information, manipulates it, and sends it to the client.

▪ **Nonparsed header.** A gateway program beginning with the **nph-** prefix indicates that the CGI application is a nonparsed header (**nph**) program. This means that results sent to the standard output by this type of application are not processed by the server, but passed directly to the client through the server.

Through these two methods, information is passed to the server. Figure 14-3 shows the relationship between these two methods in relation to the browser, the server, and your CGI application. The upper arrow represents the path of the parsed header method. The lower arrow represents the pass through using a nonparsed header program. In either case, the end result is an HTTP response sent to the browser. (See Appendix G, for information on HTTP responses.)

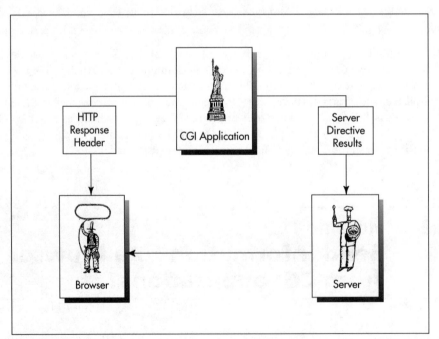

Figure 14-3 Passing of information from a gateway application to the browser

Steps

The following step-by-step procedures show how to pass information to the browser via the parsed and nonparsed header methods.

> **WARNING**
>
> It is imperative that server directives from parsed header applications and response headers from nonparsed header applications terminate with a blank line. This blank line indicates the end of the header and the beginning of any attached object.

Parsed Header

If the results generated by a CGI application are relatively simple in nature, you don't need to fine tune the response header that will be eventually passed to the browser. Use the following procedure to pass CGI information to the browser via the server.

1. Issue a server directive as the first line of your gateway application output. Servers currently support three allowable server directives:

`Content-type: type/subtype`

Location: URL

Status: code message

For example, the following line might be used in a Bourne shell script. Substitute corresponding statements used in other development languages.

`echo Content-type:  text/html`

The How It Works section describes these three server directives.

2. Follow the server directive with a blank line. For example, in a Bourne shell script, issue the following command. In other development languages, use corresponding commands.

`echo`

3. In a `Content-type` server directive, the remainder of the output is the object returned to the browser (an HTML document, a GIF image, and so on). In a Status server directive, the remainder of the output is the text of the error message returned to the browser; simple text is the safest format for such a message.

Nonparsed Header Applications

With an **nph** application, the full response header that is sent to the client must be generated and returned by your gateway program. Use the following process to generate a minimal HTTP response header. Additional response header fields that could be included are discussed in Appendix G. Nonparsed header programs tend to be slightly faster since the server need not perform any processing or make any additions.

Many browsers, but not all, can deal with less information than this minimum.

1. Issue a status line. The first line of an HTTP response header contains a specification of the protocol and version, followed by a status code, and ending with a status message. For example, `HTTP/1.0 200 OK` would be an appropriate first line. This should be the first line placed on standard output by your application. In a Bourne shell script, you could enter

```
echo "$SERVER_PROTOCOL 200 OK"
```

2. In the next line, specify the date that the current document was put together. Your gateway application should calculate this information and place it on the standard output. For example, `Date: Sat, 25-Dec-99 14:24:32 GMT`. Since all servers work according to Greenwich Mean Time (GMT), make sure that the times you generate are for this time zone. The following code segment is appropriate for generating this information in a Bourne shell script.

```
echo -n "Date: "

/usr/bin/date -u -'+%a, %d-%h-%y %T GMT'
```

3. Specify the server software and version being used. This information is found in the `SERVER_SOFTWARE` environment variable. For example, if you're using NCSA version 1.3 server software, send the line `Server: NCSA/1.3` to the standard output next. You could use the following code in a Bourne shell script.

```
echo "Server: $SERVER_SOFTWARE"
```

4. Include a MIME version field. The current version is 1.0. So, a line like `MIME-version: 1.0` should appear next. You could use the following code in a Bourne shell script.

```
echo "MIME-version: 1.0"
```

5. Add other header fields as required by the status code and the resultant data being transmitted back to the browser. (See the Comments section and Appendix G.)

6. Terminate the HTTP response header with a blank line. For example, use the following code in a Bourne shell script.

```
echo
```

7. If a `Content-type` field appears in the response header, the remainder of the output after the blank line is the object returned to the browser (an HTML document, a GIF image, and so on.).

How It Works

Your application sends its results to the standard output. If the name of your gateway program does not begin with the `nph-` prefix, the server parses and interprets the results your application places on the standard output. If your application name starts with the **nph-** prefix, the server assumes that the program is a nonparsed header program and retransmits the results from the gateway application without modification.

In the case of a parsed header application, the server reads and interprets the server directive. The remaining results placed on the standard output are interpreted based upon the server directive. Unless the **Content-type** directive is used, additional results passed to the standard output may cause problems. The server then generates an appropriate HTTP response header and attaches any associated data to it. Figure 14-4 displays this process for the three accepted server directives, which are

- **Content-type: type/subtype**: Indicates that the object in the HTTP response body is of the specified MIME type.

- **Location: URL comment**: Indicates that the requested file is in a different location. The URL specifies where the desired information is located.

- **Status: code message**: Allows you to specify an exit status for your CGI application.

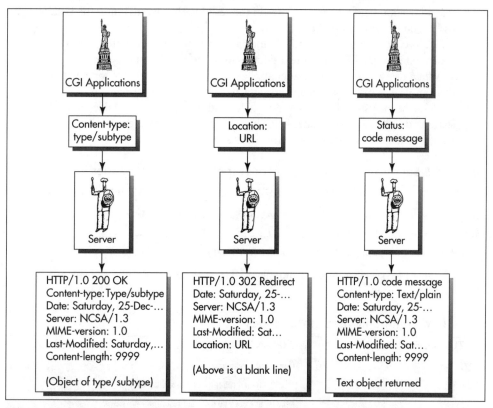

Figure 14-4 Transformation of parsed header CGI output to an HTTP response message

With respect to **nph** gateway applications, the data placed on the standard output by your application is passed directly back to the client. Therefore, your application generates a complete HTTP response header, with associated data.

In either case, the browser receives an HTTP response header and any relevant data objects.

Comments

Both methods rely on passing information to the server via the standard output. The difference is that nonparsed header gateway applications are responsible for generating an entire HTTP response header, plus any generated results from execution. CGI programs with parsed headers just provide a server directive, however, and allow the server to construct an appropriate HTTP response header. Appendix G, provides information on HTTP response header fields you can use in your nonparsed header CGI applications.

Status codes and status messages tell the browser the status of its request. Status codes range from 200 to 599. A code within the 200 to 299 range indicates a successful transaction.

A code from 300 to 399 specifies some manner of redirection. This usually implies that a Location field will appear later in the response header, defining the URL to use in lieu of the requested one.

Status codes between 400 and 599 indicate errors. The nature of the error is often explained in a small HTML or text document in the HTTP response body.

When using a nonparsed header application, you are responsible for generating the complete response header and any attached object. Using particular status codes suggests the inclusion of specific header fields and attached objects. Table 14-5 maps status codes to suggested header fields beyond the minimum suggested in the nonparsed header procedure given in the Steps section.

Table 14-5 Suggested header fields for response status categories

STATUS CODE	SUGGESTED RESPONSE INFORMATION	ATTACHED OBJECT?
200–299	Content-type, Content-Length (if known)	Yes
300–399	Location	No
400–599	Content-type, Content-Length	Yes (error message)

Table 14-6 specifies many commonly used status codes, along with an explanation of their meaning.

Table 14-6 Commonly used status codes

STATUS CODE	EXPLANATION
200	Completed successfully.
201	POST method request completed successfully.
202	Request has been queued, but results are unknown.

STATUS CODE	EXPLANATION
203	Completed, but all information was not returned.
204	No operation. Complete successful.
301	Requested data moved permanently to another location.
302	Request completed, but desired data is at another location.
400	Syntax error in request.
403	Access to requested resource is forbidden.
404	Requested URL not found.
500	Internal server error.
501	Server does not support requested method.

Aside from error codes and complete success, the status code you are most likely to use is code 204. This code indicates no response, but successful completion. An HTTP response using this code results in no change to the document currently seen in the browser. This code is handy for specifying the default action to be taken in an imagemap, or to demonstrate how a particular browser displays a link. In either case, you can specify the following gateway application as the target URL.

```
#!/bin/sh

# Indicate status followed by a blank line
echo Status:   204 No response, but successful
echo
```

COMPLEXITY
INTERMEDIATE

14.3   How do I...
Create a simple CGI application?

COMPATIBILITY: HTML, HTTP, CGI

Problem

I want to create a simple gateway application. I don't require user input data, but I do want to generate a document on the fly from information available on the server host machine. How can I do this?

Technique

This How-To shows how to write an application to generate an HTML document from data existing at the server site. The sample application uses the Bourne shell scripting language for demonstrative purposes. This language is both easy to use and reasonably portable. The technique presented should be easy to transfer to other development languages.

Steps

The next procedure documents the development and incorporation of a Bourne shell CGI script to execute a command and return the results of that command as a dynamically created HTML document. The actual commands depend on whether you are authoring in sh, Perl, TCL, or another scripting language.

1. In a text editor, create a file called `first.cgi`.

2. The script must begin with the following line specifying the execution environment:

```
#!/bin/sh
```

3. Issue a server directive to the standard output. In the case of a script written to process a command and report the output, the most likely directive you will use is Content-type. The actual type you specify should correspond to whatever type of file your application will send back to the browser.

```
echo Content-type: text/html
```

This code segment indicates that the attached file is an HTML document.

> **NOTE**
>
> How-To 14.2 goes into detail on the use of the three valid server directives.

4. Terminate the server directive with a blank line indicating that the attached object follows. Use a single echo statement to generate this blank line.

```
echo
```

5. Set the PROG variable to the program you wish to run. For example, if you wish the script to generate the local date and time on the server, use the following line:

```
PROG=/usr/bin/date
```

6. Since the server directive you used indicates that an HTML document is attached, generate the HTML-formatted output of your specified command. The following segment of code generates the beginning of an HTML document to be returned to the browser:

```
cat << EOF
<!DOCTYPE HTML PUBLIC "-//W3C//DTD HTML 3.2//EN">
<HTML>
<HEAD>
<TITLE>
EOF

echo "$PROG Response Page"

cat << EOF
</TITLE>
```

```
</HEAD>
<BODY>
<H1>
EOF

echo "$PROG Response Page"

cat << EOF
</H1>
<HR>
EOF
```

The `cat << EOF` commands cause the script to output the proceeding text until an `EOF` is reached.

7. Run the specified program on the server. You need to format the results for presentation by the browser. The following code executes the program and formats the results as the content of a `<PRE>` element.

```
echo \<PRE\>
$PROG
echo \</PRE\>
```

8. End the document by closing the `<BODY>` and `<HTML>` elements.

```
cat << EOF
</BODY></HTML>
EOF
```

9. Save this script file, and exit the editor.

10. Change permissions on the script file, if necessary, to make it executable.

11. Test the application. The results seen should start with a server directive, followed by a blank line. The blank line is followed by an attached document. The results that should appear from the execution of the script developed in this How-To should look like this:

```
Content-type: text/html

<!DOCTYPE HTML PUBLIC "-//W3C//DTD HTML 3.2//EN">
<HTML>
<HEAD>
<TITLE>
/usr/bin/date Response Page
</TITLE>
</HEAD>
<BODY>
<H1>
/usr/bin/date Response Page
</H1>
<HR>
<PRE>
Sat Dec 25 14:24:32 EDT 1999
</PRE>
</BODY></HTML>
```

12. Make the script available for use through your HTML documents. First, install the script and register it with your server. For servers like NCSA or CERN, gateway applications should be placed in a `cgi-bin` directory by default.

13. Determine the URL of your installed CGI application.

14. Refer to your gateway script as the destination for HTML links.

How It Works

Gateway applications of this type process data and generate results that are sent back to the client in some specified format. Figure 14-5 diagrams the execution of such a CGI application. The application generates an appropriate server directive, separated from the body of the message by a blank line. The object returned to the browser follows the blank line.

The script using the program `/usr/bin/date` developed in this example is on the CD-ROM, with the filename `FIRST.CGI`.

When a link specifies this gateway script as its destination, the application generates a parsed header and a message body, which are passed to the server. The server processes this information and generates a full HTTP response header to return to the client.

Figure 14-6 shows the page resulting from the activation of a link to the `first.cgi` script.

Comments

More complex methods are necessary for dealing with CGI applications that require some level of user input. These methods are investigated more deeply in later How-To's in this chapter.

For detailed information on HTTP response header information and parsed versus nonparsed headers, see How-To 14.2.

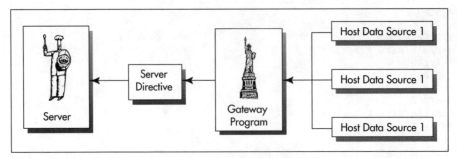

Figure 14-5 Transformation of parsed header CGI output to an HTTP response message

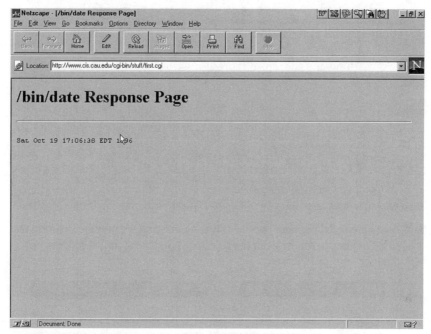

Figure 14-6 Results of activating a link to `first.cgi`

14.4   How do I...
Install a CGI application?

COMPATIBILITY: NCSA HTTPD, CERN HTTP

Problem

Once I've written my gateway application, I need to make it available. Where do I need to place the application so I can access it from an HTML document, and how do I create a reference to it?

Technique

This How-To describes standard procedures for installing CGI applications on NCSA or CERN servers. Other servers provide different means for registering allowable gateway applications. The Comments section provides useful references to information on installing gateway applications on several other servers.

NCSA and CERN servers use two installation methods: script directories and file types. NCSA allows for both types, while the CERN server allows only script directories.

> **NOTE**
>
> You may need to discuss the installation of any CGI application with your Web site administrator. CGI applications are run on the host machine and therefore represent a potential security risk.

Steps

The following sections provide detailed instructions for installing CGI applications on NCSA and CERN servers.

Installing a CGI Application in an NCSA Script Directory

You make script directory specifications in the server resource map file. The following steps describe how to install your CGI application using this method.

1. If you are installing your application to an existing script directory, skip to step 5. Otherwise, change to the directory containing the server resource map file and load the `srm.conf` file into your text editor.

> **NOTE**
>
> To specify new script directories you must have server administrator privileges.

2. Append a `ScriptAlias` directive to the `srm.conf` file. The format for this command is as follows:

```
ScriptAlias virtual_directory physical_directory
```

The virtual directory refers to the path you should put in a URL to reference this script directory. The physical directory represents the actual directory located on the machine running the server; if a relative path is specified, the `ServerRoot` is assumed to be the base path.

The following lines designate the `/usr/local/httpd/bin/` and `ServerRoot/my-cgi-bin/` directories as script directories. In URLs, refer to them as `/local/bin/` and `/mybin/`, respectively.

```
ScriptAlias    /local/bin/    /usr/local/httpd/bin/
ScriptAlias    /mybin/    my-cgi-bin/
```

Any URL specified for a link anchor or HTML form action referencing `http://www.mysite.edu/mybin/myscript` causes the server to execute `ServerRoot/my-cgi-bin/myscript`. You can have as many `ScriptAlias` directives in your configuration as you wish.

3. Save the configuration file.

4. Stop the server and restart it. This causes the server to read the altered configuration file and treat your script directories properly.

5. Move or copy your executable CGI application to a script directory. In UNIX, use the **mv** or **cp** command. For instance, to move the gateway program **first.cgi** to **/usr/local/httpd/bin**, issue the following command:

```
mv first.cgi /usr/local/httpd/bin
```

> **NOTE**
>
> To install applications in existing directories, you need write access to the script directory.

6. Make sure that the application is executable by all users since the user associated with the server needs execution access to your code. Use the following UNIX command to give read and execute privileges to all users:

```
chmod ugo+rx first.cgi
```

Installing a CGI Application in a CERN Script Directory

The CERN Web server provides a script directory mechanism for installing gateway programs. The following steps describe how to install your programs using this method.

1. If you are installing your application to an existing script directory, skip to step 5. Otherwise, change to the directory containing the server configuration file and load the **httpd.conf** file into your text editor.

> **NOTE**
>
> To specify new script directories, you must have server administrator privileges.

2. Add exec rules to this file. The format for this command is **Exec /virtual_directory/*/physical_directory/***. You may add as many script directories as you want with exec rules. The physical directory represents the location to which the server should map the virtual directory when seen in a URL. The following line designates the **/usr/local/httpd/bin/** directory as a script directory. In URLs, refer to this directory as **/local/bin/**.

```
Exec     /local/bin/*      /usr/local/httpd/bin/*
```

Any URL specified as a link anchor or HTML form action referencing **http://www.mysite.edu/local/bin/myscript** causes the server to execute **/usr/local/httpd/bin/myscript**.

3. Save the configuration file.

4. Stop the server and restart it. This causes the server to read the altered configuration file and treat your script directories properly.

5. Move or copy your executable CGI application to a script directory. In UNIX, use the **mv** or **cp** command. For instance, to move the gateway program **first.cgi** to **/usr/local/httpd/bin**, issue the following command:

```
mv first.cgi /usr/local/httpd/bin
```

> **NOTE**
>
> To install applications in existing directories, you need write access to the script directory.

6. Make sure that the application is executable by all users, since the user associated with the server needs execution access to your code. Use the following UNIX command to give read and execute privileges to all users.

```
chmod ugo+rx first.cgi
```

Installing a CGI Application Using NCSA File Type Mechanism

With this method, gateway programs can be placed anywhere. The server recognizes an application by an extension type. This type can be established across all documents on a particular server, or on an individual directory basis.

1. If you are installing your application to a directory with an access file set for CGI applications, or if your server has been configured to allow CGI applications anywhere, skip to step 4. If you are configuring the server to allow gateway applications anywhere, change to the directory containing the server resource map file, load the **srm.conf** file into your text editor, and skip to step 3. If you are configuring a single directory for gateway applications, change to the directory you are configuring and load the access control file (the default name is **.htaccess**) into your text editor. If an access file does not exist, create one using the filename specified in the server resource map file. The directive you are looking for is **AccessFileName**.

2. Insert the following line in the access control file. This line allows execution of gateway applications in this directory.

```
Options ExecCGI
```

> **NOTE**
>
> To specify execution of CGI applications in a particular directory, you need to have read and write access to the directory level access control file.

3. Insert an **AddType** directive. This directive tells the server how to interpret files with a given extension. For example, if you want all files with the extension .cgi to be treated as gateway programs, insert the following line into the access control file:

```
AddType    application/x-httpd-cgi    .cgi
```

> **NOTE**
> To specify the file type across a server, you must have server administrator privileges. For individual directories, you need to have read and write access to the directory level access control file.

4. Move or copy your executable CGI application to the desired directory. If you have set the server so that gateway programs can reside anywhere, then the only restriction is that the chosen directory must be visible to the server. In UNIX, use the **mv** or **cp** command. For instance, to move the gateway program **first.cgi** to **/usr/local/httpd/bin**, issue the command:

```
mv first.cgi /usr/local/httpd/bin/first.cgi
```

> **NOTE**
> You need to have read and write access to the directory where you wish to place your application.

5. Make sure that the application is executable by all users since the user associated with the server needs execution access to your code. Use the following UNIX command to give read and execute privileges to all users:

```
chmod ugo+rx first.cgi
```

How It Works

Both NCSA and CERN servers allow you to configure directories so that the server treats your files in these directories as gateway programs. Once you have configured directories as script directories, whenever the server sees a URL addressing the logical name for such a directory, it launches the filename attached to the URL as a CGI application. To install an application, move the executable code or script to the directory and make sure that it can be executed by the server. The procedures in this How-To show the steps required to establish script directories and install applications in them.

The other means provided by the NCSA server for installing gateway programs is by file type and modification of access control files. Access control files may appear anywhere visible to your server. They control how files in the current directory and its subdirectories are accessed. In the access control file, specify that the server treat all files ending with a particular file extension as CGI applications. Gateway applications can then be installed anyplace that is controlled by the modified access file. If the server resource map file is modified, then applications may appear wherever they are visible to the server, as long as they have the correct filename extension.

Comments

Documentation for CGI application installation for various servers can be found at the locations in Table 14-7.

Table 14-7 Common Gateway Interface documentation for various servers

SERVER	CGI INFORMATION LOCATION
NCSA	http://hoohoo.ncsa.uiuc.edu/docs/tutorials/cgi.html
CERN	http://www.w3.org/pub/WWW/Daemon/User/CGI/Overview.html
FastTrack	See online material distributed with the server
WN	http://hopf.math.nwu.edu/
MacHTTP	http://www.starnine.com/development/extending.html
WinHTTPD	http://www.city.net/win-httpd/

Installing gateway applications for a FastTrack server is almost identical to the processes described for NCSA. The actual configuration file command syntax is slightly different. However, since the administration server provides a form-based interface for configuring appropriate directories, these differences are transparent unless you configure your FastTrack server by direct configuration file modification.

COMPLEXITY
INTERMEDIATE

14.5 How do I...
Create a query document using the <ISINDEX> element?

COMPATIBILITY: CGI

Problem

I am interested in creating a searchable document. The search criterion is a simple list of terms. How do I place a query for the search terms, and information on how to access this data from my CGI application, into my document?

Technique

This How-To describes the process for developing a gateway program to manage an <ISINDEX> query document. Since <ISINDEX> documents generate query URLs by appending a query string to the current URL, CGI applications that generate and handle <ISINDEX> query documents must have two components: one to generate the query page and one to generate the response page.

When the URL is triggered, the application checks the number of command line arguments to determine whether to generate the query page or the response page.

<ISINDEX> query terms are sent to the application as command line arguments. (See How-To 14.1 for more information on how information is passed to gateway applications.) Figure 14-7 displays the approach taken with this technique.

Steps

The following procedure delineates the steps you should follow to develop your <ISIN-DEX> gateway applications. The example provided has been developed using the Bourne shell script language to run the finger utility with any arguments specified in the <ISIN-DEX> field. When developing your applications, use the appropriate constructs in your development language to accomplish the tasks demonstrated in the steps. When you have completed the procedure, you can use the URL for your <ISINDEX> application as you would any other URL (for the target of a link, an open location, and so on).

1. Open a text editor and begin writing the source for your <ISINDEX> application. Place any necessary header information in your application (script to use, header files, helper functions, and so on). In the example finger script, this step includes specification of the Bourne shell, as well as defining a variable pointing to the finger program.

```
#!/bin/sh
#Finger <ISINDEX> application
FINGER=/usr/ucb/finger
```

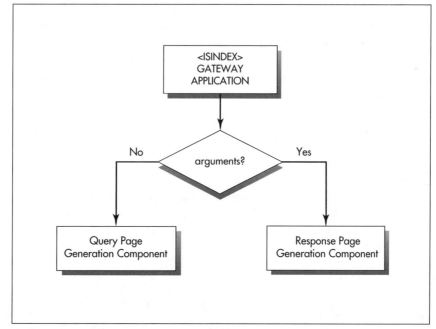

Figure 14-7 <ISINDEX> application architecture

2. Determine if any command line arguments have been passed to your application program. If no arguments are present, call the query generation component. If arguments are present, process them and call the response generation component. In the sample application, use an if statement to determine whether arguments are present. The then portion leads to the query generator, while the else (step 6) leads to the response generator.

```
# Determine if command line arguments are present.
if [ $# = 0 ]; then
```

3. Develop the query generation component. The first part of the query generation sends the Content-type server directive, followed by a blank line. Since you are using an **<ISINDEX>** element, specify **text/html** as the type. In the example, the echo command places this information on the standard output.

```
echo Content-type: text/html
echo
```

> **NOTE**
>
> If this <ISINDEX> application is a non-parsed header application (nph- prefix on the application file name), generate the full response header as described in How-To 14.2.

4. Attached to this response header, include an HTML document that has the **<ISINDEX>** element in the **<HEAD>** component. The **<HEAD>** component should also contain an appropriate title for the generated document. In the sample application, use the cat command to place this information on the standard output. (This particular cat command also places the body on the standard output in step 5.)

```
cat << EOF
<!DOCTYPE HTML PUBLIC "-//W3C//DTD HTML 3.2//EN">
<HTML>
<HEAD>
<TITLE>Finger Query</TITLE>
<<ISINDEX>>
</HEAD>
```

5. Add information relevant to the application and the proper format for submitting input text in the body of the document. In the Bourne shell file, a cat command places this information on the standard output (continued from the listing in step 4). The **EOF** command signals the end of the information.

```
<BODY>
<H1>Finger Query</H1>
<HR>
This is a "finger" query page. Enter a series of user@host entries in the
available search dialog.
```

```
<HR>
</BODY>
</HTML>
EOF
```

6. Develop a response to the query. The response to the query is like any other gateway application response. A server directive (or response header for **nph** applications) is sent, terminated with a blank line. The blank line is followed by an attached file, if required. The sample application signifies the response generation component with the else command from the **if** statement entered in step 2.

```
else
```

7. The response document is begun by sending the appropriate server directive on the standard output. As with the query component, the sample application uses the echo command to perform this task.

```
# Generate Response Document

echo Content-type: text/html
echo
```

8. Generate the attached file by processing and sending back an appropriately generated document. In the sh script example, this is done using a cat command. The processing of the arguments is embedded in the document generation process.

```
cat << EOF
<!DOCTYPE HTML PUBLIC "-//W3C//DTD HTML 3.2//EN">
<HTML>
<HEAD>
<TITLE>Finger Response</TITLE>
</HEAD>
<BODY>
<H1>Finger Response</H1>
<HR>
Input Terms Were: $*
<PRE>
EOF

$FINGER $*

cat << EOF
</PRE>
<HR>
</BODY>
</HTML>
EOF
```

9. Add any necessary closing information. In the example application developed in this procedure, the closing information is simply the termination of the **if** statement that checked the argument count.

```
fi
```

10. Save the application, and compile it, if necessary.

11. If feasible, test your application. First, run it with no arguments to see that it generates a proper HTML document with **<ISINDEX>** in the **<HEAD>**. Then, if the response component generates a readable output (for example, text or HTML), run your application with command line arguments.

12. Install your **<ISINDEX>** application as described for CGI application installation in How-To 14.4.

How It Works

When a browser first accesses the URL of your application through a link or an open location, your application launches without command line arguments (unless the author or opener has appended a query string to the URL). Your application detects that no command line arguments are present and executes the query generation component. When the user enters the desired input in the query page, the server launches the same application; however, the browser appends a query string composed of the user response to the URL. Therefore, the server converts the query string into command line arguments and launches your application. This execution of your application receives command line arguments and runs the response component of the application.

The sample application developed through this procedure can be found in file SECOND.CGI on the CD-ROM.

When a link to a URL without a query string attached associated with an **<ISINDEX>** gateway application is triggered, the server launches the application without command line arguments; therefore, the query generation component executes. For the sample application, running the query generator component results in the HTML document seen in Figure 14-8.

If you enter data in the provided query field and submit the request, the browser generates a request with the inputs attached to the URL as a query string. This URL is submitted to the server, which launches the gateway application with the items in the query string passed as command line arguments. If you launch the sample application with the query text seen in Figure 14-8, the result is a document like the one shown in Figure 14-9.

Comments

Even though the sample application was developed using the Bourne shell language, the components represented in the code can be used for **<ISINDEX>** applications written in any development language. You need to map your language's constructs into the three primary tasks specified:

- Decision

- Query generation

- Response generation

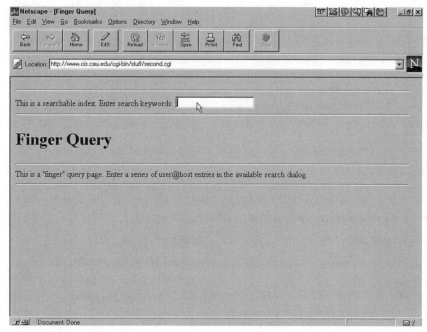

Figure 14-8 Execution of `second.cgi` without command line arguments

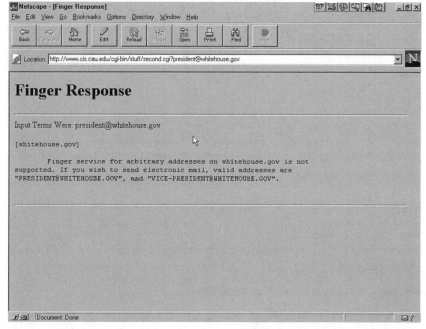

Figure 14-9 Execution of `second.cgi` with command line arguments

Steps 7 and 8 of the procedure can be modified if a different type of response is required, based upon the processing of the data. In the example script, the response from finger was presented, whether it generated a valid response or an error. In your application, you may wish to send a different response message based upon the results of processing the data. For example, if the input is processed correctly, you might send a TIFF file with a Content-type: `image/tiff`, a redirection command with a `Location:URL`, or a particular error with a `Status` directive. If an error is generated, you might want to respond with an HTML document describing the error that occurred.

The finger program is a UNIX utility that provides information concerning valid users on specified machines. The formats for acceptable command line arguments are provided in Table 14-8. Multiple command line arguments are acceptable.

Table 14-8 Information request arguments of finger

COMMAND LINE ARGUMENT	INFORMATION REQUEST
user	Information for user on current machine
user@host	Information for user on host machine
@host	List users currently on host machine

COMPLEXITY
INTERMEDIATE

14.6 How do I...
Access client data in sh CGI scripts?

COMPATIBILITY: CGI, BOURNE SHELL

Problem

For reasons of portability, I've decided to write gateway applications using Bourne shell scripts. I need to retrieve user-specified form data. The information is encoded and sent by several means. Is there an efficient mechanism for accessing the data that was originally entered?

Technique

Your first step in developing a Bourne shell application that requires user input data is the retrieval of the input data. This common task is performed by all CGI applications that require input data. This information can be in several forms:

- Query string from a `"get"` method form

- Standard input from a `"post"` method form

- Command line arguments from an `<ISINDEX>` query

This How-To provides step-by-step instructions for retrieving and accessing input data from both **"get"** and **"post"** method forms. How-To 14.5 presents a way to retrieve **<ISINDEX>** data.

Steps

To access user input data from a Bourne shell script, you develop and install a helper application that parses the input data and places it in environment variables that can be accessed by your shell script.

The helper application called **shparse** has been developed in the C language, and the first three steps involve the creation and installation of this program.

The remainder of the steps provide instruction on incorporating the helper function in your gateway scripts and offer a simple example script. If the **shparse** program has already been compiled and installed in a location visible to your sh application, you should skip ahead to step 4.

1. Copy the following files from the CD-ROM to a local directory where you will build the **shparse** program.

> **parse.h** : This file contains necessary header information.
>
> **parse.c** : This file holds the helper function and declarations for reconstructing "post" method form data.
>
> **parseget.c** : This file holds the helper function and declarations for reconstructing **"get"** method form data.
>
> **shparse.c** : This file holds the main **shparse** application.

2. Using your C compiler, compile the three C files that you have just copied in the previous step, and rename the output **shparse**. For example:

```
gcc -o shparse parse.c parseget.c shparse.c
```

3. Move the **shparse** application to a location visible to your shell gateway programs. Make sure that the file security for the **shparse** application is set for execution by all individuals who need access to it.

4. Open your Bourne shell application in your text editor.

5. Insert the following lines to specify a Bourne shell script and to read the user input data into environment variables.

```
#!/bin/sh

eval `shparse`
```

6. Develop the rest of your application. All input data appears in environment variables with the **INPUT_** prefix. The remainder of each variable name is the attribute associated with the attribute/value pair. If multiple inputs have the same attribute, they are placed in the environment individually, as **INPUT_SUF, INPUT_SUF_D1, INPUT_SUF_D2**, and so forth.

> **NOTE**
>
> If you wish to change the default prefix from INPUT_ to something else, modify the `shparse.c` file prior to compilation.

7. Test your application by running it with suitable environment variables set and providing data on the standard input, if necessary. If the application works as you expect, proceed to the next step; otherwise, debug your sh script as necessary.

8. Install your application in a suitable location. See How-To 14.4 for information on application installation.

How It Works

The first step in your CGI application is to call the **shparse** application in the manner just prescribed. Figure 14-10 shows how your Bourne shell script and the **shparse** application interact with each other and with the server.

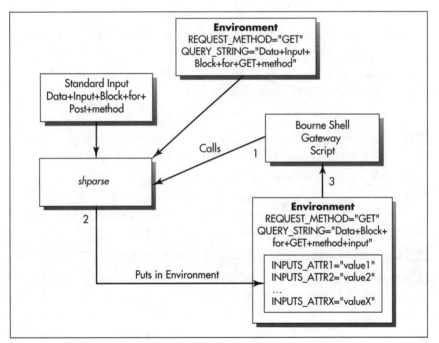

Figure 14-10 `shparse` and your Bourne shell gateway program

Once the input data has been parsed, your script can access and process this data as necessary to generate the proper response. The response is passed back to the server, and from the server to the browser. The output of your gateway application should conform to the standard specifications, as described in How-To 14.2.

Next is a sample application written using the `shparse` application developed in this How-To.

```
#!/bin/sh

eval `shparse`

echo Content-type: text/plain
echo

echo argc is $#. argv is "$*".
echo

echo Environment Variables
echo SERVER_SOFTWARE = $SERVER_SOFTWARE
echo SERVER_NAME = $SERVER_NAME
echo REQUEST_METHOD = $REQUEST_METHOD
echo HTTP_ACCEPT = "$HTTP_ACCEPT"
echo PATH_INFO = "$PATH_INFO"
echo PATH_TRANSLATED = "$PATH_TRANSLATED"
echo SCRIPT_NAME = "$SCRIPT_NAME"
echo QUERY_STRING = "$QUERY_STRING"
echo REMOTE_HOST = $REMOTE_HOST
echo REMOTE_ADDR = $REMOTE_ADDR
echo REMOTE_USER = $REMOTE_USER
echo AUTH_TYPE = $AUTH_TYPE
echo CONTENT_TYPE = $CONTENT_TYPE
echo CONTENT_LENGTH = $CONTENT_LENGTH

echo Form Inputs
echo INPUT_T1 = $INPUT_T1
echo INPUT_T2 = $INPUT_T2
echo INPUT_T3 = $INPUT_T3
```

This application displays generic environment variables, plus the environment variables `INPUT_T1`, `INPUT_T2`, `INPUT_T3`. These three environment variables are assumed to have been generated by the evaluation of the results of `shparse`. The values associated with form input fields T1, T2, and T3 are stored respectively in the previously mentioned environment variables.

Comments

These programs and scripts were developed and tested on a UNIX platform machine. Modification may be necessary, depending on the target platform.

Furthermore, complications will arise if an attribute name ends in the suffix **_DX** or if more than 10 values are associated with a particular attribute.

COMPLEXITY
ADVANCED

14.7 How do I...
Parse client data in CGI programs and scripts?

COMPATIBILITY: CGI

Problem

The browser transforms HTML form data prior to submitting it to the appropriate server, and ultimately to my gateway application. How do I process this data to regenerate the original data submitted by the user?

Technique

You have created a form to query the reader for information necessary for the generation of a dynamic document. Each entry the user makes is associated with an attribute, or name, defined in your form. The form data is passed to your application through the server. However, this information is modified in the process. Since most CGI applications need to transform and parse this data, a systematic approach to regenerating the input data is desirable.

This How-To presents a generic method suitable to break the data block passed to your gateway application into its original form. Figure 14-11 gives an overview of this processing technique.

The browser receives the data entered into HTML forms. For safety and security reasons, the browser transforms the special characters in this form data. The browser transmits this data to the server through either a **"get"** or a **"post"** method transaction. Depending on the method, your gateway application retrieves the data from the environment or standard input, respectively. You must then transform the data to restore the special characters. Your application can now proceed to processing the data and generating an HTML results page.

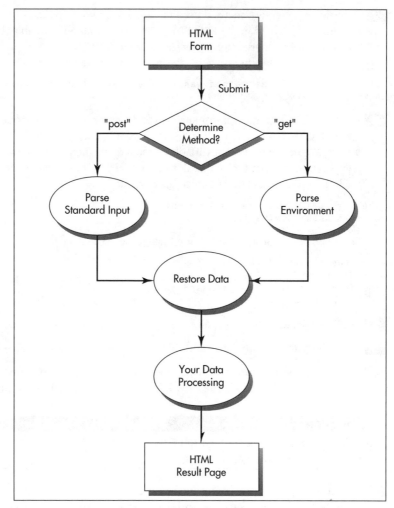

Figure 14-11 Regenerating HTML form data in gateway

Steps

The following steps allow you to parse and transform the modified data passed to your program. The original data will be placed in a specified location, with each of the attributes specified in your HTML form associated with the data the user entered.

The Comments section describes the use of this procedure with several common gateway application development languages.

1. Open the source code of your gateway application.

2. Determine the request method used to pass data to your application. This information is stored in the **REQUEST_METHOD** environment variable. In C, you retrieve this information using the **getenv** function; for example, the following line stores the method type in the **app_check** variable.

```
/* Check to determine what method was used to call this application.  */
app_check=getenv("REQUEST_METHOD");
```

3. Parse the data from the appropriate source depending upon the request method. If the request method is **"get"**, parse the data from the **QUERY_STRING** environment variable. If the request method is **"post"**, retrieve the data from the standard input. For example, in Perl, the following lines retrieve the data sent by a **"get"** request.

```
#Read the form data from the environment
$data = $ENV{ QUERY_STRING };
```

For a **"post"** request, the following lines retrieve the data.

```
#Determine the length of the POST'd data.
$len = $ENV{ CONTENT_LENGTH };
#Read the form data from the standard input
read(STDIN, $data, $len);
```

4. Separate the attribute/value pairs.

5. Break the pairs into attributes and values.

6. Restore the special characters. This process depends significantly upon your implementation language. The How It Works section describes this process.

> **NOTE**
> You can combine steps 4 through 6 if this combination yields a more suitable implementation.

7. Implement the data processing and result generation components of your gateway application. (See How-To 14.6 for an example using Bourne shell.)

8. Save your gateway application.

9. Compile your program, if necessary.

10. Test your application. You may need to set environment variables manually and supply standard input data to perform this task. Correct any errors.

11. Install your application in a suitable location. See How-To 14.4 for information on application installation.

How It Works

Your CGI application must retrieve and restore form data prior to use. When a reader triggers the Submit button for your form, the browser packages and transmits the entered data. The HTTP request type specified in the form's METHOD attribute determines how the browser sends this data.

"Post" is the preferred transmission method because a **"post"** data block does not have as many size constraints. The maximum size of the command line and maximum length of an environment variable both constrain a **"get"** method data block. With the **"get"** method, the browser transforms the form data and appends it to the URL submitted to the server. With the **"post"** method, the browser composes the information entered in a form into a data block that it passes to the server as the attached object in the HTTP request.

The server passes the data to the CGI application either as an environment variable or as standard input, for **"get"** and **"post"** requests, respectively. You must transform this data back into standard ASCII, then resolve it back into attribute/value pairs. These attribute/value pairs can then be accessed by the CGI application.

The browser transforms the input data by stringing together attribute/value pairs. The browser places an equal sign (=) between each attribute and its value, and it places an ampersand (**&**) between each pair. It converts the spaces in any attribute or value to plus signs (**+**) and converts any special characters into an escaped value (as seen in Table 14-3 in How-To 14.1.)

Therefore, breaking the data passed to the gateway program at ampersands reconstitutes the pairs, and breaking the pairs at equal signs separates the components of the pair. The restoration of each attribute or value to its original format is accomplished by examining each character and modifying it appropriately. Plus signs in the input are changed back to spaces. Escaped characters, when encountered, are converted back to their original ASCII form.

For example, the form shown next has three data fields named **"message"**, **"teacher"**, and **"topic"** that will be composed and sent to the CGI application t2. The **"post"** method will be used to pass the data to the application.

```
<!DOCTYPE HTML PUBLIC "-//W3C//DTD HTML 3.2//EN">
<HTML>
<!-- Sample Data Entry Form - Calls CGI application t2 -->
<HEAD>
<TITLE>Sample Form</TITLE>
</HEAD>
<BODY>
<H1>Sample Form</H1>
<HR>
<FORM METHOD="POST" ACTION="http://www.mysite.edu/cgi-bin/t2"
ENCTYPE="application/x-www-form-urlencoded">
Enter the Text of your message below:<BR>
<TEXTAREA NAME="message" ROWS=10 COLS=40></TEXTAREA>
<INPUT TYPE="hidden" NAME="teacher" VALUE="dsk@cau.auc.edu">
<INPUT TYPE="hidden" NAME="topic" VALUE="Miscellaneous">
<INPUT TYPE="submit" VALUE="Mail">
</FORM>
<HR>
<H6>Last Modified: March 9, 1995 by dsk@cau.auc.edu</h6>
</BODY>
</HTML>
```

Figure 14-12 shows how Prodigy's Web browser presents this form. It has a single visible input field and a Submit-type button labeled Mail. Two hidden input fields are also present.

When the button is pressed, the browser composes an input block and passes the information to the specified CGI application via the server. The data block generated for this sample form looks like this:

```
message=This+is+a+sample+of+text+input.++This+might+have%0Abeen+entered+⇐
into+the+sample+form+whose%0Asource+appears+in+figure+5%2D8%2D1.++How+will+⇐
it%0Abe+processed%3F&teacher=dsk@cau.auc.edu&topic=Miscellaneous
```

Comments

The CD-ROM contains source code in several programming languages that accomplishes the tasks specified in the preceding steps. Following are specific instructions for each of these languages.

C Implementation

The C implementation of this process requires the files **parse.h**, **parse.c**, and **parseget.c**. The file **main.c** provides you with a template to use for your C gateway program development.

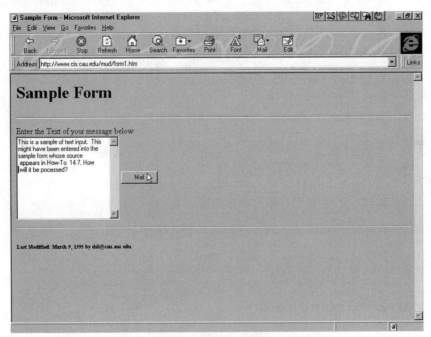

Figure 14-12 Sample form (as displayed) with input

To use these files, copy the file `main.c` to the filename that you wish to use to store your main function. This file contains the C statements necessary to parse and restore HTML form data.

Edit this file to add any includes necessary to your application, to add any variables that need to be declared, and to add the statements necessary to accomplish the remainder of your program. You access the forms data through the inputs array.

Compile the `main.c`, `parse.c`, and `parseget.c`, together with any other required C files, to generate your executable application. You can test your application by simulating `"get"` or `"post"` requests by placing suitable information in the environment and on the standard input.

For the sample form shown in Figure 14-12, the inputs array after executing the supplied code contains the data (`input_count = 3`) shown in Table 14-9.

Table 14-9 Contents of input array for Figure 14-12

ENTRY	DATA
`inputs[0].attribute`	`"message"`
`inputs[0].value`	`"This is a sample of text input. This might have\nbeen entered into the sample form whose\nsource appears in figure 5-8-1. How will it\nbe processed?"`
`inputs[1].attribute`	`"teacher"`
`inputs[1].value`	`"dsk@cau.auc.edu"`
`inputs[2].attribute`	`"topic"`
`inputs[2].value`	`"Miscellaneous"`

Multiple entries in the inputs array support multiple values for the same attribute. If the query string sent to your application were as follows:

`t1=a1&t2=a2&t1=a3`

the inputs array would store multiple entries for the same attributes. The values in the relevant variables for the query string are shown in Table 14-10. The attribute "t1" would have values of "a1" and "a3".

Table 14-10 Duplicate values example under C

VARIABLE	VALUE
`input_count`	3
`inputs[0].attribute`	`"t1"`
`inputs[0].value`	`"a1"`
`inputs[1].attribute`	`"t2"`
`inputs[1].value`	`"a2"`
`inputs[2].attribute`	`"t1"`
`inputs[2].value`	`"a3"`

C++ Implementation

The C++ implementation uses the following files from the CD-ROM: INPUTS.H, PARSE.H, PARSE.C, PARSEGET.C, and INPUTS.CPP. When creating a C++ CGI program, add these files to the compile line. These files declare and define the `Inputs` class you will use to retrieve and restore form data.

The `Inputs` class is responsible for the parsing and converting of the form data. The public interface to the class provides the necessary access mechanism for the use of HTML form input. This class provides two methods: `count` and the indexing operator `[]`. The `count` method returns the number of attribute/value pairs that the browser sent. The indexing operator receives an attribute in the form of a string and returns a value associated with that attribute. In instances of multiple values, repeated use of the indexing operator with the same attribute index cycles through all values associated with the attribute. The return of a null pointer indicates the end of the cycle. If you need to retrieve the first value instance for an attribute, you need to reset the `Inputs` object; you do this by using an empty string ("") with the indexing operator.

NOTE

To guarantee finding all values, do not attempt to access the value of a second attribute until you have cycled through all values of the first.

When you declare an object of this class in your application, all the data management is performed for you. Plus signs in the input are changed back to spaces. Escaped characters (see Table 14-3 in How-To 14.1), when encountered, are converted back to their original ASCII form. The `Inputs` object will provide you with access to the pass data through the indexing operator.

In your application program, you must add the following line to include the declaration of the `Inputs` class.

```
#include "Inputs.h"
```

You perform the retrieve and restore functions by declaring an object of class `Input`. If you pass no parameters, the default values are assumed for maximum number of pairs, length of attribute fields, and length of value fields. Specification of parameters will substitute the value given for the default. The following several lines of code provide a few sample declarations of objects.

```
Inputs inputs;                  // Take defaults
Inputs inputs(10);              // Only 10 input pairs maximum
Inputs inputs(10,64);           // Only 10 inputs and max attrib length of 64
Inputs inputs(10,64,128);       // Only 10 inputs, 64 max on attrib, 128 max
                                // On val
```

Access is provided to this data through the use of the indexing operator. The index used is the attribute for which you want to find the value. In the example shown in Figure 14-12, indexing the `Inputs` object would yield the results in Table 14-11. In this table, the ordering of accesses matters.

Table 14-11 Data access under C++ from form in Figure 14-12

VARIABLE	VALUE
inputs["message"]	"This is a sample of text input. This might have\nbeen entered into the sample form whose\nsource appears in figure 5-8-1. How will it\nbe processed?"
inputs["teacher"]	"dsk@cau.auc.edu"
inputs["teacher"]	(char *)null
inputs["topic"]	"Miscellaneous"
inputs["teacher"]	"dsk@cau.auc.edu"
inputs[""]	(char *)null
inputs["teacher"]	"dsk@cau.auc.edu"

The **Inputs** class provides a cycling method for accessing multiple values associated with an attribute. For example, the input string here would indicate that the attribute **"t1"** has values of **"a1"** and **"a3"**.

t1=a1&t2=a2&t1=a3

The resultant **Inputs** object would return the first value in the first access, the second value in the second access, and a null pointer on the third access attempt. The values in the relevant variables derived from the query string are shown in Table 14-12.

Table 14-12 C++ handling of duplicate values

VARIABLE	VALUE
inputs["t1"]	"a1"
inputs["t2"]	"a2"
inputs["t1"]	"a1"
inputs["t1"]	"a3"
inputs["t1"]	(char *)NULL

The order in which the accesses occur is significant. The cycle for the **"t1"** attribute resets at the access of the value of attribute **"t2"**. The null pointer returned in the last line indicates a full cycle through the values of attribute **"t1"**.

Perl Implementation

The Perl implementation of the data retrieval and restoration process uses the file MAIN.PL from the CD-ROM. You can use this file as a template for your gateway scripts. Copy this file to whatever name you wish for your Perl CGI application, and add the commands necessary to implement the processing and result generation portions of your script.

The Perl commands in **main.pl** provide you with the necessary retrieval and restoration of the form data. The script first checks the HTTP method used in the request.

Based upon this information, the script determines the location of the input data block. The transformation of the data occurs in the following order:

- All spaces restored
- Attribute/value pairs separated
- All ampersands (**&**) restored
- Pairs separated into attributes and values
- Special characters restored for all attributes and values
- Array inputs defined

Your commands access the form data submitted through the inputs array. Use the attribute name as the index to access the value. For example, the form shown in Figure 14-12 fills the inputs array as shown in Table 14-13.

Table 14-13 Figure 14-12 data access from Perl

VARIABLE	VALUE
inputs{message}	"This is a sample of text input. This might have\nbeen entered into the sample form whose\nsource appears in figure 5-8-1. How will it\nbe processed?"
inputs{teacher}	"dsk@cau.auc.edu"
inputs{topic}	"Miscellaneous"

COMPLEXITY
ADVANCED

14.8 How do I...
Process FILE type input from an HTML form?

COMPATIBILITY: HTML 3.2+; CGI; NETSCAPE NAVIGATOR

Problem

The browser transforms HTML form data prior to submitting it to the appropriate server, and ultimately to my gateway application. I cannot use the standard approach because the form is sending a file as input. How do I access this form data?

Technique

You have created a form to query the reader for information necessary for the generation of a dynamic document. Each entry the user makes is associated with an attribute, or name, defined in your form. The form data is passed to your application through the server. However, this information is modified in the process. Since most CGI applications need to transform and parse this data, a systematic approach to regenerating the input data is desirable.

This How-To presents a generic method suitable to break the data block passed to your gateway application into its original form. Figure 14-11 in How-To 14.7 gives an overview of the processing technique for standard gateway applications. Figure 14-13 extends this general approach to deal with HTML 3.2's new FILE input type.

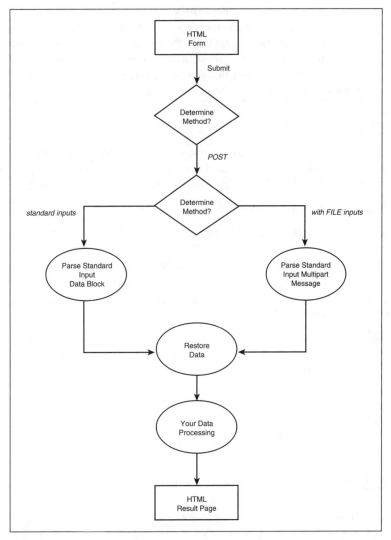

Figure 14-13 Regenerating HTML form data in gateway applications—revisited

The browser receives the data entered into HTML forms and combines this with any files selected. The browser transmits these data to the server through a **"post"** method transaction. Your gateway application retrieves the data from the standard input. You must parse the data to regenerate the attribute/value pairs. Your application can now proceed to processing the data and generating an HTML results page.

NOTE

Currently, only the Netscape Navigator browser supports this aspect of the HTML 3.2 standard. Other browser software that supports HTML 2 forms will not allow the submission of FILE type input data. Further, the submission process has not been formalized into the CGI/1.1 standard; therefore, the process described in this How-To examines the mechanism established by Netscape to convey FILE type information. Published specifications indicate Microsoft's intent to support FILE type input in the Internet Explorer browser.

Steps

The following steps allow you to parse and transform the data passed to your program. The original data will be placed in a specified location, with each of the attributes specified in your HTML form associated with the data the user entered.

1. Open the source code of your gateway application.

2. Determine the request method used to pass data to your application. This information is stored in the **REQUEST_METHOD** environment variable. In C, you retrieve this information using the **getenv** function; for example, the following line stores the method type in the **app_check** variable.

```
/* Check to determine what method was used to call this application.  */
app_check=getenv("REQUEST_METHOD");
```

3. Parse the data from the appropriate source, depending upon the request method. If the request method is **"get"**, parse the data from the **QUERY_STRING** environment variable (See How-To 14.7). If the request method is **"post"**, retrieve the data from the standard input. For a **"post"** request, the following lines retrieve the data.

```
#Determine the length of the POST'd data.
$len = $ENV{ CONTENT_LENGTH };
#Read the form data from the standard input
read(STDIN, $data, $len);
```

4. Determine the content type of the data on the standard input. This information is stored in the **CONTENT_TYPE** environment variable. In C, you retrieve this information using the **getenv** function; for example, the following line stores the content type in the **content_type** variable.

```
/* Check to determine what content type is on the standard input.  */
content_type=getenv("CONTENT_TYPE");
```

5. Separate the attribute/value pairs. If the content type is `"application/x-www-form-urlencode"`, use the procedure described in How-To 14.7. If the content type is `"multipart/form-data; boundary=some_string"`, continue with this process.

6. Find an instance of the boundary string. (See Appendix C, Multipurpose Internet Mail Extensions (MIME), for more information on the architecture of multipart MIME messages.)

7. Scan the `Content-Disposition` field immediately following the boundary string. Break the data associated with this field into component pieces. The first piece of data following the field name indicates information about the derivation of this portion of the multipart message. This data item should indicate that the component is "form-data." The remaining data items represent paired data. Among these data, a pair with the identifier `"name"` indicates the attribute name from the HTML form that is associated with the data in this portion of the multipart message. For example:

```
Content-Disposition: form-data; name="category"
```

This line indicates that the message body for this portion of the multipart message contains the value data associated with the category attribute, the data submitted by the user for the INPUT item in the HTML form with the `NAME="category"`.

8. In the situation where the Content-Disposition field contains a filename paired data entry, the body in this portion of the message represents a file submitted through a FILE type input field. If this is not the case, proceed with step 9 to parse and store the data value. The message portion header of a file submission contains an additional field indicating the content type of the field submitted. Your gateway application will need to determine a priori whether or not it can deal with file data of this content type. For example:

```
Content-Disposition: form-data; name="stuff"; filename="C:\caulogo.gif"
Content-Type: image/gif
```

The first line indicates that the message body for this portion of the multipart message contains the value data associated with the stuff attribute. On the client machine running the browser, the file submitted is named `C:\caulogo.gif`. The second line indicates that the file submitted is a GIF image. (See Appendix C, for additional information on potential MIME types.)

9. Read the blank line that separates the header portion of this part of the multipart message from the body portion.

10. Read the body portion, and dispose of the data as required by your application. A usual disposition of standard form data might be in name/value paired character arrays. File data might require an indirect method of storage, such as storing the INPUT field name and the file name as a paired character array while caching the actual file on the server's hard disk.

11. The body portion terminates with another instance of the boundary string. If this is the end of the file, continue with step 12 to process the data; otherwise, return to step 7 to process the next portion of the message.

> **NOTE**
>
> The last instance of the boundary string usually has two additional dashes appended to it.

12. Implement the data processing and result generation components of your gateway application. (See How-To 14.6 for an example using Bourne shell.)

13. Save your gateway application.

14. Compile your program, if necessary.

15. Test your application. You may need to set environment variables manually and supply standard input data to perform this task. Correct any errors.

16. Install your application in a suitable location. See How-To 14.4 for information on application installation.

How It Works

HTML form data that include submitted files require the use of the `ENCTYPE="multipart/form-data"` attribute in the `<FORM>` element. The use of this encoding type instructs Netscape Navigator (the only browser currently supporting FILE input types) to submit the HTML form data as a multipart MIME message (See Appendix C, Multipurpose Internet Mail Message (MIME).

Figure 14-14 displays a form using this type of encoding; the complete HTML source for this form is in the FILEDNLD.HTM file on the CD-ROM. The `<FORM>` element that generates the input areas on this page appears here.

```
<FORM ACTION="/cgi-bin/p" METHOD="POST" ENCTYPE="multipart/form-data">
<!-- Hidden Element -->
<INPUT TYPE="hidden" NAME="hide" VALUE="newstuff">
Please enter a password:
<INPUT TYPE="password" NAME="pw"><BR>
```

```
Please enter some text:
<INPUT TYPE="text" NAME="txt" VALUE="default text">
<P>
The following form item should be a file request.
This request uses the following input element:<BR>
&lt;INPUT TYPE=&quot;file&quot; NAME=&quot;send&quot;&gt;
<INPUT TYPE="file" NAME="send">
<P>
<INPUT TYPE="submit" VALUE="Submit Data">
</FORM>
```

Selecting the submit button seen in Figure 14-14 generated the following multipart message sent to the standard input of the specified gateway application:

Figure 14-14 Sample file download form

```
------------------------------51412919431542
Content-Disposition: form-data; name="hide"

newstuff
------------------------------51412919431542
Content-Disposition: form-data; name="pw"

adfa
------------------------------51412919431542
Content-Disposition: form-data; name="txt"

default text
------------------------------51412919431542
Content-Disposition: form-data; name="send"; ⇐
filename="C:\MSOFFICE\WINWORD\HTML3HT\CHAP2\CD\HT12\Home.htm"⇐
Content-Type: text/html
<HTML>
<HEAD>
<TITLE>Home Page of XXXXXXXXX</TITLE>
</HEAD>
<BODY>

<!-- Mark the beginning of this portion with a horizontal rule. -->
<HR>
<!-- Center your name as a level 1 header. -->
<TAB ALIGN="center"><H1>XXXXXXXX</H1>
<!-- Provide any desirable contact information. -->
999 My Street<BR>
City, ST Postalcode<BR>
E-mail: my_id@mysite.edu

<!-- Mark the beginning of this portion with a horizontal rule. -->
<HR>
<!-- Choose the heading text that you feel appropriate. -->
<H1>About Me</H1>
<!-- The formatting and information should be developed to suit your needs⇐
-->
<TAB INDENT=5>This is the first paragraph in this section about myself.
I have been at MY BUSINESS fo the past X years.
<P>
<TAB INDENT=5>I am currently working on several projects.
These projects include...

<!-- Mark the beginning of this portion with a horizontal rule. -->
<HR>
<!-- Substitute the appropriate information in your document. The date⇐
should -->
<!-- appear in a long format with the mont name written out since the⇐
order -->
<!-- conventions for date abbreviations vary. -->
```

```
Last modified on CURRENT_DATE by YOUR_NAME (YOUR_E-MAIL)

</BODY>
</HTML>
```

```
----------------------------51412919431542--
```

Your gateway application needs to parse this multipart message and extract the necessary HTML form data in the form of attribute/value data pairs and file data. The process works by repeatedly parsing the subcomponents of the message, where each subcomponent is demarked by an arbitrarily chosen boundary string, `----------------------------51412919431542` in the example.

Each subcomponent has a header portion and a body portion. The header portion contains any relevant meta-information about the body portion. The body portion contains the actual data submitted through the form. A blank line separates the header portion from the body portion.

Minimally, the header contains a disposition field which indicates how the gateway application should treat the body portion; currently, the only defined disposition is form-data. The remainder of the disposition field contains information about the HTML form input item that generated the particular subcomponent. In the case of any input type other than `FILE`, this usually simply contains the name of the input item from the form. In the case of the `FILE` input types, the disposition field also contains the filename representing the location of the submitted file on the client submitting the file. Use the presence of the filename data pair on the disposition line to clue your gateway application in to the fact that the body portion of this subcomponent contains file input data. The header portion may also contain a content-type field specifying the type of data sent in the body portion; file submission will always include this field.

The body portion of the subcomponent contains the actual data submitted by the user. For HTML form input other than file type, the body portion contains the relevant value that the user entered. Unlike a data block, this textual information is not URL encoded. In the case of file type form input, the header contains a content-type field describing the type of file sent; the body portion contains the data of the type specified. For information concerning the different types of data, see the MIME information in Appendix C.

Comments

The file P.C on the CD-ROM contains the source code for the **p** application that processes the data from the form shown in Figure 14-14. This application simply generates a `text/plain` content-type server directive (see How-To 14.2), calls a standard test application that displays the pertinent environment variables, and displays the multipart MIME message sent by the browser. Figure 14-15 displays the result of submitting the form shown in Figure 14-14.

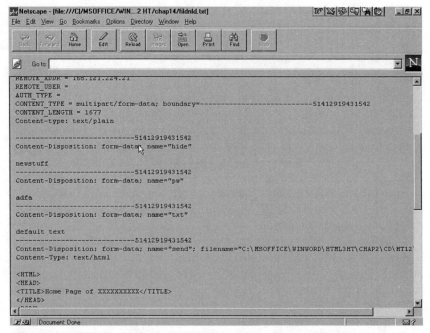

Figure 14-15 Environment variables and multipart MIME message generated

This application does not separate the input data. It is a diagnostic application for viewing any **"post"** method form submissions.

COMPLEXITY
ADVANCED

14.9   How do I...
Write a CGI application to send me e-mail?

COMPATIBILITY: CGI; C; HTML 2,3, 3.2

Problem

Some browsers support mailto resources, but not all. I want to allow people to send me e-mail through a Web page, whether their browser supports this or not. How can I generate an HTML form and gateway application to accomplish this task? What must I do to extend this capability to allow e-mail to be sent to other users?

Technique

Establishing e-mail Web pages for a specified group of users requires two gateway applications. The first generates an HTML form to gather the e-mail message to be sent. The second CGI program receives the input from this form, determines whether the target of the e-mail is in a defined set of allowed targets, sends the e-mail if appropriate, and generates a resultant HTML document. Figure 14-16 displays the interactions among the components of the developed package.

This How-To shows a step-by-step process for developing, installing, and maintaining a CGI e-mail handling package on your server.

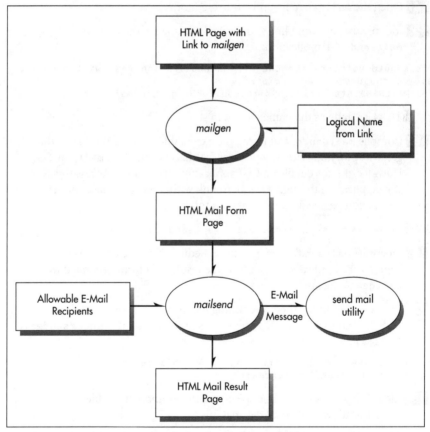

Figure 14-16 How the e-mail CGI package components interact

Steps

The C source code for the e-mail package is available on the CD-ROM in files `mailgen.c` and `mailsend.c`; you also need helper files `parse.h` and `parse.c`.

1. Change directories to the location where you wish to perform your development tasks.

2. Copy the `mailgen.c` file from the CD-ROM. This file contains the source code for the application that will generate an e-mail form for any target.

3. Choose a name for the `mailsend` component of this package.

4. Open the `mailgen.c` file in your text editor.

5. Identify the following line and modify it to specify the URL for the `mailsend` CGI application:

```
/* This should point to the URL of the application that will send the  *
 * mail to the designated recipient.                                   */
#define MAILSEND http://www.mysite.edu:8080/cgi-bin/mailsend
```

This URL reflects the name chosen in step 3.

6. Compile `mailgen.c`, and install the executable as you would any other gateway program. The default name for this executable is `mailgen`. See How-To 14.4 for details on CGI application installation. Access this gateway application through a standard link with the logical name of the destination passed as additional path information.

7. Copy files `parse.h`, `parse.c`, and `mailsend.c` from the CD.

8. Open the `mailsend.c` file in your text editor. This file contains the source code for the application that sends the results of a form generated by `mailgen` to the appropriate recipient.

9. Identify and modify the line defining the location of your server system's mailsend utility. On UNIX systems, this utility is usually either `"sendmail"` or `"smail"`.

```
/* You should specify your mail program in this define.                */
#define SENDMAIL "/usr/lib/sendmail"
```

10. Identify and modify the line specifying the location of the file containing the list of allowable e-mail destinations.

```
/* The ALLOW define specifies the location of the allowable users file.*/
#define ALLOW "/usr/local/some_directory/.allow"
```

11. Compile these three files to create the `mailsend` application. If you do not call this application `mailsend`, be sure you specified the URL of this application in step 5. You can now install `mailsend` as you would any other CGI program. See How-To 14.4 for more information on installing gateway applications. Access this gateway application through the specified action in the form generated by `mailgen`, or whatever you choose to call the application installed in step 6.

12. Begin allowing the generation of e-mail pages for selected users. Your first task at this stage is to define a group of users you wish to provide with this service. Either you or they need to establish a logical name used to refer to them within the context of this e-mail package. This logical name helps generate the mail form, as well as verifying that each user is allowed to receive mail via this application.

13. Change directories to the location where you wish to store the file of allowable e-mail recipients. This is the directory you specified in the `ALLOW` define from step 10.

14. Open the file specified in the `ALLOW` define.

15. Add a line for each e-mail recipient. A line is composed of the logical name, followed by white space, followed by the e-mail address.

16. After entering all valid recipients, add a line containing the word `"end"`.

17. Generate e-mail forms for submitting mail to users specified in the `ALLOW` file by referencing the URL of the `mailgen` CGI application. Appended to this URL should be the logical name of the mail recipient in the form of path information. For example, if the `mailgen` program were located in the `/cgi-bin` directory, and if you wished to create a link to a mail page for registered logical name `paul`, the requested URL would be `http://www.mysite.edu/cgi-bin/mailgen/paul`.

How It Works

The two programs, `mailgen` and `mailsend`, interact with each other and with the `ALLOW` file to provide a mechanism to support e-mail for a set of registered users. The e-mail package is launched when a link referencing the URL of the `mailgen` application is triggered. For example, `http://www.mysite.edu/cgi-bin/mailgen/abner` specifies the e-mail entry page associated with the logical name `abner`.

> **NOTE**
>
> You can also enter the package by sending the proper data fields to the `mailsend` application via the `"post"` HTTP method; however, in general, most users enter the package through `mailgen`.

When the link is triggered, a mail entry form is dynamically tailored to the specific logical name passed via additional path information. For example, the form displayed in Figure 14-16 was generated by a link designating logical name **dsk** as the target.

The user fills the data fields with his or her name, return address, and the body of the message. When the Submit button is pressed, the input data is sent by **"post"** method to the **mailsend** CGI application.

The **mailsend** application is responsible for processing and storing the data, as well as providing the user with a response concerning the data items in question. The input data is passed to the application through an input data block on the standard input. Then **mailsend** calls the C build function to parse and convert the attribute/value pairs.

The **mailsend** application goes through the following steps in the process of delivering mail messages.

1. Retrieves the user input data from the form. This task is performed by the procedure in How-To 14.7 for parsing HTML **"post"** method form data.

2. Opens the file of allowable mail recipients and checks for the specified logical name among those listed. If this is not present, **mailsend** returns an error document.

3. Opens a pipe to the **mailsend** utility.

4. Writes the mail message to this pipe.

5. Closes the pipe to the **mailsend** utility. This action, in effect, causes the e-mail to be sent to the specified recipient.

6. Begins generation of a response page.

7. Formats and presents the page to the user.

8. Closes the generated document.

If the data present in Figure 14-17 were submitted, then the resultant document would look like the one shown in Figure 14-18. The mail application on the server site would be responsible for handling the delivery of the mail to its destination.

Comments

The package developed in this How-To has been compiled and tested in the UNIX environment. Porting the application to other environments will require some modification.

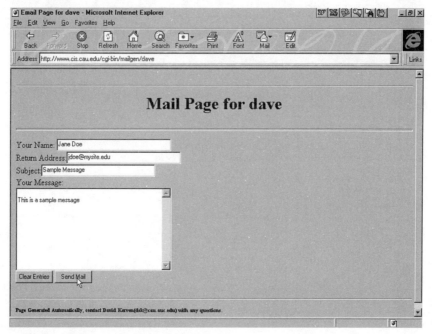

Figure 14-17 E-mail entry form

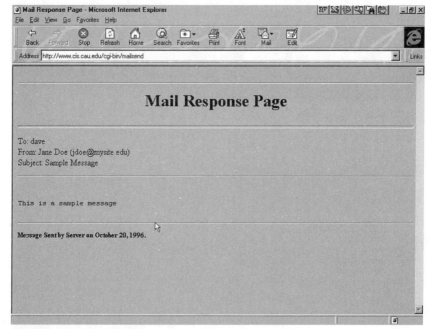

Figure 14-18 E-mail response page

PART IV
BEYOND HTML 3.2

CHAPTER 15

NAVIGATOR AND INTERNET EXPLORER HTML EXTENSIONS

15

NAVIGATOR AND INTERNET EXPLORER HTML EXTENSIONS

How do I...

The World Wide Web is changing at a remarkable rate. New browsers such as Microsoft Internet Explorer 3.0 and Netscape 3.0, with new HTML extensions, are unveiled. New technologies such as Java and VRML are introduced to the World Wide Web. The range of capabilities available to Web page authors is growing every day. This chapter examines some of the new HTML extensions and new technologies. (Because some of the content of this chapter is based on beta versions of software and rapidly evolving languages and protocols, some of this information may be out of date by the time you read this.)

15.1 Add Marquees of Scrolling Text

Text scrolling across a page is a unique way to grab the attention of a reader. This How-To shows how to use an HTML extension in Microsoft Internet Explorer 3 to create marquees of text that can scroll across the screen in a variety of styles.

15.2 Utilize TrueType and Other Fonts

Now it is possible to exercise some control over the fonts a Web page is rendered in. This How-To shows you how to set the fonts used.

15.3 Format My Web Page in Multiple Columns

You no longer need to use a table to create multiple column Web pages. This How-To shows you an alternative way to create "newspaper" style Web pages.

15.4 Insert Blank Space into My Web Page

There are times when you actually would like to have blank space (i.e., nothing) on a part of a Web page. This How-To shows you how to include blank space on a Web page.

15.5 Add Color to Tables

One way to make tables really stand out on a page is to include color cells and backgrounds. This How-To shows how easy it is to add colors to a table.

15.6 Add a Background Image to a Table

There are times when you may want to make a table a bit more exciting by adding a background image to it. This How-To shows you how to add background images to your tables.

15.7 Control Table Borders

There are times when you may want part of a table to have borders and another part either not to have borders or to have different borders. This How-To shows you how to control the borders of your tables.

15.8 Create New Windows for Linked Documents

Often it's useful to have a document that's referenced in a link in a Web page appear in a separate window so the reader can easily compare the two documents. This How-To shows how to use an HTML extension supported by Netscape 2.0 to automatically open a separate window and place the linked document there.

15.9   Use Netscape's `Client Pull`

The Netscape `Client Pull` feature provides a means for automatically loading new documents at specified time intervals. This capability provides support for slide shows as well as text-based animation. This How-To explains how to use the Netscape `Client Pull` feature in your documents.

15.10   Specify Netscape `Server Push`

With the Netscape viewer, you can develop gateway applications that provide automatically updating HTML pages. In this How-To, you will learn how to create CGI applications to generate server-pushed HTML pages.

COMPLEXITY
INTERMEDIATE

15.1   How do I...
Add marquees of scrolling text?

COMPATIBILITY: INTERNET EXPLORER 2+

Problem

I would like to bring attention to some text on my Web page by scrolling it across the page. How can I easily create a marquee of scrolling text for my page?

Technique

Microsoft's Internet Explorer 3 supports the HTML extension `<MARQUEE>`, which allows people using that browser to see marquees of text that scroll across the screen. A number of attributes for the tag allow you to control the size, scrolling `BEHAVIOR`, and color of the marquee.

Steps

Open your document and identify the text you want to use as the marquee and the location in the page for the marquee.

1. Place the `<MARQUEE>` tag at the beginning and the `</MARQUEE>` tag at the end of the text that will be in the marquee. This creates a default marquee that scrolls across the screen once. For example:

```
<MARQUEE>This is an example of a marquee</MARQUEE>
```

2. You can control the type of scrolling used with the `BEHAVIOR` attribute. The `BEHAVIOR` attribute supports three values, which are described in Table 15-1. The default value for `BEHAVIOR` is `SCROLL`.

Table 15-1 Values for the BEHAVIOR attribute in <MARQUEE>

VALUE	DESCRIPTION
ALTERNATE	Bounces the text back and forth between the two sides of the screen
SCROLL	Starts the text all the way off the screen and moves it across the marquee all the way off the screen on the other side
SLIDE	Starts the text all the way off the screen and moves it across the marquee until the text touches the margin on the other side of the screen

To create a sliding marquee, use

```
<MARQUEE BEHAVIOR=SLIDE>This is an example of a sliding
marquee</MARQUEE>
```

To create a bouncing marquee, use

```
<MARQUEE BEHAVIOR=ALTERNATE>This is an example of a bouncing
marquee</MARQUEE>
```

3. The DIRECTION attribute controls the direction the text moves across the marquee. DIRECTION can have two values: LEFT (for text scrolling from left to right) and RIGHT (for text scrolling from right to left). The default value is LEFT. To create a scrolling marquee that goes from right to left, use

```
<MARQUEE DIRECTION=RIGHT>This is an example of a marquee moving right to
left</MARQUEE>
```

4. You can control the speed of the marquee with two attributes, SCROLLAMOUNT and SCROLLDELAY. SCROLLAMOUNT sets the number of pixels between each redraw of the marquee. That is, the next time the marquee is drawn, the contents of the marquee will be moved down by the number of pixels set by the SCROLLAMOUNT attribute. The SCROLLDELAY attribute sets the delay, in milliseconds, between redraws. A marquee can be speeded up by increasing the value of the SCROLLAMOUNT attribute (moving the text a greater distance between redraws), decreasing the value of the SCROLLDELAY attribute (shortening the time between redraws), or both. For example, to create a scrolling marquee that moves the text 25 pixels between redraws, you would use

```
<MARQUEE SCROLLAMOUNT=25>This is an example of a marquee</MARQUEE>
```

To create a marquee that waits 10 milliseconds between redraws, use

```
<MARQUEE SCROLLDELAY=10>This is an example of a marquee</MARQUEE>
```

To combine the two attributes in the same marquee, use

```
<MARQUEE SCROLLAMOUNT=25 SCROLLDELAY=10>This is an example of a
marquee</MARQUEE>
```

5. You can set the number of times the marquee scrolls across the page with the LOOP attribute. To create a continuously scrolling marquee, set LOOP equal to **-1** or **INFINITE**. To create a marquee that will scroll across the screen five times, use

```
<MARQUEE LOOP=5>This is an example of a marquee that scrolls 5
times</MARQUEE>
```

To create a marquee that scrolls continuously, use

```
<MARQUEE LOOP=INFINITE>This is an example of a continuously scrolling
marquee</MARQUEE>
```

6. The **BGCOLOR** attribute sets the background color of the marquee. The attribute can be set to a hexadecimal set of red, green, and blue intensities (known as an RGB triplet), or to one of a set of special color names supported by Internet Explorer. For example, each of the following two lines creates a marquee with a red background.

```
<MARQUEE BGCOLOR="#FF0000">This is an example of a marquee with a red back-
ground</MARQUEE>
<MARQUEE BGCOLOR="Red">This is an example of a marquee with a red back-
ground</MARQUEE>
```

7. The **HEIGHT** and **WIDTH** attributes adjust the height and the width of the marquee. They can either be set equal to a specific distance in pixels, or to a percentage of the width or height of the screen. To create a marquee that is 300 pixels wide and 50 pixels high, use

```
<MARQUEE WIDTH=300 HEIGHT=50>This is an example of a marquee</MARQUEE>
```

To create a marquee that is 20 percent of the height of the screen and 75 percent of the width of the screen, use

```
<MARQUEE WIDTH=75% HEIGHT=20%>This is an example of a marquee</MARQUEE>
```

8. The **ALIGN** attribute sets the vertical alignment of the text around the marquee. **ALIGN** can have three values: **TOP** (for text aligned with the top of the marquee), **MIDDLE** (for text aligned with the middle of the marquee), and **BOTTOM** (for text aligned with the bottom of the marquee). The **ALIGN** attribute does not control the alignment of text within the marquee. For example, to align text that follows the marquee with the top of the marquee, use

```
<MARQUEE ALIGN=TOP>The text that follows this marquee will be aligned with
the top of the marquee</MARQUEE> Some text that follows the marquee.
```

9. The **HSPACE** and **VSPACE** attributes adjust the horizontal and vertical margins, respectively, of the marquee. These attributes are set equal to the size, in pixels, of the margin. For example, to create a marquee with a 10-pixel margin on the top and bottom and a 15-pixel margin on the left and right, use

```
<MARQUEE VSPACE=10 HSPACE=15>This is an example of a marquee with hori-
zontal and vertical margins</MARQUEE>
```

An example of the **<MARQUEE>** tag is shown in Figure 15-1. The HTML code used to create the figure can be found on the CD-ROM as file 15-1.HTML.

> **Scrolling Text**
>
> This is normal text.
>
> This is a sample Marquee -- wee
>
> This Marquee will scroll forever!

Figure 15-1 An example of `<MARQUEE>`

How It Works

When Internet Explorer recognizes the `<MARQUEE>` tag in a file, it creates a marquee on the page, using values from any attributes in the `<MARQUEE>` tag. The text moves across the marquee in the style defined by the attributes, or by using the default values, if no attribute values are specified.

Comments

The `<MARQUEE>` tag is currently supported only by Internet Explorer. Users with other browsers, such as Netscape and Mosaic, will be unable to see the marquee; the text will appear normally on the page. The use of long text strings in marquees and short values for the `SCROLLDELAY` attribute may slow down the user's computer, particularly a slower machine or one running other applications at the same time. You can find updated information about `<MARQUEE>` on the Web at the URL `http://www.microsoft.com/windows/ie/IE20HTML.htm`.

COMPLEXITY
INTERMEDIATE

15.2 How do I...
Utilize TrueType and other fonts?

COMPATIBILITY: INTERNET EXPLORER, NETSCAPE 3+

Problem

I'm tired of always having the same font on all my Web pages. How can I use different fonts?

Technique

Netscape 3 and Internet Explorer both recognize a `FACE` attribute in the `<FONT>`... `</FONT>` tag. By setting the `FACE` attribute to a desired font, all the following text will be rendered in either the set font or a default font if the desired font isn't available on the user's system. The form of `<FONT>` tag would be

```
<FONT FACE="font name for first choice, 2nd choice, 3rd choice">...</FONT>
```

You can also add the size and color attributes to really alter the appearance of your text. A complete tag would look like this:

```
<FONT FACE="arial" SIZE=5 COLOR="FF0000">This is big Arial if you are on a
PC</FONT>
```

Steps

The following steps show how to use different fonts in your Web documents.

1. Create a new document or open an existing document where you wish to format text in a different font.

2. Place the `<FONT>`...`<FONT>` tags around the text you wish to render differently. Include the `FACE` attribute and set it to the font you wish to use. It is best to set at least one alternative font, in case the font you wish to use isn't available on a user's system. If you wish, you can also include `SIZE` and `COLOR` attributes. For example:

```
<FONT FACE="Comic Sans MS, Courier NEW>This is my text</FONT>
```

3. View your document to make sure everything looks like you think it should. Experiment some.

How It Works

When the browser encounters the `<FONT>` tag, it will attempt to render the text between the tags in the first font listed in the `FACE` attribute; if that font is not found, it will attempt to use the second font, and so on. If no font is found that matches the one in the FACE attribute, the default font will be used.

Comments

It should be remembered that Macs and PCs use different basis system fonts. Microsoft has TrueType fonts available on its Web site for people to download. Still, it cannot be assumed that everybody will have this TrueType available to them. You can find more information on fonts at `http://www.microsoft.com/truetype/`. Figure 15-2 shows some examples of rendered fonts.

Font Face Demo

This is the default.

This is arial on a PC, Helvetica on a Mac!

ABCDEFGHIJKLMNOPQRSTUVWXYZ!

This is comic sans or NY on the Mac.

ABCDEFGHIJKLMNOPQRSTUVWXYZ!

Figure 15-2 Rendered fonts

COMPLEXITY

INTERMEDIATE

15.3 How do I...
Format my Web page in multiple columns?

COMPATIBILITY: NETSCAPE 3

Problem

I want to have more than one column on my Web page, and I would like another way of doing this besides using tables. What can I do?

Technique

You may create multiple column Web pages by using the `<MULTICOL>...<MULTICOL>` tags. Any text between these tags will be rendered in the number of columns you specify. It is even possible to nest `<MULTICOL>` tags inside of other `<MULTICOL>` tags, which creates a "newspaper" effect. The format of the `<MULTICOL>` tag is as follows:

```
<MULTICOL COL="number of columns" GUTTER="number" WIDTH="number"
```

To break down these attributes a little:

- **COL** — The number of columns you wish to render, which can be any number

- **GUTTER** — The space between columns, where the default value is 10 pixels

■ `WIDTH`   The width of all the columns associated with the tag, where width can be given in pixels or as a percentage of the screen (if no width is given, the columns will take up all the available screen)

Steps

The following steps show how to create documents with multiple columns.

1. Either open an existing document or create a new document.

2. Place `<MULTICOL>...</MULTICOL>` tags at the beginning and at the end of the selected text. Set the `COLUMN`, `GUTTER`, and `WIDTH` attributes. For example:

```
<HTML><HEAD><TITLE>Multiple Column Example</TITLE></HEAD>
<BODY>
<H2>Newspaper like</H2>
<MULTICOL COLS=2 GUTTER=10 WIDTH="100%">
.Today in the news, the President said that he is the president and he
doesn't care what congress says as well.  "He do what he pleases."<P>
Congress of course said, "well even if he is the president he still should
at least listen to us."  To which the president replied, "Leave me alone."
As you can plainly see it has been a slow news day.<P>
<H4>Sports</H4>
Scores: <BR>
8 -6 <BR>
9-5<BR>
4-3 (in 10 innings)<BR>
<P>
In other sports news. The international Olympic committee decided against
moving skiing to the summer games. Like a spokesmans said, "true the Summer
games get better exposure but we think that skiing really benefits from
snow."
</MULTICOL>
</BODY>
</HTML>
```

3. View your document to make sure it looks like you desire it to look. Experiment some with different values for the different attributes so you see how they affect the documents.

How It Works

When the browser encounters a `<MULTICOL>...</MULTICOL>` tag pair, all the text between these two tags is rendered in the number of columns the `COLUMN` attribute is set to.

Comments

By nesting `<MULTICOL>` tags inside of each other, it is very easy to create a page that has a different number of columns throughout. Examples of this are shown on the book's sample Web page at `http://www.psnw.com/~jmz5/waite/columns.html`. Figure 15-3 shows how the above example looks when rendered with Netscape 3.

COMPLEXITY
BEGINNING

15.4 How do I...
Insert blank space into my Web page?

COMPATIBILITY: NETSCAPE 3

Problem

I would like to be able to position text farther down or farther across on the screen than my current position. How can I do this?

Technique

You may insert horizontal or vertical space with the `<SPACER>` tag. The `<SPACER>` tag looks like this:

```
<SPACER TYPE="horizontal | vertical" SIZE="a number">
```

The browser will insert either horizontal or vertical space equal to the amount set in size.

Steps

The following steps show one way to insert blank space into a document:

1. Open or create a new document in which you want to include some blank space.

Newspaper like

.Today in the news, the President said that he is the president and he doesn't care what congress says as well. "He do what he pleases."

Congress of course said, "well even if he is the president he still should at least listen to us." To which the president replied, "Leave me alone." As you can plainly see it has been a slow news day.

Sports

Scores:
8 -6
9-5
4-3 (in 10 innings)

In other sports news. The international Olympic committee decided against moving skiing to the summer games. Like a spokesmans said, "true the Summer games get better exposure but we think that skiing really benefits from snow."

Figure 15-3 Multiple column Web page

2. Place a `<SPACER>` tag wherever you wish to have blank space. Set type to either **HORIZONTAL** or **VERTICAL**, and size to the amount of space you would like. For example:

```
<HTML><HEAD><TITLE>Spacer Demo</TITLE></HEAD>
<BODY BGCOLOR="FFFFFF">
<SPACER TYPE="HORIZONTAL" SIZE="50">Printed after 50 horizontal spaces.
<SPACER TYPE="VERTICAL" SIZE="50">Printed after 50 vertical spaces.
<SPACER TYPE="VERTICAL" SIZE="100">Printed after 100 horizontal spaces.
<SPACER TYPE="HORIZONTAL" SIZE="100">Printed after 100 horizontal spaces.
<P>
<SPACER TYPE="HORIZONTAL" SIZE="100">Printed after a new paragraph and 100
horizontal spaces.
</BODY>
</HTML>
```

3. View your document to make sure it looks like you want it to look. Feel free to experiment.

How It Works

When the browser encounters a `<SPACER>` tag, it inserts the proper amount of space as governed by the attributes.

Comments

As of this writing, there wasn't a lot of documentation on `<SPACER>`. Still, it is a useful tag, especially since browsers ignore multiple spaces in a row. `<SPACER>` gives you finer control over where you position text and graphics. Figure 15-4 shows how the above example looks in Netscape 3.

Figure 15-4 Web page with blank space inserted

COMPLEXITY
INTERMEDIATE

15.5   How do I...
Add color to tables?

COMPATIBILITY: NETSCAPE 3, INTERNET EXPLORER 3

Problem

I have a table on my page, but it is kind of boring. I would like to liven it up by adding some color to it. How do I do this?

Technique

Color is added to tables in the same manner as it is added to backgrounds. You may insert a **BGCOLOR** attribute in the **<TABLE>** tag to set the color of the entire table. Or you may insert a **BGCOLOR** attribute in a **<TD>** or **<TH>** tag to set the color of a particular cell. The color is set to a 6-digit hexadecimal number. Refer to the section on background colors (How-To 15.6) if you wish.

Steps

The following steps show you how to add color to your tables:

1. Create a new document or open an existing one having a table.

2. If you wish to give the table a background color, add the **BGCOLOR** attribute to the **<TABLE>** tag. For example:

```
<TABLE BGCOLOR="FF0000">
THE REST OF THE TABLE TAGS
</TABLE>
```

3. If you wish to make any individual cells different colors, add the **BGCOLOR** attribute to the cells you wish to change. For example:

```
<TD BGCOLOR="FFFFF00">This cell is a different color</TD>
```

4. View your table to make sure it looks like you want it to. Experiment with color combinations until you get just the right combinations.

How It Works

When either Netscape 2+ or Internet Explorer encounters a **<TABLE>** tag, it will look for **BGCOLOR** attributes, either in the **<TABLE>** tag itself or in **<TD>** and **<TH>** tags found within. If any **BGCOLOR** tags are found, the table or the cell will be rendered in the appropriate color.

Comments

Color can make a nice addition in any table. Figure 15-5 shows an example of color being used in a table. To see some color examples of the table, check out `http://www.psnw.com/ ~jmz5/waite/tables.html`.

COMPLEXITY
INTERMEDIATE

15.6 How do I...
Add a background image to a table?

COMPATIBILITY: INTERNET EXPLORER 3

Problem

I have a table on my page. I would really like to liven it up by adding a background to it. How do I do this?

Technique

Backgrounds are added to tables much as they are to pages. You include a **BACK-GROUND** attribute in either the **<TABLE>** or **<TD>** tag, setting the **BACKGROUND** to the URL of the image you would like to use as the background of either the entire table or of a single cell.

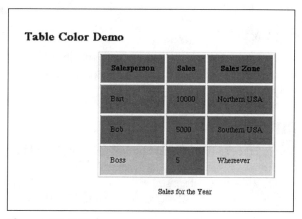

Figure 15-5 Color used in a table

Steps

The following steps show one way of adding backgrounds to your table.

1. Create or obtain a suitable image to use as a background.

2. Open an existing document or create a new one that contains a table.

3. Include a **BACKGROUND** attribute either in the **<TABLE>** tag, if you wish to use a background for the entire table, or in a specific **<TD>** tag, if you wish only a certain cell to use a background. Remember to set the URL of the **BACKGROUND** to the image you want to use. Here's an example:

```
<HTML><HEAD><TITLE>Table Width Demo</TITLE></HEAD>
<BODY BGCOLOR="FFFFFF">

<H2>Table Background Demo</H2>
<BIG>The following example shows how to add a background to a table.</BIG>

<CENTER>
<TABLE BORDER=2 BACKGROUND="slow_back.gif">
<TR><TH>Salesperson</TH><TH>Sales</TH><TH>Sales Zone</TH></TR>
<TR><TD >Bart</TD><TD>10000</TD><TD>Northern USA</TD></TR>
<TR><TD>Bob</TD><TD>5000</TD><TD>Southern USA</TD></TR>
<TR><TD>Boss</TD><TD>5</TD><TD>Whereever</TD></TR>
...
<CAPTION ALIGN="BOTTOM">Sales for the Year </CAPTION>
</TABLE>
</CENTER>
</BODY>
```

4. View your document to make sure it looks like you want it to.

How It Works

When IE encounters a **BACKGROUND** attribute in either a **<TABLE>** or **<TD>** tag, it uses the image pointed to by the attribute as the background for either the table or the cell in question.

Comments

This is a nice feature of Internet Explorer 3. It should be remembered, though, that not all images make good backgrounds. Also, remember that putting an image in a table can be tricky; if the size of the table and the background image don't correspond, your page could look a little strange. Figure 15-6 shows an example of a background image in a table.

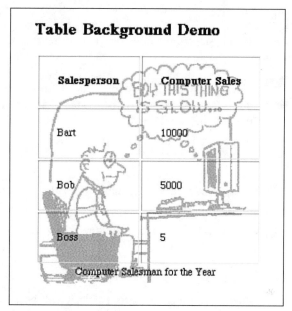

Figure 15-6 Background image in a table

COMPLEXITY
INTERMEDIATE

15.7   How do I...
Control table borders?

COMPATIBILITY: INTERNET EXPLORER 3

Problem

I have a table, but I don't want all my borders to be the same. How do I control table borders?

Technique

You may set the borders of a table by using the RULES attribute inside of a <TABLE> tag. RULES may be set to three things:

- ROW   Only rows will have borders between them.
- COLS   Only columns will have borders between them.
- NONE   Neither rows or columns will have borders.

Steps

The following steps show how easy it is to alter the borders of rows and columns in tables.

1. Create or open a document with tables.

2. Add the **RULES** attribute to the **<TABLE>** tag, setting rules to the desired value. For instance:

```
<TABLE RULES=ROWS BORDER=2>
Other table tags and text
</TABLE>
```

The above tag will create a table where the rows are bordered, but not the individual columns.

3. View your document to make sure it looks like you think it should.

How It Works

Before Internet Explorer 3 renders a table, it will check to see if the **<TABLE>** tag has a **RULES** attribute associated with it, and if it does, the browser will render the table accordingly.

Comments

Remember, so far this feature is only available with Internet Explorer. Figure 15-7 shows an example of different borders in a table.

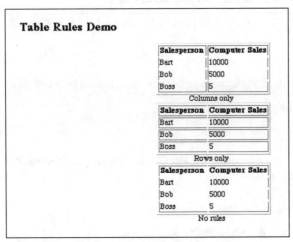

Figure 15-7 Different borders in a table

COMPLEXITY
BEGINNING

15.8 How do I...
Create new windows for linked documents?

COMPATIBILITY: NETSCAPE 2+

Problem

I would like to include a link to a document in my Web page, but instead of loading that document in the same browser window, replacing the previous page, I would like the new document to go into a separate window. Is there a way of creating new windows for linked documents?

Technique

Netscape 2+ supports the **TARGET** attribute of the anchor tag **<A>**, which identifies the name of a new window that opens, containing the new document. The **TARGET** attribute can also be used with the **<BASE>** tag to identify a default target window name for all links in a document that do not include the **TARGET** attribute.

Steps

Open your document. Identify the links that you want to have go to separate windows.

1. To send the document referenced in a link to another window, add the **TARGET** attribute and set it equal to the name of the window. For example, to send the document referenced by a link to a window named "The Widgets Page", you would enter

```
<A HREF="http://www.widgets.com/" TARGET="The Widgets Page">Go to the
Widgets Page</A>
```

2. The **TARGET** attribute can also be used in the **<AREA>** element (see How-To 15.6) in client-side imagemaps. This allows the link for a specific area of an imagemap to appear in a separate window. For example, to send the document referenced by a link in an imagemap to another window named "The Widgets Page", enter

```
<AREA SHAPE="RECT" COORD="90,90,120,95" HREF="http://www.widgets.com/"
TARGET="The Widgets Page">
```

3. The `TARGET` attribute can also be used in the `<FORM>` element. This sends the output of a form submission to a separate page. For example, to send the results of a form to a page thanking the user for filling out the form, enter

```
<FORM ACTION="results.cgi" TARGET="Thanks!">
```

4. Netscape reserves certain "magic" target names for specific purposes. The magic names and their uses are described in Table 15-2.

Table 15-2 "Magic" values for `TARGET`

NAME	DESCRIPTION
"_blank"	Loads the referenced document into a blank window
"_self"	Loads the referenced document into the same window where the anchor was selected
"_parent"	Loads the referenced document into the parent frameset of the current document
	(see How-To 15.5)
"_top"	Loads the referenced document into the full body of the window if frames
	are being used (see How-To 15.5)

For example, to load a document to a new, blank window, use

```
<A HREF="http://www.widgets.com/" TARGET="_blank">Go to the Widgets Page</A>
```

5. To send all the links on a page without the `TARGET` attribute to a specific window, add the `<BASE>` element to the header of the page (that is, within the `<HEAD>` and `</HEAD>` tags) and set the `TARGET` attribute of it equal to the name of the window. For example, to send all links without a `TARGET` attribute to a window named "Default Window", enter

```
<BASE TARGET="Default Window">
```

How It Works

When Netscape encounters a URL, an imagemap listing, or a form with the `TARGET` attribute, it creates a new window with the title of the window set to the value of the `TARGET` attribute. However, if the `TARGET` attribute is set to one of the reserved magic names, the browser executes the specific task defined by that name.

Comments

A new window is created only if a window does not already exist with a particular name. If a named window does exist, the document displayed in that window is replaced with the one currently being referenced. Names for `TARGET` must begin with a letter or number, with the exception of the magic names listed in Table 15-2. Also, the

TARGET attribute is currently supported only by Netscape. Other browsers ignore the attribute and load the documents normally. For updated information about targeted windows in Netscape, check the URL `http://www.netscape.com/assist/ net_sites/new_html3_prop.html#Target`.

COMPLEXITY
INTERMEDIATE

15.9 How do I...
Use Netscape's Client Pull?

COMPATIBILITY: HTTP/1, NETSCAPE NAVIGATOR BROWSER

Problem

I would like to create an interactive slide presentation on the Web. I need to be able to specify a default link to follow after a specified amount of time. How can I create this type of HTML 3 document?

Technique

This facility is not supported directly by HTML 3. To create a document of this type, however, you can use the **Client Pull** feature of the Netscape Navigator browser.

The **Client Pull** feature works by allowing a special use of the **<META>** element within the head of a document. You can use this element to instruct the Netscape Navigator browser to load a new document in a specified amount of time. Through this mechanism, interactive slide presentations and guided tours can be developed.

Steps

The following procedure shows how to develop documents using the **Client Pull** feature of the Netscape Navigator browser.

1. Determine the document to which you wish to add the **Client Pull** feature. This document could be the beginning of a slide show, the first frame of a character-based animation, or a document that gets updated periodically by the server system. In any case, you should open this document in your favorite text editor or HTML editor, even though most HTML editors do not support the particular element you are adding.

2. In the **<HEAD>** element of the document, add a **<META>** element. Add the following text within the **<HEAD>** element:

```
<META HTTP-EQUIV="Refresh" CONTENT=
```

3. Continue the previous line as appropriate for the situation. Table 15-3 displays the possible values for the **CONTENT** attribute.

Table 15-3 CONTENT attribute values for Refresh

VALUE	USAGE
number	Specifies delay for the current document to refresh
number; URL=URL	Specifies a URL to load after a delay

For example, if you want to reload the same document after 20 seconds, add the following text in the CONTENT field:

```
20
```

If you want the document http://www.mysite.edu/next.htm to load after a 30-second delay, include the following text in the CONTENT field:

```
"30; URL=http://www.mysite.edu/next.htm"
```

4. Terminate the <META> element with a greater-than sign (>).

5. Save the altered document. This document is now set to tell a client to pull a new document after the specified delay.

How It Works

The Client Pull feature of the Netscape Navigator browser allows a document to specify that another document be loaded in a defined amount of time. This is supported through the use of a Refresh directive built in to the head portion of an HTML document, with the use of the <META> element.

The directive includes both the new document to load and the time to wait. Figure 15-8 shows how the HTML document in the code below is displayed using the Netscape Navigator.

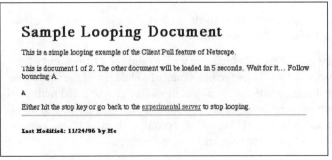

Figure 15-8 First document of pull example

```
<HTML>
<HEAD>
<META HTTP-EQUIV="Refresh"

CONTENT="5; URL=http://jasper.cau.auc.edu:8080/dsk/push-pull/doc2.htm">
<TITLE>Sample Client Pull Document 1</TITLE>
<LINK REV="made" HREF="mailto:me@mysite.edu">
</HEAD>
<BODY>
<H1>Sample Looping Document</H1>

<P>
This is a simple looping example of the Client Pull feature of Netscape.
<P>
This is document 1 of 2.  The other document will be loaded in 5 seconds.
Wait for it...  Follow the bouncing A.
<PRE>
A
</PRE>
Either hit the stop key or go back to the <A HREF="/index.htm">experimental
server</A> to stop looping.
<HR>
<H6>Last Modified: April 12, 1995 by Me</H6>
</BODY>
</HTML>
```

The document appearing in Figure 15-9 is loaded five seconds after the one that appears in Figure 15-8. These two documents loop back and forth to create the effect of a bouncing letter A. The HTML code for this second document appears below.

Figure 15-9 Second document of pull example

```
<HTML>
<HEAD>
<META HTTP-EQUIV="Refresh"
CONTENT="1; URL=http://jasper.cau.auc.edu:8080/dsk/push-pull/doc1.htm">
<TITLE>Sample Client Pull Document 2</TITLE>
<LINK REV="made" HREF="mailto:me@mysite.edu">
</HEAD>
<BODY>
<H1>Sample Looping Document</H1>

<P>
This is a simple looping example of the Client Pull feature of Netscape.
<P>
This is document 2 of 2.  The other document will be loaded in 1 second.
Wait for it...  Follow the bouncing A.
<PRE>
     A
</PRE>
Either hit the stop key or go back to the <A HREF="//www.cis.cau.auc.edu/⇐
index.htm">server</A> to stop looping.
<HR>
<H6>Last Modified: April 12, 1995 by Me</H6>
</BODY>
</HTML>
```

The only ways to stop the infinite looping are to press the Stop button on the Netscape Navigator menu bar, or to activate a link within one of the two documents.

The `Client Pull` feature is supported by allowing documents to send a refresh directive in the HTTP response; however, they do not necessarily refresh themselves. They may refresh with some other document. The use of the `<META>` element with an `HTTP-EQUIV` attribute tells the server to add the information provided in the response header that is sent back to the client when this particular document is retrieved. (See Appendix G, The Hypertext Transfer Protocol (HTTP), for more information on HTTP responses.) For example, the document appearing in Figure 15-8 would have the following line in the response header sent with the document.

```
Refresh 5; URL=http://jasper.cau.auc.edu:8080/dsk/push-pull/doc2.htm
```

This line instructs the Netscape Navigator client to refresh the current document with the one specified in the given URL. Similarly, the response header sent along with the document appearing in Figure 15-9 would include a `Refresh` directive as follows:

```
Refresh 1; URL=http://jasper.cau.auc.edu:8080/dsk/push-pull/doc1.htm
```

This in turn causes the browser to go back to the first document after one second has elapsed. These directives in the response header tell the client when and what to reload.

Comments

This feature is currently only supported by the Netscape Navigator browsers. Whether or not other browser applications will support this feature in the future is unknown. Most other browsers currently ignore the **Refresh** directive sent in the response header and, consequently, do not refresh after the specified delay.

You can also use the **Refresh** directive in response headers generated through gateway applications. This allows your CGI program to both generate a response page and load a URL after a suitable delay. (See Chapter 14, The Common Gateway Interface (CGI), for more information on CGI applications.)

COMPLEXITY
ADVANCED

15.10   How do I...
Specify Netscape Server Push?

COMPATIBILITY: CGI, NETSCAPE NAVIGATOR

Problem

The information in my document changes very frequently. I would like to update my HTML document as new information arrives. How can I create such a document?

Technique

The Netscape Navigator supports a mechanism called **Server Push** to provide this capability. Instead of a standard HTTP access as described in Appendix G, The Hypertext Transfer Protocol (HTTP), a **Server Push** keeps the connection between client and server open. When a request from the client is serviced, an initial response is made. The client/server connection is not closed until the server drops the connection. While connected, the server sends updated documents, which the browser displays as they arrive.

The **Server Push** capability is supported through the use of CGI applications that repeatedly generate and send new documents to the browser at intervals specified by the application. The initial response generated by the gateway program indicates that the response is composed of multiple documents, each of which replaces the previous one. A step-by-step process for developing such an application is given below.

Steps

You can change directories to a location where you wish to build your **Server Push** gateway program and begin the development process. The method below deals with the response generation portion of your application. The tasks performed should be accomplished using the commands in your chosen programming language.

1. Start your application by retrieving any data that the user has submitted to your gateway application. You will find a procedure for accomplishing this task in How-To's 14.6 and 14.7.

2. Decide whether the input data, if any, will be processed before, during, or after the generation of your response document. If your response depends upon the results of processing, then processing, or at least partial processing, must occur prior to response generation. If the results are directly embedded in the response, then the processing must occur during response generation. Finally, if the response is independent of the processed data, processing may occur after the response is generated. The decision on when and how processing is performed needs to be decided on an application-by-application basis. Based on this decision, intersperse the processing as appropriate among the steps below.

3. Generate the response header indicating that the document will be updated. This response uses the standard `Content-type` server directive. However, the type specified should be a `multipart/x-mixed replace; boundary=boundary_string`, where the `boundary_string` is replaced by some boundary string indicator of your choice. For example, in Perl you could use the print command as shown below.

```
print "Content-type: multipart/x-mixed-replace;boundary=WhyNot\n\n";
```

4. Send the boundary string, preceded by two dashes to signal the beginning of a response document. To begin a response document, place `--boundary_string` on the standard output. In C, you might use the `printf` command:

```
printf("--WhyNot\n");
```

5. Place the `Content-type` server directive appropriate for the document type you will be attaching on the standard output, followed by a blank line. In Perl, you could use the `puts` command to accomplish this task.

```
print "Content-type: text/plain\n";
```

6. Output your attached document in the format specified in step 5.

7. Perform whatever processing tasks are required (waiting for new data from an outside source, waiting a specified amount of time, processing the next data set). When you have performed this task and are ready to generate an update to the current document, return to step 4; the new document will replace the currently viewed one. If you are not going to generate any more updates, continue with step 8.

8. Send the boundary string surrounded by pairs of dashes, `--boundary_string--`, to the standard output. In Perl, you would use the `print` command for this task.

```
print "--WhyNot--\n";
```

9. Once your application has been developed and, if required, compiled, you can install this gateway application.

10. Reference the URL for this gateway application as you would any other CGI program.

How It Works

The use of this procedure is shown through the development of an example `Server Push` gateway application. This sample application is written in the Perl scripting language. Further, this sample `Server Push` application requires no input from the user. The purpose of this program is to provide a snapshot of the individuals logged in to the server when the document is first retrieved (see Figure 15-10) and then again 30 seconds later through the use of the finger network utility. The source for this application appears on the CD in file NPH-PUSH.CGI.

When this script is initially accessed, the document provides information about who is currently logged in to the server system, as shown in Figure 15-10. Figure 15-11 shows what is displayed 30 seconds later.

Between the generation of the first and second documents, an additional user logged in to the system. If you wanted to perform a more systematic monitoring, you could have placed the finger document generation phase in a loop.

Figure 15-10 Results of running the finger utility

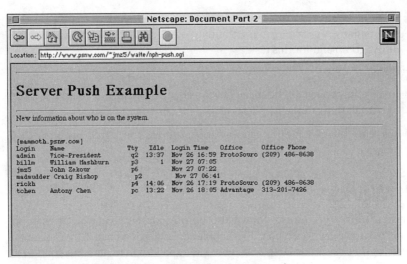

Figure 15-11 Updated finger results 30 seconds

This application follows the procedure described above. There is no input to be dealt with, and processing occurs during response generation. The initial response header is sent, signaling that the following response messages will successively replace the previous message. The boundary string is sent to signal the first document. The first message is the immediate result of the finger command, with some HTML formatting around it. To make sure the output buffer is flushed, the signal for the second document is sent. Once this document is complete, some internal processing occurs; namely, the application sleeps for 30 seconds. Finally, the second document, another HTML-formatted finger result, is sent. The overall message concludes with the boundary string, surrounded by dashes, being sent to the standard output.

Comments

When using the `Server Push` capability and buffered output, you must make sure to flush your output buffer when a particular component message is complete. If you do not, your component objects may simply appear one after the other after several have been generated. In the Perl script example described in this How-To, the line selection `(STDOUT); $|=1;` flushes the standard output after the completion of the first HTML document.

If you do not provide a termination for the multipart document response by including a final boundary string `(--boundary_string--)`, the only way to stop updating the document is to activate a link in the document or use a stop facility provided by your browser.

Finally, implementation of a **Server Push** gateway application should be done in a language that terminates the application when the user interrupts the request, with the stop facility, for example. Applications written in the Bourne shell scripting language may not terminate when an interrupt occurs, which means that server resources continue to be used even though the browser no longer requests them.

## CHAPTER 16

CASCADING STYLE SHEETS

16

CASCADING STYLE SHEETS

How do I...

HMTL is in a continuous state of evolution. New features and elements are proposed and discussed daily. Style sheets are one such proposed addition. From an historical perspective, HTML style sheets are not particularly new conceptually. They were first introduced as a potential enhancement of HTML 2 and were later included in the draft specification of HTML 3. The proposed HTML 3.2 cuts back a little with respect to full-scale inclusion of style sheets, but preliminary hooks are contained within the HTML 3.2 specification. Currently, the Amaya browser for UNIX/X11 platform and its precursor Arena, and Microsoft's Internet Explorer 3 and later, are the only browsers implementing support for this feature. But Netscape has announced plans to support a variation of style sheets in its next release (See information at URL `http://home.netscape.com/comprod/products/platform/open.html` concerning Netscape's JavaScript Style Sheets).

Style sheets serve a variety of purposes. You can attach them to a variety of Web pages to create a consistent look for a group of documents. As a Web surfer, you can create a style sheet that your browser will apply to all incoming documents. The style sheet mechanism provides a versatile means of extending, enhancing, and modifying the way browsers present Web pages.

For the remainder of this chapter, refer to Table 16-1 for units of length applicable to various aspects of the HTML style sheets that you develop.

Table 16-1 Style sheet units of length

ABBREVIATION	UNIT TYPE	DESCRIPTION
cm	centimeters	
em	ems	Width of the character m
ex	exes	Height of the character x
in	inches	
mm	millimeters	
pc	picas	1 pica = 12 points
pt	points	1 point = 1/72 inch
px	pixels	Single cell on display

> **NOTE**
> Microsoft's Internet Explorer only supports lengths in the following unit types: points (pt), inches (in), centimeters (cm), and pixels (px).

The How-To's in this chapter introduce the use of this exciting new HTML feature.

16.1 Create a Style Sheet to Alter an HTML Element

Style sheets provide a mechanism for supporting consistent style across multiple Web pages. Style sheets allow you to extend and enhance HTML elements in significant ways. This How-To shows how to build style sheets conforming to the CSS 1 standard (Cascading Style Sheets standard, level 1).

16.2   Alter an Element's Font Characteristics

Style sheets allow greater flexibility and control with respect to the size and types of fonts used to display Web pages. This How-To demonstrates the various font-related properties that you can specify using HTML 3.2 style sheets.

16.3   Alter an Element's Color

Style sheets support a significant enhancement in your ability to control the color of text displayed in your Web page. With style sheets, you can selectively choose the text color within any HTML element. This How-To provides a practical guide to using the style sheet color property.

16.4   Alter an Element's Background

HTML 3.2 only allows a single background specification for an entire page. With style sheets, you can add different backgrounds to different elements within your Web page. In this How-To, you will learn how to utilize style sheet background properties.

16.5   Alter an Element's Text Properties

Text properties allow you greater control over the presentation of textual element. In this How-To, you will learn how to utilize the various text properties available through style sheets.

16.6   Alter the Borders of an Element

Style sheets allow the specification of borders around any HTML 3.2 element. You can configure a variety of aspects of the borders including style, color, and width. This How-To provides an introduction to the use of the various border-related style sheet properties.

> **NOTE**
>
> Internet Explorer 3 does not support border properties.

16.7   Specify Layout Constraints of an Element

One of the biggest shortfalls of HTML 3.2 is the lack of flexible layout controls. Current "fixes" resort to the use of tables or lists to manage margins and spacing. Style sheets provide an effective means for specifying page layout. This How-To introduces you to the style sheet properties that support page layout.

16.8   Indicate Style Information for List Elements

HTML 3.2 supports the use of different list styles using the TYPE attributes of ordered and unordered lists (See How-To's 6.2 and 6.4). Style sheets also provide another means of specifying this list style information. In this How-To, you will learn how to specify the style of lists using style sheet properties.

> **NOTE**
> Internet Explorer 3 does not support list style properties.

16.9 Cascade HTML Style Sheets

You can combine style sheets with other style sheets as well as with HTML **\<STYLE\>** elements. This combination leads to aggregate style sheets and alternative style sheets. This How-To explains how to attach style sheets to Web pages to provide alternative and aggregate presentation styles for the page.

16.10 Add Cascading Style Information Directly to a Web Page

Besides attaching style sheets to pages, style information can be embedded directly into a Web page. This How-To details how to add style information to specific Web pages, or even a specific element within a page.

16.11 Include Style Elements and Protect Browsers Without Style Support

The information in **\<STYLE\>** elements may be misinterpreted by older browsers. In this How-To, you will learn how to reduce the potential misinterpretation of style information by those browsers that do not support **\<STYLE\>** elements.

COMPLEXITY
INTERMEDIATE

16.1 How do I...
Create a style sheet to alter an HTML element?

COMPATIBILITY: HTML 3+, INTERNET EXPLORER

Problem

I want to establish standard styles for use in many of my Web pages. I want to enhance Web pages that I retrieve to maximize the capabilities of my browser. For legal reasons, a section of all my Web pages needs to appear the same. How can I create a style sheet for my documents?

Technique

You create style sheets through a standard text editor. You specify a set of parameters and values that you want to associate with HTML elements of a particular type, such as **\<P\>** elements, or a particular class within an element, such as **\<P CLASS="red"\>**. Each style sheet may define properties for any number of elements. Each entry in a style sheet is composed of a selector indicating the HTML 3.2 element that is modified and one or more declarations indicating properties to set or modify.

Style-sheet–capable browsers read the style sheets associated with a Web page and those designated by the reader and attempt to apply the styles to the page. A cascading mechanism helps to resolve conflict among multiple applicable styles. (See How-To 16.9 for information on how to cascade style information.)

Steps

The following steps take you through the style sheet creation process. You should select the elements and properties that you want to include. A full list of properties that may modify HTML 3.2 elements is provided in the How It Works section, with additional details and specific examples provided in subsequent How-To's.

1. Open the style sheet in a text editor.

2. Use the `@import` command to import and combine existing style sheets with the current style sheet. Conflicts in declarations are resolved in favor of the declarations of the importer. Thus, to include the entries from `sheet1.css`, issue the following command:

```
@import sheet1.css -- Use entries from sheet1, but override as follows --
```

> **NOTE**
>
> Internet Explorer 3 does not support imported style sheets.

3. If you are modifying or adding a property to an existing entry, move to that entry in the sheet and proceed with step 4. Otherwise, specify the selector for the HTML 3.2 element that you want to modify. The following examples represent possible selectors.

The following selector indicates the modification of `<H1>` elements:

```
H1
```

The following selector indicates the modification of `<H1>` and `<H2>` elements:

```
H1,H2
```

The following selector indicates the modification of `red` class, `<P>` elements:

```
P.red
```

The following selector indicates the modification of `red` class elements:

```
.red
```

The following selector indicates the modification of `<H2>` elements that follow `<P>` elements:

```
(P) H2
```

NOTE

Internet Explorer 3 does not support this last selector method.

4. Include the declaration(s) for the selector within opening and closing curly braces ({ and }). For example, the following declaration indicates that the browser should draw the selected element using the color red. See How-To's 16.2 through 16.8 for information on the particular declaration types.

```
{ color: red }
```

5. Return to step 2 to continue editing; otherwise, save your style sheet.

6. Proceed to How-To 16.9 for a discussion on including the style sheet in your Web page.

How It Works

Style sheets are composed of standard text. A style sheet consists of a series of entries, each composed of a selector and a declaration. The selector indicates the HTML 3.2 element(s) affected by the properties in the declaration. A declaration may end with either a `!legal` or `!important` designation, indicating an imperative for using the particular declaration.

You may specify a selector in several forms. Selectors may specify a very narrow or very broad portion of a Web page, ranging from a particular class of an HTML element preceded by some other element to the entire page. In addition, the declarations for a selected element are inherited by those elements contained within the selected elements. For example, using HTML as the selector indicates that the declaration applies to all elements contained within the `<HTML>` element, namely the entire document. Generally, the selector falls into the following categories (brackets indicate optional user additions):

- `element`: You can select a single HTML element for which the declaration applies. For example, you might use the following selector to indicate application to `<H1>` elements:

```
H1
```

- `element1,element2,[element3,...]`: Use this form to apply the same declaration to a number of HTML elements. The following selector indicates application of the declaration to `<H1>` and `<H2>` elements:

```
H1,H2
```

- `element.class`: Use this form to specify a declaration that applies to only a particular class of a particular HTML element. Thus, the following selector specifies the application of the selector to `<P>` elements with `red` class designation:

```
P.red
```

■ `class`: Use this form to apply the same declaration to all HTML elements with the specified class. The following selector indicates that the declarations apply to all HTML elements of the `red` class:

`.red`

■ `(preceding_element1) [(preceding_element2)...] element`: Use this form to indicate that a declaration only applies when the last HTML element is contained within the specified preceding HTML elements. The following selector applies to all `<STRONG>` elements within `<P CLASS="red">` elements:

`(P.red) STRONG`

> **NOTE**
> Microsoft's Internet Explorer 3 does not support this last selector method.

Declarations specify the properties of the selector that are set by the style sheet entry. Style sheets allow modification of a large variety of properties. The current HTML 3.2 style sheet working draft specifies level 1 properties. (See `http://www.w3.org/pub/WWW/Style/` for the current status of style sheets.)

Each declaration is composed of a property and a value. The property indicates what to modify, and the value indicates the value(s) of the modification. The level 1 properties are, for the most part, stable. (For additional level 1 properties and other information, see URL `http://www.w3.org/pub/WWW/TR/WD-css1.html`.) Table 16-2 lists the categories of declarations and the How-To's which explain these categories.

Table 16-2 Using different types of declarations

DECLARATION TYPE	HOW-TO
Font-related	16.2
Foreground color	16.3
Background characteristics	16.4
Text properties	16.5
Border properties	16.6
Layout constraints	16.7
List style constraints	16.8

Web pages appear differently depending on the style sheets associated with them. In Figures 16-1 and 16-2, a different style sheet is attached to the same Web page. The source code for this page appears below.

```
<HTML>
<HEAD>
<TITLE>Style is Everything</TITLE>
<LINK TITLE="Style Sheet 1" REL=stylesheet HREF="style1.css">
</HEAD>
<BODY>
<H1>Going in Style</H1>
<P>
Putting on the Ritz
</BODY>
</HTML>
```

Figure 16-1 shows how this page appears with the following style sheet. The HTML source for this appears on the CD-ROM in file STYLE1.HTM, with the style sheet stored in STYLE1.CSS.

```
H1 { color: #F00 }
P { font-size: 16pt, color: #00F }
```

Changing the **<LINK>** element to attach the style sheet below results in the Web page seen in Figure 16-2. The HTML source for this appears on the CD in file STYLE2.HTM, with the style sheet stored in STYLE2.CSS.

```
H1 { color: #00F, background: #FFF }
P { font-size: 8pt, color: #0F0 }
```

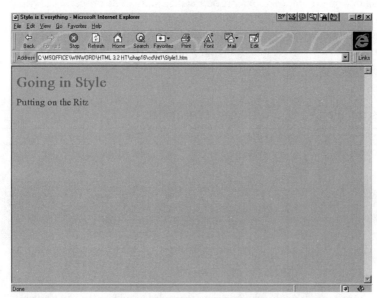

Figure 16-1 Paragraph with large font and red level 1 header

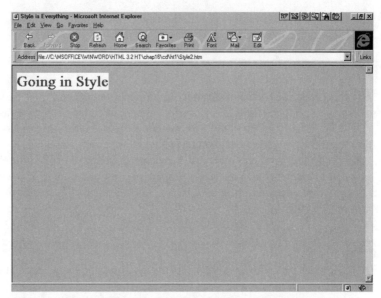

Figure 16-2 Paragraph with small font and blue level 1 header on white background

Comments

The cascading style sheet standard is currently still in the draft stages. The elements described in this How-To are fairly stable; however, they may be subject to change. For up-to-the-minute information on style sheet development, you may want to consult the evolution of the style sheet standard at `http://www.w3.org/ pub/WWW/Style/`.

The only browsers currently supporting cascading style sheets are Arena for the X-Window environment, recently superseded by the Amaya browser, and Microsoft's Internet Explorer 3, above.

COMPLEXITY
INTERMEDIATE

16.2 How do I...
Alter an element's font characteristics?

COMPATIBILITY: HTML 3+, INTERNET EXPLORER

Problem

HTML 3.2 goes farther than previous HTML standards in allowing me to control the fonts used to display my page; however, this standard falls far short of the flexibility I can get with a high powered desktop publishing environment. Is there anything I can do to close the gap?

Technique

Style sheets provide control of a variety of properties associated with the font used to display a specified HTML 3.2 element. These font choices can cover as broad a span of a page as the entire `<BODY>` element or as restricted as a single class of a narrower element type, such as all `<ADDRESS CLASS="dsk">` elements.

To specify font constraints on HTML 3.2 elements, you need to select the element(s) you want to configure and select the properties you want to alter. You will associate this style information with your Web page using the methods discussed in How-To's 16.9 and 16.10.

Steps

The following procedure walks you through the process of associating font-related style information with your Web page.

1. Select the HTML 3.2 element in your Web page, or in the broad set of documents, using the style sheet you are modifying and to which you want to apply stylistic constraints. Create an appropriate selector as described in How-To 16.1.

2. Select the font-related property that you want to alter from Table 16-3.

Table 16-3 Font-related properties

DECLARATION	DESCRIPTION
font-family	Delineates prioritized list of fonts to use
font-style	Specifies the style of the font selected
font-variant	Selects normal or small caps variations
font-weight	Indicates the weight of the font to use
font-size	Specifies the size of the font to use
font	Provides support for combination of multiple font properties

3. Use How-To's 16.9 and 16.10 to select and create the appropriate mechanism for adding this style information to the Web page(s) of your choice.

How It Works

Using style sheets, you may choose to alter any of the following font-related properties:

- **font-family:** Value: `family-name1|generic-family1 [family-name2|generic-family2...`

  The browser generally determines the default font family used to present Web pages. This property allows the specification of a prioritized list of font families to use. Replace spaces in font family names with dashes (for example, new century schoolbook becomes `new-century-schoolbook`). CSS level 1 defines the following generic family names: `cursive`, `fantasy`, `serif`, and `sans-serif`. You should generally include a generic font family at the end of your font family list. For example, use the following to establish a font list for paragraphs (`<P>` elements):

```
P { font-family: helvetica new-century-schoolbook cursive }
```

- **font-style:** Value: `italic | oblique | normal`

  This property determines the style of font that a browser uses to display the elements specified by the selector. The default value is normal. You can use this property to alter the style. For example, use the following to designate that browsers should display `<H4>` elements as italic:

```
H4 { font-style: italic }
```

- **font-variant:** Value: `small-caps | normal`

  This property determines the variant of font that a browser uses to display the elements specified by the selector. The default value is normal. You can use this property to switch between the current two allowable variants: normal and small caps. For example, use the following to designate that browsers should display `<H4>` elements as small caps:

```
H4 { font-variant: small-caps }
```

- **font-weight:** Value: `normal | bold | bolder | lighter | 100 | 200 | 300 | 400 | 500 | 600 | 700 | 800 | 900`

  The default font weight is normal. You set the weight with either a number or a relative modifier (such as bolder). The number should range from 100 to 900 corresponding to the lightest weight through the darkest. On this scale, normal corresponds to 400 and bold to 700. The lighter and bolder terms instruct the browser to lighten or darken with respect to the weight inherited from the surrounding HTML element. For example, use the following to present an entire Web page as bold:

```
HTML { font-weight: bold }
```

▣ `font-size:` Value: `length | percent | # | xx-small | x-small | small | medium | large | x-large | xx-large | smaller | larger`

The browser usually determines the default font size. You can specify a size, a percentage of the font size in the parent element, or a relative size using either a number or one of the descriptive literals above (such as smaller or larger). For example, use the following to set the font sizes of `<H5>` and `<H6>` elements, respectively:

```
H5 { font-size: 12pt }
H6 { font-size: small }
```

▣ `font:` Value: `<font-size> [ / <line-height> ] <font-family>`

Use this property as a shorthand for setting various font attributes at once. Setting a font property by itself overrides the shorthand value. For example, use the following to set the font of `<STRONG>` elements that follow `<P CLASS="script">` paragraphs:

```
(P.script) STRONG { font: 16pt/20pt cursive }
```

For more information on the font-related property of Cascading Style Sheets 1, see the current Internet draft at `http://www.w3.org/pub/WWW/TR/WD-css1.html#font-properties`.

Figure 16-3 displays the FONTS.HTM file from the CD. Figure 16-4 shows this same document in a browser without style sheet capability.

The following style sheet, FONTS.CSS on the CD, is linked to the page using the mechanism described in How-To 16.9.

```
H1 {      font-family: Braggadocio, "Comic Sans MS", sans-serif;
     font-size: 32pt
     font-weight: extra-bold
     }
P.italics {       font-style: italic;
          font-weight: light}
```

Comments

Microsoft's Internet Explorer 3 supports the following subset of the font properties specified in Table 16-3; these properties are `font-size`, `font-family`, `font-weight`, and `font-style`. In addition, the values associated with these properties do not conform in all cases to the CSS 1 standard. Consult Microsoft's style sheet guide for specific information on Internet Explorer support (`http://www.microsoft.com/workshop/author/howto/css-f.htm`).

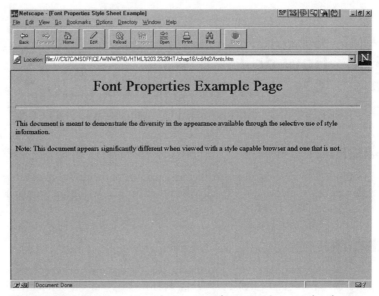

Figure 16-3 Font properties example page in a style sheet capable browser

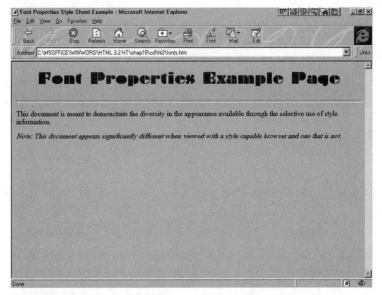

Figure 16-4 Font properties example page in a browser without style sheet capability

COMPLEXITY
INTERMEDIATE

16.3   How do I...
Alter an element's color?

COMPATIBILITY: HTML 3+, INTERNET EXPLORER

Problem

I would like browser to display different portions of the text of my Web page using different colors. How can I specify the color for text within particular HTML 3.2 elements?

Technique

Style sheets provide the color property to associate a foreground color used to draw text with a particular class, a particular HTML 3.2 element, or a particular class of a particular element.

Steps

The following procedure walks you through the process of altering the color of particular elements within your Web pages.

1. Select the HTML 3.2 element in your Web page, or in the broad set of documents using the style sheet you are modifying, to which you want to apply stylistic constraints. Create an appropriate selector as described in How-To 16.1.

2. Select the color to which you want to change this element. Table 16-4 provides the named colors supported by the CSS level 1 standard.

Table 16-4 Supported named colors

COLOR	HEXADECIMAL TRIPLET	COLOR	HEXADECIMAL TRIPLET
Black	#000000	Green	#008000
Silver	#C0C0C0	Lime	#00FF00
Gray	#808080	Olive	#808000
White	#FFFFFF	Yellow	#FFFF00
Maroon	#800000	Navy	#000080
Red	#FF0000	Blue	#0000FF
Purple	#800080	Teal	#008080
Fuchsia	#FF00FF	Aqua	#00FFFF

3. Use How-To's 16.9 and 16.10 to select and create the appropriate mechanism for adding this style information to the Web page(s) of your choice.

How It Works

You alter the color used to display the text within a particular HTML 3.2 element using the color property. Use this property to set the color for the selector; see How-To 16.1 for the different definitions of selectors. You may specify the color value in several ways. These methods include by name, by 3-tuple (three numbers corresponding to the red, green, and blue components of the desired color), or by hexadecimal value. The list of supported colors appears in Table 16-4. The proposal calls for the acceptance of RGB values as either 3-tuples or hexadecimal. For example, use any one of the following to set a red color for `<H1 CLASS="red">`:

```
H1.red { color: red }
H1.red { color: 1.0 0.0 0.0 }      /* Floating point 3-tuple */
H1.red { color: 255 0 0 }          /* One byte value 3-tuple */
H1.red { color: #F00 }          /* Single digit hexadecimal */
H1.red { color: #FF0000 }          /* Double digit hexadecimal */
```

For more information on the color property of Cascading Style Sheets 1, see the current Internet draft at URL **http://www.w3.org/pub/WWW/TR/WD-css1.html#color**.

Figure 16-5 displays a document with the following `<STYLE>` element in its `<HEAD>` element:

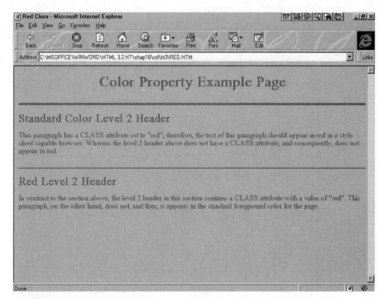

Figure 16-5 Red class

```
<STYLE>
<!--
BODY { color: teal }
.red { color: red }
-->
</STYLE>
```

This style element instructs the browser to display the text within any HTML 3.2 element that has a CLASS attribute with a value of red in the color red and all other text within element within the <BODY> element of the Web page in teal. A paragraph element and a level 2 header element make use of this style information. The file RED.HTM on the CD contains complete HTML 3.2 source for the document appearing in Figure 16-5.

Comments

Appendix H, "Color Table," provides a table of hexadecimal triplet values and the color that these values represent. Consult this table for helpful hints in coming up with appropriate color values.

You can use the color property to implement the same tricks discussed in How-To 2.11 with respect to blending and vanishing visited links. The files BLEND.HTM and VANISH.HTM on the CD implement these tricks. The style information in these Web pages uses the within document method discussed in How-To 16.10 and the cross-browser protection mechanism from How-To 16.11 to incorporate the necessary information. However, for best cross-browser performance, you are better off using the methods for these tricks from How-To 2.11 since those methods hinge upon HTML 3.2 standard features rather than style sheet capability. Figure 16-6 shows the use of the ALINK method for blending in a browser without style sheet support, while Figure 16-7 displays the style sheet method for blending in a browser without style sheet support.

Figure 16-6 Vanishing links using the ALINK attribute of the
<BODY> element

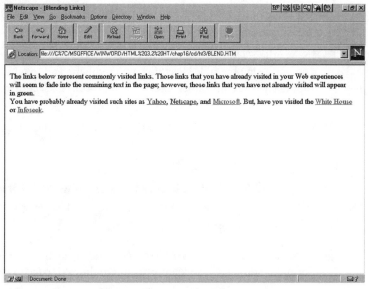

Figure 16-7 Vanishing links using the style sheet method

COMPLEXITY
INTERMEDIATE

16.4 How do I...
Alter an element's background?

COMPATIBILITY: HTML 3+, INTERNET EXPLORER

Problem

HTML 3.2 allows me to alter the background of my Web page; however, I would like more control over the background than HTML 3.2 permits. I want to specify different backgrounds for different portions of my Web page. How can I selectively modify the backgrounds of particular HTML 3.2 elements?

Technique

CSS level 1 provides the background property to support alterations of background for elements covered by selectors (as described in How-To 16.1).

Steps

The following procedure steps you through the process of altering the background of selected portions of your Web page.

1. Select the HTML 3.2 element in your Web page, or in the broad set of documents using the style sheet you are modifying and to which you want to apply stylistic constraints. Create an appropriate selector, as described in How-To 16.1.

2. Select the type of background value you want to select from the table below:

VALUE	DESCRIPTION
color	Color value for the background—either by name (see Table 16-5) or by value.
URL	Specify a background image. See the How It Works section for additional modifiers for this value type.

3. Use How-To's 16.9 and 16.10 to select and create the appropriate mechanism for adding this style information to the Web page(s) of your choice.

How It Works

You use the background property to associate a particular background with an HTML 3.2 element. The background property has the following syntax:

```
background: transparent | <color> || <url> || <repeat> || <scroll> ||
<position>
```

Set the background of an element as either a particular color, a background pattern, or transparent. The default value is transparent. You indicate a color value as described for the color property in How-To 16.3. Use a URL to indicate a background pattern; the URL should be placed within parentheses. For example, use the following to set the background of unordered lists (**<UL>**) and list elements (**<LI>**), respectively:

```
UL { background: #F00 }
LI { background: url(http://www.mysite.edu/pix/checker.gif) }
```

The background property is not inherited by contained elements per se; however, since the default background is transparent, the designated background may still apply.

If you have opted to use a background image specified by a URL, several optional modifiers can be used. These modifiers represent:

- **<repeat>:** This optional modifier may be one of the following literals: `repeat`, `repeat-x`, `repeat-y`, or `no-repeat`. If no **<repeat>** modifier is chosen, the browser will assume the default of repeat. The literals designate, respectively, whether the background image is repeated horizontally and vertically, just horizontally, just vertically, or not at all.

- **<scrolling>:** This optional modifier may be either `fixed` or `scroll`. Scroll is the default value if a scrolling modifier is not specified. This modifier indicates whether the background image should remain fixed with respect to page motion or scroll with the page, respectively. Selecting fixed is analogous to the fixed background image discussed in How-To 2.12.

- **<position>:** This optional modifier allows you to specify the position of the background image relative to the modified element. Consult `http://www.w3.org/pub/WWW/TR/WD-css1.html#background` for examples and details of specifying the image position.

For more information on the background property of Cascading Style Sheets 1, see the current Internet draft at `http://www.w3.org/pub/WWW/TR/WD-css1.html#background`.

Figure 16-8 displays a document with the following **<STYLE>** element in its **<HEAD>** element.

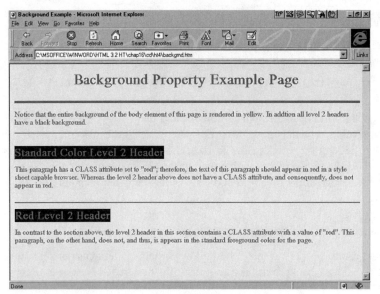

Figure 16-8 Yellow background of the body element and black background of level 2 headers

```
<STYLE TYPE="text/css">
<!--
BODY { color: teal ;
    background: yellow}
.red { color: red }
H2 { background: black}
-->
</STYLE>
```

This style element instructs the browser to display the text within any HTML 3.2 element that has a **CLASS** attribute with a value of **red** in the color red, and all other text within the **<BODY>** element of the Web page in teal. (See How-To 16.3 for information on the use of the color property.) A paragraph element and a level 2 header element make use of this style information. The background of the **<BODY>** element for this page is set to yellow while the background for level 2 header elements is set to black. The file BACKGRND.HTM on the CD contains complete HTML 3.2 source for the document appearing in Figure 16-8. For an example using an image as the background for an element, see the discussion of the button trick in the Comments section.

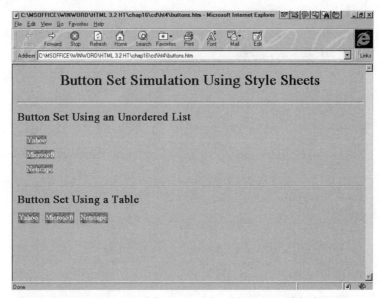

Figure 16-9 Buttons trick in a style-sheet–capable browser

Comments

One neat trick that you can do with selective backgrounds is the simulation of textured buttons. The usual method for including buttons on a page requires a separate image for each button. With style sheets, however, you can simulate a set of buttons with similar texture by creating a list or table depending on your desired layout for the buttons. You configure the elements of the list or cells of the table to use the same texture as a background image. This improves performance by requiring the reader to download a single image for all the buttons rather than one image per button.

The BUTTONS.HTM file on the CD contains an example of this usage. Figures 16-9 and 16-10 show this page in a style-sheet–capable browser and a style-sheet–incapable browser, respectively. You should note that, even in the style incapable browser, the page still appears fine with a list or table of links rather than buttons.

> **NOTE**
> Internet Explorer 3 has a slight problem with this trick with respect to previously visited links using the list format; the problem does not seem to occur with the table implementation. Hopefully, this bug will be fixed in future releases.

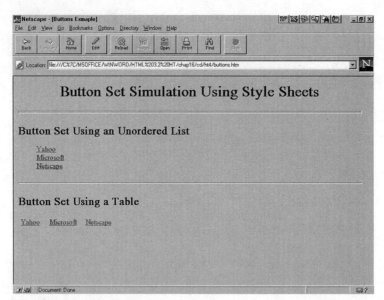

Figure 16-10 Buttons trick in a browser without style sheet capability

COMPLEXITY

INTERMEDIATE

16.5 How do I...
Alter an element's text properties?

COMPATIBILITY: HTML 3+, INTERNET EXPLORER

Problem

I would like to modify the alignment of the text associated with a particular HTML element. I want to turn off the underlining of links within my Web page. I want to configure a special class of indentations to associate with several different HTML elements in my page. How do I provide this text-related style information?

Technique

The Cascading Style Sheets level 1 standard supports a variety of properties for specifying the style of the text associated with particular HTML elements. Use the appropriate property from those listed in Table 16-5.

Table 16-5 CSS 1 text-related properties

PROPERTY	DESCRIPTION
letter-spacing	Adds space between letters of text
line-height	Specifies the height of a line of text within the targeted selector
text-align	Selects the alignment style for the text within the targeted selector
text-decoration	Places decorative effect on the text
text-indent	Indents the text a specified amount
text-transform	Performs case transformation on text
vertical-align	Positions the selected element vertically
word-spacing	Provides additional space between words

The How It Works section provides detailed information on the use of these properties.

Steps

The following procedure walks you through the process of associating text properties with HTML elements in your Web page.

1. Select the HTML 3.2 element in your Web page, or in the broad set of documents using the style sheet you are modifying, to which you want to apply stylistic constraints. Create an appropriate selector, as described in How-To 16.1.

2. Select the text property that you want to use from the Table 16-5.

3. Use How-To's 16.9 and 16.10 to select and create the appropriate mechanism for adding this style information to the Web page(s) of your choice.

How It Works

You can select to modify the style information represented by the following text-related properties defined for CSS level 1:

▪ letter-spacing: Value: normal | <length>

The default value for this property is normal. The length should be specified in terms of the units shown in Table 16-1. The actual value specified determines the space between characters in addition to the default distance. Negative values are allowable, subject to browser constraints. In addition, if the letter-spacing is specifically set to zero, the browser should refrain from attempting to justify text on a line.

■ line-height: Value: <number> | <length> | <percentage>

This property determines the distance between two adjacent baselines. The default value for this property varies among browsers. When a number is specified as the value, this number serves as a multiplier with respect to the current font height. You can also specify this distance using a length in one of the unit types presented in Table 16-1. Finally, you can indicate the distance as a percentage of the current font height. For example, the following <STYLE> element defines that <P> elements should render text with a line height equal to 150 percent of the font height:

```
<STYLE TYPE="text/css">
<!--
P { line-height: 150% }
-->
</STYLE>
```

> **NOTE**
>
> Internet Explorer 3 does not support the numeric values for this property; in addition, added line spacing to make up the line height is added above the modified element.

■ text-align: Value: left | right | center | justify

This property specifies the proper alignment for the selected element. The default value varies depending upon your browser. For example, the following example would specify an inline indication of right alignment for the indicated address:

```
<P STYLE="text-align: right">
John Q. Public
9999 Oakmore St.
Atlanta, GA 30333
<P><!-- Next Paragraph>
```

> **NOTE**
>
> Internet Explorer 3 does not support the justify values, and the default alignment is left.

■ text-indent: Value: <length> | <percentage>

Use this property to indent text associated with a particular selector. The amount of indentation can be specified as an absolute amount in one of the unit types recognized in Table 16-1 or as a percentage of the enclosing element's width. The default value of this property is zero.

■ `text-decoration:` Value: `none | [underline | overline | line-through | blink ] +`

Use this property to associate a decoration with a particular selector. For example, to create an underlined `<H2 CLASS="under">` element, use the following:

```
H2.under { text-decoration: under }
```

> **NOTE**
>
> Internet Explorer 3 only supports the values `none`, `underline`, and `line-through`.

■ `text-transform:` Value: `capitalize | uppercase | lowercase | none`

The default value of this property is none. The literal values above indicate their respective purposes. A capitalized value indicates that the first letter of each word of text in the selected element should be uppercase. The uppercase value specifies that all text should be uppercase, and the lowercase value instructs the browser to render all text in lowercase.

■ `vertical-align:` Value: `baseline | sub | super | top | text-top | middle | bottom | text-bottom | <percentage>`

Most of the potential values for the vertical-align are self-explanatory. Six of these values (`baseline`, `middle`, `sub`, `super`, `text-bottom`, and `text-top`) represent vertical alignment with respect to the parent element of the selector modified. The top and bottom values represent vertical alignment with respect to tallest and lowest elements, respectively, on the same line with the modified element. The percentage represents a percentage of the value of the line-height of the element itself.

■ `word-spacing:` Value: `normal | <length>`

As with letter spacing, the default value of this property is normal. By specifying an explicit value, you instruct the browser to add the specified amount of space in addition to the default. The actual word spacing is also influenced by the justification of the text.

For more information on the text related properties of Cascading Style Sheets 1, see the current Internet draft at `http://www.w3.org/pub/WWW/TR/WD-css1.html#text-properties`.

Figure 16-11 displays a document using several of the text-related properties discussed above. The address appearing immediately following the first horizontal rule uses the following `<P>` element to right align the text:

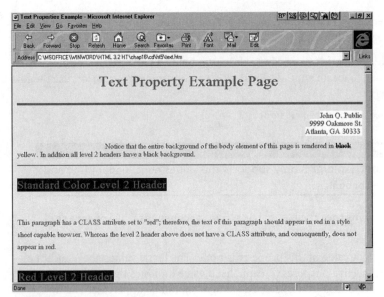

Figure 16-11 Text-related properties document

```
<P STYLE="text-align: right; color: green; background: white">
John Q. Public<BR>
9999 Oakmore St.<BR>
Atlanta, GA 30333
```

The strikethrough of the word **black** in the first paragraph uses a text-decoration property defined in the Web page's **<STYLE>** element. The **<STYLE>** element contains the following line responsible for the strikethrough in this case:

```
FONT.del { text-decoration: line-through; color: black }
```

The use of the following **<P>** element generates the double-spaced second paragraph of this page:

```
<P CLASS="red" STYLE="line-height: 20pt">
```

> **NOTE**
>
> This element uses a specified **<STYLE>** element constraint and an inline **<STYLE>** attribute.

The following specification for indented paragraphs is used to indent the first paragraph 1/4 of the width of the **<BODY>** element of this page.

```
P.indent { text-indent: 25% }
```

The file TEXT.HTM on the CD contains complete HTML 3.2 source for the document appearing in Figure 16-10.

Comments

Microsoft's Internet Explorer supports a limited set of the text-related properties. Release 3.0 supports `line-height`, `text-align`, `text-decoration`, and `text-indent` properties. Further restrictions with respect to these properties are identified above.

COMPLEXITY
INTERMEDIATE

16.6   How do I...
Alter the borders of an element?

COMPATIBILITY: HTML 3+

Problem

I would like to add borders around certain elements in my Web page. How do I indicate the size, style, and location of such borders using CSS level 1?

Technique

Use the various border properties listed in Table 16-6 to indicate borders around specific HTML 3.2 elements in your Web pages.

Steps

The following procedure walks you through the process of associating border-related style information with your Web page.

1. Select the HTML 3.2 element in your Web page, or in the broad set of documents using the style sheet you are modifying and to which you want to apply stylistic constraints. Create an appropriate selector, as described in How-To 16.1.

2. Select the border property that you want to alter from the Table 16-6:

Table 16-6 CSS 1 border properties

PROPERTY	DESCRIPTION
border	Shorthand for specifying padding constraints
border-bottom	Selects bottom padding
border-left	Sets the left padding
border-right	Specifies the right padding
border-top	Selects top padding

3. Select the border width using one of the following: `thin | medium | thick | <length>`. A `<length>` is some value in one of the units specified in Table 16-1.

4. Choose a border style from the following: `none | dotted | dashed | solid | double | groove | ridge | inset | outset`.

5. Specify the color for the border, using a color value as described in How-To 16.3.

6. Use How-To's 16.9 and 16.10 to select and create the appropriate mechanism for adding this style information to the Web page(s) of your choice.

How It Works

All the border properties work in a similar manner. After choosing the HTML 3.2 elements through selectors, you specify the particular border to alter with any necessary additional data. A border is a potentially visible band of space surrounding an element.

No matter which border property you modify, you may specify the following three types of additional data: a border width, a border style, and a color.

Border Width: Value: `thin | medium | thick | <length>`

The border width value is the first of a border property's parameters. This first value may be one of the literals (`thin`, `medium`, and `thick`) or a length in one of the unit types detailed in Table 16-1.

Border Style: Value: `none | dotted | dashed | solid | double | groove | ridge | inset | outset`

The border style is the second border property parameter. The value in the property specification should be a literal describing how the border of the element should look. `None` designates no border even if a border width had been set for this element. `Dotted` signifies the use of a dotted line to draw the border. A `dashed` value requests the use of a dashed line. `Solid` suggests the use of a solid line as the border; further, `double` indicates the use of a double line around the specified element. The `groove` and `ridge` values, respectively, connote the use of a 3D effect drawn using the element's color property value. Similarly, `inset` and `outset` paint their respective effects using the color value associated with the element modified.

Border Color: `<color>`

The third parameter of a border property is the `color` value for the element modified. The color chosen must conform to the methods of color specification discussed in How-To. 16.2.

The border property alone is a shorthand for the specification of equivalently constrained borders on all sides of an element. For more information on the border properties of Cascading Style Sheets 1, see the current Internet draft at `http://www.w3.org/pub/WWW/TR/WD-css1.html#border-top-border-right-border-bottom-border-left-border`.

Comments

Microsoft's Internet Explorer 3 does not support the border properties.

COMPLEXITY
ADVANCED

16.7 How do I...
Specify layout constraints of an element?

COMPATIBILITY: HTML 3+, INTERNET EXPLORER

Problem

HTML 3.2 provides extremely limited means of controlling the layout of its elements; either I need to "misuse" elements or layout all my elements using tables. How can I specify layout constraints for elements using the Cascading Style Sheets level 1 standard?

Technique

CSS level 1 provides a large number of layout support properties that you can use to control the layout of HTML 3.2 elements in your Web pages. Table 16-7 lists and briefly describes these layout properties.

The How It Works section provides detailed information on the detailed syntax of these layout properties.

Table 16-7 CSS 1 layout constraints

PROPERTY	DESCRIPTION
border properties	Sees How-To 16.6
clear	Specifies the clearance requirements of an element
float	Indicates where the element should float
height	Specifies the height of an element
margin	Shorthand for specifying margin constraints
margin-bottom	Selects the bottom margin

continued on next page

continued from previous page

PROPERTY	DESCRIPTION
margin-left	Sets the left margin
margin-right	Specifies the right margin
margin-top	Selects the top margin
padding	Shorthand for specifying padding constraints
padding-bottom	Selects the bottom padding
padding-left	Sets the left padding
padding-right	Specifies the right padding
padding-top	Selects the top padding
width	Specifies the width of an element

Steps

The following procedure walks you through the process of specifying layout constraints for your Web page.

1. Select the HTML 3.2 element in your Web page, or in the broad set of documents using the style sheet you are modifying and to which you want to apply stylistic constraints. Create an appropriate selector as described in How-To 16.1.

2. Select the layout constraints that you want to set from Table 16-7 above.

3. Choose any values required by the chosen layout constraint. See detailed descriptions in the How It Works section below.

4. Use How-To's 16.9 and 16.10 to select and create the appropriate mechanism for adding this style information to the Web page(s) of your choice.

How It Works

The Cascading Style Sheets level 1 standard provides a number of style properties which allow you to control the layout of HTML 3.2 elements in your Web pages. You can select to modify the style information represented by the following layout properties defined for CSS level 1:

■ clear: Value: none | left | right | both

This value specifies the layout of an element with respect to floating elements which may occupy either side of the displayed Web page. The default value for this property is none; thus, the browser should render the element next to any element floating to the left and consider any right floating elements the right boundary. Specifying any of the other values indicates that the browser should not display the configured element until beyond floating object conforming to the specified value (`left`, `right`, or `both`).

▣ `Float:` Value: `none | left | right`

This property allows you to configure an element so that browsers float the element to either the right or left margin of the page. The default value for this property is `none`, indicating that an element should not float to either margin.

▣ `Height:` Value: `<length> | auto`

Use this property to set the height of an element. You may specify the height as either auto, the default, which allows the element to size itself as required, or as a specific length in a unit mentioned in Table 16-1.

▣ `margin, margin-bottom, margin-left, margin-right, margin-top:`
Value: `<length> | <percent> | auto`

Use these properties to set the appropriate margins of the selector. The value can either be a length, a percentage of the parent element's width, or an automatic setting. Margin values may be negative. For example, to set the left margin of a list element (`<LI>`) to be 20 percent of its parent's width and the right margin to 25 percent and to set the top margin of paragraph (`<P>`) element to 12 points, use the following:

```
LI { margin-left: 20%; margin-right: 25% }
P.double { margin-top: 12pt }
```

The `margin` property is a shorthand for the other four. The `margin property` requires between one and four values representing the top, right, bottom, and left margins, respectively. If only one value is given, the value is applied to all margins. If two or three values are given, the browser should use the values specified for the opposite sides.

Figure 16-12 displays a page with the above margin constraints in a style sheet capable browser, while Figure 16-13 shows the same page in a browser without this capability. The CD contains the complete style sheet and HTML sources for these pages in the MARGINS.CSS and MARGINS.HTM files, respectively.

Figure 16-12 Layout constraint page in style sheet capable browser

Figure 16-13 Layout constraint page in browser without style sheet capability

padding, padding-bottom, padding-left, padding-right, padding-top: Value: <length> | <percent> | auto

Use these properties to set the appropriate padding of the selector. The padding represents the distance between the border of the element and the element content. The value can either be a length, a percentage of the parent element's width, or an automatic setting. Padding values may not be negative. In all other respects, these properties are configured in the same way as margins.

NOTE

Internet Explorer 3 does not support these layout properties.

◻ **Width:** Value: `<length>` | `<percent>` | `auto`

Use this property to specify the width of an element as either a specific width in a recognized unit from Table 16-1, or a percentage of the parent element's width. The default value allows the element to size itself. If applied to an inserted media type, the element should scale the object as appropriate; if this element's height property is set to auto, the default, the aspect ratio should remain the same.

NOTE

Internet Explorer 3 does not support this layout property.

For more information on the layout properties of Cascading Style Sheets 1, see the current Internet draft at `http://www.w3.org/pub/WWW/TR/WD-css1.html#box-properties`.

Comments

Of the layout constraints above, Microsoft's Internet Explorer 3 only supports the `margin-left`, `margin-right`, and `margin-top` properties.

COMPLEXITY
INTERMEDIATE

16.8   How do I...
Indicate style information for list elements?

COMPATIBILITY: HTML 3+, INTERNET EXPLORER

Problem

CSS level 1 provides more fine grained control of the style of list elements. How do I control the style of my list elements using the CSS1 `list-style` property?

Technique

The CSS1 `list-style` property allows you to control both the style and positioning of the "bullet" or number associated with individual list items. To constrain a particular list element, choose an appropriate selector and specify the style desired for this selector.

Steps

The following procedure walks you through the process of indicating list elements in style information for your Web page.

1. Select the HTML 3.2 element in your Web page or in the broad set of documents using the style sheet you are modifying and to which you want to apply stylistic constraints. Create an appropriate selector as described in How-To 16.1.

2. Select the style of the list element marker from Table 16-8:

Table 16-8 CSS 1 list styles

STYLE	DESCRIPTION
disc	Default value; filled bullet
circle	Open circle
square	Square bullet
decimal	Decimal number (1, 2, 3, 4, and so on)
lower-roman	Lowercase roman numerals (i, ii, iii, iv, and so on)
upper-roman	Uppercase roman numerals (I, II, III, IV, and so on)
lower-alpha	Lowercase alphabetic (a, b, c, d, and so on)
upper-alpha	Uppercase alphabetic (A, B, C, D, and so on)
none	No marker

3. Select the desired positioning of the list element marker. You can choose either inside or outside. The default positioning is outside.

4. Use How-To's 16.9 and 16.10 to select and create the appropriate mechanism for adding this style information to the Web page(s) of your choice.

How It Works

Cascading Style Sheets level 1 provides the list-style property to constrain the presentation of elements within ordered and unordered HTML 3.2 lists. The list-style attaches to **<LI>** HTML 3.2 elements within **<OL>** and **<UL>** elements.

This constraint may be imposed at a higher level than directly associated with <LI> elements. If an HTML 3.2 element has this property set, elements contained within that element are similarly subject to the imposed setting. For example, the following <DIV> element standardizes all list elements used within its context, unless subjected to an overriding list-style property.

```
DIV.nomark { list-style: none}
```

All list elements that would have a mark no longer have one within division elements constrained by this selector. However, more localized list-style property constraints could override this inherited style.

In addition to the type of mark used, the list-style property allows the specification of the default positioning of the indicated mark. The two potential values are inside and outside, with outside being the default value. This positioning value indicates the positioning of the mark with respect to the remainder of the text within the list element. With selection of the outside positioning, the mark appears outside all portions of the list elements, subject to the constraint. In the case of inside, the mark appears within the text of the list elements. For example, a browser might display an outside lowercase Roman numeral list as follows:

```
i.    The mark appears outside the entire
         text of the list element.
   ii.    Second such list element.
```

On the other hand, a browser might display an inside lowercase Roman numeral list as follows:

```
i.    The mark appears outside the entire
   text of the list element.
   ii.    Second such list element.
```

For more information on the list-style property of Cascading Style Sheets 1, see the current Internet draft at `http://www.w3.org/pub/WWW/TR/WD-css1.html#list-style`.

Comments

Microsoft's Internet Explorer does not as yet support this property. In addition, use of the TYPE attribute of <LI> elements as described in How-To 6.4 allows for similar control of list style.

COMPLEXITY
ADVANCED

16.9 How do I...
Cascade HTML style sheets?

COMPATIBILITY: HTML 3+, INTERNET EXPLORER

Problem

I need to associate style sheets with my Web pages. How can I do that, and how do the attached style sheets interact among themselves to resolve conflicting property specifications?

Technique

You can associate style information with your Web page in several manners:

■ You can embed the style information directly through a **STYLE** attribute.

■ You can embed the style information directly through a **<STYLE>** header element.

■ You can attach style sheets directly through **<LINK>** elements.

The first two methods involve inserting style information directly into a Web page; How-To 16.10 discusses the methods for accomplishing this. The third method, discussed in this How-To, involves creating a separate style sheet that may be linked to multiple Web pages.

Browsers combine and integrate style information determined from these sources, as well as any local style sheets. The browser follows strict rules on which style information to combine and which style information has precedence. It then uses this combined style information to present the Web page to the viewer.

Steps

The following procedures walk you through the process linking style sheets to your Web page. You can use the **<LINK>** element to attach style sheets to a Web page. This process is semantically equivalent to importing a style sheet from within a **<STYLE>** element (see How-To 16.10).

1. Create a style sheet as described in How-To's 16.1 through 16.8.

2. In a text editor, open the Web page to which you want to add a style sheet.

3. Find the **<HEAD>** element of your Web page.

4. Add a **<LINK>** element, with the HREF attribute set to the URL of the style sheet you want to attach. The **TITLE** attribute serves as the combination mechanism; all style sheets attached by **<LINK>** with the same title are combined. Therefore, set the **TITLE** attribute to indicate which group of style sheets the one you want to add should combine with. For example, to attach **sheet1.css** to the **"Company"** group of style sheets, you would add the following **<LINK>** element.

```
<LINK REL=stylesheet TITLE="Company" HREF="sheet1.css" TYPE="text/css">
```

The **REL** attribute should be set to **"stylesheet"**. The TYPE attribute should be set to **"text/css"**; currently, no other type of style sheet has been proposed.

5. Perform step 4 for each style sheet you want to attach.

6. Save your Web page.

7. Test your Web page.

How It Works

The cascading style sheet model allows you to associate stylistic information with presented Web pages. A browser generally may receive stylistic information from three sources:

■ Reader style information: A particular reader has created a style sheet (as described in How-To's 16.1 through 16.8), or the browser has built-in style constraints. In either case, the browser combines this information with incoming style information.

> **NOTE**
>
> Microsoft's Internet Explorer does not support local style sheets.

■ External style sheets: External style sheets are linked to a Web page via **<LINK>** elements. Each such style sheet is separately requested by the browser.

■ Internal style information: Web pages contain internal style information in **<STYLE>** elements and **STYLE** attributes; see How-To 16.10.

The browser accumulates style information from these three sources to derive a single set of style constraints. The first possible conflict that may arise in this process is the potential multiplicity of grouped external style sheets. This situation arises when **<LINK>** elements with different **TITLE** attributes occur in the same Web page. All external style sheets with the same **TITLE** are combined; however, the choice of which combined style sheet to use rests with the reader. The model suggests that the reader should be able to choose among the **TITLE** attributes for the desired combined style.

The model suggests the following steps in resolving conflicts whenever stylistic information is combined and applied to a particular element.

1. Remove declarations for the same property for the same selector by removing the more imported, least local declaration. Thus, if a color declaration for the <H1> element appears in both the <STYLE> element for a page and an imported style sheet, then the declaration from the <STYLE> element remains.

2. If rules for the same selector and property still exist, remove all but the declaration specified last.

3. Determine all declarations applicable to a particular element.

4. Applicable declarations are sorted by weight, with !important or !legal declarations being heavier than normal declarations.

5. Sort the applicable declarations by information origin, with incoming style information overriding reader style information.

6. Sort the applicable declarations by the detail of the selector specification. For example, a <STRONG> element appearing within an <LI> element is more specific than a <STRONG> element alone.

7. Allow specific property declarations to override a generic property. For example, specification of a font-size property would override the value from a font property.

8. If a conflict still remains, resolve the conflict in favor of the declaration declared last.

After proceeding through this resolution scheme, the browser applies the remaining declarations to the element in question.

Comments

Style sheets are currently supported only by a limited number of browsers: Arena browser for the X-Window environment (http://www.w3.org/pub/WWW/Arena/), Amaya (http://www.w3.org/), and Microsoft's Internet Explorer (http://www.microsoft.com/ie). Even these browsers do not support the selection among titled combined style sheets. Adding style sheet capability to existing browsers may lead to some discrepancies between the proposed model and the implemented solution.

You should examine http://www.w3.org/pub/WWW/Style/ for the latest status information on style sheets. The CSS level 1 specification seems relatively stable at this point. The working draft for this standard is located at http://www.w3.org/pub/WWW/TR/WD-css1.html.

COMPLEXITY
INTERMEDIATE

16.10 How do I...
Add cascading style information directly to a Web page?

COMPATIBILITY: HTML 3+, INTERNET EXPLORER

Problem

I would like to specify stylistic constraints peculiar to an individual Web page. It seems pointless for me to create an entire style sheet for use with only a single page. How can I provide style information specific to a single page within that page?

Technique

You can associate style information with your Web page in several manners:

- You can embed the style information directly through a **STYLE** attribute.

- You can embed the style information directly through a **<STYLE>** header element.

- You can attach style sheets directly through **<LINK>** elements. See How-To 16.9.

Browsers combine and integrate style information determined from these sources as well as any local style sheets. The browser follows strict rules on which style information to combine and which style information has precedence. It then uses this combined style information to present the Web page to the viewer.

> **NOTE**
> Microsoft's Internet Explorer does not support local style sheets.

Steps

The following procedures walk you through configuring style information specific to a single Web page or to a specific element within a page.

<STYLE> Element Process

You can use the **<STYLE>** element to mix and match existing style sheets with local overrides to develop a combined set of stylistic information for use with a particular Web page.

1. Open your HTML page in a text editor.

2. Locate the **<HEAD>** portion of the document.

3. If a `<STYLE>` element does not exist, create one using the following lines:

```
<STYLE TYPE="text/css">
</STYLE>
```

You will add style information between the opening and closing tags of this element.

4. Use the `@import` command to import any stand-alone style sheets. For example, to include the `sheet1.css` and `sheet2.css` style sheets, insert the following two lines in the `<STYLE>` element:

```
@import sheet1.css
    @import sheet2.css
```

> **NOTE**
>
> Internet Explorer does not support the importation of style sheets.

5. Add declarations that you want to override the declarations in the imported style sheets.

> **NOTE**
>
> Currently, Internet Explorer 3 does not support overriding linked style sheets by a `<STYLE>` element; if you need to override a linked style sheet, or a `<STYLE>` element, use the inline `<STYLE>` attribute discussed below.

6. Save the Web page.

7. Test your Web page.

`STYLE` Attribute Process

The `STYLE` attribute may be used to configure style information specific to a single element within a Web page.

1. Open your HTML page in a text editor.

2. Locate the element within the page for which you want to define style constraints.

3. If a `STYLE` attribute does not exist, create one. For example, you might use the following modified `<H1>` element to indicate a red, 32 point level 1 header.

```
<H1 STYLE ="color: red; font-size: 32pt">Red, 32 Pt Level 1 Header</H1>
```

You will add style information between the quotation marks that delimit the value of this attribute.

4. Add declarations that you want to override the declarations in the imported style sheets or **<STYLE>** element declarations. Separate each declaration with a semicolon.

5. Save the Web page.

6. Test your Web page.

How It Works

Embedded **<STYLE>** elements work in an identical fashion to attached style sheets. In fact, the style information from the **<STYLE>** element is combined with style information from one or more attached style sheets. The How It Works section in How-To 16.9 outlines the conflict resolution process to resolve conflicting style information.

<STYLE> elements provide a finer grain of control than does an attached style sheet. The particular styles chosen can be more tuned to the particular page. In fact, this is the very purpose of the **<STYLE>** element. Whereas attached style sheets can provide generic style information across a broad spectrum of Web pages, the information provided in the **<STYLE>** element can provide page-specific guidance for displaying particular HTML 3.2 elements or classes of elements.

STYLE attributes establish the finest granularity. With the **STYLE** attribute, you can individually control the style information with respect to a single HTML 3.2 element within a single Web page. The style information specified in this attribute only applies to the element in which the attribute is defined.

Comments

Internet Explorer 3's implementation of cascading style information is slightly non-standard. Microsoft's implementation places any style information provided with the following precedence, from highest to lowest:

▪ STYLE attribute

▪ Attached style sheets through **<LINK>** elements

▪ Embed the style information through a **<STYLE>** header element

The CSS 1 standard actually calls for **<STYLE>** element information to override conflicting attached style sheet information.

COMPLEXITY
BEGINNING

16.11 How do I...
Include style elements and protect browsers without style support?

COMPATIBILITY: HTML 3+, INTERNET EXPLORER

Problem

Most browsers do not support style elements in the <HEAD> of an HTML document. In fact, several of them even misinterpret and attempt to display this information as page content. How do I include style information, while maintaining cross-browser support?

Technique

Browsers that understand the <STYLE> element have no problem parsing and using information found within this element; however, older browsers, and browsers that lack style support, sometimes attempt to display the content of the <STYLE> element as Web page content.

Steps

Use the following process to modify your <STYLE> element to protect browsers that do not support this element.

1. Open your HTML page in a text editor.

2. Locate the <HEAD> portion of the document.

3. Locate the <STYLE> element within the <HEAD> element.

```
<STYLE TYPE="text/css">
/* Your Declarations */
</STYLE>
```

4. Insert comment tags around the declarations within your style element.

```
<STYLE TYPE="text/css">
<!--
/* Your Declarations */
-->
</STYLE>
```

5. Save the Web page.

6. Test your Web page.

How It Works

By surrounding the style information with an opening and closing comment tag, you can ensure that browsers that do not support **<STYLE>** elements will simply ignore the content as if it were a comment. **<STYLE>** enabled browsers, however, will parse and apply the stylistic constraints specified to the appropriate Web page content.

Comments

Even if your readers will only be using **<STYLE>** enabled browsers, you should still strongly consider the use of the comment tags. This mechanism entails minimal additional work, while protecting against future potential problems.

## CHAPTER 17

WEB PROGRAMMING WITH JAVA™ AND JAVASCRIPT™

17

WEB PROGRAMMING WITH JAVA™ AND JAVASCRIPT™

How do I...

17.1   Write a Basic Java Applet

Java™ is a new object-oriented programming language that allows designers of Web pages to create new, highly interactive pages. This How-To shows how to write a basic Java applet, or application, for use in a Web page.

17.2   Include a Java Applet in an HTML Document

Once a Java applet is written, code must be included in the Web page so that the page can access the applet. This How-To shows how to include tags so that the page can access and run the appropriate Java applet.

17.3   Pass Variables from a Web Page to an Applet

There are cases in which you will want to provide a Java applet with a set of initial values based on user input or other criteria to get the desired result. This How-To shows how to use the **<PARAM>** element in HTML 3.2 to send a set of initial values to an applet.

17.4   Find More Information About Java

There is far more to Java than what can be presented in a few How-To's. This How-To lists resources that any aspiring Java programmer will find useful while learning the language.

17.5   Improve Java Applet Download Time

A problem with Java applets is that complex applets can require a large number of calls to the server to download different classes used by the applet, slowing it down. This How-To shows two methods, one used by Netscape and the other by Internet Explorer, to improve Java applet downloading time by bundling together the classes used by the applet.

17.6   Include a Script Element

JavaScript™ is a powerful but simple scripting language that can be incorporated into Web pages, even with small snippets. This How-To shows how to include elements of JavaScript into Web pages in order to enhance their functionality.

17.7   Write a Basic JavaScript Script

JavaScript can be used to create detailed, highly interactive pages. While JavaScript is a topic suitable for an entire book, this How-To will show the basics of writing a JavaScript script.

17.8   Include a Script in a Web Page

JavaScript is a new scripting language developed by Netscape that allows users to create scripts without delving into complex languages like Perl or Java. The scripts can be included in the same document as the rest of the Web page. This How-To shows how to use the **<SCRIPT>** tag in Netscape to run JavaScript scripts.

17.9   Generate a Pop-up Dialog Using JavaScript

One of the useful applications of JavaScript is the ability to write small scripts that will generate dialog boxes that pop up on the screen with advice, warnings, or other special information. This How-To shows how to write a JavaScript script that can generate a pop-up dialog box on the user's screen.

17.10   Check an HTML Form for Required Input Fields

Another useful application of JavaScript is to create scripts that can check HTML forms and see whether all the required fields have been filled out before the form is sent to the server for processing. This How-To shows how to write a script that can check to see whether certain fields in a form have been filled out.

17.11   Find More Information on JavaScript

Like Java, there is much more to JavaScript than what can be crammed into a few How-To's. This How-To provides information on resources that will help anyone trying to learn this new scripting language.

17.12   Provide an Alternative If Scripting Is Not Supported

There are still many browsers in use on the Web which do not support JavaScript or do not have JavaScript enabled. These users need alternatives to scripts which are used on Web pages. This How-To shows how to provide alternative HTML code or CGI scripts to these users.

COMPLEXITY
INTERMEDIATE

17.1   How do I...
Write a basic Java applet?

COMPATIBILITY: NETSCAPE 2+, INTERNET EXPLORER 3

Problem

I'm interested in making my page more interactive by adding Java applets: programs that can be run from my page. However, I don't know anything about the language and don't know where to begin. How do I write a simple Java applet?

Technique

A full understanding of Java is beyond the scope of this book. Those who have written programs in C++ will find Java familiar, but others may have difficulty trying to learn the language. However, most applets have a similar structure that can be briefly described and then duplicated for other applets. This How-To shows how to create a basic but useful applet that displays the current time. How-To 17.2 shows how to incorporate the applet into an HTML document.

Steps

Open a file in a text editor. Name the file whatever you want to name the applet, appended with the suffix `.java`, such as `MyApplet.java`.

1. First, specify any libraries of routines that need to be included for the applet to run correctly. Applets in general require a library named `java.applet.Applet`. For this applet, you will need two other libraries: `java.util.Date` (which will provide a command to obtain the current time) and `java.awt.Graphics` (which includes graphics routines for displaying the results of the date on the page). Add libraries using the `import` command:

```
import java.util.Date;
import java.applet.Applet;
import java.awt.Graphics;
```

Be sure to add a semicolon (`;`) after each line, as this is the method Java uses to indicate the end of a line.

2. Java is based on creating program classes that are based on previous classes. This allows a program to call on a number of higher-level classes without explicitly referencing them in the code. The class to extend upon here is called `Applet` (which you have included by importing the `browser.Applet` library). Use the `public class` command and the name of the current applet to define a new class based on the `Applet` class:

```
public class CurrentDate extends Applet {
```

Note the open brace used at the end of the line instead of a semicolon. This indicates that the lines that follow it all belong to the class `CurrentDate`.

3. Define the current date by creating a new variable, `d`, of the class `Date`, and setting it equal to the current date, as follows:

```
Date d = new Date();
```

4. The applet now needs an initialization routine that defines an area on the page where the date is displayed. This is done with a routine called `init()`, which is public and returns no data (void). In the routine, a `resize` command defines the area, in pixels, of the page section reserved for displaying the date. For example:

```
public void init() {
resize(300,25);
}
```

5. Next, include a routine to display the date on the page. Create a graphics routine called `paint` that contains the necessary commands:

```
public void paint(Graphics g) {
```

6. To display the date, the applet must convert the information stored in the date variable into a string that can be drawn on the page. Run a function called **toString()** that converts the date variable **d** into a string, and sets it equal to a new variable **s** of class **String**:

```
String s = d.toString();
```

7. The final part of the applet is the command that prints the string containing the current date on the page. The routine **g.drawString()**, part of the **java.awt.Graphics** package imported at the beginning of the applet, does this. The command needs three values: the string, the x pixel location of the beginning of the string, and the y pixel location for the bottom of the string. For example, to print the time after the string **"Current time: "**, and place it near the top of the window, use

```
g.drawString("Current time: "+s, 5, 25);
   }
}
```

Note that since this is the last command of the applet, you need to include the closing braces for the **paint** routine and the overall class.

8. Finally, run the applet through the Java compiler. If the compiler doesn't find any errors, it produces another file that contains the executable code for the applet. The filename is the name of the applet, plus the file suffix **.class**. In this case, it creates a file named **CurrentDate.class**. The exact method of submitting the applet to the compiler varies from system to system. For example, if you use a UNIX system, enter at the prompt the command:

```
javac CurrentDate.java
```

The full code of the document is included on the CD-ROM as file CURRENT-DATE.JAVA.

How It Works

First, the browser loads any libraries of routines that might be necessary for the browser to work. A new applet is created by extending an existing **Applet** class, thereby calling upon all the parent routines to the applet. This particular applet uses a command to find the current date on the machine, converts it to a string, and then invokes a display routine to print it on the screen.

Comments

The Java language is still under development. The language will likely change more before a final, stable version is released. To keep up with the current status of the language, check the Java home page at Sun Microsystems, **http://java.sun.com**.

COMPLEXITY
INTERMEDIATE

17.2   How do I...
Include a Java applet in an HTML document?

COMPATIBILITY: HTML 3.2

Problem

I have written a Java applet and I'd like to include that applet in my Web page. How can I add a Java applet to an HTML document?

Technique

The **<APPLET>** tag is an addition to HTML 3.2 that allows you to include a Java applet in a Web page. This element allows you to specify the path to the applet, the amount of space on the screen the applet will occupy, and alternative code for those browsers that don't support Java. The **<APPLET>** tag can be used in conjunction with the **<PARAM>** tag (see How-To 17.3) to pass variable names and values to Java applets.

Steps

Open your HTML document and locate the section of document where you want to add the applet.

1. Place the **<APPLET>** and **</APPLET>** tags where you want the applet to be in your document. Set the **CODE** attribute equal to the name of the applet. For example, to insert the applet **CurrentDate.class** into a Web page, enter

```
<APPLET CODE="CurrentDate"></APPLET>
```

2. If the applet is not located in the same directory as the HTML document, use the **CODEBASE** attribute to provide the location of the applet. **CODEBASE** can be a pathname or a URL. If the applet in the last step is located in the directory **applets/new**, use

```
<APPLET CODE="CurrentDate" CODEBASE="applets/new"></APPLET>
```

3. The **WIDTH** and **HEIGHT** attributes are required for the **<APPLET>** element. They give the width and height of the applet display area in pixels. To create a display area 50 pixels wide and 75 pixels high for the applet, use

```
<APPLET CODE="CurrentDate" WIDTH=50 HEIGHT=75></APPLET>
```

4. Similar to **WIDTH** and **HEIGHT**, **VSPACE** and **HSPACE** set the vertical and horizontal margins, respectively. Set the attributes equal to the size of the margin in pixels. To insert an applet with a vertical margin of 20 pixels and a horizontal margin of 10 pixels, enter

```
<APPLET CODE="CurrentDate" WIDTH=50 HEIGHT=75 VSPACE=20 HSPACE=10></APPLET>
```

5. The **ALIGN** attribute controls the alignment of the applet. The **<APPLET>** tag's **ALIGN** supports many of the values used by the **<IMG>** element (see Chapter 8, Establishing Links). The valid values for **ALIGN** include

- **left** (left side of the screen)

- **right** (right side of the screen)

- **top** (aligns with the top of the tallest item on the line)

- **texttop** (aligns with the top of text on that line)

- **middle** (aligns the baseline of the line with the middle of the applet display)

- **absmiddle** (aligns the middle of the line with the middle of the applet display)

- **baseline** (aligns the baseline of the line with the bottom of the applet display)

- **bottom** (same as **baseline**)

- **absbottom** (aligns the bottom of the line with the bottom of the image)

For example, to align the line that follows the applet with the top of the applet display, enter

```
<APPLET CODE="CurrentDate" WIDTH=50 HEIGHT=75 ALIGN=TOP></APPLET>
```

6. The **NAME** attribute gives the applet instance a specific name for potential future reference. This is a more advanced feature that allows applets on the same page to communicate with each other. For example, to give an applet instance the name **"current"**, enter

```
<APPLET CODE="CurrentDate" WIDTH=50 HEIGHT=75 NAME="current"></APPLET>
```

7. There are two ways you can insert text that those browsers that don't support Java applets can display. One way is to use the **ALT** attribute and set it equal to a text string that explains what the applet is. For example, to include the **ALT** attribute in the preceding applet, enter

```
<APPLET CODE="CurrentDate" WIDTH=50 HEIGHT=75 ALT="This is a Java applet
that displays the current time."></APPLET>
```

Another way to do this is to place the text between the **<APPLET>** and **</APPLET>** tags. This text displays in browsers that don't support Java applets, but is ignored by those that do run applets. To revise this example using this method, enter

```
<APPLET CODE="CurrentDate" WIDTH=50 HEIGHT=75>This is a Java applet that
displays the current time.</APPLET>
```

A sample output of the **CurrentDate** applet (described in How-To 17.1) as seen in Netscape 3 is shown in Figure 17-1. The HTML code used to create the output is on the CD as file 17-1.HTML.

How It Works

For the **<APPLET>** element, the tag instructs the browser to load and run the Java applet named in the tag. The browser creates a display area for the applet on the page based on the size of the display area and the alignment of the display as specified by attributes in the tag. The browser also passes values for any applet-specific variables that the applet requires to run correctly.

Figure 17-1 An example of a Java applet

Comments

Since not all browsers support Java (particularly Microsoft Internet Explorer before version 3.0 and Netscape Navigator before 2.0, on most platforms), and not all users of Java-capable browsers have it enabled for security reasons, it's important to include some kind of alternative for those users. You can put any text, image, or other markup between the **<APPLET>** and **</APPLET>** tags, so you can be very flexible in the content you provide for the Java-disabled.

COMPLEXITY
INTERMEDIATE

17.3 How do I...
Pass variables from a Web page to an applet?

COMPATIBILITY: HTML 3.2

Problem

I need to give an applet a set of starting values for it to run properly, and those values may be different at different times I run the applet. How can I pass a variable and its value from a Web page to the applet?

Technique

HTML 3.2 includes the **<PARAM>** tag which, in conjunction with the **<APPLET>** tag (see How-To 17.2), can be used to send a value for a named variable from the page to the applet.

Steps

Open your HTML document and locate the parts of the document that contain references to Java applets that need variable values passed to them.

1. Between the **<APPLET>** and **</APPLET>** tags, enter the **<PARAM>** tag:

```
<APPLET CODE="CurrentDateTwo" WIDTH=50 HEIGHT=75>
<PARAM>
</APPLET>
```

2. Add the **NAME** attribute to the **<PARAM>** tag, and set it equal to the name of the variable in the Java applet that will receive the value:

```
<APPLET CODE="CurrentDateTwo" WIDTH=50 HEIGHT=75>
<PARAM NAME="TimeZone">
</APPLET>
```

3. Add the `VALUE` attribute to the `<PARAM>` tag and set it equal to the value that will be passed on to the named variable in the Java applet:

```
<APPLET CODE="CurrentDateTwo" WIDTH=50 HEIGHT=75>
<PARAM NAME="TimeZone" VALUE="Eastern">
</APPLET>
```

4. Repeat the process for any additional variables you want to pass on to the applet.

```
<APPLET CODE="CurrentDateTwo" WIDTH=50 HEIGHT=75>
<PARAM NAME="TimeZone" VALUE="Eastern">
<PARAM NAME="Size" VALUE="5">
</APPLET>
```

How It Works

When a browser encounters the `<PARAM>` tag within the `<APPLET>` tag, it reads in the variable name and value specified and passes that value to the named variable in the current applet.

Comments

The `<PARAM>` tag must be placed within the `<APPLET>` and `</APPLET>` tags so that the variable names and values are linked to the appropriate applet. Other information, such as alternative text, can still be included in-between the `<APPLET>` and `</APPLET>` tags.

COMPLEXITY
INTERMEDIATE

17.4 How do I...
Find more information about Java?

COMPATIBILITY: NETSCAPE 2+, INTERNET EXPLORER 3

Problem

I'm very interested in learning more about the Java language and writing applets for my Web pages. How do I find more information about Java?

Technique

As Java is a complete programming language, we can only touch upon a few key issues of the language and its use in Web applets in this book. As one might expect, though, there are a wide range of Java resources available on the Web that you can use to expand your knowledge of Java.

Steps

You may want to open your Web browser so you can look at the Java resources discussed next.

1. The first stop in any exploration of Java on the Web should be Sun's Java home page at `http://www.javasoft.com/`. Sun developed the Java language long before it was applied to the Web and has the most authoritative resources on the language and its application to Web applets.

2. If your interest is limited to finding an interesting applet for your page, one of the largest collections of applets can be found at Gamelan, `http://www.gamelan.com/`. This site has a wide variety of applets and applications, from business to entertainment. This site also lists full-fledged Java applications and links to resources to learn more about Java.

3. There are a number of sites with tutorials about Java and extensive links to other Java resources on the Web. A few of the best sites are

- `http://www.sover.net/~manx/java.html`

- `http://infoweb.magi.com/~steve/java.html`

- `http://www.digitalfocus.com/digitalfocus/faq/`

4. The more experienced Java programmer will likely find *JavaWorld* magazine, `http://www.javaworld.com/`, a useful resource. This online publication includes the latest Java news and articles to increase one's knowledge of some more advanced aspects of the language.

How It Works

These Web sites provide information, sample applets, and other documentation that you can use to build your knowledge of Java. Most of these resources include samples of Java applets online so you can see the code in action.

Comments

The Web is changing very rapidly, so it's always possible that some of the resources described here may no longer exist by the time you read this. You may want to supplement these resources with others on the Web (many more Java-related Web sites can be found using one of the popular search engines) or with a book or other documentation.

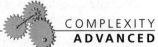

COMPLEXITY
ADVANCED

17.5 How do I...
Improve Java applet download time?

COMPATIBILITY: NETSCAPE 2+, INTERNET EXPLORER 3

Problem

I have some complex applets that call on a number of different Java classes. When I include these applets in my Web page, the applets download and run slowly because each class must download separately. How can I improve the loading time of my applets?

Technique

Netscape and Microsoft have developed their own methods of downloading a single object with all the classes required for that applet. Only a single connection is needed to download the package, allowing the applet to run faster. Unfortunately, the two methods described here are not compatible with each other. The following steps will show how to use this technique with Netscape's **ARCHIVE** attribute and Microsoft's **CAB** architecture.

Steps

Open the HTML document that includes references to Java applets.

Netscape Navigator

1. Place all the `.class` files needed for your applet into a single `.zip` file, using a Java development tool or other application.

2. Place this `.zip` file in the same directory as the applet that will use the classes in the `.zip` file.

3. Use the **APPLET** tag to place the applet in the appropriate location on the page. Include a new attribute called **ARCHIVE** and set it equal to the filename of the `.zip` file:

```
<APPLET CODE="MyApplet.class" ARCHIVE="MyApplet.zip" WIDTH=200 HEIGHT=200>
If you're reading this text, you don't have a Java-enabled browser.
</APPLET>
```

Microsoft Internet Explorer

1. Place a list of the Java `.class` files your applet needs in a file with a `.ddf` extension, such as `MyApplet.ddf`.

2. Microsoft provides a tool for Windows systems called Diamond that can create the `CAB` (for CABinet) files within Microsoft's Java development environment. From the command line, you would enter

```
diamond /f MyApplet.ddf
```

3. Once the `CAB` file (which usually has the filename extension `.cab`) has been created, it can be referenced by a Java applet in a Web page. One way is to use the `<PARAM>` tag (see How-To 17.3). The `NAME` attribute is set to `"cabbase"` and the `VALUE` attribute is set equal to the filename of the `CAB` file:

```
<APPLET CODE="MyApplet.class" WIDTH=200 HEIGHT=200>
<PARAM NAME="cabbase" VALUE="MyApplet.cab">
</APPLET>
```

4. For larger Java libraries, you can use the `<OBJECT>` element in a Web page to refer to `CAB` files. This requires using the Microsoft Java development tools to create a *unique class identifier* (`CLSID`) for the library. An example of this in a Web page is

```
<OBJECT
    CLASSID="clsid:12345678-9abc-def1-1234567890ab"
    CODEDBASE="cabs/MyApplet.cab#Version=1,0,0,12">
</OBJECT>
```

How It Works

With either the `ARCHIVE` or `CABBASE` techniques, the browser is prompted to download a single file containing all the `.class` files needed by a particular browser. This file is then uncompressed and the files stored in memory or on the disk for access by the applet.

Comments

This is a very new area, which is only starting to be supported by browsers and Java development tools. `ARCHIVE` and `CABBASE` are not recognized by versions of Netscape and Internet Explorer before 3.0. Moreover, Netscape does not yet support the `CABBASE` technique, and Internet Explorer does not yet support the `ARCHIVE` technique, reducing their usability in Web pages. Sun has just introduced a new, competing format named JAR (Java Archive). Information about this format is available at `http://www.javasoft.com/products/JDK/1.1/docs/guide/jar/jarGuide.html`.

COMPLEXITY
ADVANCED

17.6 How do I...
Include a script element?

COMPATIBILITY: NETSCAPE 2+, INTERNET EXPLORER 3

Problem

I want to be able to do more with my pages than simple HTML allows me to do. I have heard about JavaScript, and it sounds easier to use than other scripting languages. How do I go about adding a JavaScript script element in my HTML documents?

Technique

JavaScript is a powerful, fairly easy-to-use addition to the Netscape and Internet Explorer browsers. According to the Netscape press release, it "allows cross-platform scripting of events, objects and actions." You can use JavaScript to accomplish many tasks that you would have previously needed Java or Perl to perform. JavaScript is an object-based scripting language like the Java language, except that JavaScript is less extendable and simpler to use.

While JavaScript can be used to create sophisticated scripts (see How-To 17.8), elements of JavaScript can be included within HTML elements to perform specific, simple tasks, such as displaying a message in a window or displaying text when a user passes over a link. This How-To provides examples of how to include JavaScript elements in a Web page.

Steps

Open the HTML document in which you want to include JavaScript elements.

1. One way to include JavaScript elements in a Web page is to include an element that would cause the browser to go back to the previous page in the browser's history, like the **Back** button. First, create a button similar to those used with forms in Chapter 11, HTML Interactive Forms:

```
<FORM><INPUT TYPE="button" VALUE="Go to previous page"></FORM>
```

2. Now we add the JavaScript element to the **<INPUT>** tag so that it will perform the function described:

```
<FORM><INPUT TYPE="button" VALUE="Go to previous page"⇐
onClick="history.back()"></FORM>
```

Don't worry about the exact syntax used here; it will become familiar to you as you learn JavaScript. Instead, concentrate on how the JavaScript element is used in an HTML element.

3. Another example of including a JavaScript element in a Web page is the ability to use JavaScript to display alternative information whenever a user passes over a link. For example, create a link on a page:

```
<A HREF="otherpage.html">Link to another page</A>
```

4. To display something other than the URL of the link when the cursor passes over the link, you can enter something like

```
<A HREF="otherpage.html" onMouseOver="window.status='This is a link to my⇐
other page'; return true">Link to another page</A>
```

Again, don't worry about the exact syntax of the JavaScript used here, but instead focus on how it is included in the HTML tags.

An example of the use of JavaScript elements in a page is shown in Figure 17-2. The HTML code used for that figure is included on the CD as file 17-2.HTML.

How It Works

A browser that supports JavaScript will interpret JavaScript elements contained within the body of an HTML document. For these elements to be used, they must be set equal to some JavaScript attribute that signals to the browser when the JavaScript

Figure 17-2 Examples of JavaScript elements in a page

code should be executed. Some examples of these attributes are shown in How-To 17.7.

Comments

Including JavaScript elements directly into an HTML tag in a Web page is the best solution when only something simple is being done, such as brief messages or basic actions. Anything that requires more JavaScript markup to be accomplished would probably be better off in its own script, which will be described in How-To 17.8.

COMPLEXITY
ADVANCED

17.7   How do I...
Write a basic JavaScript script?

COMPATIBILITY: NETSCAPE 2+, INTERNET EXPLORER 3

Problem

I want to do more things with my pages than simple HTML allows me to. I know I could use Java or Perl, but I am looking for something a bit simpler to learn. I have heard about JavaScript, and it sounds like it will meet most of my needs. How do I go about writing a basic JavaScript script?

Technique

JavaScript is a property-based scripting language that makes use of objects. It is a small but complete, fully functional language. JavaScript does not allow you to create new objects as you can with Java. Instead, you use a group of predefined objects to accomplish your tasks.

The object hierarchy is as follows. The document object and all objects above the document are always available. All the objects below the document object are created on the fly, depending on the HTML code in the document.

For example, the following sample script has a form that contains a text field called `"name"`.

```
<INPUT TYPE="text" NAME="name" SIZE=20>
```

To refer to that text field, you must use the object name, complete with all its ancestors:

```
document.forms[0].name
```

To use the value of that text field, use

```
document.forms[0].name.value
```

As of this writing, all forms in a document are stored in a forms array. To refer to the forms, you use **"forms[0]"** for the first form, **"forms[1]"** for the second form, and so on.

Now that you have objects to use, you need to know when to use them. This is where event handlers come into play. Event handlers are the result of certain user actions, such as clicking on a button or check box, or selecting certain text.

For example, the following code causes the JavaScript function **doform()** to execute when the button defined by this tag is clicked on.

```
<INPUT TYPE="button" VALUE="Go for it" onClick="doform(this.form)">
```

The function uses the items created by **<INPUT TYPE>** tags in the current form as parameters.

The types of event handlers currently supported are

- **onFocus**: Script to run when the form element is the focus of input

- **onBlur**: Script to run on loss of input focus

- **onChange**: Script to run when a field's value is changed

- **onSelect**: Script to run when a text field is selected

- **onSubmit**: Script to run when a form is submitted

- **onClick**: Script to run when a button is clicked

Outside of objects and event handlers, JavaScript greatly resembles other programming languages you are probably already familiar with.

JavaScript has variables. To create a variable, name the variable with the **var** statement, or simply use it. For example:

```
var score
score = 0
```

Both of the these statements create a variable named **score**.

JavaScript has a set of built-in functions. It also allows the declaration of user-defined functions (brackets indicate optional user additions):

```
function name ([parameter] [, parameter] [, ..., parameter] ) {
    statements }
return
```

JavaScript has complete sets of assignment (**=**), arithmetic (**+, −, *, /**), logical (**&&, ||, !**), and comparison (**==, >, >=, <, <=, !=**) operators.

JavaScript also supports many types of control structures, such as

```
if (condition) {
    statements
} [else {
    else statements} ]
```

and

```
while (condition) {
    statements}
```

and

```
for ([initial expression;] [condition;] [update expression]) {
    statements
}
initial expression = statement | variable declaration
```

As you can see, JavaScript is a complete language. You can use different combinations of objects and event handlers along with all or some of the other features of JavaScript to create JavaScript scripts.

The keywords currently used and reserved by JavaScript are

break	continue	else	false
for	function	if	in
null	return	this	true
var	while	with	

For the latest list of all the items and features, refer to the Netscape home page at `http://home.netscape.com/`.

Steps

The following steps show one way you can create and use a JavaScript script. This is a basic script, yet it takes advantage of many of the nicer features of JavaScript. There are, of course, many other ways to create JavaScript scripts.

1. Decide what you want to do, and then decide whether JavaScript really is the best way to do it. This example uses forms to make a simple test for a user to take, and you'll need an application to test the answers sent by a form and grade the results. This is a fine application for JavaScript.

2. Create a base HTML document for your JavaScript script. For this example, use

```
<HTML>
<HEAD>
<TITLE>JavaScript Example</TITLE>
</HEAD>
<BODY>
<H2>Knowledge Tester</H2>
<HR>
<HR>
</BODY>
</HTML>
```

There's not much here yet, but it's a good start.

3. Add the form that contains the questions for the user to answer and for JavaScript to process.

```
<FORM>
Enter your name please:
```

```
<INPUT TYPE="text" NAME="yourname" SIZE=20><P>
Who's buried in Washington's grave?
<INPUT TYPE="text" NAME="question1" SIZE=15 ><P>
Roosters lay eggs (true or false)?
<INPUT TYPE="text" NAME="question2" SIZE=5 ><P>
<INPUT TYPE="button" VALUE="Go for it" onClick="doform(this.form)">
<HR>
<BR>
Result:
<INPUT TYPE="text" NAME="score" SIZE=15 >
<BR>
</FORM>
```

When viewed through a browser, this form looks like Figure 17-3.

This is a pretty typical form, except for the **onClick** event handler, which is the JavaScript extension. This causes the JavaScript **doform()** to execute when the user clicks on the button.

4. Now that you have the form to interact with, you need JavaScript to process this form. To start the script, place the **<SCRIPT>...</SCRIPT>** tags in the header of your document.

```
<SCRIPT LANGUAGE="JavaScript">
</SCRIPT>
```

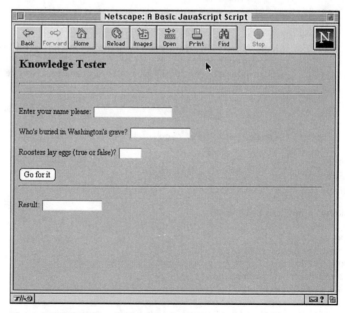

Figure 17-3 A form in JavaScript

You are placing this script in the header. Also, you want the script to contain a function that executes when the user clicks on the Forms button.

5. Define and insert the JavaScript function. Make sure that the function name is the same used when the function is called in the `<INPUT TYPE="button"...>` tag. The function used in this example is

```
function doform(form) {
    if (confirm("Are you sure "+document.forms[0].yourname.value+"?")){
        score=0
        if (document.forms[0].question1.value=="Washington"){
                score=score+1; }
            if (document.forms[0].question2.value=="false"){
                score=score+1; }
        form.score.value = (score / 2)*100
  }
 else
        alert("Please come back again.")
}
```

6. Save and name the HTML document with the JavaScript script in it. The entire document and script will look like this:

```
<HTML>
<HEAD>
<TITLE>JavaScript Demo</TITLE>
<SCRIPT LANGUAGE="JavaScript">
function doform(form) {
    if (confirm("Are you sure "+document.forms[0].yourname.value+"?")){
        score=0
        if (document.forms[0].question1.value=="Washington"){
                score=score+1; }
            if (document.forms[0].question2.value=="false"){
                score=score+1; }
        form.score.value = (score / 2)*100
  }
 else
        alert("Please come back again.")
}
</SCRIPT>
</HEAD>

<BODY>
<H2>Knowledge tester</H2>
<HR>
<FORM>
Enter your name please:
<INPUT TYPE="text" NAME="yourname" SIZE=20><P>
Who's buried in Washington's grave?
<INPUT TYPE="text" NAME="question1" SIZE=15 ><P>
Roosters lay eggs (true or false)?
<INPUT TYPE="text" NAME="question2" SIZE=5 ><P>
<INPUT TYPE="button" VALUE="Go for it" onClick="doform(this.form)">
```

```
<HR>
<BR>
Result:
<INPUT TYPE="text" NAME="score" SIZE=15 >
<BR>
</FORM>
</BODY>
</HTML>
```

7. View the document with the latest version of Netscape to make sure everything is working properly. When first executed, the screen should look like Figure 17-4. After the user answers the questions and clicks the Go for it button, the screen should resemble Figure 17-5.

8. Experiment! The best way to learn JavaScript is to change this example and see what effects your changes have. Once you are comfortable with this script, start writing your own scripts.

How It Works

When the user clicks on the Go for it button, the information in the form is sent to the `doform()` function named in the `<INPUT TYPE>` tags and defined in the header of the document.

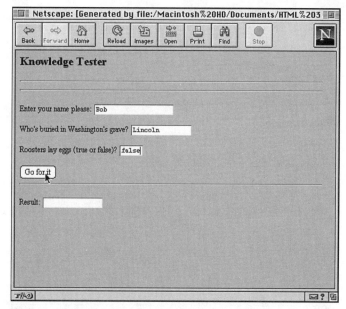

Figure 17-4 Starting the JavaScript script on the page

Four fields of information are sent to the function:

- **yourname**: Named by the first **<INPUT TYPE>** tag and referenced by **document.forms[0].yourname**

- **question1**: Named by the second **<INPUT TYPE>** tag and referenced by **document.forms[0].question1**

- **question2**: Named by the third **<INPUT TYPE>** tag and referenced by **document.forms[0].question2**

- **score**: Named by the fifth **<INPUT TYPE>** tag and referenced by **document.forms[0].score**

The value of any of these fields can be found by appending **.value** to the reference for that field, such as

```
document.forms[0].name.value
```

The first statement in the function

```
if (confirm("Are you sure "+document.forms[0].yourname.value+"?")){
```

sets up a control structure and gives the user a chance to back out. It uses the **confirm** method to display a dialog box, such as the one shown in Figure 14-12 in the user's window.

Figure 17-5 Output from the JavaScript script

The results from the dialog box are then processed by the **if** statement. If the user responds negatively (clicks no), the function executes the **else** block. In this case, that puts up a "Please come back again." message in an alert box. The function then exits, returning control to the form.

If the user responds positively, the function executes the statements under the **if** statement. These statements work as follows:

```
score=0
```

creates a variable to calculate the user's score.

The following statements

```
if (document.forms[0].question.1.value=="Washington"){
    score = score + 1; }
if (document.forms[0].question.2.value=="false"){
    score=score+1;}
```

compare the value of the information entered in the form with the correct answer. If the value equals the correct answer, then the user's score is incremented.

Finally, the user's final score is calculated by

```
document.forms[0].score.value= (score /2)*100
```

This value is placed into the score field created with the form. When the function exits, the updated score value is shown in the field.

Comments

In the old days (last year), you would have used Perl to do something like this example. Though this example is very rudimentary because it contains no error checking and is case-sensitive, you can still see how easy JavaScript makes certain tasks, such as validating forms input.

Please note: JavaScript is a vast enough topic that it could easily be the subject of a book. This section did not even go into such matters as methods or object properties. For more information on these, consult the latest Netscape documentation.

COMPLEXITY
ADVANCED

17.8 How do I...
Include a script in a Web page?

COMPATIBILITY: NETSCAPE 2+, INTERNET EXPLORER 3

Problem

I want to be able to do more with my pages than simple HTML allows me to do. I have heard about JavaScript, and it sounds easier to use than other scripting languages. How do I go about adding a JavaScript script in my HTML documents?

Technique

You can use JavaScript to accomplish many tasks that you would have previously needed Java or Perl to perform. JavaScript is an object-based scripting language like the Java language, only JavaScript is less extendable and simpler to use.

To include a JavaScript script in an HTML document, use the **<SCRIPT>** tag. The **<SCRIPT>** tag's format is

```
<SCRIPT LANGUAGE="language.name" [SRC="a URL for the script"]>
a JavaScript script
</SCRIPT>
```

In this format, **LANGUAGE** is the language the script is written in, and **SRC** is an optional attribute that gives the URL of the script to be loaded. **LANGUAGE** is mandatory unless the **SRC** attribute gives the scripting language.

Steps

The following steps give a rudimentary introduction to how you can add JavaScript scripts (see How-To 17.7) to your Web pages.

1. Create a basic HTML document using any text editor. For this example, use the very basic document that follows:

```
<HTML>
<HEAD>
<TITLE>JavaScript Demo</TITLE>
</HEAD>
<BODY>
The above line was written from a JavaScript script. And so is the
following line.
<P>
</BODY>
</HTML>
```

2. Enter the **<SCRIPT>** tags.

3. Enter the JavaScript script between the two tags. This example uses two very simple scripts that write to the screen. The script lines are

```
<SCRIPT LANGUAGE="JavaScript">
document.write("Simple demo...")
document.write("<P>")
</SCRIPT>
```

and

```
<!-- Second Script -->
<SCRIPT LANGUAGE="JavaScript">
document.write("<P>THE END...")
</SCRIPT>
```

Notice the HTML tags embedded in **write**. These function just as they would normally in HTML.

4. Save and name the document.

5. View the document to make sure it works the way you think it should. For example, look at the following:

```
<HTML>
<HEAD>
<TITLE>JavaScript Demo</TITLE>
</HEAD>
<BODY>
<!-- First Script -->
<SCRIPT LANGUAGE="JavaScript">
document.write("Simple demo...")
document.write("<P>")
</SCRIPT>
The above line was written from a JavaScript script. And so is the
following line.
<P>

<!-- Second Script -->
<SCRIPT LANGUAGE="JavaScript">
document.write("<P>THE END...")
</SCRIPT>

<!-- It may not seem like much now, as you do this without using
JavaScript, but in the next section you will see some of the power of
JavaScript. -->

</BODY>
</HTML>
```

When viewed by a browser that supports JavaScript, the example looks like Figure 17-6. A browser that does not support JavaScript only displays `The above line was written from a JavaScript script. And so is the following line.`

How It Works

A browser that supports JavaScript reads and evaluates the scripts that are embedded between the `<SCRIPT>` tags. JavaScript functions are stored but not evaluated until they are executed by events in the page.

Comments

It is possible to do a lot with JavaScript. JavaScript can be a very helpful tool when it comes to event-handling tasks such as reading and validating information from forms and responding to other types of user actions, such as clicks. JavaScript, while not as powerful as Java or Perl, is less cumbersome and therefore easier to learn and use than the other two.

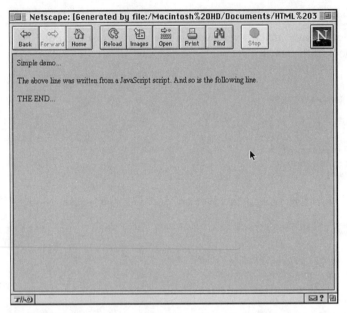

Figure 17-6 A script as seen in a JavaScript-aware browser

COMPLEXITY
ADVANCED

17.9 How do I...
Generate a pop-up dialog using JavaScript?

COMPATIBILITY: NETSCAPE 2+, INTERNET EXPLORER 3

Problem

I would like to create a simple dialog box that appears with a brief message at certain points in my Web page. How to I generate pop-up dialog boxes in JavaScript?

Technique

JavaScript provides the programmer with a number of simple ways to include a dialog box that pops up when needed. These boxes can provide a warning, a chance for the user to confirm his choice, or a way for the user to enter specific data.

Steps

Open the HTML document in which you want to add a JavaScript dialog box.

1. Identify the portion of the document in which you want to generate a dialog box. For this example, we'll create a button similar to that used in How-To 17.6:

```
<INPUT TYPE="button" NAME="Press Me">
```

2. One kind of dialog box is the alert box, which is used to provide a warning or other notice to the user. The `alert()` element in JavaScript is used to create an alert box, with the text to be displayed in the box placed within the parentheses. Use the example started in the previous step:

```
<INPUT TYPE="button" NAME="Press Me" onClick=alert('This is the wrong⇐
button to push!')>
```

3. Another kind of dialog box is the confirmation box. This is used to give the user the chance to confirm a task before it is executed, with the option to cancel. The JavaScript element `confirm()` works like the `alert()` one described in the previous step:

```
<INPUT TYPE="button" NAME="Press Me" onClick=confirm('Are you sure?')>
```

This is usually used as part of a larger script, where the value returned by the `confirm()` element (**true** or **false**) is used to direct the future action of a script.

4. A third option for a dialog box is the prompt box, which allows the user to enter a certain value that will be given to a variable in a script. The JavaScript `prompt()` element is used to create this. It takes on two values: the message displayed in the box and the default value. Use the example from step 1:

```
<INPUT TYPE="button" NAME="Press Me" onClick=prompt('Enter your favorite
number,'')>
```

As with the `confirm()` option, `prompt()` is usually used with a script to process the value entered by the user.

Examples of JavaScript dialog boxes are shown in Figures 17-7 (alert), 17-8 (confirm), and 17-9 (prompt). The HTML and JavaScript used to create these can be found on the CD as file 17-4.HTML.

How It Works

When a JavaScript-aware browser receives a JavaScript command to generate a dialog box, it will create the box depending on the type of box requested. The contents of the box depend on the data passed to the JavaScript routine, and the action taken depends on the type of dialog box generated and the option the user chooses.

Figure 17-7 An alert dialog box in JavaScript

Figure 17-8 A confirm dialog box in JavaScript

Figure 17-9 A prompt dialog box in JavaScript

Comments

Most of the examples shown here have been very simplistic. In a real JavaScript routine, the dialog boxes shown here would have been included as part of a larger function that is called somewhere on a Web page. The next section shows a slightly more sophisticated routine that does use dialog boxes as part of its operation.

COMPLEXITY
ADVANCED

17.10 How do I...
Check an HTML form for required input fields?

COMPATIBILITY: NETSCAPE 2+, INTERNET EXPLORER 3

Problem

My Web page includes a form that sends data to a CGI script on my server. To decrease the workload on my server, I would like to use JavaScript in some way to make sure the forms are completely filled out before sending them to the server. How do I have JavaScript verify that the form has been filled out before proceeding?

Technique

There is a way to include a simple JavaScript script in a Web page that can verify whether or not all the desired fields have been filled out. The script will keep the form from being sent to a CGI script if the data is not filled out, or else allow it to proceed if it is. This is a good example of a simple script that brings together some of the JavaScript aspects described earlier in this chapter.

Steps

Open an HTML document.

1. The first step is to create a simple form. For this example, the form will have only two fields, a name and an e-mail address:

```
<FORM METHOD="POST" ACTION="myscript.cgi">
Name: <INPUT TYPE="text" NAME="yourname"><BR>
E-Mail: <INPUT TYPE="text" NAME="email"><BR>
<INPUT TYPE=SUBMIT VALUE="Enter!">
</FORM>
```

2. Now we add a JavaScript attribute to the `<FORM>` tag so that when the form is submitted, the contents of the form are first passed to a JavaScript routine that will verify that all the fields in the form are filled. We will also give the form a name, which we will need for the script:

```
<FORM METHOD="POST" ACTION="myscript.cgi" NAME="theform" onSubmit="return
formCheck()">
Name: <INPUT TYPE="text" NAME="yourname"><BR>
E-Mail: <INPUT TYPE="text" NAME="email"><BR>
<INPUT TYPE=SUBMIT VALUE="Enter!">
</FORM>
```

3. Now we can set up the script in the header of the document:

```
<SCRIPT LANGUAGE="JavaScript">
</SCRIPT>
```

4. The script will have one function, called `formCheck()`, which will check the contents of the submitted forms:

```
<SCRIPT LANGUAGE="JavaScript">
function formCheck()
{
}
</SCRIPT>
```

5. For the form to be valid, both the name and e-mail address fields have to have some content in them. We can test for this by seeing whether first one field, then the other, is empty:

```
<SCRIPT LANGUAGE="JavaScript">
function formCheck()
{
```

```
        if (document.theform.yourname.value == " ")
        {
        }

        if (document.theform.email.value == " ")
        {
        }
}
</SCRIPT>
```

6. Now we have to include some action if either field is empty. One possibility is an alert dialog box that warns the user. We can also include a **return false** statement, which quits the script and keeps the form from being submitted:

```
<SCRIPT LANGUAGE="JavaScript">
function formCheck()
{
        if (document.theform.yourname.value == " ")
        {
        alert("You did not include your name. Please try again.");
        return false;
        }

        if (document.theform.email.value == " ")
        {
        alert("You did not include your e-mail address. Please try again.");
        return false;
        }
}
</SCRIPT>
```

An example of this form is shown in Figure 17-10. The HTML and JavaScript code used to generate this can be found on the CD as file 17-5.HTML.

How It Works

When the user fills out and submits the form, the browser first calls on the JavaScript function listed in the **<FORM>** tag. The form runs through a series of **if** statements, checking to see that each field has a value entered. If a field turns up empty, then a warning message is displayed by the browser and the form submission is canceled.

Comments

This form can be expanded from the simple two-field version to one with as many fields as needed. It's also possible to parse the values submitted to look for specific things, such as whether the e-mail address submitted is of proper form.

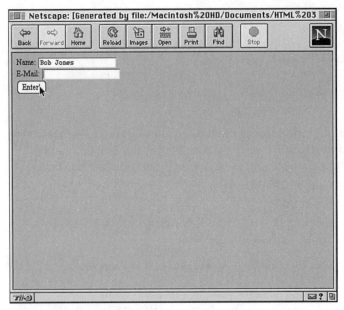

Figure 17-10 A JavaScript script checking an HTML form

COMPLEXITY
ADVANCED

17.11   How do I...
Find more information on
JavaScript?

COMPATIBILITY: NETSCAPE 2+, INTERNET EXPLORER 3

Problem

I would like to learn more about JavaScript to see how I can implement my own scripts
for my Web pages. How do I find out more information on JavaScript?

Technique

As JavaScript is much like a complete programming language, we can only touch
upon a few key issues of the language and its use in Web applets in this book. As
one might expect, though, there is a wide range of JavaScript resources available on
the Web that you can use to expand your knowledge of JavaScript.

Steps

You may want to open your Web browser to explore some of these resources.

1. Since Netscape introduced JavaScript to the Web, you might expect good JavaScript resources from the company. In fact, there is detailed information on the language and its applications in Web pages at `http:// home.netscape.com/eng/mozilla/Gold/handbook/javascript/`.

2. If you're looking for JavaScript scripts to add to your pages, you can go to the same place you might go for Java applets: Gamelan, at `http://www.gamelan.com/`. Gamelan has links to a wide variety of JavaScript scripts and general JavaScript resources.

3. Another resource for JavaScript scripts on the Web can be found at `http://www.geocities.com/SiliconValley/9000/`. A variety of different scripts, all written by the same authors, can be found here.

4. For tips on writing your own JavaScript scripts, the JavaScript Tip of the Week site at `http://webreference.com/javascript/` has a number of useful tips. You can learn script techniques like the form verification routine found in How-To 17.10.

How It Works

These Web sites provide information, sample applets, and other documentation that you can use to build your knowledge of JavaScript. Most of these resources include samples of JavaScript scripts online so you can see the code in action.

Comments

The Web is changing very rapidly, so it's always possible that some of the resources described here may no longer exist by the time you read this. You may want to supplement these resources with others on the Web (many more JavaScript-related Web sites can be found using one of the popular search engines) or with a book or other documentation.

COMPLEXITY
ADVANCED

17.12 How do I...
Provide an alternative if scripting is not supported?

COMPATIBILITY: NETSCAPE 2+, INTERNET EXPLORER 3

Problem

I'm using a number of JavaScript scripts in my Web pages, but I realize that some people do not use browsers that support it, or have turned off JavaScript. How do I provide an alternative if JavaScript is not supported on the browser?

Technique

While JavaScript can do many things, not all people are able to or desire to take advantage of it. Thus, it is important to provide alternatives to scripting so that information on the Web page is still available to those users. There are a couple ways to do this.

Steps

Open an HTML document that contains JavaScript scripts.

1. Since browsers that don't support JavaScript won't recognize that the items contained within the **<SCRIPT>** and **</SCRIPT>** tags are part of a script and not markup, it will try to print them on the screen. To avoid this, you can use a trick to make them invisible:

```
<SCRIPT LANGUAGE="JavaScript">
<!--
document.write("This will appear only on a JavaScript-enabled browser");
//-->
</SCRIPT>
```

Since HTML browsers recognize **<!--** as the beginning of a comment and **-->** as the end, it will not print what is between them. JavaScript, however, will see and process the contents of the script between the **<!--** and **-->** tags because it defines comments differently.

2. Another trick exists for displaying alternate text for JavaScript-disabled browsers. JavaScript recognizes any single line that begins with **<!--** as a comment, so it will ignore anything else on that line as a comment. Combining that with the closing HTML comment symbol, you can provide alternate text for other browsers:

```
<SCRIPT LANGUAGE="JavaScript">
<!--> <H1>This is visible only to JavaScript-disabled browsers</H1>
document.write("This will appear only on a JavaScript-enabled browser");
//-->
</SCRIPT>
```

3. Netscape introduced the `<NOSCRIPT>` tag in version 3. Designed to work analogously to `<NOFRAMES>` for framed pages, it provides alternate content for those browsers not using JavaScript:

```
<SCRIPT LANGUAGE="JavaScript">
<!--
document.write("This will appear only on a JavaScript-enabled browser");
//-->
</SCRIPT>
<NOSCRIPT>
<H1>This is visible only to JavaScript-disabled browsers</H1>
</NOSCRIPT>
```

An example of how these techniques work on browsers with JavaScript support turned on and off are shown in Figures 17-11 and 17-12, respectively. The HTML code used for both can be found on the CD as file 17-6.HTML.

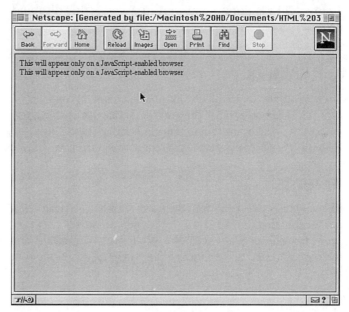

Figure 17-11 Hidden JavaScript in a JavaScript-enabled browser

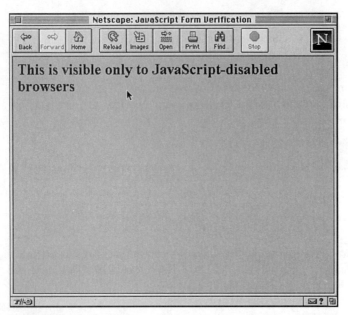

Figure 17-12 Hidden JavaScript in a JavaScript-disabled browser

How It Works

Since HTML and JavaScript use different definitions of comment beginnings and endings, it is possible to "hide" content from JavaScript-enabled or -disabled browsers by carefully applying the comment marks described here. The <NOSCRIPT> tag promises to make it easier to separate content between the two sets of users.

Comments

The <NOSCRIPT> tag was introduced in Netscape Navigator 3, so there are previous versions that support JavaScript but not the <NOSCRIPT> tag. In these cases, the browsers will not know what the <NOSCRIPT> tag means and will display the markup inside them, even though the JavaScript scripts are running!

## CHAPTER 18

DIRECT INCLUSION OF MULTIMEDIA OBJECTS

18

DIRECT INCLUSION OF MULTIMEDIA OBJECTS

How do I...

When the Web was first developed several years ago, it was a text-only medium: No pictures, no sounds, and no animations were available. The Web first started to become popular when browsers like Mosaic allowed people to view graphics embedded into pages. Since then the number of multimedia types supported by Web browsers has exploded. It's now possible to include interactive animations, high-quality music, and three-dimensional worlds into Web pages...so long as users are patient enough to wait for them to download! This chapter will look at some of the ways you can include multimedia in your Web pages. It's not possible to discuss in detail all the possible ways, but after going through this chapter, you'll understand the basics of adding multimedia to the Web.

18.1   Embed Objects Supported by Plug-Ins

Plug-ins are a way to add functionality to your Web browser by enabling it to interpret and display different types of files, including sounds and videos. This How-To shows how to reference a multimedia file in a Web page so that a user with the appropriate plug-in will be able to view it.

18.2   Directly Incorporate Windows-Supported Information Types into a Web Page

Microsoft Internet Explorer supports an expanded version of embedding multimedia objects that includes Windows-supported information types and even Java applets. This How-To shows how to use the `<OBJECT>` tag to include these elements in a Web page.

18.3   Include a Video in My Web Page

Animations can make a Web page more entertaining or useful. However, they require the use of an external application that will display animations, which not all Web users may have. This How-To shows how to use an HTML extension in Microsoft Internet Explorer 3 to add an inline video in AVI format to your Web page, and how to embed other types of videos into pages that can be viewed by Internet Explorer or Netscape Navigator.

18.4   Add Sound Tracks to My Web Page

A sound track can add to the multimedia experience of viewing a page. However, there is no standard way to have a sound play in the background while reading a Web page. This How-To shows how you can use an HTML extension in Microsoft Internet Explorer 2 and later to play sound tracks in the background, and how to embed a sound into a page that can be interpreted by Netscape and Microsoft.

18.5   Include a Director Application

Macromedia Director is a multimedia authoring application in wide use by many designers. Macromedia has released Shockwave, a plug-in for Web browsers that allows users to view specially prepared Director movies in Web pages. This How-To shows how to convert a Director movie into the correct format and how to include it on a Web page.

18.6   Add Web Links to a Director Application

One advantage of Shockwave movies is that you can include links to other Web pages within them, adding an additional degree of interactivity. This How-To shows how to include Web links into a Director movie that can be viewed on a Web page with Shockwave.

18.7 Include an Astound/Studio M Application in a Web Page

Another multimedia application in wide use outside the Web is Astound, as well as its sibling product, Studio M. It is now possible to include Astound and Studio M presentations into Web pages with the use of special player and creator software. This How-To addresses how to include versions of these presentations in your Web pages.

18.8 Embed a VRML Space

Virtual Reality Modeling Language (VRML) is a popular way of creating three-dimensional spaces, or worlds, on the Web. Both Microsoft Internet Explorer and Netscape Navigator support a number of methods of including these spaces on a Web page. This How-To shows how to include a VRML space on a Web page.

18.9 Include a Multimedia Object to Maximize Cross-Browser Support

Both Microsoft and Netscape have developed their own ways of including multimedia objects on Web pages, and these methods are not always compatible with each other or with other Web browsers. This How-To looks at ways to include multimedia objects in a way that is supported by the widest variety of browsers.

COMPLEXITY
INTERMEDIATE

18.1 How do I...
Embed objects supported by plug-ins?

COMPATIBILITY: MICROSOFT INTERNET EXPLORER, NETSCAPE NAVIGATOR

Problem

I have a multimedia file that is supported by a browser plug-in that I want to include on a Web page. How do I write the HTML so that the browser will load the file and display it on the screen with the plug-in?

Technique

Both Microsoft Internet Explorer and Netscape Navigator support the `<EMBED>` tag, which allows multimedia applications supported by plug-ins to be downloaded and displayed by the user. The syntax of the `<EMBED>` tag is very similar to the `<IMG>` tag discussed in Chapter 9, Using Images in Your Documents.

Steps

Open the HTML document to which you want to add the multimedia objects. Identify the objects you want to add and the locations on the page to add them.

1. At the location of the HTML document where you want to place the object, add the `<EMBED>` tag.

```
<P> My multimedia object is below:</P>
<EMBED>
```

2. Include the `SRC` attribute and set it equal to the URL of the object. The URL can be a local reference or a full URL to an object on another site.

```
<P> My multimedia objects are below:</P>
<EMBED SRC="widget.mov">
<EMBED SRC="http://www.widgets.com/widget.mov">
```

3. As with images, you can use the `HEIGHT` and `WIDTH` attributes to set the height and width of the image in pixels.

```
<P> My multimedia objects are below:</P>
<EMBED SRC="widget.mov" HEIGHT="50" WIDTH="50">
<EMBED SRC="http://www.widgets.com/widget.mov" HEIGHT="100" WIDTH="175">
```

4. For browsers that don't support plug-ins, or for users who don't have the appropriate plug-in installed, the `ALT` attribute can be used to display alternative text.

```
<P> My multimedia objects are below:</P>
<EMBED SRC="widget.mov" HEIGHT="50" WIDTH="50" ALT="My widget movie">
<EMBED SRC="http://www.widgets.com/widget.mov" HEIGHT="100" WIDTH="175"
ALT="Their widget movie">
```

5. In addition to these attributes, there are a number of other attributes, specific to the object and the plug-in, that can be added. These attributes provide additional information on how the file should be displayed, such as whether and how many times it should loop, how the file should be started, and more. Some of the additional attributes will be discussed in How-To's elsewhere in the chapter.

How It Works

When a browser encounters an `<EMBED>` tag, it loads the file and determines the MIME type it has. The MIME information explains to the browser what kind of file is being downloaded. The browser then checks for the plug-in that corresponds with that MIME type and uses that plug-in, if available. If no corresponding plug-in exists, an error message is usually displayed, and the multimedia file is not displayed on the screen. The user then has the option of finding and downloading the appropriate plug-in, if one exists for that browser and operating system.

Comments

Embedded files can't be displayed unless the appropriate plug-in exists on the user's system. This places the burden of finding and maintaining a collection of plug-ins on the browser user, who will often only have the time, disk space, or general inclination to keep plug-ins for major file formats (like sounds, videos, Shockwave, and so on). You will want to keep this in mind if you're planning to use a more obscure file format that requires a specialized plug-in that many users may not have.

COMPLEXITY
INTERMEDIATE

18.2 How do I...
Directly incorporate Windows-supported information types into a Web page?

COMPATIBILITY: MICROSOFT INTERNET EXPLORER

Problem

I would like to include a file in a Windows-specific format into my Web page. How can I write the HTML so the file can be included and viewed by people using specific browsers?

Technique

Microsoft Internet Explorer supports the **<OBJECT>** element, which allows Web page designers to include a variety of multimedia and other files, including Java applets. **<OBJECT>** has been designed to eventually replace **<EMBED>** and **<APPLET>** and become the primary way to include multimedia files and applications in Web pages.

Steps

Open your HTML document. Locate the files you want to include as multimedia objects in the page, and their location in the page.

1. Enter the **<OBJECT>** tag where you want to locate the object on the page. A closing tag, **</OBJECT>**, is required, although no content needs to exist between the two tags.

```
<P>Here is my multimedia object:</P>
<OBJECT></OBJECT>
```

2. The CODEBASE attribute is used to define the code base, or location, of the object. The attribute is set equal to the URL of the file.

```
<P>Here is my multimedia object:</P>
<OBJECT CODEBASE="myfile.class"></OBJECT>
```

3. Similarly, the DATA attribute is set equal to the URL that defines the data for the object.

```
<P>Here is my multimedia object:</P>
<OBJECT CODEBASE="myfile.class" DATA="data.class"></OBJECT>
```

4. Like the <IMG> tag, <OBJECT> accepts attributes like ALIGN, HEIGHT, WIDTH, HSPACE, VSPACE, BORDER, and USEMAP.

```
<P>Here is my multimedia object:</P>
<OBJECT CODEBASE="myfile.class" DATA="data.class" HEIGHT=100 WIDTH=75
ALIGN=CENTER></OBJECT>
```

5. The STANDBY attribute can be included and set equal to a text message to be displayed by the browser while waiting for the object to load.

```
<P>Here is my multimedia object:</P>
<OBJECT CODEBASE="myfile.class" DATA="data.class" HEIGHT=100 WIDTH=75
ALIGN=CENTER STANDBY="Object loading...please wait"></OBJECT>
```

6. While there doesn't need to be any content between the <OBJECT> and </OBJECT> tags, you can place any valid HTML markup there to be displayed by a browser that does not support the <OBJECT> tag.

```
<P>Here is my multimedia object:</P>
<OBJECT CODEBASE="myfile.class" DATA="data.class" HEIGHT=100 WIDTH=75
ALIGN=CENTER STANDBY="Object loading...please wait">You need to use a browser
which supports OBJECT to see this file</OBJECT>
```

How It Works

If a browser supports the <OBJECT> tag, it will load the corresponding file and display it according to the values set in the attributes contained within the <OBJECT> tag. If a browser doesn't support the <OBJECT> tag, it will display whatever markup is contained between the <OBJECT> and </OBJECT> tags.

Comments

Currently only Internet Explorer supports the <OBJECT> tag, which limits its usefulness on the Web. The tag may be more widely supported, though, and even become a part of a future HTML standard down the road. Until that time, you will need to look into workarounds for other browsers. How-To 18.9 will help you do this.

COMPLEXITY
INTERMEDIATE

18.3 How do I...
Include a video in my Web page?

COMPATIBILITY: MICROSOFT INTERNET EXPLORER, NETSCAPE
NAVIGATOR

Problem

I have a video clip that I would like to include in my Web page so that the video displays on the screen as the user reads the page. Is there a way to include a video on my Web page?

Technique

Both Netscape Navigator and Microsoft Internet Explorer support embedded video, using the appropriate plug-ins. In addition, Internet Explorer supports inline AVI videos natively, which allows them to be played on the page instead of by an external application or with a plug-in. The browser supports attributes that allow you to control the size of the video display, the number of times it plays, and when to start the video.

Steps

Find the video clip you want to include in the page. Open your document and find the location where you want to add the video clip.

Embedded Video for Plug-Ins (Netscape and Internet Explorer)

1. Insert the `<EMBED>` tag in the area of the document where you want to place the video. Set the `SRC` attribute equal to the URL of the video file.

```
<P>Here is a animation of the planet Mars:</P>
<EMBED SRC="mars.mov">
```

2. To reserve an area of the window for the video, include the `HEIGHT` and `WIDTH` attributes and set them equal to the size of the video image, in pixels.

```
<P>Here is a animation of the planet Mars:</P>
<EMBED SRC="mars.mov" HEIGHT="150' WIDTH="150">
```

3. For people unable to load or view the video, include the `<ALT>` tag and set it equal to some text describing the video.

```
<P>Here is a animation of the planet Mars:</P>
<EMBED SRC="mars.mov" HEIGHT="150' WIDTH="150" ALT="Video of Mars">
```

4. If the video you are using is a QuickTime video, there are several other attributes you can include in the `<EMBED>` tag. If you want the video to loop around and play again after finishing, set the `LOOP` attribute equal to `TRUE`.

```
<P>Here is a animation of the planet Mars:</P>
<EMBED SRC="mars.mov" HEIGHT="150' WIDTH="150" ALT="Video of Mars" LOOP=TRUE>
```

Otherwise you can set `LOOP` equal to `FALSE`.

5. For the video to play automatically when loaded, include the `AUTOPLAY` attribute equal to `TRUE`. As with the `LOOP` attribute, this also can be set to `FALSE` if you don't want the video to start automatically.

```
<P>Here is a animation of the planet Mars:</P>
<EMBED SRC="mars.mov" HEIGHT="150' WIDTH="150" ALT="Video of Mars" LOOP=TRUE
AUTOPLAY=TRUE>
```

6. If you want a control panel to appear so users can stop, start, and scan through the video, set the `CONTROLLER` attribute equal to `TRUE`. Otherwise, this can be set to `FALSE`.

```
<P>Here is a animation of the planet Mars:</P>
<EMBED SRC="mars.mov" HEIGHT="150' WIDTH="150" ALT="Video of Mars" LOOP=TRUE
AUTOPLAY=TRUE CONTROLLER=TRUE>
```

7. If you are using an AVI video and a plug-in like ClearVideo (formerly CoolFusion), there are other attributes you can add to the `<EMBED>` element. The equivalent of `CONTROLLER` is `SHOWCONTROLS`, which can be set to `TRUE` (to display a control panel) or `FALSE`.

```
<P>Here is a animation of the planet Mars:</P>
<EMBED SRC="mars.avi" HEIGHT="150" WIDTH="150" SHOWCONTROLS=TRUE >
```

8. You can assign specific commands to the video based on mouse clicks within the image. `ONLBUTTONDOWN` allows you to assign a command, like `"pause"` or `"play"`, to the left mouse button, while `ONLDOUBLECLK` does the same when the left mouse button is double-clicked. For example, to assign a single left button click to pause the video and a double click to start the video over, enter

```
<P>Here is a animation of the planet Mars:</P>
<EMBED SRC="mars.avi" HEIGHT="150" WIDTH="150" SHOWCONTROLS=TRUE
ONLBUTTONDOWN="pause" ONLDOUBLECLK="play repeat">
```

Inline AVI Video (Internet Explorer)

1. Use the `<IMG>` tag (see Chapter 9, Using Images in Your Documents) to insert the video. Set the attribute `DYNSRC` (for "Dynamic Source") equal to the name of the video. `DYNSRC` can be a filename, a full path, or a URL to the video file. For example, to include a video with the filename `mars.avi`, enter

```
<IMG DYNSRC="mars.avi">
```

If the video is accessible by HTTP from `www.widgets.com` in the directory `videos/mars.avi`, enter

```
<IMG DYNSRC="http://www.widgets.com/videos/mars.avi">
```

2. For those browsers that don't support AVI videos, you can specify an image to be shown in its place. To do this, set the `SRC` attribute equal to the filename of the image. In the example from the last step, to add a reference to an image called `mars.gif`, you would enter

```
<IMG DYNSRC="mars.avi" SRC="mars.gif">
```

3. Use the `START` attribute to tell the browser when to start playing the video. `START` can have two values, `FILEOPEN` and `MOUSEOVER`. If `START` is set equal to `FILEOPEN`, the video starts playing as soon as the file has finished loading. If `START` is set equal to `MOUSEOVER`, the video will not start playing until the user moves the mouse cursor over the animation. The default value is `FILEOPEN`. To insert a video that doesn't start playing until the user moves the cursor over the video, use

```
<IMG DYNSRC="mars.avi" SRC="mars.gif" START=MOUSEOVER>
```

It's possible to use both `FILEOPEN` and `MOUSEOVER` for the `START` attribute. In this case, the video will play as soon as the file loads, and again each time the cursor passes over the video. To do this, enter

```
<IMG DYNSRC="mars.avi" SRC="mars.gif" START=FILEOPEN,MOUSEOVER>
```

4. You can add a set of video controls beneath the video clip with the `CONTROLS` attribute. For example, to add a set of video controls to a clip, use

```
<IMG DYNSRC="mars.avi" SRC="mars.gif" CONTROLS>
```

5. The number of times the video displays can be set with the `LOOP` attribute. The `LOOP` attribute can be set to the number of times the video is played. Setting `LOOP` equal to `INFINITE` or `-1` plays the video continuously. To play a video clip five times, use

```
<IMG DYNSRC="mars.avi" SRC="mars.gif" LOOP=5>
```

To play the video continuously, use

```
<IMG DYNSRC="mars.avi" SRC="mars.gif" LOOP=INFINITE>
```

6. The `LOOPDELAY` attribute controls the amount of time the browser waits before replaying a video. Set the `LOOPDELAY` attribute to the number of milliseconds the browser waits after the end of the video before replaying it. For example, to wait two seconds between replays of a continuously looping video, use

```
<IMG DYNSRC="mars.avi" SRC="mars.gif" LOOP=INFINITE LOOPDELAY=2000>
```

A sample of a movie included in a Web page (in this case, a QuickTime movie embedded into Netscape) is shown in Figure 18-1.

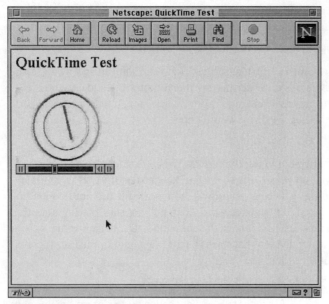

Figure 18-1 A QuickTime movie in a Web page

How It Works

When an `<EMBED>` element is encountered on a Web page, the browser checks the MIME type of the file referenced in the element. If the file is of a type supported by plug-ins installed with the browser, the file is downloaded and displayed, and the browser passes on the values of any attributes to the plug-in. If the file format is not supported by any plug-ins on the user's computer, an error message is displayed and video is not shown.

When Internet Explorer identifies the `DYNSRC` attribute in the `<IMG>` tag, it loads the video file specified by that attribute. The browser then displays the video, using the values provided by any attributes or the default values.

Comments

If you use the `<EMBED>` method, note that a typical user will likely only have a few plug-ins of the most common type installed on his or her computer, so the user may not be able to view videos not in common formats (like AVI, MPEG, and QuickTime). You may want to convert your video to one of these formats to maximize the number of people able to view your work.

Besides the attributes just mentioned, you can use other `<IMG>` attributes. See Chapter 9, Using Images in Your Documents, for a full discussion of the attributes supported by `<IMG>`. Currently, only Internet Explorer 2 supports inline AVI video, so users using other browsers will be able to see only the image referenced in the SRC attribute.

You can provide a link to the animation (in AVI or another format) that people with other browsers can see with an external application. For example, to include a link to an MPEG version of an animation, enter

```
<A HREF="mars.mpg"><IMG DYNSRC="mars.avi" SRC="mars.gif"></A>
```

You can find updated information about including AVI videos on the Web at the URL `http://www.microsoft.com/workshop/author/newhtml/default.htm`.

COMPLEXITY
INTERMEDIATE

18.4 How do I...
Add sound tracks to my Web page?

COMPATIBILITY: MICROSOFT INTERNET EXPLORER, NETSCAPE NAVIGATOR

Problem

I would like to include some music that will play on the user's computer when he or she reads my page. How can I include a sound track on my Web page?

Technique

Both Microsoft Internet Explorer and Netscape Navigator support the use of the `<EMBED>` tag to include sound files. This method relies on plug-ins to play the sound file. Microsoft's Internet Explorer 2 and above also supports the HTML extension `<BGSOUND>`, which allows users to add sounds that will play in the background for those who are using that browser. Other browsers may treat this like any other unsupported HTML element. The browser supports a number of different sound formats and allows you to control the number of times the sound is played.

Steps

Identify the appropriate sound for your page and open the document that contains the HTML code for the page.

Embedded Sound for Plug-Ins (Netscape and Internet Explorer)

1. Insert the `<EMBED>` tag in the page. Set the `SRC` attribute to the URL of the sound file.

```
<BODY>
<EMBED SRC="sound.mid">
</BODY>
```

2. There are other attributes you can add to the **<EMBED>** tag that are relevant to sound files. To have the sound start automatically when loaded, include the **AUTOSTART** attribute and set it equal to **TRUE**. **AUTOSTART** can also be set to **FALSE** in the opposite case.

```
<BODY>
<EMBED SRC="sound.mid" AUTOSTART=TRUE>
</BODY>
```

<BGSOUND> **Tag (Internet Explorer)**

1. Insert the **<BGSOUND>** tag in the body of the page. The location of the tag within the body is not important; the sound will be played as soon as the page is loaded, regardless of the location of the tag. No closing tag is required.

```
<BODY>
<!-- text and HTML markup tags -->
<BGSOUND>
<!-- more text and HTML markup tags -->
</BODY>
```

2. To identify the name of the sound file, include the attribute **SRC** and set it equal to the name of the file. For example, to include a file named **bam.wav**, use

```
<BODY>
<!-- text and HTML markup tags -->
<BGSOUND SRC="bam.wav">
<!-- more text and HTML markup tags -->
</BODY>
```

3. Like many other HTML tags, you can specify the full pathname of the file or include a URL that goes to a sound file on another computer. For example, if the sound file is located in the directory **sounds/loud**, use

```
<BODY>
<!-- text and HTML markup tags -->
<BGSOUND SRC="sounds/loud/bam.wav">
<!-- more text and HTML markup tags -->
</BODY>
```

If the file is accessible by HTTP from the computer **www.widgets.com** in the same directory as this example, you would enter

```
<BODY>
<!-- text and HTML markup tags -->
<BGSOUND SRC="http://www.widgets.com/sounds/loud/bam.wav">
<!-- more text and HTML markup tags -->
</BODY>
```

4. To play the sound more than once, you can use the LOOP attribute. Set the attribute equal to the number of times you want the sound played. To play the sound from the last step three times, enter

```
<BODY>
<!-- text and HTML markup tags -->
<BGSOUND SRC="sounds/loud/bam.wav" LOOP=3>
<!-- more text and HTML markup tags -->
</BODY>
```

5. To continuously play a sound in the background, set the LOOP attribute equal to INFINITE. Setting LOOP equal to −1 has the same effect. To make the sound in the last example play continuously, enter

```
<BODY>
<!-- text and HTML markup tags -->
<BGSOUND SRC="sounds/loud/bam.wav" LOOP=INFINITE>
<!-- more text and HTML markup tags -->
</BODY>
```

How It Works

When an <EMBED> element is encountered on a Web page, the browser checks the MIME type of the file referenced in the element. If the file is of a type supported by plug-ins installed with the browser, the file is downloaded and played, and the browser passes on the values of any attributes to the plug-in. If the file format is not supported by any plug-ins on the user's computer, an error message is displayed and the sound is not played.

When Internet Explorer loads a page that contains the <BGSOUND> tag, it loads the sound file specified by the SRC attribute. The browser then plays the sound the number of times indicated by the LOOP attribute. The browser will play the sound once if the LOOP attribute is missing.

Comments

If you use the <EMBED> method, note that a typical user will likely only have a few plug-ins of the most common type installed on his or her computer, so the user may not be able to play sound files not in common formats.

As of this writing, Internet Explorer supports three sound formats: WAV, AU, and MID (MIDI). Sound files in other formats will not be played by Internet Explorer. Note that <BGSOUND> is an HTML extension supported only by Internet Explorer. Other browsers, such as Netscape and Mosaic, will skip over the tag and not load or play the specified sound. You can find updated information about <BGSOUND> on the Web at the URL http://www.microsoft.com/ie/.

COMPLEXITY

INTERMEDIATE

18.5 How do I...
Include a Director application?

COMPATIBILITY: MICROSOFT INTERNET EXPLORER, NETSCAPE
NAVIGATOR, DIRECTOR

Problem

I have a multimedia presentation I have created using Macromedia Director. I want to include this on my Web site and have people view it, even if they don't have a copy of Director. How can I include a Director application in my Web page and make it visible to as many people as possible?

Technique

Macromedia has introduced Shockwave, a method of including Director movies on a Web page. Shockwave consists of two parts: an application called Afterburner that compresses Director movies into a special format, and a browser plug-in called Shockwave that can read the Afterburner-compressed files and display them in the browser. This method allows designers to create high-quality interactive multimedia applications that can include sound and video, and can even react to user input.

Steps

Within Director, create a standard Director movie for your specific project, and save it as a Director file.

1. Drag the icon for the Director movie onto the icon for Afterburner, or start up Afterburner, and use it to locate the Director movie you want to convert.

2. When prompted, give the file name for the compressed file. This file name should end in `.dcr` (as in `movie.dcr`) to help identify the file as a Shockwave file.

3. Place the converted file into the appropriate directory on your Web server.

4. Now open the HTML document in which you want to include the Shockwave movie.

5. At the appropriate location in the file, insert the `<EMBED>` tag and include the `SRC` attribute, setting it equal to the URL of the Shockwave movie.

```
<P>Here is a Shockwave movie:</P>
<EMBED SRC="movie.dcr">
```

6. You can also include the `HEIGHT` and `WIDTH` attributes to reserve space in the browser window for the movie.

```
<P>Here is a Shockwave movie:</P>
<EMBED SRC="movie.dcr" HEIGHT=150 WIDTH=275>
```

7. The `ALT` attribute can also be included to display alternative text if the browser can't show the Shockwave movie (if, for example, a user has a text-only browser or does not have the Shockwave plug-in).

```
<P>Here is a Shockwave movie:</P>
<EMBED SRC="movie.dcr" HEIGHT=150 WIDTH=275 ALT="My shockwave movie!">
```

8. The `ALIGN` attribute can also be used to align the Shockwave movie onto a particular side of the browser window, taking as its values the same values as the `<IMG>` element.

```
<P>Here is a Shockwave movie:</P>
<EMBED SRC="movie.dcr" HEIGHT=150 WIDTH=275 ALT="My shockwave movie!"
ALIGN=LEFT>
```

A screen shot of the process of "burning" a Director movie into a Shockwave file is shown in Figure 18-2.

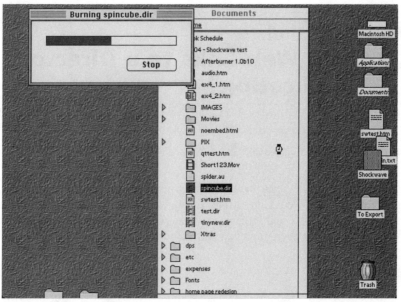

Figure 18-2 "Burning" a Shockwave movie from a Director movie

How It Works

The Afterburner application reads in a Director movie and then compresses it to create a smaller file (which takes less time to transfer across the net.) On the user's end, when he or she encounters a page with a Shockwave movie referenced in an <EMBED> tag, the browser checks to see if the Shockwave plug-in is available. If the plug-in is available, the movie is downloaded and the plug-in used to uncompress the movie and display it within the browser window. If the plug-in is not available, an error message is displayed and the movie is not shown.

Comments

The only current way to create Shockwave movies is through Director, a powerful, but rather expensive multimedia application. If you don't have Director, you can still include Shockwave movies created elsewhere, but you cannot create your own. Also, while Afterburner does a good job compressing Director movies, the files can still be rather large and take considerable time to download, especially for people with slower modems. Keep file size in mind when creating Shockwave movies.

COMPLEXITY
ADVANCED

18.6 How do I...
Add Web links to a Director application?

COMPATIBILITY: MICROSOFT INTERNET EXPLORER, NETSCAPE
NAVIGATOR, DIRECTOR

Problem

I've created a Director movie that I plan to convert into a Shockwave movie to include on my Web page. I would like to have the movie include links to other Web pages within the movie itself, so that the user can click on something in the movie and automatically go to that page. How do I add Web links to a Director application?

Technique

You can use Lingo, a scripting language built into Director, to include links to Web pages for specific parts of the movie. This can become quite complicated depending on the sophistication of the movie, but in this case we will provide a simple example that shows the essentials of including Web links in a Director/Shockwave movie.

Steps

Open your Director movie in Director. (This How-To assumes you have Director, which is essential in the creation of Shockwave movies.)

1. Select the cast member (portion of the movie, such as graphic element) to serve as the link. The element you choose will depend on the type and number of links you plan to include in your movie.

2. Double-click on that cast member to open it in the Paint window.

3. Select the script button, in the menu bar in the top center of the Paint window. This will open a new script window that you can edit.

4. In the script window, enter

```
on mouseUp
    goToNetPage("test.html")
end
```

where `"test.html"` is replaced with the URL of the page you want to link.

5. Close the script window, then close the Paint window. Save the movie in Director format and, if you are finished with any other modifications to the movie, quit Director.

6. The Director movie can then be converted into Shockwave format using the process described in How-To 18.5. The completed Shockwave file will have the link to the page embedded in it, which will be activated when the user clicks on that element of the movie.

A screen shot of the process of including the script in the Director movie is shown in Figure 18-3.

How It Works

When a user clicks in a linked portion of a Shockwave movie, the Shockwave plug-in looks up the URL referenced in the script for that element. The plug-in then passes the URL on to the browser, which will leave the current page for the new page.

Comments

Links in a Shockwave movie are relative to the location of the movie, not to the page itself. Thus, when using links, the Shockwave creator must be careful to specify the path to the desired document relative to the location of the movie, not the page where the movie was shown.

Figure 18-3 Including a Web script in a Director movie

COMPLEXITY
ADVANCED

18.7   How do I...
Include an Astound/Studio M application in a Web page?

COMPATIBILITY: MICROSOFT INTERNET EXPLORER, NETSCAPE NAVIGATOR

Problem

I have a multimedia presentation that I created in Astound. I would like to include this on a Web page, but I want to make it as easy as possible for Web browsers to display the presentation. How do I include this presentation in a Web page?

Technique

Astound, a multimedia presentation package, and Studio M, a related multimedia program, are both popular applications by Astound, Inc. (formerly Gold Disk) that are used to create presentations for display on other computers or in print. Recently, Astound unveiled a technique for including Astound presentations directly on the Web, as an alternative to Shockwave. It combines compressed presentation files, like Shockwave, with a Java-based viewer that does not require a plug-in.

Steps

Create your multimedia presentation in either Astound or Studio M.

1. Save the project in either application as self-contained and purge any unused resources, to minimize the size of the file.

2. If you plan on installing the application over the network, start up your Internet connection. If you plan to save the file to the local disk and are using Windows 3.1, you will need to start your TCP/IP program so that the installer application will work correctly, even if you're not planning to start a network connection.

3. Start the Astound Web Installer (`AII.EXE`), available from the Astound Web site (`http://www.astoundinc.com/awp/awi.html`).

4. In the dialog box that appears, select the Astound or Studio M presentation you want to place on the Web.

5. Select the installation option you want: installation on the local disk or over the network. If you choose to install on the local disk, you will be prompted for the location on the disk where the file should be saved. If you choose to place the file on a remote server over the Internet, you will be prompted for the URL of that location.

6. The Web Installer utility also offers the option to create a Web page that includes a link to the converted file. You can select that or the No Web Page option, which will not create or modify any Web pages.

7. At this point, the Web Installer creates the file and stores it in the appropriate location.

8. If you did not choose to have the installer create a Web page with a link to the file, you can add a link to the Web page(s) of your choice. If you want the file to play in the entire browser window, you can add a simple hypertext link to the file:

```
<A HREF="project.ASN">My Astounding presentation</A>
```

9. However, if you want to embed the file within a Web page, you can use the `<EMBED>` command, as with previous multimedia examples. Place the `<EMBED>` tag in the appropriate place on the page and set the `SRC` attribute equal to the URL of the file.

```
My Astounding presentation:
<EMBED SRC="project.ASN">
```

10. You can reserve space for the file in the browser window by including the `HEIGHT` and `WIDTH` attributes and setting them equal to the size of the file screen, in pixels.

```
My Astounding presentation:
<EMBED SRC="project.ASN" HEIGHT=100 WIDTH=125>
```

How It Works

The Web Installer program converts an Astound or Studio M file into a format suited for distribution over the Internet. This includes adding a small (20 K) Java applet that replaces the need for a plug-in to display the file. When a browser encounters an ASN file in a Web page, it loads the file, which includes the Java applet. The applet serves as the player for the multimedia file on the screen.

Comments

While the ASN files don't require a separate plug-in to be viewed, they do require that a browser have Java enabled in order to view the presentation. If the browser is not Java-aware or the user has turned off Java, the presentation cannot be viewed. Also, the Web Installer program was, as of this writing, available only for Windows. A Macintosh version is reportedly under development.

COMPLEXITY
ADVANCED

18.8   How do I...
Embed a VRML space?

COMPATIBILITY: MICROSOFT INTERNET EXPLORER, NETSCAPE
NAVIGATOR

Problem

I have created a three-dimensional world using VRML that I would like to share with people on the Web. I would prefer to have them be able to view it directly from their Web browsers and not have to start a separate VRML browser to view it. How do I embed a VRML space into a Web page?

Technique

A number of different methods exist for embedding VRML (Virtual Reality Modeling Language) spaces, or worlds, into Web pages. Most require that some kind of plug-in be installed on the user's machine, although Microsoft Internet Explorer provides a more seamless approach to including VRML spaces within Web pages.

Steps

Create a VRML space in the application of your choice, and place it on your Web server in the appropriate location. Open an HTML document in which you want to include the VRML space and locate the portion of the document where the VRML space will go.

1. Netscape Navigator 3 comes with the Live3D plug-in, which can be used to display VRML spaces embedded in documents. To embed a VRML space in a document that can be read by Live3D, use the **<EMBED>** tag and set the **SRC** attribute equal to the URL of the VRML file:

```
Here is a VRML space:
<EMBED SRC="myspace.wrl">
```

2. You can reserve space for the VRML display on the screen by including the **HEIGHT** and **WIDTH** attributes and setting them equal to the size of the VRML display area, in pixels.

```
Here is a VRML space:
<EMBED SRC="myspace.wrl" HIGHT=300 WIDTH=400>
```

3. There are a number of other VRML plug-ins that will work with Netscape and Internet Explorer, including Cosmo Player, CyberHub Client, Topper, VR Scout, Vrealm, and WIRL. Most of these plug-ins are supported for Windows 95 and Windows NT only, although there is increasing support for the Macintosh and UNIX systems. All of these use similar **<EMBED>** commands to support displaying VRML spaces, but some may use proprietary attributes that may be of interest. Check out these plug-ins. The Netscape site has a detailed, updated list of VRML and other plug-ins, with links to their sites for more information. How-To 10.10 also has additional information.

4. Internet Explorer 3 supports a more seamless approach to including VRML spaces in Web sites. Simply use the **<IMG>** tag and set the **VRML** attribute equal to the location of the VRML space.

```
Here is a VRML space:
<IMG VRML="myspace.wrl">
```

5. You can still use the **SRC** attribute and set it equal to a regular image. The normal image will appear on browsers that don't support the **VRML** attribute in the **<IMG>** tag (that is, every browser except Internet Explorer 3 and later versions).

```
Here is a VRML space:
<IMG VRML="myspace.wrl" SRC="stillpic.gif>
```

6. As with any other case of the **<IMG>** tag, you can include **WIDTH** and **HEIGHT** attributes and include alternative text in the **ALT** attribute for browsers that don't support or aren't loading images of any kind.

```
Here is a VRML space:
<IMG VRML="myspace.wrl" SRC="stillpic.gif" HEIGHT=300 WIDTH=400 ALT="VRML
space">
```

How It Works

As with other instances of `<EMBED>`, when the browser encounters an `<EMBED>` tag, it checks the MIME type of the file being requested with the available plug-ins installed with the browser. If a suitable plug-in exists, the VRML space is downloaded and displayed in the browser window. If no plug-in that supports VRML can be found, an error message is shown by the browser and the VRML space is not displayed.

Microsoft Internet Explorer has built-in support for VRML spaces. If the `VRML` attribute is found in an `<IMG>` tag, that VRML space is loaded and displayed instead of a normal image. For other browsers, the `VRML` attribute is ignored and the normal image, as specified by the `SRC` attribute, or the `ALT` text, if no other image is available, is shown in its place.

Comments

VRML spaces can become very complex and large, and hence the files can take some time to download. Take this into account when designing Web pages: People may not have the patience to wait several minutes for a VRML space to download.

COMPLEXITY
ADVANCED

18.9 How do I...
Include a multimedia object to maximize cross-browser support?

COMPATIBILITY: MICROSOFT INTERNET EXPLORER, NETSCAPE
NAVIGATOR

Problem

I have a multimedia file that I want to include in a Web page. How can I write the HTML for the file so that it can be viewed in the largest possible number of browsers?

Technique

Since different browsers support different tags for multimedia files, it takes a little effort to write HTML so that the file can be viewed in a number of different browsers. One important trick is the `<NOEMBED>` tag, which can be used to designate HTML markup to be displayed if the file requested in the `<EMBED>` tag cannot be used.

Steps

Open your HTML document and locate the areas where files are embedded or otherwise included.

1. After an `<EMBED>` tag, you can place a `<NOEMBED>...</NOEMBED>` pair of tags, and place HTML markup to display if the file requested in the `<EMBED>` file cannot be displayed. For example, to display alternative markup if a browser does not support `<EMBED>`:

```
<EMBED SRC="myspace.wrl" HIGHT=300 WIDTH=400>
<NOEMBED>
<EM>You need a VRML plug-in to view this</EM>
</NOEMBED>
```

2. If the browser does not support an inline version of a particular file using the `<EMBED>` command, you can add a link to a version of the file within the `<NOEMBED>` content and allow the user to view the file using an outside helper application, if any.

```
<EMBED SRC="myspace.wrl" HIGHT=300 WIDTH=400>
<NOEMBED>
<EM><A HREF="myspace.wrl">Check out my VRML space</A></EM>
</NOEMBED>
```

3. Other objects can be placed within the `<NOEMBED>` region, such as `<OBJECT>`. This allows for support by browsers that can use the `<OBJECT>` content but cannot handle the `<EMBED>` files. This can be especially useful since Netscape supports `<EMBED>` and `<NOEMBED>`, but not `<OBJECT>`, while Microsoft Internet Explorer supports `<EMBED>` and `<OBJECT>`, but not `<NOEMBED>`.

```
<EMBED SRC="myspace.wrl" HIGHT=300 WIDTH=400>
<NOEMBED>
<OBJECT CODEBASE="myspace.class">
</NOEMBED>
```

An example of a Web browser that shows the text in the `<NOEMBED>` tag because it doesn't support `<EMBED>` is shown in Figure 18-4. In this particular case, the browser is from America Online for the Macintosh.

How It Works

If a browser supports the `<EMBED>` command, it will ignore the content contained between the `<NOEMBED>` and `</NOEMBED>` tags. However, browsers that do not support `<EMBED>` will ignore it and the `<NOEMBED>` commands, allowing the content between the `<NOEMBED>` and the `</NOEMBED>` tags to be displayed. This content can include text, images, other embedded files, and any other valid HTML markup.

Figure 18-4 An example of the use of `<NOEMBED>`

Comments

If a browser supports the `<EMBED>` command, but not the type of file requested, it should not display what is contained between the `<NOEMBED>` and `</NOEMBED>` tags. In that case nothing will be displayed. Thus, it's useful to describe any embedded files in "plain view" in the document, not hidden in a `<NOEMBED>` region that might not be displayed.

CHAPTER 19

FRAMES

19

FRAMES

How do I...

Frames are nonstandard additions to HTML, added to Netscape's browser and then adopted by the Internet Explorer. They are powerful features that allow a page to be broken into many different sections that, while related, operate independently of each other.

19.1   Include Frames in My Web Page

Frames are a way in Netscape and Explorer to divide the browser window into a number of independent sections, each displaying a separate document. A link in a document in one frame can load a document in another frame. This How-To discusses how to create frames in a Web page and link documents to different frames.

19.2   Make Frames Go Away

Many times, frames are fine for some information, but limit the view for other information. This How-To shows how to link from a page in a frame to a page without a frame.

19.3   Use One Frame to Index Another That Will Display the Contents

One of the most common uses for frames is to split the screen into two columns. One column is a table of contents or an index. The other column is content based on what the user selects in the first column. This How-To shows one way to accomplish this.

19.4   Add a Floating Frame to My Web Page

Internet Explorer allows the creation of in-line frames—frames that float on a Web page just as an image does. This How-To shows how you can create in-line frames.

19.5   Create a Borderless Frame

There are times when you want a frame on a page, but you don't want that frame to have a border. This How-To shows you how to create frames without borders.

19.6   Create Frames with Borders Between Them

You may now and then want to separate frames with a color border. This How-To shows you how to create frames with a color border between them.

19.7   Minimize Work When Maintaining Frame and Non-Frame Versions of My Pages

You are creating pages for browsers that support frames, yet since you don't want to ignore people on older browsers, you are also maintaining non-frame versions of your pages. This How-To will help you minimize the work.

COMPLEXITY
ADVANCED

19.1 How do I...
Include frames in my Web page?

COMPATIBILITY: NETSCAPE 2, INTERNET EXPLORER 2

Problem

I see some pages around the Web where the screen is broken into separate windows or frames. How can I add frames to my documents?

Technique

Frames are created through the use of frame documents, which in turn are created by using **<FRAMESET>** tags and **<FRAME>** tags. Frame documents are not all that different from regular HTML documents. In frame documents, the **<FRAMESET>** container is used in place of a **<BODY>** container. The **<FRAMESET>** container describes the different HTML "sub" documents that will make up the frames on the page.

The basic structure of a frame document is

```
<HTML>
<HEAD>
</HEAD>
<FRAMESET>
other FRAMESETS or FRAME tags or NOFRAME tags
</FRAMESET>
</HTML>
```

The **<FRAMESET>...</FRAMESET>** tags are used as the container of the frame document, and also to define the size of the frames. The tag has two attributes, **ROWS** and **COLS**. **ROWS** describes the numbers of rows of the screen to be allocated to each frame. **COLS** describes the number of columns of the screen that each frame in the document will be allocated. These numbers may be given as an absolute number or a percentage value, or an ***** may be used to indicate that the corresponding frame should receive all the remaining space. For example:

```
<FRAMESET ROWS="50%, 25%,25%>
```

creates three frames. The first frame is twice as long as the other two frames.

```
<FRAMESET COLS=150,*>
```

creates two frames. The first has a fixed column width of 150 pixels; the second receives the remaining part of the screen.

It is possible to nest **<FRAMESET>...</FRAMESET>** tags inside of other **<FRAMESET>...</FRAMESET>** tags in order to create all sorts of effects.

The second tag used to create frames is the **<FRAME>** tag. It defines a frame within a frameset and has six possible attributes. The **<FRAME>** tag syntax is

```
<FRAME SRC="url" NAME="window_name" MARGINWIDTH="value"
MARGINHEIGHT= "value" SCROLLING="yes|no|auto" {NORESIZE}>
```

SRC is the URL of the source document to be displayed in this frame.

NAME is an optional attribute that assigns a name to a frame so that the frame may be used by links in other documents. All names must begin with an alphanumeric character. The following names are reserved, though, as they have special meanings:

- **_blank-->**: Always load this link into a new, unnamed window.

- **_self-->**: Always load this link over itself.

- **_parent-->**: Always load this link of its parent or itself if it has no parent.

- **_top-->**: Always load this link at the top level or itself if it is at the top level.

MARGINWIDTH: An optional attribute used to set the width of the margins of the frame. If used, the value is in pixels.

MARGINHEIGHT: The same as **MARGINWIDTH**, except that it controls the upper and lower margins of the frame.

SCROLLING: Used to describe whether the frame should have a scroll bar. Setting this attribute to **yes** means the frame always has a scroll bar. Setting the attribute to **no** means the frame never has a scroll bar. Use of the **auto** setting displays a scroll bar when needed. This is an optional attribute, with **auto** being the default.

NORESIZE: An optional attribute. If a **NORESIZE** appears in the tag, the user will not be able to change the size of the frame. By default, all frames can be resized.

For example:

```
<FRAME SRC="http://www.myserver.com/title.html" NORESIZE>
```

loads the document retrieved at **www.myserver.com/title.html** into the defined frame. Because of the **NORESIZE** attribute, the user cannot change the size of this frame.

Finally, the **<NOFRAME>...</NOFRAME>** tag may be used in conjunction with the other frame tags. Use the **<NOFRAME>** tag to provide alternative information to browsers that are non-frame-capable clients. A frame-capable client ignores all items found inside the **<NOFRAME>** tag.

For example:

```
<NOFRAME>
The information on the page makes use of frame technology. For best results,
use the latest version of Netscape.
</NOFRAME>
```

This code causes the message between the tags to be displayed by any browser that cannot render frames.

Steps

The following steps show one way that you can add frames to your documents.

1. Think about the number of frames you want to use in your document and the screen layout. It may help to design the initial screen layout on paper. This example contains three documents in three frames: a header in a top frame, and two equally sized frames underneath on left and right parts of the screen. These frames contain a graphic and a description, respectively.

A quick sketch of the layout:

```
|          Header          |

|   Graphic    |   Description    |
|   frame      |   frame          |
```

2. Compose the individual documents that will make up the individual frames. This example has three frames, therefore three separate documents. Each document is as follows:

A very simple header document, `header.html`:

```
<HTML>
<!-- header.html -->
<!-- This document is used as the header frame for the frameset -->
<HEAD><TITLE>Cartoons</TITLE></HEAD>
<BODY>
<center>
<H1>A Cartoon</H1>
Enhanced with Netscape 2.0 Frames
</center>
</BODY>
</HTML>
```

The document `picture.html` contains the graphic you want to show in the second (left side) frame:

```
<HTML>
<HEAD><TITLE>A toon</TITLE></HEAD>
<!-- picture.html -->
<!-- this document simply loads a picture -->
<BODY>
<IMG ALIGN=CENTER SRC="slow.GIF">
<P><small>My favorite cartoon<Sup>1
<P>
1</SUP>By Jz</small>
</BODY>
</HTML>
```

Finally, `facts.html` contains the information you want to show in the
third (right side) frame:

```
<HTML>
<!-- facts.html -->
<!-- simple document that contains information to be shown in a frame -->
<HEAD><TITLE>Facts</TITLE></HEAD>
<BODY>
<H2>Some notes about cartoons</H2>
Cartoons have been around for a long time.  Almost as soon as papers
first came into existence, cartoons started popping up in them.  Today
comics can be found in almost any language known to man.
<P>
Cartoons serve many functions:
<UL><LI>To entertain
<LI>To enlighten
<LI>To inform
</UL>
Or some combination of all three.
<P>
A good source of cartoons on the web is
<A HREF="http://www.phlab.missouri.edu/~c617145/comix.html">
Comics 'n Stuff</A>
<P>
<P>
</BODY>
</HTML>
```

These three documents are all quite simple, but when combined into
frames on a screen, they can be quite effective.

3. Create the document that will hold the three frames. This can be done with
any text editor. This document will begin and end like any other HTML
document, with the **<HTML>** tags.

4. Define the first frameset. This is done with the **<FRAMESET>** tag:

```
<FRAMESET ROWS="70,*">
```

This tag, in effect, splits the screen into two horizontal sections. The first
section is 70 rows long. The remaining section occupies the rest of the
screen.

5. Add the first frame with the **<FRAME>** tag:

```
<FRAME SRC="header.html" NORESIZE>
```

This tag causes the document **header.html** to display in the first frame,
the one designated to be 70 rows long. The user cannot resize this frame.

6. Add a second frameset that will be nested into the first frameset. This is
done with

```
<FRAMESET COLS="50%,*">
```

This tag creates another frameset in the area of the screen not occupied by the `header.html` frame. This new frameset consists of two frames of equal size.

7. Add the second and third documents to their respective frames.

```
<FRAME SRC="picture.html" MARGINHEIGHT=0 MARGINWIDTH=4 SCROLLING=no ⇐
NAME="toon">
<FRAME SRC="facts.html" NAME="story" NORESIZE>
```

This works just as the `<FRAME>` tag did in step 5, only these frames are included in the second frameset.

8. Close the two framesets.

```
</FRAMESET>
</FRAMESET>
```

9. Include some information for browsers that do not support frames. This is done by inserting information between `<NOFRAME>...</NOFRAME>` tags. The information included here can be anything from a simple message to a non-frame version of your document. For a sample of this, you may view the entire document, shown at the end of this section.

10. Save and name the document. For this example, use `toon_dem.html`. The entire document:

```
<HTML>
<TITLE>About Cartoons</TITLE>

<!-- Create the first frameset and load the first frame -->

<FRAMESET ROWS="70,*">
<FRAME SRC="header.html" MARGINHEIGHT=0 MARGINWIDTH=0 SCROLLING="no" NORESIZE>

<!-- Create the second frameset and load the second and third frames -->

<FRAMESET COLS="50%,*">
<FRAME SRC="picture.html" MARGINHEIGHT=0 MARGINWIDTH=4 SCROLLING=no ⇐
NAME="toon">
<FRAME SRC="facts.html" NAME="story" NORESIZE>

</FRAMESET>
</FRAMESET>
<NOFRAME>

<!-- The following is used by non-frame-aware browsers -->

<H2>Cartoons</H2>
<IMG ALIGN=LEFT SRC="slow.GIF">
Cartoons have been around for a long time.  Almost as soon as papers
first came into existence cartoons started popping up in them.  Today
comics can be found in almost any language known to man.
<P>
Cartoons serve many functions:
```

continued on next page

continued from previous page

```
<UL><LI>To entertain
<LI>To enlighten
<LI>To inform
</UL>
Or some combination of all three.
<P>
A good source of cartoons on the web is
<A HREF="http://www.phlab.missouri.edu/~c617145/comix.html">
Comics 'n Stuff</A>
<HR>
Note:this is one of my favorite cartoons<P>
</NOFRAME>

</HTML>
```

11. View the document to make sure it looks the way you think it should. Figure 19-1 shows how the sample document looks when viewed by a browser that supports forms.

12. Just to be cautious, view your document with a browser that does not support frames, to see if it looks okay. Figure 19-2 shows what the sample document looks like when seen through an older version of Netscape.

13. Experiment with different frame settings.

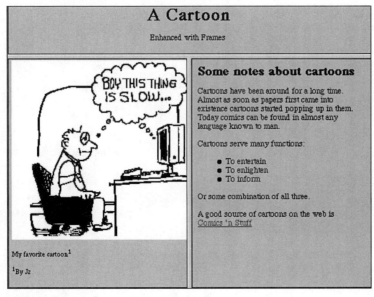

Figure 19-1 A frames demonstration

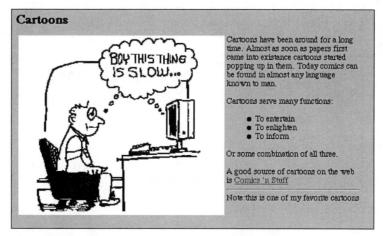

Figure 19-2 The sample document when viewed with Netscape 1.1

How It Works

The first `<FRAMESET>` tag splits the screen into two parts: a top section with a length of 70 pixels and a bottom section that occupies the remaining portion of the screen. The first `<FRAME SRC>` tag loads the `header.html` document into the top frame. The next `<FRAMESET>` tag splits the remaining section of the screen into two equal frames. The next two `<FRAME SRC>` tags load the `picture.html` and the `facts.html` documents into these frames. When a frames-aware browser encounters these tags, it renders the documents in three separate frames.

The `<NOFRAME>` tags render information on browsers that do not support frames.

Comments

Frames are a new, dynamic, and powerful addition to HTML. This example gives a general overview of frames. It only covers the basics. If you are interested in exploring frames further, check the latest online documentation at the Netscape home page: `http://home.netscape.com/`.

It should also be noted here that frames, while being powerful tools, are not part of the HTML standard, as of this writing. They are in fact only supported by the latest version of the Netscape browser. If you want to create HTML documents that look relatively the same from one browser to the next, you probably do not want to use frames.

19.2 How do I...
Make frames go away?

COMPATIBILITY: NETSCAPE 2, INTERNET EXPLORER

Problem

Frames are great for some things, but they really limit what my readers can see for other things. Can I make a page in a frame link to another page that is not in a frame?

Technique

To create a link from a frame to a page that is not in a frame, you use the **TARGET** attribute. The **TARGET** attribute is attached to the **<A HEF>...</A>** tag with the form:

```
<A HREF="URL    TARGETt="name">
```

where **TARGET** is either the name of a frame (as assigned in a **<FRAME>** tag) or **TARGET** can be set to one of these special values:

SPECIAL VALUES FOR TARGET ATTRIBUTES	
`_top`	This will cause the URL specified in the HREF to load into the entire browser window, thus removing any frames.
`_blank`	This will cause the URL specified in the HREF to load into a new unnamed browser.
`_self`	This will cause the URL specified in the HREF to load over the current window.
`_parent`	This will cause the URL specified in the HREF to load into the frameset's parent window.

For this example, we will be using the **_top** setting.

Steps

The following steps show one way to create links from frames to documents not in frames.

1. Create a document that contains frames.

2. In one of the frames, include a **<A HREF>** tag with a **TARGET** attribute set to **_top**. For example:

```
<A HREF="index.html"> target=_top>Home</A>
```

3. Check your document to make sure it works the way you think it should.

How It Works

When the browser references a link with the **TARGET** set to **_top**, it places the contents of that link in a new window. Thus, any frames you may have had on the referring page are not used.

Comments

The next section shows this tag at work. Note that, although the use of frames may be a more advanced concept, removing frames is actually quite simple.

COMPLEXITY
INTERMEDIATE

19.3 How do I...
Use one frame to index another that will display the contents?

COMPATIBILITY: NETSCAPE 2, INTERNET EXPLORER

Problem

One thing I see a lot of people doing with frames is splitting the browser window into two sections. One section contains an index of table of contents. The second section contains corresponding information that will pop up after selecting something from the first window. How can I do this?

Technique

To create an index or a table of contents that allows users a choice of options, then updates or displays whatever they choose in another corresponding window, you use the **<FRAMESET>** element to split the screen into two separate frames. Create one frame that will contain the specified information, and label this frame with the name attribute in the **<FRAME>** tag. For example:

```
<FRAME  SRC="info.html" NAME="ifno">
```

Create another frame. This frame will contain links to the first frame. To make sure this information loads in the first frame, you specify the frame's name in the **<A HREF>** tag. For example:

```
<A  HREF="links.html" TARGET="info:>Information</A>
```

Steps

The following steps show one way to create an index that displays information in another frame.

1. Decide on the layout you wish to use. For this example, we will be using a very simple two frame structure. The frame on the left will hold an index—in this case, cartoons to choose from. The frame on the right will contain the results of the selection.

2. Decide on a name for the frame you wish the information to appear in, once something is selected in the index. For this example, we will use the name "toon".

3. Create the base document that will hold the **<FRAMESET>** and **<FRAME>** tags. The document will look like the following:

```
<HTML>
<TITLE>Frames</TITLE>
<FRAMESET COLS="25%,*">
<BODY BGCOLOR="FFFFFF">
<NOFRAMES>
You need frames for this example
</NOFRAMES>
<FRAME SRC="toon_list.html"  MARGINHEIGHT=0 MARGINWIDTH=0 SCROLLING="yes"
NORESIZE>
<FRAME SRC="slow.gif" NAME="toon">
</BODY>
</FRAMESET>
</HTML>
```

4. Create the HTML document that will act as the index. Make sure each of the links that should display its information in the **"toon"** frame includes **toon** in the target. For example:

```
<HTML> <TITLE>Choices</TITLE> <BODY BGCOLOR="FFFFFF">
<H3>Pick a toon</H3>
<UL>
<A Href="cc/cc1001.GIF"  target="toon">October  1st</A><P>
<A Href="cc/cc1002.GIF"  target="toon">October  2nd</A><P>
<A Href="cc/cc1003.GIF"  target="toon">October  3rd</A><P>
<A Href="cc/cc1004.GIF"  target="toon">October  4th</A><P>
<A Href="cc/cc1007.GIF"  target="toon">October  7th</A><P>
<A Href="cc/cc1008.GIF"  target="toon">October  8th</A><P>
<A Href="cc/cc1009.GIF"  target="toon">October  9th</A><P>
<A Href="cc/cc1010.GIF"  target="toon">October  10th</A><P>
<A Href="cc/cc1011.GIF"  target="toon">October  11th</A><P>
<A Href="cc/cc1012.GIF"  target="toon">October  12th</A><P>
</UL>
<A Href="index.html" target=_top>Home</A>
</HTML>
```

5. View the document to make sure it looks and acts like you think it should. Figure 19-3 shows a two frame example.

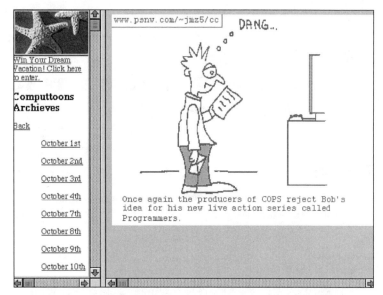

Figure 19-3 Two frames: one that is an index and the other that shows the results of that index

How It Works

When the browser encounters an **<A HREF> </A>** tag in a frame, if that tag contains a target that is a different frame, the results of the **<A HREF></A>** tag will be displaying in the targeted frame.

Comments

This example could have been smoother if, instead of only displaying the GIF in the **toon** frame, we had created an HTML file for each **toon** pointed to by the **TOON_LIST** frame. This way it would have been possible to add background colors and links.

This How-To is given an Intermediate complexity as, once you understand the concept of frames creating this sort of display, it is not all that complex.

19.4 How do I...
Add a floating frame to my Web page?

COMPATIBILITY: INTERNET EXPLORER 3

Problem

When I'm using Internet Explorer, I notice that sometimes I come across frames that seem to be in the middle of non-framed documents. How can I add these "floating" frames to my pages?

Technique

Internet Explorer allows you to treat frames of HTML code much like you would an image, by allowing you to insert the frame into a document and align text to it. The tag used for this is `<IFRAME>...</IFRAME>`. The attributes for `<IFRAME>` are

`ALIGN=LEFT|CENTER|RIGHT`

`FRAMEBORDER=1|0` (1 for border)

`HEIGHT`

`WIDTH`

`MARGINHEIGHT`

`MARGINWIDTH`

`NAME="name to use in TARGET"`

`SRC="URL"`

`SCROLLING="yes|no"`

All the size attributes are in pixels.

Steps

Follow these steps to add in-line (floating) frames to your Explorer documents:

1. Decide on the layout of the document. For this example, we will be using a document that contains a list of links to cartoons. Once the user selects a cartoon from this list, it is displayed in an in-line frame.

2. Create the document that will hold the in-line frame.

3. Add the `<IFRAME>...<IFRAME>` tag. Make sure to set the `NAME` and `HEIGHT` and `WIDTH` attributes. For example:

```
<IFRAME SRC="slow.gif"> Name="itoon" Align="right" Width=384
Height=288></IFRAME>
```

4. Add the appropriate links to the document, making sure the `TARGET` attribute is set to the name of the `IFRAME`. For example:

```
<A Href="cc/cc1001.GIF" target="itoon">Ocotber 1st</A>
```

5. Check the documents to make sure everything looks and works like you think it should. Figure 19-4 shows one example.

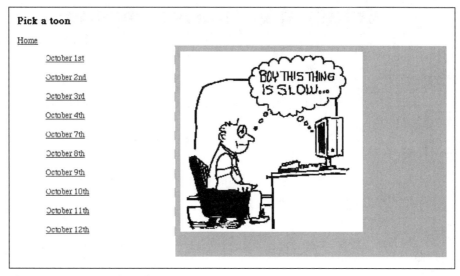

Figure 19-4 An in-line frame

How It Works

When Internet Explorer encounters an `<IFRAME>...</IFRAME>` tag, it creates a frame in the document and places whatever is pointed to by the `SRC` attribute into that frame. The whole process works very much like loading an image or graphic into a document.

Comments

Notice that the `<IFRAME>...</IFRAME>` tag needs to be closed. Also, in the future, there may be a difference between in-line and floating frames, but as of this writing they seem to be one and the same. My guess would be that the reason that the `<IFRAME>` tag is an open tag is that it is meant to allow Web designers to someday build frames "on the fly" by entering tags and text between the `<IFRAME>` tags, much like forms work.

It would be nice if Netscape had the ability to recognize in-line frames.

COMPLEXITY
BEGINNING

19.5   How do I...
Create a borderless frame?

COMPATIBILITY: INTERNET EXPLORER

Problem

I would like to use frames, but I don't want them to have any borders. How do I accomplish this?

Technique

To create frames without borders, use the `FRAMEBORDER` attribute in a `<FRAME>` or `<IFRAME>...</IFRAME>` tag, and set it to `0`.

Steps

Follow these simple steps to create a frame without a border.

1. Find or create a document with frames.

2. Decide on which frames you wish to make borderless.

3. Set the `FRAMEBORDER` attribute to 0 in the `<FRAME>` tag.

`<FRAM\E   SRC="slow.gif" NAME="toon" FRAMEBORDER=0>`

4. View the document to make sure it works and looks like you think it should. Figure 19-5 shows a document with frames without borders.

How It Works

When Internet Explorer encounters a `<FRAME>` or `<IFRAME>` tag, it checks to see if that tag contains a `FRAMEBORDER` attribute. If it does and if the attribute is set to 0, then no border is displayed for that frame.

Comments

The `<FRAMEBORDER>` tag can help create seamless pages with frames. Notice that though frames may be a more advanced concept, removing their borders is quite simple.

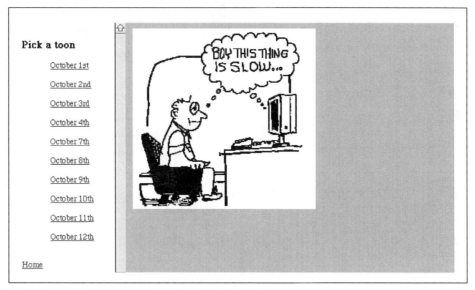

Figure 19-5 Document with a borderless frame

COMPLEXITY
INTERMEDIATE

19.6   How do I...
Create frames with borders between them?

COMPATIBILITY: INTERNET EXPLORER

Problem

I would like to separate my frames with a color border. How do I accomplish this?

Technique

To create frames with a color border between them in Explorer, you use the combination of **FRAMESPACING** and **FRAME BORDER** in the **<FRAMESET>** tag. You also use either **BACKGROUND** or **BGCOLOR** attributes in **<BODY>** tag. Setting **FRAMESPACING** to a number greater than **0** will result in space between frames. This allows any background or background color set in the **<BODY>** tag to display.

Steps

The following steps show how to create documents with frames that have colored borders between them.

1. Decide on the layout of your document.

2. Create the document that will hold the frames. Make sure that you include a **<BODY>** tag and set the **BGCOLOR** to the color of the border you wish to place between the frames. For example:

```
<BODY BGCOLOR="0000FF">
```

3. Add the **<FRAMESET>** tag to the document. Make sure to include the **FRAMESPACING** attribute and set it to a significant number of pixels. For example:

```
<FRAMESET COLS="25%",*" FRAMEBORDER=0 FRAMESPACING=20>
```

4. Add the **<FRAME>** tags to the document. The final document will now resemble, at least in structure:

```
<HTML>
<TITLE>Frames</TITLE>
<BODY BGCOLOR="0000FF">
<FRAMESET COLS="25%,*" FRAMEBORDER=0 FRAMESPACING=20>
<FRAME SRC="toon_list.html"  MARGINHEIGHT=0
MARGINWIDTH=0 SCROLLING="yes" BORDERCOLOR="FF00FF" NORESIZE>
<FRAME SRC="slow.gif" NAME="toon" FRAMEBORDER=0>
</FRAMESET>
</BODY>
</HTML>
```

5. View the document to make sure it looks and acts the way you intended. Figure 19-6 shows a sample document with a colored border between frames.

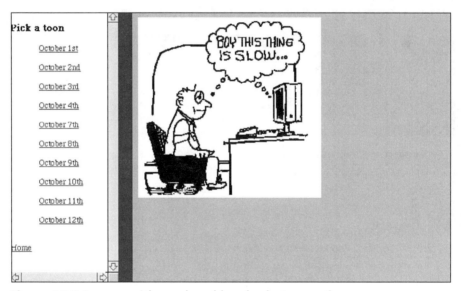

Figure 19-6 Frames with a colored border between them

How It Works

By setting `FRAMESPACING` to a significant number of pixels, space is created between frames, thereby letting the background color set in the `<BODY>` tag be seen.

Comments

By using `FRAMESPACING` and `FRAMEBORDER`, you can create some neat effects. The document used in this example will display only a blank blue background when viewed with Netscape.

COMPLEXITY
INTERMEDIATE

19.7 How do I...
Minimize work when maintaining frame and non-frame versions of my pages?

COMPATIBILITY: NETSCAPE 2, INTERNET EXPLORER

Problem

My pages use frames, but I am also using the `<NOFRAMES>` tag to also display versions of my pages without frames. I find this is a lot of work. What can I do to minimize this work?

Technique

Creating framed and non-framed versions of your pages can be quite time-consuming, but with a little planning, you can minimize the work.

Steps

The following steps show some techniques you may use when working with both framed and non-framed versions of your pages.

1. Take time to plan out your design so the non-framed version is as close to the framed version as possible. With a little forethought, it is possible to copy and paste changes from one to the other.

2. Record somewhere what frame files correspond to what non-framed versions.

3. Give the framed files and their corresponding non-frame files similar names.

How It Works

A little planning, design work and record keeping in the beginning stages can save a lot of time in the later updating stages.

Comments

Other techniques that might be possible are to use INCLUDE files to hold your text in both the frame and non-frame files. This would allow you to simply update the INCLUDE file. The downside to this is that many servers do not support INCLUDE files. Even if a sever does support INCLUDE files, they can put an added drain on the system, so this might be an extravagant use of INCLUDE files.

Perl programmers might be able to create scripts that would allow them to easily update a series of related framed and non-framed files.

A final note on frames: Many of these examples may be found on the accompanying Web page at `http://www.psnw.com/~jmz5/waite/frames`.

## CHAPTER 20

UNSUPPORTED, PROPOSED HTML FEATURES

20

UNSUPPORTED, PROPOSED HTML FEATURES

How do I...

The HTML standard has evolved over time. This evolution has led to the proposal and development of a myriad of possible HTML elements. Despite the development of an HTML 3.2 proposed standard, individuals and software manufacturers are constantly proposing or incorporating modifications to the proposed standard.

Chapters 15 through 19 address many elements of these types, particularly those that popular browsers implement. This chapter discusses many additional elements that are implemented only, if at all, in an exceedingly limited manner. The HTML 3.0 standard defined most of these elements; however, they do not appear in the HTML 3.2 proposed standard. Even so, with the way HTML evolves, these elements could potentially be resurrected, either by a future HTML standard or by the incorporation of support for the element into a popular browser. The fact that a particular element is not part of the "standard" has not seemed to discourage browser developers from creating their own browser-specific extended dialects.

With this in mind, you should be wary of using these features in your Web pages and expecting generic browsers to display them in any particular manner. Most browsers simply ignore unrecognized HTML elements, so in general, their inclusion should not adversely impact the presentation of your Web page. The How-To's in this chapter examine these elements, providing step-by-step instructions for using them within your Web pages. However, considering the nature of these elements, each How-To attempts to present alternatives that conform to the proposed HTML 3.2 standard.

20.1   Mark an Abbreviation or Acronym

In your document, you may refer to a number of abbreviations or acronyms that may require special formatting. This simple How-To explains how to use HTML tags to mark these items.

20.2   Tag Computer Commands and Arguments

In the course of writing your page, you may want to insert brief sections of computer commands or arguments. This How-To explains how you can format these text elements in HTML.

20.3   Identify a Proper Name

You may wish to identify proper names in your document, either for formatting purposes or to make the names easily extractable by indexing programs. This simple How-To explains how to identify proper names using HTML tags.

20.4   Denote Inserted or Deleted Text

Bills, contracts, and other legal documents often include sections that have been inserted or deleted since they were originally drawn up. This How-To explains how to easily include references to inserted or deleted sections of text.

20.5   Create a Multicolumn List

You may have information you would like to display in a series of lists, side by side, such as a comparison of the characteristics of different items. This How-To will explain how to use the WRAP attribute for bulleted lists in HTML 3 to create multicolumn lists.

20.6 Specify the Language Context for the Remainder of a Web Page

The WWW, as the name implies, is world-wide in scope. Developing multilingual documents is a growing concern in HTML. Several proposed mechanisms provide support for specifying the language of a particular Web page. In the How-To, you will learn how to use these mechanisms for selecting a language for a Web page.

20.7 Place an Embedded Quotation

Often you have a quotation you would like to insert into a document. This is very simple to do manually, but HTML provides more sophisticated ways of inserting quotations in pages, including using different quotation marks for different languages. This simple How-To explains how to add an embedded quotation to your page.

20.8 Align Text with Tabs

HTML provides elements to support the alignment of the textual content of your HTML documents. This How-To describes these elements, explains their usage, and provides concrete examples. In this How-To, you will learn how to add horizontal alignment elements to your HTML pages.

20.9 Insert Cautionary Notes

The HTML 3.0 standard introduced a mechanism for incorporating admonishments, such as warnings, cautions, and notes, into your Web page. This How-To details this process.

20.10 Add a Footnote

Scholarly works require that an author designate the source of an original idea or quotation. HTML 3.0 provides a means of specifying such footnotes. Where feasible, HTML 3.0 suggests such footnotes use pop-up windows to display the relevant information. In this How-To, you will learn how to add pop-up footnotes within your Web pages.

20.11 Place a Mathematical Equation in My Web Page

If your page covers topics in math, science, or engineering, you may need to display special mathematical symbols not available in normal ASCII text. This How-To explains how to insert various types of mathematical symbols, including characters, vectors, and matrices, in your page, and how to properly format complex mathematical equations.

20.12 Insert an Array into a Math Element

If your page covers topics in math, science, or engineering, you may run across the need to display mathematical arrays. This How-To explains how to insert arrays into your Web pages.

20.13   Change the Shape of a Link

Links have been limited to text and other objects, but HTML 3 provides a way to create a link within a part of an image by specifying the location and shape of the area in an image to serve as a link. This How-To shows how to create links of different shapes and embed them in images using HTML 3.

COMPLEXITY
BEGINNING

20.1   How do I...
Mark an abbreviation or acronym?

COMPATIBILITY: HTML 3

Problem

I have a page that includes a number of abbreviations and acronyms. I would like to call attention to them, but I don't require a specific physical style. Is there a generic way to call attention to these items in HTML?

Technique

HTML 3 supports two tags, **<ABBREV>** and **<ACRONYM>**, that can be used to mark abbreviations and acronyms, respectively. The physical style used for these items varies from browser to browser.

Steps

Open your document and locate the text you want to identify as an abbreviation or an acronym.

1. To identify an abbreviation, place the **<ABBREV>** tag at the beginning of the abbreviation and **</ABBREV>** at the end of the abbreviation:

```
The paper by Smith <ABBREV>et al.</ABBREV> shows how this can be done.
```

2. To identify an acronym, place the **<ACRONYM>** tag at the beginning of the abbreviation and **</ACRONYM>** at the end of the acronym:

```
The National Aeronautics and Space Administration, or
<ACRONYM>NASA</ACRONYM>, was founded in 1958.
```

How It Works

When a browser encounters either an **<ABBREV>** or an **<ACRONYM>** element, it formats the text contained between the opening and closing tags accordingly. The actual physical style applied to the text contained within these tags will be controlled by the browser viewing the document. Neither element creates a visual effect in Netscape's Navigator or Microsoft's Internet Explorer.

Comments

Because formatting applied to the **<ABBREV>** and **<ACRONYM>** tags will vary from browser to browser, it may be bold, italics, or something else entirely. Thus, it's better to refer to acronyms or abbreviations by content rather than by style. Because they are additions to HTML 3, neither **<ABBREV>** nor **<ACRONYM>** is supported by older browsers. Further, these elements do not appear in the HTML 3.2 standard, but browsers may choose to support them as nonstandard elements.

The original intent of these elements was to provide a logical character effect without necessarily any visual effect. For this purpose, no easy alternative is available in the current 3.2 standard, but since no visual effect is intended, the nonconforming use of these elements will not hurt the appearance of your Web page in most browsers.

COMPLEXITY
BEGINNING

20.2   How do I...
Tag computer commands and arguments?

COMPATIBILITY: HTML 1,2

Problem

On my page I would like to highlight names of computer programs and their arguments. I would like to format these samples differently than the standard text is formatted. How can I do this in HTML?

Technique

The HTML example style element **<XMP>** allows you to mark example text. Use it to display computer commands and arguments. The text tagged by **<XMP>** is usually shown in a fixed-width font.

> **NOTE**
>
> The `<XMP>` element is not recommended for current use. Refer to Chapter 3, Adding HTML Physical Character Effects, and Chapter 4, Adding HTML Logical Character Effects, for potentially more appropriate HTML 3.2 elements.

Steps

To specify example text, place the `<XMP>` tag at the beginning of the text and the `</XMP>` tag at the end of the text. For example:

```
At the prompt enter the command <XMP>lpr output.txt</XMP>.
```

How It Works

When a browser encounters an `<XMP>` element, it places everything between the opening and closing tags in example style. Such text is usually rendered in a fixed-width font, but font style can vary among browsers. Both Netscape's Navigator and Microsoft's Internet Explorer currently support this element. Figure 20-1 displays the following document as rendered by Internet Explorer.

Figure 20-1 Example element displaying a command and its arguments

```
<HTML>
<HEAD>
<TITLE>Sample Stop/Restart Server</TITLE>
</HEAD>
<BODY>
Stop and restart the server by entering:<BR>
<XMP>
kill -1 SERVER_PROCESS_ID
</XMP>
</BODY>
</HTML>
```

The HTML source for this document also appears on the CD-ROM in the XMP.HTM file.

Comments

The specification of HTML 2 deprecates the use of this element. This deprecated specification also appears in the HTML 3 and 3.2 specifications. Some older browsers and HTML documents may use this element. However, in general, you should select a more appropriate element from those discussed in Chapter 3 and 4. For the particular task of computer commands and arguments, consider the elements described in How-To 4.5.

COMPLEXITY
BEGINNING

20.3   How do I...
Identify a proper name?

COMPATIBILITY: HTML 3

Problem

I would like to call attention to the names of people and to other proper names in my pages. The names do not necessarily have to be highlighted, but someone running an indexing program through my pages should be able to pull out the names easily. How can I do this in HTML?

Technique

HTML 3 provides two new tags, **<AU>** and **<PERSON>**, that can be used to identify the names of people as well as other proper names. **<AU>** identifies an author, while **<PERSON>** identifies any person (or other proper name).

Steps

Open your document and locate the text you want to identify as a proper name.

1. To identify the name of an author, place **<AU>** at the beginning of the name and **</AU>** at the end of the name:

```
<AU>William Faulkner</AU> wrote many novels set in Mississippi.
```

2. To identify the name of a person, place **<PERSON>** at the beginning of the name and **</PERSON>** at the end of the name:

```
<PERSON>Ronald Reagan</PERSON> was the 40th president of the United States.
```

How It Works

When a browser encounters either an **<AU>** or a **<PERSON>** tag, it does nothing to alter the style of the text; these tags simply identify names for outside indexing programs. Neither Netscape's Navigator nor Microsoft's Internet Explorer supports a visual effect for either of these elements.

Comments

The **<AU>** and **<PERSON>** tags are only supported by HTML 3, so neither the older, pre-HTML 3 browsers nor the post-HTML 3 browsers can take advantage of them. These tags are primarily used by programs that scan HTML files and index their contents. These elements do not appear in the HTML 3.2 standard, but certain browsers and applications may make use of them.

The original intent of these elements was to provide a logical character effect without necessarily any visual effect. For this purpose, no easy alternative is available in the current 3.2 standard, but since no visual effect is intended, the nonconforming use of these elements will not hurt the appearance of your Web page in most browsers.

COMPLEXITY
BEGINNING

20.4 How do I...
Denote inserted or deleted text?

COMPATIBILITY: HTML 3

Problem

I'm putting some legal documents on my Web page, and I would like to point out where sections of the text have been amended, either by additions of new sections or deletions of old sections. Is there a way I can easily mark this in HTML?

Technique

HTML 3 provides two tags, **<INS>** and **<DEL>**, that allow you to mark sections of text that have been inserted or deleted from the original version of a document. As with other content styles, the physical rendering of the text depends on the browser.

Steps

Open your document and locate the text you would like to display as inserted or deleted text.

1. To mark text that has been inserted, place **<INS>** at the beginning of the inserted text and **</INS>** at the end of the inserted text:

```
His latest contract called for $3.5 million a year <INS>and a beachfront
condo</INS>.
```

2. To mark text that has been deleted, place **<DEL>** at the beginning of the section that has been deleted and **</DEL>** at the end of the text:

```
The people on the team now include John, Jane, <DEL>Bob,</DEL> and Arnold.
```

How It Works

When a browser encounters an **<INS>** or a **<DEL>** element, it formats the text contained within the tags according to the style programmed into the browser. This style may vary from browser to browser. Neither Netscape's Navigator nor Microsoft's Internet Explorer supports a visual effect for either of these elements.

Comments

The **<INS>** and **<DEL>** elements don't actually insert or delete text; rather, they point out where text has been added to or removed from a document. These features were added only to HTML 3, so pre-HTML 3 and post-HTML 3 browsers do not support these tags. These elements do not appear in the HTML 3.2 standard.

The original intent of these elements was to provide a logical character effect without necessarily any visual effect. You could, however, use some standard physical effects to indicate insertions or deletions. Deletions might be addressed using the strike through element discussed in How-To 3.7. A physical effect for insertions is not so directly apparent. As a convention within an authoring group, insertions might be tagged as bold (How-To 3.1), italic (How-To 3.2), colored with a specific color (How-To 3.5), or underlined (How-To 3.6). Such a decision should reflect the needs of the organization adopting the change (for example, if color changes are standard in documents developed, then some other option might be a better choice to indicate insertions). Figure 20-2 displays several of these potential alternatives. The HTML code for this document appears in the INSDEL.HTM file on the CD.

COMPLEXITY
INTERMEDIATE

20.5 How do I...
Create a multicolumn list?

COMPATIBILITY: HTML 3

Problem

I have a set of data I would like to display as a list. The data includes a number of different quantities, and I would like to display them side by side to make it easier for the reader to compare them. I don't want this to look like a table, though. How could I do this in HTML?

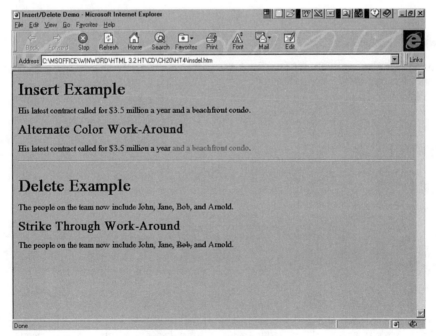

Figure 20-2 Insertion and deletion alternatives

Technique

In HTML 3, the **WRAP** attribute added to a bulleted list will wrap list items across the screen into a set of columns. You can combine this with other attributes, such as **BLANK**, to create unmarked multicolumn lists.

Steps

Open your document. Identify the locations in your document where you want to include a list.

1. First, place the items you want to include in the list in your document, using carriage returns to separate the items for clarity:

```
Red Sox
Cubs
Royals
Dodgers
Indians
Angels
White Sox
```

2. Place an **<LI>** tag in front of each list item:

```
<LI>Red Sox
<LI>Cubs
<LI>Royals
<LI>Dodgers
<LI>Indians
<LI>Angels
<LI>White Sox
```

3. To create a list in which the items go across the screen and then down, use the **<UL>** and **</UL>** tags with the attribute **WRAP="horiz"**:

```
<UL WRAP=HORIZ>
<LI>Red Sox
<LI>Cubs
<LI>Royals
<LI>Dodgers
<LI>Indians
<LI>Angels
<LI>White Sox
</UL>
```

4. To create a list in which the items go down the page before starting a new column, use the attribute **WRAP="vert"**:

```
<UL WRAP=VERT>
<LI>Red Sox
<LI>Cubs
<LI>Royals
<LI>Dodgers
<LI>Indians
<LI>Angels
<LI>White Sox
</UL>
```

How It Works

When an HTML 3-compliant browser reads the **WRAP** attribute, it formats the list items that follow it according to the attribute's value. If the **WRAP** attribute is set to **"horiz"**, it places the list items across the screen in a row until the end of the window is reached, then it starts a new row. When the **WRAP** attribute is set to **"vert"**, it places list items down the screen until it reaches the bottom of the window, and then it starts a new column.

Comments

In a multicolumn list, the number of columns and the contents of each are controlled solely by the browser, not by the text. If you want explicit control over the layout of a multicolumn list, it would be better to set it up as a table, which provides explicit control over layout. Chapter 5, Tables, discusses tables in detail. The **WRAP** attribute of the **<UL>** element does not appear in the HTML 3.2 standard.

As previously mentioned, the clearest alternative to create the desired effect of this attribute is to format the list data as an HTML **<TABLE>** element rather than as a list. See Chapter 5, for further information on the creation and organization of HTML tables. Figure 20-3 displays several of these potential alternatives. The HTML code for this document appears in the WRAP.HTM file on the CD.

COMPLEXITY
BEGINNING

20.6   How do I...
Specify the language context for the remainder of a Web page?

COMPATIBILITY: HTML 3, NETSCAPE NAVIGATOR,
INTERNET EXPLORER

Problem

I am developing Web pages for an international audience. I need to provide multiple languages in my pages. How do I specify the appropriate character set to display the information in a particular language?

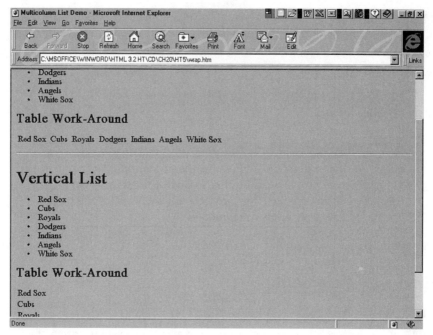

Figure 20-3 Multicolumn list alternative

Technique

A proposed addition to the HTML 3.2 standard is the inclusion of the **LANG** element and attribute. Most other HTML 3.2 elements would support the use of **LANG** as an attribute.

Using the **LANG** attribute, you may select the appropriate language to use within the current HTML element. Using the **LANG** element, you may select the appropriate language to use over a specified range of your Web page.

Steps

The following steps walk you through the process of specifying a language using the **LANG** element or attribute, as appropriate. If you only want to change the language of an existing Web page element, use the **LANG** attribute. If you want to alter the language specification for a larger portion of the document, use the **LANG** element.

Adding a LANG attribute

1. Open the Web page that you want to modify in a text editor.

2. Move the cursor to the end of the opening tag of the element that you wish to modify.

3. Add the **LANG** attribute to this tag. The values associated with this attribute are the class and subclass strings that represent the desired language. Examine, for example, this level 1 header element:

```
<H1> ä "   </H1>
```

For display in Hebrew, you might add the following **LANG** attribute.

```
<H1 LANG="ISO8859-8"> ä "   </H1>
```

> **NOTE**
>
> HTML documents will only appear in the appropriate language in an application properly configured to deal with the alternate language. If the application is not properly configured, the page displayed will likely appear meaningless.

4. Save the document.

Adding a LANG **element**

1. Open the Web page that you want to modify in a text editor.

2. Move the cursor to the point just prior to where you want to specify the language change.

3. Insert a **<LANG>** element opening tag with a **LANG** attribute, as described in step 3 of the preceding procedure. For example, an opening tag to indicate the choice of the Cyrillic character set might appear as:

```
<LANG LANG="KIO8-R">
```

> **NOTE**
>
> HTML documents will only appear in the appropriate language in an application properly configured to deal with the alternate language. If the application is not properly configured, the page displayed will likely appear meaningless.

4. Move the cursor to the point where you want the language change to end, and insert a **</LANG>** element closing tag.

```
</LANG>
```

5. Save the document.

How It Works

Browser applications display Web pages according to the character set specified in their configurations. Viewers may alter this default manually in most browsers. However, the **LANG** element and attribute assume that browsers eventually may support dynamic selection of character sets relevant to portions of a Web page.

An author specifies this linguistic shift as appropriate to the particular page authored. The specification may be at several levels of granularity: a single element, a portion of the page, or the entire Web page.

> **NOTE**
>
> A limited number of current browsers support the entire Web page level of granularity.

The two finer grains of specification are the province of the **LANG** attribute and element. Specifying a language with respect to an entire page is briefly discussed in the Comments section. In general, browsers should select the rendering language based upon proximity of the language specification to the text. The closest **LANG** attribute, whether in a **LANG** element or in another enclosing element, takes precedence. If the particular language is not supported by the browser, the browser should use the next closest. This selection process continues outward from the current element until the author-defined document-level language selection; this language serves as a default when no other language selection applies. If the browser does not support this default language, the browser should use the default language configured by the reader.

In the case of the **LANG** element, a **LANG** attribute of this element is also required. Whenever you use a **LANG** attribute, the value associated with the attribute is the name of the desired language. The current proposal for language naming is RFC 1766. Feel free to consult this reference; check a Web search tool for a current location. Under this standard, you compose a language name of a base type, optionally followed by a dash and a subtype. For example, **EN** represents the English language base type. From this base type, **EN-US** and **EN-UK** might, respectively, represent the United States and United Kingdom variants of the English language.

Some browsers, however, may simply opt for the use of particular character set designations as the appropriate value. IANA maintains a listing of currently registered character sets in a subdirectory of URL `ftp://ftp.isi.edu/in-notes/iana/assignments/`.

Comments

Currently, the **LANG** attribute is only a proposed addition to the standard. The WWW Consortium maintains current information on this developing standard, and additional information on the further internationalization of HTML and the Web, at `http://www.w3.org/pub/WWW/International/`.

Currently, neither Netscape's Navigator nor Microsoft's Internet Explorer supports this attribute. However, both browsers do support limited selection of character sets through the inclusion of a character-set parameter in the `Content-type` field in the response header returning a document. Authors may selectively add such a field using the **<META>** element. For example, the following **<META>** element would indicate use of the ISO8859-8 character set (Hebrew), as seen in Figure 20-4:

```
<META HTTP-EQUIV="Content-Type" CONTENT="text/html; charset=iso-8859-8">
```

Depending on the particular language, a browser may require manual adjustment of the character set encoding and font choice. For additional information on internationalization using Netscape, see URL `http://home.netscape.com/people/ftang/i18n.html`. For additional information on internationalization using Internet Explorer, see URL `http://www.microsoft.com/ie/most/howto/multi.htm`.

COMPLEXITY
INTERMEDIATE

20.7   How do I...
Place an embedded quotation?

COMPATIBILITY: HTML 3

Problem

I want to include a quotation in my page. However, I would like the browser to do the work of including the appropriate quotation marks for a given language. How can I embed this quotation using HTML?

Figure 20-4 Use of the Hebrew character set

Technique

HTML 3 introduces the `<Q>` tag, which places quotation marks around the tagged text. By adding the `LANG` attribute, it is possible to tell the browser to use the quotation marks specific to a certain language.

Steps

1. To insert an embedded quotation, place the `<Q>` tag at the beginning of the text and `</Q>` at the end of the text:

```
Hamlet said, <Q>To be, or not to be, that is the question.</Q>
```

2. To use the quotation marks from a specific language, insert the `LANG` attribute in the `<Q>` tag and set it equal to a language. Languages are usually referred to by a two-letter abbreviation, such as `EN` for English, `FR` for French, `DE` for German, and the like. The following line of code calls for the use of English (specifically, American English, which is represented by `EN-US`) quotation marks:

```
Hamlet said, <Q LANG="EN-US">To be, or not to be, that is the question.</Q>
```

To render the quotes as used in German, the code would look like this:

```
Hamlet said, <Q LANG="DE">To be, or not to be, that is the question.</Q>
```

How It Works

When a browser encounters a `<Q>` tag, it replaces the `<Q>` and `</Q>` tags with opening and closing quotes, respectively. The text and the quotes are also rendered in italics. It uses the quotes for the language specified by the `LANG` attribute, or the default quotes if none is given.

Comments

The `<Q>` tag was introduced in HTML 3, and removed from HTML 3.2, so it is not supported by many browsers. While the `<Q>` tag may be useful for rendering quotation symbols, especially for other languages, it may be simpler just to add the quote symbols manually, if they are available. As of this writing, neither Navigator nor Internet Explorer support quotation symbols used in nonEnglish languages. Further, this element generates no visual effect in either browser.

This element does not appear in the new HTML 3.2 standard. The `<BLOCKQUOTE>` element described in How-To 7.8 provides a potential alternative. Figure 20-5

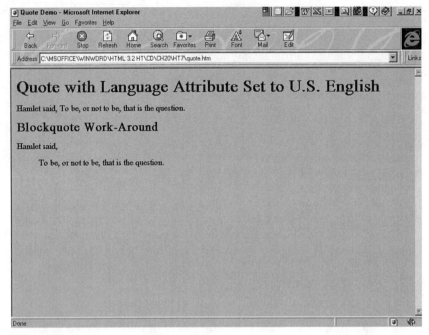

Figure 20-5 Quotation alternative

displays several of these potential alternatives. The HTML code for this document appears in the QUOTE.HTM file on the CD.

COMPLEXITY
INTERMEDIATE

20.8 How do I...
Align text with tabs?

COMPATIBILITY: HTML 3

Problem

I would like to control the horizontal spacing in my document. I want to be able to specify where I want items to appear, and whether the items are centered, left justified, or right justified. With HTML 3, how can I specify this type of formatting information?

Technique

There are several ways to specify horizontal alignment of text.

Center element: This element began as a Netscape Navigator extension, but the HTML 3.2 standard has adopted it. A center element is added like any other element. Use the procedure defined in How-To 7.3.

Table element: This element allows for the fine control of the horizontal and vertical positioning of information and data. Use the procedures described in Chapter 5 and Chapter 7, Managing Document Spacing, to align text and data using tables.

Tab elements: Tab elements are used to establish horizontal tabs in your HTML document. Since tabs are part of the HTML 3 specification, they are more likely to be understood and rendered than a center element.

Steps

Use the following steps to set and use tabs within an HTML document. These tabs enable you to align text within the body of your HTML documents.

1. Open the HTML document you wish to edit in your favorite text editor. (See How-To 2.4 on editing environments.) If your HTML editor allows you to create **<TAB>** elements with macro or menu options, follow the instructions for the editor.

2. Place the insertion point where you wish to place the **<TAB>** element within your document.

3. Insert the appropriate **<TAB>** element in your document. **<TAB>** elements are empty and therefore do not require a closing tag. Use the following table to select the proper **<TAB>** element for your use.

TAB ELEMENT FORMAT	PURPOSE
`<TAB ID="name">`	Sets a tab at the current location default aligned left
`<TAB ID="name" ALIGN="alignment">`	Sets a tab with a particular alignment
`<TAB TO="name">`	Jumps to the specified tab location
`<TAB INDENT=x>`	Indents x en spaces
`<TAB ALIGN="right">`	Places remainder of the line flush right
`<TAB ALIGN="center">`	Centers text between margins
`<TAB ALIGN="left">`	Places text flush to the left

4. Save your document, or continue editing. If you wish to add additional **<TAB>** elements, return to step 2.

How It Works

You can align text horizontally with tabs. The **<TAB>** element supports the followng attributes:

- **ALIGN="alignment"**: This specifies the alignment of the tab. This attribute has one of four values: **"left"**, **"right"**, **"center"**, and **"decimal"**. These values determine how text is situated with respect to the tab.

- **DP="c"**: This attribute specifies the character to be used by a decimal tab to align text. The default value is the period. However, if you wished to align a tab with another character, you would include this attribute with the desired tab character as a value. For example, if you included **DP="$"** in the **<TAB>** opening tag, the tab would align along the dollar sign.

- **ID="name"**: This associates a name with a specific horizontal tab location. You can use the value associated with **ID** as the value of a **TO** attribute. In effect, using the **ID** attribute sets a tab at the named location. See the examples provided next.

- **INDENT="x"**: This allows the specification of a leading indent. The integer value associated with this attribute specifies the number of en spaces to indent a particular line. This attribute should not be used in conjunction with a **TO** attribute.

- **TO="name"**: Like **ID**, this takes a name as a value. The value indicates the horizontal position for the browser to tab forward to before rendering the text.

To indent several lines of text, use a **<TAB>** element with the **INDENT** attribute set. For example, the following code indents the specified line 5 en spaces. The **
** element is used to force a line break at the location where the element appears. (Refer to How-To 7.4 for further information on the line break element.)

```
This line has no indentation.<BR>
<TAB INDENT=5>This line is indented 5 en spaces.
```

The resulting text looks like this:

```
This line has no indentation.
    This line is indented 5 en spaces.
```

Use a **<TAB>** element with an **ID** attribute to set tab locations. If you want a tab stop with other than left alignment, use the **ALIGN** attribute to specify the alignment.

For example, use the following code to specify a left-aligned tab after the word **"bear"**. The second line represents a line indented right below the first.

```
We will watch the bear <TAB ID="bear"> walk through<BR>
<TAB TO="bear> the woods and take joy in this delight.
```

This would be rendered by browsers as follows:

```
We will watch the bear walk through
                        the woods and take joy in this delight.
```

If you use the **ALIGN** attribute without a **TO** attribute, the tab overrides the default alignment with respect to the margins of the page. If no paragraph elements are used, then this default alignment is left. If paragraph elements are used, you can set a default alignment for a particular paragraph using the same **ALIGN** attribute values as specified for a tab. (Refer to How-To 7.4 for further information on the paragraph element.)

```
<P ALIGN="center">
This line is centered.<BR>
So is this one.<BR>
<TAB ALIGN="left">This one is left justified.<BR>
Back to center.
```

This would appear in a browser as

```
                    This line is centered.
                       So is this one.
This one is left justified.
                       Back to center.
```

If you use a **<TAB>** element with both an **ALIGN** attribute and a **TO** attribute, the text following the tab is placed at the tab stop identified as the **TO** value and aligned as specified in the **ALIGN** value. The **DP** attribute allows you to define the character to align around. The default is the decimal point.

```
I will set my <TAB ID="here"> at this point.<BR>
<TAB ALIGN="decimal" TO="here">$500.00<BR>
<TAB ALIGN="decimal" TO="here">$1000.00<BR>
<TAB ALIGN="decimal" TO="here">approx $50.00
```

These lines appear as

```
I will set my at this point.
        $500.00
       $1000.00
 approx $50.00
```

The tab in this case is aligned around the decimal point.

Comments

A more complete discussion of the paragraph element is provided in How-To 7.4. This element can be used to establish the default horizontal alignment for a block of lines. The <TAB> element is not currently supported by any popular browsers. Further, it does not appear in the proposed HTML 3.2 standard. Unless use of the <TAB> element is mandatory, strongly consider using a <TABLE> element as a more powerful alternative.

COMPLEXITY
BEGINNING

20.9 How do I...
Insert cautionary notes?

COMPATIBILITY: HTML 3

Problem

I want to deliver a warning to readers of my Web page. The message needs to stick out somehow and grab the reader's attention.

Technique

HTML 3 provides the <NOTE> element to support the specification of messages admonishing the reader of a page. You use this element by including it and the appropriate note text within the context of the Web page.

Steps

The following procedure provides step-by-step instructions for including a note as an admonishment within a Web page.

1. Open your Web page in a text editor.

2. Move your cursor to the position where you want the note to appear.

3. Insert a note element opening tag. The key attribute that should also appear in this tag is the CLASS element. The value of this attribute represents the type of note desired by the author. The following table summarizes these potential values and their respective purposes.

CLASS VALUE	NOTE TYPE
note	General purpose note
warning	Provides the reader with a warning
caution	Cautions the user against inappropriate actions

4. Optionally, add an **SRC** attribute and value. Add this attribute if you want an image displayed as part of the note or if you want to override the browser's default image associated with a message of a given **CLASS**. The actual use of the **SRC** attribute may vary among different browsers.

5. Type the text of the note.

6 Insert a closing note tag.

7. Save the document.

How It Works

When a browser encounters a **<NOTE>** element, the browser should set the note off from the remainder of the page in such a way as to draw the reader's attention to the warning provided. The Arena browser associated a particular image with each of the potential note classes.

Comments

This element does not appear in the new HTML 3.2 standard. Further, this element is not directly supported by either Netscape Navigator or Microsoft Internet Explorer.

As an alternative, an author could use the indentation created through the "misuse" of a definition list or a block quote. (Refer to How-To 6.8 for more information on the proper use of a definition list or How-To 7.8 on block quotations.) This definition list mimics the appropriate indentation for a note. However, in this situation, the author would need to explicitly include an indicative image rather than count on an appropriate default image associated with the note's **CLASS** attribute. So for a warning note, the following might be an appropriate HTML 3.2-supported alternative:

```
<DL>
<DD>
<!-- An appropriate image inclusion using the IMG or OBJECT element as
appropriate -->
Warning: You are entering a restricted area. If you are seeing this
message, you have gone too far.
Please report yourself to the nearest re-education center. War is peace.
</DL>

<BLOCKQUOTE>
<!-- An appropriate image inclusion using the IMG or OBJECT element as
appropriate -->
Warning: You are entering a restricted area. If you are seeing this
message, you have gone too far.
Please report yourself to the nearest re-education center. War is peace.
</BLOCKQUOTE>
```

The file NOTE.HTM on the CD contains the complete source for a simple Web page including this note. Figure 20-6 displays this document.

COMPLEXITY
BEGINNING

20.10 How do I...
Add a footnote?

COMPATIBILITY: HTML 3

Problem

Often scholarly works require the use of footnotes to properly credit original ideas and quotes. Authors also use footnotes to clarify cryptic portions of a literary work. How do I add a footnote to a Web page?

Technique

The HTML 3.0 standard provides the **<FN>** element to support the inclusion of footnotes in your Web page. You place the footnote material within the bounds of the opening and closing tag of the element. The intent in the specification of this element is that the material should appear as a pop-up window when the reader triggers

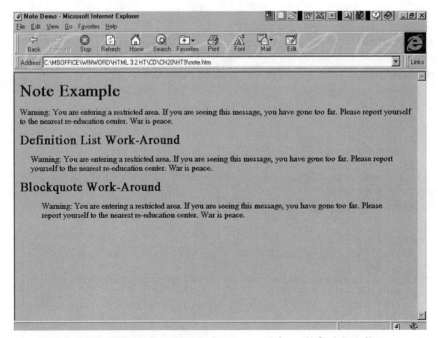

Figure 20-6 Mimicking a <NOTE> element with a definition list

a link referencing the particular footnote. The target of the link is a named location within the current Web document. The named location is a specific **<FN>** element.

Steps

This following procedure provides a stepwise approach to the inclusion of footnotes within your Web page.

1. Open your Web page in a text editor.

2. Move to the end of the body portion of your Web page.

3. Insert an **<FN>** element opening tag. Choose a value for the **ID** attribute of this tag that is unique within the scope of this Web page.

4. Add the text of the footnote.

5. End the footnote text with an **<FN>** element closing tag.

6. Locate the text in your page that will reference a footnote, and move the insertion point to just before this location. For example, you could create a footnote text referencing William Shakespeare with the following footnote element.

```
<FN ID="fn1">William Shakespeare</FN >
```

7. Insert an anchor around this text. The target (**HREF** attribute) of this anchor should name a location within the current document (a value beginning with a pound [#] sign). For example, if you wanted to link the phrase "To be, or not to be…" to a footnote, you might use the following anchor attribute around the phrase.

```
<A HREF="#fn1">To be, or not to be ... </A>
```

This would link the quote to the footnote with an **ID** of **fn1**.

8. Save the document.

How It Works

The footnote element provides you with a mechanism to specify text that should appear in a pop-up window when a reader triggers the link attached to that footnote. The **<FN>** element delimits the text that appears in the pop-up window. The link locates the footnote text in the same manner as a named location within a document is found. Once the location is found, the browser determines that the target of the link is a footnote rather than a named document location. Once the browser makes this determination, it can display the footnote contents appropriately.

Comments

Since this element does not appear in the HTML 3.2 proposed standard and since neither Navigator nor Internet Explorer support this element, you should seriously consider the available alternatives to this element. HTML 3.2 provides several alternate approaches to this task.

- Use anchor elements rather than footnote elements.

- Use a scripted procedure to produce the desired footnote.

- Use a Java application to support a pop-up message.

See Chapter 17, Web Programming with Java and JavaScript, for some of the basics of Java and JavaScript programming. The first alternative uses anchors rather than the footnote element. The references within the document do not change, but instead of **<FN>** tags, use **<A>** tags around the intended footnote. Where the footnote element used an **ID** attribute in the opening tag, the anchor opening tag should use a **NAME** attribute.

COMPLEXITY
INTERMEDIATE

20.11 How do I...
Place a mathematical equation in my Web page?

COMPATIBILITY: HTML 3

Problem

The material I want to include on my page contains a number of mathematical formulas that are difficult to show using normal text characters. I would like to show these equations as text, without having to resort to graphics. How can I format mathematical equations in HTML?

Technique

HTML 3 includes a number of elements that can be used to format mathematical equations in the text of a page. The **<MATH>** element is used to identify equations, and tags contained within the **<MATH>** tag are used to format the equation. With these tags, it is possible to display complicated equations with subscripts and superscripts, square roots, vectors and other special symbols. Other tags can be used to display integrals, summation symbols, and other mathematical symbols. Unfortunately, these commands do not exist in HTML 2 (or HTML 3.2), so older and newer browsers can't recognize them and, thus, can't format the text correctly.

Steps

Open your document and locate the areas in the document where you would like to place mathematical formulas. Type plain-text versions of the formulas now to guide you later, when you add the HTML **<MATH>** tags.

1. To identify any equation, place the **$** tag at the beginning of the function and the **$** tag at the end of the function:

```
The equation for kinetic energy is <MATH>E = 1/2mv2</MATH>
The function of the curve is <MATH>y = (3 + x)/(5 - 2x)</MATH>
```

2. As discussed in Chapter 3, you can use the **<SUP>** and **<SUB>** tags for superscripts and subscripts, respectively. However, within the **$** and **$** tags, you can use shortcuts for those tags: **^** for **^{** and **}**, and **_** for **_{** and **}**:

```
The equation for kinetic energy is <MATH>E = 1/2mv^2^</MATH>
The line can be represented by the equation <MATH>y = c_0_ + c_1_*x</MATH>
```

3. To express fractions, you can use the **<BOX>** and **<OVER>** tags. Place **<BOX>** at the beginning of the fraction, **</BOX>** at the end of the fraction, and **<OVER>** where the division between the numerator and denominator occurs. Within the **<MATH>** tag, you can substitute **{** (the left brace) for **<BOX>** and **}** (the right brace) for **</BOX>**:

```
The equation for kinetic energy is <MATH>E =
<BOX>1<OVER>2</BOX>mv^2^</MATH>
The equation for kinetic energy is <MATH>E = {1<OVER>2}mv^2^</MATH>
```

4. To place fractions and other mathematical equations in parentheses, brackets, braces, or horizontal lines, use the **<BOX>** tag and the desired symbol. Use the **<LEFT>** tag at the beginning of the expression, just after the symbol, and the **<RIGHT>** tag at the end of the expression, just before the closing symbol:

```
<MATH>{(<LEFT>3+x<OVER>5-2x<RIGHT>)}</MATH>
<MATH>{[<LEFT>3+2x<OVER>5-2x<RIGHT>]}</MATH>
<MATH>{|<LEFT>3+2x<OVER>5-2x<RIGHT>|}</MATH>
<MATH>{&ltbrace;<LEFT>3+2x<OVER>5-2x<RIGHT>&rtbrace;}</MATH>
```

Note that in order to display something within braces, you must use the special characters **&ltbrace;** and **&rtbrace;** for the left brace and right brace symbols, respectively.

5. HTML 3 also provides a number of tags you can use within the `<MATH>` element to display special modified characters such as vectors, dots, and bars:

Special mathematical symbols in HTML

TAG	DEFINITION
`<VEC>`	Displays a vector over a character
`<BAR>`	Displays a horizontal bar over a character
`<DOT>`	Displays a single dot over a character
`<DDOT>`	Displays a double dot over a character
`<HAT>`	Displays a hat (carat) (^) over a character
`<TILDE>`	Displays a tilde (~) over a character

For example:

```
The equation for kinetic energy is <MATH><VEC>E</VEC> =
1/2m<VEC>v</VEC>^2^</MATH>
```

```
The average value of x, <MATH><BAR>x</BAR></MATH>, was 42.
```

6. The `<SQRT>` tag places the text found between it and the `</SQRT>` tag inside the square root symbol. A more general form is the `<ROOT>` tag, which, along with the `<OF>` tag, places the text between the `<OF>` and `</ROOT>` tags inside the root symbol and places the text located between the `<ROOT>` and `<OF>` in the area of the root symbol used to designate the power of the root (**2** for square root, **3** for cube root, and so on):

```
The Pythagorean theorem states that <MATH>c = <SQRT>a^2^ + ⇐
b^2^</SQRT></MATH>
```

```
The radius of a sphere with volume V is
<MATH><ROOT>3<OF>{3V<OVER>4pi}</ROOT></MATH>
```

Examples of the various mathematical styles are shown in Figure 20-7. The code is also available on the CD as file MATH.HTM.

How It Works

The `<MATH>` tag alerts the browser that the text contained within the `<MATH>` and `</MATH>` tags requires special formatting, including symbols that have different meanings within the `<MATH>` tags than they have in normal text. The special tags encountered within the `<MATH>` tags are then converted into appropriate graphics and spacing, according to the specifications of the browser.

Comments

Because this mathematical notation is only available in HTML 3, people using pre-HTML 3 browsers will not be able to see the appropriate graphics and spacing, which may render some equations more confusing than if they had been left as plain text.

Figure 20-7 Use of math elements in a Web page

Keep this in mind when creating your documents. Also, as of this writing, not all of the mathematical elements had been incorporated into Arena, the HTML 3 testbed browser; the browser did not yet support roots and some special characters. Neither Netscape Navigator nor Microsoft Internet Explorer supports mathematical symbols of any kind at this time. Work in the area of supporting mathematical symbols through HTML is currently continuing. The World Wide Web Consortium provides the most current information on work in this area.

COMPLEXITY
INTERMEDIATE

20.12 How do I...
Insert an array into a math element?

COMPATIBILITY: HTML 3

Problem

The material I want to include on my page contains mathematical matrices that are difficult to show using normal text characters. I would like to show these matrices as text, without having to resort to graphics. How can I format mathematical matrices in HTML?

Technique

HTML 3 includes a number of elements that can be used to support the inclusion of matrices within the context of a **<MATH>** element. The **<MATH>** element is used to identify and to format the mathematical constructs within a Web page. Within the **<MATH>** element, HTML 3.0 provides the **<ARRAY>**, **<ROW>**, and **<ITEM>** elements to create and manage matrices. Unfortunately, these commands do not exist in HTML 2, so older browsers can't recognize them and thus can't format the text correctly.

Steps

Open your document and locate the areas in the document where you would like to place your array.

1. To identify any matrix/array, place the **$** tag at the beginning of the matrix and the **$** tag at the end:

2. To create an array, use the **<ARRAY>** tag to define the beginning of an array, and **</ARRAY>** to mark the end of the array. Within these tags, the **<ROW>** tag marks the beginning of a new row in the array, and **<ITEM>** marks a new entry in the array:

```
<ARRAY>
    <ROW><ITEM>a<ITEM>b
    <ROW><ITEM>c<ITEM>d
</ARRAY>

<ARRAY>
    <ROW><ITEM>a<ITEM>b<ITEM>c
    <ROW><ITEM>d<ITEM>e<ITEM>f
</ARRAY>
```

3. To align the array within the window, use the **ALIGN** attribute within the **<ARRAY>** tag:

```
<ARRAY ALIGN=CENTER>
    <ROW><ITEM>a<ITEM>b
    <ROW><ITEM>c<ITEM>d
</ARRAY>
```

4. To align columns in the array, use the **COLDEF** attribute within the **<ARRAY>** tag. This attribute uses a capital letter to signify the alignment for each column in the array: **L** for left, **C** for center, **R** for right. For example, to align the first two columns in the center, but align the third column on the right, enter

```
<ARRAY COLDEF="CCR">
    <ROW><ITEM>a<ITEM>b
    <ROW><ITEM>c<ITEM>d
</ARRAY>
```

Examples of the various mathematical styles are shown in Figure 20-7. The code is also available on the CD as file MATH.HTM. The arena browser displayed used in Figure 20-7 does not support **<ARRAY>** elements.

How It Works

The **<MATH>** tag alerts the browser that the text contained within the **$** and **$** tags requires special formatting, including symbols that have different meanings within the **<MATH>** tags than they have in normal text. The special tags encountered within the **<MATH>** tags are then converted into appropriate graphics and spacing according to the specifications of the browser.

Specifically, the **<ARRAY>**, **<ROW>**, and **<ITEM>** elements allow you to control the specific layout of a desired matrix. Each row of the intended matrix starts with a **<ROW>** element open tag; by default, the next **<ROW>** open tag ends the current row. Use the **<ITEM>** element to delimit the individual items within a row of the matrix. All **<ROW>** elements are within the scope of the enclosing **<ARRAY>** element. The array element supports several attributes within its opening tag:

- **ALIGN**: The **ALIGN** attribute describes the placement of the matrix with respect to the text immediately preceding or following it. The acceptable values for this attribute are **top**, **bottom**, and **middle**. These values hold the same meanings that they do in the context of embedded image alignment as described in How-To 9.3.

- **COLDEF**: The **COLDEF** attribute takes a string as its value. This string may contain the following characters: **+**, **−**, **=**, **C**, **L**, and **R**. The combination of such characters determines the formatting of the columns in the matrix. The **+**, **−**, and **=** signs instruct the browser to place the sign used between columns of the matrix. The **C**, **L**, and **R** values indicate that a particular column of the matrix should be center, left, and right aligned, respectively.

> **NOTE**
>
> An **ALIGN** attribute used for a particular **<ITEM>** element will override the alignment suggested in the **COLDEF** string.

■ **LABELS**: This attribute requires no value. It indicates to the browser that the first column and the first row of data represent header information rather than actual data. When you use this tag, the first **<ITEM>** in the first **<ROW>** element is ignored; however, this item must be present and not empty for proper management.

Comments

Current browsers do not support the **<MATH>** element; consequently, the **<ARRAY>** element and its sub-elements are also not supported. Research continues into the development of suitable elements to include mathematics within Web pages. For current information on this topic, refer to the HTML Activity Statement at URL **http://www.w3.org/**.

COMPLEXITY
INTERMEDIATE

20.13   How do I...
Change the shape of a link?

COMPATIBILITY: HTML 3

Problem

I would like to define a certain area of a figure on my page as a link to a specific document. I don't want to go though the hassle of creating an imagemap, though. Is there a way to accomplish this using HTML 3?

Technique

The HTML 3 **SHAPE** attribute permits links of different shapes and sizes to be included in figures (using the new HTML 3 **<FIGURE>** tag). **SHAPE** lets you do many of the same things an imagemap (Chapter 9, Using Images in Your Documents) does, but without the need to create a separate map file or deal with CGI scripts.

Steps

Open your document. Also, load an image with a viewer that allows you to get the pixel locations on the image so that you can specify image locations in the links.

1. First, decide what areas on the image will serve as links. These areas can be circles, rectangles, or even complex polygons. Note the pixel locations of the areas: the x coordinate increases to the right, and the y coordinate increases downwards.

2. Create a list of links, as described in How-To 8.16. For each link, include the **SHAPE** attribute. The **SHAPE** attribute can take on the forms shown in Table 20-1.

Table 20-1 SHAPE attribute types

ATTRIBUTE	DESCRIPTION
`circle x,y,r`	A circle centered at the point (x,y) with radius r.
`rect x,y,w,h`	A rectangle of width w and height h with its upper left corner at (x,y).
`polygon x1,y1,x2,y2,...`	A polygon that consists of lines linking the points $(x1,y1)$, $(x2,y2)$, and so on. The polygon is closed by a line linking the last set of points to the first set.
default	The background of the figure, which includes those points not inside a circle, rectangle, or polygon.

For example, a simple list consisting of a circle, rectangle, and triangle (three-point polygon), as well as a default link for the rest of the figure, might look like this:

```
<UL>
    <LI><A SHAPE="circle 10,10,5" HREF="page1.html">Page 1</A>
    <LI><A SHAPE="rect 30,20,10,5" HREF="page2.html">Page 2</A>
    <LI><A SHAPE="polygon 50,40,40,40,40,30" HREF="page3.html">Page 3</A>
</UL>
```

See Figure 20-8 for an example of how this would look.

3. This list of shaped links is then incorporated into a figure, using the HTML 3 `<FIGURE>` tag. An example using the list might look like this:

```
<FIG SRC="book.gif">
    <UL>
        <LI><A SHAPE="circle 10,10,5" HREF="page1.html">Page 1</A>
        <LI><A SHAPE="rect 30,20,10,5" HREF="page2.html">Page 2</A>
      <LI><A SHAPE="polygon 50,40,40,40,40,30" HREF="page3.html"> ⇐
Page 3</A>
    </UL>
</FIG>
```

How It Works

The **SHAPE** attribute defines an area on the image as a link. If a reader selects that part of the image, the link is activated the way any other link would be. This works just as an imagemap would, but without the need to create a separate map file of the image or write a script to interpret the imagemap.

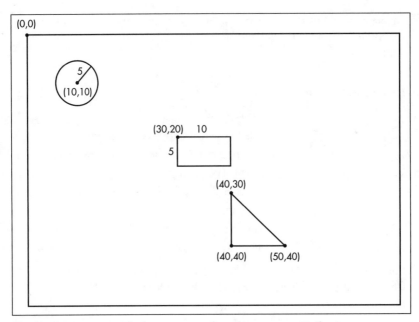

Figure 20-8 A sample imagemap for the SHAPE attribute

Comments

If a person selects an area of an image where two or more links overlap, the browser finds the link whose center is closest to the selected point and chooses it. If the default link is not created in the figure, any part of the figure outside the linked areas is not active and is not linked to other documents.

## CHAPTER 21

SOME OF THE BEST
SITES ON THE WEB

21

SOME OF THE BEST SITES ON THE WEB

A book on HTML isn't complete without some reference to pages on the Web that are cool. The following, while by no means all-encompassing, is a list of some of the best and coolest spots on the Web. The criteria for inclusion were two:

- Visual interface

- Behind-the-scenes HTML

The description of each Web page listed here includes a discussion of why its visual interface deserves mention and what HTML was used to make the page truly outstanding. Hopefully, perusing the pages in this chapter will give you inspiration for your own Web pages.

The Spot

URL: `http://www.thespot.com/`
Owner: Fattal & Collins
Webmaster: Troy Bolotnick
Purpose: Entertainment

The Spot centers around the "adventures" in the lives of a bunch of young, good-looking people. Love it or loathe it, The Spot is one of the most active sites on the World Wide Web. The Spot is also one of the slickest spots on Web; it is a fine example of what a little imagination and lots of expert coding can do. Figure 21-1 shows a clip from The Spot.

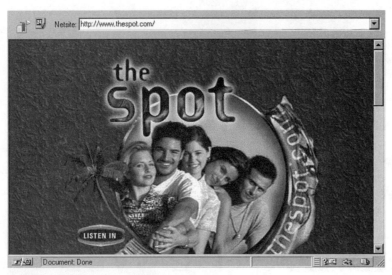

Figure 21-1 The Spot's main menu

The look and feel of The Spot is great. It is easy for anyone to navigate to wherever one wishes to go.

The Spot makes great use of tables in a monthly calendar that lets you read the daily diary entries of the inhabitants of The Spot. You name a technique and The Spot uses it.

The Spot came under a lot of fire when it first arrived on the spot (sorry) for pretending to be a real place. The creators have now come clean, so to speak, with Spot Tech, which explains how The Spot works. Like it or not, The Spot is one of the most popular and well-executed sites on the Web.

The Heart: A Virtual Exploration

URL: http://sln.fi.edu/biosci/heart.html
Owner: The Franklin Institute
Webmaster: webteam@sln.fi.edu
Purpose: Education

The Heart: A Virtual Exploration is a fine example of education on the Web. It takes a topic that could be quite daunting, such as the human heart, and breaks it down into easy-to-understand pieces. It is a great example of things to come. Figure 21-2 shows The Heart's top page.

The amount and level of information here is very impressive. There are definitions, graphics, explanatory text, and activities. It makes learning about the heart painless and fun.

There really is nothing cool going on behind the scenes here. The one downside of this page is that it doesn't use any advanced techniques to deliver information.

Figure 21-2 The top page of The Heart

For example, the activities, a series of tests, would be a lot more fun to do if they were done with a form and made interactive.

The Heart is a great site for information and learning, but it could be given a little pizzazz by incorporating some forms and imagemaps.

The Dominion

URL: http://www.scifi.com
Owner: The SciFi Channel
Webmaster: Jamie Biggar
Purpose: Entertainment

The Dominion, or The Sci Fi Channel's Web site, is one the older but still cooler sites on the Web. It is the place to go for all the latest info on what's happening in the world of sci fi. Figure 21-3 shows The Dominion.

From the opening page on, you are greeted with simple yet smart backgrounds, animated icons, and a nice Java script that tells you the number of days you have left until the Millennium.

The Dominion makes use of about every HTML trick in the book: backgrounds, tables, imagemaps, the works. You can maneuver successfully throughout its vast pages with menu bars. The site offers chat b-boards and has even hosted an online conference. This is truly a great Web site.

This site was nominated for the 1996 Still Cool Site of the Year. Check it out and you will see why.

Figure 21-3 The Dominion

The Uncanny X-Page

URL: `http://www.mallorn.com/~m-blase/xpage/`
Owner: Marty Blase
Webmaster: Marty Blase
Purpose: Information and entertainment

The Uncanny X-Page is devoted totally to the world's most popular mutants: Marvel Comic's X-men. The page, which is not sanctioned by Marvel, is a nice example of what a lot of dedication and work can produce. It is the definitive source of X-information. Figure 21-4 shows the X-Page title page when viewed with Netscape 2.

The pages are loaded with graphics and choices. Each separate topic has its own menu bar. The background image is also good.

This was one of the first nonNetscape-owned pages to make use of frames; the table of contents always stays in a window while another window shows whatever information you have chosen.

This page is not put together by a professional Web team, but from its look and feel, you could never tell. It certainly is as nice to look at and fun to read (if you're a fan) as anything on the Web.

People On-Line

URL: `http://pathfinder.com/people/toc.html`
Owner: *People Magazine* (*Time Life*)
Webmaster: `74774.1513@compuserve.com`
Purpose: Infotainment

The online version of the very popular *People Magazine*. All the glitz and glamour of the magazine translate well to the Web. Figure 21-5 shows a sample "cover."

Figure 21-4 The Uncanny X-Page—Notice the use of frames

Figure 21-5 The cover of People On-Line

This page has a very nice look and feel. Many of the same images from the paper magazine make their way to the electronic version, and for some reason the look and feel of the electronic version is better. There is even a part of the site that is updated daily with all the latest celeb news and entertainment news.

This page makes great use of graphics and imagemaps. The screens are well laid out and condensed. There is also a nice built-in keyword search that lets you find related articles.

A great mix of information, slick presentation, and smooth layout makes this one of the best conversions from paper to electronics on the Web.

The Heather Locklear Internet Fan Club

URL: `http://www.riv.be/garyfs/index.html`
Owner: Gary F. Spradling
Webmaster: Gary F. Spradling
Purpose: A tribute from the president of the fan club

There are hundreds of pages on the Web devoted to actors and actresses. The Heather Locklear page, which is maintained by Gary F. Spradling, is certainly one of the best. If you want information on or photos of this very popular actress, this is the place to come. Figure 21-6 shows the Heather Locklear Internet Fan Club.

The graphics look smooth and the layout is clean and easy to look at. This is also one of few sites on the Web that allow you to register so you can be informed when the site is updated. The site contains everything you probably need to know about Heather Locklear.

Notice the excellent background image and choice of colors. It is one of the first sites to take advantage of Microsoft's Internet Explorer.

This is an amazing, well-executed job by a devoted fan. It looks as good and professional as anything you'll find on the Web.

The Point

URL: `http://www.pointcom.com/`
Owner: Point Communications
Questions: `editor@pointcom.com`
Purpose: Index of leading sites on the Web

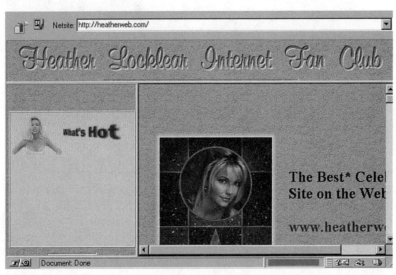

Figure 21-6 The Heather Locklear Internet Fan Club (`index2.html`)

The Point is one of the premier index sites on the Web. While other index sites tend to list many sites, The Point only lists reviews of sites it considers to be in the top 5 percent of all Web sites. It is a well-executed and valuable reference. Figure 21-7 shows The Point's reviews menu.

The Point is one of the best-looking and easy-to-navigate index sites. The writing makes many of the listings more fun to read than your average index.

In addition to the visual interface, it's also obvious that lots of thought went into the layout and design of this. The authors made good use of graphical imagemaps.

ESPNET SportsZone

URL: `http://espnet.sportszone.com/`
Owner: ESPN
Webmaster: Starware
Purpose: Complete sports updates and information

If you want to know anything about sports, this is the place to check first. All major sports are covered, with standings, scores, and articles. There is even a section devoted to some of the less major sports. This is a fine sports reference. Figure 21-8 shows the ESPNET SportsZone's home page.

ESPNET has a nice design and layout, easy to look at and easy to navigate. Even the ads look cool.

Notice the great use of tables and imagemaps in the various tables of contents and menu bars. The scripting is also impressive: The "up-to-the-minute" scores really are pretty much up to the minute.

One of the finest sites on the Web, this is a great blend of information and presentation and is what all sites should strive for.

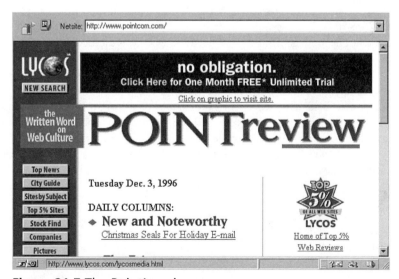

Figure 21-7 The Point's reviews menu

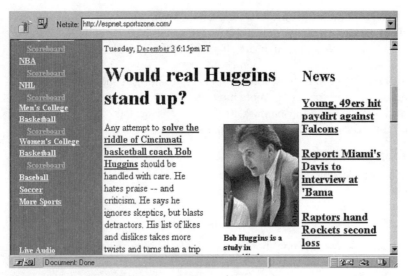

Netsite: http://espnet.sportszone.com/

Scoreboard
NBA
Scoreboard
NHL
Scoreboard
Men's College Basketball
Scoreboard
Women's College Basketball
Scoreboard
Baseball
Soccer
More Sports

Live Audio

Tuesday, December 3 6:15pm ET

Would real Huggins stand up?

Any attempt to solve the riddle of Cincinnati basketball coach Bob Huggins should be handled with care. He hates praise -- and criticism. He says he ignores skeptics, but blasts detractors. His list of likes and dislikes takes more twists and turns than a trip

Bob Huggins is a study in

News

Young, 49ers hit paydirt against Falcons

Report: Miami's Davis to interview at 'Bama

Raptors hand Rockets second loss

Document: Done

Figure 21-8 The ESPNET SportsZone home page

Webaholics Top 50 Links List

URL: `http:/cns-web.cns.ohiou.edu/~rbarrett/webaholics/favlinks/entries.html`
Owner: Rich Barrette
Webmaster: Rich Barrette
Purpose: A fun place to promote a site

Do you have a site that you think is cool and that you would like to share with the world? That's the **purpose** of the Webaholics Top 50 Links List. It is a list that simply consists of 50 links added interactively by readers. Once added, a link starts at number one, then gets bumped down as other links are added. Figure 21-9 shows a standard Top 50 list.

The visual interface just consists of a list of links. Since that is the purpose of this site, listing the links is all that is necessary.

The code behind the scenes is very impressive. This page makes good use of forms and CGI scripting. You enter your URL with a form, and then it is instantaneously added to the top of the list while it bumps off the 50th item.

This page shows how simple design and a little programming can make for a fun and informative stop.

WebComics Daily

URL: `http://www.webcomics.com/`
Owner: David de Vitry
Webmaster: David de Vitry
Purpose: Entertainment for comics lovers

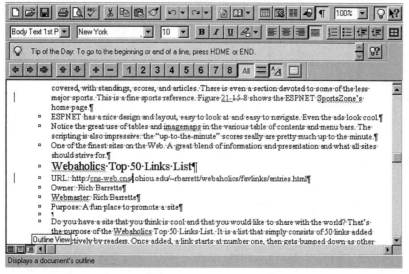

Figure 21-9 The Top 50 list

If you are interested in seeing the actual comics that appear on the Web, WebComics Daily is a good, graphics-intensive alternative to those lists of links. WebComics inlines the various daily comics from all over the Web into five easy-to-read pages. Figure 21-10 shows a typical page from WebComics Daily.

This page has a great design with a simple, yet effective, graphical tool bar. The choice of comics is nicely laid out on the top of each page. Each tool is labeled clearly.

Figure 21-10 A typical page from WebComics Daily

This is no easy task, collecting the URLs of all the daily strips on the Web and then inlining them all in one well-organized, easy-to-read "magazine." This site also makes fine use of backgrounds to give it a really cool feel.

It has got to be a labor of love on Mr. de Vitry's part to create such a fine Web resource. Be forewarned, though; this is not a stop for someone with a slow connection.

SEDS Internet Space Warehouse

URL: `http://www.seds.org/`
Owner: Students for the Exploration and Development of Space, University of Arizona Chapter
Webmaster: Chris Lewicki at `<webmaster@seds.org>`
Purpose: Information about and images of astronomy, space exploration

If you are interested in learning about astronomy and seeing some intergalactic images, check out SEDS. Figure 21-11 shows the SEDS home page.

Visitors to the SEDS home page are greeted with a view of the planet Earth taken from a hypothetical camera on the surface of the moon. Above it, a list of links allows users to learn more about the organization, study the planets, or look up images of planets, stars, and spacecraft.

The page uses an ingenious combination of normal links and imagemaps. A list of links is grouped together in the center of the page. Above and below the links are imagemaps that provide access to some of the same resources listed in the text links, as well as to new links. The designers also spent a great deal of time organizing the comprehensive archive of space images and providing a graphical interface that allows users to see thumbnails of the full images, as well as a search index for finding a particular image.

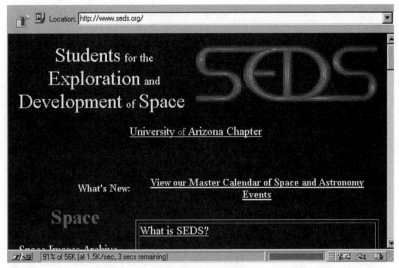

Figure 21-11 The SEDS home page

If you're accessing the Web through a slow connection, the use of lots of images may make accessing the site frustrating. However, if you have any interest in space, or an interest in a well-designed, graphics-rich Web page, the SEDS Internet Space Warehouse is a must-see.

boston.com

URL: `http://www.boston.com/`
Owner: *The Boston Globe*
Webmaster: Dave Margulius at `<margulius@globe.com>`
Purpose: Information about Boston

Planning a trip to Boston? If so, make sure you visit boston.com before you leave. Figure 21-12 shows the boston.com home page.

A very basic page greets visitors to boston.com, with a handful of links to different resources. The information on the other side of those links, though, is enough to answer anyone's questions about Boston. Visitors can read the current issue of *The Boston Globe*, check out restaurant reviews, search classified ads, and take part in online discussions.

Load the boston.com page. Now reload it. If everything's working, the featured links you saw the first time should have been replaced with a different set. The site uses a CGI script to generate the HTML code for the home page on the fly, randomly selecting the featured links from a list. The site has power: Redundant Sun SPARCstation 20 servers run the Netsite commerce server from Netscape and access 40-gigabyte RAID disks. The site has a T3 connection to the Internet so that it can handle heavy traffic with ease.

The boston.com site provides one-stop shopping for information about the Boston area. The site emphasizes information and keeps graphics and imagemaps

Figure 21-12 The boston.com home page

down to a minimum, so that those using text-based browsers or who have turned off image loading can still make good use of the pages.

Amazon.com Books

URL: `http://www.amazon.com`
Owner: Amazon.com Books
Webmaster: `webmaster@amazon.com`
Purpose: Selling books

Looking for a book to buy? Try Amazon.com books. Figure 21-13 shows the Amazon.com home page.

Amazon.com, which modestly bills itself as "Earth's biggest bookstore," offers a catalog of one million titles. A search engine allows users to search the catalog by title, author, subject, or key word. You can add (and remove) books from a "shopping basket," and arrange for payment when you're ready to buy them.

CGI scripts generate dynamic HTML documents, so that when you return to the home page, a different book may be advertised than on your original visit. The search engine for the book catalog is very efficient; it can scan through the contents of the catalog and return an HTML document with the results of the search in only a few seconds.

Amazon.com shows how to combine a large catalog of information with a Web page and search engine to allow visitors to quickly find the information they need.

Red Dirt Shirt

URL: `https://hoohana.aloha.net/~reddirt/`
Owner: Red Dirt Shirts
Webmaster: `reddirt@aloha.net`
Purpose: T-shirt catalog

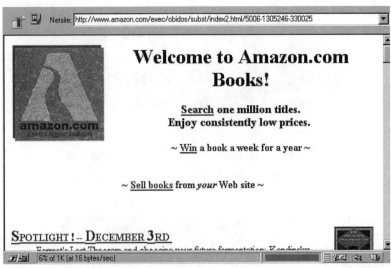

Figure 21-13 The Amazon.com home page

Looking for a T-shirt? Red Dirt Shirts has their catalog online. Figure 21-14 shows the Red Dirt Shirt home page.

The home page itself is not remarkable, but the list of "cool shirts" for sale shows a good way to create a catalog page on the Web. Small graphical images of the shirts are combined in a form so that people can see the variety of shirts available and immediately select those they want to buy.

The site uses a secure server from Netscape to provide safer transaction of credit card information for those using the Netscape browser (note the different protocol in the URL for the secure site: `https` instead of `http`).

The Red Dirt Shirts page shows how a catalog of merchandise can be simply and effectively created on the Web.

Switchboard

URL: `http://www2.switchboard.com`
Owner: Coordinate.com
Webmaster: `webmaster@switchboard.com`
Purpose: Information

Looking for a somebody or some business? If they have a listed phone number in their name, you can find them here. Figure 21-15 shows the Switchboard home page.

Graphically, Switchboard is nothing out of the ordinary; it is a nice, well done home page. It has a simple but tasteful design. There are some nice clean icons on the top of the page that serve as a menu. There are also text versions of the icons until the graphical menu loads. It is all clean and simple, but nothing to make you go wow! It is the interface that makes this site so good.

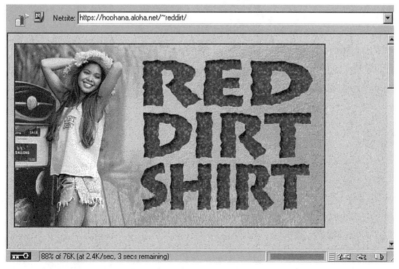

Figure 21-14 The Red Dirt Shirt home page

Figure 21-15 Switchboard home page

The site uses forms interacting through CGI with a very extensive database. The database contains the names of just about everybody in the United States who has a listed phone number. You enter the information about the person or persons you are looking for by filling in the proper fields of the form. Switchboard then gives you a list of all the people who match your criteria.

Switchboard is one of the more useful sites on the Web.

AltaVista

URL: http://altavista.digital.com
Owner: Digital Computing
Webmaster: suggestions.altavista@pa.dec.com
Purpose: Searching

Looking for a Web site on, well, anything? If so, AltaVista should be the first place you look. Figure 21-16 shows the AltaVista home page.

The home page is very simple. It basically consists of a form where you enter a phrase to search for. The phase may be text or even a specific URL or part of a URL (which is really useful if you are trying to find sites that link to you).

The home page may be simple; the results aren't. After you enter the phrase you are looking for, AltaVista will search its very, very extensive database and return any Web pages that have content that match the phrase you entered. The matching pages are returned to you in groups of 10 or so, with the URL and some text from the page where a match is found. Clicking on the URL or the title will bring you to the page.

AltaVista is, if not the best, then one of the best searching mechanisms on the Web.

Figure 21-16 The AltaVista home page

A

HTML QUICK REFERENCE

This appendix lists the tags used in various versions of HTML, divided by subject, for quick reference when you're working on a page. References to the How-To's that describe the tags in greater detail are included. Tags that are available only in HTML 3 and/or Netscape are noted in the definition; otherwise, the tag is from HTML 2. If a tag has an attribute that can be included in the tag, it is shown in an indented list below the tag. An ellipsis (**...**) is used to indicate where text can be placed between tags. Text in italics indicates a variable that should be replaced with the appropriate filename, key word, or number.

Document Basics

These tags provide the basic structure for an HTML document.

ELEMENT	HOW TO	DEFINITION
`<BODY>...</BODY>`	2.8	Marks the beginning and end of the body of an HTML document
`BACKGROUND = URL`	2.12	Specifies the image to be used as background
`BGCOLOR = color`	2.9	Specifies color for background (*color* can be a name or a hexadecimal number)
`TEXT = color`	2.10	Specifies color for the text
`LINK = color`	2.11	Specifies color for links on a page
`ALINK = color`	2.11	Specifies color for active links on a page
`VLINK = color`	2.11	Specifies color for visited links on a page

continued on next page

continued from previous page

ELEMENT	HOW TO	DEFINITION
`LEFTMARGIN = n`		Specifies the distance between the left side of the document and the left edge of the browser window (Microsoft)
`TOPMARGIN = n`		Specifies the distance between the top of the document and the top of the browser window (Microsoft)
`BGPROPERTIES = FIXED`		Fixes the location of the background image (that is, doesn't let it scroll)
`<HEAD>...</HEAD>`	2.6	Marks the beginning and end of the header of an HTML document
`<HTML>...<HTML>`	2.6	Marks the beginning and end of an HTML document
`<TITLE>...</TITLE>`	2.6	Identifies the title of an HTML document (used in the heading)
`<!--...-->`	2.7	Makes a comment in an HTML document
`<!DOCTYPE HTML info>`		Defines the DTD used for this document (`info` is the name of the DTD)
`<META>`		Provides meta-information about a document
`HTTP-EQUIV = name`		The header of the HTTP file relevant to the data in the `<META>` document
`CONTENT = name`		The data associated with the named HTTP header
`NAME = name`		A description of the document
`URL = URL`		A URL associated with the meta-information

Physical Text Styles

These tags allow you to change the physical style of text in your document, that is, change how the text is displayed for the user.

ELEMENT	HOW-TO	DEFINITION
`<B>...</B>`	3.1	Makes text bold
`<BIG>...</BIG>`	3.4	Puts text in a large-print font
`<BASEFONT SIZE=n>`	3.4	Sets the default font size for the document
`<BLINK>...</BLINK>`		Makes blinking text (Netscape)
`<FONT >...</FONT>`	3.4	
`SIZE = n`		Changes the font size by a value n (n can be any number from 1 to 7, or a positive or negative number to indicate an offset from the base font size)
`COLOR = color`		Changes the font color (`color` can be a name or a hexadecimal number)
`FACE = font name`		Changes the font style to the font(s) named, provided the fonts exist on the local system (Microsoft/Netscape)
`<I>.../I>`	3.2	Italicizes text

ELEMENT	HOW-TO	DEFINITION
<MARQUEE>...</MARQUEE>	15.1	Inserts a marquee of moving text (Microsoft)
ALIGN = *align*		The alignment of text surrounding the marquee (LEFT, CENTER, RIGHT, TOP, MIDDLE, BOTTOM)
BEHAVIOR = *behavior*		How the text moves (SCROLL, SLIDE ALTERNATE)
BGCOLOR = *color*		Background color of the marquee (*color* can be a name or a hexadecimal value)
DIRECTION = *direction*		Direction the text scrolls (LEFT, RIGHT)
HEIGHT = *n*		Height of the marquee (pixels)
WIDTH = *n*		Width of the marquee (pixels)
HSPACE = *n*		Amount of horizontal space around the marquee
VSPACE = *n*		Amount of vertical space around the marquee
LOOP = *n*		Scrolls the marquee *n* times
SCROLLDELAY = *n*		Number of milliseconds between each update
SCROLLAMOUNT = *n*		Amount text has moved in one update
<S>...</S>	3.7	Puts text in a strikethrough font (HTML 3), also </STRIKE>...</STRIKE> (Netscape))
<SMALL>...</SMALL>	3.4	Puts text in a small-print font (HTML 3)
_{...}	3.8	Puts text in a subscript (HTML 3)
^{...}	3.8	Puts text in a superscript (HTML 3)
<TT>...</TT>	3.3	Puts text in a teletype (fixed-width) font
<U>...</U>	3.6	Underlines text

Content Text Styles

These tags allow you to change the content style of the text in your document, that is, change the implied meaning of the text.

ELEMENT	HOW-TO	DEFINITION
<ADDRESS>...</ADDRESS>	4.8	Specifies the author, contact information, and so on, of the page
<CITE>...</CITE>	4.3	Specifies a citation
<CODE>...</CODE>	4.5	Includes code (from a computer program)
<DFN>...</DFN>	4.4	Specifies a definition
<EM>	4.2	Emphasizes text
<H*n*>...</H*n*>	4.1	Identifies the heading for a document (*n* can be a whole number between 1 (largest heading) and 6 (smallest heading))
ALIGN = *alignment*		Sets the alignment of the heading (*alignment* can be LEFT, CENTER, RIGHT, or JUSTIFY) (HTML 3/Netscape)

continued on next page

continued from previous page

ELEMENT	HOW-TO	DEFINITION
\<KBD>...\</KBD>	4.7	Identifies input or output from a computer
\<SAMP>...\</SAMP>	4,6	Specifies a sample of literal characters
\<STRONG>.../STRONG>	4.2	Strongly emphasizes text
\<VAR>...\</VAR>	4.5	Specifies a variable

Document Spacing

These tags control the spacing in your document.

ELEMENT	HOW-TO	DEFINITION
\<BLOCKQUOTE>...\</BLOCKQUOTE>	7.7	Creates a quotation block
\ 	7.4	Inserts a line break
CLEAR = *alignment*		Clears text wrap (*alignment* can be LEFT, RIGHT, or ALL)
\<CENTER>...\</CENTER>	7.3	Centers text (same as \<DIV ALIGN=CENTER>)
\<DIV>...\</DIV>	7.8	Marks a division in a Web page
ALIGN = *alignment*		Alignment of division (LEFT, CENTER, RIGHT)
\<HR>	4.1	Adds a horizontal line
ALIGN = *alignment*		Alignment of the line (*alignment* can be LEFT, RIGHT, or CENTER)
SIZE = *n*		Specifies the thickness of the line
NOSHADE		Makes the line black
WIDTH = *n%*		Specifies the width of the line (*n* can be any number from 0 to 100)
COLOR = *color*		Color of the line (Microsoft) (*color* can be a name or a hexadecimal number)
\<MULTICOL>...\</MULTICOL>	15.3	Creates multicolumn text (Netscape 3)
COLS = *n*		Number of columns
GUTTER = *n*		Number of pixels between columns
WIDTH = *n*		Width of each column
\<NOBR>...\</NOBR>	7.5	Marks text that should not have a line break included (Microsoft/Netscape)
\<P>...\</P>	7.4	Creates a paragraph
ALIGN = *alignment*		Alignment of the paragraph (*alignment* can be LEFT, CENTER, or RIGHT)
\<PRE>...\</PRE>	7.6	Identifies preformatted text
WIDTH = *n*		Width of text in characters

ELEMENT	HOW-TO	DEFINITION
`<SPACER>`	15.4	Creates horizontal or vertical space (Netscape 3)
TYPE = *type*		Type of spacer to use (*type* can be HORIZONTAL, VERTICAL, or BLOCK)
SIZE = *n*		Size of hortizontal or vertical spacer
WIDTH = *n*		Width of block spacer
HEIGHT = *n*		Height of block spacer
ALIGN = *alignment*		Alignment of block spacer (*alignment* can be LEFT, CENTER, or RIGHT)
`<WBR>`		Includes a soft line break within a nonbreaking line

Tables

These tags allow you to create tables in HTML 3 or Netscape.

ELEMENT	HOW-TO	DEFINITION
`<CAPTION>...</CAPTION>`	5.2	Identifies the table caption
ALIGN = *alignment*		Alignment of the caption (*alignment* can be TOP or BOTTOM)
`<TABLE>...</TABLE>`	5.1	Defines a table
BORDER = *n*		Shows the lines of the table to the specified thickness
ALIGN = *alignment*		Alignment of the table (*alignment* can be BLEEDLEFT, LEFT, CENTER, RIGHT, BLEEDRIGHT, or JUSTIFY)
WIDTH = *n*		Fixed width of the entire table (*n* is any number)
BGCOLOR = *color*	15.5	Defines the color of the background of the table (*color* can be a name or a hexadecimal number) (Microsoft/Netscape)
BORDERCOLOR = *color*	15.5	Defines the color of a table border (Microsoft)
BORDERCOLORLIGHT = *color*	15.5	Defines the color of the light portion of a 3D table border (Microsoft)
BORDERCOLORDARK = *color*	15.5	Defines the color of the dark portion of a 3D table border (Microsoft)
BACKGROUND = *URL*	15.6	Defines the location of the background image for a table (Microsoft)
CELLSPACING = *n*	5.9	Sets the spacing between cells in a table
CELLPADDING = *n*	5.10	Sets the spacing between cell contents and borders
COLS = *n*		Sets the number of columns in a table (Microsoft)
FRAME = *frame*	15.7	Defines the type of outside table border to show (*frame* can be VOID, ABOVE, BELOW, HSIDES, LHS, RHS, VSIDES, BOX, or BORDER) (Microsoft)
RULES = *rule*	15.7	Defines the type of inside table border to show (*rule* can be NONE, GROUPS, ROWS, COLS, ALL) (Microsoft)
`<TH>...</TH>`, `<TD>...</TD>`	5.3, 5.4	Defines a table heading `<TH>` or a data table entry `<TD>`

continued on next page

continued from previous page

ELEMENT	HOW-TO	DEFINITION
ALIGN = *alignment*		Alignment of entries in a row (*alignment* can be LEFT, CENTER, or RIGHT)
VALIGN = *alignment*		Vertical alignment of table row entries (*alignment* can be TOP, MIDDLE, BOTTOM, or BASELINE)
ROWSPAN = *n*		Number of table rows the cell should cover
COLSPAN = *n*		Number of table columns the cell should cover
NOWRAP		Turns off word wrapping in the table cell
WIDTH = *n*		Width of the cell, in pixels or percent
HEIGHT = *n*		Height of the cell, in pixels
<TR>...</TR>	5.6	Starts a new row in the table
<TBODY>...</TBODY>		Defines the table body (Microsoft)
<THEAD>...</THEAD>		Defines the table head (Microsoft)
<TFOOT>...</TFOOT>		Defines the table foot (Microsoft)

Lists

These tags allow you to create a number of different types of lists in your document.

ELEMENT	HOW-TO	DEFINITION
<OL>...</OL>	6.1	Creates an ordered (numbered) list
COMPACT		Displays a compacted version of the list
TYPE = *type*	6.2	Specifies the type of numbering used (*type* can be A, a, I, i, or 1)
START = *n*	6.2	Starting number of the list
<UL>...</UL>	6.3	Creates an unordered (bulleted) list
COMPACT		Displays a compacted version of the list
TYPE = *type*		Specifies the type of bullet to use (*type* can be CIRCLE, DISC, or SQUARE)
<DL>...</DL>	6.8	Creates a glossary list
COMPACT		Displays a compacted version of the list
<MENU>...</MENU>	6.6	Creates a menu list
COMPACT		Displays a compacted version of the list
<DIR>...</DIR>	6.7	Creates a directory list
COMPACT		Displays a compacted version of the list
<DT>	6.8	Identifies a defined term in a glossary list
<DD>	6.8	Identifies a definition in a glossary list
<LI>	6.1, 6.3, 6.6, 6.7	Identifies a list item in <OL>, <UL>, <MENU>, or <DIRECTORY>
TYPE = *bullet type*		Specifies the type of bullet to use for this and subsequent list entries in a bulleted list (*bullet type* can be CIRCLE, DISC, or SQUARE)

ELEMENT	HOW-TO	DEFINITION
TYPE = *number type*		Specifies the type of numbering used for this and subsequent list entries in an ordered list (*number type* can be A, a, I, i, or 1)
VALUE = *n*		Starting number of this and later entries in a numbered list (*n* is any integer)

Links

These tags allow you to create links to Web pages, FTP and Gopher sites, and other Internet resources.

ELEMENT	HOW-TO	DEFINITION
`<A>...</A>`	8.5-8.14	Defines an anchor for a link
HREF = *URL*		Specifies the destination of the link, using its URL
NAME = *name*		Specifies the name of a section of a document for later use in links
SHAPE = *shape*	7.16	Shape of a link embedded in a figure (HTML 3) (*shape* can be `circle x,y,r`; `rect x,y,r,h`; `polygon x1,y1,x2,y2, ,xn,yn`; or `default`)
TARGET = *target*	19.1	Specifies the target window for a link
TITLE = *title*		Title that appears when a link is selected
`<BASE HREF=URL>`	8.3	Defines the base URL of the relative links in a document (located in the header of the document)
`<LINK>`	8.4	Defines the relationship between the current document and other documents
REL		Type of relationship between the current document and other documents
REV		Reverse relationship between other documents and the current one
HREF = *URL*		URL of the reference

Images

These tags allow you to incorporate images into your pages.

ELEMENT	HOW-TO	DEFINITION
`<IMG>`	9.2	Includes an inline image
ALIGN = *alignment*	9.3	Alignment of the image (*alignment* can be TOP, MIDDLE, BOTTOM, LEFT, or RIGHT)
ALIGN = *alignment*	9.3	Alignment of the image (Netscape) (*alignment* can be LEFT, RIGHT, TEXTTOP, ABSMIDDLE, BASELINE, or BOTTOM)
ALT = *"text"*	9.4	Text description of the image
BORDER = *n*		Size of the picture border, in pixels
HEIGHT = *n*	9.5	Fixed height of the image

continued on next page

continued from previous page

ELEMENT	HOW-TO	DEFINITION
WIDTH = *n*	9.5	Fixed width of the image
HSPACE = *n*		Horizontal runaround space, in pixels
VSPACE = *n*		Vertical runaround space, in pixels
ISMAP	9.13	Declares the image to be an image map
SRC = *graphic filename*		Filename of the image
LOWSRC = *graphic filename*	9.10	Filename of a low-resolution version of the image (Netscape)
USEMAP = *URL*		URL of a client-side image map for the image
<MAP>...</MAP>	9.14	Collection of links for a client-side image map
NAME = *name*		Name of the image map
<AREA>	9.14	Link in a client-side image map
COORDS = *coords*		Coordinates defining the location of the link
HREF = *URL*		Destination of the link
NOHREF		Makes the region inactive in the image map
SHAPE = *shape*		Type of shape for the link (*shape* can be RECT, CIRC, POLY, DEFAULT)
ALT = "*text*"		Alternative text for the link
TARGET = *target*		Destination window of the link (Microsoft)

Forms

These tags allow you to create forms that include different types of inputs; they also specify what to do with the results of the form when submitted.

ELEMENT	HOW-TO	DEFINITION
<FORM>...</FORM>	11.1	Defines a form
ACTION = *URL*		Location (URL) of the script that will process the form results
METHOD = *method*		Method of sending the form input (*method* can be GET or POST)
ENCTYPE = *enctype*		Encoding type for the form data
<INPUT>		Creates an input area of the form
TYPE =		Type of form input
CHECKBOX	11.3	Check box
FILE	11.7	Allows user to attach a file
ACCEPT = "*text*"		Limits the range of acceptable files
HIDDEN		Invisible input
IMAGE	11.9	Returns information on where the user clicked on the image
RADIO	11.4	Radio button

ELEMENT	HOW-TO	DEFINITION
PASSWORD	11.5	Password
TEXT	11.2	Single-line text input
SUBMIT	11.1	Button to submit the form input
RESET	11.1	Button to reset the form input
NAME = *name*		Name of this input variable, as seen by the script (but not displayed in the form)
SIZE = *n*		Defines the size of the text display for a TEXT form
MAXLENGTH = *n*		Maximum length of a TEXT input item
VALUE = "*text*"		Value used to initialize HIDDEN and TEXT fields
DISABLED		Disables the field to prevent text from being entered
CHECKED		Initializes a field in a CHECKBOX or RADIO to be selected
SRC = *graphic filename*		Specifies the image filename for IMAGE, SUBMIT, and RESET
ALIGN = *align*		Alignment of form element (*align* can be TOP, MIDDLE, BOTTOM, LEFT, or RIGHT)
<ISINDEX>		Defines a searchable index
ACTION = *URL*		Specifies the gateway program to be used (Microsoft)
PROMPT = "*text*"		Specifies the text to be shown before the prompt (Microsoft)
<OPTION>	11.6	Specifies an option in a <SELECT> menu form
DISABLED		Disables the entry to prevent its selection
SELECTED		Initializes the entry to be selected
<SELECT>...</SELECT>	11.6	Creates a menu of selections
NAME = *name*		Name of the input variable, as seen by the script (but not displayed in the form)
MULTIPLE		Permits multiple selections to be made from the menu
DISABLED		Disables the menu to prevent selections
WIDTH = *n*		Fixed width of the menu (Netscape)
HEIGHT = *n*		Fixed height of the menu (Netscape)
SIZE = *n*		Height of the menu
<TEXTAREA>...</TEXTAREA>	11.8	Creates a multiline text input area for a form (any text located between the tags becomes the initial value for the form)
NAME = *name*		Name of the input variable, as seen by the script (but not displayed in the form)
ROWS = *n*		Number of rows down the text area should be
COLS = *n*		Number of columns across the text area should be
DISABLED		Disables the menu to prevent input

Frames

These tags let you create a variety of different types of frames in a document.

ELEMENT	HOW-TO	DEFINITION
`<FRAMESET>`	19.1	Defines a set of frames in a document (Microsoft/Netscape)
`COLS = n`		Creates column-oriented frames (n is a set of pixel widths or percentages)
`ROWS = n`		Creates row-oriented frames (n is a set of pixel widths or percentages)
`FRAMEBORDER = 0,1`	19.2	Turns on (1) or off (0) frame borders (Microsoft)
`FRAMEBORDER = YES,NO`	19.2	Turns on or off frame borders (Netscape)
`BORDER = n`	19.2	Thickness of frame borders (Netscape)
`BORDERCOLOR = color`	19.2	Color of border (color can be a name or hexadecimal number) (Netscape)
`FRAMESPACING = n`		Defines space between frames (Microsoft)
`<FRAME>`	19.1	Defines a frame (Microsoft/Netscape)
`ALIGN = align`		Alignment of frame or surrounding text (Microsoft) (align can be LEFT, CENTER, RIGHT, TOP, or BOTTOM)
`FRAMEBORDER = 0,1`	19.2	Turn on (1) or off (0) frame borders (Microsoft)
`FRAMEBORDER = YES,NO`	19.2	Turn on or off frame borders (Netscape)
`MARGINHEIGHT = n`		Defines the margin height of frame, in pixels (Microsoft)
`MARGINWIDTH = n`		Defines the margin width of frame, in pixels (Microsoft)
`NAME = name`		Defines target name for the frame
`SCROLLING = YES,NO`		Turns scrolling on or off
`SRC = URL`		Defines the URL for the frame
`<IFRAME>...</IFRAME>`	19.4	Defines a floating frame (Microsoft)
`ALIGN = align`		Aligns a frame or surrounding text (align can be LEFT, CENTER, RIGHT, TOP, or BOTTOM)
`FRAMEBORDER = 0,1`	19.2	Turns on (1) or off (0) frame borders
`MARGINHEIGHT = n`		Defines the margin height of the frame, in pixels (Microsoft)
`MARGINWIDTH = n`		Defines the margin width of the frame, in pixels (Microsoft)
`NAME = name`		Defines target name for the frame
`SCROLLING = YES,NO`		Turns scrolling on or off
`SRC = URL`		Defines the URL for the frame
`HEIGHT = n`		Defines the height of a floating frame
`WIDTH = n`		Defines the width of a floating frame
`<NOFRAMES>...</NOFRAMES>`	19.7	Defines alternative text for those not using frames-enabled browsers

Multimedia

These tags allow you to include Java applets, JavaScript scripts, and other multimedia elements into your Web pages.

ELEMENT	HOW-TO	DEFINITION
`<APPLET>...</APPLET>`	17.2	Includes a Java applet
`ALIGN = align`		Defines the alignment of the applet (`align` can be LEFT, CENTER, or RIGHT)
`CODE = file`		Defines the filename of the applet
`CODEBASE = URL`		Defines the URL to the applet
`HEIGHT = n`		Defines the height of the applet
`WIDTH = n`		Defines the width of the applet
`HSPACE = n`		Defines the horizontal space around the applet
`VSPACE = n`		Defines the vertical space around the applet
`NAME = name`		Defines the name of the applet to identify it to other applets on the page
`PARAM NAME = name`		Defines an applet-specific argument from an HTML page (Microsoft)
`<EMBED>`	18.1	Includes a multimedia object (Microsoft/Netscape)
`HEIGHT = n`		Defines the height of the object
`WIDTH = n`		Defines the width of the object
`NAME = name`		Defines the name of the object to identify it to other objects on the page
`SRC = URL`		Defines the URL of the object
`<NOEMBED>...</NOEMBED>`	18.10	Defines alternative text for browsers that don't support embedded objects (Netscape)
`<OBJECT>...</OBJECT>`	18.2	Includes a multimedia object (Microsoft)
`ALIGN = align`		Defines the alignment of the object (`align` can be BASELINE, CENTER, LEFT, MIDDLE, RIGHT, TEXTBOTTOM, TEXTMIDDLE, or TEXTTOP)
`BORDER = n`		Defines the width of the object border
`CLASSID = URL`		Defines the class ID for ActiveX controls
`CODEBASE = URL`		Defines the URL for the code base of the object
`CODETYPE = type`		Defines the media type of the object
`DATA = URL`		Defines the location of data for the object
`DECLARE`		Declares an object without starting it
`HEIGHT = n`		Defines the height of the object
`HSPACE = n`		Defines the horizontal space around the object

continued on next page

continued from previous page

ELEMENT	HOW-TO	DEFINITION
NAME = *URL*		Defines the name of the object if submitted in a form
SHAPES		Specifies that the object has shaped hyperlinks
STANDBY = *"Message"*		Defines a message to display while the object is loading
TYPE = *type*		Defines the media type for the object data
USEMAP = *URL*		Defines a client-side image map to be used
VSPACE = *n*		Defines the vertical space around the object
WIDTH = *n*		Defines the width of the object
<PARAM>	17.3	Defines parameters to pass to a Java applet
NAME = *name*		Defines the name of the variable
VALUE = *value*		Defines the value to pass to the applet
VALUETYPE = *type*		Specifies how to interpret the data (*type* can be DATE, REF, or OBJECT) (Microsoft)
TYPE = *type*		Defines the media type (Microsoft)
<BGSOUND>		Includes a sound to play in the background (Microsoft)
SRC = *URL*		Defines the URL of the sound file
LOOP = *n*		Defines the number of times to play the sound
<STYLE>...</STYLE>	16.10	Includes a style sheet (Microsoft)
<SPAN>...</SPAN>		Applies style information to part of a document (Microsoft)
STYLE = *style*		Defines the style to be used
<SCRIPT>...</SCRIPT>	17.8	Includes a script (Microsoft/Netscape)
LANGUAGE = *language*		Defines the language of the script
SRC = *URL*		Defines the URL of the script (Netscape)
<NOSCRIPT>...</NOSCRIPT>	17.12	Defines alternative markup for browsers that don't support the script

B

WWW RESOURCES

This book can't go into full detail on every WWW and HTML topic, nor can it provide information on every WWW browser, server, or related application. This appendix is a brief list of information available on the Web and elsewhere on the Internet that will allow you to study in greater detail some of the topics addressed in the book, and also allow you to find Web-related software for your use.

> **NOTE**
>
> The following URLs were accurate when this appendix was written. However, URLs often change and Web sites sometimes disappear, so some of the sites listed may no longer be valid.

Basic Information on WWW and HTML

The World Wide Web (W3) Consortium

`http://www.w3.org/`

Home to general information on the World Wide Web and links to all areas of WWW and HTML.

The WWW Section of Yahoo!

`http://www.yahoo.com/Computers/World_Wide_Web`

Links to hundreds of pages regarding WWW and HTML.

Indexes

ALIWEB

`http://web.nexor.co.uk/public/aliweb/aliweb.html`

> A searchable database of Web pages based on descriptions of sites by their creators.

AltaVista

`http://altavista.digital.com/`

> A powerful search engine for finding Web pages and Usenet postings.

HotBot

`http://www.hotbot.com/`

> A Web search engine sponsored by HotWired.

InfoSeek

`http://www.infoseek.com/`

> Another good search engine for scanning the Web.

Lycos

`http://www.lycos.com/`

> An extensive database of Web pages with sophisticated search tools.

OpenText

`http://www.opentext.com/`

> An extensive database of Web sites.

TradeWave Galaxy

`http://www.einet.net/`

> A subject-based guide to Web pages (formerly EINet Galaxy).

W3 Search Engines

`http://cuiwww.unige.ch/meta-index.html`

> A page with links to a number of WWW search engines.

WebCrawler

`http://webcrawler.com/`

> A search engine that uses its own index or checks the Web in real time to answer queries.

World Wide Web Worm (WWWW)

`http://wwww.cs.colorado.edu/wwww/`

> A searchable database that can find Web pages by title or URL.

Yahoo!

`http://www.yahoo.com/`

> A popular, extensive database of Web pages.

Browsers

Text-Based

Agora

`http://www.w3.org/hypertext/WWW/Agora/Overview.html`

> A browser that uses e-mail to transfer pages, for those without full Internet access.

Emacs W3

`http://www.cs.indiana.edu/elisp/w3/docs.html`

> An Emacs subsystem that can run WWW documents.

Line Mode Browser

`http://www.w3.org/hypertext/WWW/LineMode/`

> A line-based (as opposed to screen-based) browser for dumb terminals.

Lynx

`http://www.cc.ukans.edu/about_lynx/about_lynx.html`

> A screen-based text browser for UNIX, VMS, and DOS systems.

Macintosh

Cyberdog

`http://cyberdog.apple.com/`

A multifaceted Internet tool, including Web browser, that uses Apple's OpenDoc technology.

Enhanced Mosaic (Spyglass)

`http://www.spyglass.com/products/browser.html`

An enhanced version of NCSA's Mosaic, marketed solely to other companies.

Microsoft Internet Explorer

`http://www.microsoft.com/ie/`

Microsoft's powerful and increasingly popular Web browser.

Mosaic for Macintosh

`http://www.ncsa.uiuc.edu/SDG/Software/MacMosaic/MacMosaicHome.html`

The Macintosh version of the Mosaic browser.

Netscape Navigator

`http://home.netscape.com/`

The Macintosh version of the very popular Netscape Navigator browser.

NeXTSTEP

OmniWeb

`http://www.omnigroup.com/Software/OmniWeb/`

A Web browser marketed by Omni Development, Inc.

UNIX (X Windows)

Amaya

`http://www.w3.org/hypertext/WWW/Amaya`

A combination browser and editor from the World Wide Web Consortium.

Arena

http://www.w3.org/hypertext/WWW/Arena/

A prototype HTML 3 Web browser developed by the World Wide Web Consortium.

Chimera

http://www.unlv.edu/chimera/

A small Web browser whose capabilities can be extended by users.

Enhanced Mosaic (Spyglass)

http://www.spyglass.com/products/browser.html

An enhanced version of NCSA's Mosaic, marketed solely to other companies.

Mosaic for X Window

http://www.ncsa.uiuc.edu/SDG/Software/XMosaic/

The X Window version of the Mosaic browser.

Netscape

http://home.netscape.com/

The X Window version of the very popular Netscape Navigator browser.

Viola

http://marble.ebay.gnn.com/proj/viola/violaHome.html

A Web browser created using the Viola hypermedia language.

Windows

Cello

http://www.law.cornell.edu/cello/cellotop.html

An old but once-popular Web browser.

Enhanced Mosaic (Spyglass)

http://www.spyglass.com/products/browser.html

An enhanced version of NCSA's Mosaic, marketed solely to other companies.

Galahad

http://www.mcs.com/~jvwater/main.html

An off-line Web browser.

Microsoft Internet Explorer

`http://www.microsoft.com/ie/`

Microsoft's powerful and increasingly popular Web browser.

Mosaic for Windows

`http://www.ncsa.uiuc.edu/SDG/Software/WinMosaic/HomePage.html`

The Windows version of the Mosaic browser.

Netscape

`http://home.netscape.com/`

The Windows version of the very popular Netscape Navigator browser.

SlipKnot

`http://www.interport.net/slipknot/slipknot.html`

A graphical Web browser that does not require a SLIP or PPP connection or TCP/IP.

Servers

Macintosh

MacHTTP

`http://www.biap.com/machttp_info.html`

A Web server program now superseded by WebSTAR.

WebSTAR

`http://mac-1.qdeck.com/webstar/`

An enhanced, commerical version of MacHTTP.

OS/2

GoServe
`http://www2.hursley.ibm.com/goserve/`

A server program that supports the Web and Gopher protocols.

UNIX

CERN/W3C HTTPD

http://www.w3.org/hypertext/WWW/Daemon/Status.html

A server program developed at CERN and available for most versions of UNIX.

Jungle

http://catless.ncl.ac.uk/Programs/Jungle/

A server written using the tcl/tk programming toolkit.

NCSA HTTPD

http://hoohoo.ncsa.uiuc.edu/docs/Overview.html

A server program written at NCSA.

Netscape Servers

http://home.netscape.com/comprod/mirror/server_download.html

A suite of commercial server programs created by Netscape.

PHTTPD

http://www.signum.se/phttpd/

A free, fast Web server program for computers running the Solaris (SunOS) operating system.

Plexus

http://www.bsdi.com/server/doc/plexus.html

A public domain Web server written in Perl.

WN

http://hopf.math.nwu.edu/

A Web server that incorporates navigation features and conditionally served files.

VAX/VMS

VAX/VMS server

http://kcgl1.eng.ohio-state.edu/www/doc/serverinfo.html

A Web server program created at Ohio State.

Windows

HTTPS (Windows NT)

`http://www.w3.org/hypertext/WWW/HTTPS/Status.html`

A Web server program available for Intel-based systems and the DEC/Alpha.

WebSite (NT and Windows95)

`http://website.ora.com/`

A Web server, with an included Enhanced Mosaic browser, that runs on 386 and higher machines.

Windows HTTPD (Windows 3.1)

`http://www.city.net/win-httpd/`

A small and very fast Web server based on NCSA HTTPD.

HTML Editors

Macintosh

Arachnid

`http://sec-look.uiowa.edu/about/projects/arachnid-page.html`

An HTML editor that won a 1995 Apple Enterprise Award.

BBEdit

`http://www.barebones.com/bbedit.html`

A popular, powerful Macintosh text editor with HTML capabilities.

Claris Home Page

`http://www.claris.com/products/clarispage/`

A WYSIWYG Web page tool that allows you to create pages without having to manually edit HTML.

GNNPress

`http://www.tools.gnn.com/press/index.html`

A multiplatform Web page design tool.

HoTMetaL PRO

http://www.sq.com/products/hotmetal/hmp-org.htm

A commerical HTML editor with a less powerful but free version also available.

HTML Editor

http://dragon.acadiau.ca/~giles/HTML_Editor/Documentation.html

A semi-WYSIWYG HTML editor.

HTML Grinder

http://www.matterform.com/grinder/

An HTML editor that uses special plug-in modules to handle sophisticated tasks.

HTML-HyperEditor

http://www.lu.se/info/Editor/

An HTML editor written as a HyperCard stack that supports special characters used in other languages.

PageMill

http://www.adobe.com/prodindex/pagemill/overview.html

A powerful WYSIWYG editor that creates Web pages without requiring manual HTML editing.

PageSpinner

http://www.algonet.se/~optima/pagespinner.html

An HTML editor that supports many of the newest HTML extensions.

World Wide Web Weaver/HTML Web Weaver

http://www.miracleinc.com

A set of commercial and shareware HTML editors.

UNIX

A Simple HTML Editor (ASHE)

ftp://ftp.cs.rpi.edu/pub/puninj/ASHE/README.html

An HTML editor written in C using Motif and the NCSA HTML Widget.

City University HTML Editor

`http://web.cs.city.ac.uk/homes/njw/htmltext/htmltext.html`

A free, easily configurable HTML editor written using the Andrew toolkit.

GNNPress

`http://www.tools.gnn.com/press/index.html`

A multiplatform Web page design tool.

Symposia

`http://www.grif.fr/prod/sympro.html`

A Web design application for UNIX and Windows.

tkHTML

`http://www.cobaltgroup.com/~roland/tkHTML/tkHTML.html`

An HTML editor written using the tcl/tk toolkit.

Web Magic

`http://www.sgi.com/Products/WebFORCE/WebMagic/index.html`

A powerful Web page creation tool for users of SGI machines.

Windows

FrontPage

`http://www.microsoft.com/msoffice/frontpage/default.htm`

Microsoft's Web page and site development application.

GNNPress

`http://www.tools.gnn.com/press/index.html`

A multiplatform Web page design tool.

HomeSite

`http://www.dexnet.com/homesite.html`

A full-featured shareware Web page designer.

HoTMetaL PRO

http://www.sq.com/products/hotmetal/hmp-org.htm

A commerical HTML editor, with a less powerful but free version also available.

HotDog

http://www.sausage.com/

An HTML editor with a Windows 95-style interface that supports HTML 3 tags and Netscape extensions.

HTML Assistant Pro

http://www.brooknorth.com/istar.html

A commerical HTML editor based on a popular shareware editor.

HTML Writer

http://lal.cs.byu.edu/people/nosack/index.html

An HTML editor that allows you to edit more than one document at a time.

InContext Spider

http://www.incontext.ca/products/spider1.html

A commercial Web page tool that supports advanced HTML features.

Symposia

http://www.grif.fr/prod/sympro.html

A Web design application for UNIX and Windows.

Webber

http://www.csdcorp.com/webber.htm

An HTML editor that includes a validator program to look for invalid HTML markup.

WebMedia Publisher

http://www.wbmedia.com/publisher/

A Web page tool that supports the latest Microsoft and Netscape HTML extensions.

Web Wizard

`http://www.halcyon.com/webwizard/index.html`

An HTML editor available in 16-bit and 32-bit versions.

HTML Document Development

HTML 2.0 Specification

`http://www.w3.org/hypertext/WWW/MarkUp/html-spec/index.html`

A full description of the final draft of HTML 2.

HTML 3.2 Draft Specification

`http://www.w3.org/pub/WWW/MarkUp/`

A full description of the current draft of HTML 3.2.

HTML Style Guide

`http://www.w3.org/hypertext/WWW/Provider/Style/Overview.html`

Tim Berners-Lee's excellent guide to designing WWW documents.

NetSpace Guide for HTML Developers

`http://netspace.org/netspace/wwwdoc.html`

Lots of links to documents on creating effective HTML documents.

Subjective Electronic Information Repository

`http://cbl.leeds.ac.uk/nikos/doc/repository.html`

Links to hundreds of WWW development documents.

URL Descriptions

`http://www.w3.org/hypertext/WWW/Addressing/Addressing.html`

Definitions of the various types of URLs, as well as discussion of URNs and URIs.

WWW Development Page (Virtual Library)

`http://www.charm.net/~web/Vlib/`

Links to a wide range of HTML development documents.

Net Tips for Writers and Designers

http://www.dsiegel.com/tips/

Design tips for effective Web pages from a leading designer.

Frames Tutorial

http://www.newbie.net/frames/

A step-by-step tutorial for creating pages using frames.

Common Gateway Interface (CGI)

CGI Documentation

http://hoohoo.ncsa.uiuc.edu/cgi/

Information on the Common Gateway Interface, including CGI scripts in programs.

CGI Programs (Perl)

http://www.seas.upenn.edu/~mengwong/perlhtml.html

A library of commonly used CGI routines, written in Perl.

Forms and Imagemaps

NCSA Forms Documentation

http://hoohoo.ncsa.uiuc.edu/cgi/forms.html

Information on using forms in conjunction with CGI scripts.

Image Maps: CERN HTTPD

http://www.w3.org/hypertext/WWW/Daemon/User/CGI/HTImageDoc.html

A tutorial for creating imagemaps for the CERN HTTPD server program.

Image Maps: NCSA HTTPD

http://hoohoo.ncsa.uiuc.edu/docs/tutorials/imagemapping.html

A tutorial for creating imagemaps for the NCSA HTTPD server program.

Scripting and Multimedia

ActiveX

ActiveX Development Information

`http://www.microsoft.com/intdev/`

Microsoft's guide to its ActiveX resources.

ActiveX Examples

`http://www.rollins-assoc.com/fvbs.html`

Examples of ActiveX and Visual Basic applications for the Web.

Java

Sun's Java Information

`http://java.sun.com/`

Java information from Sun, the company that created the language.

Gamelan Java Applets

`http://www.gamelan.com/`

A repository of hundreds of Java applets.

JavaWorld

`http://www.javaworld.com/`

An online magazine for the beginning or experienced Java user.

Java Links

`http://www.sover.net/~manx/java.html`

Links to Java resources across the Web.

Steve's Java Resources

`http://infoweb.magi.com/~steve/java.html`

More information about Java on the Web.

Digitalfocus

`http://www.digitalfocus.com/digitalfocus/faq/`

Frequently asked questions about Java and other links.

JavaScript

Netscape JavaScript Information

`http://home.netscape.com/eng/mozilla/Gold/handbook/javascript/`

JavaScript information from the company that brought it to the Web.

Gamelan JavaScript Scripts

`http://www.gamelan.com/`

A repository of many JavaScript scripts.

JavaScript Scripts

`http://www.geocities.com/SiliconValley/9000/`

A set of useful JavaScript scripts by the same set of authors.

JavaScript Tip of the Week

`http://webreference.com/javascript/`

Numerous tips and tricks on using JavaScript.

Babyak's JavaScript Resources

`http://www.epix.com/~mbabyak/`

Links to JavaScript resources across the Web.

Shockwave

Macromedia Shockwave Information

`http://www.macromedia.com/shockwave/`

Shockwave information and tools to create and view Shockwave files.

VRML

VRML FAQ

`http://vag.vrml.org/VRML_FAQ.html`

Frequently asked questions and resources on Virtual Reality Modeling Language.

VRML Respository

`http://www.sdsc.edu/vrml/`

Links to VRML browsers and viewers, development applications, and VRML sites.

NSCA VRML Information

`http://www.ncsa.uiuc.edu/General/VRML/VRMLHome.html`

More information on VRML.

WWW Usenet Newsgroups

Browsers

`comp.infosystems.www.browsers.mac`

Disussion about Macintosh browsers.

`comp.infosystems.www.browsers.ms-windows`

Discussion about Microsoft Windows browsers.

`comp.infosystems.www.browsers.x`

Discussion about X Window browsers.

`comp.infosystems.www.browsers.misc`

Discussion about other classes of browsers.

Document Authoring Groups

`comp.infosystems.www.authoring.cgi`

Discussion of CGI applications.

`comp.infosystems.www.authoring.html`

Discussion of HTML markup.

`comp.infosystems.www.authoring.images`

Discussion of the use of images in WWW documents.

`comp.infosystems.www.authoring.misc`

Discussion of other questions about document creation not covered in the groups already mentioned.

Servers

`comp.infosystems.www.servers.mac`

Discussion about Macintosh servers.

`comp.infosystems.www.servers.ms-windows`

Discussion about Microsoft Windows servers.

`comp.infosystems.www.servers.unix`

Discussion about UNIX servers.

`comp.infosystems.www.servers.misc`

Discussion about other classes of servers.

Other Discussion and Announcement Groups

`comp.infosystems.www.advocacy`

Discussion (and arguments) about various WWW applications and products.

`comp.infosystems.www.announce`

Announcement (no discussion permitted) of new and improved WWW sites.

`comp.infosystems.www.misc`

Discussion about WWW topics not covered by any of the newsgroups already mentioned.

WWW Mailing Lists

`www-talk@info.cern.ch`

Discussion about WWW among experts. To subscribe, e-mail `listserv@info.cern.ch` with the line `subscribe www-talk Your Name` in the body of the message. Subscription requests can also be sent to `www-talk-request@info.cern.ch` to be processed by a human.

`www-announce@info.cern.ch`

Used for "low-volume" announcements of products and services. Use the `listserv` address to subscribe (replace `www-talk` in the body with `www-announce`), or e-mail `www-announce-request@info.cern.ch`.

C

MULTIPURPOSE INTERNET MAIL EXTENSIONS (MIME)

World Wide Web clients, such as browsers and servers, use MIME protocol to communicate information about the type of data requested and sent via HTTP. The sections of this appendix describe MIME and explain how it is used in the World Wide Web environment.

What Is MIME?

The Multipurpose Internet Mail Extensions (MIME) were developed as an extension to the Internet mail protocol to provide for incorporation of multimedia objects. The original definition for Internet mail dealt primarily with the transmission and reception of plain text messages. This mail protocol, as defined in RFC 822 (for more information, see `http://www.w3.org/pub/WWW/Protocols/rfc822/0verview.html`), specified several message header elements that provided direction for routing of the mail messages. The development of this protocol provided a standard that all Internet mail programs could use.

The Internet mail protocol, however, left message content largely unmentioned, assuming that most messages would be simple text. In today's world of Internet mail, complex, multipart, and multimedia messages are becoming commonplace. MIME was developed to support these types of complex mail messages. It does so by adding suitable header fields to describe message content and delimit multimedia objects. A standard such as MIME is necessary to provide for interoperability among

Internet mail programs that support complex mail messages. For example, the following message represents a multipart message containing text, audio, and PostScript components:

```
MIME-Version: 1.0
Content-type: multipart/mixed; boundary=SomeString

--SomeString
Content-type: text/plain
Text message body

--SomeString
Content-type: audio/basic
An audio object

--SomeString
Content-type: application/postscript
A postscript object

--SomeString--
```

(For an official list of registered media types, see URL `ftp://ftp.isi.edu/in-notes/iana/assignments/media-types`.)

The headers define the MIME version and the kind of message being sent. In this case, the message is specified as `multipart/mixed`, with an indication that the string will be used to delimit the subcomponents. Each subcomponent has individual *type/subtype* specifications to describe the content of the particular subcomponent. The delimiter string marks the beginning and end of a subcomponent as well as marking the termination of the message. For more details on MIME, see the specification contained in RFC 1521, which is available at `http://sunsite.auc.dk/RFC/rfc/rfc1521.html`.

MIME Content-type **Header and the Web**

The portion of MIME protocol that is of central interest to HTML document developers is the `Content-type` header field. The World Wide Web environment uses MIME content-type information in several ways. Table C-1 specifies a set of the more commonly used MIME types that may be encountered in that environment.

Table C-1 MIME types commonly or specifically used with the World Wide Web

MIME TYPE/SUBTYPE	DESCRIPTION	COMMON FILE EXTENSIONS
application/acad	AutoCAD file	dwg
application/arj	ARJ archive file	arj
application/clariscad	ClarisCAD file	CCAD
application/dxf	AutoCAD DXF file	dxf
application/excel	Microsoft Excel	xl
application/mac-binhex40	Binhex archive format	hqx

MIME TYPE/SUBTYPE	DESCRIPTION	COMMON FILE EXTENSIONS
application/msword	Microsoft Word	doc
application/mswrite	Microsoft Write	wri
application/octet-stream	Binary data	bin
application/oda	Office Document Architecture	oda
application/pdf	Adobe Acrobat PDF format	pdf
application/postscript	PostScript document	ps eps
application/rtf	Rich Text format	rtf
application/set	French CAD standard	set
application/x-csh	C shell script	csh
application/x-cpio	POSIX CPIO format	cpio
application/x-director	Macromedia Director files	dir dcr dxr
application/x-dvi	Device-Independent format	dvi
application/x-gtar	GNU tar format	gtar
application/x-gzip	GNU zip format	gz gzip
application/x-hdf	NCSA HDF data	hdf
application/x-latex	LaTeX document	latex
application/x-mif	FrameMaker MIF files	mif
application/x-netcdf	Net Common Data Format	cdf nc
application/x-pl	Perl script	perl pl
application/x-sh	Sh shell script	sh
application/x-shar	Shell archive	shar
application/x-stuffit	Macintosh Stuffit archive	sit sea
application/x-tcl	Tcl script	tcl
application/x-tex	TeX document	tex
application/x-texinfo	TexInfo format	texinfo texi
application/x-troff	troff document	t tr troff
application/x-troff-man	troff with man macros	man
application/x-troff-me	troff with me macros	me
application/x-troff-ms	troff with ms macros	ms
application/x-ustar	POSIX tar format	ustar
application/x-wais-source	WAIS source	src
application/x-winhelp	Windows Help format	hlp
application/zip	Zip compressed document	zip
audio/basic	Basic audio file (8-bit PCM)	au snd
audio/x-aiff	AIFF audio file	aiff aif

continued on next page

continued from previous page

MIME TYPE/SUBTYPE	DESCRIPTION	COMMON FILE EXTENSIONS
audio/x-pn-realaudio	RealAudio	ra ram
audio/x-pn-realaudio-plugin	RealAudio plug-in	rpm
audio/x-wav	Microsoft audio format	wav
image/gif	GIF image	gif
image/ief	Image exchange format	ief
image/jpeg	JPEG image	jpeg jpg jpe
image/pict	PICT image	pict
image/tiff	TIFF image	tiff tif
image/x-portable-anymap	Portable image format	pnm
image/x-portable-bitmap	Portable Bitmap format	pbm
image/x-portable-graymap	Portable Grayscale image format	pgm
image/x-portable-pixmap	Portable Pixmap format	ppm
image/x-rgb	RGB image	rgb
image/x-xwindowdump	X Window dump	xwd
image/x-xbitmap	X bitmap	xbm
image/x-xpixmap	X pixelmap	xpm
message/rfc822	MIME message	mime
multipart/mixed	Multipart messages	
multipart/x-zip	PKZIP archive	zip
multipart/x-gzip	GNU Zip archive	gz gzip
text/html	HTML text	html htm
text/plain	Normal text (ASCII)	txt
text/richtext	MIME Rich Text format	rtx
text/tab-separated-values	Text with tab-separated values	tsv
text/x-setext	Structure enhanced text	etx
video/mpeg	MPEG format video	mpeg mpg mpe
video/msvideo	Microsoft Video format	avi
video/quicktime	QuickTime format video	qt mov
video/x-sgi-movie	SGI format movie	movie
x-world/x-vrml	VRML virtual environment	wrl wrz

In addition, the World Wide Web environment defines several other experimental and nonstandard MIME content types. Table C-2 lists some of them, along with references to the How-To's within this book that describe these particular MIME content types.

Table C-2 World Wide Web–specific MIME types

MIME TYPE/SUBTYPE	DESCRIPTION	HOW-TO REFERENCE
application/x-www-form-urlencode	Encoding for form data	11.1, 14.1
application/x-www-pem-request	PEM authorization request	13.10
application/x-www-pem-reply	PEM authorization reply	13.10
applicaiton/x-www-pgm-request	PGM authorization request	13.10
application/x-www-pgm-reply	PGM authorization reply	13.10
application/x-httpd-cgi	CGI applications	
	(cgi filename extension)	14.4
magnus-internal/parsed-html	NS FastTrack parsed HTML	13.4
magnus-internal/cgi	NS FastTrack executable CGI	14.4
multipart/form-data	Alternate form data method	11.7, 14.8
multipart/x-mixed-replace	Netscape Server Push	15.10
text/x-server-parsed-html	NCSA parsed HTML	13.4

The categories specified in these tables are not a complete list of MIME content types, but they do cover a large percentage of common types. The WWW-specific types described are all nonstandard MIME content types and may not be suitable for all clients, servers, and client/server combinations.

The HTTP protocol specifies the content types of HTTP requests and responses using MIME type/subtype designations. (See Appendix G, "The Hypertext Transfer Protocol [HTTP].") When a client issues a **GET** request of an HTTP server, the server sends a **Content-type** field in the header of its response indicating the type of information enclosed in the response body. When a client issues a **POST** request, it includes a **Content-type** field in the request header specifying the format of the data being sent to the server:

```
Content-type: application/x-www-form-urlencoded
```

or

```
Content-type: multipart/form-data
```

Content-type fields for both MIME and HTTP are composed of the header name, **Content-type**, and at least two fields specifying a type and a subtype:

```
Content-type: type/subtype
```

The type specification can be chosen from the following list:

- ▪ **application**: The file needs to be processed or manipulated in some manner by the recipient. For example, a PostScript object should be sent to an appropriate PostScript viewer.

- ▪ **audio**: The file is an audio object. This object should be rendered using the appropriate software and hardware, if available. If a suitable rendering environment is unavailable, many browsers allow the reader to save the object to a file.

■ **extension-token**: This refers to a type beginning with the **x-** prefix. Use this prefix for all experimental, nonstandard, or private types. For example, the **x-world** type specifies a virtual environment.

■ **image**: The file is an image of some type and should be treated appropriately.

■ **message**: The file conforms to a different message standard, such as RFC 822.

■ **multipart**: The file is composed of multiple objects, each having its own respective type and subtype. The multipart type requires another header element specifying a boundary string to delimit the various component objects.

■ **text**: The message body is composed of text. This text may be in a variety of formats. For example, the text could be an HTML document or a plain text document.

■ **video**: The message body contains a video component. The object should be displayed using appropriate hardware and software.

The second portion of the **Content-type** header field is the subtype. The subtype is used to provide a more detailed specification of the content. For example, the content type **text/plain** represents a plain text file. The content type **text/html** designates an HTML page. The variety of subtypes precludes the delineation of all possible subtypes, but Tables C-1 and C-2 provide a good subset of World Wide Web–related content types, both type and subtype.

MIME and the Web Client

Web clients use MIME content types to determine which external viewer to launch when a server sends it a given document. When a client sends a request to an HTTP server, the server's response includes a response header, and possibly a message body, depending on the results of the request. One of the fields in the response header is **Content-type**, which specifies the content type of the response's message body.

Similarly, Gopher servers provide information concerning message content FILL (message data type in a Gopher framework). However, when local files are accessed or an FTP transaction occurs, no information concerning the type of information being accessed is available. Therefore, the client must determine the type and present the information in an appropriate manner. The mechanism used by most browsing software is to determine the type based upon the filename extension of the object accessed. Table C-1 provides a list of the most commonly used MIME types with respect to World Wide Web transactions. For the types specified in Table C-2, specific configuration instructions for browsers to support these types are provided in the referenced How-To's. For example, the **multipart/x-mixed-replace** type is currently only supported by the Netscape browser and requires no additional configuration, whereas the **x-www-local-exec** type requires a modification of the browser's configuration files.

Browsers usually maintain a database of file extensions and their associated MIME types. This database is accessed by the client whenever a file needs to be resolved into a type prior to being displayed to the user. This information can usually be modified and extended by the user through configuration control. For example, to modify the MIME database in MacWeb, you modify part of the program resource fork accessible via a pulldown menu in the application. On the other hand, modification of the database for X Window Mosaic involves editing the `mime.types` file.

MIME and the Web Server

Servers also base content-type determination on file-type extensions. When a client makes a request, the server determines the `Content-type` field to use in the response header based on the filename extension of the file. Thus, files on the server with a `.tif` extension generate a `Content-type: image/tiff` field in the response header. Similarly, files with the `.htm` extension are sent with a `Content-type: text/html` in the server's response header.

Additional extensions can be identified to map to the same content type. For example, both the `.htm` and `.html` extensions may signify an HTML document; this is particularly true of PC servers that are limited to three-character file extensions. Whenever additional extensions or new types need to be added to the server, the MIME types database for the server needs to be updated. For the NCSA HTTPD and Netscape FastTrack servers, this database is contained in the `mime.types` file in the `conf` subdirectory.

If the server cannot resolve a filename extension to a type, or if the requested file does not have a filename extension, the server sends a default type in the response header. Many servers use `text/plain` as a default type; however, depending on the server, this default type might be configurable. For example, the `DefaultType` directive in the server resource map file will set this default type for an NCSA HTTPD server.

D

UNIX QUICK REFERENCE

Even though you may be creating your documents on a Windows or Macintosh system, you will find that many aspects of HTML, such as directory paths in URLs, are borrowed directly from UNIX. Despite its reputation as a user-unfriendly operating system, basic UNIX commands can be easily learned and used. In fact, if you have used DOS on a PC before, you will find UNIX very similar (but with some differences). Here's a brief list of UNIX commands that may be of use to you.

Changing Directories

To change from the current directory to a subdirectory, type

```
cd directoryname
```

To change from the current directory to a subdirectory several levels down, type

```
cd directoryname1/directoryname2/directoryname3
```

> **NOTE**
> UNIX uses forward slashes to separate directory names, unlike DOS, which uses backslashes.

To change from the current directory to the parent directory (one level up), type

```
cd ..
```

To change from the current directory to a directory several levels up, type

```
cd ../../..
```

To change to a directory that branches off from a common parent directory, type

```
cd ../directoryname
```

To go to your home directory, regardless of your current location, type

```
cd
```

Listing the Contents of a Directory

To list the contents of a directory, simply type

```
ls
```

To display a long listing, including the filename, size, date created or modified, and owner, type

```
ls -l
```

To list all files, including hidden files (whose filenames begin with a period), type

```
ls -a
```

To place symbols beside specific names (a / after directory names, or an * after executable files), type

```
ls -F
```

Moving and Deleting Files and Changing Filenames

To change the name of a file from file1 to file2, type

```
mv file1 file2
```

To move file1 to a subdirectory, type

```
mv file1 directoryname/file1
```

To move file1 to a parent directory, type

```
mv file1 ../file1
```

To move a group of files that begin with the name "file" to a subdirectory, type

```
mv file* directoryname/
```

To delete a file named file1, type

```
rm file1
```

To delete the entire contents of a directory, type

```
rm *
```

(Use this command with care. Once you delete a file, it's gone for good.)

Creating and Removing Directories

To create a subdirectory in the current directory, type

```
mkdir directoryname
```

To remove an empty subdirectory from the current directory, type

`rmdir directoryname`

To remove a subdirectory and all the files and directories contained within it, type

`rm -r directoryname`

Setting File and Directory Permissions

To change the permissions on a file to allow or prevent others from accessing it, type

`chmod nnn filename`

To change the permissions on all files in a directory to allow or prevent others from accessing them, type

`chmod nnn directoryname`

where *nnn* are three digits that define how a file or directory can be accessed by various users. The first digit represents the user, the second digit the user's group (a subset of users on the computer system), and the third digit all users on a system. The various number values the digits usually take are

0 No access
4 Read-only access
5 Read and executable access
6 Read and write access
7 Read, write, and executable access

For example, to make a file readable, writable, and executable for yourself, but only readable and executable for other users, type

`chmod 755 file1`

or to allow all users to read and write to a document, type

`chmod 666 file2`

HTML STYLE GUIDE

Suggestions for Do's and Don'ts

The Web is a wide open, freewheeling place. There are no set rules that govern what a person should or shouldn't do with his or her pages. Much of what appears on a page is left to a combination of the creator's individual style and the browser's pre-determined set of standards. The following Do's and Don'ts are meant only as guidelines and suggestions for creating readable, nonfrustrating home pages.

Do's

The following Do's, while certainly not carved in stone, will help make your pages more readable. They are general enough to apply to almost any page.

- Label your pages. With search utilities and Web crawlers, readers can find your pages in any number of ways. Help them locate your pages by using a label to identify each page.

- List an author somewhere on your pages, preferably on the top or bottom. Take credit for the work you put into your pages.

- Use informative titles in `<TITLE>` tags. This allows users to easily jump to where they want to go in their "history list." This also makes it easy for users to add your pages to their hotlists.

- Give readers an idea of how complete your pages are. It sometimes seems as if 90 percent of the Web is always under construction and the other 10 percent isn't working. It's a good idea to let readers know the current state of your pages. However, "under construction" should not be synonymous with "Lots of stuff here doesn't work."

- Give an e-mail address where users may contact you if they have comments or problems.

- Give warnings with any links that lead to explicit documents or images. Not everybody on the Web is as open-minded as you are.

- Give warnings with any links that lead to large images or documents. It's a considerate touch to label links with the size of documents or images. This way, users have a general idea of how long it may take for the document to load.

- A last-modified date is always good to have. It lets readers know how current your information is.

- A creation date on your page, while not essential, is certainly a nice feature. It lets readers know how long you've been around.

- If you include browser-specific tags (such as the Netscape enhancements) in your documents, add a statement to the document so that people who don't use the browser in question know why things look so strange.

- Use the **ALT** attribute with the **<IMG>** tag so that people with nongraphical browsers can get an idea of what they could be seeing.

- When loading images, use the **WIDTH** and **HEIGHT** attributes in the **<IMG>** tag. This will shorten the time the images need to load.

- When possible, make smaller images such as icons with backgrounds that are transparent. They look cleaner and more professional that way.

- Remember you are writing an electronic document, not a paper document. Things that look fine on paper, such as multiple columns, may not work so well on a scrollable document. The medium is different. It is up to you to figure out how you want to make the most out of that difference.

- If you think your document is something people might be interested in printing and referring to later, make a nonhypertext copy available for people to print.

- If you are using frames, make sure you also use the **<NOFRAMES>...</NOFRAMES>** tags to either have a non-frame version, or at least tell readers using browsers that don't support frames that your pages use frames. Also, try not to go too frame-crazy. While frames are a powerful tool, they can also be abused—used in places where instead of being a navigational aid, they become a real distraction and/or space waster.

- Take some time to "optimize" any graphics you may have. A little work with a program such as Photoshop and you may be able to reduce a graphic's size without hurting its quality.

■ Try to use proper (or at least understandable) grammar and syntax. It will make your pages smoother to read. Try to have several people proofread your pages.

■ Before you do any actual encoding of your documents into HTML, outline your page's structure. Remember, learning HTML is easy. The hard part is designing your pages so that people can easily access the information you are providing.

Don'ts (General)

The following is a list of suggestions of what to avoid on your Web pages. These are very general suggestions meant to work with any pages.

■ Don't use links to documents that don't exist. There is nothing more frustrating than the message

```
Error Code XXX file not found.
```

■ Don't insult your readers unless they have a pretty good idea when they come to your page that they could get insulted.

■ Don't copy images from somebody else's page unless you get their permission first.

■ Avoid anchoring links to words that are device-dependent and don't really describe what the link leads to. For instance:

```
You may <A HREF="manual.html">Click here</A> for users manual.
```

Instead, try to use

```
A <A HREF="manual.html">User's manual</A> is available.
```

■ Don't include trailing blanks or punctuation marks in tags. It doesn't look nice. For example:

```
Here is <A HREF="mydoc.html">my document!</A>
```

Instead, this could be:

```
Here is <A HREF="mydoc.html">my document</A>!
```

It is a simple change, but it looks much cleaner.

■ Don't load your page with a lot of big images unless you are certain that most of your readers will have fast (ISDN or better) connections. As a general rule of thumb, remember that a page with 60K of text and graphics will take around a minute to load over a 14.4 connection. Another general rule of thumb is not to use graphics of over 40K on a page.

■ Be careful with animated GIFs. One or two can go a long way; any more than that can really overpower a browser. Also, try to avoid GIFs that loop forever; certain versions of Netscape may have cache problems with this.

Don'ts (Conservative)

The following is a list of conservative don'ts. The authors don't usually follow these don'ts, but other more purist types do. They are presented so that you may decide whether you wish to follow them or not.

▪ Don't use browser-specific tags and elements. Using too many browser-specific tags makes a document unreadable to somebody not using that browser. There are people out there who don't like the way Netscape incorporates tags into their browsers either not supported by HTML 3 or supported in a different manner.

▪ Don't use more than one or two horizontal rules per page.

▪ Don't use graphic lines (colored or horizontal lines with pictures in them); they needlessly slow down the server.

▪ Don't use heading levels out of order. In other words, don't do something like the following:

```
<HTML>
<HEAD><TITLE>Bad example?</TITLE></HEAD>
<BODY>
<H4>Going!</H4>
<H2>Going!!</H4>
<H1>Gone!</H1>
</BODY>
</HTML>
```

▪ Don't use a lot of bold, italics, or exclamation marks. Italics seem to be especially hard to read with some browsers.

▪ Don't put a lot of WORDS IN CAPITALS. Usually there is no need to shout on the Web.

▪ Don't change the default colors of the text and links.

Making Your Page Shine

Follow these suggestions if you wish to make your pages more memorable.

▪ Use a distinct background, but just make sure it is not too large.

▪ Start your page with a nice graphic logo. Take a little time with a good graphics program to optimize the image by using a minimal number of colors and, if possible, anti-aliasing.

▪ Center titles.

▪ Don't be afraid to use icons or images to make your page more readable and more pleasing to the eye. Even if you are not an artist, there are plenty of sites around that offer icons to be downloaded. Since these sites change often, it's best to search for icons or consult a big index such as Yahoo!, the Whole Internet Catalog, or AltaVista.

■ Take time to plan the navigational aids you use in your pages. It's a good idea to include a navigational marker at the top or bottom of each page. The marker can contain the basic Next, Previous, Top of Server, and Home Page links.

■ Plan and structure your links. Ideally, you want to set up your documents so that readers have numerous ways of finding information, but you want to avoid cluttering your pages with excess or redundant links. It takes practice, common sense, and experimentation to work out the optimal blend of information and links to that information.

SUMMARY OF SELECTED SERVER SOFTWARE

Described here are some of the HTTP servers available. Each description concludes with a reference to a URL where additional and up-to-date information can be found.

The servers listed are those most commonly used. If none of these is suitable, examine URL `http://www.yahoo.com/Computers_and_Internet/Software/Internet/World_Wide_Web/Servers/` for an up-to-date list of available server software.

UNIX

This platform has the greatest variety of servers available. Since the original HTTP servers were developed on this platform, most new developments and enhancements appear first on UNIX servers. Several popular UNIX servers are discussed here.

Apache Server

The Apache server is a freeware server based upon NCSA HTTPD. This application is one of the more popular Web servers.

The server software is available as source code or precompiled binaries. The software architecture is extremely modular, which allows for very selective control over the features available in a particular compilation of the server.

This product supports the standard CGI/1.1 interface for handling gateway applications. A variety of modules support many standard and experimental

authentication mechanisms. A modification of this software is available for supporting
SSL connections (see URL `http://www.algroup.co.uk/Apache-SSL`).
    Further information on the Apache server is available at the URL

`http://www.apache.org`

CERN HTTP Server

One of the best features of this server is its ability to act as a proxy server, allowing
you to run a server and access outside servers through an Internet firewall. Further,
this software is fully CGI/1.1 compliant and comes packaged with a variety of gateway applications, including active image support. This server supports `HEAD`, `GET`,
`POST`, and `PUT` client requests. Several How-To's in Chapter 13, Handling Server Security,
provide information on specific configuration tasks with respect to the CERN
server. For information as well as the software itself, use this URL:

`http://www.w3.org/hypertext/WWW/Daemon/Status.html`

GN

This freeware server software provides both HTTP and Gopher service. Use is restricted per the standard GNU license (`http://hopf.math.nwu.edu/docs/Gnu_License`).
Security is handled through domain or IP address restrictions on a per-directory basis,
or over the entire server. However, user authentication is not supported. Unlike most
other servers, the default is to deny access to information unless explicit permission
is given. Installation and configuration of this server is similar in many ways to creating a standard Gopher server. Therefore, those familiar with Gopher should
have an easier time installing this package. The server supports `GET`, `HEAD`, and `POST`
requests. Further information on this server is available at the following URL:

`http://hopf.math.nwu.edu:70/`

NCSA HTTPD

This application, available freely from the National Center for Supercomputing
Applications, supports `GET`, `HEAD`, and `POST` HTTP requests. Security is provided
for host filtering through specification of domains or IP addresses; in addition, password security is supported. These measures provide access protection at the
directory level. Server-side includes and directives are supported via a parsed
HTML type that is processed by the server prior to transmission to a browser. (See
How-To 13.4 for additional information on server side includes and directives.) Several
How-To's in Chapter 12, Server Basics, and Chapter 13, Handling Server Security,
provide additional information on the use of this server. This software and relevant
information can be found at this URL:

`http://hoohoo.ncsa.uiuc.edu/docs/Overview.html`

Netscape Servers

The Netscape Communications Corporation markets two server packages: the
FastTrack server, an upgrade of its Communications Server; and the Enterprise Server,

an enhancement of its Commerce Server. The primary difference between these two applications is the level of security capabilities and the suite of power tools packaged with the server. Both servers support the basic, digest, and Kerberos authentication and directory/file-level domain and address restrictions, as well as encrypted SSL connections, but the Enterprise Server supports more extensive security measures and additional administrative and programmatic support capabilities. These servers are fully CGI/1.1 compliant, and they support a variety of package-specific components. Both applications support GET, HEAD, PUT, and POST requests. Several How-To's in Chapter 12, Server Basics, and Chapter 13, Handling Server Security, provide information on the configuration and use of these servers. Additional information is available at the following URL:

```
http://home.netscape.com/
```

WN

This is another freeware HTTP server application distributed under the GNU license (`http://hopf.math.nwu.edu/docs/Gnu_License`). It provides a variety of cutting-edge features that are both useful and experimental. WN provides security features that include IP address and domain restrictions, user authentication support by password, and digest authentication process. Like GN, the default access to documents is to deny access. This package is fully CGI/1.1 compliant, and it also includes a full suite of built-in search capabilities. Server-side includes are supported, as well as conditional server includes. GET, HEAD, and POST requests are currently supported. Further information can be found at this URL:

```
http://hopf.math.nwu.edu
```

VMS

Currently, only two servers have been developed for the VMS platform. The first of these is a port of the CERN HTTP server. The second was developed for the VMS platform. Thus, this server is reputedly better adapted to the VMS environment.

CERN HTTP Server

This is a port of the popular UNIX server. The features are identical to the original package. This server software can be found at the URL

```
http://delonline.cern.ch/delphi$www/public/vms/distribution.html
```

Cheetah Cross-Platform Server

The Cheetah server is a commercial product available for a variety of platforms, including OpenVMS 6.1 or later. This server provides support for many features of the UNIX servers including authentication, basic and digest, and it also provides CGI/1.1 support. Additional information and an evaluation copy are available through this URL:

```
http://www.tgv.com/public/cheetah/cheetah_welcome.html
```

DECthread HTTP Server

As a native VMS server, this software is reputed to better exploit the features of the VMS operating system than the CERN server. The DECthread server was developed using the DECthreads model, which should lead to significantly faster access than the CERN server, particularly when multiple simultaneous requests are made. This server is CGI compliant and comes equipped with a variety of useful gateway applications. Finally, the server supports GET and HEAD requests. Information and software can be found at the URL

`http://kcgl1.eng.ohio-state.edu/www/doc/serverinfo.html`

Windows NT and Windows 95

Several server software options are available for these platforms. They support a large variety of standard features while being in an environment comfortable for Windows NT and Windows 95 users. Several of these servers are described here.

HTTPS

This server supports GET, HEAD, and POST client requests. It is CGI compliant; however, it does not support either access control or user authentication security. Additional information about this product is available at URL

`http://emwac.ed.ac.uk/html/internet_toolchest/https/CONTENTS.HTM`

Microsoft Servers

Microsoft supports two levels of Web servers: a personal Web server (PWS) and a more powerful commercial Web server, the Internet Information Server (IIS).

IIS provides three servers in one for the Windows NT platform. This server supports the HTTP, FTP, and Gopher protocols. Server security is fully integrated with the NT security model. Further, IIS supports encrypted connections using SSL. Gateway applications written in Perl are supported, as well as integrated support for ActiveX-based embedded object controls. The Internet Service Manager provides administration of IIS through any machine with network access to the server. This server is freely available through Microsoft at this URL:

`http://www.microsoft.com/infoserv/`

Microsoft has recently released a small-scale Web server product, PWS, for its Windows 95 platform. This server supports Internet information dissemination via the HTTP and FTP protocols. This new server product is available with Microsoft's Internet Explorer Starter Kit. Consult the following URL for download and installation information:

`http://www.microsoft.com/ie/isk/pws.htm`

Netscape Servers

Netscape markets servers for the Windows NT and 95 platforms that provide the same capabilities as the servers described in the UNIX section. Both the Enterprise Server and the FastTrack server are available. See Netscape's home page for more information on these products:

`http://home.netscape.com`

Website

The Website server is a commercial package developed by the O'Reilly and Associates publishing firm. The package runs on both the Windows NT and 95 platforms. The basis for this application is the WinHTTP server developed for the Windows 3.1 platform. Website is CGI compliant and supports `GET`, `HEAD`, and `POST` requests. Beyond standard CGI, it has some additional capabilities to run Windows applications such as Excel and Visual Basic within HTML documents. For security, both basic authentication, and IP address and domain restrictions are supported. The following specifies the minimum running requirements for this application:

- 80386 or higher processor

- VGA or better display

- 3.5" disk drive

- 12+MB RAM (16MB suggested)

- At least 5MB of free hard disk space

- Windows NT 3.5 or 95 with TCP/IP connectivity

An enhanced version that supports increased security, WebSite Professional, is also available. This enhanced version provides for encrypted connections using either SSL or SHTTP.

Additional information and ordering information is available through the URL

`http://website.ora.com/`

OS/2

Several server packages have been developed for OS/2. This section describes three of them—Apache, GoServe, and HTTPD. URLs specifying up-to-date information are provided at the end of each description. For more information on OS/2 server options, use URL

`http://www.yahoo.com/Computers_and_Internet/Software/Internet/`
`World_Wide_Web/Servers/OS_2/`

Apache for OS/2

This server is a port of the popular UNIX freeware server of the same name. This port provides most of the features and capabilities of its parent. To download this server or to view additional information, consult URL

`http://www.slink.com/ApacheOS2/`

GoServe

The GoServe package supports both HTTP and Gopher protocols. This product is distributed freely under the IBM OS/2 Employee Written Software program and is subject to the IBM license agreement (`http://ww2.hursley.ibm.com/goserve/license.txt`) for OS/2 Tools. The server supports HTTP/1.0, including `GET`,

HEAD, and POST requests. Further, CGI standards for gateway applications are included. Security is provided by the basic authentication package. Directory access security is provided by domain and address restrictions. Some proposed HTTP/1.1 features have been added.

Additional information concerning this package can be found at URL

```
http://www2.hursley.ibm.com/goserve
```

OS2HTTPD

This port of the NCSA HTTPD server to the OS/2 platform supports many of the original's features. Currently, it does not support encrypted connections through SSL or SHTTP. For further information on this product, see URL

```
ftp://ftp.netcom.com/pub/kf/kfan/overview.html
```

Macintosh

Currently, the only HTTP server available for Macintosh users is the MacHTTP server, also now known as WebSTAR.

MacHTTP (WebSTAR)

This server will run on a Macintosh running the System 7 operating system with at least 8 megabytes of RAM. MacTCP is also required. MacHTTP will service GET, HEAD, and POST requests. It also supports a number of built-in search capabilities, but use of these features requires that AppleScript be installed. This server is CGI compliant and loads AppleScript, MacPerl, HyperCard, or custom applications developed with its own set of AppleEvents.

MacHTTP supports several security features. Access control can be limited on a domain or machine basis by restricting access to particular IP addresses or domain specifications. In addition, folder- and document-level security can be established through username and password access control. MacHTTP is the shareware version of this product.

WebStar is the commercial version of this server. It supports a variety of enhancements over its shareware predecessor. These improvements include quicker response time, increased capacity, support for additional security, and other advanced features. The price tag for WebStar is consequently higher than for MacHTTP.

How-To 13.8 examines issues in configuring security for a MacHTTP server. You can find registration information and download an evaluation copy of MacHTTP from the following URL:

```
http://www.starnine.com
```

Windows 3.1

Several server packages have been developed for the Windows and Windows for Workgroups environments. These servers are fairly full featured, but they suffer from a lack of true multitasking and task separation. The WinHTTPD server package is briefly described here.

WinHTTPD

This port of the NCSA HTTPD UNIX server to the Windows environment retains many of the features supported by its UNIX parent. The server supports **GET**, **HEAD**, and **POST** method requests, CGI 1.1 compliance, directory-level access control via domain restriction and the basic authentication package, and automatic directory indexing.

WinHTTPD supports gateway applications written as DOS batch files, Visual Basic programs, and Perl scripts. A variety of such programs have been developed and are available for this platform.

For commercial use, this package requires a registration fee. Further information, restrictions, and the software itself are available at URL

```
http://www.city.net/win-httpd
```

G

THE HYPERTEXT TRANSFER PROTOCOL (HTTP)

The Hypertext Transfer Protocol (HTTP) was developed as the standard exchange protocol for use with the World Wide Web. This is the language that is spoken between Web clients and Web servers.

Client/server communication can be viewed as a telephone conversation between two individuals. However, the vocabulary and grammar of the conversation are restricted to the HTTP language. The conversation is started by a client (a Web browser) dialing the exchange of the desired server. When the server picks up the connection, the client starts the conversation by making a request, stating its requirements and a description of itself. The server responds with an answer to the request, followed by a description of itself and the results of the request. At this point, the conversation ends, and the phone receiver is placed back on the hook.

These conversations are very structured. Each party speaks only once in a particular conversation involving a single request and a single response. What this means in a Web sense is that, if you attempt to load an HTML document with four inline images, your client will have to hold five discrete conversations to load the entire document: one to request the base document followed by four more to retrieve the images.

Further, clients and servers have exceedingly limited memories of previous conversations. Thus, if you have entered information in an HTML form, this data is passed to the appropriate gateway application (see Chapter 14, The Common Gateway Interface [CGI]). However, the server simply acts as a translator passing on the information. It does not keep a copy of this information. Therefore, many gateway applications encode this information back into the documents that they generate as hidden input fields. If they did not, the same information would need to be requested at several levels of nested HTML forms.

Each conversation between a client and a server is composed of four parts:

- Open connection

- Request

- Response

- Close connection

This HTTP communications process is shown in Figure G-1 and explained in detail.

Open Connection

The first stage of HTTP communications involves the client requesting a connection to a particular server. If a port number is given, the client will attempt to connect to that port; otherwise, the default port number 80 is used for the connection. For example, if you request that a server open the URL list in the following code, the client attempts to establish a connection with the **www.mysite.edu** machine at port 8080.

```
http://www.mysite.edu:8080/new/index.htm
```

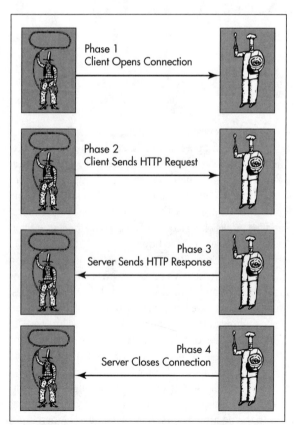

Figure G-1 HTTP communication process

HTTP Request

Once a connection has been established, the client sends an HTTP request. An HTTP request is composed of two parts: the request header and the request body.

The request header also contains two components. The first line of the header contains the method field. In the case of the example in this appendix, a simple GET method request would be generated. The method field that might be associated with this request appears as follows:

```
GET /new/index.htm HTTP/1.0
```

The remainder of the header is a series of attributes describing the client and its capabilities to the server. For example, the following might be the remainder of the request header sent for retrieving the document in this appendix:

```
Accept: text/plain
Accept: text/html
...
Accept: */*
User Agent: Mozilla/1.1N (X11; I; SunOS 4.1.3_U1 sun4m)
```

The request header ends with a blank line. The remainder of the request is the request body.

The body of a request is often empty. When it is not, it is most frequently used to send an encrypted actual request, to send input data via a POST method request, or to provide the information entity for a PUT method request. The header and body are separated by a blank line. This blank line must be included even if a request body is empty. The blank line is a signal to the server that the request header component is ended.

The first line of the request header is the method line. This line follows the format specified here:

```
Method          Identifier          Version
```

The *Method* is the HTTP method that the client wishes to use; Table G-1 presents several commonly used methods. (For a comprehensive list of methods, you may want to examine `http://www.w3.org/pub/WWW/Protocols/HTTP/Methods.html`.) The *Identifier* is the path to the information to use with the specified method. The *Version* field states the protocol and version of the protocol being used, most often HTTP/1.0.

Table G-1 Commonly used HTTP/1.0 requests

METHOD	EXPLANATION
GET	Retrieves the information entity specified by the identifier
HEAD	Retrieves the header information concerning the information entity specified by the identifier
PUT	Places the information contained in the request body at the location specified by the identifier
POST	Passes the information contained in the request body to the entity specified by the identifier and returns the results

The method line is followed by a series of attributes supplied by the client that the server may use as desired. Table G-2 presents a description of several commonly used HTTP/1.0 attributes. (For more information about additional attributes, you may want to reference URL `http://www.w3.org/pub/WWW/Protocols/HTTP/HTRQ_Headers.html`.)

Table G-2 Commonly used HTTP/1.0 request header directives

ATTRIBUTE	EXPLANATION
`Accept: type/subtype`	Describes the MIME types of the documents supported by the client making the request. Each such MIME type should be declared in an `Accept` element. The asterisk (*) may be used as a wildcard.
`Content-length: number`	The number of bytes contained in the request body.
`Content-type: MIME`	Specifies the MIME type of file contained in the request body.
`UserAgent: string`	Tells the server the specific type of client making the request.

No request body is necessary for a **GET** method request. The body will depend upon the request type. For example, if the client makes a **PUT** method request, the body will contain the information entity to place on the server. The request body may be used when secure transactions are required. In this case, the request body contains the encrypted request.

> **NOTE**
>
> The request header is terminated with a blank line whether or not a request body follows.

HTTP Response

The server follows up a request with a suitable response. The response also contains two parts: a header and a body.

As in a request, the response header has two components. The first line of the response header is the status line. The status line includes the HTTP version, a status code, and a status message.

The status line has the following format:

Version   *StatusCode*   *StatusMessage*

The *Version* represents the version of HTTP used for the communication (usually HTTP/1.0). The *StatusCode* and *StatusMessage* inform the client of the results of a request. A complete listing of standard status codes and messages is provided at URL `http://www.w3.org/pub/WWW/Protocols/HTTP/HTRESP.html`. Some of the more commonly used status codes and messages are presented in Table G-3. The status codes are three-digit numbers that can be categorized in terms of the first digit of the code.

▪ If the first digit is **1**, the result is informational.

▪ If the first digit is **2**, the request was understood and successfully completed.

▪ If the first digit is **3**, additional actions are required to complete the request.

▪ If the first digit is **4**, an error was found in the client's request.

▪ If the first digit is **5**, the client sent a valid request, but the server was unable to fulfill the request.

Table G-3 Commonly used HTTP/1.0 status codes and messages

CODE	MESSAGE
200	Completed successfully.
201	Created. Server-side resource created through either PUT or POST request.
202	Request has been queued, but results are unknown.
203	Completed, but all information was not returned.
204	No content. No new information available. Client should not alter current document.
301	Moved permanently. Requested information moved to another location.
302	Request completed, but desired data is at another location.
304	Not modified. Document that was requested conditionally based upon modification date has not been modified. Client should not alter current document.
400	Syntax error in request.
403	Forbidden. Authorization to access requested information not allowed.
404	Not found. Information requested was not found at the location specified.
500	Internal server error. The server encountered a problem and was unable to service the request.
501	Server does not support requested method.

So for the retrieval started in the example, the following status line might be generated:

```
HTTP/1.0 200 OK
```

The status line is followed by a series of attributes describing both the document being retrieved as well as the server providing the document.

Table G-4 displays many of the commonly used response header attributes. A complete specification of the HTTP response headers for HTTP/1.0 can be found at URL `http://www.w3.org/pub/WWW/Protocols/HTTP/Object_Headers.html`.

Table G-4 Commonly used HTTP/1.0 response header directives

ATTRIBUTE	EXPLANATION
Public: *methods*	Describes the nonstandard methods that this server supports
Content-Length: *number*	The number of bytes contained in the response body

continued on next page

continued from previous page

ATTRIBUTE	EXPLANATION
Content-type: *MIME*	Specifies the MIME type of the information entity contained in the response body
Date: *date*	The date and time the request was serviced
Title: *string*	The title of the document that was requested
Server: *string*	Tells the client the specific type of server responding
WWW-Link: *links*	Provides the client with information from the <LINK> element of the HTML 3 document retrieved

The following is a sample set of attributes:

```
Date: Sunday, 17-Dec-1995 11:30:00 GMT
Server: NCSA/1.4.1
MIME-version: 1.0
Content-type: text/html
Last-modified: 16-Jun-1995 10:35:39 GMT
Content-Length: 247
```

The response header ends with a blank line.

The remainder of the response is the body. This contains the actual data being transferred. This could be an HTML 3 document, a GIF image, or any other document type supported by the server.

Close Connection

The conversation is complete, and the connection between the server and the client is closed.

The HTTP standard, like the HTML standard, is continuing to develop. The HTTP/1.1 standard is currently under consideration. The proposed new standard would support many additional features and request types. If you are interested in the progress of HTTP/1.1, you should examine the information at URL **http://www.w3.org/pub/WWW/Protocols/**. Links on this page provide access to the latest information on HTTP development.

H

COLOR TABLE

HTML Color Table

The following table lists some of the more popular colors and their RGB values. These values may be used to change background color, text color, and link colors. The values are given in hexadecimal, where the first two digits represent the red value, the next two the green, and the last two the blue. Each red, green, or blue value may go from **00** (none of that color) to **FF** (all of that color).

COLOR	RRGGBB
White	FFFFFF
Red	FF0000
Green	00FF00
Blue	0000FF
Magenta	FF00FF
Cyan	00FFFF
Yellow	FFFF00
Black	000000
Aliceblue	F0F8FF
Aquamarine	70DB93
Backer's Chocolate	5C3317
Blue Violet	9F5F9F
Brass	B5A642

continued on next page

continued from previous page

Bright Gold	D9D919
Brown	A62AA2
Bronze	8C7853
Bronze II	A67D3D
Cadet Blue	5F9F9F
Cool Copper	D98719
Copper	B87333
Coral	FF7F00
Cornflower Blue	42426F
Dark Brown	5C4033
Dark Green	2F4F2F
Dark Green Copper	4A766E
Dark Olive Green	4F4F2F
Dark Orchid	9932CD
Dark Purple	871F78
Dark Slate Blue	6B238E
Dark Slate Gray	2F4F4F
Dark Tan	97694F
Dark Turquoise	7093DB
Dark Wood	855E42
Dim Gray	545454
Dusty Rose	856363
Feldspar	D19275
Firebrick	8E2323
Forest Green	238E23
Gold	CD7F32
Goldenrod	DBDB70
Gray	C0C0C0
Green Copper	527F76
Green Yellow	93DB70
Hunter Green	215E21
Indian Red	4E2F2F
Khaki	9F9F5F
Light Blue	C0D9D9
Light Gray	A8A8A8
Light Steel Blue	8F8FBD
Light Wood	E9C2A6
Light Green	32CD32

Mandarin Orange	E47833
Maroon	8E236B
Medium Aquamarine	32CD99
Medium Blue	3232CD
Medium Forest Green	6B8E23
Medium Goldenrod	EAEAAE
Medium Orchid	9370DB
Medium Sea Green	426F42
Medium Slate Blue	7F00FF
Medium Spring Green	7FFF00
Medium Turquoise	70DBDB
Medium Violet Red	DB7093
Medium Wood	A68064
Midnight Blue	2F2F4F
Navy Blue	23238E
Neon Blue	4D4DFF
Neon Pink	FF6EC7
New Midnight Blue	00009C
New Tan	EBC79E
Old Gold	CFB53B
Orange	FF7F00
Orange Red	FF2400
Orchid	DB70DB
Pale Green	8FBC8F
Pink	BC8F8F
Plum	EAADEA
Quartz	D9D9F3
Rich Blue	5959AB
Salmon	6F4242
Scarlet	8C1717
Sea Green	238E68
Semi-Sweet Chocolate	6B42226
Sienna	8E6B23
Silver	E6E8FA
Sky Blue	3299CC
Slate Blue	007FFF
Spicy Pink	FF1CAE
Spring Green	00FF7F

continued on next page

continued from previous page

Steel Blue	236B8E
Summer Sky	38B0DE
Tan	DB9370
Thistle	D8BFD8
Turquoise	ADEAEA
Very Dark Brown	5C4033
Very Light Gray	CDCDCD
Violet	4F2F4F
Violet Red	CC3299
Wheat	D8D8BF
Yellow Green	99CC32

INTERNET EXPLORER 3.0: A FIELD GUIDE

A new day dawned. The sun reached its fingers over the digital outback. The mighty Navigators (*Netscapus navigatorus*)—a species that reproduced like rabbits and ran nearly as fast—covered the landscape. Yonder, on a cliff that seemed to be beyond the horizon, a trembling new creature looked out over the Internet jungle. This strange new creature, calling itself the Explorer (*Microsoftus interneticus explorus*), sniffed around, considering whether it should enter the fragile ecosystem. Netscape gators gnashed their teeth, but the Explorers were not daunted. Explorer was a formidable beast. It became a part of the jungle and thrived. And even though it began as a mere pup, it evolved and it evolved and it evolved.

Now the jungle is rife with two intelligent species.

What follows is a guide to domesticating Internet Explorer. You will learn how to care for your Explorer and even how to teach it tricks. Before long, you shall find truth behind the old axiom that the Explorer is man's (and woman's) best friend.

Introducing Explorer to Your Ecosystem

Whether you're running Windows NT or Windows 95, installing Explorer is easy. Explorer's own installation program makes setup a breeze, and you need only to select the appropriate file on the CD-ROM to launch this installer. Make sure the CD-ROM included with this book is in the CD-ROM drive; then, depending upon your system, follow the directions below for either Windows 95 or Windows NT.

Windows 95 Installation

1. Click the Start button in the lower left corner of your screen.

2. Click on the Run... option in the Start menu. A dialog box similar to the one shown in Figure I-1 appears.

3. Using the Run dialog box, type in a pathname and specify the location of the Explorer installation program. IE301M95.EXE is in the CD's \Explorer directory, so if your CD-ROM drive is designated as D:, you'd type

`d:\explorer\ie301m95.exe`

If your CD-ROM drive has a different designation letter, type in the appropriate drive designation letter in place of **d:**.

4. After typing the proper pathname, click the OK button to start the Explorer's installation program. Depending upon your system, it may take a moment to load.

5. Once the installation program loads, follow the on-screen prompts to set up Explorer on your computer.

Windows NT 4 Installation

1. Click the Start button in the lower left corner of your screen.

2. Click on the Run... option in the Start menu. A dialog box similar to the one shown in Figure I-2 appears.

3. Using the Run dialog box, type in a pathname and specify the location of the Explorer installation program. MSIE30M.EXE is in the CD's \Explorer directory, so if your CD-ROM drive is designated as D:, you'd type:

`d:\explorer\ie301mnt.exe`

Figure I-1 The Windows 95 Run dialog box

Figure I-2 The Windows NT Run dialog box

If your CD-ROM drive has a different designation letter, type in the appropriate drive designation letter in place of **d:**.

4. After typing the proper pathname, click the OK button to start the Explorer's installation program. Depending upon your system, it may take a moment to load.

5. Once the installation program loads, follow the on-screen prompts to set up Explorer on your computer.

Once you've run the installation, you'll need to restart your system. You can then click on the Internet icon on your desktop. If you've already selected an Internet provider with Windows dial-up networking, you'll be connected. If not, you'll be walked through the dial-in process. You'll need to enter the phone number of your Internet provider, your modem type, and other related information. Ultimately, you'll be taken to Microsoft's home page, where you can register your Explorer and find out about its latest features.

> **NOTE**
>
> The Explorer is a constantly evolving animal. For the latest updates, plug-ins, and versions, be sure to regularly check out Microsoft's neck of the woods at http://www.microsoft.com/ie/.

Explorer Components

Explorer is more than a plain-Jane Web browser. As you work through the installation, you'll be able to choose a variety of components. You can select the following add-ons:

- **Internet Mail**. This is a comprehensive e-mail package. Using simple icons, you can write and read your mail off-line and then log on quickly to send and receive your latest batch of correspondence. See Figure I-3.

- **Internet News**. This is a window that lets you browse through thousands of newsgroups, read through the threads, and post your own messages. The News system is very easy to use. You can easily keep track of your favorite topics and automatically update with the latest news.

- **ActiveMovie**. This feature of Explorer lets you watch all sorts of video clips—MPEG, AVI, and QuickTime formats. It even supports a special streaming version of video that downloads movies as you watch them, letting you view video with little delay. The ActiveMovie system also lets you listen to all popular formats of audio files—AU, WAV, MIDI, MPEG, and AIFF. This makes it easy to add background sound to Web pages.

- **VRML Support**. This feature is a separate module that lets you download and coast through Virtual Reality Modeling Language worlds. This allows you to explore true 3D landscapes and objects.

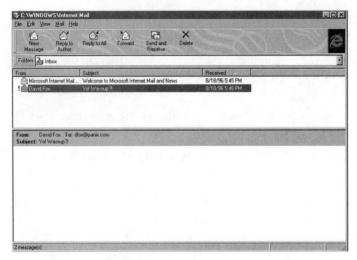

Figure I-3 The Internet Mail main window

■ **NetMeeting**. This is a full-featured package that lets you hold entire meetings over the Internet. You can chat with one person or with dozens. If you have a microphone, you can use the Internet phone feature to hold voice conversations with other people. You can share applications. For example, you and a client can edit the same word processing document together. A whiteboard feature lets you draw on a "digital blackboard" that can be updated live across the Internet.

■ **HTML Layout Control**. This tool lets Web page publishers create spiffy versions of HTML pages, the way professional designers would lay out a magazine page or a newspaper. Designers can choose exactly where to place elements within a Web page. You can make objects transparent and layer objects over each other, which helps make a Web page eye-catching yet uncluttered.

The Nature of the Beast

Internet Explorer features very up-to-date HTML. It supports HTML 3.2, including the following:

■ **Frames**. These break up the Web page window into several areas. For example, you can keep an unchanging row of navigation controls along the top of the page while constantly updating the bottom. You can use borderless frames, which split up the page without making it seem split. A special type of frame known as the *floating frame* lets you view one Web page within another.

▣ **Cascading Style Sheets**. This allows all your Web sites to have the same general look and feel.

▣ **Tables**. You can create or view all sorts of fancy tables, with or without graphics, borders, and columns.

▣ **Embedded Objects**. Internet Explorer can handle Java applets, ActiveX controls, and even Netscape plug-ins. These objects are discussed later, in the Symbiotic Partners section of this appendix.

▣ **Fonts**. Explorer supports many fonts, allowing Web pages to have a variety of exciting designs.

From the get-go, Internet Explorer has included a few special bells and whistles. For example, it's easy to create and view marquees across Web pages. This lets you scroll a long, attention-drawing message, similar to a tickertape, that puts a great deal of information in a very small space.

Training the Explorer

By its very nature, the Explorer is a friendly beast. You can access the full range of the Explorer's talents by pushing its buttons. These buttons, which appear in the toolbar at the top of the screen as depicted in Figure I-4, are as follows:

▣ **Back**. Use this to return to the Web page you've just come from. This will help you retrace your steps as you take Explorer through the Internet maze.

▣ **Forward**. Use this after you've used the Back button, to jump forward again to the page from which you began.

▣ **Stop**. If a Web page is taking too long to load, press this button. Any text and graphics will immediately stop downloading.

▣ **Refresh**. If your Web page is missing some graphics, or if you've previously stopped its loading using the Stop button, you can reload it using Refresh.

▣ **Home**. This takes you to your pre-set home page. By default, this is Microsoft's main Web page, but you can set your home to any page you like. See the Taming the Beast section.

▣ **Search**. This takes you to a special page that allows you to search for a Web page, using a number of cool search engines. See the Hunting Skills section.

▣ **Favorites**. This button lets you access a list of your favorite Web sites. See the Favorite Haunts section.

▣ **Print**. This allows you to print out the current Web page, allowing you to keep a perfect hard copy of it.

▣ **Font**. Find yourself squinting at a Web page? Just click here to zoom in. The font size will grow several degrees. Too big now? Click a few more times and the size will shrink once again.

Figure I-4 A cosmetic look at Explorer

Mail. This will launch the Internet Mail program, which allows you to send and receive e-mail and to access newsgroups.

PLAYING FETCH

Your Explorer is a devoted friend. It can scamper anywhere within the Internet, bringing back exactly what you desire.

If you know where you want to go, just type the URL into Explorer's Address box at the top of the screen. If you like, you can omit the `http://` prefix. The Web page will be loaded up. You can also search for a page or load up a previously saved page.

You can now click on any *hyperlink*—an underlined or colored word or picture—to zoom to that associated Web page or Internet resource. Some hyperlinked graphics may not be obvious. Explorer will tell you when you are positioned over a valid hyperlink, because the cursor will change into a pointing finger. Continue following these links as long as you like. It's not uncommon to start researching knitting needles and end up reading about porcupines.

> **NOTE**
>
> If you're an aspiring Web page writer, you might want to take a peek at the HTML source code to see how that page was created. Just select View, Source.

HUNTING SKILLS

If you want to find Web pages dealing with a specific category, the Explorer makes it easy to find them. Click the Search button. The Search screen will appear, as in Figure I-5. You can search for more than Web pages. With Explorer, it's easy to find

- Phone numbers, ZIP codes, and addresses

- Information on a number of topics—health, home, education, consumer affairs, finance, weather, sports, travel, and so on

- References—maps, a dictionary, a thesaurus, quotations, and an encyclopedia

- Online books, newspapers, and magazines

> **TIP**
>
> You can also quickly hunt for any idea, word, or category. Simply type GO in the Address box at the top of the screen, followed by the word or phrase you want to search for.

Figure I-5 The Search screen

FAVORITE HAUNTS

It's easy to keep track of the Web pages you visit most. When you want to save a page for future reference, simply click the Favorites button or choose the Favorites menu item. Select the Add To Favorites option. The current Web page will now be added to the list of favorites, which appears each time you click on the Favorites button or menu.

After a while, your list of favorites will get long and cluttered. It's simple to keep track of huge lists of favorites—just put them into separate folders. Organize your favorites, as shown in Figure I-6, by selecting Favorites, Organize Favorites.

To create a new folder, click on the New Folder icon (the folder with the little glint on it) at the top of the window. Now drag and drop your Web page bookmarks into the appropriate folders. You can also move, rename, or delete a folder by selecting it and using the corresponding buttons at the bottom of the screen.

TIP

You can even include or attach a favorite Web document within an e-mail message, the way you would attach any other file.

NOTE

On Windows systems, the Favorites list is actually a folder within your Windows directory. This reflects a Microsoft trend—treating the entire World Wide Web as just another folder to explore on your desktop. Eventually, you'll be able to drag and drop documents across the Internet as easily as you would within your own hard drive.

Figure I-6 Organizing the Favorites list

MEMORY

Internet Explorer keeps track of every Web page you visit. This is kept in a vast History list. You can view the entire History list, in chronological order, by clicking the View History button. Just click on any page you'd like to revisit.

> **NOTE**
>
> The History list is cleared every 20 days—you can set this value within the Navigation properties sheets.

TAMING THE BEAST

Now that you and your Explorer are getting acquainted, why not tame it so that it acts and looks exactly like you want? Select View, Options and pick a tab at the top of the window to customize the following properties:

- **General**. The general properties sheet is illustrated in Figure I-7. Since multimedia content (such as sounds, movies, and graphics) takes longer to load in Web pages, you can choose to not load certain media types. You can also easily customize the color of the text and hyperlinks. Finally, you can decide how little or how much information appears in your toolbar.

> **NOTE**
>
> You can change the size and position of your toolbar simply by clicking on its borders and dragging it to a desired location.

Figure I-7 The general properties sheet

Connection. You can adjust your connections settings, as shown in Figure I-8, by clicking on this tab. This lets you choose your Internet provider. If you're connecting to the Internet through a network firewall, you can also set your proxy server information here.

Navigation. You can customize which page you'd like to use as your starting home page. Just enter its URL in the Address box here.

Programs. This allows you to set which programs you'd like to use for e-mail and for Usenet news. By default, you can use Microsoft's Internet Mail and Internet News, which are included with Explorer. You can also tell Explorer how to handle various types of files by selecting the File Types button. It allows you to designate which program or plug-in should be launched whenever Explorer comes across various unfamiliar file formats.

Security. You are able to customize how securely documents will be handled by Explorer. If you want to keep your computer extremely safe, you may tell Explorer not to download possible security risks such as ActiveX controls, Java applets, or other plug-ins. Another nice feature is a Content Advisor. Click on Settings; the Content Advisor window will appear as in Figure I-9. You may now decide which Web pages to skip, based on adult language, nudity, sex, or violence. Many questionable Web pages are written with certain tags so that the pages can be weeded out by people who don't want to see them. This is a great option to use if your kids surf the Internet, or if your sensibilities are easily offended. To turn ratings on, click on the Enable Ratings button. You can also lock this window with a password.

Figure I-8 The connection property sheet.

Figure I-9 The Content Advisor window

■ **Advanced**. This properties sheet lets you customize when Internet Explorer will issue warnings. This is useful if you deal with sensitive information and want to know which Web pages are secure and which are not. You can also set a number of other advanced Java and Security options here.

SYMBIOTIC PARTNERS

Explorer includes many of the latest Web technologies. These make your Web pages sing, dance, and even act as entire applications. The line between what a computer can do in general and what a computer can do over the Internet is thinning.

ACTIVEX

Microsoft's proprietary ActiveX technology lets you drop controls into your Web pages. Controls are software components such as specialized buttons, input forms, graphics viewers, sound players, and so forth.

When you load a page with an ActiveX control, Explorer will check if you already have that control on your system. If not, you'll be asked whether you'd like to download it. You'll be told whether the control has been authenticated by Microsoft. If the control is secure, it'll automatically be downloaded and installed for you. The resulting Web page may look more like a software program than a Web page. Don't be surprised to find all new types of buttons, such as the up and down arrow controls in Figure I-10.

SCRIPTS

Internet Explorer allows Web page writers to add different types of scripts right into the source code of the Web page itself. This means you can get instantaneous feedback and control of the Web browser, ActiveX controls, Java applets, and other plug-ins. This makes interactivity fast and easy. Internet Explorer supports Visual Basic, Scripting Edition and JavaScript languages.

Figure I-10 Loading a page with an ActiveX control

JAVA

Finally, Explorer fully supports the popular Java language. Java is a programming language that lets you write full applications that run directly within your Web browser. Java is great for writing games, graphics demonstrations, databases, spreadsheets, and much more.

TOTAL MASTERY

Now that you are fully in control of Explorer, you can learn, work, and have fun using it with the greatest of ease. Wandering through the Internet faster than ever, you are ready to investigate new paths of adventure with your trusty, obedient Explorer guiding you every step of the way.

INDEX

M

MacHTTP (WebSTAR) server, 890
    domain/address security, 529, 531-533
        host filtering, 530
        passwords, 530-531
    Web site, 854
Macintosh
    browser Web sites, 852
    editor Web sites, 856-857
    servers
        installing documents, 466-469
        Web sites, 854
        WebSTAR, see MacHTTP
        WinHTTPD, 891
Macromedia Director applications
    embedding, 748-750
    linking, 750-752
magazines (People On-Line Web site), 824-825
magenta color, 899
mailing lists (Web sites), 865
Mailto tag (URL), 272
Main Menu commands (Internet Connections;
  America Online), 8
mandarin orange color, 901
MAP tag, 313-315, 844
Margin (style sheets), 681
MARGINHEIGHT attribute (FRAME tag), 764
MARGINWIDTH attribute (FRAME tag), 764
maroon color, 901
MARQUEE tag attributes, 623, 839
    ALIGN, 625
    BEHAVIOR, 623-624
    BGCOLOR, 625
    DIRECTION, 624
    HEIGHT, 625
    HSPACE, 625
    SCROLLAMOUNT, 624
    SCROLLDELAY, 624
    VSPACE, 625
    WIDTH, 625
marquees, creating, 623-626
Marvel Comics X-Men (Uncanny X-page) Web site,
  824-825
Mask directives, 511-513
Material node, 369
math
    equations, creating, 810-813
    matrices, creating, 813-816
MATH tag, 810-813
matrices, creating, 813-816
medium aquamarine color, 901
medium blue color, 901

medium forest green color, 901
medium goldenrod color, 901
medium orchid color, 901
medium sea green color, 901
medium slate blue color, 901
medium spring green color, 901
medium turquoise color, 901
medium violet red color, 901
medium wood color, 901
menu lists
    creating, 189-191
    nested, 199-200
MENU tag, 190-191, 842
menus (pulldown), creating, 402-404
META tag, 55, 60, 639-643, 838
METHOD attribute (FORM tag), 389
Microsoft
    browsers *see* browsers
    servers, *see* servers
Microsoft's style sheet guide Web site, 662
midnight blue color, 901
MIME, 867-868
    clients, 872-873
    RFC 1521, 868
    RFC 822 Web site, 867
    servers, 873
    types, 341, 868, 871
        encryption, 554
        servers, registering, 461-465
Mm2html converter, 43
Modelers (VRML), 364-367
Mosaic, 12, 15
Mosaic Web site, 852-854
MPEGs
    application support, 345
    converting formats, 345-347
    linking, 344
MpegUtil program, 347
Ms2html converter, 43
MULTICOL tag, 628-629, 840
Multicolumn lists, creating, 794-796
multimedia
    Astound/Studio M, embedding, 752-754
    browser support, 756-758
    Director applications
        embedding, 748-750
        linking, 750-752
    embedding
        OBJECT tag, 739-740
        plug-ins, 737-739
    extensions, 328-329

929

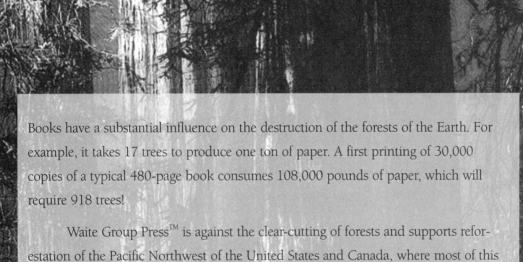

Books have a substantial influence on the destruction of the forests of the Earth. For example, it takes 17 trees to produce one ton of paper. A first printing of 30,000 copies of a typical 480-page book consumes 108,000 pounds of paper, which will require 918 trees!

Waite Group Press™ is against the clear-cutting of forests and supports reforestation of the Pacific Northwest of the United States and Canada, where most of this paper comes from. As a publisher with several hundred thousand books sold each year, we feel an obligation to give back to the planet. We will therefore support organizations that seek to preserve the forests of planet Earth.

Message from the
Publisher

WELCOME TO OUR NERVOUS SYSTEM

Some people say that the World Wide Web is a graphical extension of the information superhighway, just a network of humans and machines sending each other long lists of the equivalent of digital junk mail.

I think it is much more than that. To me, the Web is nothing less than the nervous system of the entire planet—not just a collection of computer brains connected together, but more like a billion silicon neurons entangled and recirculating electro-chemical signals of information and data, each contributing to the birth of another CPU and another Web site.

Think of each person's hard disk connected at once to every other hard disk on earth, driven by human navigators searching like Columbus for the New World. Seen this way the Web is more of a super entity, a growing, living thing, controlled by the universal human will to expand, to be more. Yet, unlike a purposeful business plan with rigid rules, the Web expands in a nonlinear, unpredictable, creative way that echoes natural evolution.

We created our Web site not just to extend the reach of our computer book products but to be part of this synaptic neural network, to experience, like a nerve in the body, the flow of ideas and then to pass those ideas up the food chain of the mind. Your mind. Even more, we wanted to pump some of our own creative juices into this rich wine of technology.

TASTE OUR DIGITAL WINE

And so we ask you to taste our wine by visiting the body of our business. Begin by understanding the metaphor we have created for our Web site—a universal learning center, situated in outer space in the form of a space station. A place where you can journey to study any topic from the convenience of your own screen. Right now we are focusing on computer topics, but the stars are the limit on the Web.

If you are interested in discussing this Web site or finding out more about the Waite Group, please send me e-mail with your comments, and I will be happy to respond. Being a programmer myself, I love to talk about technology and find out what our readers are looking for.

Sincerely,

Mitchell Waite

Mitchell Waite, C.E.O. and Publisher

200 Tamal Plaza
Corte Madera, CA 94925
415-924-2575
415-924-2576 fax

Website:
http://www.waite.com/waite

CREATING THE HIGHEST QUALITY COMPUTER BOOKS IN THE INDUSTRY

Waite Group Press

Come Visit
WAITE.COM
Waite Group Press
World Wide Web Site

Now find all the latest information on Waite Group books at our new Web site, **http://www.waite.com/waite.** You'll find an online catalog where you can examine and order any title, review upcoming books, and send e-mail to our authors and editors. Our FTP site has all you need to update your book: the latest program listings, errata sheets, most recent versions of Fractint, POV Ray, Polyray, DMorph, and all the programs featured in our books. So download, talk to us, ask questions, on **http://www.waite.com/waite.**

The New Arrivals Room has all our new books listed by month. Just click for a description, Index, Table of Contents, and links to authors.

The Backlist Room has all our books listed alphabetically.

The People Room is where you'll interact with Waite Group employees.

Links to Cyberspace get you in touch with other computer book publishers and other interesting Web sites.

About WGP • New Arrivals • Backlist Room • People Room • FTP • Order • Subject Room • Links to Cyberspace

The FTP site contains all program listings, errata sheets, etc.

The Order Room is where you can order any of our books online.

The Subject Room contains typical book pages that show description, Index, Table of Contents, and links to authors.

World Wide Web:

COME SURF OUR TURF—THE WAITE GROUP WEB

http://www.waite.com/waite
Gopher: gopher.waite.com
FTP: ftp.waite.com

This is a legal agreement between you, the end user and purchaser, and The Waite Group®, Inc., and the authors of the programs contained in the disk. By opening the sealed disk package, you are agreeing to be bound by the terms of this Agreement. If you do not agree with the terms of this Agreement, promptly return the unopened disk package and the accompanying items (including the related book and other written material) to the place you obtained them for a refund.

SOFTWARE LICENSE

1. The Waite Group, Inc. grants you the right to use one copy of the enclosed software programs (the programs) on a single computer system (whether a single CPU, part of a licensed network, or a terminal connected to a single CPU). Each concurrent user of the program must have exclusive use of the related Waite Group, Inc. written materials.

2. The program, including the copyrights in each program, is owned by the respective author, and the copyright in the entire work is owned by The Waite Group, Inc. and they are therefore protected under the copyright laws of the United States and other nations, under international treaties. You may make only one copy of the disk containing the programs exclusively for backup or archival purposes, or you may transfer the programs to one hard disk drive, using the original for backup or archival purposes. You may make no other copies of the programs, and you may make no copies of all or any part of the related Waite Group, Inc. written materials.

3. You may not rent or lease the programs, but you may transfer ownership of the programs and related written materials (including any and all updates and earlier versions) if you keep no copies of either, and if you make sure the transferee agrees to the terms of this license.

4. You may not decompile, reverse engineer, disassemble, copy, create a derivative work, or otherwise use the programs except as stated in this Agreement.

GOVERNING LAW

This Agreement is governed by the laws of the State of California.

LIMITED WARRANTY

The following warranties shall be effective for 90 days from the date of purchase: (i) The Waite Group, Inc. warrants the enclosed disk to be free of defects in materials and workmanship under normal use; and (ii) The Waite Group, Inc. warrants that the programs, unless modified by the purchaser, will substantially perform the functions described in the documentation provided by The Waite Group, Inc. when operated on the designated hardware and operating system. The Waite Group, Inc. does not warrant that the programs will meet purchasers' requirements or that operation of a program will be uninterrupted or error-free. The program warranty does not cover any program that has been altered or changed in any way by anyone other than The Waite Group, Inc. The Waite Group, Inc. is not responsible for problems caused by changes in the operating characteristics of computer hardware or computer operating systems that are made after the release of the programs, nor for problems in the interaction of the programs with each other or other software.

THESE WARRANTIES ARE EXCLUSIVE AND IN LIEU OF ALL OTHER WARRANTIES OF MERCHANTABILITY OR FITNESS FOR A PARTICULAR PURPOSE OR OF ANY OTHER WARRANTY, WHETHER EXPRESS OR IMPLIED.

EXCLUSIVE REMEDY

The Waite Group, Inc. will replace any defective disk without charge if the defective disk is returned to The Waite Group, Inc. within 90 days from date of purchase.

This is Purchaser's sole and exclusive remedy for any breach of warranty or claim for contract, tort, or damages.

LIMITATION OF LIABILITY

THE WAITE GROUP, INC. AND THE AUTHORS OF THE PROGRAMS SHALL NOT IN ANY CASE BE LIABLE FOR SPECIAL, INCIDENTAL, CONSEQUENTIAL, INDIRECT, OR OTHER SIMILAR DAMAGES ARISING FROM ANY BREACH OF THESE WARRANTIES EVEN IF THE WAITE GROUP, INC. OR ITS AGENT HAS BEEN ADVISED OF THE POSSIBILITY OF SUCH DAMAGES.

THE LIABILITY FOR DAMAGES OF THE WAITE GROUP, INC. AND THE AUTHORS OF THE PROGRAMS UNDER THIS AGREEMENT SHALL IN NO EVENT EXCEED THE PURCHASE PRICE PAID.

COMPLETE AGREEMENT

This Agreement constitutes the complete agreement between The Waite Group, Inc. and the authors of the programs, and you, the purchaser.

Some states do not allow the exclusion or limitation of implied warranties or liability for incidental or consequential damages, so the above exclusions or limitations may not apply to you. This limited warranty gives you specific legal rights; you may have others, which vary from state to state.

MACMILLAN COMPUTER PUBLISHING USA

A VIACOM COMPANY

Technical ---- Support:

If you cannot get the CD/Disk to install properly, or you need assistance with a particular situation in the book, please feel free to check out the Knowledge Base on our Web site at **http://www.superlibrary.com/general/support**. We have answers to our most Frequently Asked Questions listed there. If you do not find your specific question answered, please contact Macmillan Technical Support at **(317) 581-3833**. We can also be reached by email at **support@mcp.com**.

SATISFACTION REPORT CARD

Please fill out this card if you wish to know of future updates to
HTML 3.2 Plus How-To, or to receive our catalog.

First Name: _____ **Last Name:** _____

Street Address: _____

City: _____ **State:** _____ **Zip:** _____

E-Mail Address _____

Daytime Telephone: (   ) _____

Date product was acquired: Month   **Day**   **Year**   **Your Occupation:**

Overall, how would you rate *HTML 3.2 Plus How-To*?

☐ Excellent ☐ Very Good ☐ Good
☐ Fair ☐ Below Average ☐ Poor

What did you like MOST about this book? _____

_____

_____

What did you like LEAST about this book? _____

_____

_____

Please describe any problems you may have encountered with installing or using the disk: _____

_____

How did you use this book (problem-solver, tutorial, reference...)?

_____

What is your level of computer expertise?

☐ New ☐ Dabbler ☐ Hacker
☐ Power User ☐ Programmer ☐ Experienced Professional

What computer languages are you familiar with? _____

_____

Please describe your computer hardware:

Computer _____ Hard disk _____
5.25" disk drives _____ 3.5" disk drives _____
Video card _____ Monitor _____
Printer _____ Peripherals _____
Sound Board _____ CD-ROM _____

Where did you buy this book?

☐ Bookstore (name): _____
☐ Discount store (name): _____
☐ Computer store (name): _____
☐ Catalog (name): _____
☐ Direct from WGP ☐ Other _____

What price did you pay for this book? _____

What influenced your purchase of this book?

☐ Recommendation ☐ Advertisement
☐ Magazine review ☐ Store display
☐ Mailing ☐ Book's format
☐ Reputation of Waite Group Press ☐ Other

How many computer books do you buy each year? _____

How many other Waite Group books do you own? _____

What is your favorite Waite Group book? _____

_____

Is there any program or subject you would like to see Waite Group Press cover in a similar approach? _____

_____

Additional comments? _____

_____

_____

Please send to: **Waite Group Press**
                       200 Tamal Plaza
                       Corte Madera, CA 94925

☐ **Check here for a free Waite Group catalog**

**BEFORE YOU OPEN THE DISK OR CD-ROM PACKAGE ON THE
FACING PAGE, CAREFULLY READ THE LICENSE AGREEMENT.**

Opening this package indicates that you agree to abide by the license agreement found in the back of this book. If you do not agree with it, promptly return the unopened disk package (including the related book) to the place you obtained them for a refund.